Multicultural Education in a Pluralistic Society

EIGHTH EDITION

DONNA M. GOLLNICK
National Council for Accreditation of Teacher Education

PHILIP C. CHINN
California State University, Los Angeles

Merrill
is an imprint of

Upper Saddle River, New Jersey
Columbus, Ohio

Library of Congress Cataloging-in-Publication Data

Gollnick, Donna M.
  Multicultural education in a pluralistic society / Donna M. Gollnick, Philip C. Chinn.
—8th ed.
    p. cm.
  Includes bibliographical references and index.
  ISBN 978-0-13-613899-0 (alk. paper)
  1. Multicultural education—United States. 2. Social sciences—Study and teaching
(Elementary)—United States. 3. Pluralism (Social sciences)—Study and teaching
(Elementary)—United States. 4. Social Sciences—Study and teaching (Secondary)—United
States. 5. Pluralism (Social sciences,—Study and teaching (Secondary)—United States.
I. Chinn, Philip C., 1937– II. Title.
  LC1099.3.G65 2009
  370.117—dc22

                                                              2007042747

Vice President and Executive Publisher: Jeffery W. Johnston
Executive Editor: Darcy Betts Prybella
Development Editor: Amy J. Nelson
Editorial Assistant: Nancy J. Holstein
Project Manager: Sarah N. Kenoyer
Production Coordinator: Mary Tindle, S4Carlisle Publishing Services
Design Coordinator: Diane C. Lorenzo
Cover Design: Jason Moore
Cover Image: Jupiter Images
Operations Specialist: Susan W. Hannahs
Director of Marketing: Quinn Perkson
Marketing Coordinator: Brian Mounts

This book was set in Garamond by S4Carlisle Publishing Services. It was printed and bound by R. R.
Donnelley & Sons Company. The cover was printed by Phoenix Color Corp.

Photo Credits: David Young-Wolff/PhotoEdit Inc., pp. 1, 41; Stock Connection/Fotosearch.com, LLC,
p. 84; Stewart Cohen/Jupiter Images–Blend Images, p. 122; Scott Cunningham/Merrill, p. 161; Michael
Newman/PhotoEdit Inc., p. 199; Lushpix/Fotosearch.com, LLC, p. 234; Comstock Images/Jupiter
Images–Comstock Images, p. 287; M. Antman/The Image Works, p. 337; Anne Vega/Merrill, p. 375.

Pearson Education Ltd.   Pearson Education Australia Pty. Limited
Pearson Education Singapore Pte. Ltd.   Pearson Education North Asia Ltd.
Pearson Education Canada, Ltd.   Pearson Educación de Mexico, S.A. de C.V.
Pearson Education–Japan   Pearson Education Malaysia Pte. Ltd.

Merrill
is an imprint of

10 9 8 7 6 5 4 3 2
ISBN-13: 978-0-13-613899-0
ISBN-10:   0-13-613899-3

To Dr. Asa Hilliard III (Baffour Amankwatia II) for his leadership and commitment to improving the education of African American children and teaching them to understand, appreciate, and be inspired by their African roots.

To my daughter, Michele M. Clarke, and her four-year-old students who begin school excited about learning and with hope for their futures.
DMG

To Sophie, Elodie, Calvin, Stephanie, Shelby, and Carson, my hope for the next generation to make a difference.
PCC

Preface

Introduction

The eighth edition of *Multicultural Education in a Pluralistic Society* introduces readers to diversity, helps them understand the social and educational issues faced by a diverse nation, and guides them to think critically and reflectively regarding their decisions as a teacher in a classroom.

Diversity in the Twenty-First Century

As we begin the twenty-first century, the United States is a multicultural nation comprised of indigenous peoples, such as the American Indians, Aleuts, Eskimos, and Hawaiians, and those who themselves or whose ancestors arrived as immigrants from other countries. These groups of individuals represent different ethnicities, races, classes, religions, and native languages. In addition, they differ in gender, sexual orientation, age, and physical and mental abilities. They have come from different parts of the world and now live as part of regional cultures within the United States. As we move further into this century, the population will become increasingly more diverse. By 2020, children of color will comprise nearly half of the school-aged population. As the ethnic composition of the United States changes, so will the religious landscape as new immigrants bring their religions from Africa, the Middle East, and Asia. They also bring diverse languages, values, and ideas that are reshaping U.S. society.

The culture and the society of the United States are dynamic. They are in a continuous state of change. Unless teachers are able to understand the role of race, class, and gender in their students' lives, it will be difficult to teach them effectively.

What Impact Does Multicultural Education Have on Teaching?

Education that is multicultural provides an environment that values diversity and portrays it positively. Students' gender, age, race, ethnicity, native language, religion, class, or disability should not limit their educational and vocational options. Educators have the responsibility to help students contribute to and benefit from our democratic society. Effective instructional strategies do not evolve solely from the teacher's culture. They are drawn from the cultures of students and their communities. The integration of multicultural education throughout the curriculum helps students and teachers think critically about institutional racism, classism, sexism, ablism, ageism, and homophobia. Hopefully, educators will help their students develop both individual and group strategies to overcome the debilitating effects of these societal scourges.

About the Eighth Edition

Students in undergraduate, graduate, and in-service courses will find this text helpful in examining social and cultural conditions that influence education. It provides the foundation for understanding diversity and using this knowledge effectively in classrooms and schools. Other social services professionals will find it helpful in understanding the complexity of cultural backgrounds and experiences as they work with families and children.

Cultural Identity

As in previous editions, we approach multicultural education with a broad perspective of the concept. Using culture as the basis for understanding multicultural education, we present descriptions of eight groups that impact the identity of students and teachers: ethnicity and race, class and socioeconomic status, gender and sexual orientation, exceptionality, language, religion, geography (that is, the places we live), and age. These groups are critical in understanding pluralism and multicultural education. Thus, this text examines these groups and the ways in which educators can develop education programs to help all students learn.

Equity in Classrooms

We also emphasize the importance of an equitable education for all students. Educators should not fight against sexism without also fighting racism, classism, homophobia, and discrimination based on abilities, age, religion, and geography. Schools can eradicate discrimination in their own policies and practices if educators are willing to confront and eliminate their own racism, sexism, and other biases. To rid our schools of such practices takes a committed and strong faculty. The eighth edition helps readers develop the habit of self-reflection that will help them become more effective teachers in classrooms that provide equity for all students.

How the Text Is Organized

Multicultural Education in a Pluralistic Society provides an overview of the different cultural groups to which students belong. The first chapter examines the pervasive influence of culture, the importance of understanding our own and our students' cultural backgrounds and experiences, and the evolution of multicultural education. The following eight chapters examine ethnicity and race, class and socioeconomic status, gender and sexual orientation, exceptionality, language, religion, geography, and age. The final chapter contains recommendations for using culturally responsive and social justice pedagogies in the implementation of education that is multicultural. All of the chapters in this edition have been revised and reorganized to reflect current thinking and research in the area. In particular, the first chapter provides the foundational framework that supports our thinking about multicultural education. The final chapter integrates critical pedagogy with research on teaching effectively. Each chapter opens with a scenario to place the topic in an educational setting.

Multiple Perspectives

We have tried to present different perspectives on a number of issues in the most unbiased manner possible. We are not without strong opinions or passion on some of the issues. However, in our effort to be equitable, we do attempt to present different perspectives on the issues and allow the reader to make his or her own decisions. There are some issues related to racism, sexism, handicappism, and so on, that are so important to the well-being of society that we do provide our positions, which we recognize to be our biases.

Attention to Language

Readers should be aware of several caveats related to the language used in this text. Although we realize that the term *American* is commonly used to refer to the U.S. population, we view *American* as including other North and South Americans as well. Therefore, we have tried to limit the use of this term when referring to the United States. Although we have tried to use the terms *black* and *white* sparingly, data about groups often have been categorized by the racial identification, rather than by national origin such as African or European American. In many cases, we were not able to distinguish ethnic identity and have continued to use *black, white,* or *persons of color.* We have limited our use of the term *minority* and have focused more on the power relationships that exist between groups. In previous editions we used the term *Hispanic.* In this edition we have tried to use *Latino,* which appears to be the preferred term for individuals with a Spanish-speaking heritage who have immigrated from countries as diverse as Mexico, Cuba, Argentina, Puerto Rico, Belize, and Colombia.

What Is New in the Eighth Edition?

Chapter on Geography

This important new chapter explores the impact of geography on our cultural identity. It begins with a discussion of the role of immigration in populating this nation, the political control of where immigrants came from, and its impact on education. Regional cultures, the diversity of the population, and education in the South, New England, the Middle Atlantic, Midwest, Great Plains, Southwest, and West are described. The impact of globalization on population groups and its educational implications complete the discussion of geography.

New Topics

Expanded attention to sexual orientation, non-Western religions, and Evangelicals capture issues at the forefront of our constantly changing society.

Experience and Apply

myeducationlab

Your Class. Your Career. Everyone's Future.

"Teacher educators who are developing pedagogies for the analysis of teaching and learning contend that analyzing teaching artifacts has three advantages: it enables new teachers time for reflection while still using the real materials of practice; it provides new teachers with experience thinking about and approaching the complexity of the classroom; and in some cases, it can help new teachers and teacher educators develop a shared understanding and common language about teaching. . . ."[1]

As Linda Darling-Hammond and her colleagues point out, grounding teacher education in real classrooms—among real teachers and students and among actual examples of students' and teachers' work—is an important, and perhaps even an essential, part of training teachers for the complexities of teaching today's students in today's classrooms. For a number of years, we have heard the same message from many of you as we sat in your offices learning about the goals of your courses and the challenges you face in teaching the next generation of educators. Working with a number of our authors and with many of you, we have created a website that provides you and your students with the context of real classrooms and artifacts that research on teacher education tells us is so important. Through authentic in-class video footage, interactive simulations, rich case studies, examples of authentic teacher and student work, and more, **MyEducationLab** offers you and your students a uniquely valuable teacher education tool.

Licensure Test Prep

1. A middle school teacher is trying to interest girls in the field of science. He has ensured that boys and girls work together in groups to conduct the day's experiment. Which of the following is a sign of inequitable participation of the girls and boys that may affect how they feel about science?
   A. All students appear engaged in planning the experiment and observing the results.
   B. Some of the boys are disengaged and a couple of girls are talking among themselves about social issues.
   C. Boys have gathered the equipment for the experiment and are conducting the experiment while the girls record notes about the steps and results.
   D. Girls and boys score about the same on the assessment related to the experiment.

Go to the *Homework and Exercises* section in Chapter 4 of MyEducationLab and select *Licensure Test Prep* to complete this exercise.

MyEducationLab is easy to use! Wherever the MyEducationLab logo appears in the text, you and your students can follow the simple link instructions to access the MyEducation-Lab resource that corresponds with the chapter content. These include:

Video: Authentic classroom videos show how real teachers handle actual classroom situations.

Homework & Exercises: These assignable activities give students opportunities to understand content more deeply and to practice applying content. The following features are located in this section: *Pause to Reflect, Focus your Cultural Lens: Debate, Video Insights, Licensure Test Prep Activities,* and *Observe and Learn: Lessons in Action.*

---

1. Darling-Hammond, l., & Bransford, J., Eds. (2005). *Preparing Teachers for a Changing World.* San Francisco: John Wiley & Sons.

Building Teaching Skills: These assignments help students practice and strengthen skills that are essential to quality teaching. Within each chapter, additional application exercises encourage the reader to walk through and reflect on the teacher's actions illustrated in the *Critical Incidents in Teaching* text feature.

Case Studies: A diverse set of robust cases drawn from some of our best-selling books further expose students to the realities of teaching and offer valuable perspectives on common issues and challenges in education.

Student & Teacher Artifacts: Authentic student and teacher classroom artifacts are tied to course topics and offer practice in working with the actual types of materials encountered every day by teachers.

Individualized Study Plan: Your students have the opportunity to take pre- and post-tests before and after reading each chapter of the text. Their test results automatically generate a personalized study plan, identifying areas of the chapter they must reread to fully understand chapter concepts. They are also presented with interactive multimedia exercises to help ensure learning. The study plan is designed to help your students perform well on exams and to promote deep understanding of chapter content.

Readings: Specially selected, topically relevant articles from ASCD's renowned *Educational Leadership* journal expand and enrich students' perspectives on key issues and topics.

Other Resources:

Lesson & Portfolio Builders: With this effective and easy-to-use tool, you can create, update, and share standards-based lesson plans and portfolios.

News Articles: Looking for current issues in education? Our collection offers quick access to hundreds of relevant articles from the New York Times Educational News Feed.

MyEducationLab is easy to assign, which is essential to providing the greatest benefit to your student.   Visit www.myeducationlab.com for a demonstration of this exciting new online teaching resource.

NEW! Observe and Learn: Lessons in Action

To illustrate chapter content, this new feature directs students to MyEducationLab to see nine multicultural lesson plans come to life in real classrooms across the country through video segments. The feature's questions are also located online for student convenience.

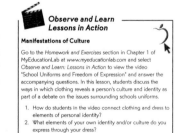

Observe and Learn
Lessons in Action

Manifestations of Culture

Go to the *Homework and Exercises* section in Chapter 1 of MyEducationLab at www.myeducationlab.com and select *Observe and Learn: Lessons in Action* to view the video "School Uniforms and Freedom of Expression" and answer the accompanying questions. In this lesson, students discuss the ways in which clothing reveals a person's culture and identity as part of a debate on the issues surrounding schools uniforms.

1. How do students in the video connect clothing and dress to elements of personal identity?
2. What elements of your own identity and/or culture do you express through your dress?
3. Have you ever felt that one of your students was inappropriately dressed in school? What about one of your colleagues? If so, what—if anything—did you say/do?
4. How might your views regarding dress in school affect what you do in your future classroom?

Critical Incidents in Teaching

- This feature presents both real-life and hypothetical situations that occur in schools or classrooms providing readers with the opportunity to examine their feelings, attitudes, and possible actions or reactions to each scenario. This feature occurs at least once in each chapter.

- Problem-solving exercises located on MyEducationLab help facilitate and sharpen readers' critical thinking skills and their ability to reflect when they need to make informed decisions.

CRITICAL INCIDENTS IN TEACHING

Celebrating Ethnic Holidays

Esther Greenberg is a teacher with Asian and African American students in an alternative education class. Ms. Greenberg's college roommate was Chinese American and she remembers fondly her visit to her roommate's home during the lunar New Year. She remembers how the parents and other Chinese adults had given all the children, including her, money wrapped in red paper, which was to bring all of the recipients good luck in the New Year. Ms. Greenberg thought that it would be a nice gesture to give the students in her class the red paper envelopes as an observance of the upcoming lunar New Year. Since she was unable to give the students money, she took gold-foil covered coins (given to Jewish children) and wrapped these coins in red paper to give to her students.

Unfortunately, on the lunar New Year's Day, all of the African American students were pulled out of class for a full day of testing. All of the remaining students were her Asian students. When she passed out the red envelopes, the students were surprised and touched by her sensitivity to a cherished custom.

When her administrator was told what Ms. Greenberg had done, he became enraged. He accused her of favoritism to the Asian students and of deliberately leaving out the African American students. When she tried to convince him otherwise, he responded that she had no right to impose Asian customs on African American students. She responded that this was an important Asian custom, and that the Asian students had participated in the observance of Martin Luther King's birthday. However, he continued his attack saying that this was Asian superstition bordering on a religious observance. She was threatened with discipline.

Questions for Classroom Discussion

1. Were Esther Greenberg's actions inappropriate for a public school classroom? If so, why? If no, why not? Was this a violation of the principles of church and state?

2. Did Ms. Greenberg create problems for herself by giving out the red envelopes when the African American students were absent from class? Did this create an appearance of favoritism of one racial group over the other?

3. How could Ms. Greenberg have handled the situation to make it a pleasing experience to all concerned?

4. Was the administrator the one who was out of line, and was Ms. Greenberg simply a victim?

Building Teaching Skills

Go to the *Building Teaching Skills* section in Chapter 1 of MyEducationLab at *www.myeducationlab.com* and select *Critical Incidents in Teaching: Celebrating Ethnic Holidays* to complete this exercise.

NEW! Licensure Test Prep

At the end of each chapter are sample test items that are similar in format to those readers will find on licensure tests. They are designed to help readers think about one or more of the issues raised in the chapter.

Licensure Test Prep

1. Which of the following topics is most likely to be included in the traditional Western curriculum that ignores socioeconomic groups that are not advantaged?
    A. Labor movements in the coal mines of Appalachia that pitted workers against owners.
    B. The struggles of Mexican American farmworkers in California and the Southwest.
    C. The conditions that led to the fall of the stock market and the Great Depression in 1929.
    D. Affirmative action which has helped improve the salaries and wages of women over the past 30 years.

Go to the *Homework and Exercises* section in Chapter 3 of MyEducationLab and select *Licensure Test Prep* to complete this exercise.

Explore Your Beliefs

Five New ABC News Video Insights

The **Video Insights: ABC News** DVD (packaged in this text) helps readers explore additional current issues in multicultural education today. Five new videos have been added, for a total of 14. Each video feature in the text provides a synopsis of the video segment, along with thought-provoking questions that challenge readers to consider the real-life experiences presented. Readers are invited to submit their responses online via MyEducationLab. See page xxxi for a complete description of all ABC News videos.

VIDEO INSIGHTS

Smart Kid, Tough School

In recent years, more and more attention has been given to the deteriorating condition of many of the nation's schools. Surely, students who are educated in such surroundings do not receive an education equal to the education given to students who attend schools with greater financial and community resources. Cedric Jennings, a star student from a high school in the poorest section of Washington, DC, saw this confirmed when he enrolled in a summer program for gifted students of color, only to find that the students from higher-income neighborhoods were better prepared academically. Yet, when scholarship offers to attend expensive prep schools came his way, Cedric refused them and returned to his old high school for his senior year. Why do you think Cedric decided to return to Ballou High School?

Imagine you were a teacher at an inner-city school like the high school profiled in the video segment.

1. How would you try to instill a sense of the value of an education in students in a world where being smart is not always valued by their peers?
2. How would your own class background affect your ability to relate to the students?
3. What could you do in your classroom on a day-to-day basis to help eradicate the crippling effects of class differences?

Go to the Video Insights DVD and watch the *Smart Kid, Tough School* video segment. Then, go to the *Homework and Exercises* section in Chapter 3 of MyEducationLab and select *Video Insights: Smart Kid, Tough School* to answer these questions.

FOCUS YOUR CULTURAL LENS: DEBATE

Is Full Inclusion Feasible for All Children with Disabilities?

The Individuals with Disabilities Education Act is a federal law that requires the placement of students with disabilities in the least restrictive environment. This means that these students should be placed in settings in or as close to a general education setting as is feasible for them. What is the least restrictive setting for a child with a disability? Is it feasible to place every child with a disability in a general education setting? Are there realistically adequate resources to do this? Do we have the skill and the will to make it work?

For
- Full inclusion for all children with disabilities is a moral and ethical issue. It is as immoral to segregate a child because of his or her disability as it is to segregate children because of the color of their skin.
- The least restrictive environment that is feasible for every child is a general education classroom. We have the know-how to deliver quality educational services for every child in an inclusive general education classroom.
- The fact that we do not have adequate fiscal resources is not the fault of the child with a disability. If we don't have the resources, then we need to find ways to get them.

Against
- Full inclusion may work for some students with disabilities, but it makes no sense to insist on it for every student regardless of the disability or the degree of impairment.
- Some students with disabilities lack the maturity, the cognitive ability, the social skills, or adequate behaviors to function in general education.
- Until the Federal Government makes good on its commitment to fully fund IDEA, there will never be adequate resources to successfully implement full inclusion for all children with disabilities.
- Even if there were the fiscal resources, there simply are not enough professionally prepared personnel to provide the type of services needed for successful inclusion of every child.

Questions

1. Are there some students who should never be considered for general education placement?
2. If the Federal Government mandates special education for all children, commits itself to funding 40% of the cost, and continues to renege on the full funding, should school districts be forced to fully implement IDEA?
3. Is excluding children with disabilities from being fully included in general education morally and ethically comparable to excluding children because of race?

Go to the *Homework and Exercises* section in Chapter 5 of MyEducationLab and select *Focus Your Cultural Lens* to answer these questions.

Data is from VIDEO: Special Education Inclusion, Wisconsin Education Association Council, undated. Retrieved from www.weac.org/resource/june96/speced.htm

Focus Your Cultural Lens: Debate

Located in every chapter, this feature presents a controversial school issue with *for* and *against* statements for readers to consider. Questions guide readers to critically analyze both sides of the issue and encourage them to take a side by posting their responses via MyEducationLab.

Pause to Reflect

Located several times in each chapter, this feature encourages readers to reflect on how the issue being discussed relates to their everyday life as teachers. It asks readers to complete an activity, collect data, or it poses questions about the topic. Feature questions are linked to MyEducationLab.

Pause to Reflect 1.1

To work effectively with the heterogeneous student populations found in schools, educators need to understand and feel comfortable with their own cultural roots. How would you describe your cultural background?

- From what countries did you or your ancestors come?
- How long has your family lived in the United States?
- How would you describe the experiences your family has had in the United States?

Go to the *Homework and Exercises section in Chapter 1 of MyEducationLab at www.myeducationlab.com* and select *Pause to Reflect 1.1* to answer these questions.

Chapter-Opening Classroom Scenarios

Each chapter opens with a classroom scenario to place the chapter content in an educational setting. Questions at the end of each scenario encourage readers to think about the scenario and guide them to reflect on the decisions they would make.

Chapter 5

EXCEPTIONALITY

No otherwise qualified handicapped individual in the United States . . . shall, solely by reason of his [or her] handicap, be excluded from the participation in, be denied benefits of, or be subjected to discrimination under any program or activity receiving federal financial assistance.

SECTION 504, PL 93-112 (VOCATIONAL REHABILITATION ACT, 1993)

Calvin Behler, a third-grade teacher at the Martin Luther King Elementary School, has been asked to see the principal, Erin Wilkerson, after the students leave. Dr. Wilkerson explains that the school is expanding their **full inclusion** program in which children including those with severe disabilities are fully integrated into general education classrooms. Congruent with school district policy, King Elementary is enhancing its efforts to integrate special education students into general education settings. Behler's classroom is one of four additional general education classrooms, which will have special education placed in the next few weeks. "What this will involve, Cal, is two students with severe disabilities. One is a child with Down's syndrome who has **developmental disabilities** (characterized by severe delays in the acquisition of cognitive, language, motor, and social skills). He has some severe learning problems. The other child has normal intelligence but is nonambulatory, with limited speech and severe cerebral palsy."

"You will be assigned a full-time aide with a special education background. In addition, Bill Gregg, the inclusion specialist, will assist you with instructional plans and strategies. What is important is that you prepare the students in your class and the parents so that a smooth transition can be made when these students come into your class in January, in just two and a half months. I'd like you and Bill to map out a plan of action and give it to me in two weeks."

Reflections

1. What should Behler and Gregg's plan of action include?
2. When students with severe disabilities are integrated into general education classrooms, do they detract from the programming of nondisabled students?
3. Are the students with disabilities potentially a disrupting influence in the classroom?
4. Do general education teachers like Calvin Behler have adequate training and background to accommodate students with disabilities in their classrooms?
5. Should they be integrated, regardless of the degree of disability?

Students with Disabilities and Those Who Are Gifted and Talented

A significant segment of the population in the United States is made up of exceptional individuals. The Centers for Disease Control and Prevention (CDC, 2005) reports that the U.S. Census Bureau indicates that there are over 50 million individuals in the United States with some type of disability. The National Center for Education Statistics (2005) reports a total of approximately 6.3% or 3 million gifted and talented students. When we factor in adults, millions more would be added to the total. Every day, educators come into contact with exceptional children and adults. They may be students in our classes, our professional colleagues, our friends and neighbors, or people we meet in our everyday experiences.

Exceptional people include both individuals with disabilities and gifted individuals. Some, particularly persons with disabilities, have been rejected by society. Because of their unique social and personal needs and interests, many exceptional people become part of a cultural group composed of individuals with similar exceptionalities. For some, this cultural identity is by ascription; they have been labeled and forced into enclaves by virtue of the residential institutions where they live. Others may live in the same communities or even neighborhoods by their own choosing. This chapter will examine the exceptional individual's relationship to society. It will address the struggle for equal rights and the ways the treatment of individuals with disabilities often parallels that of oppressed ethnic minorities.

Supporting Materials

For Students

NEW! MyEducationLab

The eighth edition of this text includes access to MyEducationLab, available at www.myeducationlab. com. See page vii for a full description of MyEducationLab.

Video Insights: ABC News Videos on DVD

Packaged with every copy of this text and connected to the text's ABC News *Video Insights* feature. Readers are able to view the videos as they read the chapter. See page xxxi for a complete video list.

For Instructors

This text has the following ancillary materials to assist instructors in their attempts to maximize learning for all students. The following materials are located on the **Instructor Resource Center** at www.pearsonhighered.com.

- **Instructor's Manual/Media Guide with Test Bank**—provides chapter-by-chapter instructional material. The manual provides concrete suggestions to promote interactive teaching and actively involve students in learning.
- **Computerized Test Bank**—questions give professors electronic access to the test questions printed in the Instructor's Manual. Instructors can manage their courses and gain insight into their students' progress and performance by creating and customizing exams.
- **PowerPoint Slides**—designed as an instructional tool, presentations are provided for each chapter and can be used to present and elaborate on chapter content.
- **Video Insights: ABC News Video DVD**—packaged with this text, offers students a look into the controversial issues that surround education today. See page xxxi for the DVD's table of contents.

Instructor Resource Center

Instructor's one-time registration at the **Instructor Resource Center** opens the door to Pearson's premium digital resources listed above. There are no additional forms to fill out. You will receive one username and password that will allow you to access new titles and/or editions. Contact your Pearson Representative to register today, and maximize your time at every stage of your course preparation.

Acknowledgments

The preparation of any text involves the contributions of many individuals in addition to those whose names are found on the cover.

We wish to thank Maria Gutierrez for assistance once again in researching and manuscript development. We extend a special thanks to Dr. Muzammil H. Siddiqi, Director of the Islamic Society of Orange County, California, who provided suggestions in the development of the overview of Islam and conducted a thorough review of that section for accuracy. We also thank Jeptha Greer for his review of portions of the manuscript and Dr. Frances Kuwahara Chinn for her continuous support and assistance throughout the manuscript development. The assistance, patience, encouragement, and guidance of our editors, Darcy Betts and Amy Nelson, are sincerely appreciated.

We wish to thank the following reviewers, whose recommendations were used to improve this edition: Vincenne Revilla Beltran, Point Park University; Juanita Chang Benioni, Utah Valley State College; Kam Chi Chan, Purdue University North Central; Paul A. Flores, Azusa Pacific University; Emiliano Gonzalez, University of St. Thomas; Theresa Garfield, Palo Alto College; Valerie Hill-Jackson, Texas A&M University; Michael Jennings, University of Texas-San Antonio; Kimberly P. Joyce, University of Richmond; Thomas E. Lehman, Tallahassee Community College; Nyaradzo Mvududu, Seattle Pacific University; and Angela López Pedrana, University of Houston-Downtown.

Brief Contents

Contents

Note: Every effort has been made to provide accurate and current Internet information in this book. However, the Internet and information posted on it are constantly changing, and it is inevitable that some of the Internet addresses listed in this textbook will change.

Special Features

Critical Incidents in Teaching

Video Insights

Observe and Learn: Lessons in Action

Focus Your Cultural Lens: Debate

ABC News

Video Library

The ABC News Video Library titled *Video Insights: ABC News* is packaged on the DVD with this text.

This video library challenges students to explore chapter topics through ABC News segments focusing on multicultural issues. *Video Insights* features within each chapter offer a short summary of each episode and ask students to think about and respond to questions relating to the video and chapter content.

School Busing

In this video segment, you will see proponents of busing in Oklahoma City and in other cities across the country say their children have been subjected to segregated settings within integrated schools. African American children are often assigned to remedial classes or lower academic tracks and do not get exposure to the services and resources that other students receive. In addition, because these schools are not close to home, it is difficult for parents to be involved or even present if there is a problem or an emergency at school.

Chapter 1, Page 32
Running Time: 6:32 minutes

Acting White

This ABC News video segment discusses how some African American students have attributed academic achievement to "acting white." They attack achieving students for excelling in school, speaking Standard English, listening to the "wrong" music, or having white friends. They see the academic high achievers as being traitors or disloyal to their race. By adopting values common to the dominant culture, these students are seen as trying to ignore their own racial history and experiences. As a result, many African American students do not study as hard as European American students and do not choose the more challenging advanced placement courses. Latino students have indicated that they too have experienced this same phenomenon.

Chapter 2, Page 63
Running Time: 14:03 minutes

Smart Kid, Tough School

This ABC News video segment discusses how students who are educated in deteriorating schools do not receive an education equal to the education given to students who attend schools with greater financial and community resources. This segment features Cedric Jennings, a star student from a high school in the poorest section of Washington, DC. Cedric saw this confirmed when he enrolled in a summer program for gifted minority students, only to find that the students from higher-income neighborhoods were better prepared academically. Yet, when scholarship offers to attend expensive prep schools came his way, Cedric refused and returned to his old high school for his senior year.

Chapter 3, Page 111
Running Time: 19:09 minutes

The Secret Life of Boys

In this video segment, you will see that boys have a more difficult time showing emotion and feelings. By the age of 5 it's often difficult to tell if something is bothering a little boy, because he has already learned to mask his feelings. In addition, while boys are conditioned to keep their feelings and emotions inside, girls are supported and expected to share and discuss their feelings with others. Does this difference have an outward effect? Some researchers say yes; this emotional repression leads to boys acting out more in school and being labeled with learning disorders and behavior problems more often than girls. Often, culture determines the appropriate activities in which boys and girls participate.

Chapter 4, Page 124
Running Time: 15:34 minutes

The Fairer Sex?

In this video segment, a man and a woman decide to see for themselves whether men and women are treated differently in otherwise identical situations, such as buying a car, getting clothes dry cleaned, setting a tee time at a golf course, and interviewing for a job. Using hidden cameras, they document that women often suffer from a subtle and insidious kind of discrimination, the kind of discrimination that is difficult to quantify and even more difficult to prove.

Chapter 4, Page 144
Running Time: 17:05 minutes

Jessica Parks Surmounts Her Obstacles

In this video, the accomplishments of a truly remarkable young woman, Jessica Parks, are highlighted. Born without arms, she has accomplished more than many individuals without disabilities, and far more than her parents, physicians, and educators could have imagined. Educators (including special educators) often predetermine in their minds what children with disabilities will or will not be able to accomplish, and limit their access to educational programs. This is often a mistake, which can even lead to lawsuits. In this video, we can see why the courts will almost always side with the student and his or her parents if the schools refuse to allow the student the opportunity to demonstrate the ability to perform in a general education class.

Chapter 5, Page 176
Running Time: 10:41 minutes

Against the Odds: Three Children with Autism

This ABC News video segment introduces us to a family with three children with autism. The family has found a highly specialized treatment program, which has had a profoundly positive impact on these children. However, the program requires tuition of more than $170,000 a year for the three children. The family has exhausted their life savings on tuition. The Individuals with Disabilities Education Act (IDEA) requires schools to provide for the educational needs of children with disabilities. The U.S. Supreme Court has ruled that the schools are required to provide a basic floor of opportunity for children with disabilities, but are not required to provide them with the best possible education. With the private schooling, these three children seem to be thriving. The public schools are reluctant to pay the tuition to the private clinic.

Chapter 5, Page 180
Running Time: 22:29 minutes

American Spoken Here

This ABC News video segment discusses American accents. In this information age where everyone is a phone call, an e-mail, or a flight away from another, it would seem logical that the different accents and dialects around the country might merge into one, but research from the University of Pennsylvania tells a different story. You will see how American accents are becoming more and more distinct from one another.

Chapter 6, Page 207
Running Time: 7:10 minutes

Battle Between Faith and Science

This video shows how a community in Pennsylvania has been split by religious differences and the teaching of evolution and intelligent design. The debate was fueled by the school board adopting a book that indicated evolution was a theory, and creationism a fact. Although God was not mentioned in the book, many Christians agreed with its thesis. A lawsuit against the school board determined what the school system could require.

Chapter 7, Page 250
Running Time: 19:42 minutes

Standing Alone

Although the Supreme Court voted in 1963 to remove prayer from schools, the issue is still not settled. In some areas of the country, where religious diversity is minimal, this ruling is effectively ignored. Other districts have agreed to a "moment of silence" for the purpose of moral reflection. Still others are locked in battle over this issue, like the high school choir in Utah, an area with a large Mormon population, that refused to honor the wishes of Rachel, its single Jewish member, to sing fewer religious songs.

Chapter 7, Page 275
Running Time: 12:53 minutes

Immigration Wars

This video segment reports that President George W. Bush proposed to improve security at the Mexican border by deploying thousands of National Guard troops to assist Border Patrol agents. Some residents along the Mexico and Arizona border can't wait for federal support. They have armed themselves to patrol the border and prevent undocumented persons from crossing. Not all politicians and Southwest residents agree with the President's proposal nor the minutemen who are currently guarding the border.

Chapter 8, Page 350
Running Time: 8:41 minutes

The In Crowd and Social Cruelty

This video segment shows how socially cruel children can be. Popularity and its impact on friendship and peer relationships are explored. The video indicates that bullying takes place on the playground every day. Yet teachers seem to either ignore it or are oblivious to it.

Chapter 9, Page 350
Running Time: 38:00 minutes

Action, Reaction, and Zero Tolerance

This video segment explores practices schools have adopted to prevent school shootings like at Columbine High School in Colorado. School authorities are understandably cautious to the point of establishing zero tolerance rules. However, some of the rules are so stringent that some students are reported and arrested for actions that should not result in arrest, discipline, or punishment.

Chapter 9, Page 358
Running Time: 19:31 minutes

The Reunion

In this video segment, the alumni of a kindergarten class in Shaker Heights, Ohio, meet again at a reunion where they discuss their experiences as the students who voluntarily integrated the elementary school in 1960. They talk about being best friends across races in and out of school when they were young. Relationships changed when they moved to a junior high school with students from formerly segregated schools. At the height of the Civil

Rights Movement, they began to segregate themselves as they developed their identities with their own ethnic groups. The video ends by interviewing Shaker Heights High School students 40 years later who talk about race in their school today.

Chapter 10, Page 390
Running Time: 39:01 minutes

Observe and Learn

Videos

The *Observe and Learn: Lessons in Action* chapter features (Chapters 1, 3, 4, 5, 6, and 7) direct students to the MyEducationLab (www.myeducationlab.com). There, students will view videos that illustrate chapter concepts and bring nine multicultural lesson plans to life in real classrooms across the country. The videos explore all grade levels and all types of multicultural topics.

School Uniforms and Freedom of Expression
High School, Social Studies

In this video clip, a high school Social Studies class brainstorms ways that people visually express identity. The teacher provides students with an assortment of current court cases involving students and dress. Students work in groups to connect their understandings of constitutional law with their own cultural backgrounds and beliefs to come up with rulings on the cases. As you watch the video, notice how the teacher makes consistent reference throughout the lesson to her students and their experiences relating to the issue of dress and expression of identity in school.

Chapter 1, Page 16
Running Time: 13:56 minutes

The 14th Amendment of Our Schools
High School (10th grade), Social Studies

In this video clip, high school Social Studies students read, discuss, and debate two court cases dealing with 14th amendment issues. After reading the cases, students divide into two large groups, one for each case, that take responsibility for understanding the case and presenting the details to the rest of the class. Students learn about issues affecting immigrant groups by relating issues like tuition, taxes, and quality of education to their own contexts. As you watch the video, notice how the teacher breaks down complicated issues into concepts that these sophomore students can both understand and relate to their own lives.

Chapter 1, Page 31
Running Time: 18:32 minutes

The Universal Declaration of Human Rights
High School, Social Studies

In this video clip, a high school Social Studies class, focusing on model United Nations, discusses the Universal Declaration of Human Rights. The class first discusses the nature of human rights, then students break into groups to make posters that report human rights violations around the world. Students make important connections to a variety of issues that often reflect their home cultures and religious beliefs. They also engage in interdisciplinary learning by connecting to a variety of subject areas in this lesson. As you watch the video, notice how students bring their home cultures into the discussions.

Chapter 1, Page 34
Running Time: 13:31 minutes

We Are in the Dumps with Jack and Guy
Elementary

In this video clip, elementary school students begin by brainstorming the word "home" then read a Maurice Sendak picture book about homelessness, poverty, and other sensitive issues. Following the reading, students meet in groups to write and illustrate a nursery rhyme about homelessness that mimics the rhyme structure of the book they just read. As you watch the video, notice how the teacher connects the topic in the story to the lives of the students in his class.

Chapter 3, Page 95
Running Time: 13:26 minutes

Am I Blue?
Middle School (8th grade), English Language Arts

In this video clip, eighth grade English Language Arts students read a short story entitled "Am I Blue?" that deals with issues such as homophobia, gay bashing, and sexual identity. Students discuss the events in the book while unpacking the meaning of terms like "gay" and "homophobic" and comments such as "that's so gay." As you watch the video, notice how the teacher incorporates students' experiences and current events into the discussion in order to connect the story to the students' lives.

Chapter 4, Page 136
Running Time: 21:11 minutes

Rosalind Franklin: The Other Discoverer of DNA
Middle School (6th grade), Gifted and Talented Physical Science

In this video clip, a class of sixth grade students learns about scientist Rosalind Franklin, who was not originally credited for her important contributions to the discovery of DNA. As students are told about Dr. Franklin's work, they assume that the teacher is talking about a male scientist. When it is revealed that Dr. Watson was a woman, students are surprised and then discuss their reactions.

As you watch the video, notice how the teacher sets up the discussion so that students make their own assumptions about the gender of Rosalind Franklin. Notice also how the teacher leads the subsequent discussion about the lack of credit that Dr. Franklin received in her lifetime.

Chapter 4, Page 141
Running Time: 19:59 minutes

FDR's Secret
Elementary

In this video clip, elementary school students brainstorm reasons someone might hide a disability, then explore the life and presidency of Franklin Delano Roosevelt, focusing on the question: "Was FDR successful at hiding his disability?" The teacher attends to students with different learning styles by providing photographs and historical cartoons of FDR and then asks small groups to come to their own answer to the question. As you watch the video, notice how the teacher connects a general discussion of disabilities to a specific case such as FDR's as a means of providing students with the opportunity to discuss this issue.

Chapter 5, Page 175
Running Time: 11:15 minutes

Talking with Your Body
Elementary (2nd grade)

In this video clip, a class of second grade students discusses non-verbal communication (gestures and facial expressions) and explores its meanings across cultures. Students are asked to predict if particular gestures are rude or not and then create their own greeting gestures. As you watch the video, notice how the teacher handles students' responses to the gesture assignment, especially one student who unwittingly demonstrates a rude gesture for the class.

Chapter 6, Page 215
Running Time: 13:32 minutes

Geometry and Tessellation in Islamic Art
Middle School, Computers

In this video clip, middle school students view examples of architectural sites in India as the teacher points out instances of geometric patterns and tessellations in the images. The teacher explains how these shapes carry important religious significance in Islamic art. After a computer demonstration, students are allowed to create their own computer images using a drawing program. As you watch the video, notice how the teacher expands the lesson and connects to the real-world by encouraging students to explore beyond the classroom.

Chapter 7, Page 257
Running Time: 14:22 minutes

Chapter 1

FOUNDATIONS OF
MULTICULTURAL
EDUCATION

Equality is the heart and essence of democracy, freedom, and justice.

A. PHILIP RANDOLPH, Civil Rights Leader, 1942

You are just beginning your first teaching position in a nearby urban area. Like many new teachers in an urban area, you were offered the job only a few weeks before school started. You had never been to that part of the city but were sure you could make a difference in the lives of students there. You quickly learn that many students have single parents, many of whom work two jobs to make ends meet. Almost all of the students are eligible for free lunch. The families of some students do not speak English at home, but the principal says the students speak English. You are disappointed in the condition of the school, and your classroom in particular, but have been assured it will be re-painted during one of the vacation periods.

When students arrive on the first day, you are not surprised that a large proportion of them are from families who immigrated from Central America during the past two decades. The population includes some African American students and a few European American students. You did not realize that the class would include a student who had just moved from Bulgaria and spoke no English and that the native language of two students was Farsi. You have taken a few Spanish courses but know little or nothing about the language or cultures of Bulgaria and Iran. You wonder about the boy with the black eye but guess that he has been in a fight recently.

Reflections

1. What assumptions about these students and their academic potential did you make as you read this brief description?
2. How has your own cultural background prepared you to teach this diverse group of students?
3. What might you want to learn about students' cultures to assist them in learning?
4. What kind of challenges are you likely to confront during this year?
5. What do you wish you had learned in college to help you be a better teacher in this school?
6. Where should you go for assistance in working with students whose native language is not English?
7. Are you glad that you accepted this teaching assignment? Why or why not?

Diversity in the Classroom

Educators today are faced with an overwhelming challenge to prepare students from diverse populations and backgrounds to live in a rapidly changing society and a world in which some groups have greater societal benefits than others because of race, ethnicity, gender, class, language, religion, ability, geography, or age. Schools of the future will become increasingly diverse. Demographic data on birthrates and **immigration** indicate that the number of Asian American, Latino, and African American children is increasing. More than four of 10 students in P–12 schools today are students of color (U.S. Department of Education, 2006). By 2020, they are projected to be nearly half of the elementary and secondary population. However, the race and sex of their teachers match neither the student population nor the general population; 84% of the teachers are European American and 75% are female (U.S. Census Bureau, 2006).

Latinos, Asian Americans, American Indians, and African Americans already comprise more than half of the student population in Arizona, California, the District of Columbia, Hawaii, Louisiana, Mississippi, New Mexico, and Texas (Snyder, Tan, & Hoffman, 2006). European Americans make up less than one fourth of the student population in many of the nation's largest school districts (Dalton, Sable, & Hoffman, 2006). Although the U.S. Census Bureau (2006) reports that only 17% of U.S. children live below the official poverty level, 41% of the fourth graders are eligible for free or reduced-price lunch programs in the nation's schools (U.S. Department of Education, 2006). African American and Latino students are more likely than other students to be concentrated in high poverty schools (U.S. Department of Education, 2006). The number of students with disabilities who are being served by special programs has increased from 4.3 million in 1987 to 6.7 million or nearly 14% of the school population in 2005 (U.S. Department of Education, 2006).

See Chapter 2 for more information about students from diverse ethnic groups and Chapter 3 for details on students from low-income families.

It is not only ethnic and racial diversity that is challenging schools. During the past 35 years, new waves of immigrants have come from parts of the world unfamiliar to many Americans. With them have come their religions, which seem even stranger to many Americans than the new immigrants. While small groups of Muslims, Hindus, Buddhists, and Sikhs have been in the country for many decades, only recently have they and their religions become highly visible. Even Christians from Russia, Hong Kong, Taiwan, Korea, and the Philippines bring their own brand of worship to denominations that have strong roots in this country. The United States has not only become a multicultural nation, it has also become a multireligious society. In earlier years, most religious minority groups maintained a low and almost invisible profile. As the groups have become larger, they have become more visible, along with their houses of worship (Eck, 2000).

For more information on the religions that students bring to schools, see Chapter 7.

These religious differences raise a number of challenges for educators. The holidays to be celebrated must be considered, along with religious codes related to the **curriculum,** appropriate interactions of boys and girls, dress in physical education classes, and discipline. Immigrant parents value the importance of education for their children, but they do not always agree with the school's approaches to teaching and learning, nor accept the public school's secular **values** as appropriate for their family. Values are the qualities that parents find desirable and important in the education of their children, and include areas such as morality, hard work, and caring, often with religious overtones. Working collaboratively with parents and communities will become even more critical in providing education equitably to all students.

Pause to Reflect 1.1

To work effectively with the heterogeneous student populations found in schools, educators need to understand and feel comfortable with their own cultural roots. How would you describe your cultural background?

- From what countries did you or your ancestors come?
- How long has your family lived in the United States?
- How would you describe the experiences your family has had in the United States?

Go to the *Homework and Exercises* section in Chapter 1 of MyEducationLab at *www.myeducationlab.com* and select *Pause to Reflect 1.1* to answer these questions.

Educators also must understand the cultural setting in which the school is located to develop effective instructional strategies. They must help their students become aware of cultural differences and inequalities in the nation and in the world. One goal is to help students affirm cultural differences while realizing that individuals across **cultures** have many similarities.

Teachers will find that students have individual differences, even though they may appear to be from the same cultural group. These differences extend far beyond intellectual and physical abilities. Students bring to class different historical backgrounds, religious beliefs, and day-to-day experiences that guide the way they behave in school. The cultures of some students will be mirrored in the school culture. For others, the differences between home and school cultures will cause dissonance unless the teacher can integrate the cultures of the students into the curriculum and develop a supportive environment for learning. If the teacher fails to understand the cultural factors in addition to the intellectual and physical factors that affect student learning and behavior, it will be difficult to help students learn.

Multicultural education is an educational strategy in which students' cultures are used to develop effective classroom instruction and school environments. It supports and extends the concepts of culture, diversity, equality, social justice, and democracy into the school setting. An examination of the theoretical precepts and practical applications of these concepts will lead to an understanding of the development and practice of multicultural education.

Multicultural Education

Not all students can be taught in the same way because they are not the same. Their cultures and experiences influence the way they learn and interact with their teachers and peers. They have different needs, skills, and experiences that must be recognized in developing educational programs. Each student is different because of physical and mental abilities, gender, ethnicity, race, language, religion, class, sexual orientation, geography, and age. Students behave differently in school and toward authority because of cultural factors and their relationship to the dominant society. As educators, we behave in certain ways toward students because of our own cultural experiences within the power structure of the country. Multicultural education is a concept that incorporates the diversity of students and equality in education. **Equality** ensures that students are provided the same access to the benefits of society regardless of their group memberships.

When educators are given the responsibilities of a classroom, they need the knowledge and skills for working effectively in a diverse society. The following fundamental beliefs and assumptions support multicultural education, a strategy for accomplishing this goal:

- Cultural differences have strength and value.
- Schools should be models for the expression of human rights and respect for cultural and group differences.
- **Social justice** and equality for all people should be of paramount importance in the design and delivery of curricula.
- Attitudes and values necessary for the continuation of a democratic society can be promoted in schools.
- Schooling can provide the knowledge, skills, and **dispositions** (i.e., values, attitudes, and commitments) to help students from diverse groups learn.
- Educators working with families and communities can create an environment that is supportive of multiculturalism.

Many concepts support multicultural education. The relationships and interactions among individuals and groups are essential to understanding and working effectively with students from groups different than the teachers. Educators should understand **racism, sexism,** prejudice, discrimination, oppression, powerlessness, power, inequality, equality, and stereotyping. Multicultural education includes various components that often manifest themselves in courses, units of courses, and degree programs. They include ethnic studies, global studies, bilingual education, women's studies, human relations, special education, and urban education. Let's examine how multicultural education evolved over the past century.

Evolution of Multicultural Education

Multicultural education is not a new concept. Its roots are in the establishment of the Association for the Study of Negro Life and History. Through their research and books on the history and culture of African Americans, Carter G. Woodson, W. E. B. DuBois, Charles C. Wesley, and other scholars were the pioneers of ethnic studies. Woodson founded the *Journal of Negro History* and the *Negro History Bulletin* to disseminate research and curriculum materials. These materials were integrated into the curricula of segregated schools and the historically black colleges and universities, allowing these students to be empowered by the knowledge of their own history (J. A. Banks, 2004).

By the 1920s some educators were writing about and training teachers in intercultural education. The intercultural movement during its first two decades had an international emphasis with antecedents in the pacifist movement. Some textbooks were rewritten with an international point of view. Proponents encouraged teachers to make their disciplines more relevant to the modern world by being more issue oriented. One of the goals was to make the dominant population more tolerant and accepting toward first- and second-generation immigrants in order to maintain national unity and social control (C. A. M. Banks, 2004). However, issues of power and inequality in society were ignored. The interculturalists supported understanding and appreciation of diverse groups, but did not promote collective ethnic identities that were the focus of ethnic studies.

Following the Holocaust and World War II, tensions among groups remained high. Jewish organizations such as the Anti-Defamation League and the American Jewish Committee provided leadership for improving intergroup relations and reducing the anti-Semitic sentiment that existed at the time. National education organizations and progressive educational leaders such as Hilda Taba and Lloyd A. Cook promoted intergroup relations in schools to develop tolerance for new immigrants, African Americans, and other groups of color. Like the earlier intercultural movement, many intergroup educators had adopted the goal of assimilating immigrants and people of color into dominant society (J. A. Banks, 2004). Some programs focused on understanding the "folk" culture of these groups. Others were directed at native-born European Americans and their prejudice and discrimination against other groups. There was disagreement among the supporters of intergroup relations about the degree that they should promote an understanding of the culture and history of ethnic groups (C. A. M. Banks, 2004). Historian David Tyack (2003) found this movement to be one in which "oppression became reduced to stereotyping and separate ethnic identity was to be dissolved as painlessly as possible" (p. 81).

By the 1960s desegregation was being enforced in the nation's schools. At the same time, cultural differences were being described as deficits. Students of color and whites from low-income families were described as culturally deprived. Their families were blamed for not providing them with the **cultural capital** or advantages such as wealth and education that would help them succeed in schools. Programs like Head Start, **compensatory education**, and special education were developed to make up for these shortcomings. Not surprisingly, those classes were filled with students of color, in poverty, or with disabilities—the children and youth who had not been privileged in society and whose own cultures seldom found their way into textbooks and the school's curriculum.

In the 1970s oppressed groups were described as culturally different to acknowledge that they had a culture but that it was different from the culture of the **dominant group.** The goal of this approach was to teach the culturally different to develop the cultural patterns of the dominant society so that they could fit into the mainstream (Sleeter & Grant, 2006). Students with disabilities were still primarily segregated from their able-bodied peers.

The civil rights movement of the 1960s and 1970s brought a renewed interest in ethnic studies, discrimination, and intergroup relations. Racial and ethnic pride emerged from oppressed groups, creating a demand for African American and other ethnic studies programs in colleges and universities across the country. Similar programs were sometimes established in secondary schools. However, students and participants in ethnic studies programs were primarily members of the group being studied. Programs focused on their own ethnic histories and cultures with the objective of providing students with insights to and instilling pride in their own ethnic backgrounds. Most of these programs were ethnic-specific, and only one ethnic group was studied. Sometimes the objectives included an understanding of the relationship and conflict between the ethnic group and the dominant population, but seldom was a program's scope multiethnic.

Concurrent with the civil rights movement and the growth of ethnic studies, emphasis on intergroup or human relations again emerged. Often, these programs accompanied ethnic studies content for teachers. The objectives again were to promote intergroup, and especially interracial, understanding to reduce or eliminate stereotypes. This approach emphasized the affective level—teachers' attitudes and feelings about themselves and others (Sleeter & Grant, 2006).

With the growth and development of ethnic studies came a realization that those programs alone would not guarantee support for the positive affirmation of diversity and differences in this country. Students from the dominant culture also needed to learn the history, culture, and contributions of other groups. Thus, ethnic studies expanded into multiethnic studies. Teachers were encouraged to develop curricula that included the contributions of oppressed groups along with those of the dominant group. Textbooks were rewritten to represent more accurately the multiethnic nature of the United States and world. Students were to be exposed to perspectives of diverse groups through literature, history, music, and other disciplines integrated throughout the general school program. Curriculum and instructional materials were to reflect multiple perspectives, not just the single master narrative of the dominant group.

During this period, other groups that had suffered from institutional discrimination called their needs to the attention of the public. These groups included women, persons with low incomes, persons with disabilities, English language learners (ELL), and the elderly. Educators responded by expanding multiethnic education to the more encompassing concept of multicultural education. This broader concept focused on the different groups to which individuals belong, with an emphasis on the interaction of race, ethnicity, class, and gender in their cultural identities. It also called for the elimination of discrimination based on group membership. No longer was it fashionable to fight sexism without simultaneously attacking racism, classism, homophobia, and discrimination against all children, the elderly, and persons with disabilities.

CRITICAL INCIDENTS IN TEACHING _____

Celebrating Ethnic Holidays

Esther Greenberg is a teacher with Asian and African American students in an alternative education class. Ms. Greenberg's college roommate was Chinese American and she remembers fondly her visit to her roommate's home during the lunar New Year. She remembers how the parents and other Chinese adults had given all the children, including her, money wrapped in red paper, which was to bring all of the recipients good luck in the New Year. Ms. Greenberg thought that it would be a nice gesture to give the students in her class the red paper envelopes as an observance of the upcoming lunar New Year. Since she was unable to give the students money, she took gold-foil covered coins (given to Jewish children) and wrapped these coins in red paper to give to her students.

Unfortunately, on the lunar New Year's Day, all of the African American students were pulled out of class for a full day of testing. All of the remaining students were her Asian students. When she passed out the red envelopes, the students were surprised and touched by her sensitivity to a cherished custom.

When her administrator was told what Ms. Greenberg had done, he became enraged. He accused her of favoritism to the Asian students and of deliberately leaving out the African American students. When she tried to convince him otherwise, he responded that she had no right to impose Asian customs on African American students. She responded that this was an important Asian custom, and that the Asian students had participated in the observance of Martin Luther King's birthday. However, he continued his attack saying that this was Asian superstition bordering on a religious observance. She was threatened with discipline.

Questions for Classroom Discussion

1. Were Esther Greenberg's actions inappropriate for a public school classroom? If so, why? If no, why not? Was this a violation of the principles of church and state?
2. Did Ms. Greenberg create problems for herself by giving out the red envelopes when the African American students were absent from class? Did this create an appearance of favoritism of one racial group over the other?
3. How could Ms. Greenberg have handled the situation to make it a pleasing experience to all concerned?
4. Was the administrator the one who was out of line, and was Ms. Greenberg simply a victim?

Building Teaching Skills

Go to the *Building Teaching Skills* section in Chapter 1 of MyEducationLab at *www.myeducationlab.com* and select *Critical Incidents in Teaching: Celebrating Ethnic Holidays* to complete this exercise.

Multicultural Education Today

The 1990s were characterized by the development of standards, which led to debates between fundamentalists and multiculturalists. The fundamentalists argued that history standards should stress what they believed are the foundations of democracy—patriotism and historical heroes. The multiculturalists promoted the inclusion of diverse groups and multiple perspectives in the standards. The U.S. Senate was drawn into the history standards fray in 1995, voting 99 to 1 to abort the history standards developed by a widely respected group of historians who had promoted the inclusion of diverse groups (Symcox, 2002). In English language arts, groups disagreed about the literature to which students should be exposed, some arguing for multiple perspectives and others arguing that such literature might promote values they could not support.

Multicultural education is sometimes criticized as focusing on differences rather than similarities among groups. On the other side it is criticized for not adequately addressing issues of power and oppression that keep a number of groups from participating equitably in society. At least three schools of thought push multiculturalists to think critically about these issues: critical pedagogy, antiracist education, and critical race theory (Sleeter & Bernal, 2004). Critical pedagogy focuses on the culture of everyday life and the interaction of class, race, and gender in contemporary power struggles. Antiracist education is the strategy supported in Canada and a number of European countries to eliminate racist practices such as tracking, inequitable funding, and segregation in schools. Critical race theory also focuses on racism in challenging racial oppression, racial inequities, and white privilege (Ladson-Billings, 2004). Multicultural education as presented in this text attempts to incorporate critical pedagogy, antiracist education, and critical race theory as different groups are discussed. Multicultural education includes **critical thinking** about these and other issues to ensure that education serves the needs of all groups equitably.

Still, after eight decades of concern for civil and human rights in education, racism persists. Educators struggle with the integration of diversity into the curriculum and provision of equality in schools. Some classrooms may be desegregated and mainstreamed, and both boys and girls may now participate in athletic activities. However, students are still labeled

Although the Supreme Court ruled that schools should be desegregated in 1954, students in many classrooms today are from the same racial, ethnic, or language group.

© Patrick White/Merrill

as at risk, developmentally delayed, underprivileged, lazy, and slow (Tyack, 2003). They are tracked in special classes or groups within the classroom based on their real and perceived abilities. A disproportionate number of students who are African American, Mexican American, Puerto Rican, American Indian, and some Asian/Pacific American groups score below European American students on national standardized tests. The number of students of color, low-income students, and girls participating in advanced science and mathematics classes is not proportionate to their representation in schools. They too often are offered little or no encouragement to enroll in advanced courses that are necessary to be successful in college.

Some reformers are calling a good education a fundamental civil right (Spring, 2001; Tyack, 2003). In a country that champions equal rights and the opportunity for an individual to improve his or her conditions, educators are challenged to help all students achieve academically. At the beginning of the twenty-first century, the standards movement focused on identifying what every student should know and be able to do. The federal legislation for elementary and secondary schools, *No Child Left Behind* (NCLB), requires standardized testing of students to determine how effective a school is in helping students learn. It mandates that test scores be reported to the public by "race, gender, English language proficiency, disability, and socio-economic status" (U.S. Department of Education, 2001, p. 10). The goal of NCLB is to improve the academic achievement of all students. Students in low-performing schools may transfer to a higher-performing school to improve their chances of passing tests if their school is low-performing for three years.

A large number of students who are not European American or are from low-income families are not meeting proficiency standards in the current high-stakes testing environment. Only 42% of African American, 46% of Latino, and 48% of American Indian fourth graders scored at the basic level or higher on the reading test of the National Assessment of Educational Progress (NAEP) in 2005 as compared to 76% of the white fourth graders (NAEP, 2007). Forty-six percent of low-income students scored at the basic level or higher as compared to 77% of students from families with higher incomes. The pattern is similar on the eighth-grade mathematics test as shown in Figure 1.1.

Multicultural Proficiencies for Teachers

States and school districts expect teachers to have **proficiencies** or the specific knowledge, skills, and dispositions related to multicultural education by the time they finish a teacher education program. With *No Child Left Behind*, they are obligated to hire teachers who can help low-income students, students of color, English language learners, and students with disabilities meet state standards.

State standards for teacher licensure reflect the national standards in Table 1.1, which were developed by the Interstate New Teacher Assessment and Support Consortium (INTASC). Each of the 10 INTASC standards is further explicated by statements of the knowledge, dispositions, and performances that new teachers should be able to demonstrate for a state license to teach. Many of these multicultural proficiencies are discussed in this text; others will be addressed in other teacher education courses. For example, the INTASC standards (1992) that address multicultural proficiencies state that new teachers should:

- Know about areas of exceptionality in learning—including learning disabilities, visual and perceptual difficulties, and special physical or mental challenges. (Standard 3)
- Know about the process of second language acquisition and about strategies to support the learning of students whose first language is not English. (Standard 3)

FIGURE 1.1   NAEP 8th Grade Mathematics 2005 by Race and Ethnicity.

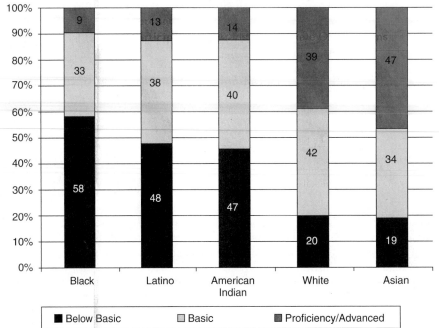

Data from the National Assessment of Educational Progress. (2007). Washington, DC: National Center for Education Statistics, U.S. Department of Education. Retrieved on May 20, 2007, from www.nces.ed.gov/nationsreportcard/nde/viewresults.asp

- Understand how students' learning is influenced by individual experiences, talents, and prior learning, as well as language, culture, family, and community values. (Standard 3)
- Have a well-grounded framework for understanding cultural and community diversity and know how to learn about and incorporate students' experiences, cultures, and community resources into instruction. (Standard 3)
- Understand how cultural and gender differences can affect communication in the classroom. (Standard 6)
- Understand how factors in the students' environment outside of school (e.g., family circumstances, community environments, health and economic conditions) may influence students' life and learning. (Standard 10)

In working with students who come from different ethnic, racial, language, and religious groups than the teacher, the development of dispositions that are supportive of diversity and differences is important. Students quickly become aware of the educators who respect their cultures, believe they can learn, and value differences in the classroom. Examples of dispositions that the INTASC standards (1992) expect teachers to have developed include:

- Appreciating multiple perspectives and conveying to learners how knowledge is developed from the vantage point of the knower. (Standard 1)
- Believing that all children can learn at high levels and persisting in helping all children achieve success. (Standard 3)
- Being sensitive to community and cultural norms. (Standard 3)
- Making students feel valued for their potential as people, and helping them learn to value each other. (Standard 3)

TABLE 1.1   INTASC* Standards for New Teachers

1. The teacher understands the central concepts, tools of inquiry, and structures of the discipline(s) he or she teaches and can create learning experiences that make these aspects of subject matter meaningful for students.
2. The teacher understands how children learn and develop, and can provide learning opportunities that support their intellectual, social, and personal development.
3. The teacher understands how students differ in their approaches to learning and creates instructional opportunities that are adapted to diverse learners.
4. The teacher understands and uses a variety of instructional strategies to encourage students' development of critical thinking, problem solving, and performance skills.
5. The teacher uses an understanding of individual and group motivation and behavior to create a learning environment that encourages positive social interaction, active engagement in learning, and self-motivation.
6. The teacher uses knowledge of effective verbal, nonverbal, and media communication techniques to foster active inquiry, collaboration, and supportive interaction in the classroom.
7. The teacher plans instruction based upon knowledge of subject matter, students, the community, and curriculum goals.
8. The teacher understands and uses formal and informal assessment strategies to evaluate and ensure the continuous intellectual, social, and physical development of the learner.
9. The teacher is a reflective practitioner who continually evaluates the effects of his/her choices and actions on others (students, parents, and other professionals in the learning community) and who actively seeks out opportunities to grow professionally.
10. The teacher fosters relationships with school colleagues, parents, and agencies in the larger community to support students' learning and well-being.

Reprinted with permission from Council of Chief State School Officers. (1992). Model standards for beginning teacher licensing, assessment, and development: A resource for state dialogue. Washington, DC. http://www.ccsso.org/content/pdfs/corestrd.pdf

- Understanding how participation supports commitment, and being committed to the expression and use of democratic values in the classroom. (Standard 5)
- Appreciating the cultural dimensions of communication, responding appropriately, and seeking to foster culturally sensitive communication by and among all students in the class. (Standard 6)
- Being committed to using assessment to identify student strengths and promoting student growth rather than denying students access to learning opportunities. (Standard 8)

As a new teacher, you should be able to demonstrate in your teaching the knowledge and dispositional proficiencies outlined above. The portfolio activities at the end of each chapter will provide opportunities for you to begin to collect artifacts related to your proficiency for working with a diverse student population and delivering education that is multicultural. The portfolio activities at the end of each chapter indicate the INTASC standard for which the activity may provide evidence. These artifacts could become part of the portfolio that you are developing in your teacher education program. They may be a valuable part of the portfolio that you present to a future employer, showing that you have developed the knowledge, skills, and dispositions appropriate for working effectively with a diverse student population. Finally, you may be able to further develop and refine these portfolio entries for national certification later in your teaching career.

Most state licensure tests include questions related to multicultural education in a combination of short-answer and multiple-choice questions. The Praxis II series of tests by the Educational Testing Service (ETS) include a test of your knowledge of (1) the subject that

Pause to Reflect 1.2

As you progress through your teacher education program, you will be expected to work with students from diverse groups in field experiences, student teaching, and/or your own classroom. How close are you to meeting the following INTASC proficiencies related to multicultural education?

Proficiency	Already Met	Partially Met	Not Met
• Know about areas of exceptionality in learning—including learning disabilities, visual and perceptual difficulties, and special physical or mental challenges.	☐	☐	☐
• Know about the process of second language acquisition and strategies to support the learning.	☐	☐	☐
• Understand how students' learning is influenced by language, culture, family, and community values.	☐	☐	☐
• Know how to learn about and incorporate students' experiences, cultures, and community resources into instruction.	☐	☐	☐
• Understand how cultural and gender differences can affect communication in the classroom.			
• Appreciate multiple perspectives.			
• Believe that all children can learn at high levels.	☐	☐	☐
• Be sensitive to community and cultural norms.	☐	☐	☐

Go to the *Homework and Exercises* section in Chapter 1 of MyEducationLab at *www.myeducationlab.com* and select *Pause to Reflect 1.2* to answer these questions.

you plan to teach and (2) learning and teaching. The second test addresses four categories: students as learners, instruction and assessment, communication techniques, and teacher professionalism. Each of these four categories includes content related to multicultural education. Some states have developed their own licensure tests with National Evaluation Systems (NES) or another testing company, but they address similar categories related to professional and pedagogical knowledge. At the end of each chapter you will have the opportunity to practice a test item that is similar to one that you may find on the licensure test that you will be required to pass before you can teach.

Reflecting on Multicultural Teaching

Throughout these chapters you will have the opportunity to pause and reflect on issues related to diversity and multicultural education. You may want to respond to the questions in your journal or on the book's Homework and Exercises section of MyEducationLab at www.myeducationlab.com. Teachers who reflect on and analyze their own practice report that their teaching improves over time (National Board for Professional Teaching Standards, 2001). You are encouraged to begin to develop the habit of reflecting on your practice now and to include in that reflection the multicultural proficiencies mentioned above.

From the first day of student teaching, you should begin to reflect on your effectiveness as a teacher. Are you actually helping students learn the subject and skills you are teaching? An important part of teaching is to ask what is working and what is not. Good teachers are able to change their teaching strategies when students are not learning. They do not leave any student behind, drawing on the experiences and cultures of their students to make the subject matter relevant to them. Self-reflection will be a critical skill for improving your teaching.

You can begin to develop skills for reflection while you are preparing to teach. Many teacher education programs require teacher candidates to keep journals and develop portfolios that include reflection papers. Videotaping lessons that you teach will allow you to critique your knowledge of the subject matter, interactions with students, and managing a class. The critique could be expanded to look for multicultural proficiencies. You may find it valuable to ask a colleague to periodically observe you while you are teaching and provide feedback on your multicultural proficiencies. Honest feedback can lead to positive adjustments in our behavior and attitudes.

Multicultural education requires an understanding of five basic concepts that support it: culture, cultural identity, pluralism, equality, and social justice. These foundational areas are discussed in the remaining sections of this chapter.

Culture

Until early in the twentieth century, the term culture was used to indicate the refined ways of the elite and powerful. People who were knowledgeable in history, literature, and the fine arts were said to possess culture. No longer is culture viewed so narrowly. It helps define who we are. It influences our knowledge, beliefs, and values. It provides the blueprint that determines the way we think, feel, and behave. What appears as the natural and only way to learn and to interact with others is determined by our culture. Generally accepted and patterned ways of behavior are necessary for a group of people to live together. Culture imposes order and meaning on our experiences. It allows us to predict how others will behave in certain situations.

Culturally determined norms guide our language, behavior, emotions, and thinking; they are the do's and don'ts of appropriate behavior within our culture. Although we are comfortable with others who share the same culture because we know the meaning of their words and actions, we often misunderstand the cultural cues of persons from different cultures. Culture is so much a part of us that we do not realize that not everyone shares our way of thinking and behaving. This could be, in part, because we may never have been in cultural settings different from our own. This lack of knowledge often leads to our responding to differences as personal affronts, rather than simply cultural differences. These misunderstandings may appear insignificant to an observer, but they can be important to participants. Examples include how loud is too loud, how late one may arrive at an event, and how close one can stand to another without being rude or disrespectful.

Pause to Reflect 1.3

It is normal for people to experience some cultural discontinuity when they visit another country or a new city or a neighborhood in which the inhabitants are ethnically different from themselves.

- In what settings have you found that you did not know the cultural norms and were at a loss as to how to fit in?
- How often have you been in such settings?
- Why did you feel uncomfortable?
- How were you able to overcome your awkwardness?
- How could you become more comfortable in cultural settings different than your own?

Go to the *Homework and Exercises* section in Chapter 1 of MyEducationLab at *www.myeducationlab.com* and select *Pause to Reflect 1.3* to answer these questions.

Characteristics of Culture

We all have culture, but how did we get it? One of the characteristics of culture is that it is learned. We were born into the culture of our parents or caretakers. The way a baby is held, fed, bathed, dressed, and talked to is culturally determined and begins the process of learning the family's culture. The process continues throughout life as we interact with members of our own and other cultures.

Two similar processes interact as one learns how to act in society: **enculturation** and **socialization.** Enculturation is the process of acquiring the characteristics of a given culture and becoming competent in its language and ways of behaving and knowing. Socialization is the general process of learning the social norms of the culture. Through this process, we internalize social and cultural rules. We learn what is expected in social roles, such as mother, husband, student, and child, and in occupational roles such as teacher, banker, plumber, custodian, and politician.

Enculturation and socialization are processes initiated at birth by parents, siblings, nurses, physicians, teachers, and neighbors. These varied instructors may not identify these processes as enculturation or socialization, but they demonstrate and reward children for acceptable behaviors. We learn how to behave by observing and participating in society and culture, learning the patterns of the cultures in which we are raised.

Because culture is so internalized, we tend to confuse biological and cultural heritage. Our cultural heritage identity is not innately based on the culture in which we are born. For example, Vietnamese infants adopted by Italian American, Catholic, middle-class parents will share a cultural heritage with middle-class Italian American Catholics, rather than with Vietnamese. Observers, however, will continue to identify these individuals as Vietnamese Americans, because of their physical characteristics and a lack of knowledge about their cultural experiences.

A second characteristic of culture is that it is shared. Shared cultural patterns and customs bind people together as an identifiable group and make it possible for them to live together and function with ease. An individual in the shared culture is provided with the context for identifying with the group that shares that culture. Although there may be some disagreement about certain aspects of the culture, there is a common acceptance and agreement about most aspects. Actually, most points of agreement are outside our realm of awareness. For example, we do not usually realize that the way we communicate with each other and the way we raise children are part of culture.

Third, culture is an adaptation. Cultures accommodate environmental conditions and available natural and technological resources. Thus, Eskimos who live with extreme cold, snow, ice, seals, and the sea develop a culture different from that of Pacific Islanders, who have limited land, unlimited seas, and few mineral resources. The culture of urban residents differs from that of rural residents, in part, because of the resources available in the different settings. The culture of oppressed groups differs from that of the dominant group because of power relationships within society.

Finally, culture is a dynamic system that changes continuously. Some cultures undergo constant and rapid change; others are very slow to change. Some changes, such as a new word or new hairstyle, may be relatively small and have little impact on the culture as a whole. Other changes have a dramatic impact. For instance, the introduction of technology into a culture has often produced changes far broader than the technology itself. Such changes may also alter traditional customs and beliefs. For example, the use of the computer has led to changes in the way we communicate with each other for business and personal purposes. It has even changed the way a number of people meet each other. Instead of blind dates, they are matched by a computer dating service with people they may want to meet.

Our cultures are adapted to the environments in which we live and work. While the environment in rural areas is characterized by space and clean air, urban dwellers adapt to smog, crowded conditions, and public transportation.

New York Convention & Vistors Bureau

Manifestations of Culture

The cultural patterns of a group are determined by how the people organize and view the various components of culture. Culture is manifested in an infinite number of ways through social institutions, lived experiences, and the individual's fulfillment of psychological and basic needs. To understand how extensively our lives are affected by culture, let's examine a few of these manifestations.

Our values are initially determined by our culture. They influence the importance of prestige, status, pride, family loyalty, love of country, religious belief, and honor. Status symbols differ across cultures. For many families in the United States, accumulation of material possessions is a respected status symbol. For others, the welfare of the extended family is of utmost importance. These factors, as well as the meaning of morality or immorality, and the use of punishment and reward, and the need for higher education are determined by the value system of the culture.

Culture also manifests itself in nonverbal communication patterns. The meaning of an act or an expression must be viewed in its cultural context. The appropriateness of shaking hands, bowing, or kissing people on greeting them varies across cultures. Culture also determines the manner of walking, sitting, standing, reclining, gesturing, and dancing. We must remind ourselves not to interpret acts and expressions of people from a different cultural group as wrong or inappropriate just because they are not the same as our own. These behaviors are culturally determined.

Observe and Learn — Lessons in Action

Manifestations of Culture

Go to the *Homework and Exercises* section in Chapter 1 of MyEducationLab at www.myeducationlab.com and select *Observe and Learn: Lessons in Action* to view the video "School Uniforms and Freedom of Expression" and answer the accompanying questions. In this lesson, students discuss the ways in which clothing reveals a person's culture and identity as part of a debate on the issues surrounding schools uniforms.

1. How do students in the video connect clothing and dress to elements of personal identity?
2. What elements of your own identity and/or culture do you express through your dress?
3. Have you ever felt that one of your students was inappropriately dressed in school? What about one of your colleagues? If so, what—if anything—did you say/do?
4. How might your views regarding dress in school affect what you do in your future classroom?

Language itself is a reflection of culture and provides a special way of looking at the world and organizing experiences that is often lost in translating words from one language to another. Many different sounds and combinations of sounds are used in the languages of different cultures. Those of us who have tried to learn a second language may have experienced difficulty in verbalizing sounds that were not part of our first language. Also, diverse language patterns found within the same language group can lead to misunderstandings. For example, one person's "joking" is heard by others as serious criticism or abuse of power; this is a particular problem when the speaker is a member of the dominant group and the listener is a member of an oppressed group or vice versa.

Although we have discussed only a few daily patterns determined by culture, they are limitless. Among them are relationships of men and women, parenting, choosing a spouse, sexual relations, and division of labor in the home and society. These patterns are shared by members of the culture and often seem strange and improper to nonmembers.

Language is discussed in more depth in Chapter 6.

Ethnocentrism

Because culture helps determine the way we think, feel, and act, it becomes the lens through which we judge the world. As such, it can become an unconscious blinder to other ways of thinking, feeling, and acting. Our own culture is automatically treated as innate. It becomes the only natural way to function in the world. Even common sense in our own culture is naturally translated to common sense for the world. Other cultures are compared with ours and are evaluated by our cultural standards. It becomes difficult to view another culture as separate from our own—a task that anthropologists attempt when studying other cultures.

This inability to view other cultures as equally viable alternatives for organizing reality is known as **ethnocentrism.** Although it is appropriate to cherish one's culture, members sometimes become closed to the possibilities of difference. These feelings of superiority over other cultures can become problematic in interacting and working effectively and equitably with members of other cultures. The inability to view another culture through its cultural lens, rather than through one's own cultural lens, prevents an understanding of the second culture. This inability can make it difficult to function effectively in a second culture. By overcoming one's ethnocentric view of the world, one can begin to respect other cultures and even learn to function comfortably in more than one cultural group.

Chapter 10 includes recommendations for becoming familiar with cultural groups other than your own.

Cultural Relativism

Never judge another man until you have walked a mile in his moccasins. This North American Indian proverb suggests the importance of understanding the cultural backgrounds and experiences of other persons, rather than judging them by our own standards. The principle of cultural relativism is to see a culture as if WE are a member of the culture. In essence, it is an attempt to view the world through another person's cultural lens. It is an acknowledgement that another person's way of doing things, while perhaps not appropriate for us, may be valid for him or her. This ability becomes more essential than ever in the world today as countries and cultures become more interdependent. In an effort to maintain positive relationships with the numerous cultural groups in the world, we cannot afford to ignore other cultures or to relegate them to an inferior status.

Within our own boundaries are many cultural groups that historically have been viewed and treated as inferior to the dominant Western European culture that has been the basis for most of our institutions. These intercultural misunderstandings occur even when no language barrier exists and when large components of the major culture are shared by the people involved. These misunderstandings often happen because one group is largely ignorant about the culture of another group and gives the second culture little credibility. One problem is that members of one group are, for the most part, unable to describe their own cultural system, let alone another. These misunderstandings are common among the various groups in this country and are accentuated by differential status based on race, gender, class, language, religion, and ability.

Cultural relativism suggests that we need to learn more about our own culture than is commonly required. That must be followed by study about, and interaction with, other cultural groups. This intercultural process helps one know what it is like to be a member of the second culture and to view the world from that point of view. To function effectively and comfortably within a second culture, that culture must be learned.

Cultural Identity

Groups in the United States have been called **subsocieties** or **subcultures** by sociologists and anthropologists because they exist within the context of a larger society in which political and social institutions are shared along with some traits and values of the dominant culture. These groups provide the social identity for their members, allowing them to have distinctive cultural patterns while sharing others with members of the dominant culture. At the same time, there is no essential or absolute identity such as female or male, American or recent immigrant, or Buddhist or Jew. Our identities in any single group are influenced by our historical and lived experiences and membership in other groups.

Numerous groups exist in most nations, but the United States is exceptionally rich in the many distinct groups that make up the population. Group identity is based on traits and values learned as part of our ethnicity, religion, gender, sexual orientation, age, class or socioeconomic status, native language, geographic region, place of residence (e.g., rural or urban), and abilities or exceptional conditions, as shown in Figure 1.2. Each of these groups has distinguishable cultural patterns shared with others who identify themselves as members of that particular group. Although they share certain characteristics of the dominant culture with most of the U.S. population, members of these groups also have learned cultural traits, discourse patterns, ways of learning, values, and behaviors characteristic of the groups to which they belong.

Individuals sharing membership in one group may not share membership in other groups. For example, all men are members of the male culture, but not all males belong to the same ethnic, religious, or class group. On the other hand, an ethnic group may be composed of both males and females with different religious and socioeconomic backgrounds.

The interaction of these various group memberships within society begins to determine an individual's cultural identity. Membership in one group can greatly influence

FIGURE 1.2 Cultural identity is based on membership in multiple groups that continuously interact and influence each other. Identity within these groups is affected by interaction with the dominant group and power relations among groups in society.

From Johnson, James, A., Diann L. Musial, et al. Introduction to the foundations of American Education, 13e. Published by Allyn and Bacon, Boston, MA. Copyright © 2005 by Pearson Education. Reprinted by permission of the publisher.

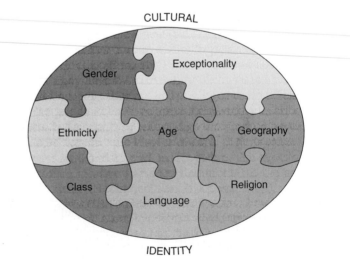

the characteristics and values of membership in other groups. For instance, some fundamentalist religions have strictly defined expectations for women and men. Thus, membership in the religious group influences, to a great extent, the way a female behaves as a young girl, teenager, bride, and wife, regardless of her ethnic group. One's economic level will greatly affect the quality of life for families, especially the children and elderly in the group.

This interaction is most dynamic across race, ethnicity, class, and gender relations. The feminist movement, for example, was primarily influenced early on by white, middle-class women. The labor movement had an early history of excluding workers of color and women, and their causes; in some areas, this antagonism continues. Membership in one group often conflicts with the interests of another as is the case when people feel forced to declare their primary identity by race rather than gender, class, or sexual orientation.

One cultural group may have a greater influence on identity than others. This influence may change over time and depends on life experiences. We can shed aspects of our culture that no longer have meaning, and we can also adopt or adapt aspects of other cultures that were not inherent in our upbringing. Identity is not fixed. Alternative views of self and culture can be learned as **cultural borders** are crossed (Kuper, 2000).

The degree to which individuals identify with the groups of which they are members and the related cultural characteristics determines, to a great extent, their individual cultural identities. For example, a 30-year-old, middle-class, Catholic, Polish American woman in Chicago may identify strongly with being Catholic and Polish American when she is married and living in a Polish American community. However, other group memberships may have a greater impact on her identity after she has divorced, moved to an ethnically diverse neighborhood, and becomes totally responsible for her financial well-being. Her femaleness and class status may become the most important representations in her identity as portrayed in Figure 1.3.

The interaction of these cultural groups within society is also important. Most political, business, educational, and social institutions (e.g., the courts, the school system, the city government) have been developed and controlled by the dominant group. The values and practices that have been internalized by the dominant group also are inherent within these institutions. Members of oppressed groups are usually beholden to the dominant group to share in that power.

Assimilation policies to force children to adopt the dominant culture have been promoted in schools as the values of the dominant group are reflected in school rules and the **informal curriculum** that guides the expected behaviors and attitudes of students. The children of immigrants and persons of color are expected to learn the dominant culture. To be successful in school they are expected to communicate and behave according to the dominant cultural norms. In the past, Americanization programs for immigrants have not only taught English, but also reinforced the meaning of being American. The virtues of being American and being patriotic continue to be reinforced in many schools, especially in times of crisis such as 9/11 and conflicts with other nations.

Understanding the importance of your group memberships to your identity helps answer the question "Who am I?" An understanding of other groups will help answer the question "Who are my students?" The various groups that educators are likely to confront in a classroom are examined in detail in Chapters 2 through 9.

FIGURE 1.3   Cultural identity is adapted and changed throughout life in response to political, economic, educational, and social experiences that either alter or reinforce one's status or position in society. Membership in some cultural groups may take on more importance than others at different periods of life, as shown here for a woman when she was 30 years old and married, and again when she was 35, divorced, and a single mother.

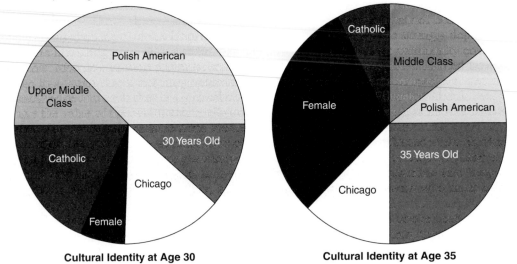

Cultural Identity at Age 30   **Cultural Identity at Age 35**

Pause to Reflect 1.4

Think about the cultural groups to which you belong. How important is your membership in the groups discussed above in your cultural identity? Identify their importance by drawing a circle similar to Figure 1.3 and indicating the degree of importance each has. After you have completed your circle, answer the following questions:

- What cultural groups are most important in your identity? Why?
- Why do some groups have little importance to your identity at this time?
- How has discrimination or the lack of it impacted the group memberships that are most important to you? Why?

Go to the *Homework and Exercises* section in Chapter 1 of MyEducationLab at *www.myeducationlab.com* and select *Pause to Reflect 1.4* to answer these questions.

FOCUS YOUR CULTURAL LENS: DEBATE

Should Patriotism Be a School Requirement?

What does it mean to be an American? Many schools are revitalizing the teaching of patriotism in elementary schools. First graders in some schools are being taught to love their country along with reading and writing. Greenbriar East Elementary School in Fairfax County outside of Washington, DC, hosts an annual Patriotic Salute in which their diverse student population sings "God Bless America," "This Land Is Your Land," and "We're Glad We Live in the U.S.A." Patriotic programs have included essay contests on being an American and assemblies to honor veterans. Other schools avoid interjecting patriotism into their curriculum, viewing it as a personal responsibility.

At times of crisis such as 9/11 and armed conflicts with other nations, state legislators and school board members are sometimes inclined to require students to recite the Pledge of Allegiance, sing the national anthem, or participate in patriotic activities on a daily or regular basis. However, these practices begin to infringe on the rights of groups and do not have unanimous support in all communities. For instance, the Supreme Court declared early last century that Jehovah Witness students could not be forced to say the Pledge of Allegiance.

Do you think patriotism should be required in schools?

For
- Students need to understand what it means to be American.
- Schools have an obligation to help students embrace American democracy.
- Students need to learn to appreciate the United States.

Against
- Civics instruction should be about personal responsibility, not instilling patriotism.
- Democracy is about making informed, thoughtful choices.
- Loving your country is not something that should be indoctrinated.

Questions

1. Why do some school districts feel obligated to push patriotism in their schools?
2. How might schools address issues of good citizenship without offending parents who find the focus on patriotism inappropriate?
3. What do you think is an appropriate balance between helping students be good citizens and overt patriotism?

Go to the *Homework and Exercises* section in Chapter 1 of MyEducationLab at *www.myeducationlab.com* and select *Focus Your Cultural Lens* to answer these questions.

Adapted from Kalita, S. M. (2004, June 8). A blending of patriotism, native pride: In diverse Fairfax school, civics starts in 1st grade. *The Washington Post*, p. B. 01.

Cultural Borders

Each of us belongs to multiple cultures (e.g., ethnic, religious, and socioeconomic groups) that help define us. As long as those differences have no status implications in which one group is treated differently from another, conflict among groups is minimal. Unfortunately, cultural borders are often erected between groups, and crossing them can be easy or difficult. What is valued on one side of the border may be denigrated on the other side. For example, speaking both Spanish and English may be highly rewarded in the community, but using Spanish in some schools is not tolerated.

Educators establish cultural borders in the classroom when all activity is grounded in the teacher's culture alone. As we learn to function comfortably in different cultures, we may be able to move away from a single perspective linked to cultural domination. We may be able to cross cultural borders, bringing the students' cultures into the classroom as well.

Biculturalism and Multiculturalism

Individuals who have competencies in, and can operate successfully in, two or more different cultures are border crossers; they are bicultural or multicultural and are often bilingual or multilingual as well. Having proficiencies in multiple cultures allows a broad range of abilities on which to draw at any given time, as determined by the particular situation.

Because we participate in more than one cultural group, we have already become proficient in multiple systems for perceiving, evaluating, believing in, and acting according to the patterns of the various groups in which we participate. We often act and speak differently when we are in the community in which we were raised than when we are in a professional setting. We behave differently on a night out with members of our own sex than we do at home with the family. People with competencies in several cultures develop a fuller appreciation of the range of cultural competencies available to all people.

Many members of oppressed groups are forced to become **bicultural** to work or attend school and participate effectively in their own ethnic community. Different behaviors are expected in the two settings. To be successful on the job usually requires proficiency in the ways of the dominant group. Because most schools reflect the dominant society, students are forced to adjust (or act white) if they are going to be academically successful. In contrast, most middle-class whites find almost total congruence between the culture of their family, schooling, and work. Most remain monocultural throughout their lives. They do not envision the value and possibilities of becoming competent in a different culture.

Becoming knowledgeable of other cultural groups is discussed in Chapter 10.

In our expanding, diverse nation, it is critical that educators themselves become at least bicultural. Understanding the cultural cues of several ethnic groups, especially oppressed groups, improves our ability to work with all students. It also helps us to be sensitive to the importance of these differences in teaching effectively.

Pluralism in Society

Although many similarities exist across cultures, differences exist in the ways people learn, the values they cherish, their worldviews, their behavior, and their interactions with others. There are many reasonable ways to organize our lives, approach a task, and use our languages and dialects. It is when we begin to see our cultural norms and behaviors not just as one approach, but as superior to others, that differences become politicized.

Differing and unequal power relations have a great impact on individuals' and groups' ability to define and achieve their own goals. These differences among and within groups can lead not only to misunderstandings and misperceptions, but also to conflict. Cultural differences sometimes result in political alliances that respond to the real and perceived realities of domination or subordination faced by the group. The result may be strong feelings of patriotism or group solidarity that expand into armed conflicts across nations, tribes, religious communities, or ethnic groups. Feelings of superiority of one's group over another are sometimes reflected in anti-Semitic symbols and actions, cross burnings, gay bashing, and sexual harassment.

Conflicts between groups are usually based on the groups' differential status and value in society. The alienation and marginalization that many powerless groups experience can lead them to accentuating their differences, especially to separate themselves from the dominant group. Groups sometimes construct their own identities in terms of others. For example, European Americans often do not think of themselves as white, except as different from blacks. Males define themselves in opposition to female. Many European American men have been socialized to see themselves as being at the center of a world in which they are privileging themselves in relation to others—women and African Americans.

In developing an understanding of differences and **otherness,** we can begin to change our simplistic binary approaches of us/them, dominant/subordinate, good/bad, and right/wrong. We begin to realize that a plurality of truths are as reasonable as our own. We seek out others for dialogue and understanding, rather than speak about and for them. We can begin to move from exercising power over others to sharing power with them.

The Dominant Culture

U.S. political and social institutions have evolved from an Anglo-Saxon or Western European tradition. The English language is a polyglot of the languages spoken by the various conquerors and rulers of Great Britain throughout history. The legal system is derived from English common law. The political system of democratic elections comes from France and England. The middle-class value system has been modified from a European system. Even our way of thinking, at least the way it is rewarded in school, is based on Socrates' linear system of logic.

Formal institutions, such as governments, schools, social welfare, banks, and businesses, affect many aspects of our lives. Because of the strong Anglo-Saxon influence on these institutions, the dominant cultural influence on the United States also has been identified as Anglo-Saxon, or Western European. More specifically, the major cultural influence on the United States, particularly on its institutions, has been White, Anglo-Saxon, and Protestant (WASP). But no longer is the dominant group composed only of WASPs. Instead, most members of the ethnically diverse middle class have adopted traditionally WASP characteristics and values that provide the framework for the dominant culture.

Although most of our institutions still function under the strong influence of their WASP roots, many other aspects of American life have been influenced by the numerous cultural groups that have come to comprise the U.S. population. Think about the different food we eat, or at least try: Chinese, Indian, Mexican, soul food, Italian, Caribbean, and Japanese. Young people of many cultures choose clothing that is influenced by hip-hop and black culture. But, more important are the contributions made to society by individuals from different groups in the fields of science, the arts, literature, athletics, engineering, architecture, and politics.

Although the United States has an agrarian tradition, the population now is primarily located in metropolitan areas and small towns. The country has mineral and soil wealth,

Members of Congress do not yet represent the diversity of the nation's population.

elaborate technology, and a wealth of manufactured goods. Mass education and mass communication are ways of life. Americans are regulated by clocks and calendars, rather than by seas and the sun. Time is used to organize most activities of life. Most Americans are employees whose salaries or wages are paid by large, complex, impersonal institutions. Work is done regularly, purposefully, and sometimes grimly. In contrast, play is fun—an outlet from work. Money is the denominator of exchange. Necessities of life are purchased, rather than produced. Achievement and success are measured by the quantity of material goods purchased. Religious beliefs are concerned with general morality.

The overpowering value of the dominant group is **individualism,** which is characterized by the belief that every individual is his or her own master, is in control of his or her own destiny, and will advance and regress in society only according to his or her own efforts (Bellah, Madsen, Sullivan, Swidler, & Tipton, 1996). This individualism is grounded in the Western worldview that individuals can control both nature and their destiny. Traits that emphasize this core value include industriousness, ambition, competitiveness, self-reliance, independence, appreciation of the good life, and the perception of humans as separate from, and superior to, nature. The acquisition of such possessions as the latest technology gadget, cars, boats, and homes measures success and achievement.

Another core value is **freedom,** which is defined by the dominant group, however, as not having others determine their values, ideas, or behaviors (Bellah et al., 1996). Relations with other people inside and outside their group are often impersonal. Communications may be very direct or confrontational. Many members of the dominant group rely more on associations of common interest than on strong kinship ties. The nuclear family is the basic kinship unit. Values tend to be absolute (e.g., right or wrong, moral or immoral), rather than range along a continuum of degrees of right and wrong. Personal life and community affairs are based on principles of right and wrong, rather than on shame,

Pause to Reflect 1.5

How much do you know about the power you have because of your race? Circle your responses to the following questions?

• Can you turn on the television or open the newspaper and see people of your race widely represented?	Yes	No
• Can you speak in public to a male group without putting your race [or gender] on trial?	Yes	No
• Can you perform well on a project without being called a credit to your race?	Yes	No
• Are you ever asked to speak for all people of your race?	Yes	No
• Can you be reasonably sure that if you ask to talk to "the person in charge," you will find a person of your same race?	Yes	No
• When you are stopped for a traffic violation, do you have to worry that you have been racially profiled?	Yes	No
• When you shop, are you followed around by a clerk or security person?	Yes	No

Go to the *Homework and Exercises* section in Chapter 1 of MyEducationLab at *www.myeducationlab.com* and select *Pause to Reflect 1.5* to answer these questions.

Adapted from McIntosh, P. (2004). White privilege: Unpacking the invisible knapsack. In M. L. Anderson & P. H. Collins (Eds.), *Race, class, and gender* (pp. 103–108.). Belmont, CA: Wadsworth.

dishonor, or ridicule. Youthfulness is emphasized in advertisements and commercials. Men and women use Botox and have plastic surgery to try to maintain their youthfulness. Many U.S. citizens, especially if they are middle-class, share these traits and values to some degree. They are patterns that are privileged in institutions such as schools. They are values to which the dominant society expects all citizens to adhere.

Privilege. Most male members of the dominant group do not usually think about themselves as white, financially secure, Christian, English-speaking, or heterosexual. They have not seen themselves as **privileged** in society and do not view themselves as oppressors of others. Most schools and teachers do not recognize the inequality, racism, and powerlessness that work against the success of students of color, girls, English language learners, non-Christians, students from low-income families, and students with disabilities. Most members of the dominant group have not had the opportunity to explore their own European ethnicity and privileged position in society. They often have not studied or interacted with groups to which they do not belong. Therefore, they have been unable to locate themselves within the continuum of power and inequality in society.

In contrast to whites, members of oppressed groups are constantly confronted with the difference of their race, language, class, religion, gender, disability, and/or homosexuality. The degree of identification with the characteristics of the dominant culture depends, in part, on how much an individual must interact with society's formal institutions for economic support and subsistence. The more dependence on these institutions, the greater the degree of sharing, or of being forced to adopt, the common traits and values of the dominant group.

These opposing perspectives are situated in one's real or perceived position of privilege or lack of privilege in society. They have led, in recent years, to public debates on college campuses about affirmative action to ensure diversity as well as diversity in the common core of the college curriculum. Members of oppressed groups argue that their cultures are not reflected in a curriculum that includes primarily the great books of Western European thought. The traditionalists, who are predominantly representatives of the dominant group, often invoke nationalism and patriotism in their calls to retain the purity of the Western **canon** and promote homogeneity in society. However, proponents of a common core curriculum that includes the voices of women, people of color, and religions other than Christianity also include many members of the dominant group who value differences and multiple perspectives.

The question appears to be whose culture will be reflected in the elementary and secondary, as well as college, curriculum. Those who call for a curriculum and textbooks that reflect only their history and experiences view their culture as superior to all others. Thus, they and their culture become privileged over others in schools. They do not see themselves as different; to them, diversity refers only to members of other groups in society. To be successful, members of the dominant group are not required to learn to function effectively in a second culture as are members of oppressed groups. The privileged curriculum reinforces this pattern. It is the members of the oppressed groups who must learn the culture and history of the dominant group without the opportunity to study their own cultural group or to validate the importance of their own history and lived experiences. It is as if they do not belong. This feeling may lead to **marginalization** and **alienation** from school as students are not accepted by the dominant group and do not feel a part of the school culture.

See Chapter 10 for strategies for incorporating diverse groups and multiple perspectives into the curriculum.

Acculturation.   Many groups that immigrated during the twentieth century have become acculturated or adopted the dominant group's cultural patterns. Although some groups have tried to maintain the original culture, it is usually in vain as children go to school and participate in the larger society. Continuous and firsthand contacts with the dominant group usually result in subsequent changes in the original cultural patterns of either or both groups. The rapidity and success of the **acculturation** process depends on several factors, including location and discrimination. If a group is spatially isolated and segregated (whether voluntarily or not) in a rural area, as is the case with many American Indians on reservations, the acculturation process is very slow. Unusually marked discrimination such as that faced by oppressed groups, especially African Americans, American Indians, and Mexican Americans, deprives group members of educational and occupational opportunities and primary relationships with members of the dominant group (Alba & Nee, 2003; Rumbaut & Portes, 2001). The discrimination makes it more difficult to acculturate if they choose to do so.

It is important to note that acculturation is determined, in part, by the individual or family as they decide how much they want to dress, speak, and behave like members of the dominant group. After conducting a longitudinal study of immigrants in southern California and southern Florida, Rumbaut and Portes (2001) found three acculturation patterns among immigrants: consonant, dissonant, and selective. In consonant acculturation, parents and children learn the language and culture of the community in which they live at approximately the same time. In dissonant acculturation, children learn English and the new culture while parents retain their native language and culture, often leading to conflict within the family and decreasing parental authority. Fluent bilingualism in the second generation is an outcome of selective acculturation in which the children of immigrants learn the dominant culture and language, but retain significant elements of their native culture.

Members of many groups, however, have little choice if they want to share the American dream of success. Many people have had to give up native languages and behaviors or hide them at home. However, acculturation does not guarantee acceptance by the dominant group. Most members of oppressed groups, especially those of color, have not been permitted to assimilate fully into society even though they have adopted the values and behaviors of the dominant group.

Assimilation

Assimilation occurs when a group's distinctive cultural patterns either become part of the dominant culture or disappear as the group adopts the dominant culture. **Structural assimilation** occurs when the dominant group shares primary group relationships with the second group, including membership in the same cliques and social clubs; members of the two groups intermarry; and the two groups are treated equally within society. Assimilation appears to be relevant for voluntary immigrants, particularly if they are white, but does not apply to **involuntary immigrants** who were forced to come to this country through slavery or conquest of the area in which they lived. These families have been in the country for generations and not allowed to fully assimilate, especially at the structural level.

White European immigrants usually become structurally assimilated within a few generations after arriving in this country. Marriage across groups is fairly common across white ethnic groups and Judeo-Christian religious affiliations. Nearly one of three Asian Americans and 30% of Latinos marry outside of their group. However, only 2% of whites and 4% of African Americans were marrying outside their group at the end of the twentieth century (Alba, 2000). Acculturation has neither eliminated prejudice and discrimination nor led to large-scale intermarriage with the dominant group. If the assimilation process is effective, it leads to the disappearance of a cultural group that is distinct from the dominant group, and, in the process, changes the dominant group as well.

When Portes and Rumbaut (2001) studied the second generation of recent immigrants, they found that the degree of their assimilation differed. The history and experiences of the first-generation immigrant varied across and within groups. The pace of acculturation among parents and children as described above influenced assimilation with consonant acculturation being the most rapid. A critical factor is the cultural and economic barriers faced by second-generation youth. Young people who can see upward mobility in their future are more likely to assimilate. Some groups have greater family and community resources for confronting the barriers that society establishes for immigrants. "In a high-technology society, immigrant families who bring large volumes of human and cultural capital obviously have an advantage over low-wage laborers with little formal schooling" (Alba & Nee, 2003, p. 15).

Governmental support of new immigrants also has an influence on a group's desire and ability to assimilate (Portes & Rumbaut, 2001). Some groups have been actively encouraged to immigrate and have been warmly welcomed by society. Favored refugee groups include the Vietnamese and Cubans. Other immigrant groups such as Chinese, Middle Easterners, and Europeans have been passively accepted by society without favoritism, but also with limited discrimination. Discrimination based on race has made it difficult for many Haitians, Mexican Americans, and Central Americans to easily assimilate into the dominant culture. The immigrants and their children in this last group are likely to confront segmented or downward assimilation in which they are not able to improve their economic status (Alba & Nee, 2003; Rumbaut & Portes, 2001). Low educational attainment of immigrant children in these excluded groups is affected by the persistence of racial discrimination, the growing inequality of workers, and the consolidation of oppressed populations in the inner city (Portes & Rumbaut, 2001).

Some immigrant groups try to preserve their native cultures; others have assimilation as their goal. Nevertheless, assimilation does not characterize the contemporary U.S. scene. We are a nation of many cultural groups distinguished by our ethnicity, gender, class, language, age, and religion. At the same time, America's desire to assimilate different cultural groups affects the nation's political, social, and educational policies and practices.

Cultural Pluralism

A society organized according to a theory of **cultural pluralism** allows two or more distinct groups to function separately and equally without requiring any assimilation of one into the other. Refusing or not being permitted to assimilate into the dominant American culture, many immigrants and ethnic groups maintain their own unique ethnic communities and enclaves. For most oppressed ethnic and religious groups, primary-group contacts have been maintained within the group, rather than across cultural groups as required in structural assimilation. Cross-cultural contacts occur primarily at the secondary level in work settings and political and civic institutions. Members of oppressed groups develop institutions, agencies, and power structures for services within their ethnic communities—enclaves such as Little Italy, Chinatown, Harlem, Korea Town, East Los Angeles, and Amish and Hutterite communities. In some places, persons who are blind or deaf have established communities in which they feel comfortable with others who have the same disability.

The commitment to the value of cultural pluralism is not broadly supported by individuals and groups in society. American Indian nations within the United States come the closest to reflecting cultural pluralism in that they have their own political, economic, and educational systems. For most American Indians, however, the economic, political, and educational opportunities do not approach equality with the dominant group. In a cultural pluralistic society, the retention of diverse ethnic and religious groups would be promoted in schools and society. In a culturally plural society, power and resources would be shared somewhat equitably across groups.

The problem is that dominant groups are not usually willing to share their power and wealth with others. Some critics of the system believe that the dominant group uses a strategy of divide and conquer to keep ethnic groups segregated and fighting among themselves for the few resources available. Others believe that a societal goal should be the integration of diverse groups and the promotion of more equality across groups through a united front. Still others believe that individuals should be able to maintain their ethnic identities while participating in the common culture. These beliefs are not necessarily discrete from one another; for example, society could be integrated, but members would not be required to relinquish their ethnic identities. At the same time, an integrated society can lead to greater assimilation in that primary contacts across cultural groups are more likely.

Equality and Social Justice in a Democracy

The United States is a **democracy** in which people participate in their government by exercising their power directly or indirectly through elected representatives. Schools and the mass media teach us that our democracy is one to be emulated by the rest of the world. A democracy should promote the good of all its citizens. Thus, the Constitution was fashioned with a coherent set of "checks and balances" to limit the systematic abuse of power. **Egalitarianism**—the belief in social, political, and economic rights and privileges for all people—is espoused as a key principle on which democracy is based. All citizens are expected to have a voice. Power should be shared among groups, and no one group should continuously dominate the economic, political, social, and cultural life of the country. Society and government, though not perfect, are promoted as allowing mass participation and steady advancement toward a more prosperous and egalitarian society.

One strength of a democracy is that citizens bring many perspectives, based on their own histories and experiences, to bear on policy questions and practices. Thus, to disagree is acceptable as long as we are able to communicate with each other openly and without fear of reprisal. Further, we expect that no single right way will be forced on us. For the most part, we would rather struggle with multiple perspectives and actions and determine what is best for us as individuals within this democratic society.

At the same time, a democracy expects its citizens to be concerned about more than just their own individual freedoms. In the classic *Democracy and Education,* philosopher and educator John Dewey (1916/1966) suggested that the emphasis should be on what binds us together in cooperative pursuits and results, regardless of the nation or our group alliance and membership. He raised concern about our possible stratification into separate classes and called for "intellectual opportunities [to be] accessible to all on equitable and easy terms" (p. 88).

The emphasis on individualism in the dominant culture provides a dilemma for educators who promote democratic practice. In many classrooms, individualism is supported through competitive activities in which individual achievement is rewarded. A democratic classroom promotes working together across groups. Responsibility and leadership are shared by students and teachers as students practice being active participants in a democratic setting.

Democratic classrooms are discussed in more depth in Chapter 10.

Both individualism and equality have long been central themes of political discourse in a democratic society. The meaning of equality within our society varies according to one's assumptions about humankind and human existence. At least two sets of beliefs govern the ideologies of equality and inequality. The first accepts inequality as inevitable and promotes **meritocracy,** which is a system based on the belief that an individual's achievements are due to their own personal merits and that the people who achieve at the highest levels deserve the greatest social and financial rewards. It stresses the right of access to society's resources as a necessary condition for equal rights to life, liberty, and happiness. The focus is on individualism and the individual's right to pursue happiness and obtain personal resources. The second set of beliefs supports a much greater degree of equality across groups in society. Persons who believe in equality care about people who have fewer resources and develop policies that allow more people to share in the nation's wealth.

Meritocracy is also discussed in Chapter 3.

This dilemma forces some people to promote some equality while preventing any real equity from occurring. Affirmative action, for example, is viewed by its critics as evidence of group welfare gaining precedence over individual achievement. The outcry against affirmative action suggests that racism no longer exists and that decisions about employment, promotion, and so forth are no longer influenced by racism and sexism. Whites filing reverse discrimination cases believe that their individual rights to an education at a select school, a promotion, or a job should be based solely on their individual achievement. They believe that other factors such as income (or lack of), ethnicity, race, or gender should not be valued in the process. They overlook the fact that they have been privileged throughout their lives because of their race and family income. Even though egalitarianism is an often-espoused goal of democracy in the United States, the inequities that actually exist in society are continually overlooked.

Individualism and Meritocracy

Proponents of meritocracy accept the theories of sociobiology or functionalism or both, in which inequalities are viewed as natural outcomes of individual differences. They believe that everyone has the opportunity to be successful if they just work hard enough. They give little credit to family conditions, such as being born in a wealthy family, as a head start for success. Members of oppressed groups usually are seen as inferior, and their hardships blamed on their personal characteristics rather than societal constraints or discrimination.

For more information on racism, see Chapter 2. The overrepresentation of some students in special education is discussed in Chapter 5.

The belief system that undergirds meritocracy has at least three dimensions that are consistent with dominant values. First, the individual is valued over the group. The individual has the qualities, ambitions, and talent to achieve at the highest levels in society. Popular stories promote this ideology as they describe the poor immigrant who arrived on U.S. shores with nothing, set up a vegetable stand to eke out a living, and became the millionaire owner of a chain of grocery stores.

The second dimension stresses differences through competition. IQ and achievement tests are used throughout schooling to help measure differences. Students and adults are rewarded for outstanding grades, athletic ability, and artistic accomplishment.

Students do not start life with an equal chance to succeed. Because of family income and wealth, some students have access to resources and experiences in their homes, communities, and often schools that are not available to most low-income students.

© Masterfile Royalty Free Division

The third dimension emphasizes internal characteristics, such as motivation, intuition, and character that have been internalized by the individual. External conditions, such as racism and poverty, are to be overcome by the individual; they are not accepted as contributors to an individual's lack of success.

Equal educational opportunity, or equal access to schooling, applies meritocracy to education. All students are to be provided with equal educational opportunities that supposedly will give them similar chances for success or failure. Proponents of this approach believe it is the individual's responsibility to use those opportunities to his or her advantage in obtaining life's resources and benefits. Critics of meritocracy point out that children of low-income families do not start with the same chances for success in life as children from affluent families. Even the most capable of these students do not have equal educational opportunities if the schools they attend lack the challenging curriculum and advanced placement classes typically found in middle-class and affluent communities. Thus, competition is unequal from birth. The chances of the affluent child being educationally and financially successful are much greater than for the child from a low-income family. Those with advantages at birth are almost always able to hold onto and extend those advantages throughout their lifetimes.

Observe and Learn
Lessons in Action

Equality

Go to the *Homework and Exercises* section in Chapter 1 of MyEducationLab at *www.myeducationlab.com* and select *Observe and Learn: Lessons in Action* to view the video "The 14th Amendment and Our Schools" and answer the accompanying questions. In this lesson, students take a firsthand exploration of constitutional rights by exploring the 14th Amendment and applying it to their own school context.

1. What issues did students in the video raise after reading the two Supreme Court cases? Did any of the students' comments surprise you? If so, which ones?
2. Do you agree with school choice? Why or why not?
3. What was your own high school context like in terms of socioeconomic status and class?
4. How might your views regarding school choice and the socioeconomic status of your students affect what you do in your future classroom?

Equality

With the persistence of racism, poverty, unemployment, and inequality in major social systems such as education and health, many persons have found it difficult to reconcile daily realities with the publicized egalitarianism that characterizes the public rhetoric. These persons view U.S. society as comprised of institutions and an economic system that represents the interests of the privileged few, rather than the pluralistic majority. Even where institutions, laws, and processes have the appearance of equal access, benefit, and protection, they are almost always enforced in highly discriminatory ways. These patterns of **inequality** are not the product of corrupt individuals as such, but rather are a reflection of how resources of economics, political power, and cultural and social dominance are built into the entire political-economic system.

Even in the optimistic view that some degree of equality can be achieved, inequality is also expected. Not all resources can be redistributed so that every individual has an equal amount, nor should all individuals expect equal compensation for the work they do. The underlying belief, however, is that there need not be the huge disparities of income, wealth, and power that currently exist. Equality does suggest fairness in the distribution of the conditions and goods that affect the well-being of all children and families. It is

VIDEO INSIGHTS
School Busing

For decades the remedy for segregation has been school busing. The goals of integrating schools have been racial balance and access to better schools, new equipment, and new opportunities for all students. Now some African American families are criticizing the busing experiment as a failure and are requesting a "separate but equal" education for their children in their own neighborhoods.

In this video segment, you will see proponents of this movement in Oklahoma City and in other cities across the country say their children have been subjected to segregated settings within integrated schools. African American children are often assigned to remedial classes or lower academic tracks and do not get exposure to the services and resource that other students receive. In addition, because these schools are not close to home, it is difficult for parents to be involved or even present if there is a problem or an emergency at school.

1. After viewing this video segment, how have your views on busing changed?
2. Are the people who support this movement to neighborhood schools forsaking the efforts of the countless individuals who have worked so hard for integration in our schools?
3. History has shown us that "separate but equal" has not worked. Is this because separate, by definition, is not equal?
4. What are your views on the issue of "separate but equal"?
5. Do you think we now have the resources, support, and technology to make "separate but equal" a reality?

Go to the Video Insights DVD and watch the *School Busing* video segment. Then, go to the *Homework and Exercises* section in Chapter 1 of MyEducationLab at *www.myeducationlab.com* and select *Video Insights: School Busing* to answer these questions.

fostered by policies for full employment, wages that prevent families from living in poverty, and child care for all children.

Critics decry the perceived socialism as being against the democratic foundations that undergird the nation. They believe that equality of resources and societal benefits would undermine the capitalist system that allows a few individuals to acquire the great majority of those resources. They warn that equality of results would limit freedom and liberty for individuals.

Equality is more than just providing oppressed group members with an equal chance or equal opportunity. One proposal is that equal results should be the goal. These results might be more equal achievement by students of both oppressed and dominant groups and similar rates of dropping out of school, college attendance, and college completion by different ethnic, racial, gender, and class populations.

Traditionally, the belief has been that education can overcome the inequalities that exist in society. The role of education in reducing the amount of occupation and income inequality may be limited, however. School reform has not yet led to significant social changes outside the schools. Equalizing educational opportunity has had very little impact on making

Pause to Reflect **1.6**

How do you view equality in society and schooling? Check the statements below that best describe your perceptions.

- The ablest and most meritorious, ambitious, hardworking, and talented individuals should acquire the most, achieve the most, and become society's leaders.
- The individual is more important than the group.
- The U.S. economic system represents the interests of a privileged few, rather than those of the pluralistic majority.
- Huge disparities of income, wealth, and power should not exist in this country.
- It is the student's responsibility to get as much out of school as possible.
- Differences measured on standardized tests are more important than similarities.
- External conditions, such as racism and poverty, should be overcome by the individual.
- Students from all cultural groups can be academically successful.
- Tracking of students promotes inequality.
- Teachers can make a difference in the academic success of students.

Which of these statements are most related to a belief in meritocracy, and which to a belief in equality?

Go to the *Homework and Exercises* section in Chapter 1 of MyEducationLab at *www.myeducationlab.com* and select *Pause to Reflect 1.6* to answer these questions.

---

adults more equal. Providing equal educational opportunities for all students does not guarantee equal results at the end of high school or college. It does not yet provide equal access to jobs and income across groups. It may be that programs for equal educational opportunity have not overcome the academic and economic disparities that existed among families. To ensure equality in schools students in impoverished schools would be guaranteed to have teachers who are as highly qualified as the teachers in wealthy school districts. Equality requires financial support for providing quality instruction in environments that are conducive to learning by all students. More, not less, money may be needed to ensure equity in educational results by the children of dominant groups and other groups.

Social Justice

Social justice is another element of democracy that expects citizens to provide for those persons in society who are not as advantaged as others. Dewey (1966) called for social justice when he said, "What the best and wisest parent wants for his [or her] own child, that must the community want for all of its children. Any other ideal for our schools is narrow and unlovely; acted upon, it destroys our democracy" (p. 3). In schools, social justice requires a critique of practices that interfere with equity across groups. Social and economic inequities that prevent students from learning and participating effectively in schools must be confronted (Apple, 2004).

Observe and Learn
Lessons in Action

Social Justice

Go to the *Homework and Exercises* section in Chapter 1 of MyEducationLab at *www.myeducationlab.com* and select *Observe and Learn: Lessons in Action* to view the video "The Universal Declaration of Human Rights" and answer the accompanying questions. In this lesson, students examine the role of the United Nations in promoting human rights, diversity, international understanding, and humanitarian affairs through its U.N. Convention—the Universal Declaration of Human Rights (UDHR). Violations of human rights in the form of lack of freedoms and economic and social inequalities are addressed.

1. What kinds of issues did the students document in their posters? Were most of the issues local or global? Why do you think this was the case?
2. What are some of the human rights issues that most interest/trouble/concern you at this time?
3. How might your understanding of various human rights issues affect what you do in your future classroom?

Enormous disparities exist between the very wealthy and the very poor. The very wealthy have accumulated vast resources while the very poor cannot even meet their basic needs. They are unable to obtain the barest essentials for shelter, food, or medical care. Some suffer from lack of heat in the winter and lack of cooling in very hot summers. Every year, there are reports of elderly, low-income people who die from exposure to excessive heat or cold. This reality is inconceivable for many Americans who simply turn their thermostats to the precise temperature that will meet their comfort level. Every day children from poor families come to school with insufficient sleep because of the physical discomforts of their homes, with inadequate clothing, and with empty stomachs. Tens of thousands suffer from malnutrition and no dental care. When they are sick, many go untreated. Under these conditions, it is difficult, at best, to function well in an academic setting.

Civil unrest has almost always been precipitated by the disenfranchised who have no realistic hope of extricating themselves from lives of despair. Children of affluent members of society do not typically form street gangs; they are usually too busy enjoying the good life that prosperity brings. The street gangs of New York, Chicago, and Los Angeles are comprised almost exclusively of young individuals who are poor, embittered, and disenfranchised.

Those who have the power to bring about meaningful change in society are usually the more affluent. They have the resources and connections to make things happen. To bring about truly meaningful change requires paradigm shifts. Even the middle class may be reluctant to make changes if a change in the status quo diminishes their position. Changes are usually supported only if they provide benefits to the dominant group or do not affect them negatively.

Meaningful change in society requires a universal social consciousness. It requires, to some extent, a willingness of the citizenry to explore the means of redistributing some of the benefits of a democratic society. Effective redistribution would require that some who have considerable wealth provide a greater share in the effort to eliminate poverty and its concomitant effects. The end result could be a society in which everyone has a decent place to sleep, no child goes to school hungry, and appropriate health care is available to all.

Obstacles to Equality and Social Justice

Prejudice and **discrimination** stem from a combination of several factors related to us and them. Persons who are prejudiced have an aversion to members of a group other than their own. Discrimination leads to the denial of the privileges and rewards to members of oppressed groups. Prejudice can result when people lack an understanding of the history, experiences, values, and perceptions of groups other than their own. Members of groups are **stereotyped** when others apply to them generalizations about the group without consideration of individual differences within the group.

Prejudice.   Prejudice manifests itself in feelings of anger, fear, hatred, and distrust about members of a certain group. These attitudes are often translated into fear of walking in the group's neighborhood, fear of being robbed or hurt by others, distrust of a merchant from the group, anger at any advantages that others may be perceived as receiving, and fear that housing prices will be deflated if someone from that group moves next door.

Some members of all groups possess negative stereotypes of others. For example, many African Americans and Latinos believe that whites are bigoted, bossy, and unwilling to share power. In a two-year study of teachers in a staff development project, Sleeter (1992) found that many white teachers "associated people of color—and particularly African Americans and Latinos—with dysfunctional families and communities, and lack of ability and motivation" (p. 162). These negative stereotypes may describe some members of a group, but have been unfairly extended as characteristics of all members of the group.

Although prejudice may not always directly hurt members of a group, it can be easily translated into behavior that does harm them. An ideology based on aversion to a group and perceived superiority undergirds the activities of groups such as the neo-Nazis, Ku Klux Klan, skinheads, and other white racist groups. A prejudiced teacher may hold high academic expectations for students of one group and low expectations for students of another group. Such prejudice could lead to inappropriate placement of students in gifted or special education programs.

The overrepresentation of students of color in special education is discussed in Chapter 5.

Discrimination.   Whereas prejudice is based on attitudes, discrimination focuses on behavior. Discrimination occurs at two levels: individual and institutional. Individual discrimination is attributed to, or influenced by, prejudice. Individuals discriminate against a member of a group because they have strong prejudicial, or bigoted, feelings about the group, or they believe that society demands they discriminate. For example, realtors, personnel managers, receptionists, and membership chairpersons all work directly with individuals. Their own personal attitudes about members of certain groups can influence whether a house is sold, a job is offered, a loan is granted, an appointment is made, a meal is served, or a membership is granted. The action of these individuals can prevent others from gaining the experiences and economic advantages that these activities offer.

An individual has less control in the other form of discrimination. Institutional discrimination cannot be attributed to prejudicial attitudes. It refers to inequalities that have been integrated into the system-wide operation of society through legislation and practices that ensure benefits to some groups and not to others. Laws that disproportionately limit immigration to people from specific countries are one example. Other examples include practices that lead to a disproportionately large number of African Americans being incarcerated, single low-income mothers being denied adequate prenatal care, and children in low-income neighborhoods suffering disproportionately from asthma as a result of poor environmental conditions in their neighborhoods.

We have grown up in a society that has inherently discriminated against persons of color and women since the first European Americans arrived. Throughout our lives, we have participated in societal institutions, including schools, Social Security, transportation, welfare, and housing patterns. We often do not realize the extent to which members of different groups receive the benefits and privileges of these institutions. Because we may believe that we have never been discriminated against, we should not assume that others do not suffer from discrimination.

Many individuals might argue that institutional discrimination no longer exists because today's laws require equal access to the benefits of society. As a result, they believe that individuals from all groups have had equal opportunities to be successful. They fight against group rights that lead to what is perceived as preferential treatment of the members of one group over them as individuals. The government is usually accused of going too far in eliminating discrimination against historically oppressed groups by supporting affirmative action, contracts set aside for specific groups, special education, and legislation for women's equity. Opponents to these programs charge that such programs lead to reverse discrimination.

However, criteria for access to the "good life" are often applied arbitrarily and unfairly. A disproportionately high number of persons of color have had limited opportunities to gain the qualifications for skilled jobs or college entrance or have the economic resources to purchase a home in the suburbs. As businesses and industries move from the city to the suburbs, access to employment by those who live in the inner city is limited. A crucial issue is not the equal treatment of those with equal qualifications, but the accessibility to the qualifications and jobs themselves.

The consequences are the same in individual and institutional discrimination. Members of some groups do not receive the same benefits from society as the dominant group. Individuals are harmed by circumstances beyond their control because of their membership in a specific group. The role of teachers and other professional educators requires that they not discriminate against any student because of his or her group memberships. This consideration must be paramount in assigning students to special education and gifted classes and in giving and interpreting standardized tests. Classroom interactions, classroom resources, extracurricular activities, and counseling practices must be evaluated to ensure that discrimination against students from various groups does not occur.

Summary

Multicultural education is an educational strategy that incorporates cultural differences and provides equality and social justice in schools. For it to become a reality in the formal school situation, the total environment must reflect a commitment to multicultural education. The diverse cultural backgrounds and group memberships of students and families are as important in developing effective instructional strategies as are their physical and mental capabilities. Further, educators must understand the influence of racism, sexism, and classism on the lives of their students and ensure that these are not perpetuated in the classroom.

Culture provides the blueprint that determines the way an individual thinks, feels, and behaves in society. We are not born with culture, but rather learn it through enculturation and socialization. It is manifested through society's institutions, lived experiences, and the individual's fulfillment of psychological and basic needs.

Historically, U.S. political and social institutions have developed from a Western European tradition and still function under the strong influence of that heritage. At the same time, many aspects of American life have been greatly influenced by the numerous cultural groups that make up the U.S. population. The dominant culture is based on its White, Anglo-Saxon, Protestant roots and the core values of individualism and freedom with which many middle-class families identify. Assimilation is the process by which groups adopt and change the dominant culture. Schools have traditionally served as the transmitter of the dominant culture to all students regardless of their cultural backgrounds.

Individuals also belong to a number of groups with cultural patterns that differ from that of the dominant group. Cultural identity is based on the interaction and influence of membership in groups based on ethnic origin, race, religion, gender, sexual orientation, age, class, native language, geographic region, and abilities. Membership in one of those groups can greatly affect one's identity with the others. Some religions, for example, dictate the norms for the behavior of men and women, children and adults, as well as the treatment of members of other groups. The theory of cultural pluralism promotes the maintenance of the distinct differences among cultural groups.

A democracy provides social justice for all of its people. Egalitarianism and equality have long been espoused as goals for society, but they are implemented from two perspectives. The emphasis on individualism is supported in a meritocratic system in which everyone is alleged to start out equally, but the most deserving will end up with the most rewards. Equality, in contrast, seeks to ensure that society's benefits and rewards are distributed more equitably among individuals and groups. Prejudice and discrimination continue to be obstacles to equality.

PROFESSIONAL PRACTICE FOR EDUCATORS

Questions for Discussion

1. How does multicultural education differ from multiethnic studies and intercultural or intergroup education?
2. What is the danger of stereotyping students on the basis of their membership in only one of their cultural groups?
3. Why is multicultural education as important to students of the dominant culture as to students of other cultures?
4. What impact does culture have on the way one lives?
5. How does ethnicity, gender, and religion interact in determining one's cultural identity? Why might one's cultural identity change over time?
6. What are the implicit and explicit differences between dominant and oppressed groups?
7. How might an understanding of cultural borders help teachers understand differences in classroom settings?
8. How do meritocracy and individualism conflict with the ideal of equality?

Portfolio Activities

1. Write a reflective paper that describes your cultural identity and the social and economic factors that have influenced it. Refer to your circle of cultural identity (Pause to Reflect 1.4) to get you started.
2. Develop a lesson plan for the subject and level you plan to teach that presents the topic from multiple perspectives. Include a summary of the perspectives to be presented, why they were selected, and how the different perspectives strengthen the lesson. (INTASC Standard 1)

3. Select one of the schools in which you are observing this semester to develop a case study of the cultural norms prevalent in the community served by the school. In your case study indicate the diversity of the community and the cultural norms that are reflected in the school. Teachers, parents, and students should be interviewed during the development of the case study. In addition, your observations of students should inform your case. (INTASC Standard 3)

Licensure Test Prep

The following passages are taken from a debate about the advantages and disadvantages of multicultural education. Read the two sides of the debate and answer the two questions that follow.

Why multicultural education is desirable

Multicultural education is a strategy that builds on the cultural backgrounds of students and their families to engage them in learning. It includes the experiences and histories of their cultures as well as the dominant culture of the country. It helps students develop their own self-esteem as well as linking their knowledge and backgrounds to the subject being taught. Multicultural education is not just for new immigrants and students of color as many people think. It is also important that middle-class European American students know about the histories, struggles, and contributions of other groups. In multicultural education the cultures of all students are respected and valued and drawn upon by teachers to plan lessons. The different learning styles of students are considered as lessons are planned and their work is assessed with the goal of helping all students learn at high levels.

Why multicultural education is misguided

When educators stress differences among groups rather than similarities, as they do in multicultural education, the approach is misguided. The focus of education should be to ensure that students learn English and understand the history and culture of the United States to unify the population. Focusing on differences and conflicts between the government and American Indians, African Americans, Latinos, Asian Americans, women, gays and lesbians, Jews, Muslims, low-income families, and English language learners will only divide the country into competing groups. A good teacher can help all students learn regardless of their cultural differences. Adapting instruction to different groups of students only limits the amount and quality of instruction that the average student receives in the classroom.

1. The first passage suggests which of the following is an essential element of multicultural education?
   A. The development of students' self-esteem.
   B. The inclusion of students' cultures throughout the curriculum and instruction.
   C. The maintenance of students' native languages.
   D. The acceptance of European American culture.

2. The second passage regards which of the following goals as essential for a good education?
   A. Accommodating instruction to students' learning styles and needs.
   B. Providing accurate information about the diverse groups that comprise the U.S. population.

    C. Focusing on similarities among diverse groups.

    D. Ensuring that students learn the common culture of the United States.

Go to the *Homework and Exercises* section in Chapter 1 of MyEducationLab at *www.myeducationlab.com* and select *Licensure Test Prep* to complete this exercise.

Suggested Readings

Apple, M. W. (2004). *Ideology and curriculum* (3rd ed.). New York: RoutledgeFalmer.

The politics of the school curriculum are the focus of this insightful account of the cultural, political, and economic influences on education. This edition includes a chapter on the challenges facing schools after 9/11.

Au, W., Bigelow, B., & Karp, S. (2007). *Rethinking our classrooms: Teaching for equity and justice.* Milwaukee, WI: Rethinking Schools.

This handbook for educators includes creative teaching ideas, compelling classroom narratives, and hands-on examples of ways teachers can promote the values of community, justice, and equality while building academic skills. It includes essays, poems, student handouts, and annotated resources.

Banks, J. A., & Banks, C. A. M. (Eds.). (2004). *Handbook of research on multicultural education* (2nd ed.). San Francisco: Jossey-Bass.

This comprehensive handbook provides broad coverage of the history as well as current trends, research issues, and knowledge construction of multicultural education. Well-known scholars address ethnic groups, immigrants, language issues, academic achievement, intergroup education, higher education, and international perspectives.

hooks, b. (1994). *Teaching to transgress: Education as the practice of freedom.* New York: Routledge.

Using passion and politics, this teacher promotes education that helps students cross racial, sexual, and class boundaries in the practice of freedom.

Tyack, D. (2003). *Seeking common ground: Public schools in a diverse society.* Cambridge, MA: Harvard University Press.

Beginning with the establishment of public schools in each township in the eighteenth century, this historian traces the debates that have guided the incorporation of diverse populations in schools into the twenty-first century.

References

Alba, R. D. (2000). Assimilations' quiet tide. In S. Steinberg (Ed.), *Race and ethnicity in the United States: Issues and debates* (pp. 211–222). Malden, MA: Blackwell.

Alba, R., & Nee, V. (2003). *Remaking the American mainstream: Assimilation and contemporary immigration.* Cambridge, MA: Harvard University Press.

Apple, M. W. (2004). *Ideology and curriculum* (3rd ed.). New York: RoutledgeFalmer.

Banks, C. A. M. (2004). Intercultural and intergroup education, 1929–1959: Linking schools and communities. In J. A. Banks & C. A. M. Banks (Eds.), *Handbook of research on multicultural education* (2nd ed., pp. 753–781). San Francisco: Jossey-Bass.

Banks, J. A. (2004). Multicultural education: Historical development, dimensions, and practice. In J. A. Banks & C. A. M. Banks (Eds.), *Handbook of research on multicultural education* (2nd ed., pp. 3–29). San Francisco: Jossey-Bass.

Bellah, R. N., Madsen, R., Sullivan, W. M., Swidler, A., & Tipton, S. M. (1996). *Habits of the heart: Individualism and commitment in American life.* Berkeley, CA: University of California Press.

Dalton, B., Sable, J., & Hoffman, L. (2006). *Characteristics of the 100 largest public elementary and secondary school districts in the United States: 2003–04* (NCES 2006-329). Washington, DC: U.S. Department of Education, National Center for Education Statistics.

Dewey, J. (1966). *Democracy and education: An introduction to the philosophy of education.* New York: Free Press. (Original work published 1916)

Eck, D. L. (2000). Religious pluralism in America in the year 2000. In E. W. Linder, *Yearbook of American and Canadian churches 2000.* Nashville, TN: Abingdon Press.

Interstate New Teacher Assessment and Support Consortium. (1992). *Model Standards for Beginning Teacher Licensing, Assessment, and Development: A Resource for State Dialogue.* Washington, DC: Council of Chief State School Officers.

Kuper, A. (2000). *Culture: The anthropologists' account.* Cambridge, MA: Harvard University Press.

Ladson-Billings, G. (2004). New directions in multicultural education: Complexities, boundaries, and critical race theory. In J. A. Banks & C. A. M. Banks (Eds.), *Handbook of research on multicultural education* (2nd ed., pp. 50–65). San Francisco: Jossey-Bass.

National Assessment of Educational Progress. (2007). Washington, DC: National Center for Education Statistics, U.S. Department of Education. Retrieved on May 20, 2007, from http://nces.ed.gov/nationsreportcard/nde/viewresults.asp

National Board for Professional Teaching Standards. (2001). *The impact of national board certification on teachers: A survey of national board certified teachers and assessors.* Arlington, VA: Author.

Portes, A., & Rumbaut, R. G. (2001). *Legacies: The story of the immigrant second generation.* Berkeley, CA: University of California Press.

Rumbaut, R. G., & Portes, A. (2001). *Ethnicities: Children of immigrants in America.* Berkeley, CA: University of California Press.

Sleeter, C. E. (1992). *Keepers of the American dream: A study of staff development and multicultural education.* London: Taylor & Francis.

Sleeter, C. E., & Bernal, D. D. (2004). Critical pedagogy, critical race theory, and antiracist education. In J. A. Banks & C. A. M. Banks (Eds.), *Handbook of research on multicultural education* (2nd ed., pp. 240–258). San Francisco: Jossey-Bass.

Sleeter, C. E., & Grant, C. A. (2006). *Making choices for multicultural education: Five approaches to race, class, and gender* (5th ed.). New York: John Wiley & Sons.

Snyder, T. D., Tan, A. G., & Hoffman, C. M. (2006). *Digest of education statistics 2005* (NCES 2006-030). U.S. Department of Education, National Center for Education Statistics. Washington, DC: U.S. Government Printing Office.

Spring, J. (2001). *Protecting cultural and language rights: An educational rights amendment to the U.S. constitution.* Keynote Presentation at Annual Meeting of the National Association for Multicultural Education in Arlington, VA.

Symcox, L. (2002). *Whose history? The struggle for national standards in American classrooms.* New York: Teachers College Press.

Tyack, D. (2003). *Seeking common ground: Public schools in a diverse society.* Cambridge, MA: Harvard University Press.

U.S. Census Bureau. (2006). *Statistical Abstract of the United States: 2006* (126th ed.). Washington, DC: U.S. Government Printing Office.

U.S. Department of Education. (2001). *No Child Left Behind Act of 2001.* (www.ed.gov/nclb/overview/intro/presidentplan/proposal.pdf). Washington, DC: U.S. Government Printing Office.

U.S. Department of Education, National Center for Education Statistics. (2006). *The condition of education 2006* (NCES 2006-071). Washington, DC: U.S. Government Printing Office.

Chapter 2

ETHNICITY AND RACE

Nobody recognizes I am Vietnamese because when they look at me they think I am Chinese. They cannot recognize who I am.

MY LIEN NGUYEN, Student, 1996

Denise Williams had become increasingly aware of the racial tension in the high school in which she teaches, but she did not expect the hostility that erupted between some black and white students that Friday. In the week that followed, the faculty decided they had to do more to develop positive interethnic and interracial relations among students. They established a committee to identify consultants and other resources to guide them in this effort.

Ms. Williams, however, thought that neither she nor her students could wait for months to receive a report and recommendations from the committee. She was ready to introduce the civil rights movement in her social studies class. It seemed a perfect time to promote better cross-cultural communications. She decided that she would let students talk about their feelings.

She soon learned that this topic was not an easy one to handle. African American students expressed their anger at the discriminatory practices in the school and the community. Most white students did not believe that there was any discrimination. They believed there were no valid reasons for the anger of the African American and Latino students and that if they just followed the rules and worked harder, they would not have their perceived problems. She thought the class was getting nowhere. In fact, sometimes the anger on both sides was so intense that she worried a physical fight would erupt. She was frustrated that the class discussions and activities were not helping students understand their stereotypes and prejudices. At times, she thought students were just becoming more polarized in their beliefs. She wondered whether she could do anything in her class to improve understanding, empathy, and communications across groups.

Reflections

1. What factors contribute to racial and ethnic conflict in some schools?
2. What racial groups are most likely to see themselves in the school curriculum?
3. How can a classroom reflect the diversity of its students so that they all feel valued and respected?
4. What were the positive and negative outcomes of the steps taken by Ms. Williams?
5. What would you have done to improve cross-cultural relations among class members?

Ethnic and Racial Diversity

The United States is an ethnically and racially diverse nation comprised of nearly 300 **ethnic groups** whose members can identify the national origins of their ancestors. First Americans make up less than 1.5% of the total U.S. population today with 561 federally recognized tribal entities that are **indigenous** or native to the United States (Bureau of Indian Affairs, 2007). Individuals born in Africa, Asia, Australia, Canada, Central America, Europe, Mexico, and South America comprise 12% of the population (U.S. Census Bureau, 2006). Family members and ancestors of the remaining 86.5% of the population also immigrated to the United States from around the world over the past 500 years.

Many people forget that the United States was populated when explorers from other nations arrived on its shores. As more and more Europeans arrived, American Indians were not treated as equal citizens in the formation of the new nation. Eventually, most First Americans were forcibly segregated from the dominant group and, in many cases, forced to move from their geographic homelands to reservations in other parts of the country. This separation led to a pattern of isolation and inequities that remains today. The atrocities and near genocide that resulted from the treatment of Native Americans have been ignored in most historical accounts of U.S. history. Not until 2000 did an official of the

U.S. government apologize for the Bureau of Indian Affairs' "legacy of racism and inhumanity that included massacres, forced relocations of tribes and attempts to wipe out Indian languages and cultures" (Kelley, 2000, p. 1).

Today, 2.9 million citizens identify themselves as American Indian or Alaska Native only; another 1.6 million indicate they have multiple ethnic heritages, one of them being American Indian or Alaska Native (U.S. Census Bureau, 2006). Forty percent of the Native American population belongs to one of six tribes: Cherokee, Navajo, Latin Native American, Choctaw, Sioux, or Chippewa (U.S. Census Bureau, 2006).

Native Hawaiians have experiences similar to other indigenous populations around the world. In 1894, Queen Liliuokalani of Hawaii was overthrown by a group of white sugar planters, to gain control of the Island and further their interests. The American minister sent to Hawaii by President Grover Cleveland reported the overthrow to be illegal, and the President agreed that the monarchy should be restored. However, annexationists' interests prevailed. A white president of the Republic of Hawaii was recognized immediately by the U.S. government. Hawaii was vital to the interests of the United States, and eventually became a territory and then the fiftieth state. Today, Native Hawaiians remain near the bottom of the socioeconomic ladder in Hawaii, and while a few are provided with homestead land during their lifetime, relatively few can afford to own their own homes. As with African American students in the continental United States, disproportionate numbers of Hawaiian children are placed in Hawaii's special education classes.

Although most of the first European settlers were English, the French, Dutch, and Spanish also established early settlements. After the consolidation and development of the United States as an independent nation, successive waves of Western Europeans joined the earlier settlers. Irish, Swedish, and German immigrants came to escape economic impoverishment or political repression in the countries in which they were born. These early European settlers brought with them the political institutions that would become the framework for our government. The melding of these Northern and Western European cultures over time became the dominant culture to which other immigrant groups strived or were forced to assimilate.

Africans were also among the early explorers of the Americas and later part of the foreign settlers in the early days of colonization. By the eighteenth century, Africans were being kidnapped and sold into bondage by slave traders. As involuntary immigrants, this group of Africans underwent a process quite different from the Europeans who voluntarily **emigrated**. Separated from their families and homelands, robbed of their freedom and cultures, Africans developed a new culture out of their different African, European, and Native American heritages and their unique experiences in this country. Early on, the majority of African Americans lived in the South where today they remain the majority population in many counties. When industrial jobs in northern, eastern, and western cities began to open up to them between 1910 and 1920, many migrated north—a pattern that was repeated in the 1940s and 1950s. By the beginning of the twenty-first century, the trend had reversed with a growing number of African Americans from northern states moving south.

Another factor that contributed to African American migration to the North was the racism and political terror that existed in much of the South at that time. Even today, a racial ideology is implicit in the policies and practices of institutions. It continues to block significant assimilation of many African Americans into the dominant society. Although the **civil rights** movement of the 1960s reduced the barriers that prevented many African Americans from enjoying the advantages of the middle class, the number of African Americans, especially children, who remain in poverty remains disproportionately high.

Figures on African Americans and other groups in poverty are presented in Chapter 3.

Mexican Americans also occupy a unique role in the formation of the United States. Spain was the first European country to colonize Mexico and the western and southwestern United States. In 1848, the U.S. government annexed the northern sections of the Mexican Territory, including the current areas of Texas, Arizona, New Mexico, and southern California. The Mexican and Native Americans living within that territory became an oppressed minority in the area in which they had previously been the dominant population. The labor of Mexicans has been persistently sought by farmers and businesses over the past century. Once they arrived, they were treated with hostility, limiting them to low-paying jobs and a subordinate status. Dominant supremacy theories based on color and language have been used against them in a way that, even today, prevents many Mexican Americans from assimilating fully into the dominant culture.

The industrial opening of the West in the mid-1800s signaled the need for labor that could be met through immigration from Asia. Chinese worked the plantations in Hawaii. Chinese, Japanese, and Filipinos were recruited to provide the labor needed on the West Coast for mining gold and building railroads.

By the end of the nineteenth century industries in the nation's cities required more labor than was available. Immigrants from the impoverished eastern and southern European countries were enticed to accept jobs primarily in midwestern and eastern cities. Into the early twentieth century, many immigrants arrived from nations such as Poland, Hungary, Italy, Russia, and Greece. The reasons for their immigration were similar to many earlier immigrants: devastating economic and political hardship in the homeland and demand for labor in the United States. Many immigrants came to the United States with the hope of sharing the better wages and living conditions they thought existed here. But many found conditions here worse than they had expected. Most were forced to live in substandard housing near the business and manufacturing districts where they worked. These urban ghettos grew into ethnic enclaves in which they continued to use their native language and maintain the culture of their native lands. To support their social and welfare needs, ethnic institutions often were established. Many of the dominant racist policies that had been used against African Americans, Mexican Americans, and Native Americans earlier also were applied to these immigrants. The difference was that their offspring were able to assimilate into the dominant culture during the second and third generations.

Immigration

Throughout history the U.S. Congress has prohibited the immigration of different national or ethnic groups on the basis of the racial superiority of the older, established immigrant groups that had colonized the nation. As early as 1729, immigration was being discouraged. In that year, Pennsylvania passed a statute that increased the head tax on foreigners in that colony. Some leaders, including Benjamin Franklin, worried that Pennsylvania was in danger of becoming a German state. The 1790 Naturalization Act, which allowed only whites to be U.S. citizens, declared that an immigrant could become a citizen after several years of residency.

In the nineteenth century, native-born citizens again began to worry about their majority and superiority status over entering immigrant groups. This movement, known as **nativism** restricted immigration and protected the interests of native-born citizens. It was an extreme form of ethnocentrism and **nationalism** requiring loyalty and devotion to the United States over all other nations.

Ethnocentrism was discussed in greater detail in Chapter 1.

In 1882, the Chinese Exclusion Act was passed to halt all immigration from China. Congress viewed Chinese in the same way as other groups of color, but the economic boom was coming to an end and they were no longer needed. The Chinese in the United States at that time were denied citizenship.

The Dillingham Commission reported in 1917 that all immigrants should be able to pass a literacy test. The nativists received further support for their views when Congress passed the Johnson-Reed Act in 1924, establishing annual immigration quotas to disproportionately favor immigrants from Western European countries. It also stopped all immigration from Japan. The Johnson-Reed Act was not abolished until 1965 when a new quota system was established, dramatically increasing the number of immigrants allowed annually from the Eastern Hemisphere and reducing the number from the Western Hemisphere as shown in Figure 2.1.

Congressional leaders and presidential candidates during the 1980s promoted a "get tough" approach to immigration, calling for greater control of the U.S. borders. However, the 1986 Immigration Reform and Control Act actually expanded immigration by allowing visas to persons born in countries adversely affected by the 1965 law—Europeans. Immigration policies are again under attack by a number of citizens who believe that immigration, especially unauthorized immigration, needs to be controlled. Congress was considering new legislation in 2007, including a guest worker program that would allow people from other countries temporary authorization to work in the United States.

Today's immigrants enter the country by what Martin and Midgley (2006) characterize as three doors: "a front door for legal immigrants, a side door for legal temporary migrants, and

FIGURE 2.1   Immigration from Selected Countries and Continents since 1961.

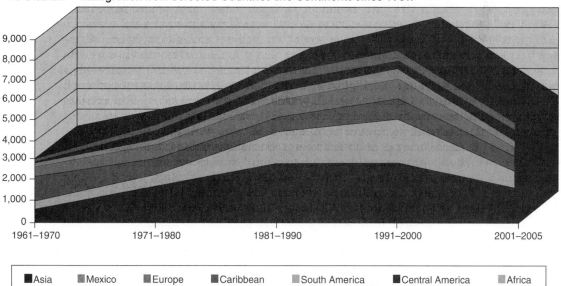

From the U.S. Census Bureau. (2006). *Statistical Abstract of the United States: 2007* (126th ed.). Washington, DC: U.S. Government Printing Office.

a back door for the unauthorized" (p. 4). Legal immigrants come in through four major routes. Family sponsorship is the primary path to immigration, representing approximately 65% of the legal immigrants. Family members who are U.S. citizens can petition the federal government to admit their relatives; there are no caps on the number of visas available for immediate family members. The second-largest group of immigrants (22%) have come to the United States at the request of their employers. They include workers with "'extraordinary ability' in the arts or sciences or multinational executives, skilled and unskilled workers, and such special categories as athletes, ministers, and investors" (Martin & Midgley, 2006, p. 4). Refugees and **asylees** make up the third group. The fourth group is for diversity immigrants—a system that allows people from countries with relatively few immigrants to enter a lottery for one of the 50,000 available slots.

As people from all over the world joined American Indians in populating this nation, they brought with them cultural experiences from their native countries. Just because individuals have the same national origins, however, does not mean that they have the same history and experiences as others. The time of immigration, the place in which groups settled, the reasons for emigrating, their socioeconomic status, and the degree to which they are affected by racism and discrimination interact to form a new ethnic group that differs from those who came before and will come afterward. You will see these differences in schools as students whose family has been in the United States for several generations do not always warmly welcome new immigrant students from the same country.

Refugees

Refugees are the persons recognized by the federal government as being persecuted in their home country because of race, religion, nationality, or membership in a specific social or political group. Between 1991 and 2005, more than 1.5 million immigrants were admitted as refugees from the countries shown in Figure 2.2. As a result of governmental immigration and refugee policies, the U.S. population from various national and ethnic groups has been controlled, but has become increasingly diverse, in part, because of the diversity of the refugees being admitted.

Undocumented Immigrants

Not all immigrants are authorized to be in the country. People from other countries enter the United States as travelers or on student or other special visas. Some of them extend their stay; others never go home. However, most of the undocumented immigrants cross borders illegally. One of three of all foreign-born residents is undocumented (Martin, 2006).

The status of many of these immigrants is later reclassified as legal because they meet the requirements for employment-based visas, refugees, or being sponsored by a family as allowed by law. They may also become legal immigrants through amnesty or similar programs periodically enacted by Congress. About 56% of the undocumented immigrants are from Mexico, and 22% are from other parts of Latin America (Martin, 2006). The number of undocumented immigrants continues to increase. Two of three have been in the United States for less than 10 years; 40% less than five years (Passel, 2006).

In *Plyler v. Doe* (1982), the U.S. Supreme Court ruled that undocumented children have the right to seek a public education. Educators cannot require students or parents to declare

FIGURE 2.2   Home Countries of Refugees Entering the United States since 1991.

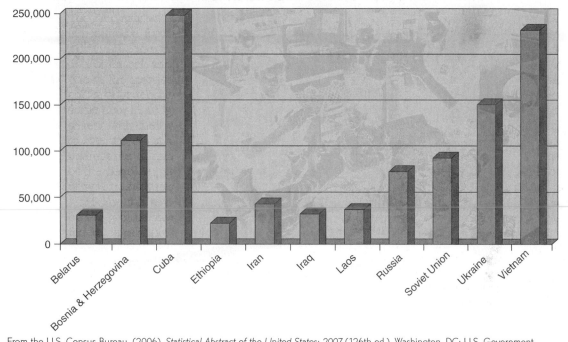

From the U.S. Census Bureau. (2006). *Statistical Abstract of the United States: 2007* (126th ed.). Washington, DC: U.S. Government Printing Office.

their immigration status, and they cannot make inquiries that might expose such status. For example, parents cannot be forced to provide social security numbers to school districts.

A Changed Landscape

The immigration rate during most of the past decade has been around 1 million annually (U.S. Census Bureau, 2006). If immigrants continue to be admitted at the same rate in the last half of this decade as the first half, the number will exceed the 1990s immigration rate. Nearly 60% of the foreign-born population lives in California, New York, Florida, or Texas (U.S. Census Bureau, 2006). Most immigrants settle in urban areas, comprising more than one of four residents in the cities shown in Figure 2.3.

Immigration to nonmetropolitan areas is often dependent on job availability and perceived quality of life. As a result, schools in more rural states across the country do include students from different cultures and with languages other than English. Approximately half of the immigrants in rural areas do not have a high school degree (Jensen, 2006), lowering the **cultural capital** that students bring to school.

As in the past, emotions about immigration policies are dividing restrictionists from immigration supporters. Many citizens value multiculturalism and bilingualism, recalling that their ancestors once were immigrants who entered the country with a culture and often language different from the dominant group. Other citizens view the growing cultural and language diversity as dangerous to the continuation of the "American" culture for which they and their ancestors have fought. In some states and school districts, they have led the

FIGURE 2.3 Immigrants in Major Cities in 2004.

From the U.S. Census Bureau. (2006). *Statistical Abstract of the United States: 2007* (126th ed.). Washington, DC: U.S. Government Printing Office.

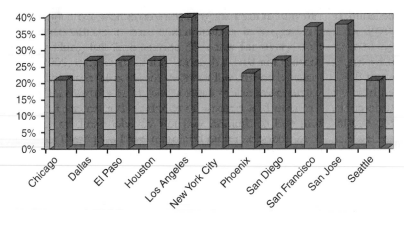

Pause to Reflect 2.1

You are likely to have one or more students in your classroom whose family recently immigrated from another country. They are likely to be English language learners. What experience do you have with persons who are new immigrants?

- What immigrant families were in your community when you were in elementary and secondary schools?
- What interactions did you have with immigrant families and their children?
- What interactions have you had in college with students from countries other than the United States?
- How would you characterize the educational participation and potential of immigrant students with whom you have interacted?

Go to the *Homework and Exercises* section in Chapter 2 of MyEducationLab and select *Pause to Reflect 2.1* to answer these questions.

movement to declare English as the official language and fight against bilingual signs and documents, which they see as promoting bilingualism. In some communities they picket places where undocumented day workers meet potential employers. Some towns are restricting housing and jobs only to those persons who can prove they are authorized.

Restrictionists charge that immigrants, especially undocumented ones, are a drain on the social welfare system as they seek education for their children and medical assistance for their family members. To control the perceived drain on their state budget, Californians passed Proposition 187 in 1994 to deny services to undocumented immigrants and their families. Although the Proposition was later found to be in violation of the Supreme Court's 1982 ruling in *Plyler v. Doe*, efforts to restrict public services, including education, continue in other states. For example, Virginia legislators are trying to drive "illegals" out of the state by denying public benefits to undocumented immigrants. In 2006 and 2007, they proposed bills to deny in-state tuition for attending public colleges and universities to the children of undocumented immigrants (Craig, 2007).

Education Background of Immigrants

The education level of immigrants varies greatly. The percent of the foreign-born population with bachelor's degrees is nearly equal to the native-born population at 17% and 18%, respectively. Nearly 10% of the foreign-born population has advanced degrees as do native-born citizens. At the other end of the economic scale, 33% of foreign-born adults do not have a high school degree—almost three times as many as the native-born population (U.S. Census Bureau, 2006). Studies of immigrants indicate that those with the social or cultural capital of higher education and higher economic status are more likely to be accepted by dominant society and allowed to assimilate into the middle class (Portes & Rumbaut, 2001).

Civil Rights

Members of oppressed groups sometimes coalesce to fight against the harsh economic and political realities and injustices imposed on them. These movements for their democratic rights and economic justice invariably lead to a rise in community solidarity based on race or national origins. The fight for civil rights has led to the reduction of overt discrimination and exclusion that kept many citizens from having access to the basic necessities and benefits of society. The events that initiated these changes in schools and broader society are outlined in the next section.

The Civil Rights Movement

The fight for civil rights by ethnic and racial groups has a long history in the United States. Native Americans fought to maintain their rights, culture, languages, and lands as foreigners appropriated their homelands. African slaves revolted against their owners. Free blacks decried the discrimination and violence they faced in the North. Martin Delaney led a

Members of different ethnic and racial groups join forces to protest for civil rights.

Mark Richards / PhotoEdit Inc.

Black Nationalist movement in the mid-1800s for black liberation. In the early twentieth century Mexican American miners in Arizona led a strike for better working conditions and pay equal to that of European American miners. Across the Southwest, Mexican Americans established ethnic organizations to fight exploitation and support those who were in dire straits. Chinese and other immigrants used the courts to overturn the 1790 Naturalization Law that excluded them from citizenship (Takaki, 1993).

Although individuals and groups continued to push the government for civil rights throughout the twentieth century, the movement exploded in the 1950s and 1960s when large numbers of African Americans in the South challenged their oppressed status. Rosa Parks defied authorities in 1955 when she sat in the whites-only section at the front of the bus in Montgomery, Alabama, sparking a boycott of the public transportation system for over a year, leading to the desegregation of the transportation system. Beginning in 1960, students from North Carolina A&T University and other historically black colleges sat at lunch counters that were for whites only, challenging **Jim Crow laws** that forced whites and persons of color to use different public accommodations such as water fountains, restrooms, hotels, and restaurants. The Congress of Racial Equality (CORE), the Student Nonviolent Coordinating Committee (SNCC), and the Black Panthers Party organized young people to fight the injustices African Americans faced daily.

Under the leadership of Fannie Lou Hamer, African American Democrats from Mississippi challenged the seating of the all-white delegation at the 1964 Democratic National Convention. Although the African American delegates were not seated, their courage led to a growing number of ethnically and racially diverse delegates in the years that followed. Facing arrest and beatings, racially mixed Freedom Riders boarded buses to break the segregation pattern in interstate travel. African Americans, sometimes joined by European Americans, marched for freedom and established Freedom Schools across the South. The March on Washington in 1963, in which Martin Luther King, Jr. made his famous "I Have a Dream" speech, inspired African Americans to continue the fight for their civil rights. But the violence against them continued. Less than a month after the March to Washington, four girls were killed when a bomb exploded in the basement of their black church in Montgomery, Alabama. Congress finally responded by passing the 1964 Civil Rights Act and the 1965 Voting Rights Act, which banned discrimination in schools, employment, and public accommodations and secured the voting rights of African Americans.

The call for "Black Power" brought attention to the history and contributions of African Americans to society. Black studies and other ethnic studies programs were established in colleges and universities. Educators and textbook publishers were pushed to rewrite books to accurately reflect the multiethnic history of the United States. Yet, societal changes did not necessarily follow. Although legislation guaranteed equality for all racial groups, many European Americans continued to fight against the desegregation of schools and other public facilities. Frustrations with the dominant group's lack of progress led African Americans and members of other oppressed groups to identify even more strongly with other members of their ethnic group to fight discrimination and inequality with a unified voice. These struggles continue today not only in this country, but throughout the world.

Brown v. Board of Education

Schools have long been at the center of civil rights movements. At one time children of color were not allowed to attend school. Later they were not allowed to attend schools with white children, leading to a system of desegregated schools in which students of color

Pause to Reflect 2.2

How much do you know about the civil rights struggles during the 1950s and 1960s? Check your knowledge on 12 questions at www.civilrightsteaching.org/mythbusterquiz.htm.

Go to the *Homework and Exercises* section in Chapter 2 of MyEducationLab and select *Pause to Reflect 2.2* to answer these questions.

The importance of *Brown v. Board of Education* in the education of exceptional students is discussed in Chapter 5.

were delegated to schools without the books and resources to which most white children had access. Desegregation continued in many states until more than a decade after the Supreme Court unanimously declared that separate but equal schooling was not equal in its 1954 *Brown v. Board of Education* decision.

The 1954 decision was the result of four cases before the Supreme Court: *Briggs v. Elliott* in South Carolina, *Davis v. County School Board of Prince Edward County* in Virginia, *Gebhart v. Belton* in Delaware, and *Brown v. Board of Education of Topeka* in Kansas. These cases were addressed together in the 1954 decision of *Brown v. Board of Education.* A fifth case, *Bolling v. Sharpe,* settled a year later, declared that the federal government could not segregate schools in the District of Columbia. The Supreme Court returned to the implementation of *Brown v. Board of Education* in 1955 when it sent

Linda Brown and her family were the plaintiffs in one of the four cases that led to the Supreme Court decision on *Brown v. Board of Education* in 1954.

Getty Images, Inc.

all school integration cases back to the lower courts and asked states to desegregate "with all deliberate speed." Nevertheless, segregation continued in many states until more than a decade after the Supreme Court decision. Later courts called for the desegregation of metropolitan areas, busing students across city lines to ensure integration.

Many segregated school districts and universities took years to begin to integrate their schools. The fierce resistance of many whites in many communities required the use of the National Guard to protect African American students who were entering white schools for the first time. Many whites established private schools or moved to the suburbs where the population was primarily European American to avoid sending their children to schools with African Americans. Some communities like Farmville, Virginia, closed their schools rather than desegregating them. As segregated public schools became desegregated, many African American teachers and principals lost their jobs. The composition of schools did change in the three decades following the *Brown* decision. In the mid-1960s only 2% of the African American students in the United States attended integrated schools. By the late 1980s, 45% of them were in integrated schools.

Other ethnic groups also used the courts to demand an equitable education for their children. In *Gong Lum v. Rice* in Mississippi in 1927 a Chinese American girl sought the right to attend a white school by arguing that she was not black. The court ruled she was not white, giving the school the authority to determine the race of their students (Willoughby, 2004). A Mexican American student was allowed to attend an integrated school in California in the 1940s as a result of *Mendez v. Westminster* (Willoughby, 2004). In 1974 Chinese American students in San Francisco won the right to have their first language used in instruction in *Lau v. Nichols.* The *Brown* decision also served as the precursor for federal laws that supported educational equity for girls and women in **Title IX,** passed in 1972, and persons with disabilities in Section 504 of the Rehabilitation Act in 1973.

By the mid-1980s the courts began lifting the federal court sanctions that had forced schools to integrate, stating that the federal requirements were meant to be temporary to overcome **de jure segregation.** Now that schools were no longer segregated by race, the easing of sanctions allowed school districts to return to neighborhood schools. Because of **de facto segregation** in communities, the students in many neighborhood schools were comprised of students of the same race, returning integration to pre-1970 levels. At the beginning of the twenty-first century, researchers Orfield and Frankenberg (2004) found that

> Black students are the most likely racial group to attend what researchers call "apartheid schools," schools that are virtually all non-white and where poverty, limited resources, social strife and health problems abound. One-sixth of America's black students attend these schools.
>
> Whites are the most segregated group in the nation's public schools. Only 14% of white students attend multiracial schools (where three or more racial groups are present).
>
> Latino students are the most segregated minority group in U.S. schools. They are segregated by race and poverty; immigrant Latinos also are at risk of experiencing linguistic segregation.
>
> Asian American students are the most integrated group in the nation's public schools. Three-fourths of Asian Americans attend multiracial schools. (p. 58)

Many educators and commentators claim that the two 2007 Supreme Court rulings against using race to determine where students attend schools have essentially halted desegregation. The milestones in the desegregation and resegregation of schools are chronicled in Table 2.1.

TABLE 2.1 Milestones in Desegregating and Resegregating Schools

1896	The Supreme Court authorizes segregation in *Plessy v. Ferguson,* finding Louisiana's "separate but equal" law constitutional.
1940	A federal court requires equal salaries for African American and white teachers in *Alston v. School Board of City of Norfolk.*
1947	In a precursor to the *Brown* case, a federal appeals court strikes down segregated schooling for Mexican American and white students in *Westminster School Dist. v. Méndez.* The verdict prompts California Governor Earl Warren to repeal a state law calling for segregation of Native American and Asian American students.
1950	Barbara Johns, a 16-year-old junior at Robert R. Moton High School in Farmville, Va., organizes and leads 450 students in an anti-school segregation strike.
1954	In a unanimous opinion, the Supreme Court in *Brown v. Board of Education* overturns *Plessy* and declares that separate schools are "inherently unequal." The Court rules that the federal government is under the same duty as the states and must desegregate the Washington, D.C., schools in *Bolling v. Sharpe.*
1955	In *Brown II,* the Supreme Court orders the lower federal courts to require desegregation "with all deliberate speed."
1956	Tennessee Governor Frank Clement calls in the National Guard after white mobs attempt to block the desegregation of a high school.
	The Virginia legislature calls for "massive resistance" to school desegregation and pledges to close schools under desegregation orders.
1957	More than 1,000 paratroopers from the 101st Airborne Division and a federalized Arkansas National Guard protect niine African American students integrating Central High School in Little Rock, Ark.
1958	The Supreme Court rules that fear of social unrest or violence, whether real or constructed by those wishing to oppose integration, does not excuse state governments from complying with *Brown* in *Cooper v. Aaron.*
	Ten thousand young people march in Washington, D.C., in support of integration.
1959	Officials close public schools in Prince Edward County, Va., rather than integrate them.
	Twenty-five thousand young people march in Washington, D.C., in support of integration.
1960	In New Orleans, federal marshals shield 6-year-old Ruby Bridges from an angry crowd as she attempts to enroll in school.
1964	The Civil Rights Act of 1964 is adopted. Title IV of the Act authorizes the federal government to file school desegregation cases. Title VI of the Act prohibits discrimination in programs and activities, including schools, receiving federal financial assistance.
	The Supreme Court orders Prince Edward Country, Va., to reopen its schools on a desegregated basis in 1964.
1965	In *Green v. County School Board of New Kent County* the Supreme Court orders states to dismantle segregated school systems "root and branch." The Court identifies five factors—facilities, staff, faculty, extracurricular activities, and transportation—to be used to gauge a school system's compliance with the mandate of *Brown.*
1969	The Supreme Court declares the "all deliberate speed" standard is no longer constitutionally permissible and orders the immediate desegregation of Mississippi schools in *Alexander v. Holmes County Board of Education.*
1971	The Court approves busing, magnet schools, compensatory education and other tools as appropriate remedies to overcome the role of residential segregation in perpetuating racially segregated schools in *Swann v. Charlotte-Mecklenburg Board of Education.*

(continued)

TABLE 2.1 Milestones in Desegregating and Resegregating Schools (continued)

1972	The Supreme Court refuses to allow public school systems to avoid desegregation by creating new, mostly or all-white "splinter districts" in *Wright v. Council of the City of Emporia* and *United States v. Scotland Neck City Board of Education.*
1973	The Supreme Court rules that states cannot provide textbooks to racially segregated private schools to avoid integration mandates in *Norwood v. Harrison.* The Supreme Court finds that the Denver school board intentionally segregated Mexican American and African American students from white students in *Keyes v. Denver School District No. 1.* The Supreme Court rules that education is not a "fundamental right" and that the Constitution does not require equal education expenditures within a state in *San Antonio Independent School District v. Rodriguez.*
1974	The Supreme Court blocks metropolitan-wide desegregation plans as a means to desegregate urban schools with high minority populations in *Milliken v. Bradley.* The Supreme Court rules that the failure to provide instruction to those with limited English proficiency violates Title VI's prohibition of national origin, race, or color discrimination in school districts receiving federal funds in *Lau v. Nichols.*
1978	A fractured Supreme Court declares the affirmative action admissions program for the University of California Davis Medical School unconstitutional because it set aside a specific number of seats for African American and Latino students. The Court rules that race can be a factor in university admissions, but it cannot be the deciding factor in *Regents of the University of California v. Bakke.*
1982	The Supreme Court rejects tax exemptions for private religious schools that discriminate in *Bob Jones University v. U.S.* and *Goldboro Christian Schools v. U.S.*
1986	For the first time, a federal court finds that once a school district meets the *Green* factors, it can be released from its desegregation plan and returned to local control in *Riddick v. School Board of the City of Norfolk, Virginia.*
1991	Emphasizing that court orders are not intended "to operate in perpetuity," the Supreme Court makes it easier for formerly segregated school systems to fulfill their obligations under desegregation decrees in *Board of Education of Oklahoma City v. Dowell.*
1992	In *Freeman v. Pitts* the Supreme Court further speeds the end of desegregation cases, ruling that school systems can fulfill their obligations in an incremental fashion.
1995	The Supreme Court sets a new goal for desegregation plans in *Missouri v. Jenkins:* the return of schools to local control.
1996	A federal appeals court prohibits the use of race in college and university admissions, ending affirmative action in Louisiana, Texas, and Mississippi in *Hopwood v. Texas.*
2001	White parents in Charlotte, N.C., schools successfully seek an end to the desegregation process, barring the use of race in making student assignments.
2003	The Supreme Court upholds diversity as a rationale for affirmative action programs in higher education admissions, but concludes that point systems are not appropriate in *Gratz v. Bollinger* and *Grutter v. Bollinger.* A federal district court case affirms the value of racial diversity and race-conscious student assignment plans in K–12 education in *Lynn v. Comfort.*
2007	The more conservative Supreme Court struck down the use of race in determining schools for students in *Parents Involved in Community Schools Inc. v. Seattle School District* and *Meredith v. Jefferson County (Ky.) Board of Education.*

Information through 2003 reprinted with permission from Holladay, J. (2004, Spring). *Brown v. Board* Timeline: School Integration in the United States. *Teaching Tolerance, 25,* 42 56.

The goal of desegregation has changed from the physical integration of students within a school building to the achievement of equal learning opportunities and outcomes for all students. Court cases today are examining the unequal access of students of color to qualified teachers, advanced mathematics and science classes, gifted classes, and adequately funded schools. Civil rights groups are asking why students of color are disproportionately represented in nonacademic and special education classes and why the rates for school suspension and dropping out of school vary for different ethnic groups. As schools become more segregated again, educators have a greater responsibility for ensuring that all students learn regardless of the ethnic and racial composition of the school. Teachers will also have the responsibility for helping students understand that the world in which they are likely to work is multiethnic and multiracial, unlike the school they may be attending.

Ethnicity

Many definitions have been proposed for the term **ethnic group.** Some writers describe ethnic identity as national origin, religion, and race. In some cases, the definition has been expanded to include gender, class, and lifestyles. The most basic definition focuses on an individual's national origins.

A nation is a historically constituted, stable community of people formed on the basis of a common language, territory, economic life, and culture. Through wars and political realignments, nations change over time because boundaries are moved (or removed) as a result of political negotiations. However, new boundaries do not always translate into new national identities; it may take generations for such a conversion.

Ethnic identity is determined by the native countries of our ancestors. We all belong to one or more ethnic groups. For those of us born in the United States, one of our ethnic groups is American. The national origins of our ancestors are reflected in our ethnic identification (e.g., German American or Chinese American). A common bond with an ethnic group is developed through family, friends, and neighbors with whom the same intimate characteristics of living are shared. These are the people invited to baptisms, marriages, funerals, and family reunions. They are the people with whom we feel the most comfortable. They know the meaning of our behavior; they share the same language and nonverbal patterns, traditions, and customs. **Endogamy** (that is, marriage within the group), segregated residential areas, and restriction of activities with the dominant group help preserve ethnic cohesiveness across generations. The ethnic group also allows for the maintenance of group cohesiveness. It helps sustain and enhance the ethnic identity of its members. It establishes the social networks and communicative patterns that are important for the group's optimization of its position in society.

The character of an ethnic group changes over time, becoming different in a number of ways from the culture in the country of origin. Members within ethnic groups may develop different attitudes and behaviors based on their experiences in the United States and the conditions in the country of origin at the time of emigration. Recent immigrants may have little in common with other members of their ethnic group whose ancestors immigrated a century, or even 20 years before. Ethnic communities undergo constant change in population characteristics, locations, occupations, educational levels, and political and economic struggles. All of these aspects affect the nature of the group and its members as they become Americans with ethnic roots in another country.

CRITICAL INCIDENTS IN TEACHING

Student Conflict Between Family and Peer Values

Win Tek Lau is a sixth-grade student in a predominantly white and African American Southern community. He and his parents emigrated from Hong Kong 4 years ago. His uncle an engineer at a local high-tech company, had encouraged Wing Tek's father to immigrate to this country and open a Chinese restaurant. The restaurant is the only Chinese restaurant in the community, and it was an instant success. Mr. Lau and his family have enjoyed considerable acceptance in both their business and their neighborhood. Wing Tek and his younger sister have also enjoyed academic success at school and appear to be well liked by the other students.

One day when Mrs. Baca, Wing Tek's teacher, called him by name, he announced before the class, "My American name is Kevin. Please, everybody call me Kevin from now on." Mrs. Baca and Wing Tek's classmates honor this request, and Wing Tek is "Kevin" from then on.

Three weeks later, Mr. And Mrs. Lau made an appointment to see Mrs. Baca. When the teacher made reference to "Kevin," Mrs. Lau said, "Who are you talking about? Who is Kevin? We came here to talk about our son, Wing Tek."

"But I thought his American name was Kevin. That's what he asked us to call him," Mrs. Baca replied.

"That child," Mrs. Lau said in disgust, "is a disgrace to our family."

"We have heard his sister call him by that name, but she said it was just a joke," Mr. Lau added. "We came to see you because we are having problems with him in our home. Wing Tek refuses to speak Chinese to us. He argues with us about going to his Chinese lessons on Saturday with the other Chinese students in the community. He says he does not want to eat Chinese food anymore. He says that he is an American now and wants pizza, hamburgers, and tacos. What are you people teaching these children in school? Is there no respect for family, no respect for our cultures?"

Mrs. Baca, an acculturated Mexican American who was raised in East Los Angeles, began to put things together. Wing Tek, in his attempt to ensure his acceptance by his classmates, had chosen to acculturate to an extreme, to the point of rejecting his family heritage. He wanted to be as "American" as anyone else in the class, perhaps more so. Like Wing Tek, Mrs. Baca had acculturated linguistically and in other ways, but she had never given up her Hispanic values. She knew the internal turmoil Wing Tek was experiencing.

Questions for Classroom Discussion

1. Is Wing Tek wrong in his desire to acculturate?
2. Are Mr. and Mrs. Lau wrong in wanting their son to maintain their traditional family values?
3. What can Mrs. Baca do to bring about a compromise?
4. What can Mrs. Baca do in the classroom to resolve the problem or at least to lessen the problem?

Building Teaching Skills

Go to the *Building Teaching Skills* section in Chapter 2 of MyEducationLab and se-lect *Critical Incidents in Teaching: Student Conflict Between Family and Peer Values* to complete this exercise.

Pause to Reflect 2.3

Some U.S. citizens trace their roots to the indigenous American Indians; some are first-generation immigrants who were born outside the United States. However, most of the population has lived in the country for generations although their ancestors emigrated from another country.

- How would you describe your ethnicity?
- Do you participate in any ethnic clubs or activities?
- How assimilated is your family into the dominant culture?
- What kind of discrimination does your ethnic group face in everyday life?
- How has your ethnic background influenced your behavior, attitudes, and values?

Go to the *Homework and Exercises* section in Chapter 2 of MyEducationLab and select *Pause to Reflect 2.3* to answer these questions.

Ethnic Identity

A person does not have to live in the same community with other members of the ethnic group to continue to identify with the group. Many second- and third-generation children move from their ethnic communities, integrating into the suburbs or other urban communities—a move that is easier to accomplish if they look white and speak standard English. Although many Americans are generations removed from an immigrant status, some continue to consciously emphasize their ethnicity as a meaningful basis of their identity. They may organize or join ethnic social clubs and organizations to revitalize their identification with their national origin. They can be ethnic when they want to be. It is characterized by a nostalgic allegiance to the culture of one's ancestral homeland. As the dominant society allows members of an ethnic group to assimilate, particular ethnic groups become less distinct. Ethnicity then becomes voluntary for group members—a process much more likely to occur when members are no longer labeled as ethnic by society.

The European heritages with which the most people identify are German (17%), Irish (12%), English (10%), Italian (6%), Polish (3%), and French (3%) (U.S. Census Bureau, 2006). Twenty-two percent of the population reported multiple ancestries because they identify with two or more national origins (U.S. Census Bureau, 2006). They may identify with one ethnic group more than others, or they may view their ethnicity as just American. However, teachers and others with whom students interact may continue to respond to them primarily on the basis of their identifiable ethnicity.

An individual's degree of ethnic identity is influenced early in life by whether or not family members recognize or promote ethnicity as an important part of their identity. Sometimes, the choice about how ethnic one should be is imposed, particularly for members of oppressed ethnic groups. When the ethnic group believes that strong and loyal ethnic identity is necessary to maintain group solidarity, the pressure of other members of the group makes it difficult to withdraw from the group. For many members of the group, their ethnic identity provides them with the security of belonging and knowing who they are. Their ethnic identity becomes the primary source of identification, and they feel no need to identify themselves differently. In fact, they may find it emotionally very difficult to sever their primary identification with the group.

Many individuals and families in the United States maintain ties with their ethnic group by participating in family and cultural traditions.

Jeff Greenberg/PhotoEdit Inc.

Some families fight the assimilative aspects of schooling that draw children into adopting the dress, language, music, and values of their peers from the dominant culture. Immigrant families, families with origins other than Europe, and families who are either not Christian or conservative Christians may fight acculturation and assimilation in an effort to maintain the values, beliefs, and codes of behavior that are important in their cultures.

Group Assimilation

Historically, oppressed groups have been segregated from the dominant group and have developed enclaves in cities and suburbs that help members maintain a strong ethnic identity. Chinatown, Little Italy, Harlem, and Little Saigon are examples of ethnic enclaves in the nation's cities. The suburbs also include pockets of families from the same ethnic groups. Throughout the country are small towns and surrounding farmland where the population comes from the same ethnic background, all the residents being African American, German American, Danish American, Anglo American, or Mexican American. The members of these communities may be culturally encapsulated, so that most of their primary relationships, and many of their secondary relationships, are with members of their own ethnic group. They may not have the opportunity to interact with members of other ethnic groups or to recognize or share the richness of a second culture that exists in another setting. They may never learn how to live with people who speak a different language or dialect, eat different foods, and value things that their own ethnic group does not value. They often learn to fear or denigrate individuals from other ethnic groups primarily because the ways of others are not familiar. White ethnic groups are particularly vulnerable to knowing only their own group and its culture. Unlike their white counterparts, most people of color are forced out of their ethnic encapsulation to achieve social and economic mobility. Many secondary relationships are with members of other ethnic groups because they work with or for members of the dominant group.

Identifying the degree of students' assimilation into the dominant culture may be helpful in determining appropriate instructional strategies. Such information can help the educator understand students' values, particularly the students' and their families' expectations for school. It also allows teachers to more accurately determine the learning styles of students so that their teaching style can be adapted to individual differences. The only way to know the importance of ethnicity in the lives of students is to listen to them. Familiarity and participation with the community from which students come also help the educator know the importance of ethnicity to students and their families.

Race

Are racial groups also ethnic groups? In the United States, many people use the two terms interchangeably. Racial groups include many ethnic groups, and ethnic groups may include members of more than one racial group. Race is a concept that was developed by physical anthropologists to describe the physical characteristics of people in the world more than a century ago—a practice that has now been discredited. It is not a stable category for organizing and differentiating people. Instead, it is a social-historical concept dependent on society's perception that differences exist and that these differences are important. Some theorists suggest that race, as used in the United States, is equivalent to **caste** in other countries. Throughout U.S. history, racial identification has been used by policymakers and much of the population to classify groups of people as inferior or superior to other racial groups, resulting in discrimination, and inequality against persons of color.

Many persons with Northern and Western European ancestry have traditionally viewed themselves as the natural, rightful leaders of the United States and the world. Until 1952, immigrants had to be white to be eligible for naturalized citizenship. At one time, slaves and American Indians were perceived as so inferior to the dominant group that each individual was counted by the government as only a fraction of a person. Chinese immigrants in the late nineteenth century were charged an additional tax. When Southern and Eastern Europeans immigrated in the late nineteenth and early twentieth centuries, they were viewed by nativists as members of an inferior race. However, these Europeans were eligible for citizenship because they were white; persons from most other continents were not eligible. Arab American immigrants, for example, had to have the courts rule that they were white so they could become citizens.

In 1916, Madison Grant's *The Passing of the Great Race* detailed the U.S. racist ideology. Northern and Western Europeans of the **Nordic race** were identified as the political and military geniuses of the world. Protecting the purity of the Nordic race became such an emotional and popular issue that laws were passed to severely limit immigration from any region except Northern European countries. **Miscegenation** laws in many states prevented the marriage of whites to members of other races until the U.S. Supreme Court declared the laws unconstitutional in 1967. However, nativism reappeared in the 1990s in resolutions, referenda, and legislation in a number of states that denied education to undocumented immigrants, restricted communication to the English language, and limited prenatal care and preschool services that were available to low-income families who are disproportionately of color.

Identification of Race

Once race identification became codified in this country, it was acceptable, even necessary at times, to identify oneself by race. It allows tracking of the participation of groups

FIGURE 2.4   Pan-ethnic and Racial Composition of the United States in 2005.

From the U.S. Census Bureau. (2006). *Statistical Abstract of the United States: 2007* (126th ed.). Washington, DC: U.S. Government Printing Office.

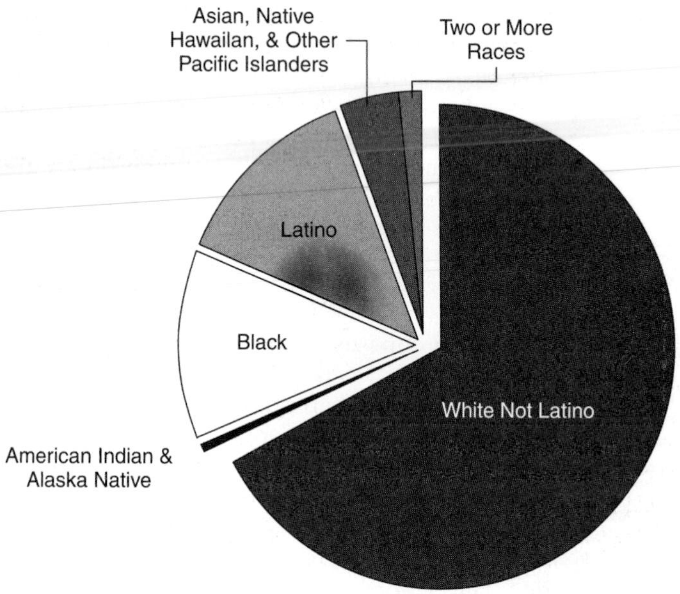

in schools, colleges, and professional fields to determine discriminatory outcomes. Federal forms and reports classify the population on the basis of a mixture of racial and pan-ethnic categorizations as shown in Figure 2.4.

A problem with identifying the U.S. population by such broad categories is that they tell little about the people in these groups. Whether a person was born in the United States or is an immigrant may have significance in how he or she identifies himself or herself. These pan-ethnic classifications impose boundaries that do not always reflect how group members see themselves. Some students rebel against having to identify themselves in this way and refuse to select a pan-ethnic identity.

Although non-Latino whites are numerically dominant in the United States, whites belong to many different ethnic groups. Neither the ethnic identification nor the actual racial heritage of African Americans, which may be a mixture of African, European, and American Indian, is recognized. Latinos represent different racial groups and mixtures of racial groups, as well as distinct ethnic groups whose members identify themselves as Mexican Americans, Puerto Ricans, Spanish Americans, and Cuban Americans. This category also includes persons with roots in numerous Central and South American countries. When Latinos were asked to declare their race as black or white in the 2000 census, many rejected the classification and declared their race as Hispanic.

The pan-ethnic classification of Asian and Pacific Islander Americans includes both individuals whose families have been here for generations and those who are first-generation immigrants. Many do not have much more in common than that their countries of origin are part of the same continent. They are "Bangladeshi, Bhutanese, Bornean, Burmese, Cambodian, Celbesian, Cernan, Chamorro, Chinese, East Indian, Filipino, Hawaiian, Hmong, Indonesian, Japanese, Korean, Laotian, Okinawan, Samoan, Sikkimese, Singaporean, Sri Lankan, and Vietnamese" (Young & Pang, 1995, p. 5). The majority of Asians in the United States today are immigrants from the educated middle or upper middle class.

African Americans range in skin color along a continuum. It is not the color of their skin that defines them, but their identification with their African heritage. They have become a single pan-ethnic group because they share a common history, language, economic life, and culture that have developed over centuries of living in the United States. They are a cohesive group, in part, because of continuing discrimination as reflected in racial profiling by police, segregated schools and housing, and treatment in shopping centers and on the job (National Conference for Community and Justice, 2006). Because individuals appear to be African American is not an indication that they always identify themselves as African Americans. Some identify themselves as black; others with a specific ethnic group—for example, Puerto Rican or Somalian or West Indian. Africans who are recent immigrants generally identify themselves ethnically by their nation or tribe of origin.

The number of persons with multiracial backgrounds is growing. Although only 1% of the population identified their race as "two or more races" in 2005, the number of interracial marriages has more than tripled since 1980 (U.S. Census, 2006). The belief of the racial superiority of whites is reflected in cases of mixed racial heritage. Individuals of black and white parentage are usually classified as black, not white; those of Japanese and white heritage usually are classified as Asian American.

Many whites see themselves as raceless. They are the norm against which everyone else is "other." They can allow their ethnicity to disappear because it is not a determinant of their life chances especially after their family has been in the United States for a few generations. They believe that their social and economic conditions are based totally on their own individual achievement, not assisted by their race. They cannot understand why members of other groups do not experience the same success. They usually deny that racial inequality has any impact on their ability to achieve. They seldom acknowledge that white oppression of people of color around the world has contributed to the subordinate status of those groups. Most whites are unable to acknowledge that they are privileged in our social, political, and economic systems. The study of whiteness exposes the privilege and power it bestows on its members in the maintenance of an inequitable system.

Racial Diversity

Over the next few decades, whites will comprise less and less of the U.S. population. More than one third of the nation is currently African American, Latino, Asian American, and American Indian. These groups will comprise almost 40% of the population by 2020, and 50% of the population by 2050 (U.S. Census Bureau, 2004).

Pause to Reflect 2.4

Although race has no scientific significance in describing people, it is a social construct that endures in the United States to classify groups. It is nearly impossible to be colorblind.

- How would others describe your race?
- Do you view some racial groups more positively than others? Which ones?
- What has influenced your perceptions of your own group and others?
- How comfortable do you feel with handling issues of race in the classroom?

Go to the *Homework and Exercises* section in Chapter 2 of MyEducationLab and select *Pause to Reflect 2.4* to answer these questions.

Two variables contribute to the population growth of persons of color. Approximately 40% of the 2.8 million increase in the U.S. population in 2005 was the result of immigration. Eighteen percent of the immigrants came from Europe and Canada. The remaining immigrants came from Asia (36%), Africa (8%), Oceania (1%), South America (9%), Mexico (14%), Central America (4%), and the Caribbean (9%) (U.S. Census Bureau, 2006). The second variable is the birthrate. In the baby boom years of 1946 to 1964, the U.S. total fertility rate was 2.9 children per woman, leading to an increase in the population. Today that rate is 2.0 as compared to 1.4 in Europe and 2.7 in the world (Population Reference Bureau, 2006). The differential rate among racial and ethnic groups contributes to differing growth patterns. White women in the United States are having an average of 2.0 children, Asian Americans and Pacific Islanders 1.9, American Indians and Alaska Natives 1.7, African Americans 2.0, and Latinos 2.8 (U.S. Census Bureau, 2006).

Racial Identity

Racial identity is influenced by one's family and by the people who look like us in newspapers, on television, and in movies. How racial groups are stereotyped influences the interactions between members of different racial groups. If a group is seen as aggressive and violent, the reaction of the second group may be fear and protection. The construct of whiteness by many students of color may be based on distrust of whites that has grown out of their own or their communities' lived experiences. Unlike most whites, persons of color see the privilege of whiteness and, in many cases, have suffered the consequences of their lack of privilege and power in society. Their oppression by the dominant group is often a unifying theme around which persons of color coalesce (Tatum, 2003).

The racial identity of groups evolves with education and life experiences, but may be suppressed at any stage before full development (Cross, 1992; Helms, 1990; Tatum, 2003). Psychologist William E. Cross (1992) identified six stages in the racial development of African Americans. Black children develop a belief that white is better based on their knowledge and interaction with the dominant culture. Adolescent youth often experience an event that makes them acutely aware of racism and more conscious of the significance of race in society. During this period, they are often angry about the stereotyping and racism they are experiencing or see others experience. Acceptance by their African American peers becomes very important, and **acting white** or hanging with whites is frowned upon. In young adulthood—often when in college—an African American develops a "strong desire to surround oneself with symbols of one's racial identity, and actively seek out opportunities to learn about one's own history and culture, with the support of same-race peers" (Tatum, 2003, p. 76). The next stage of development is internalization in which individuals are secure with their own race and able to develop meaningful relationships with whites who respect their racial identity. In the last stage individuals have a very positive sense of their racial identity and develop a commitment to the issues of African Americans as a group.

Whites also go through developmental stages as they develop their racial identity and abandon racism. At the beginning, whites usually do not recognize the significance of race. They accept the common **stereotypes** of persons of color and do not believe that racism pervades society. As they become aware of white racism and privilege, they become uncomfortable and feel guilt, shame, and anger about racism. They begin to recognize that they are prejudiced. In the next stage, they become silent about racism and are frustrated at being labeled a member of a group, rather than an individual. As they become more aware of

VIDEO INSIGHTS

Acting White

Almost every African American student in any school can define "acting white." Underachieving black students often attribute academic achievement as acting white, and attack achieving students for excelling in school, speaking Standard English, listening to the "wrong" music, or having white friends. Some African American students may perceive the achieving students as being traitors or disloyal to their race because of these behaviors. By adopting values common to the dominant culture, they are seen as trying to behave like whites and ignoring their own racial history and experiences as a result, many black students do not study as hard as achieving white students and do not choose the more challenging advanced placement courses. Latino students have indicated that they too have experienced this same phenomenon. This is a major problem for students of color who want to achieve academically, or go on to higher education.

1. Must these students learn to function biculturally and bidialectally to be successful in school?
2. What can we as educators do to address this problem?

Go to the Video Insights DVD and watch the *Acting White* video segment. Then, go to the *Homework and Exercises* section in Chapter 2 of MyEducationLab and select *Video Insights: Acting White* to answer these questions.

institutional racism, they begin to unlearn their own racism. In this stage they are often self-conscious and feel guilty about their whiteness. The development of a positive white identity allows them to move beyond the role of the victimizer, causing their feelings of guilt and shame to subside. In the last stage, they become an ally to persons of color and are able to confront institutional racism and work toward its elimination (Helms, 1990).

Elementary and secondary students will be at different stages of developing their racial identity. They may be angry, feel guilty, be ethnocentric, or be defensive—behaviors and feelings that may erupt in class as Denise Williams found in the vignette that opened this chapter. Educators must remember that students of color face societal constraints and restrictions that seldom affect white students. Such recognition is essential in the development of instructional programs and schools to effectively serve diverse populations who as yet do not share equally in the benefits that education offers.

Racism

A crucial fact in understanding racism is that many whites see themselves as better than persons and groups of color, and as a result exercise their power to prevent people of color from securing the prestige, power, and privilege held by them. Many members of the dominant group do not acknowledge the existence of external impingements that make it much more difficult for people of color to shed their subordinate status than it was for their own European ancestors. They ignore the fact that some people of color have adopted the cultural values and standards of the dominant group to a greater degree than many white ethnic groups. Yet, discriminatory policies and practices prevent them from sharing equally with whites in society's benefits. In addition, the opportunities to gain qualifications with which people of color could compete equally with whites have been severely restricted throughout most of U.S. history.

Many whites declare they are not racist. They listen to rap music, dress like black urban youth, and respect African American athletes. They argue that they have never discriminated against a person of color and that they cannot be blamed for events of 40 or 200 years ago. They take no responsibility for society's racism.

Whites have little or no experience with discrimination and often do not believe that members of other racial groups are discriminated against. In a national survey by the National Conference for Community and Justice (2006) on the state of intergroup relations in the United States, 32% of the African Americans reported incidents of discrimination in the past month, as compared with 9.5% of the whites, 21% of the Latinos, and 22.5% of the Asian Americans. Where the discrimination occurred during the past month differed by group, as shown in Table 2.2.

Blacks and whites have different perceptions of how persons of color are treated in society. Nearly three in five African Americans are dissatisfied with how they are treated (Saad, 2004). They are twice as likely as whites to believe that their children do not receive equal educational opportunities in schools (Ludwig, 2004). The fact that whites do not acknowledge the discrimination that blacks know from experience contributes to the racist policies and practices that exist in schools and society.

Intergroup Relations

Interethnic and interracial conflict is certainly not new in the United States, although the intensity of such conflicts has been mild compared to that in many other nations. Oppressed people in this country have a history of resistance, however, as shown in revolts organized by slaves, riots after particularly egregious actions of police or others, and strikes by workers. American Indian and white conflicts were common in the European American attempt to subjugate the native peoples.

What are the reasons for continued interethnic conflict? Discriminatory practices have protected the superior status of the dominant group for centuries. When other ethnic groups try to share more equitably in the rewards and privileges of society, the dominant group must concede some of its advantages. As long as one ethnic or racial group has an institutional advantage over others, some intergroup conflict will exist.

TABLE 2.2   Discrimination in Daily Life by Group

	While Shopping	At Work	In a Restaurant, Bar, or Theater	At Place of Worship	Other
Whites	4%	3%	4%	1%	3%
Blacks	20%	14%	12%	1%	9%
Latinos	8%	6%	3%	1%	3%
Asian Americans	14%	11%	8%	0%	10%

Data from National Conference for Community and Justice. (2006). *Taking America's pulse III: A survey of intergroup relations.* New York: Author.

Competition for economic resources can also contribute to intergroup conflict. As economic conditions become tighter, fewer jobs are available. Discriminatory practices in the past have forced people of color into positions with the least seniority. When jobs are cut back, disproportionately high numbers of persons of color are laid off. The tension between ethnic groups increases as members of specific groups determine that they disproportionately suffer the hardships resulting from economic depression. Conflict sometimes occurs between oppressed groups when they are forced to share limited societal resources, such as affordable housing and access to quality education programs.

In a Gallup Poll on satisfaction with the state of race relations, only 44% of the persons of color were satisfied as compared to 56% of the whites (Carlson, 2004). Most whites think that they and persons of color have equal job opportunities, but the majority of Latinos and African Americans disagree (Carroll, 2006). The negative view of blacks is based on their perceptions that conflict and tension with whites is relatively high, discrimination continues to affect their life chances, few opportunities for improving their social conditions are available, and they lack political and social influence (National Conference for Community and Justice, 2006). Most whites recognize that persons of color do not have the same opportunities as they, but the percentage who acknowledge these differences is smaller than any other group. Neither whites nor blacks are very optimistic about dramatically improving race relations; 44% of the whites and 55% of the blacks believe that they will always be a problem (Ludwig, 2004).

During the past 50 years, educational strategies have been developed to reduce and overcome intergroup conflicts. These strategies have focused on training teachers to be effective in intergroup or human relations; on attempting to change the prejudicial attitudes of teachers; on fighting institutional discrimination through affirmative action and civil rights legislation; on encouraging changes in textbooks and other resources to more accurately reflect the multiethnic nature of society; and on attempting to remove discriminatory behavior from classroom interactions and classroom practices. All of these strategies are important to combat prejudice and discrimination in the educational setting. Alone or in combination, however, the strategies are not enough, but that does not diminish the need for professional educators to further develop the strategies. It is not a sign of failure, but a recognition that prejudice, discrimination, and racism are diseases that infect all of society.

Hate Groups

White privilege is sometimes taken to the extreme as members try to protect their power by preaching hate against other groups. Since World War II, overt acts of prejudice have decreased dramatically. In the early 1940s, the majority of whites supported segregation of and discrimination against, blacks. Today, most whites support policies against racial discrimination and prejudice.

Nevertheless, intolerance of other groups and violence against them continues. Many communities have experienced hate crimes against people of color, non-Christians, and gays and lesbians that still include cross burnings and swastika graffiti. The Southern Poverty Law Center reports that:

- Every hour someone commits a hate crime.
- Every day at least eight blacks, three whites, three gays, three Jews, and one Latino become hate crime victims.
- Every week a cross is burned. (Southern Poverty Law Center, 2005, p. 1)

Over 9,000 hate crimes were reported in 2004, but many victims do not report the crimes because of fear of retaliation or the belief that nothing will be done. Although most hate crimes were historically committed in the South against African Americans and Jews, the majority today occur in the North and West (Southern Poverty Law Center, 2005).

The Southern Poverty Law Center reported the existence of 844 hate group chapters in the United States with the majority located east of the Mississippi River (Potok, 2004). While freedom of speech, guaranteed by the First Amendment, is one of the most cherished values in the country, it is also one of the variables that contributes to the proliferation of hate groups. Each individual's freedom of speech is guaranteed, and this includes those who express messages of hate in their speeches, writings, and now on the Internet. The message of hate groups is attractive to some citizens who want to blame others for their misfortunes. However, only 5% of the hate crimes are committed by members of these groups. Most are committed by young males who have adopted the hate rhetoric, but don't usually act from a deeply held ideology (Southern Poverty Law Center, 2005).

Recruitment efforts by hate groups often target areas of the country that have experienced economic and racial change, such as a factory layoff or increased diversity in a school as a result of desegregation. Other recruits are sometimes angry about economic conditions that have led to the loss of jobs in their communities. Rather than blaming corporations that are economizing and moving jobs to sources of cheaper labor, they blame African Americans, women, Arabs, Jews, or the government. Hate group organizers convince new recruits that it is members of other groups who are taking their jobs and being pandered to by government programs. A student contact in a school can provide information about the mood and anger of students that might make a school a potential candidate for recruitment (Youth and Hate, 1999).

Pause to Reflect 2.5

Hate groups exist in a number of communities and schools and colleges can be recruiting grounds for members. Respond to the questions below to describe conditions in your community that might contribute to recruitment efforts.

	Very	Somewhat	Not at All
1. How prevalent do you think racism is in your college?	☐	☐	☐
2. How prevalent do you think racism is in your home community?	☐	☐	☐
3. How likely is it that a hate group would be established in your home community?	☐	☐	☐
4. How well do different racial groups get along on your campus?	☐	☐	☐
5. How well do different racial groups get along in your home community?	☐	☐	☐

Go to the *Homework and Exercises* section in Chapter 2 of MyEducationLab and select *Pause to Reflect 2.5* to answer these questions.

Many of the hate groups have developed sophisticated websites and support an ultra-violent white power music industry (Southern Poverty Law Center, 2004). Some hate groups have links on their websites that are developed primarily for school-age youngsters. Some contain cartoons, others crossword puzzles for children. All contain a message of hate. Because so many children have become proficient in the use of computers and in surfing the web, it has become imperative for parents and educators to be able to recognize online hate and to be able to minimize the risks to their children and students. Software that will block or filter hate group websites is available through Internet providers and software dealers.

Classroom Focus

At the beginning of the twenty-first century, Latinos replaced African Americans as the largest non-European group in the United States. The number of Latino students has also surpassed the number of African American students in schools. Figure 2.5 shows how the diversity of school-aged children and youth has changed over the past 18 years. The majority of the population in many urban schools is comprised of students of color. White students are projected to comprise less than half of the student population by 2050. These demographics obviously have a profound impact on schools throughout the United States.

FIGURE 2.5   The Changing Diversity of the K–12 Student Population.

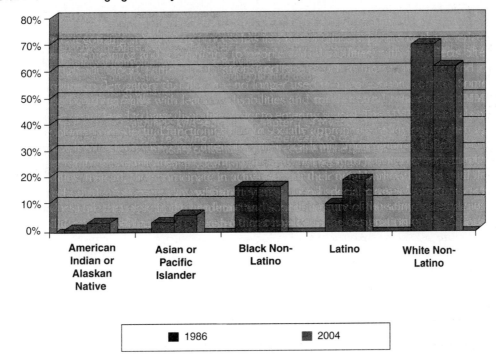

From Strizedk, G. A., Pittsonberger, J. L., Riordan, K. E., Lyter. D. M., & Orlofsky, G. F. (2006). *Characteristics of school, districts, teachers, principals, and school libraries in the United States: 2003–2004 schools and staffing survey* (NCES 2006-313 Revised). U.S. Department of Education, National Center for Education Statistics. Washington, DC: U.S. Government Printing Office.

FIGURE 2.6 Student Diversity by State.

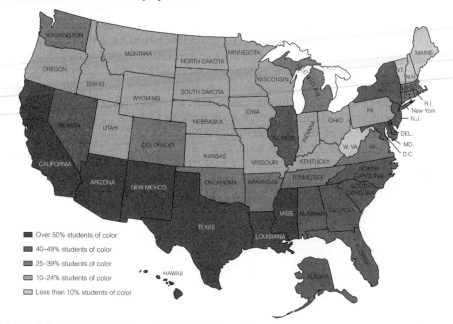

From Snyder, T. D., Tan, A. G., & Hoffman, C. M. (2006). *Digest of Education Statistics 2005* (NCES 2006-030). U.S. Department of Education, National Center for Education Statistics. Washington, DC: U.S. Government Printing Office.

Some states and areas of the country are much more diverse than others; for example, the West has the largest concentration (57%) of students of color; the Midwest the least (26%). Students of color now comprise over half of the student population in eight states as shown in Figure 2.6. The highest concentration of African American students is in the South (25%); Latinos make up 39% of the students in the West (U.S. Department of Education, 2006).

Ethnicity and race play an important role in the lives of many students and communities. Membership in oppressed groups has a significant impact on students' perceptions of themselves and their behavior and performance in school. Ethnicity and race are significant for educators because their cultural background and experiences may be incongruent with the cultural experiences of students. Teachers themselves may stereotype students who have a racial or ethnic background different than their own. The majority of teachers are white females who are charged with teaching the majority of students of color. Figure 2.7 shows that teachers of color are in short supply in the nation's schools. Therefore, it is critical that white teachers become aware of the cultures of the students in the schools to which they are assigned.

This incongruence may contribute to students not feeling their cultures are reflected in school, sometimes leading to their dropping out of school or not participating in meaningful ways. More students of color than white students are not actively engaged in their schoolwork, too often dropping out of school, in part, because they don't see the payoff in education. Only 79% of 18- to 21-year-olds have graduated from high school with Asian Americans having the highest graduation rates from both high school and college (U.S. Census Bureau, 2006). The percentage of students who actually graduate from high school on time (that is, four years after they enter high school) is much less, ranging from

FIGURE 2.7   Pan-Ethnic and Racial Diversity of K–12 Teachers and Students.

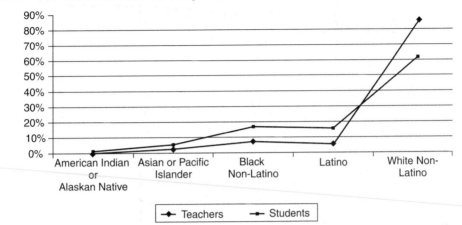

From Strizek, G. A., Pittsonberger, J. L., Riordan, K. E., Lyter, D. M., & Orlofsky, G. G. (2006). *Characteristics of schools, districts, teachers, principals, and school libraries in the United States: 2003–2004 schools and staffing survey* (NCES 2006-313 Revised). U.S. Department of Education, National Center for Education Statistics. Washington, DC: U.S. Government Printing Office.

47% to 56% for American Indians, African Americans, and Latinos to 76% and 77% for European and Asian Americans, respectively (Education Trust, 2006).

Acknowledging Race and Ethnicity in Schools

Teachers often declare that they are color-blind—they do not see a student's color and treat all students equally regardless of race. The problem is that **color blindness** helps maintain white privilege because it fails to recognize the existence of racial inequality in schools (Gallagher, 2003). Teachers do not usually confront issues of race in schools and classrooms, in part because race is not supposed to matter. Teachers' discomfort becomes intertwined with their own uncertainties about race and their possible complicity in maintaining racial inequities.

Race and ethnicity do matter to many students and their families, and do have an impact on communications and interactions with teachers. Students of color are reminded by others of their race on almost a daily basis as they face discriminatory practices and attitudes. Rather than pretending that race and ethnicity do not exist, teachers should acknowledge the differences and be aware of ways culture can influence learning. Equity does not mean sameness; students can be treated differently, as long as the treatment is fair and appropriate, to accomplish the goal of student learning.

The ethnic communities to which students belong provide the real-life examples teachers should draw on to teach. Knowing students' ethnic and cultural experiences and how subject matter interacts with students' reality are important in designing effective strategies to engage students in learning. Successful teachers ensure that students learn the academic skills needed to compete effectively in the dominant workplace. In the process they acknowledge and respect the ethnicity of their students and the community in which the school is located to prevent students from becoming alienated from their homes, their community, and their culture. A disproportionally large number of students of color are not learning what is needed to perform at accepted levels on standardized tests. In fact, the achievement of many students of color decreases the longer they stay in school. Educators should do everything possible to ensure this fact is not a reality in their classroom.

FOCUS YOUR CULTURAL LENS: DEBATE

Should Proms Be Segregated?

Many schools in communities with diverse populations are racially and ethnically integrated. Developing positive cross-cultural communications and interactions has long been a goal of schools that are seriously trying to integrate. However, practices in schools are not supportive of this goal when students are segregated in bilingual classes, advanced placement courses, special education classes, and gifted programs when students from one racial or ethnic group are disproportionately over- or underrepresented. Students often separate themselves by their racial or ethnic group at lunchtime in the school cafeteria, in after-school activities, in their choices of extracurricular activities, and in work groups in the classroom. The integration of another school tradition is being threatened in a number of communities. Students who do not feel welcome at their high school prom are organizing their own proms for students from the same racial, ethnic, religious, sexual orientation, or disability group (Richard, 2004). Schools in the South that have for years sponsored segregated proms for black and white students have been assailed for not integrating this social event. Does support for segregated events fly in the face of the goal for integration or support the preferences of each racial, ethnic, or other group?

For

- Students from the same racial or ethnic group prefer to attend proms with members of their own groups because they like the same music and food.
- Integrated proms favor one group's preference for music and refreshments over another, which does not treat groups equally.

Against

- School-sponsored events like a prom should support the school's goal for integration in all of its activities.
- The separation of groups in social situations like a prom exacerbates poor intergroup relations.

Questions

1. Why do some students not feel welcome at their high school proms?
2. What could school officials do to ensure that the needs of a diverse group of students are met at school proms and other school activities?
3. When would you be in favor of a segregated prom? Why?

Go to the *Homework and Exercises* section in Chapter 2 of MyEducationLab and select *Focus Your Cultural Lens* to answer these questions.

Reference: Richard, A. (2004, May 10). Alternative proms gain in popularity. *Education Week, XXIII* (37), 1, 19.

Confronting Racism in Classrooms

A first step in confronting racism in schools is to realize that racism exists and that, if teachers are white, they have benefited from it. This is not an easy process as discussed earlier in the section on racial identity. We often resist discussion of race and racism because we must eventually confront our own feelings and beliefs. Once teachers believe that discrimination exists in society and the school, they are more likely to believe students of color when they report incidents of racism or discrimination. They stop making excuses for the perpetrators or explaining that the action of the perpetrator was not really racist.

Students often resist participating in discussions about race and racism. In predominantly white college classrooms, Tatum (2003) found three sources of resistance:

1. Race is considered a taboo topic for discussion, especially in racially mixed settings.
2. Many students, regardless of racial group membership, have been socialized to think of the United States as a just society.
3. Many students, particularly white students, initially deny any personal prejudice, recognizing the impact of racism on other people's lives but failing to acknowledge its impact on their own.

Many teachers do not feel comfortable handling students' resistance to these topics, in part, because they are not always confident of their own stances on race. Because students are at different levels in their own racial identity, many of them cannot address these issues as rationally as the teacher might desire. Some will personalize the discussion. Some will be emotional or confrontive. Others will be uncomfortable or silent. Just because the topic is difficult to address does not mean it should be ignored. Teachers should break the silence about race and develop the courage to work at eliminating racism in their own classrooms and schools. One step is to help students think critically about race and social justice for all students.

Teachers should not ignore the racism that exists in the policies and practices of their schools. They should intervene when students call each other names that are racist. Students should be helped to understand that racist language and behavior are unacceptable and will not be tolerated in schools. When students use derogatory terms for ethnic group members or tell ethnic jokes, teachers should use the opportunity to discuss attitudes about those groups. Students should not be allowed to express their hostility to other group members without being confronted. When teachers allow students to treat others with disrespect, they are partners in the perpetuation of racism. These overt acts can be confronted and stopped, but the more difficult task will be to identify and eliminate racist practices in schools.

A teacher's challenge is to seriously confront these issues at a personal level before entering a classroom. If teachers believe that persons of color are intellectually inferior, they will find it difficult to have high expectations for the academic achievement of those students. Although the developmental stages differ for members of oppressed and dominant groups because of their own lived encounters with racism and oppression (Cross, 1992), it is important that all educators seek opportunities to confront these issues in their own lives. Once in the classroom, they will be in the position to help students grapple with these topics and their own feelings. The goal should be to attack racism and oppression in daily life, rather than reinforce it in the classroom.

Race and Ethnicity in the Curriculum

School environments should help students learn to participate in the dominant society while maintaining connections to their distinct ethnicities if they choose. Respect for and support of ethnic differences will be essential in this effort. As educators, we cannot afford to reject or neglect students because their ethnic backgrounds are different from our own. We are responsible for making sure all students learn to think, read, write, and compute so that they can function effectively in society. We can help accomplish this goal by accurately reflecting ethnicity and race in the curriculum and positively using it to teach and interact with students.

Pause to Reflect 2.6

Students from some groups are more privileged in schools than other groups. Check your knowledge by indicating whether the statements below are true or false.

1. European American students are more likely to have social capital than students of color.	True	False
2. Families of color value education.	True	False
3. The parents of European American students take greater responsibility for their children's learning than do the parents of African Americans and Latinos.	True	False
4. College admissions favor European American students.	True	False
5. Equity exists in the course-taking patterns of European American, African American, and Latino students in high school.	True	False
6. White students are more likely to be in rigorous, challenging classrooms.	True	False

Go to the *Homework and Exercises* section in Chapter 2 of MyEducationLab and select *Pause to Reflect 2.6* to answer these questions.

Traditionally, the curriculum of most schools has been centered in the dominant culture. It is based on the knowledge and perspective of the West (Northern and Western Europe). The inherent bias of the curriculum does not encourage candid admissions of racism and oppression within society. In fact, it supports the superiority of Western thought over all others and provides minimal or no introduction to the non-Western cultures of Asia, Africa, and South and Central America. Information on, and perspectives of, other groups are sometimes added as a unit during a school year. Some schools have replaced this traditional curriculum with one based on the culture of students and communities. Multicultural education, on the other hand, encourages a culturally responsive curriculum in which diversity is integrated throughout the courses, activities, and interactions in the classroom.

Ethnic Studies. Ethnic studies courses introduce students to the history and contemporary conditions of one or more ethnic groups. Many universities and some high schools have ethnic studies programs, such as African American, Asian American, American Indian, and Latino Studies, in which students can major. These courses and programs allow for in-depth exposure to the social, economic, and political history of a specific group. They are designed to correct the distortions and omissions that prevail in society about a specific ethnic group. Events that have been neglected in textbooks are addressed, myths are dispelled, and history is viewed from the perspective of the ethnic group, as well as the dominant group. Prospective teachers and other professional school personnel who have not been exposed to an examination of an ethnic group different from their own should take such a course or undertake individual study.

Traditionally, ethnic studies have been offered as separate courses that students elect from many offerings in the curriculum. Seldom have they been required courses for all students. Although the information and experiences offered in these courses are important to members of the ethnic groups, students from other ethnic groups also need to learn about others and the multiethnic nation and world in which they live.

Ethnocentric Curriculum.   Some immigrant groups have their own schools, with classes often held in the evenings or on Saturdays, to reinforce their cultural values, traditions, and the native language. Today other ethnic groups are establishing their own charter or private schools with curriculum that is centered around the history and values of their own ethnic group. Some American Indian tribes have established tribal-controlled public schools in which the traditional culture serves as the social and intellectual starting point. Although most of these schools are located in rural American Indian communities, some urban areas have created magnet American Indian schools with similar goals.

Some African American communities support an **Afrocentric curriculum** to challenge Eurocentrism and tell the truth about black history. They are designed to improve students' self-esteem, academic skills, values, and positive identity with their ethnic group. At the core of this approach is an African perspective of the world and historical events. These schools are often in urban areas with large African American student populations.

Some parents, educators, and community activists who believe that public schools were not effectively serving their children have established urban, ethnocentric, and grass-roots charter schools. These schools place the ethnic culture of the enrolled students at the center of the curriculum; they are Afrocentric, Chicano-centric, or American Indian-centric, emphasizing what is known, valued, and respected from their own cultural roots.

Multiethnic Curriculum.   A **multiethnic curriculum** permeates all subject areas at all levels of education, from preschool through adult education. All courses reflect accurate and positive references to ethnic diversity. The amount of specific content about groups varies according to the course taught, but an awareness and a recognition of the multiethnic population is reflected in all classroom experiences.

Bulletin boards, resource books, and films that show ethnic and racial diversity constantly reinforce these realities, although teachers should not depend entirely on these resources for instructional content about groups. Too often, persons of color are studied only during a unit on African American history or American Indians. Too often, they are not included on reading lists or in the study of biographies, labor unions, or the environment. Students can finish school without reading or seeing anything written or produced by females and males of color. If ethnic groups are included only during a unit or a week focusing on a particular group, students do not learn to view them as an integral part of society. They are viewed as separate, distinct, and inferior to the dominant group. A multiethnic curriculum prevents the distortion of history and contemporary conditions. Without it, the perspective of the dominant group becomes the only valid curriculum to which students are exposed.

An educator has the responsibility for ensuring that ethnic groups become an integral part of the total curriculum. This mandate does not require the teacher to discuss every ethnic group. It does require that the classroom resources and instruction *not* focus solely on the dominant group. It requires that perspectives of ethnic groups and the dominant group be examined in discussions of historical and current events. For example, one should consider the perspectives of Mexican and American Indians as well as the dominant group in a presentation and discussion of the westward movement of European Americans in the eighteenth and nineteenth centuries. It requires students to read literature by authors from different ethnic and racial backgrounds. It expects that mathematics and science will be explored from an American Indian as well as a Western perspective. The contributions of different ethnic groups are reflected in the books that are used by students, in the movies they view, and in the activities in which they participate.

Multiethnic education includes learning experiences to help students examine their own stereotypes about and prejudice against ethnic and racial groups. These are not easy topics to address but should be a part of the curriculum beginning in preschool. At all levels, but particularly in junior high and secondary classrooms, students may resist discussion of these issues. Teachers can create a safe classroom climate by establishing clear guidelines for such discussions.

Development of a multiethnic curriculum requires the educator to evaluate textbooks and classroom resources for ethnic and racial content and biases. Although advances have been made in eliminating ethnic biases and adding information about ethnic and racial groups in textbooks, many older textbooks are still used in classrooms. Biased books should not prevent the teacher from providing multiethnic instruction. Supplementary materials can fill the gap in this area. The biases and omissions in the texts can be used for discussions of the experiences of groups. None of these instructional activities will occur, however, unless the teacher is aware of and values ethnic differences and their importance in the curriculum.

Closing the Achievement Gap

After working with African American students in schools for many years, Professor Janice Hale (2001) has concluded that "inferior educational outcomes are tolerated for African American children day in and day out, in inner-city, suburban, and private school settings" (p. xx). The data on student achievement supports Hale's conclusion. African American students, as well as Latino and American Indian students, are not meeting standards as measured on the standardized tests required in most states. As a result, a disproportionately large number of students of color are not being promoted to the next grade, not graduating from high school, and dropping out of school.

The Role of Assessment.   Schools conduct widespread testing of students to determine if they are meeting the standards established by states. Tests are trumpeted as measures of competence to move from one grade to another, graduate from high school, enter upper-division college courses, earn a baccalaureate, and become licensed to teach. Overwhelmingly, promoters suggest that anyone who cannot pass the appropriate test certainly cannot be qualified to move on to further study. Thus, student performance on state tests has become the primary measure of quality in the nation's schools with sanctions if students are not making **adequate yearly progress (AYP)** or the minimum level of student performance required by the federal legislation, "No Child Left Behind." Teachers and principals sometimes lose their jobs if students do not perform at expected levels. Unfortunately, many teachers spend much of their instructional time teaching to the test, which limits their teaching of a number of subjects that are not tested and limits helping students develop critical thinking skills. For further information on how students of different races and ethnic groups are performing in your state or school district, visit the website of Education Trust at www2.edtrust.org.

Standardized tests have limited the access of many students to more rigorous study at all educational levels and may prevent them from entering the professions they desire. Testing has also led to the assignment of disproportionately large numbers of students of color to special education programs for the mentally retarded, learning disabled, and emotionally disturbed.

Between 1970 and 1990, student performance on national tests improved, with the largest gains being made by students of color (Education Trust, 2003). The progress came

Testing is a mainstay of school culture today as students are tested annually to determine if they meet state standards.

Scott Cunningham/Merrill

to a halt in the 1990s, and the achievement gap between whites and most students of color remains wide. Why do students from oppressed groups score lower than dominant group members on standardized tests? Studies indicate that:

- Low-income and students of color are more likely to be taught a low-level curriculum with low standards for performance (Barth, 2003).
- Over 6 of 10 white students complete Algebra II as compared to 52% of African American and 45% of Latino students; the gap is even greater for chemistry (Barth, 2003).
- African American and Latino high-school graduates are much less likely than whites and Asian Americans to go to college (Education Trust, 2006).
- Students in high poverty and high minority schools are more likely to be taught by teachers without a major or minor in the subject being taught (Education Trust, 2006).

Should it be a surprise that many students of color do not perform as well as white students when they have not taken advanced mathematics and science courses or had teachers who majored in those subjects? In urban schools in which students of color are overrepresented, teachers are less likely to be fully licensed than in schools with middle-class white students. Advanced courses in mathematics and science are not always available in the schools attended by a large number of students of color. Students must have access to such courses and qualified teachers to study the content on which they will be tested.

As educators, we must be careful not to label students of color intellectually inferior because their standardized test scores are low. These scores too often influence a teacher's expectations for the academic performance of students in the classroom. Standardized test scores can help in determining how assimilated into the dominant culture and how affluent one's family may be, but they provide less evidence of how intelligent a person is. Many other factors can be used to provide information about intelligence—for example, the ability to think and respond appropriately in different situations.

What should be the purposes of assessments? Rather than use tests to sort students on the basis of income, ethnicity, and family characteristics, assessments could be used *for* student learning to help understand what students know so that curriculum and activities can be designed to increase their knowledge and skills. Tests can provide information that will help improve student learning. Assessments that use observations, portfolios, projects, and essays provide evidence of what students know in many different ways. They are designed to promote complex and engaged learning.

Educators are capable of making valid decisions about ability on the basis of numerous objective and subjective factors about students. If decisions about the capabilities of students of color match exactly the standardized scores, educators should reevaluate their responses and interactions with students. Testing results today are making differences in the life chances for many students, especially those of color and from low-income families. Therefore, educators cannot afford to use assessments in unfair and inequitable ways.

Who Is Responsible for Closing the Gaps?   When students do not achieve at levels expected, many teachers do not take responsibility. They blame the students, their parents, or the economic conditions of the community rather than seriously reflecting on why students in their classroom are not learning and what might be changed to help them learn. A number of research studies report that teacher effectiveness is more important in student achievement than a student's race, poverty, or parent's education (Carey, 2004; Sanders & Rivers, 1996). In other words, effective teachers matter. Students who have been assigned the most effective teachers for three years in a row perform at much higher levels than the students who were in the classrooms of the least effective teachers for three years. With effective teachers, low-achieving students become high achievers (Education Trust, 2003).

Many teachers do not allow students to fail. There are many examples of good teachers who have helped students with low test scores achieve at advanced levels. African American and Latino students have performed at the same level as other students in mathematics and other subjects after teachers raised their expectations and changed their teaching strategies. Project SEED, the Algebra Project, and the Marcus Garvey School in Los Angeles are examples of programs that are successful in ensuring that African American students achieve at high levels (Hilliard, 2003). The Education Trust (2005) has identified a number of schools that are ensuring that their students of color are achieving at high levels. In these schools teachers and administrators:

- Clearly focus on academics;
- Embrace external standards and benchmarks;
- Provide all students a rigorous curriculum that prepares students for college;
- Have consistently high expectations for all students; and
- Provide extra instruction to students when they need it.

Students are not always inactive participants in their academic achievement. They are not always engaged with the schoolwork. They do not always do their homework. Some researchers have found that many working-class boys and students of color develop resistance or oppositional patterns to handle their subordination status within schools (Ogbu, 2003; Solomon, 1988; Willis, 1977). These patterns often take the form of breaking school rules and norms, belittling academic achievement, and valuing manual over mental work. These students may equate schooling with acting white or middle class. Although middle-class African American students perform academically better than their working-class peers, they do not do as well as white students, which some researchers attribute to this oppositional process.

Not all students of color adopt an oppositional form, and not all groups are equally affected. As a group, Asian American students have high achievement records in mathematics and science and attend college at rates disproportionately higher than other groups. One explanation is that Asian American adults are overrepresented in professional occupations, which results in incomes above that of most other groups of color. The economic advantages in the home backgrounds of many of these students contribute to their high levels of achievement and participation in mathematics and science. Generally, the cultural group values mathematics and science skills, and families provide experiences that encourage their development.

Desegregation and Intergroup Relations

The most integrated schools today are in rural and small town areas. The most segregated schools are located in central cities of large urban areas and the suburban rings closest to cities. Segregated schools for students of color usually serve impoverished communities, and, as before the 1954 *Brown* decision, are most often providing unequal educational opportunities to their clientele. Charter and private schools tend to be even more segregated than public schools. This segregation guarantees that most white students have little contact with students of color except in the South and Southwest (Orfield & Lee, 2004).

Courts are beginning to expect states to equalize educational outcomes for all students (Carroll, Fulton, Abercrombie, & Yoon, 2004). The courts continue to hear cases alleging unequal resources for the education of students of color. Many middle-class families are very involved in their children's schools, ensuring that they are staffed by highly qualified teachers and offer a challenging curriculum. The problem is that they are less likely to be concerned about the quality of education for other people's children, particularly the children of parents with whom they never interact.

While schools are becoming more segregated, the courts are acknowledging the importance of diverse student populations in educational settings. In a recent affirmative

When students of different ethnic groups have the opportunity to develop interpersonal relationships, racial and ethnic relations are likely to be improved.

Barbara Schwartz/Merrill

action case regarding the practices at the University of Michigan (*Grutter v. Bollinger*, 2003), Justice Sandra Day O'Connor said in the majority opinion that "Numerous studies show that student body diversity promotes learning outcomes, and better prepares students for an increasingly diverse workforce and society, and better prepares them as professionals" (p. 8). However, two Supreme Court decisions in 2007 ruled against voluntary diversity plans that assigned students to schools by their race in Seattle and Louisville.

Another outgrowth of *Brown v. Board of Education* was the need for intergroup relations to assist students and teachers in respecting each other and working together effectively. This need continues today. Even within desegregated schools, students are often segregated in classes, the cafeteria, and activities. In a survey of students, Williams (2003) found that schools contributed to placing people into categories. One third of the students said it was hard to make friends with students in other groups. Four of ten students said that their group had rejected someone from another group. To ensure that students interact with students from other ethnic and racial groups, educators have to consciously plan for this outcome. A number of national groups have developed programs to encourage cross-cultural communications. The Southern Poverty Law Center's project, Mix It Up at Lunch, for example, challenges schools to mix students from different groups during the lunch hour. More than 3,000 schools are now participating in the project, which is described at www.mixitup.org.

Small-group teams and cooperative learning promote both learning and interracial friendships. Engaging parents in school activities and decision making helps decrease the dissonance between school and home. Students should have equal access to the curriculum, advanced courses, qualified teachers, and activities to develop high-order thinking skills. They should see themselves in the curriculum and in textbooks. Practices such as tracking and pull-out programs are barriers to providing equal access and improving intergroup relations. Multicultural education is a critical component in the continued effort to integrate schools and improve intergroup relations.

Summary

Almost from the beginning of European settlement in the United States, the population has been multiethnic, with individuals representing many American Indian and European nations, later to be joined by Africans, Latinos, and Asians. Primary reasons for immigration were internal economic impoverishment and political repression in the countries of origin and the demands of a vigorous U.S. economy that required a growing labor force. The conditions encountered by different ethnic groups, the reasons they came, and their expectations about life here differed greatly and have led ethnic groups to view themselves as distinct from each other.

Persons of color have had to fight for their civil rights throughout U.S. history. During the 1950s and 1960s African Americans were successful in removing Jim Crow laws that allowed states to segregate public schools and accommodations. Their efforts led to the passage of the 1964 Civil Rights Act and 1965 Voting Rights Act and spawned civil rights actions for women, Latinos, Asian Americans, American Indians, and persons with disabilities.

Ethnicity is a sense of peoplehood based on national origin. Although no longer useful in describing groups of people, the term race continues to be used in this country to classify groups of people as inferior or superior. Its popular usage is based on society's perception that racial differences are important—a belief not upheld by scientific study. Members of oppressed groups experience discriminatory treatment and often are relegated to relatively low-status positions in society.

The school curriculum has traditionally represented the dominant culture as the focus of study. Since the 1970s, ethnic studies have been added to curricula as an extension or special segment that provides in-depth study of the history and contemporary conditions of one or more ethnic groups. Some ethnic groups have established schools or programs in traditional schools that center the curriculum on their ethnicity. A multiethnic approach is broader in scope in that it requires ethnic content to permeate the total curriculum. Understanding ethnicity is an advantage in developing effective teaching strategies for individual students.

Educators should examine how they are administering and using standardized tests in the classroom. Too often, testing programs have been used for the purpose of identifying native intelligence and thus sorting people for education and jobs. If disproportionately large numbers of students of color are scoring poorly on such tests and being placed in special classes as a result, the program must be reviewed.

Desegregation is a process for decreasing racial/ethnic isolation in schools. Although early desegregation efforts focused on ensuring that black and white students attended the same schools, increasing numbers of students of color attend predominantly minority schools. The emphasis is on ensuring the academic achievement of all students and eliminating the inequities in educational opportunities. Intergroup activities in schools help students develop cross-cultural communications skills, thus getting to know students from different ethnic and racial groups.

PROFESSIONAL PRACTICE FOR EDUCATORS

Questions for Discussion

1. Why is membership in an ethnic group more important to some individuals than to others?
2. What factors cause members of oppressed groups to view ethnicity differently from dominant group members?
3. How different and similar were the immigration patterns of Africans, Asians, Central Americans, Europeans, and South Americans during the past four centuries?
4. Why have the changes made during the Civil Rights Movement of the 1950s and 1960s not eliminated the income and educational gaps between groups?
5. Why does race remain such an important factor in the social, political, and economic patterns of the United States?
6. What characteristics might an educator look for to determine a student's ethnic background and the importance it plays in that student's life?
7. How would you use the ethnicity and race of your students to teach a lesson in the subject that you are planning to teach?
8. What are the advantages and disadvantages of the following approaches: ethnic studies, ethnocentric education, and integration of ethnic content?

9. Why is the use of standardized tests so controversial? What are the dangers of depending too heavily on the results of standardized tests?

10. Why do school officials seek teachers who believe that all students can learn?

Portfolio Activities

1. Develop a lesson that reflects an integrative approach to incorporating multiethnic content. The lesson should be for the subject and level (for example, elementary or secondary) that you plan to teach. (INTASC Standard 3)

2. As you observe schools, record practices in classrooms, the halls, the cafeteria, extracurricular activities, and the main office that might be perceived as racist by persons of color. Write a paper for your portfolio that describes these practices, why they could be considered racist, and how the school could change them. (INTASC Standard 3)

3. Analyze the performance of students on required standardized scores in one or more of the schools you are observing. Discuss the results based on the race or ethnicity of students in the school and indicate your conclusions. (Note: Schools are required by the federal legislation, "No Child Left Behind," to disaggregate data by race and ethnicity.) (INTASC Standard 8)

Licensure Test Prep

Ms. Stewart teaches English language arts to sophomores at a high school whose students are primarily African American and Latino. All students will have to pass the state test to graduate. The school superintendent has expressed concern about low academic performance on achievement tests at Ms. Stewart's school. Teachers in the English Department have challenged themselves to improve the literacy performance of their students. One of the department's objectives is to make the curriculum more relevant to students by incorporating their experiences and cultures. Ms. Stewart is planning a unit that will assess comprehension, analysis, and writing skills. She can select a single short story or multiple ones as the focus of the unit. Her major concern is how to engage the students in the unit so they improve their skills.

Short Answer Questions

1. Describe two strategies for integrating the ethnic experiences of the community into the curriculum.

2. Explain how each of these strategies would help students improve their literacy skills.

Go to the *Homework and Exercises* section in Chapter 2 of MyEducationLab and select *Licensure Test Prep* to complete this exercise.

Suggested Readings

Arboleda, T. (1998). *In the shadow of race: Growing up as a multiethnic, multicultural, and "multiracial" American*. Mahwah, NJ: Lawrence Erlbaum.

This personal chronicle of the author's struggle to identify his ethnicity and race when they do not fit society's categories provides insights into institutionalized notions of race, culture, ethnicity, and class.

Bigelow, B., & Peterson, B. (Eds.). (1998). *Rethinking Columbus: The next 500 years*. Milwaukee, WI: Rethinking Schools.

This book calls for a replacement of the murky legends of Columbus with a more honest sense of who we are and why we are here. It also discusses the courageous struggles and lasting wisdom of indigenous peoples.

Fox, H. (2006). *"When race breaks out": Conversations about race and racism in college classrooms*. New York: Peter Lang.

Although the focus of this book is on the college classroom, it is a helpful guide to thinking about how to discuss issues of race in the classroom, including examples of how different teachers have handled students who are angry, guilty, silent, or defensive.

Jackson, C. (2007). *The ABCs of hip hop*. Montgomery, AL: Teaching Tolerance. Available at www.tolerance.org/teach/activities/activity.jsp?ar=815

Hip-hop can be used to engage students in new ways to explore tolerance and anti-bias. This resource includes an exploration of the political and social contexts of hip-hop and lesson plans for using it in the classroom.

Lee, E., Menkart, D., & Okazawa-Rey, M. (Eds.). (1998). *Beyond heroes and holidays: A practical guide to K–12 anti-racist, multicultural education and staff development*. Washington, DC: Network of Educators on the Americas.

This interdisciplinary guide for educators, students, and parents includes lessons and readings on racism, transforming the curriculum, tracking, parent/school relations, and language policies.

Moses, R. P., & Cobb, C. E. (2002). *Radical equations: Civil rights from Mississippi to the algebra project*. Boston: Beacon Press.

Civil rights leader Robert Moses has transformed the grassroot organizing of parents, teachers, and students into a program that successfully teaches algebra to middle-school students. Building on the civil rights movement in the South, the authors describe the Algebra Project, which has helped students of color create a culture of literacy around algebra.

Southern Poverty Law Center. (2005). *Ten ways to fight hate* (3rd ed.). Montgomery, AL: Author. Available at www.tolerance.org/pdf/ten_ways.pdf

This guide provides 10 principles for fighting hate and includes inspiring stories of how people have pushed hate out of their communities.

Teaching Tolerance. (Published by the Southern Poverty Law Center, 400 Washington Ave., Montgomery, AL 36104). For a complimentary copy, go to www.tolerance.org/teach/magazine. This semiannual magazine provides teachers with resources and ideas to promote harmony in the classroom. Articles are written from the perspectives of multiple ethnic groups. It is available at no cost to teachers.

References

Barth, P. (2003, Winter). A common core curriculum for the new century. *Thinking K–16, 7*(1), 3–19. Retrieved on May 28, 2007, from www2.edtrust.org/NR/rdonlyres/26923A64-4266-444B-99ED-2A61D5F14061F/0/k16_winter2003.pdf

Brown v. Board of Education, 349 U.S. 294, at 300 (1955).

Bureau of Indian Affairs. (2007, March 22). Indian entities recognized and eligible to receive services from the United States Bureau of Indian Affairs. *Federal Register, 72*(55), 13648.

Carey, K. (2004, Winter). *The real value of teachers: Using new information about teacher effectiveness to close the achievement gap*. Washington, DC: The Education Trust.

Carlson, D. (2004, February 17). *As blacks mark history, satisfaction gap persists*. Princeton, NJ: Gallup Organization.

Carroll, J. (2006). *Whites, minorities differ in views of economic opportunities in U.S.* Princeton, NJ: Gallup Organization. Retrieved May 27, 2007, from www.galluppoll.com/content/?ci=23617&pg=1

Carroll, T. G., Fulton, K., Abercrombie, K., & Yoon, I. (2004). *Fifty years after Brown v. Board of Education: A two-tiered education system.* Washington, DC: National Commission on Teaching and America's Future.

Craig, T. (2007, February 2). House proposes tough laws; Senate objects to some. *The Washington Post*, p. B05.

Cross, W. E., Jr. (1992). *Shades of black: Diversity in African American identity.* Philadelphia: Temple University Press.

The Education Trust. (2003). *African American achievement in America.* Washington, DC: Author. Retrieved on May 28, 2007, from www2.edtrust.org/NR/rdonlyres/9AB4AC88-7301-43FF-81A3-EB94807B917F/0/AfAmer_Achivement.pdf

The Education Trust. (2005, November). *Gaining traction, gaining ground: How some high schools accelerate learning for struggling students.* Washington, DC: Author.

The Education Trust. (2006, Fall). *Education watch: The nation: Key education facts and figures.* Washington, DC: Author. Retrieved on May 27, 2007, from www2.edtrust.org/edtrust/summaries2006/USA.pdf

Gallagher, C. A. (2003). Color-blind privilege: The social and political functions of erasing the color line in post race America. *Race, Gender & Class, 10*(4), 22–37.

Grutter v. Bollinger, 1235 Ct. 2325 (2003).

Hale, J. E. (2001). *Learning while black: Creating educational excellence for African American children.* Baltimore, MD: The Johns Hopkins University Press.

Helms, J. A. (Ed.). (1990). *Black and white racial identity development: Theory, research, and practice.* Westport, CT: Praeger.

Hilliard, III, A. G. (2003). No mystery: Closing the achievement gap between Africans and excellence. In T. Perry, C. Steele, & A. G. Hilliard, III (Eds.), *Young, gifted, and black: Promoting high achievement among African-American students* (pp. 131–165). Boston: Beacon Press.

Jensen, L. (2006). New immigrant settlements in rural America: Problems, prospects, and policies. Durham, NH: Carsey Institute, University of New Hampshire.

Kelley, M. (2000, September 8). Indian affairs head makes apology. Associated Press.

Ludwig, J. (2004, April 27). *Race and education: The 50th anniversary of Brown v. Board of Education.* Princeton, NJ: Gallup Organization. Retrieved on May 27, 2007, from www.galluppoll.com/content/?ci=11521&pg=1

Martin, P. (2006, April 11). *The battle over unauthorized immigration to the United States.* Washington, DC: Population Reference Bureau. Retrieved on February 4, 2007, from www.prb.org/Articles/2006/TheBattleOverUnauthorizedImmigrationtotheUnitedStates.aspx

Martin, P. & Midgley, E. (2006). Immigration: Shaping and reshaping America (Revised and Updated 2nd ed.). *Population Bulletin, 61*(4), 1–28.

National Conference for Community and Justice. (2006). *Taking America's pulse III: A survey of intergroup relations.* New York: Author.

Ogbu, J. U. (2003). *Black American students in an affluent suburb: A study of academic disengagement.* Mahwah, NJ: Lawrence Erlbaum.

Orfield, G., & Frankenberg, E. (2004, Spring). Where are we now? *Teaching Tolerance, 25,* 57–59.

Orfield, G., & Lee, C. (2004, January). *Brown at 50: King's dream or Plessy's nightmare?* Cambridge, MA: The Civil Rights Project, Harvard University.

Passel, J. (2006). The size and characteristics of the unauthorized migrant population in the United States. *PEW Hispanic Center Research Report 61.* Retrieved on February 11, 2007, from http://pewhispanic.org/reports/report.php?ReportID=61

Plyler v. Doe, 457 U.S. 202 (1982).

Portes, A., & Rumbaut, R. G. (2001). *Legacies: The story of the immigrant second generation.* Berkeley, CA: University of California Press.

Potok, M. (2004, Summer). The year in hate. *Intelligence Report, 113,* 29–32.

Saad, L. (2004, January 19). *Blacks lag behind whites in life satisfaction.* Princeton, NJ: Gallup Organization. Retrieved on May 27, 2007, from www.galluppoll.com/content/?ci=10258&pg=1

Sanders, W. I., & Rivers, J. C. (1996). *Cumulative and residual effects of teachers on future student academic achievement.* Knoxville, TN: University of Tennessee Value-Added Research and Assessment Center.

Solomon, R. P. (1988). Black cultural forms in schools: A cross-national comparison. In L. Weis (Ed.), *Class, race, and gender in American education* (pp. 249–265). Albany: State University of New York Press.

Southern Poverty Law Center. (2004). *White power music: Music manufacturer boots Resistance Records.* Retrieved July 15, 2004, from www.splcenter.org/intel/intelreport/article.jsp?aid=96

Southern Poverty Law Center. (2005). *Ten ways to fight hate* (3rd ed.). Montgomery, AL: Author.

Takaki, R. (1993). *A different mirror: A history of multicultural America.* Boston: Little, Brown.

Tatum, B. D. (2003). *"Why are all the black kids sitting together in the cafeteria?" And other conversations about race.* New York: Basic Books.

U.S. Census Bureau. (2004). *U.S. interim projections by age, sex, race, and Hispanic origin.* Retrieved on May 26, 2007, from www.census.gov/ipc/www/usinterimproj/natprojtab01a.pdf

U.S. Census Bureau. (2006). *Statistical Abstract of the United States: 2006* (126th ed.). Washington, DC: U.S. Government Printing Office.

U.S. Department of Education, National Center for Education Statistics. (2006). *The condition of education 2006* (NCES 2006-071). Washington, DC: U.S. Government Printing Office.

Williams, D. (2003, Fall). Mixitup: Students bridge social boundaries on mix it up at lunch day. *Teaching Tolerance, 24,* 44–47.

Willis, P. E. (1977). *Learning to labor: How working-class kids get working-class jobs.* Farnborough, UK: Saxon House.

Willoughby, B. (2004, Spring). Beyond black and white. *Teaching Tolerance, 25,* 45.

Young, R. L., & Pang, V. O. (1995, Winter). Asian Pacific American students: A rainbow of dreams. *Multicultural Education, 3*(2), 4–7.

Youth and Hate. (1999, Fall). *Intelligence Report* (Southern Poverty Law Center), *96,* 24–27.

CLASS AND SOCIOECONOMIC STATUS

*W*e are obliged to make sure that every child gets a healthy start in life. With all of our wealth and capacity, we just can't stand by idly.

COLIN POWELL, Former Secretary of State, 2000

While he was still in college, Tomas Juarez decided he wanted to work with children from low-income families. He began his teaching career, however, in a culturally diverse suburban school. The school had been built only a few years before and included state-of-the-art science labs. Students were proficient with computers; they even helped Mr. Juarez develop his skills. Most of the students participated in extracurricular activities, and their parents were active in school affairs. More than 90% of the previous graduating class had enrolled in postsecondary programs. It was a pleasure to work with a team of teachers who planned interesting lessons based on a constructivist approach, engaged students in the content, and developed higher-order thinking skills.

After a few years, Mr. Juarez decided he was ready to take on the challenge of an inner-city school where most students were members of oppressed groups. As soon as he stepped into his new school, he realized that he had been spoiled in the suburbs.

First, the smell wasn't right and the halls were dirty even though it was the beginning of the school year. The room that was to be his classroom did not have enough chairs for all of the students who had been assigned to the class. Not only did the room look as if it had not been repainted for 20 years, but several windowpanes were covered with a cardboard-like material, and numerous ceiling tiles were missing. His first thought was that both he and the students would be exposed to asbestos and lead poisoning. Outside, the playground was uninviting. There was no grass, the stench from local factories was overpowering, and the football field did not even have goalposts.

During Mr. Juarez's first few weeks, he found that the students were terrific. They were enthusiastic about being back in school. He had only enough textbooks for half the class, however, and no money in the budget to purchase more. Supplies were limited, and most of the audiovisual equipment had been stolen the previous year and never replaced.

Reflections

1. Why were conditions at Mr. Juarez's new school so much different from those in the suburban school?

2. How can a teacher overcome environmental conditions that are not supportive of effective learning?

3. What are the chances of the new students being academically successful at the same level as his students in the suburban school?

4. Why are students in the urban school more likely to drop out, become pregnant, and not attend college?

5. Why has society allowed some students to go to school under such appallingly poor conditions?

Class Structure

"**Class** is a system that differentially structures group access to economic, political, cultural, and social resources" (Andersen & Collins, 2007, p. 72). It determines the schools we attend, the stores in which we shop, the restaurants at which we eat, the community in which we live, and the jobs to which we have access. Class is socially constructed by society and its institutions, determining the relationships between families and persons who have little or limited financial resources and those who are wealthy.

The two views of equality in U.S. society that were outlined in Chapter 1 suggest different class structures across the country. One view accepts the existence of different socioeconomic levels or classes in society. It also strongly supports the notion that one can be socially mobile and can move to a higher class by getting an education and working hard. Groups that have not yet achieved upper-middle-class status are viewed as less capable. The hardships faced by low-income families are blamed on their lack of middle-class values and behaviors. The individual is at fault for not moving up the class ladder—a phenomenon called blaming the victim.

In the second view of U.S. society, distinct class divisions are recognized. Those individuals and families who own and control corporations, banks, and other means of production comprise the privileged upper class. The professional and managerial elite have not only accumulated wealth; they also are able to ensure that their needs are supported by legislative representatives whom they have elected (American Political Science Association, 2004). Persons who earn a living primarily by selling their labor make up the middle and working classes. Another class includes those persons who are unable to work or who can find work only sporadically. Although some individuals are able to move from one class level to another, opportunities for social mobility are limited. Those who control most of the resources and those who have few of the resources are dichotomous groups in a class struggle.

Most people are caught in the socioeconomic strata into which they were born, and the political-economic system helps them remain there. Certainly some individuals have been socially and economically mobile. Stories about athletes, coaches, movie stars, and singers are recounted during sporting events and in newspaper and television reports. Few people, however, have abilities that translate into the high salaries of elite stars of the entertainment world. A college education is the most reliable step for moving from a low-income to a middle-class and higher status.

Family background has been found to account for a large part of the variation in educational and occupational attainment. The opportunity to achieve equally is thwarted before one is born. Individuals born into a wealthy family are likely to achieve wealth; individuals born into a low-income family will have much more difficulty achieving wealth no matter how hard they try. Families usually do everything possible to protect their wealth to guarantee that their children maintain the family's economic status. The inequalities that exist in society often lead to the perpetuation of inequalities from one generation to the next.

Class Identity

Most people, if asked, could identify themselves by class. They may not strongly vocalize their identity with a specific class, but they participate socially and occupationally within a class structure. Their behavior and value system may be based on a strong ethnic or religious identification, but that specific identification is greatly influenced by their economic circumstances. The first generation of a group that has moved to the **middle class** may continue to interact at a primary level with friends and relatives who remain in the working class. Differences in friends, communities, and jobs, however, often lead to the reduction of those cross-class ties over time.

Most U.S. citizens exhibit and articulate less concern about class consciousness than many of their European counterparts. Nevertheless, many have participated in class actions, including teachers, such as strikes or work stoppages to further the interests of the class to which they belong. Class consciousness, or solidarity with others at the same socioeconomic level, may not be so pronounced here because overall improvement in the standard of living has occurred at all levels, especially during the period from 1940 to the early 1970s and again in the 1990s. In addition, the dominant cultural values and belief systems hold individuals personally responsible for their class position.

Pause to Reflect 3.1

Think about the community in which you grew up and the class of your family and other members of the community.

- How would you describe the class of your family?
- In which class do the majority of your neighbors fall?
- What was the class of the majority of students in your high school?
- How did class influence your educational aspirations and those of your high school peers?

Go to the *Homework and Exercises* section in Chapter 3 of MyEducationLab and select *Pause to Reflect 3.1* to answer these questions.

Social Stratification

Social stratification ranks individuals and families on the basis of their income, education, occupation, wealth, and power in society. Many people accept and follow socially defined behavior based on their occupation, race, gender, and class. However, civil rights organizations, including women's groups, try to combat the institutionalized acceptance and expectation of unequal status across groups.

Inequality results, in part, from differential rankings within the division of labor. Different occupations are evaluated and rewarded unequally. Some jobs are viewed as more worthy, more important, more popular, and more preferable than others. People who hold high-ranking positions have developed common interests for maintaining their positions and the accompanying power. They have established policies and practices to restrict others' chances of obtaining the same status—a key to establishing and maintaining a system of stratification.

Many people in the United States receive high or low rankings in the social stratification system on the basis of characteristics over which they have no control. Women, people with disabilities, the elderly, children, and people of color often receive low-prestige rankings. **Ascribed status**—one's assignment to groups at birth—affects who is allowed entrance into the higher-ranking socioeconomic positions. However, not all white, able-bodied men achieve a high-ranking position. They are found at all levels along the continuum, from being homeless to being a billionaire, but they and their families are overrepresented at the highest levels. Conversely, members of most oppressed groups can be found at all levels of the continuum, with a few at the top of the socioeconomic scale.

Socioeconomic Status

How is economic success or achievement measured? The economic condition of persons and groups is measured with a criterion called **socioeconomic status (SES).** It serves as a composite of the economic status of a family or unrelated individuals on the basis of occupation, educational attainment, and income. Related to these three factors are wealth and power, which also help determine an individual's SES but are more difficult to measure.

These five determinants of SES are interrelated. Although inequality has many forms, these factors are probably the most salient for an individual because they affect how one lives. A family's SES is usually observable—in the size of their home and the part of town in which they live, the schools their children attend, or the clubs to which the parents belong. Many educators place their students at specific SES levels on the basis of similar observations about their families, based on the way students dress, the language they use, and their eligibility for free or reduced lunch.

Income

Income is the amount of money earned in wages or salaries throughout a year. One way to look at income distribution is by dividing the population into fifths; the lowest one fifth earns the lowest income, and the highest one fifth earns the highest income. Figure 3.1 shows the percentage of total income earned by each fifth of the population, and the total wealth held by each fifth. The top fifth of the population earned 48% of the total income, whereas the bottom fifth earned 4% of the total income. High incomes are reserved for the privileged few. The 5% of U.S. families with the highest incomes earned 21% of the total income earned by all families (U.S. Census Bureau, 2006b).

Many people view this income inequity as a natural outcome of the American way. Those people who have contributed at high levels to their professions or jobs are believed to deserve to be paid more for their effort. People at the lower end of the continuum are either unemployed or work in unskilled jobs and thus are not expected to receive the same economic rewards. The difference between these two ends of the continuum can be quite large, however. Chief executive officers (CEOs) of the largest 350 U.S. companies earned an average compensation of $11.6 million in 2004, including salary, stocks, and other incentives (Anderson, Cavanagh, Collins, & Benjamin, 2006). At the other end of the scale, people earning the minimum wage receive less than $11,000 annually. When jobs were being moved outside the United States, the salaries of most CEOs increased. If the average production worker's annual pay had increased as quickly as CEO pay since 1990, the worker "would have made $108,138, compared to the actual average of $28,314. Similarly, if the federal minimum wage had grown at the same rate as CEO pay, it would have been $22.61 in 2005, instead of $5.15." (Anderson et al., 2006, p. 32). International studies

FIGURE 3.1   Distribution of Family Income and Wealth in the United States by Fifths of the Population.

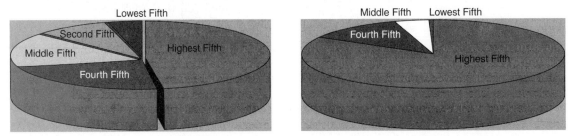

(Income) From U.S. Census Bureau. (2006). *Statistical abstract of the United States: 2007* (126th ed.). Washington, DC: U.S. Government Printing Office. (Wealth) Rose, S. J. (2000). *Social stratification in the United States.* New York: New Press.

report that the gap between high and low wages is greater in the United States than in most other industrialized countries. This situation is further exacerbated by the lack of tax policies to readjust somewhat the disparities; in fact, the rich are paying fewer taxes than in the past (Anyon, 2005).

Between World War II and 1973, the growth of the U.S. economy allowed incomes of workers at all levels to increase at a faster rate than expenditures. Many middle-income families were able to purchase homes, cars, boats, and luxuries for the home; often, money was left over for savings. One way to examine the continuum of income is to use **median income,** which is the number at which half of the group earns more and the other half earns less. During this period, the annual median income of all people 14 years of age and older nearly tripled, from $1,787 to $5,004. The standard of living for most of the population was markedly better in 1973 than in 1940. Beginning in 1973, however, the cost of living (the cost of housing, utilities, food, and other essentials) began to increase faster than income. Except for the wealthy, all families felt the financial pressure. No longer did they have extra income to purchase nonessentials. No longer was one full-time worker in a family enough to maintain the same standard of living. The 1990s brought another upswing in the economy. By 2004, the median annual income of a family was $54,061. When both husband and wife worked, the median income of married couples was $76,814 (U.S. Census Bureau, 2006b).

Income sets limits on the general lifestyle of a family, as well as on their general welfare. It controls the consumption patterns of a family—the number and quality of material possessions, housing, consumer goods, luxuries, savings, and diet. It allows families to save money for college educations and the purchase of new cars. However, most low-income and middle-income families are barely able to cover their expenses from one paycheck to the next. If they lose their job, they could be homeless within a few months. Higher incomes provide security for families who do not need to worry about paying for the essentials and have access to health care and retirement benefits.

Wealth

Although the difference in income among families is great, an examination of income alone does not indicate the vast differences in the way families live. Income figures show the amount of money earned by a family for their labors during one year, but the figures do not include the amount of money earned from investments, land, and other holdings. They do not present the **net worth** of a family. The **wealth** of a family includes savings accounts, insurance, corporate stock ownership, and property. Wealth provides a partial guarantee of future income and has the potential of producing additional income and wealth. However, for most families, the majority of family wealth comes from the equity value of their homes and the residual value of household goods. Approximately 20% of U.S. households have zero or negative wealth (Collins & Veskel, 2004).

Whereas income can be determined from data gathered on federal income tax forms by the Internal Revenue Service, wealth is difficult to determine from these or any other standard forms. However, the distribution of wealth is concentrated in a small percentage of the population. The wealthiest 10% of the population had a median net worth of $1.3 million in 2001; the median net worth of the bottom fifth of the population was $1,100 (Keenan, 2003). The wealthiest 1% of the population accumulated more than half of the new financial wealth created between 1983 and 2001 while the bottom 80% of the population accumulated 5% (Teller-Elsberg, Folbre, Heintz, & The Center for Popular Economics, 2006). Figure 3.1 shows how wealth is distributed across fifths of the population.

CRITICAL INCIDENTS IN TEACHING

Differences in Socioeconomic Status

The middle school in a rural community of 9,000 residents has four school-sponsored dances each year. At the Valentine's dance, a coat-and-tie affair, six eighth-grade boys showed up in rented tuxedos. They had planned this together, and their parents, among the more affluent in the community, thought it would be "cute" and paid for the rentals. The final dance of the year is scheduled for May, and it, too, is a coat-and-tie dance. This time, rumors are circulating around school that "everyone" is renting a tux and that the girls are getting new formal dresses. The parents of the three boys are, according to the grapevine, renting a limousine for their sons and their dates. These behaviors and dress standards are far in excess of anything previously observed at the middle school.

Several students, particularly those from lower socioeconomic backgrounds, have said they will boycott the dance. They cannot afford the expensive attire, and they claim that the ones behind the dress-up movement have said that only the nerds or geeks would show up in anything less than a tux or a formal gown.

Questions for Classroom Discussion

1. Should the school administration intervene? Why or why not?
2. Should the limo-renting parents be contacted? Why or why not?
3. Should the matter be discussed in the homerooms? In a school assembly? Why or why not?
4. Should the May dance be canceled? Why or why not?
5. Should limits be set on the dress for school dances? Could the school legally enforce limits?
6. Can and should an issue be made of the hiring of limousine services for middle school students?

Building Teaching Skills

Go to the *Building Teaching Skills* section in Chapter 3 of MyEducationLab and select *Critical Incidents in Teaching: Differences in Socioeconomic Status* to complete this exercise.

The wealthiest nations in the world are the United States, Canada, and Western Europe, but inequities across groups continue to exist in these countries. The world's wealth is held by a few people. For example, the 225 richest people in the world have a combined wealth equal to the annual income of the poorer half of the world population (Smith, 2000). The difference between the economic lives of populations in the wealthiest and poorest countries in the world is shocking in its magnitude. The average person in the richest countries is more than 100 times wealthier than a person in the poorest countries (Smith, 2003).

Wealth ensures some economic security for its holders even though the amount of security depends on the amount of wealth accumulated. It also enhances the power and prestige of those who possess it. Great wealth accrues power, provides an income that allows luxury, and creates values and lifestyles that are very different from the rest of the population. Wealth also gives great economic advantages to children in these families who can attend the best schools, travel widely, and not worry about medical and health needs.

Occupation

Income, for most people, is determined by their occupation. Generally speaking, income is a fair measure of occupational success—both of the importance of the occupation to society and of one's individual skill at the job. In addition to providing an income, a person's job is an activity that is considered important. Individuals who are unemployed often are stigmatized as noncontributing members of society who cannot take care of themselves. Even individuals with great wealth often hold a job although additional income is unnecessary. Just over half of today's workforce is comprised of **white-collar** workers—people who do office work. The percentage of service workers is growing, although the percentage who are private household workers continues to decline. Between now and 2014, most of the 10 fastest growing occupations are in the following health and computer fields:

1. home health aides,
2. network systems and data communications analysts,
3. medical assistants,
4. physician assistants,
5. computer software engineers, applications,
6. physical therapist assistants,
7. dental hygienists,
8. computer software engineers, systems software,
9. dental assistants, and
10. personal and home care aides (U.S. Census Bureau, 2006b).

In addition, some education positions are among the fastest growing occupations. Preschool teachers are 21st on the list, followed by college faculty. Many of the jobs on this list require no postsecondary preparation (for example, retail salespersons, home health aides, waiters, and medical assistants) (U.S. Census Bureau, 2006b).

The type of job one holds is the primary determinant of income received, providing a relatively objective indicator of a person's SES. The job usually indicates one's education, suggests the types of associates with whom one interacts, and determines the degree of authority and responsibility one has over others. It gives people both differing amounts of compensation in income and differing degrees of prestige in society.

Occupational prestige is often determined by the requirements for the job and by the characteristics of the job. The requirements for an occupation with prestige usually include more education and training. Job characteristics that add to the prestige of an occupation are rooted in the division between mental and manual labor. When the prestige of an occupation is high, fewer people gain entry into that occupation. When the prestige of an occupation is low, employees are allotted less security and income, and accessibility to that occupation is greater. Occupations with the highest prestige generally have the highest salaries.

Education

The best predictor of occupational prestige is the amount of education one acquires. Financial compensation is usually greater for occupations that require more years of education.

The type of jobs one holds impacts one's socioeconomic status. Low-wage jobs make it difficult if not impossible to move into the middle class.

© Laima Druskis/PH College

For example, medical doctors and lawyers remain in school for several years beyond a bachelor's degree program. Many professionals and other white-collar workers have completed at least an undergraduate program. Craft workers often earn more money than many white-collar workers, but their positions require specialized training that often takes as long to complete as a college degree.

A great discrepancy exists among the incomes of persons who have less than a high school education and those who have completed professional training after college. The median income of a male who had not completed high school in 2003 was $18,990; if he had completed four years of college or more, it was $55,751. The differential for a female was $10,786 and $35,125 (U.S. Census Bureau, 2006b).

Education is rightfully viewed as a way to enhance one's economic status. However, impressive educational credentials are more likely to be achieved as a result of family background, rather than other factors. High school graduates whose parents have at least a bachelor's degree are more likely to enroll in postsecondary education (U.S. Department of Education, 2006). The higher the socioeconomic level of students' families, the greater the students' chances of finishing high school and college. Students enrolled in college soon after high school graduation ranged in 2005 from 59% of those from families with annual incomes of less than $36,539 to 87% of those from families with incomes of more than $98,433. College graduation rates ranged from 12% for students at the lower income level to 73% for the top income level as shown in Figure 3.2 (Family Income and Higher Education Opportunity, 2006).

The conditions under which low-income students live sometimes make it difficult for them to go to school instead of going to work. They often begin higher education by attending community colleges. The greater the income of families, the greater the chances that their children will have books, magazines, and newspapers available in the home; that they will have attended plays or concerts; and that they will have traveled beyond the region in which they live. Even the colleges that students attend are influenced more by the SES of the family than by the academic ability of the student. Many students simply cannot afford to attend private colleges and instead choose state colleges and universities or

FIGURE 3.2 High School Graduates Enrolled and Completing College by Family Income.

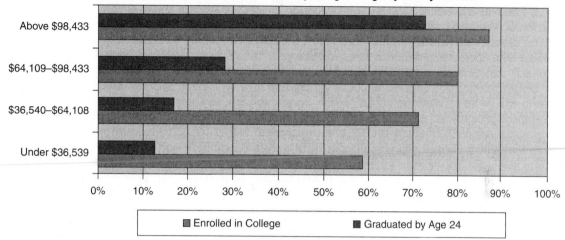

Data from Family Income and Higher Education Opportunity: 1970 to 2005. (2006, December). *Postsecondary Education Opportunity*, No. 174.

Pause to Reflect 3.2

Think about your future job as a teacher. The following questions will help you consider why you are choosing this career.

- How interesting, meaningful, challenging, or routine do you expect teaching to be? What do you think you will like the most about teaching?
- How much control will you have over your environment?
- What salary do you expect to make? How will a teacher's salary influence your lifestyle?
- Why do you want to be a teacher? Is your reason similar to the reasons your colleagues have chosen teaching as a career?

Go to the *Homework and Exercises* section in Chapter 3 of MyEducationLab and select *Pause to Reflect 3.2* to answer these questions.

community colleges. Thus, a student's socioeconomic origins have a substantial influence on the amount and type of schooling received and, in turn, the type of job obtained.

Power

Individuals and families who are at the upper SES levels exert more power than those at any other level. These individuals are more likely to sit on boards that determine state and local policies, on boards of colleges and universities, and on boards of corporations. They determine who receives benefits and rewards in governmental, occupational, and community affairs. Groups and individuals with power control resources that influence their lives and the lives of others. Groups or individuals with little power do not have the means to get what they need or the access to the people who could influence their interests. They continually obtain fewer of society's benefits, in part, because they lack accessibility to sources of power.

Persons with higher incomes are more likely to participate in national and local politics. They are also much more likely to vote in presidential elections. A study by the American Political Science Association (APSA) (2004) found that 90% of individuals in families with an income over $75,000 vote as compared to half of the individuals in families earning under $15,000. Voting and contributing financially to political candidates provides power to influence votes. The political scientists who wrote the APSA report found that "citizens with lower or moderate incomes speak with a whisper that is lost on the ears of inattentive government officials while the advantaged roar with a clarity and consistency that policymakers readily hear and routinely follow" (p. 1). This power is reflected in legislative action that benefits persons, families, and corporations with money. APSA reports that "recent research strikingly documents that the votes of U.S. senators far more closely correspond with the policy preferences of each senator's rich constituents than with the preferences of the senator's less-privileged constituents" (p. 14).

Education is not exempt from the exercise of power. California's Proposition 13, which was enacted in 1978 to limit real estate taxes, has had a dramatic effect on the quality of education in the state. Once among the top rated states with regard to student achievement, California now lags behind many states in student achievement scores. With limited funding, many schools must survive without the services of support personnel such as librarians and adequate numbers of school counselors. Many have limited and decaying facilities. At the same time, other schools have excellent facilities, adequate support staff, and up-to-date technology for teachers and students. These inequities are due, in part, to the fact that schools in affluent communities have private foundations where parents and other citizens can raise millions of dollars to support school programs. Wealth and affluence in California and other parts of the country can create an uneven playing field for many students.

Power relationships also exist between teachers and students. Teachers and administrators wield power over students by controlling the knowledge dispensed (predominantly grounded in a Western European worldview) and the acceptable behaviors, thoughts, and values for experiencing success in schools. Fewer teachers today are totally **authoritarian;** a growing number of teachers use cooperative learning rather than lecture and competitive strategies. Nevertheless, the curriculum is controlled by teachers, school boards, and national standards. In high-income schools, families have greater influence on their schools. Parents are able to financially contribute to the hiring of teachers for programs like music and art that many school districts can no longer afford. They will not tolerate the hiring of unqualified or poor teachers. On the other end of the income spectrum, families have little input into who teaches their children and cannot afford to contribute resources to maintain a full and desirable curriculum.

Class Differences

Many Americans identify themselves as middle class. It is an amorphous category that often includes everyone who works steadily and is not a member of the upper class. It ranges from well-paid professionals to service workers. Most white-collar workers, no matter what their salary, see themselves as middle class. Manual workers, in contrast, may view themselves as working class, rather than as middle class even though their incomes and cultural values may be similar to many white-collar workers.

Despite the popular myth, most people in the United States are not affluent. A medium budget representing a reasonably comfortable life for a family requires about $40,000 (Anyon, 2005; National Center for Children in Poverty, 2006). The family may be buying a home, but would not be able to accumulate any significant savings. This budget compares to the federal government's poverty line of $9,645 for one person and $19,307 for a family of four. Nearly 37 million people or 12.7% of the total population live in poverty by federal standards, but almost one of three U.S. families earned less than $35,000 in 2004 (U.S. Census Bureau, 2006b). Many of these individuals identify themselves as middle class but are unable to obtain the material goods and necessities to live comfortably. In this section we will explore the different classes and socioeconomic levels of the population.

The Unemployed and Homeless

The portion of the population who suffers the most from the lack of a stable income or other economic resources is the unemployed and homeless. The long-term poor fall into this group; many others are temporarily in poverty because of a job loss or family illness. Of the individuals classified as living in poverty, only 2.2% are persistently poor as measured by living in poverty for at least eight out of the last ten years (Rose, 2000).

The hard-core unemployed have seldom, if ever, worked and often lack the skills to find and maintain a job. The number of unemployed persons was over 5 million in 2005 or 4% of the civilian workforce (U.S. Census, 2006b), but this number does not include the discouraged workers who have given up looking for work and are no longer included in the government's report of the unemployed. Disproportionately, families in poverty are headed by single mothers, who are more likely than married women to be in poverty for more than two years.

Members of this group have become socially isolated from the dominant society. They usually are not integrated into, or wanted in, the communities of the other classes. Recommendations to build low-income housing, homeless shelters, or halfway houses in middle-class communities often result in vocal outrage from the residents. Some analysts think the lack of integration has exacerbated the differences in behavior between members of the underclass and those of other classes.

During the past two decades, the number of homeless persons and families has increased dramatically. Children and families live on the streets of our cities, comprising a large portion of today's homeless population as shown in Figure 3.3. Because almost all cities report more homeless people than shelter space, the number housed nightly in shelters undercount the actual number of

Observe and Learn — *Lessons in Action*
The Unemployed and the Homeless

Go to the *Homework and Exercises* section in Chapter 3 of MyEducationLab and select *Observe and Learn: Lessons in Action* to view the video "We Are in the Dumps with Jack and Guy" and answer the accompanying questions. The children's picture book *We Are All in the Dumps with Jack and Guy* by Maurice Sendak contains powerful illustrations and addresses serious topics such as poverty, homelessness, and child abuse. In this lesson, students discuss these issues and share their thoughts about what makes a home a home.

1. How did students react to the book? Did the teacher seem to encounter any problems in sharing the book with his students? If so, what were they?
2. What was your reaction to the book? Do you think that it was an appropriate choice for use in an elementary school? Why?
3. How might you present the book in your future classroom? How might your view on poverty and homelessness affect what you do in your future classroom?

FIGURE 3.3   Who Are the Homeless in Our Cities?

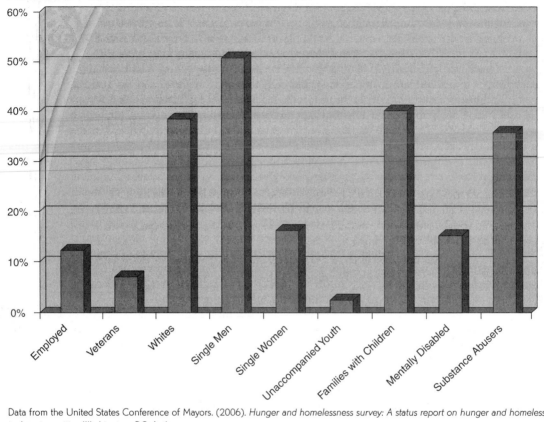

Data from the United States Conference of Mayors. (2006). *Hunger and homelessness survey: A status report on hunger and homelessness in American cities.* Washington, DC: Author.

homeless people. Approximately 3.5 million people have been homeless at some time during the year, and 1.35 million of them are children (National Law Center on Homelessness and Poverty, 2004). Many of the homeless work, but at such low wages they are unable to afford housing.

Why are people homeless? Poverty and the lack of affordable housing are the primary reasons for homelessness. The federal definition of affordable housing is rent equal to 30% of one's income. If a person makes the minimum wage, his or her household would have to include more than two people earning minimum wage to afford a two-bedroom apartment in most parts of the country. Over half of the expenditures for many low-income families with children is spent on housing, leaving little to cover all other expenses such as health care, child care, or other basic necessities. The Joint Center for Housing Studies of Harvard University (2007) reports that "one in seven US households is severely housing cost-burdened" (p. 25).

Domestic violence is another cause of homelessness because women who are escaping violent relationships do not always have another place to go. Other homeless people are without a place to stay because facilities do not exist to care for persons with mental disabilities. Some persons who are dependent on drugs or alcohol have lost their jobs, can't keep a job that earns enough to pay for their housing, or have become estranged

An increasing number of homeless adults, families, and children are found in communities around the country.

© Laima Druskis/PH College

from their families. In 23 cities 30% of the homeless are families with children (U.S. Conference of Mayors, 2006). Some teenagers leave home because of family problems, economic problems, or residential instability, often ending up homeless on city streets.

Between 500,000 and 1.3 million children and youth are homeless during a year (Levin-Epstein & Greenberg, 2003). Some homeless students do not attend school for extended periods of time, and they are not as healthy as other children. Many have not received immunizations that are expected in childhood. They experience higher rates of asthma, ear infections, stomach problems, and speech problems than other children (Books & Polakow, 2001). They have more mental health problems such as anxiety, depression, and low self-esteem. They suffer from hypothermia and are often hungry or lacking adequate nutrition. Further, they are more likely to have been abused or neglected by parents and other adults (National Center on Family Homelessness, 2007).

The **McKinney-Vento Homeless Assistance Act** requires public schools to provide educational rights and protections for homeless children and youth, including students who are living with relatives or friends because they have lost their housing. The law requires school districts to provide transportation for homeless students to stay in their schools of origin if requested by their parents or guardians. A school cannot deny enrollment to homeless students because they do not have their school records, immunization records, proof of residency, or other documents. The McKinney-Vento Act ensures that homeless students have access to schooling and are not denied services because of circumstances beyond their control. The school district's liaison for homeless students should serve as an advocate for them, assisting them in accessing available services in the school system and community.

The unemployed and homeless suffer from economic insecurity and from social, political, and economic deprivation. When they hold full-time jobs, they are of the lowest prestige and income levels. The jobs are often eliminated when economic conditions tighten or jobs move to the suburbs, resulting in unemployment again. The work for which they are hired is often the dirty work—not only physically dirty but also dangerous, menial, undignified, and degrading.

Many stereotypical notions about the poor need to be overcome for teachers to effectively serve students from low-income families. These students should not be blamed if they show acceptance, resignation, and even accommodation to their poverty as they learn to live with their economic disabilities.

Some anthropologists and sociologists who have studied the relationship between cultural values and poverty status have proposed a theory of a culture of poverty. They assert that the poor have a unique way of life that has developed as a reaction to their impoverished environment. This thesis suggests that people in poverty have a different value system and lifestyle that is perpetuated and transmitted to other generations.

Critics of the culture of poverty thesis believe that the cultural values of this group are much like those of the rest of the population but have been modified in practice because of situational stresses. This explanation suggests that the differences in values and lifestyles are not passed from one generation to the next, but rather are their adaptations to the experience of living in poverty.

The Working Class

The occupations pursued by the **working class** are those that require manual work for which income varies widely, depending on the skill required in the specific job. The factor that is most important in the description of the working class is the subordination of members to the capitalist control of production. These workers do not have control of their work. They do not give orders; they take orders from others. They have been hurt the most because of job losses resulting from technological advances and the movement of jobs to other countries. The working class comprises 40% of the employed population with jobs shown in Figure 3.4 (U.S. Census Bureau, 2006b).

Over the past few decades, jobs have shifted from the manufacturing sector to service jobs in protective services (police and firefighters), food services, health services, cleaning services, and personal services (hairdressers and early childhood assistants). The number of temporary, part-time, and contract jobs is expanding. Most of these jobs provide low wages and no health care or retirement benefits (Collins & Veskel, 2004).

The income of these workers varied in 2005 from an average hourly wage of $7.42 in food services to $29.03 for the manufacturing of motor vehicles (U.S. Census Bureau, 2006b) or salaries ranging from under $16,000 to over $60,000, which provide very different standards of living. Although the income of the working class is equal to and sometimes higher than that of white-collar workers, they have less job security. Work is more sporadic, and unemployment is unpredictably affected by the economy. Jobs are uncertain because of displacement as a result of technology, which often results in more stringent educational requirements. Fringe benefits available to these workers are often not as good as those offered to other workers. Vacation time is usually shorter, health insurance available less often, and working conditions more dangerous.

People at the low end of the wage scale are the working poor. They do the jobs that most persons with more education refuse to do. Although they sometimes work one or more jobs at minimum wages of $6.55 per hour, they can't pull themselves out of poverty. Critics of current economic and social policies ask why the minimum wage remains so low that people who earn it fall below the government's poverty line (Rank, 2004; Shipler, 2004; and Shulman, 2003). A number of local jurisdictions have set a minimum wage that is higher than the federal level. Although union workers generally receive higher incomes and have negotiated health care and retirement benefits, many low-income workers do not join unions or they work in states or companies that aggressively discourage union membership.

FIGURE 3.4   U.S. Population in Working Class Jobs.

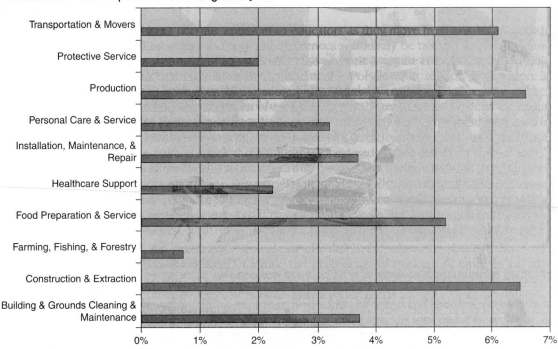

From the U.S. Census Bureau. (2006). *Statistical abstract of the United States: 2007* (126th ed.). Washington, DC: U.S. Government Printing Office.

Blue-collar workers are engaged primarily in manual work that is routine and mechanical. The education required for most of these jobs is not as high as for white-collar jobs that are not mechanical and less routine. Without additional training, it becomes difficult to move into a higher-level position. Blue-collar workers generally perceive themselves as hardworking and honest, and as performing important work for society. They want to be successful and often hope that their children will not have to spend their lives in the same kind of job.

The Middle Class

The incomes of Americans who are popularly considered middle class vary greatly. For the purpose of this discussion, families are classified as middle class if their annual incomes fall between $40,000 and $85,000—about 37% of all families in 2004 (U.S. Census Bureau, 2006b). Although some members of the middle class have comfortable incomes, many have virtually no wealth. Many live from paycheck to paycheck, with little cushion against the loss of earning power through catastrophe, recession, layoffs, wage cuts, or old age. At various periods in their life cycle, some members fall into poverty for brief periods of time. Many families have found it necessary for both husband and wife to work to make ends meet.

The jobs held by the middle class differ greatly, especially in income compensation. Overall, middle-class workers earn a median income above that of most blue-collar workers, except for skilled workers and many operatives. The median income of sales workers was

$32,344 in 2005; workers who provide administrative support in offices earned less at $28,600. Teachers and other educators had a median income of $41,496 (U.S. Census Bureau, 2006b). As a group, these workers have greater job security and better fringe benefits than many blue-collar workers, but higher education is often required.

Some white-collar jobs are as routine and boring as many blue-collar jobs; others are highly interesting and challenging. Still others are extremely alienating in that employees cannot control their environments. Some employees perceive their work as meaningless, are socially isolated from coworkers, and develop low levels of self-esteem. The type of job and the environment in which it is performed vary greatly for workers with white-collar jobs. Members of this class appear to believe strongly in the Protestant work ethic. They generally adhere to a set of beliefs and values that are inherent in the good life. Although they are only slightly better off economically than their blue-collar counterparts, they live or try to live a more affluent lifestyle.

The Upper Middle Class

Professionals, managers, and administrators are the elite of the middle class. They represent the status that many upward mobile families are trying to reach. Their income level allows them to lead lives that are, in many cases, quite different from those of white-collar and blue-collar workers. They are the group that seems to have benefited most from the nation's economic growth. Although at a level far below the upper class, the **upper middle class** are the affluent middle class.

The professionals who best fit this category are those who must receive professional or advanced degrees and credentials to practice their professions. One of every five workers has a professional or related job. Judges, lawyers, architects, physicians, college professors, teachers, computer programmers, and scientists are the professionals. Excluding teachers and social services occupations, most professionals earn far more than the median income of $46,904 reported in the census for this category (U.S. Census Bureau, 2006b). They may be classified as members of the upper middle class, many earning over

Pause to Reflect 3.3

Perceptions of others develop early in life and are corrected or reinforced on the basis of one's experiences throughout life.

- What images do you conjure up when you think of the homeless, the working class, and the middle class?
- Which characteristics are positive, and which are negative?
- Why are your perceptions value laden?
- What must you watch for in your own perceptions to ensure that you do not discriminate against students from one of these groups?

Go to the *Homework and Exercises* section in Chapter 3 of MyEducationLab and select *Pause to Reflect 3.3* to answer these questions.

$85,000 annually. They usually own a home and a new car and are able to take vacations to other parts of the country and abroad (Rose, 2000).

This group also includes managers and administrators, who make up 14% of the employed population. They are the successful executives and businesspeople, who are very diverse and include the chief executive officers of companies, presidents of colleges, and owners and administrators of local nursing homes. Those who are the most affluent make up the middle and upper management in financing, marketing, and production. The gap between men's and women's earnings is greater for managers and administrators than for professionals. As reported earlier in this chapter, the administrators of large corporations earn salaries far above this level; their salaries and fringe benefits place them in the upper class.

The incomes and opportunities to accumulate wealth are higher for this group than the bulk of the population. Members of this class play an active role in civic and voluntary organizations. Their occupations and incomes give them access to policymaking roles within these organizations. They are active participants in political processes and thus are major recipients of public benefits. Of all the groups studied so far, this one holds the greatest power.

The occupations of the people in this group play a central role in their lives, often determining their friends as well as their business and professional associates. Their jobs allow autonomy and a great amount of self-direction. Members of this group tend to view their affluence, advantages, and comforts as universal, rather than as unique. They tend to believe that their class includes almost everyone (Rose, 2000). They believe in the American dream of success because they have achieved it.

The Upper Class

High income and wealth are necessary characteristics for entering the **upper class** as well as being accepted by those persons who are already members. Within the upper class, however, are great variations in the wealth of individual families.

The upper class is comprised of two groups. One group includes the individuals and families who control great inherited wealth; the other group includes top-level administrators and professionals. Prestige positions, rather than great wealth, allow some families to enter or maintain their status at this level. The upper class includes persons with top-level and highly paid positions in large banks, entertainment corporations, and industrial corporations. It also includes those who serve as primary advisors to these positions and government leaders—for example, corporate lawyers.

The disparity between the income and wealth of members of this class and members of other classes is astounding. In 1980, for example, chief executive officers earned about 42 times as much as the average worker in their companies. In 1990, the pay ratio reached 107:1. By 2006, it had increased to 411 (Anderson et al., 2006). The number of people reporting incomes of more than a million dollars has grown dramatically since the 1980s. This increase in the size of the upper class has occurred, in part, because of the income received from increased rent, dividends, and interest payments available to the holders of financial assets, such as property and stock.

Wealth and income ensure power. The extremely small portion of the population that holds a vastly disproportionate share of the wealth also benefits disproportionately when resources are distributed. The power of these people allows them to protect their wealth. The only progressive tax in this country is the federal income tax, in which a greater percentage of the income is taxed as the income increases. Loopholes in the tax laws provide benefits to those whose unearned income is based on assets. What does this mean in terms of advantage to the rich? Tax laws in the 1980s were regressive, resulting in a decline in the taxes of higher-income families. The 1990s saw more progressive taxes in which the taxes of higher-income families rose in comparison to the taxes of low-income families. The tax cuts of 2001 reduced taxes for everyone, but more so for high-income families. Families in the bottom fifth of income earners received an average annual tax reduction of $81. However, the wealthiest 1% experienced an average savings of $42,618 (Teller-Elsberg et al., 2006). Thus, tax relief has been more beneficial to the rich than to those with the lowest incomes.

Although families with inherited wealth do not represent a completely closed status group, they do have an overrepresentation of Anglo, Protestant members who were born in the United States. They tend to intermarry with other members of the upper class. They are well-educated, although a college degree is not essential. The educational mark of prestige is attendance at elite private prep schools and prestigious private colleges and universities. Greater assimilation of lifestyles and values has occurred within this class than in any other. Although diversity exists within the group, members of the upper class may be the most homogeneous group, and they are likely to remain so as long as their cross-cultural and cross-class interactions are limited.

Interaction of Class with Race and Ethnicity, Gender, and Age

Poverty is most likely to be a condition of the young, persons of color, women, full-time workers in low status jobs, and the illiterate. Many of the individuals in poverty are members of the 7.9 million families living in poverty—10% of all U.S. families (U.S. Census Bureau, 2006b). The population groups that suffer the most from poverty are shown in Figure 3.5.

FIGURE 3.5   Population Below the Poverty Level.

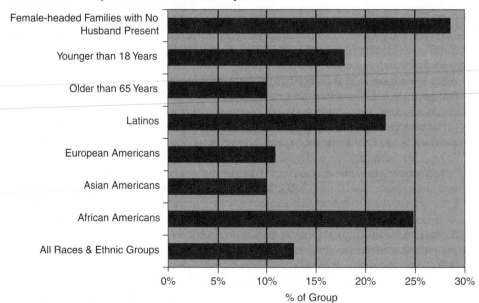

From the U.S. Census Bureau. (2006). *Statistical abstract of the United States: 2007* (126th ed.). Washington, DC: U.S. Government Printing Office.

Many low-income people do have full-time, year-round jobs but are not paid wages high enough to move their families out of poverty. Nearly 9 million households with an income of less than $25,000 have at least one member who works full-time, year-round; another 4 million families have members who work part-time or full-time for part of the year (U.S. Census Bureau, 2006b). The working poor are disproportionately located in service and retail trade occupations. It is difficult for them to rise above poverty when the minimum wage is low and part-time jobs are often the only jobs available.

Income inequality is higher in the United States than any other industrialized country. International studies report that the United States has the highest poverty rates and social policies that limit opportunities for moving out of poverty. Although workers in the United States work more hours per year, low-income families have a lower standard of living than workers in other countries. Other industrialized countries have stronger unions, higher minimum wages, and generous benefits, including more vacation days. The social policies of other countries provide a social safety net for families through maternity leave, family leave, universal health care, and child care for its children (Mishel, Bernstein, & Schmitt, 2003).

The poor are a very heterogeneous group. They do not all have the same values or lifestyles. They cannot be expected to react alike to the conditions of poverty. To many, their ethnicity or religion is the most important determinant of the way they live within the economic constraints of poverty. To others, the devastating impact of limited resources is the greatest influence in determining their values and lifestyles, which are limited severely by the economic constraints that keep them in poverty.

Race and Ethnic Inequality

With the exception of many Asian American groups, people of color are more likely to experience economic deprivation. African American families earned 65% ($35,158) of the median income of white families ($54,061), Latinos 65% ($35,401), and Asian American and Pacific Islander families 121% ($65,482) (U.S. Census Bureau, 2006b). Pacific Americans comprise only 10% of the Asian/Pacific American group, but they are disproportionately represented in poverty—a fact that is obscured by the overall panethnic category of Asian Americans. When families with married couples are compared, the gap between groups becomes smaller, but not equal.

Although more whites are in poverty than any other group, the percentage of whites in poverty is less than any other group other than Asian Americans. Of the white population, 8% fall below the poverty level, compared with 23% of African Americans, 21% of Latinos, and 7% of Asian Americans (U.S. Census Bureau, 2006a). Considerable diversity exists among Asian Americans as with other groups. For example, some Asian Americans—primarily families from the second wave of Southeast Asian immigrants—live in abject poverty. One of the reasons is that persons of color are more likely to be concentrated in low-paying jobs as shown in Figure 3.6. The percentage of African Americans in the higher-paying and higher-status jobs is much lower than whites. Although both absolute and relative gains in the occupational status of African Americans have been made during the past 40 years, they and Latinos are still heavily overrepresented in the semiskilled and unskilled positions.

This inequitable condition is perpetuated by several factors. Persons in poverty are more likely not to have graduated from high school. Students of color drop out of school in greater proportions than white students, limiting their income potential. Dropout rates are also related to family income. High school graduation rates range from 69% for those

FIGURE 3.6   Occupations of Ethnic Groups[1].

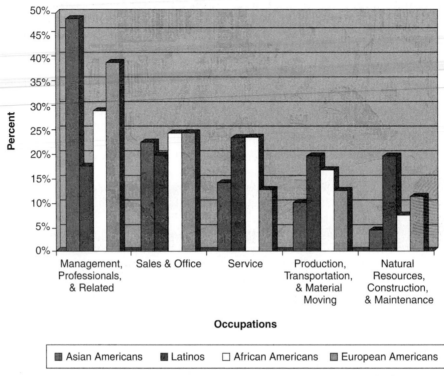

Occupations

■ Asian Americans   ■ Latinos   □ African Americans   ■ European Americans

[1]The figure shows the percentages of each group employed in an occupational category (e.g., 28% of all employed African Americans work as managers or professionals).

From the U.S. Census Bureau. (2006). *Statistical abstract of the United States: 2007* (126th ed.). Washington, DC: U.S. Government Printing Office.

from families earning less than $36,539 annually to 93% for those from families earning more than $98,434 (Family Income and Higher Education Opportunity, 2006).

Unemployment for people of color is higher than for European Americans. Less than 4% of the white population was unemployed in 2005, compared with 7.5% of African Americans and 4.8% of the Latinos. For 20- to 24-year-olds, the differences were greater, with 7.2% of whites, 18.3% of blacks, and 8.6% of Latinos unemployed (U.S. Census Bureau, 2006b). Discrimination against African Americans and Latinos is still widespread, contributing to unemployment and lack of participation in the labor market.

The historical experiences of ethnic groups have had a great impact on their gains in SES. For example, the absolute class position (income, occupation, rate of employment) of African Americans improved as a result of their migration to America's large cities where they could find jobs paying higher wages during the first half of the twentieth century. Their educational attainments have narrowed the formerly enormous gap between blacks and whites with regard to completion of high school; median number of school years completed; and, to a lesser degree, standardized test scores and prevalence of college attendance.

Racial and ethnic groups are discussed in Chapter 2.

Other oppressed groups with a disproportionately low SES have had different historical experiences than African Americans but suffer similarly from discrimination. Mexican Americans are highly overrepresented as farm laborers, one of the lowest-status occupations. Many American Indians have been isolated on reservations, away from most occupations except those lowest in prestige, and the numbers of such positions are limited. Asian Americans, who as a group have a high educational level and a relatively high SES, often reach middle-management positions but then face a glass ceiling that prevents them from moving into upper management.

Gender Inequality

As a group, women earn less and are more likely to suffer from poverty than any other group, with women of color suffering the greatest oppression. The reasons for such inequality, however, have very different origins from inequality based on race and ethnicity. Institutional discrimination based on gender is based on a patriarchal society in which women have been assigned to traditional roles of mother and wife and, if they had to work outside the home, to jobs in which subordination was expected. This status has limited their job opportunities and has kept their wages low. Overt discrimination against women has resulted in the use of gender to determine wages, hiring, and promotion of individuals by using mechanisms similar to those that promote inequality for members of other oppressed groups.

Refer to Chapter 4 for a more in-depth discussion of the income difference between males and females.

Seventy-one percent of women between the ages of 20 and 64 were working in the civilian workforce in 2005, as compared with 85% of the men (U.S. Census Bureau, 2006a). Regardless of their race and ethnicity, women participate in the labor force at about the same rate. European and African American women in this age range are more likely to work than Latino women at rates of 69%, 68%, and 59%, respectively.

To maintain an adequate or desirable standard of living today, both husband and wife in many families work. The difference that two incomes contribute to the way a family lives is obvious. The percentage of married women and white women in the workforce increased dramatically in the last half of the twentieth century. Only 16.7% of all married women worked outside the home in 1940. By 2005, 59% did. Seventy-five percent of married women with children under 18 years of age are working outside the home (U.S. Census Bureau, 2006b).

Historically, the sexual division of labor has been fairly rigid. The roles of women were limited to reproduction, childrearing, and homemaking. When they did work outside the home, their jobs were often similar to roles in the home—that is, caring for children or the sick. Jobs were stereotyped by gender. As recently as 2005, women comprised more than 90% of the traditional female occupations and less than 10% of the traditional male jobs shown in Table 3.1. The jobs in which women predominate are accompanied by neither high prestige nor high income. People in the category of professionals such as teachers and nurses do not compete in income or prestige with architects and engineers. Women continue to be overrepresented as clerical and service workers and underrepresented as managers and skilled workers.

Even within the same occupation groups, salaries between women and men differ. Table 3.2 compares their salaries for selected jobs. In 2005, the income of women was 81% of men's (U.S. Bureau of Labor Statistics, 2006). At the same time, the gap between low-income and high-income groups has led to growing inequality among women. Both men and women at the bottom of the income scale are losing ground. Women who enter

TABLE 3.1   Occupations in Which Women Are Most Likely and Least Likely to Participate

Traditionally Female Occupations	Percent Participation	Traditionally Male Occupations	Percent Participation
Secretaries & administrative assistants	97.3	Tool & die makers	1.1
Preschool & kindergarten teachers	97.7	Logging workers	1.7
Dental hygienists	97.1	Automotive mechanics	1.8
Dental assistants	96.1	Carpenters	1.9
Dietitians & nutritionists	95.3	Surveying and mapping technicians	2.7
Word processors & typists	95.0	Crane & tower operators	2.8
Child care workers	94.8	Construction & extractive occupations	3.0
Licensed practical nurses	93.4	Firefighters	3.3
Receptionists & information clerks	92.4	Aircraft mechanics & service technicians	4.5
Occupational therapists	92.9	Truck drivers	4.5
Registered nurses	92.3	Airplane pilots & flight engineers	5.2
Speech-language pathologists	92.0	Mechanical engineering	5.8
Hairdressers & cosmetologists	92.0	Construction managers	6.3
Payroll & timekeeping clerks	91.4	Electrical & electronic engineers	7.1
Bookkeeping, accounting, & auditing clerks	91.3	Grounds maintenance workers	7.5
Teacher assistants	90.9	Engineering managers	9.5

From the U.S. Census Bureau. (2006). Statistical abstract of the United States: 2007 (126th ed.). Washington, DC: U.S. Government Printing Office.

TABLE 3.2   Comparison of Women's and Men's Median Salaries in Selected Job Occupations in 2005

Occupation	Women's Annual Salary	Men's Annual Salary	Women's Salaries as Percentage of Men's
Construction & extraction	$24,960	$31,512	79%
Management, business, & financial operations	$44,055	$60,684	77%
Farming, forestry, & fishing	$17,004	$20,176	84%
Installation, maintenance, & repair	$35,932	$36,712	98%
Education, training, & library	$39,156	$49,920	79%
Protective services	$26,728	$37,908	70%
Sales	$25,116	$39,624	63%
Architects & engineering	$49,140	$58,916	84%

From the U.S. Bureau of Labor Statistics. (2006). Highlights of women's earnings in 2005 (Report 995). Washington, DC: U.S. Department of Labor.

traditionally male jobs with low-paying jobs are not increasing their chances of moving into the middle class. Highly educated women are the ones who have made absolute wage gains during this period.

With the exception of professional and doctoral degrees, more women (56%) are enrolled in higher education than men (44%). In addition, a greater percentage of women graduate than men, and they are closing the gap in professional schools. In 2004, women received 49% of all law degrees, 46% of all medical degrees, and 34% of all theological degrees (U.S. Census Bureau, 2006b). Compared with the earnings of men with the same education, however, women continue to earn less. Women with a bachelor's degree earned $31,309 compared to men's $50,916 in 2005. Men with professional degrees earned $88,530 while women earned only $48,536.

Women, especially those who are the heads of households, are more likely than men to fall below the poverty level. Twenty-eight percent of families maintained by women with no spouse presently earn an income below the official poverty level (U.S. Census Bureau, 2006b). The large number of families in this group is a result of a combination of low-paying jobs and an increase in divorces, separations, and out-of-wedlock births. When compared with male households where the spouse is absent, women without spouses earn only 67% of the median income of men (U.S. Census Bureau, 2006b).

Pause to Reflect 3.4

Throughout the next week, systematically record the types of jobs that men and women hold in your community. You might use a table such as this:

Type of Job	Number of Women	Number of Men

- What are the similarities?
- Were you surprised by your findings?
- If so, what in particular surprised you?

At the end of the week, analyze the data to determine whether men and women hold the same or similar jobs. What are the differences? What are the economic implications for the women and men in your study?

Go to the *Homework and Exercises* section in Chapter 3 of MyEducationLab and select *Pause to Reflect 3.4* to answer these questions.

Age Inequality

The highest incidence of poverty occurs for young people as shown in Figure 3.7. Eighteen percent of the nation's children under 18 years old are in poverty (U.S. Census Bureau, 2006b). However, nearly two of five children live in low-income families (National Center for Children in Poverty, 2006).

Both women and men tend to earn their maximum income between the ages of 45 and 54. The median income of persons who are 14 to 19 years old is lower than for any other group, primarily because most of these persons are just beginning to enter the workforce at the end of this period and some may not enter for several more years, especially if they attend college. Income then increases steadily for most people until after they reach 55 years of age. The income of women remains fairly constant throughout much of their working lives, whereas the income for a large percentage of men increases dramatically during their lifetimes.

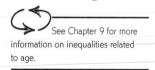

See Chapter 9 for more information on inequalities related to age.

Children's class status depends on their families, and they have little or no control over their destiny during their early years. A higher percentage of children are in poverty in the United States than in European countries (Luxembourg Income Study, 2007). International studies show that U.S. children in high- and middle-income families have a higher standard of living than children in other industrialized countries. However, children in low-income families are at least one third worse off than children in other countries (Rank, 2004). In schools, poverty is tracked by the number of students eligible for free or reduced lunches. In 2005 41% of U.S. fourth graders were eligible for this program, but the percentage of Latino (73%), African American (70%), and American Indian (65%) students was much higher than whites (24%). African American and Latino students are almost 10 times

FIGURE 3.7 Persons in Poverty by Age, Race, and Ethnicity.

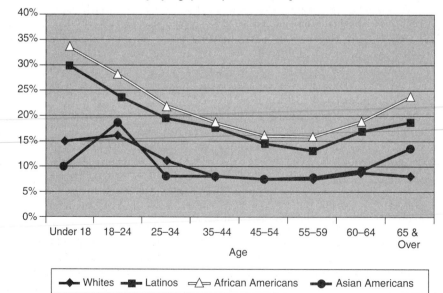

From the U.S. Census Bureau. (2006). *Statistical abstract of the United States: 2007* (126th ed.). Washington, DC: U.S. Government Printing Office.

more likely than white students to attend high poverty schools in which more than 75% of the students are eligible for free or reduced lunches (U.S. Department of Education, 2006).

Students from low-income families often begin kindergarten with lower cognitive skills than their peers in families with middle and high incomes. To compound the problem, low SES kindergartners begin their schooling in the worst public schools with low-quality teaching and discriminatory practices such as ability grouping (Lee & Burkam, 2002). These children will be disadvantaged in developing their adult earning power by inferior schooling, an oppressive financial environment, and poor health.

To prevent poverty after age 65, individuals must plan throughout their working lives to defer or save income that can be used for support once they stop earning regular incomes. Social security benefits provide some support to the elderly, and often these benefits are the only support available. Some workers participate in pension plans that provide an income after a lifetime of work, but many employees, especially blue-collar and low-level white-collar workers, do not have the opportunity to participate in such programs. Some people work on a cash basis (e.g., house cleaners) where their employers do not report their employment and do not pay taxes. As a result, they have no social security. Some must continue to work as long as they are physically able, well beyond normal retirement age.

In a society in which high ranking is given to individuals who either control wealth or are productive in the labor force, persons who do not contribute to this production are assigned a low status. Many elderly persons receive financial and medical support from the government, making them nonproductive drawers on the nation's wealth. Often, they are accorded little deference and instead face impatience, patronization, and neglect by people still in the workforce.

Classroom Focus

Many social reformers, educators, and parents view education as a powerful device for achieving social change and the reduction of poverty. From the beginning of the public school movement in the early nineteenth century, low incomes and immorality were believed to result from inadequate education. Thus, children from low-income families were encouraged to attend charity schools and public common schools to learn the Christian values that would help them learn the discipline for working. By the 1960s, many students from low-income families still were not achieving academically at the same levels as their more economically advantaged peers and continued to drop out of school at higher rates. As part of President Lyndon Johnson's War on Poverty in the 1960s, the federal government attempted to decrease poverty through the establishment of Head Start, Title I (compensatory education), Upward Bound, Job Corps, Neighborhood Youth Corps, and other educational programs. However, test scores of students from low-income groups have not improved as much as expected nor has economic inequality of families greatly decreased.

This lack of progress in overcoming the effects of poverty on students should not suggest that educational reforms are not worthwhile. Some changes make schooling more attractive to students and even increase the achievement of many individual students. In a number of states educational resources have become more equitably distributed as a result of court cases. Nevertheless, the intended goal of increasing income equity and eliminating poverty has not been realized. More than school reform will be required to raise the academic achievement of low-SES students. The social and economic conditions of their lives must be improved through higher wages and social policies that support low-income families (Rothstein, 2004).

Different social-historical interpretations of education explain the role of schools in society and the degree to which this goal and others are met. Two views are prevalent. In one view schools are an agent of social reform that can improve the chances of economic success for its graduates. The second view concludes that schools exist as agents of the larger social, economic, and political context, with the goal of inculcating the values necessary to maintain the current socioeconomic and political systems.

Supporters of the first view are much more benign in their description of the role of schools in helping students become socially mobile. They are optimistic that social reform can be achieved by providing low-income students with more effective schools. The other view sees schools as preparing students to work efficiently at their jobs in corporate organizations. The needs of business and industry are met by preparing students from low-income families for low-wage jobs that will be managed by college graduates from middle- and high-income families.

Rather than provide equal educational opportunity, many schools perpetuate existing social and economic inequities in society. In this section, we examine four areas that influence the inequities that exist in schools: teacher expectations, tracking, curriculum, and the funding of schools.

Teacher Expectations

Most classrooms are heterogeneous in terms of student gender and the SES of their families. Unfortunately, some teachers assign academic expectations to students based on their membership in these groups. Students not classified as middle class are sometimes viewed as not able to achieve at high academic levels. Most of these students are greatly harmed by such expectations. In contrast, students from the upper middle class usually benefit from a teacher's judgments because they are expected to perform better in school, are treated more favorably, and perform at a higher level in most cases.

In junior high school, students from low-income families typically take fewer courses in mathematics and science, which contributes to later differences in college enrollments

Some inner-city schools are squeezed between office buildings and housing units, leaving small playgrounds that differ greatly from those in suburban and rural areas.

© Peter Buckley/JPH College

VIDEO INSIGHTS

Smart Kid, Tough School

In recent years, more and more attention has been given to the deteriorating condition of many of the nation's schools. Surely, students who are educated in such surroundings do not receive an education equal to the education given to students who attend schools with greater financial and community resources. Cedric Jennings, a star student from a high school in the poorest section of Washington, DC, saw this confirmed when he enrolled in a summer program for gifted students of color, only to find that the students from higher-income neighborhoods were better prepared academically. Yet, when scholarship offers to attend expensive prep schools came his way, Cedric refused them and returned to his old high school for his senior year. Why do you think Cedric decided to return to Ballou High School?

Imagine you were a teacher at an inner-city school like the high school profiled in the video segment.

1. How would you try to instill a sense of the value of an education in students in a world where being smart is not always valued by their peers?
2. How would your own class background affect your ability to relate to the students?
3. What could you do in your classroom on a day-to-day basis to help eradicate the crippling effects of class differences?

Go to the Video Insights DVD and watch the *Smart Kid, Tough School* video segment. Then, go to the *Homework and Exercises* section in Chapter 3 of MyEducationLab and select *Video Insights: Smart Kid, Tough School* to answer these questions.

and vocational choices. In many schools with large numbers of low-income populations, advanced courses in these subjects may be offered, but not with the same academic rigor as in the more advantaged schools. Thus, low-income students who are achieving at a level equal to students from the dominant group are stifled in their attempts to move to higher levels in the advanced courses available at their schools. It is no wonder that they score less well on standardized assessments. They have not had the opportunity to take the same high-level courses as their middle-class peers.

Ethnographic studies of schools document how students are classified, segregated, and taught differently, starting with their first days in school. Most teachers can identify the personal characteristics of students that will lead to academic success. They then develop instruction and interactions with their students that ensure that the students will, in fact, behave as the teachers expect—a phenomenon called the **self-fulfilling prophecy.** The kindergarten teacher who divides her class into three reading and mathematics groups by the third week of school has limited knowledge about the academic abilities of the students. Too often, the groups are organized by nonacademic factors. Students in the highest group may be dressed in clean clothes that are relatively new and well pressed. They interact well with the teacher and other students, are quite verbal, and use standard English. Students in the lower two groupings may be poorly dressed and smell badly. They use a dialect; and their families appear to be less stable than those of students in the highest group. If the teacher's goal is to spend time with students in the lower group to ensure that they develop language and reading skills they will need to be successful in the first grade and their skills become less distinguishable from students in the higher groups, this grouping strategy would be successful. The problem is that many teachers do not expect the students identified as having lower academic ability at the beginning of the year to perform at high levels by the end of the year. The result is that students in the highest group continue to perform better academically and behave in a more acceptable manner than students in the other two groups. As the teacher had projected, these students are more successful throughout their schooling than students from lower socioeconomic levels.

When teachers make such judgments about students, they are taking the first step in preventing students from having an equal opportunity for academic achievement. Rather than ensure that students have access to an egalitarian system, such classification and subsequent treatment of students ensures the maintenance of an inequitable system. This action is not congruent with the democratic belief that all students can learn and should be provided equal educational opportunities.

In helping to overcome the stigma of poverty, educators must consciously review their expectations for students. Students' feelings of low esteem should not be further exacerbated by teachers. Seeing students as individuals, rather than as members of a specific socioeconomic group, may assist educators in overcoming the **classism** that exists in the school and the community. Information about a student's family background can be used in understanding the power of environment on a student's expression of self; it should not be used to rationalize stereotypes and label students. Educators should become aware of any prejudices they themselves hold against members of lower socioeconomic groups and work to overcome their biases. Otherwise, discriminatory practices will surface in the classroom in the form of self-fulfilling prophecies that harm students and perpetuate societal inequities.

Inner-city schools are populated by many low-income and working-class students whose environment outside the school is very different from that of students in most suburban schools. For many students, schools are safe places as compared to the abuse and crime that may be part of the daily lives of students in a neighborhood characterized by poverty. These students have strengths that are not recognized or supported by many educators. Many are very resilient under conditions that provide obstacles to their well-being and academic achievement. Although it is essential to ensure that all students learn the subject matter, how these skills are taught should vary, depending on the environment in which students live—a factor greatly dependent on the family's SES. Helping students achieve academically in schools that serve students from low-income families requires competent educators with "commitment, enthusiasm, compassion, solidarity, and love" (Noguera, 2003, p. 21).

How can the development of negative and harmful expectations for students be prevented? Teachers, counselors, and administrators can unconsciously fall into such behavior because they have learned that poverty is the fault of the individual. As a result, students are blamed for circumstances beyond their control. Instead, educators should see as a challenge the opportunity to provide these students with the knowledge and skills to overcome poverty. Educators should select approaches they would use for the most gifted students. The goal should be to improve the educational experiences for students who previously would have been tracked into the low-ability classes. Too many teachers blame the students, their families, and their communities for students not learning rather than examining and changing their own teaching practices to improve student learning. Effective teachers do make a difference.

Equality in the achievement of students could be increased by raising the level of instructional content and instructional discourse in all courses at all levels. Achievement is improved when teachers help students interact with the academic content through discussion and **authenticity**—relating the content to students' prior experiences and real-world applications. These strategies work for all students, not just those in the advanced placement and honors courses.

Tracking

Tracking students into different groups or classes based on their intellectual abilities is a common educational practice. Teachers often divide the class into smaller groups for instructional purposes. These groups could have a heterogeneous makeup with each group containing girls and boys from different ethnic groups and students who are currently high and low achievers. These groups are often characterized by students helping each other. In other cases, teachers assign students to a group based on their perception of the students' academic abilities, which may be based on students' latest standardized test scores. Teachers may use different instructional strategies in these groups and have different expectations for learning outcomes. Tracking also occurs when students are assigned to classes based on their perceived intellectual abilities or other characteristics such as speaking a language other than English or having a disability. Middle and high school students either choose or are assigned to college preparatory, vocational, general, and advanced courses based, in great part, on how their teachers or counselors judge their future potential. Some students are placed in gifted courses or programs and others in courses that are clearly meant for low-ability students.

Supporters of tracking argue that separating students based on their perceived abilities allows teachers to better meet the needs of all students. Critics argue that tracking and homogeneous grouping based on ability is discriminatory and prevents many students from developing their intellectual and social potential.

Tracking is an area in which class matters. High ability appears to be more closely related to family background and SES than intellectual potential (Ball, 2003; Brantlinger, 2003; Welner, 2001). Students whose families are already privileged benefit most from tracking. Students in the gifted and advanced programs are academically challenged in their courses with enrichment activities that encourage them to develop their intellectual and critical thinking skills. At the other end of the learning spectrum, the learning environment is often uninviting, boring, and not challenging. Rather than preparing these students to move to higher-level courses, these courses keep them at the lowest levels of academic achievement.

Educational researchers continue to find that simply being in the low-ability group diminishes students' achievement (Lucas, 1999; Welner, 2001). Such students are provided with fewer and less effective opportunities to learn than other students. Critical thinking tasks are reserved for the high-ability groups. Oral recitation and structured written work are common in low-ability groups. Students are exposed to low-status knowledge at a slower pace than their peers in higher-ability groups, helping them fall further behind in subjects like mathematics, foreign languages, and sciences.

Teachers in low-ability classrooms spend more time on administration and discipline and less time actually teaching. As one might expect, student behavior in low tracks is more disruptive than in higher-level groups. However, this probably happens, in part, because students and teachers have developed behavioral standards that are more tolerant of inattention, and not because of students' individual abilities. To compound the problem, the more experienced and more successful teachers are disproportionately assigned to the higher-ability groups. Unfortunately, many teachers generally view high-track students positively and low-track students negatively.

Disproportionately large numbers of students from lower socioeconomic levels are assigned to low-ability groups beginning very early in their school careers. Even more tragic is the fact that the number of students from low-income families who are classified as being mentally challenged is disproportionately high. This inequitable classification places students of color in double jeopardy because they also disproportionately suffer from poverty.

Tracking has become a second-generation segregation issue that has led to the practice being challenged in courts (Welner, 2001). In many schools with diverse student populations, students have been resegregated based on race, class, and language into separate tracks within the school. White middle-class students have disproportionately high representation in gifted and talented programs while African Americans, Latinos, students from low-income families, and English language learners comprise the majority of the students in low-ability classrooms. For the most part, the courts have agreed with the plaintiffs that tracking students into low-ability courses and programs is a discriminatory practice that limits their educational opportunities and potential for later occupational and economic success. Even when students and parents are encouraged to choose courses, a school district may be liable for discriminatory action if parents have not been appropriately informed of required prerequisites for advanced courses. Other discriminatory practices that are being considered by courts today are the inadequate preparation of low-income students and students of color to pass standardized tests and the assignment of unqualified teachers to the schools in which these students are concentrated.

Some courts have ordered school districts to detrack their schools (Welner, 2001). Other schools have voluntarily made this decision to improve the education of students who have traditionally been assigned to the low tracks. However, dismantling tracking systems in schools is not an easy undertaking. Some teachers fight detracking, in part, because they do not believe that heterogeneous groupings contribute to the learning of all students. They may believe that gifted students will suffer if they are integrated with students who do not perform at the same academic level.

Middle-class parents, especially upper-middle-class parents, often fight efforts to detrack schools. According to Welner (2001), this resistance occurs "because detracking is fundamentally redistributive—altering how schools allocate their most precious resources, including time, teachers, materials, and high-achieving students" (p. xiii). Some parents whose children are most likely to be in the high-ability or gifted tracks fight the integration of their children with others. Many of these parents believe that their achievements should be passed on to their children by ensuring that they receive the highest-quality education possible. To prevent detracking, these parents employ strategies to hold on to the privilege that their children can gain from their education. They use their power to force administrators to respond to their demands. They have been known to threaten to remove their children from public schools and hold out for other special privileges for their children. At times, they co-opt parents from the middle class to support their stand. Nevertheless, some schools have been able to detrack their schools with the goal of improving the education of all students regardless of the socioeconomic level or race of their parents.

Curriculum for Equality

The curriculum should reflect accurately the class structure and inequities that exist in the United States. The existence of nearly half the population is not validated in the curricula of most schools. Curriculum and textbooks usually focus on the values and experiences of a middle-class society. They highlight the heroes of our capitalist system. They usually ignore the history and heroes of the labor struggle in this country, in which laborers

FOCUS YOUR CULTURAL LENS: DEBATE
Detracking

Data in many schools show that the children of upper-middle-class families are overrepresented in high-ability programs for the gifted and talented and underrepresented in low-ability special education and general education courses. School officials are being pushed by the courts to change their practices that segregate students by SES or race. One of the remedies for eliminating these discriminatory practices is detracking or dismantling tracks for students based on ability as determined by standardized tests or teachers' perceptions. Some teachers and middle-class parents resist the move to a single track in which students from different ability groups are mixed.

Opinions about these strategies differ. Some people believe that detracking will provide greater equality of opportunity across economic and racial groups; opponents believe that it will lead to a lower quality of education overall. Some pros and cons for detracking are listed below:

For
- Eliminates discrimination against students from low-income families and students of color.
- Integrates students from different ability levels.
- Encourages classroom instruction that is challenging and interesting for low-income as well as upper-middle-class students.
- Supports a classroom environment in which high-ability students learn while assisting peers who may not be at the same academic level.
- Provides low-SES students greater access to good teachers, improving their chances for learning at higher levels.

Against
- Is not fair to high-ability students who need to be challenged at advanced levels.
- Makes it more difficult for teachers to provide appropriate instruction for all students whose abilities differ greatly.
- May lead to pressure from upper-middle-class parents who may withdraw their children from public schools.
- Waters down the curriculum for high-ability students.
- Prevents high-ability students from participating in gifted and talented programs and advanced level courses that will give them the advantage needed to be admitted to elite colleges and universities.

Questions
1. How do schools ensure that the voices of low- and middle-income families are included in discussions about detracking and the provision of educational equity in schools?
2. How does detracking schools contribute to the provision of equal educational opportunity?
3. What other steps could school officials take to provide low-income students greater access to advanced courses?
4. What are your reasons for supporting or not supporting detracking strategies in schools?

Go to the *Homework and Exercises* section in Chapter 3 of MyEducationLab and select *Focus Your Cultural Lens* to answer these questions.

resisted and endured under great odds to improve their conditions. They do not discuss the role of the working class in the development of the nation. The inequities based on the income and wealth of one's family are usually neither described nor discussed. In classrooms, students should learn of the existence of these differences. They should understand that the majority of the population does not live the middle-class myth.

Often overlooked are the experiences that students bring to the classroom. School is not the only place where students learn about life. Differences in school behavior and knowledge among students from dissimilar socioeconomic levels are strongly dependent on the knowledge and skills needed to survive appropriately in their community environments. Most low-income students, especially those in urban areas, have learned how to live in a world that is not imaginable to most middle-class students or teachers. Yet, the knowledge and skills they bring to school are not always valued. Educators should recognize the value of the community's informal education in sustaining its own culture and realize that formal education is often viewed as undermining that culture.

Students need to see some of their own cultural experiences reflected in the curriculum. They need to see ordinary working people as valued members of society. These students and their families need to be helped to see themselves as desirable and integral members of the school community, rather than as second-class citizens who must learn the ways of the more economically advantaged to succeed in school.

Educators should become cognizant of the materials, films, and books used in class. If students never see their communities in these instructional materials, their motivation and acceptance may be limited. All students should be encouraged to read novels and short stories about people from different socioeconomic levels. When studying historical or current events, they should examine the events from the perspective of the working class and those in poverty, as well as from the perspective of the country's leaders. Teaching can be enhanced by drawing examples from experiences with which students are familiar, especially when the experiences are different from the teacher's own.

All students, no matter what their SES, should be helped to develop strong and positive self-concepts. Many students do not realize the diversity that exists in this country, let alone understand the reasons for the diversity and the resulting discrimination against some groups. Most middle-class children believe that most persons live like their families. Educators are expected to expand their students' knowledge of the world, not to hide from them the realities that exist because of class differences.

In a classroom in which democracy and equity are important, social justice should inform the curriculum. Low-income students should receive priority time from teachers and have access to the necessary resources to become academically competitive with middle-class students.

Finally, all students should be encouraged to be critical of what they read, see, and hear in textbooks, through the mass media, and from their parents and friends. The curriculum should encourage the development of critical thinking and problem-solving skills. Unfortunately, schools traditionally have talked about the democratic vision but have been unwilling to model it. Students and teachers who become involved through the curriculum in asking why the inequities in society exist are beginning to practice democracy.

School Funding

At the beginning of this chapter, Mr. Juarez found great differences in the conditions of schools in the inner-city and the suburbs. These inequities are greatly exacerbated by the fact that the current system for funding schools mirrors these inequities. Education is

Pause to Reflect 3.5

New teachers are often assigned to teach in schools with large numbers of students from low-income families. Think about how you will help students see themselves in the curriculum.

- How will you ensure that your low-income students will not be marginalized in the curriculum?
- What projects might your students engage in to learn more about equality and inequality based on socioeconomic differences?
- What courses have you taken that help you understand the inequities in society? What did they address?

Go to the *Homework and Exercises* section in Chapter 3 of MyEducationLab and select *Pause to Reflect 3.5* to answer these questions.

supported by local property taxes, which supply about 44% of all school funds. State support averages about 49%, and federal support is around 7% (Karp, 2003). The U.S. spends less on education than many other industrialized countries, ranking 12th in a study by the Organization for Economic Cooperation and Development (Karp, 2003). Another international study rated the United States last among developed countries in the gap between the quality of schools for high- and low-income students (National Commission on Teaching and America's Future, 2004). The few U.S. students who live in high-income communities within generous states attend public schools funded at $15,000 or more per student per year. Students in low-income communities within states that are less financially able or willing are supported by $3,000 or less per year in funding for their schools. In a study of schools in the state of New York, for example, researchers found that "New York State has a two-tiered public school system: one for the more affluent, who enjoy the privileges of a relatively sound educational environment, and the other for the least privileged" (National Commission on Teaching and America's Future, 2004, p. 37).

Researchers and policymakers disagree as to how much money is needed by schools to improve academic achievement. In a reanalysis of data from studies on this relationship, University of Chicago researchers concluded that higher per-pupil expenditures, better teacher salaries, more educated and experienced teachers, and smaller class and school sizes are strongly related to improved student learning (Greenwald, Hedges, & Laine, 1996). If we agree that more money would help reduce the inequities across groups in schools and that greater resources are needed in low-wealth school districts, what areas would provide the greatest payoff for improved student achievement? Slavin (1995) recommends smaller class sizes, prekindergarten programs for four-year-olds, tutoring for students having difficulty, cooperative learning, family support systems, and extensive staff and teacher development for delivering effective programs.

Summary

Socioeconomic status (SES) is a composite of the economic status of a family or unrelated individuals, based on income, wealth, occupation, educational attainment, and power. It is a means of measuring inequalities based on economic differences and the way families live as a result of their economic well-being. Families range from the indigent poor to the very rich. Where a family falls along this continuum affects the way its members live, how they think and act, and the way others react to them. Although a family may actively participate in other cultural groups centered around ethnicity, religion, gender, exceptionality, language, or age, the class to which a family belongs is probably the strongest factor in determining how one lives.

Social stratification is possible because consistent and recurring relationships exist among people who occupy different levels of the social structure. Persons of color, women, the young, the elderly, and individuals with disabilities are disproportionately represented at the low end of the social stratification system.

The United States can be divided into classes based on income and occupation. The income and wealth that keep families at one of these levels vary greatly. Individual choice is most limited for those persons who are in poverty and who can barely meet essential needs. Whereas ethnic and religious diversity exists at all levels, the upper class is the most homogeneous. Persons of color and women who head families are overly represented at the lowest SES level. Class consciousness is strongest among the upper classes, whose members know the value of solidarity in the protection and maintenance of their power and privilege.

Disproportionately large numbers of students from lower SES levels are assigned to low-ability groups in their early school years. Educators should consciously review their expectations for students and their behavior toward students from different SES levels to ensure that they are not discriminating. Instructional methods and teaching strategies may vary greatly, depending on the environment in which students live. It is essential that all students be provided with a quality education.

Educators also need to pay attention to the curriculum. Too often, low-income students are placed in remedial programs because of discriminatory testing and placement. In addition, the curriculum does not serve students well if it reflects only the perspective of middle-class America. Low-income students need to see some of their own cultural experiences reflected in the curriculum, in addition to learning about the dominant group.

Financial support for more equitable funding of schools, no matter where they are located or which students attend them, is likely to reduce the achievement gap between groups of students. The current property tax system for supporting schools gives the advantage to families with high incomes.

PROFESSIONAL PRACTICE FOR EDUCATORS

Questions for Discussion

1. How does social stratification differentially affect groups in society?
2. Why is social mobility unreal for many members of society?
3. What role does education play in maintaining or changing the SES of the population?
4. What socioeconomic factors make it difficult for members of the underclass to improve their conditions?
5. Why do the professional and managerial workers, who comprise the upper middle class, have more power in society?

6. What is the relationship of class and race in maintaining economic inequities?
7. Why have schools not been able to eliminate poverty in this country?
8. How does a self-fulfilling prophecy prevent some students from achieving at high levels?
9. How might the tracking of students perpetuate inequalities in schools and society?
10. How can teachers ensure that students from low-income and working-class families are able to achieve academically at the same level as other students?

Portfolio Activities

1. Visit a school in an economically depressed area of your community or a nearby city and another school in a community that serves students from the upper middle class. Record the differences in the physical environment, aesthetics, school climate, resources for students, and attitudes of faculty and students. Write a paper comparing the two schools and analyzing the reasons for the differences you have observed. (INTASC Standard 2)
2. Develop a lesson plan that positively recognizes the socioeconomic differences in society, reflecting the experiences of low-income families and other persons who do not have an adequate income to live comfortably. The lesson should be for the subject and level (for example, elementary or secondary) that you plan to teach. (INTASC Standard 3)
3. Volunteer to tutor at a homeless shelter or after-school program for students from low-income families and record your feelings about the children and settings as journal entries. Your entries could include your feelings on going to the shelter or program for the first time, the strengths of the children with whom you work, and your learnings about the obstacles that students face outside of school. (INTASC Standards 2, 3, and 10)

Licensure Test Prep

1. Which of the following topics is most likely to be included in the traditional Western curriculum that ignores socioeconomic groups that are not advantaged?
   A. Labor movements in the coal mines of Appalachia that pitted workers against owners.
   B. The struggles of Mexican American farmworkers in California and the Southwest.
   C. The conditions that led to the fall of the stock market and the Great Depression in 1929.
   D. Affirmative action which has helped improve the salaries and wages of women over the past 30 years.

Go to the *Homework and Exercises* section in Chapter 3 of MyEducationLab and select *Licensure Test Prep* to complete this exercise.

Suggested Readings

Anyon, J. (2005). *Radical possibilities: Public policy, urban education, and a new social movement.* New York: Routledge.

Examining economic and public policies that contribute greatly to the disparities in income, standards of living, and schools in urban areas, Anyon confronts educational injustice. She argues that pressures for educational reform through a social movement will lead to more educational and economic justice in urban America.

hooks, b. (2000). *Where we stand: Class matters.* New York: Routledge.

Drawing on her girlhood experiences in Kentucky and later life in New York City, bell hooks reflects on the ways class and race are intertwined in our lives. The meaning of poverty and wealth are explored.

Kozol, J. (1991). *Savage inequalities: Children in America's schools.* New York: Crown.

These descriptions of rich and poor schools are a powerful statement on the class and racial inequities that exist in the nation's schools. Interwoven with the stories of students and educators is an analysis of the inadequacy of the current funding of schools.

The New York Times Correspondents. (2005). *Class matters.* New York: Times Books, Henry Holt & Co.

By interviewing Americans at different class levels, reporters of *The New York Times* bring reality to the meaning of class. These stories about the lives of individuals and families across the country show the differences that SES makes in their lives and health.

Noguera, P. (2003). *City schools and the American dream: Reclaiming the promise of public education.* New York: Teachers College Press.

Drawing on his research in schools in the San Francisco area and Richmond, Dr. Noguera explores what it will take for students in urban schools to achieve at the levels expected in standards. He describes schools that have worked against the odds to succeed.

Shulman, B. (2003). *The betrayal of work: How low-wage jobs fail 30 million Americans.* New York: New Press.

This portrait of workers who are employed full-time in jobs that pay poverty wages provides insights into the struggles of people who work hard, but are not moving up the social mobility ladder.

References

American Political Science Association. (2004). *American democracy in an age of rising inequality.* Washington, DC: Author.

Andersen, M. L., & Collins, P. H. (2007). *Race, class, and gender: An anthology* (6th ed.). Belmont, CA: Thomson Wadsworth.

Anderson, S., Cavanagh, J., Collins, C., & Benjamin, E. (2006). *Executive excess 2006: Defense and oil executives cash in on conflict* (13th Annual CEO Compensation Survey). Washington, DC: Institute for Policy Studies and Boston: United for a Fair Economy.

Anyon, J. (2005). *Radical possibilities: Public policy, urban education, and a new social movement.* New York: Routledge.

Ball, S. J. (2003). *Class strategies and the education market: The middle classes and social advantage.* New York: RoutledgeFalmer.

Books, S., & Polakow, V. (2001, Fall). Introduction to special issue: Poverty and schooling. *Educational Studies, 32*(3), 259–263.

Brantlinger, E. (2003). *Dividing classes: How the middle class negotiates and rationalizes school advantage.* New York: RoutledgeFalmer.

Collins, C., & Veskel, F. (2004). Economic apartheid in America. In M. L. Andersen & P. H. Collins (Eds.), *Race, class, and gender: An anthology* (5th ed., pp. 127–139). Belmont, CA: Wadsworth/Thomson.

Family Income and Higher Education Opportunity: 1970 to 2005. (2006, December). *Postsecondary Education Opportunity*, No. 174.

Greenwald, R., Hedges, L. V., & Laine, R. D. (1996, Fall). The effect of school resources on student achievement. *Review of Educational Research, 66*(3), 361–396.

Joint Center for Housing Studies of Harvard University. (2007). *The state of the nation's housing: 2007.* Cambridge, MA: Author. Retrieved on June 14, 2007, from www.jchs.harvard.edu/publications/markets/son2007/son2007.pdf

Karp, S. (2003, Fall). Money, schools and justice: State-by-state battle for funding equity gets mixed results. *Rethinking Schools, 18*(1), 26–30.

Keenan, F. (2003, February 3). It's still rich man, poor man. *Business Week Online.* Retrieved November 9, 2004, from www.businessweek.com/magazine/content/03_05/c3818066.htm

Lee, V. E., & Burkam, D. T. (2002). *Inequality at the starting gate: Social background differences in achievement as children begin school.* Washington, DC: Economic Policy Institute.

Levin-Epstein, J., & Greenberg, M. H. (Eds.). (2003). *Leave no youth behind: Opportunities for Congress to reach disconnected youth.* Washington, DC: Center for Law and Social Policy.

Lucas, S. R. (1999). *Tracking inequality: Stratification and mobility in American high schools.* New York: Teachers College Press.

Luxembourg Income Study. (2007). *Poverty rates for children by family type.* Retrieved September 15, 2006, from www.lisproject.org/keyfigures/childpovrates.htm

Mishel, L., Bernstein, J., & Schmitt, J. (2003). *The state of working America: 2002/2003.* Armonk, NY: Economic Policy Institute.

National Center for Children in Poverty. (2006). *Basic facts about low-income children: Birth to age 18.* New York: Author. Retrieved on June 3, 2007, from www.nccp.org/publications/pub_678.html

The National Center on Family Homelessness. (2007). *America's homeless children.* Newton Centre, MA: Author. Retrieved on June 5, 2007, from www.familyhomelessness.org/pdf/fact_children.pdf

National Commission on Teaching and America's Future. (2004). *Fifty years after Brown v. Board of Education: A two-tiered education system.* Washington, DC: Author.

The National Law Center on Homelessness and Poverty. (2004, January). *Homelessness in the United States and the human right to housing.* Washington, DC: Author.

Noguera, P. (2003). *City schools and the American dream: Reclaiming the promise of public education.* New York: Teachers College Press.

Rank, R. (2004). *One nation, underprivileged: Why American poverty affects us all.* London: Oxford University Press.

Rose, S. J. (2000). *Social stratification in the United States.* New York: New Press.

Rothstein, R. (2004). *Class and schools: Using social, economic, and educational reform to close the black-white achievement gap.* Washington, DC: Economic Policy Institute.

Shipler, D. K. (2004). *The working poor: Invisible in America.* New York: Alfred A. Knopf.

Shulman, B. (2003). *The betrayal of work: How low-wage jobs fail 30 million Americans.* New York: New Press.

Slavin, R. (1995, Summer). Making money make a difference. *Rethinking Schools, 9*(4), 10, 23.

Smith, D. (2000). *The state of the world atlas.* New York: Penguin.

Smith, D. (2003). *The Penguin state of the world atlas* (7th ed.). New York: Penguin.

Teller-Elsberg, J., Folbre, N., Heintz, J., & The Center for Popular Economics. (2006). *U.S. economy: Field guide to the U.S. economy.* New York: New Press.

U.S. Bureau of Labor Statistics. (2006). *Highlights of women's earnings in 2005* (Report 995). Washington, DC: U.S. Department of Labor.

U.S. Census Bureau. (2006a). *2005 American community survey.* Washington, DC: Author. Retrieved on June 3, 2007, from www.factfinder.census.gov/servlet/STTable?_bm=y&-geo_id=01000US&-qr_name=ACS_2005_EST_G00_S2301&-ds_name=ACS_2005_EST_G00

U.S. Census Bureau. (2006b). *Statistical abstract of the United States: 2007* (126th ed.). Washington, DC: U.S. Government Printing Office.

U.S. Conference of Mayors. (2006). *Hunger and homelessness 2006.* Washington, DC: Author.

U.S. Department of Education, National Center for Education Statistics. (2006). *The condition of education 2006.* Washington, DC: Author.

Welner, K. G. (2001). *Legal rights, local wrongs: When community control collides with educational equity.* Albany, NY: State University of New York Press.

Chapter 4

GENDER AND SEXUAL ORIENTATION

No person shall, on the basis of sex, be excluded from participation in, be denied the benefits of, or be subjected to discrimination under any education program or activity receiving federal financial assistance.

TITLE IX (EDUCATION AMENDMENTS, 1972)

Abdul Rashid planned to introduce ecology to his science class. Since school began seven months ago, he has not been able to interest most of the girls in the science content. Most of his female students are capable of understanding and using science, but they show little interest. Sometimes he thinks they just do not want to upstage the boys in the class. He knows that some of them should be in an advanced science class because they score extremely well on the written tests, but they show little interest in class discussions and experiments.

To introduce ecology, he decided to try a different approach. Perhaps he could relate the subject to something meaningful in their lives—maybe even their families' or their own social activities. He wanted to find examples they would care about. He decided to focus on the toxic chemicals found in the creek that runs behind many of their homes. Premature births in that area are being blamed on the chemical dumping that has been going on for more than 20 years.

Reflections

1. Why do most of the girls in Mr. Rashid's class appear to be uninterested in science?
2. What are the participation rates of females in advanced mathematics and science courses?
3. What are the reasons for the lack of participation in science by girls and young women?
4. How might Mr. Rashid's approach to ecology engage the girls?
5. What would you do to increase the interest and participation of females in science and mathematics?

Male and Female Differences

Although some differences exist between males and females, the popular, and sometimes "scientific," beliefs about these differences have often prevented equality across the sexes. At the beginning of the twentieth century, some scientists and many laypersons thought that men were intellectually superior to women and therefore generally more capable of professional and administrative work. They believed that women's nature made it imperative that men give orders and women take orders in the workplace. Because their physical strength was not comparable to that of men, women were also deemed unsuitable for many manual or working-class jobs, except for the most menial and the lowest paid. Well-adjusted women were expected to be married homemakers, performing services for the family without remuneration.

Even though there is now clear evidence that women and men do not differ in intelligence, the percentage of men in the best-paying and most demanding professional jobs is disproportionately higher than the percentage of women in those jobs. Because of technological advances, brute strength is usually no longer a requirement for most manual jobs, but the percentage of women in those jobs still falls far behind that of men. Nevertheless, gender equality still does not exist in many workplaces and homes.

Biological Determinism

Researchers continue to debate how much of the differences between females and males is due to biology and how much is due to socialization and culture. Most of us can easily identify physical differences between men and women by appearance alone. Girls tend to have lighter skeletons and different shoulder and pelvic proportions. Although the proportion of different hormones in the body differs by gender, boys and girls have similar hormonal

VIDEO INSIGHTS
The Secret Life of Boys

abc NEWS

Boys will be boys. This is a belief espoused by many—in schools, in homes, in the media, by society as a whole—but does it ring true? Do boys and girls act differently because of genetics, or are their behaviors learned from society?

In this video segment you will see that boys have a more difficult time showing emotion and feelings. By the age of 5 it's often difficult to tell if something is bothering a little boy because he has already learned to mask his feelings. In addition, while boys are conditioned to keep their feelings and emotions inside, girls are supported and expected to share and discuss their feelings with others. Does this difference have an outward effect? Some researchers say yes; this emotional repression leads to boys acting out more in school and being labeled with learning disorders and behavior problems more often than girls.

Often, culture determines the appropriate activities in which boys and girls participate. After watching the video segment, where do you stand on this discussion?

1. Do you notice little boys being treated differently than girls? Give some examples.
2. How do you interact differently with boys and girls?
3. How will you monitor yourself more closely as you interact with children?

Go to the Video Insights DVD and watch *The Secret Life of Boys* video segment. Then, go to the *Homework and Exercises* section in Chapter 4 of MyEducationLab and select *Video Insights: The Secret Life of Boys* to answer these questions.

---

levels and similar physical development during the first eight years of life. The onset of puberty marks the difference in hormonal levels of estrogen and testosterone that control the physical development of the two sexes. At this time, the proportion of fat to total body weight increases in girls and decreases in boys. The differences in physical structure contribute to a female's diminished strength, lower endurance for heavy labor, greater difficulty in running or overarm throwing, and better ability to float in water. However, environment and culture can also influence the extent of these physical differences for both males and females. Thus, the characteristics listed above can be altered with good nutrition, physical activity, practice, and different behavioral expectations.

Because of society's expectations for different behaviors by males and females, it is difficult to determine how many of the differences are actually biological. Some may result from different cultural expectations and lived experiences, rather than from different biological makeup. For example, gender differences in the incidence of cardiovascular disease is decreasing as more women enter jobs associated with stress.

Prior to the twentieth century, intelligence was equated with the size of the brain. Because men's brains were larger than women's, scientists of the time concluded that women were not as intelligent as men, and thus, inferior to them. Today we know that brain size is related to body size, not to intelligence. When Alfred Binet developed the first intelligence test at the beginning of the twentieth century, no differences were found in the general intelligence between the sexes. However, many studies have found some gender differences in mathematical, verbal, and spatial skills (Cassidy, 2007).

Some researchers attribute these differences to biological determinism, especially hormones affecting hemispheric specialization in the brain. The right hemisphere of the

TABLE 4.1   Advantages that Boys and Girls Receive in Schools

Advantages to Boys	Advantages to Girls
Greater athletic support and funding	Greater involvement in extracurricular activities
Attention-getting classroom behavior	Higher academic performance
Mathematics and science test scores	Reading and writing test scores
SAT scores for college admission	Higher educational aspirations
Not prone to eating and other psychological disorders	Fewer learning and behavioral disorders
Few problems caused by teen pregnancy	Fewer discipline problems
Fewer victims of sexual abuse	Fewer victims of school violence
Classrooms that privilege boys	Classroom organization that supports girls' learning

Adapted from Gurian, M. (2001). *Boys and girls learn differently!: A guide for teachers and parents.* San Francisco: Jossey-Bass.

cerebral cortex controls spatial relations and the left hemisphere controls language and other sequential skills. Females tend to favor the left hemisphere associated with speaking, reading, and writing. Males are reported to have greater right-hemisphere specialization, which leads to better performance on tests of spatial visualization and higher achievement in mathematics and science. However, some boys and some girls lean toward the hemisphere that is usually identified with the opposite sex (Gurian, 2001).

Proponents of brain-based differences argue that understanding these differences will help teachers understand why boys behave the way they do in classrooms and lead to appropriate instruction. Gurian (2001) reports that boys are more likely to be **deductive** in their conceptualizations; they begin with the general and move to the details. Girls, on the other hand, are more likely to be **inductive,** beginning with the details to figure out the general. Boys are more easily bored. They need more physical space for learning. Movement stimulates the boys' brains and helps them manage and relieve impulsive behavior. Girls, on the other hand, more easily master **cooperative learning,** in which students work together on a learning project. Table 4.1 outlines the advantages that their favored brain hemisphere gives to boys and girls.

Other researchers attribute many of the differences between females and males to socialization patterns in childrearing and schooling, rather than biological factors. They argue that girls and boys can learn to use the other hemisphere of their brain so that they can better perform the skills associated with that hemisphere. These debates focus on the nature versus nurture controversy on what causes the differences between boys and girls. A more balanced view of the causes of sex differences gives credit to the interaction of both nature and nurture.

Cultural Influences on Gender

Generally, sex is used to identify an individual as male or female based on biological differences. **Gender,** on the other hand, defines the characteristics of femininity and masculinity that are determined by culture. Women are often equated with nature and men with culture, which controls and transcends nature (Shaw & Lee, 2007). Nature is associated with childbearing, childrearing, and nurturing, which, in the past, kept them near the home.

Culture determines the appropriate activities in which boys and girls should participate.

Larry Fleming/PH College

Men had the freedom to move beyond the home to hunt and seek resources for supporting the family. These patterns have evolved into the current cultural patterns in which women are the predominant workers in the nurturing professions of teaching and health care, whereas men are overrepresented as corporate leaders, engineers, and construction workers. No research shows that women cannot do men's work and that men cannot be successful nurturers.

Although few differences separate men and women, the two are often segregated. Students are sometimes segregated by sex in school activities. Women and men congregate separately at social gatherings. They dress and groom differently. They participate in gender-specific leisure activities. Most members of each sex have stereotypical perceptions about themselves and the other sex.

Males are assigned a higher status in society than women. It is reflected in the prestige of the jobs held by men and women, the income earned, and the limited economic rewards associated with housework and childrearing. However, the range of social and economic differences within one gender is as great as it is between the genders. Some women are economically and socially better off than many men.

Men are also affected by culture's view of gender, which places value on masculine characteristics. Masculinity is often measured by a man's independence, assertiveness, leadership, self-reliance, and emotional stability. "Real" men are supposed to be tough, confident, and self-reliant as well as aggressive and daring (Flood, 2001; Mansfield, 2006). However, the focus on these masculine characteristics diminishes the importance of the inner lives and feelings of males (Flood, 2001; Kindlon & Thompson, 2000). **Homophobia**—the irrational fear of or aversion to homosexuals—is powerful in pushing boys to meet these expected stereotypes because they worry about being labeled as gay or a sissy and being harassed (Flood, 2001). As a result, they sometimes go overboard in proving their masculinity.

Pause to Reflect 4.1

There is no consensus on whether differences between females and males are due primarily to biology or culture. Check your perceptions by responding to the statements below.

• Girls can learn masculine traits and vice versa.	True	False
• Boys are pressured to behave in stereotyped ways.	True	False
• Women elementary teachers are contributing to the feminization of boys.	True	False
• Elementary classrooms should be changed to support boys by providing activities based on their need for more space and action.	True	False
• Boys and girls should be segregated for instructional purposes.	True	False

Go to the *Homework and Exercises* section in Chapter 4 of MyEducationLab and select *Pause to Reflect 4.1* to answer these questions.

Many men do not fit the male stereotype. They are empathetic and caring rather than tough and assertive. Even white men sometimes suffer from discrimination, especially in divorce courts and child-custody battles. Some conservatives argue that men are losing their masculinity, and are being harmed as they become more feminine. Life is not easy for young men as shown in the statistics indicating "climbing suicide rate, binge drinking, steroid use, undiagnosed depression, academic underachievement, and the disproportionate representation of boys among car crash victims" (Kindlon & Thompson, 2000, p. viii). However, psychologists Kindlon and Thompson (2000) do not contribute these problems to a reduction of the differences between the sexes. Instead, they find that boys have not been encouraged to be emotionally literate so that they can be themselves rather than develop a culturally determined gender identity with little room for divergence.

Gender Identity

Most people take their gender identity for granted and do not question it because it agrees with their biological identity. One's recognition of the appropriate gender identity occurs unconsciously early in life. It becomes a basic anchor in the personality and forms a core part of one's self-identity. By the age of 2 years, children realize that they are either boys or girls and begin to learn their expected behaviors. By the time they enter school, children have clear ideas about gender. Most children know that girls and boys behave differently based on behaviors and language reinforced at home. Many are prepared to strive for conformity with these gender-stereotyped roles. However, some people's gender identity does not match their sex. They identify themselves as the opposite sex, both sexes, no sex, or somewhere in between. **Transgender** individuals may cross-dress or have surgery to physically become the sex with which they identify.

Socialization

Appropriate gender behavior is reinforced in magazines, on television, in play with peers, and with gender-specific toys. In this socialization process, children develop social skills and a sense of self in accordance with socially prescribed roles and expectations. Appropriate gender behavior is reinforced throughout the life cycle by social processes of approval and disapproval, reward and punishment.

It is not only parents and relatives who socialize children. When a child enters school, the socialization process continues. Generally, schools convey the same standards for gender roles as the dominant culture. The attitudes and values about appropriate gender roles are embedded in the curriculum of schools. Elementary schools tend to imitate the mothering role, with a predominance of female teachers and an emphasis on obedience and conformity. In classrooms, boys and girls receive different feedback and encouragement for their work, but the patterns are similar to those used at home. Girls and young women are encouraged to be well-behaved and make good grades. Males are less well-behaved and do not achieve academically as well as females prior to puberty. Many working-class males develop patterns of resistance to school and its authority figures because it is considered feminine and emphasizes mental rather than manual work (Dolby, Dimitriadis, & Willis, 2004).

Children are also active participants in the socialization process. Play groups are often determined by the sex of the children. Even when girls and boys play the same game, they often play it differently with the boys being more aggressive. However, not all boys and girls follow the socially acceptable ways of their sex. Not all boys participate in large-group activities and are aggressive. The forgotten boys whose voices have been silenced and marginalized may follow behavior patterns generally associated with girls. The same is true for girls; not all follow the gender-specific behaviors expected of their sex. Nevertheless, most girls and boys do choose to be engaged in separate activities as youngsters. They develop a sense of gender as a dichotomy and opposition when they divide themselves into academic and athletic competitions that pit boys against girls. Cooperative projects in classrooms in which girls and boys work together can undermine this opposition if the students share the work rather than one gender always dominating.

School playgrounds reflect the importance placed on male as compared to female activities. The space required to play baseball, soccer, basketball, and kickball is much greater than that for girls' jump rope, foursquare, and bar tricks. Some girls may play the boys' sports with them, but almost no boys join the girls' games. When boys do engage in girls' games like jump rope, it is usually to disrupt the game, not to be equal participants.

In our society, women are supposed to be feminine and men masculine, with minimal crossover tolerated. Generally, females are allowed more flexibility in their gender identification than males. Even young girls receive positive attributes from acting like boys by being physically active, participating in sports, and rejecting feminine stereotypical behavior. On the other hand, boys are often ostracized when they join in girls' games, act effeminate, and don't engage in the same sports as most males. Unlike girls who have crossed gender lines, boys suffer loss of prestige.

Gender is no longer being viewed in the traditional bipolar fashion as if masculine and feminine traits never coexist in an individual. We exhibit the traits of one or the other as appropriate in a specific situation or setting. The dilemma is that not all of us, especially males, are encouraged to be ourselves when our behavior is counter to society's norms of gender identity. Some persons with physical disabilities may have significant emotional challenges related to perceptions of their perceived masculinity or femininity. Some physical disabilities may preclude participation in athletics when there are social expectations of male participation in activities such as softball, soccer, and so on. Disabilities may also become problematic if they preclude employment that requires physical abilities. Females with certain disabilities may also face challenges with society's emphasis on "the body beautiful, body whole," affecting perceptions of their perceived femininity.

Stereotyping of Gender Roles

Although gender roles are gradually changing, they continue to be projected stereotypically in the socialization process. Stereotyping defines the male and female roles narrowly and as quite distinct from one another. Men and women become automatically associated with the characteristics and roles with which they are constantly endowed by the mass media. Careers are not the only areas in which stereotyping occurs. Female and male intellectual abilities, personality characteristics, physical appearance, social status, and domestic roles have also been stereotyped. Persons who differ from the stereotype of their group, especially gays and lesbians, are often ostracized by the dominant group. Such role stereotyping may deny individuals the wide range of human potential that is possible.

In many families today, both wife and husband work. Although a growing number of men assist with childrearing and household chores, working mothers often have the primary responsibility for these activities in addition to their paid employment. Unable to depend on a male wage earner, a growing number of women who are divorced or widowed, especially if they have children, take on the roles of both parents. Although both men and women now work in a variety of careers and share many roles and activities that were formerly gender-typed, many of them retain their traditional gender roles.

Television is one of the perpetuators of gender stereotyping. By the time of high school graduation, the average child will have spent more hours in front of the television than in a classroom. The ideals and ideas of dominant America are incorporated into program development as symbolic representations of American society. On television, beauty can count for more than intelligence. Adult working women are portrayed, but strong, intelligent, working-class women are generally invisible. Female heroines are not social workers, teachers, or secretaries. A number of men's and women's magazines portray the two sexes stereotypically. Most newspapers have style pages that include articles on fashion, food, and social events—pages specifically written for what is believed to be the interests of women. Women's magazines often send contradictory messages by indicating that women should both be successful in their chosen professions and exhibit all of the positive feminine attributes of beauty, caring, and housekeeping. Working mothers are supposed to be supermoms who not only work, but are devoted mothers who meet the needs of their children like stay-at-home mothers do. The men's pages of newspapers are the sports and business sections, in which competition and winning are stressed. Male athletes receive the headlines and majority of the print in these sections. The athletic performances of women seldom make the front page.

Whereas adults read newspapers, magazines, and books, children spend much of their reading time with textbooks. How do the genders fare in the resources used in classrooms across the nation? Studies show that great improvements have been made. Textbooks are not as racist and sexist as in the past, and perspectives are better balanced. However, teachers still need to be cognizant of the gender and ethnicity of the authors being read by students.

In contemporary society, male and female traditional roles are practiced interchangeably in a growing number of families. Both men and women work in nontraditional careers and share many of the formerly gender-typical roles. In many communities, one no longer has to have rigid feminine or masculine characteristics, behavior, or job options. It is

Pause to Reflect 4.2

Gender identity is a continuum of traits and behaviors that range from very feminine to very masculine. What are your thoughts about your own and others' gender identity?

- Where do you fall along a continuum of gender identity?
- What people have had an influence on the development of your gender identity?
- How do you and your friends identify people who act like the opposite sex?
- Which sex suffers the most from behaving like the opposite sex? Why?

Go to the *Homework and Exercises* section in Chapter 4 of MyEducationLab and select *Pause to Reflect 4.2* to answer these questions.

becoming easier to have both. More couples are sharing the role of wage earner. A growing number of men are sharing more equally in the responsibilities of childrearing and home-making; sometimes they are the stay-at-home parent. In the future more men and women will be able to choose roles with which they are comfortable, rather than have to accept a gender role determined by society.

We are living in an era of changing norms in which old, unequal roles are being rejected by many people. These changes are resulting in many new uncertainties in which the norms of the appropriate gender role are no longer so distinct. As new norms develop, more flexible roles, personalities, and behaviors are evolving for both females and males.

Interaction of Gender with Ethnicity, Race, and Religion

The degree to which a student adheres to a traditional gender identity is influenced by the family's ethnicity, class, and religion. For many women of color, racial discrimination has such an impact on their daily lives and well-being that gender is often secondary in their identity. In some religions, gender identity and relations are strictly controlled by religious doctrine. Thus, gender inequality takes on different forms among different ethnic, class, and religious groups.

The degree to which traditional gender roles are accepted depends, in large part, on the degree to which the family maintains the traditional patterns and the experiences of their ethnic group in this country. Puerto Rican, Mexican American, Appalachian, and American Indian families that adhere to traditional religious and cultural patterns are more likely to encourage adherence to rigid gender roles than families that have adopted bicultural patterns.

Women in African American families have developed a different pattern. Historically, they have worked outside the home and are less likely to hold strict traditional views about their roles. They have learned to be both homemakers and wage earners. Unlike many middle-class European American women, middle-class African American women do not necessarily perceive marriage as a route to upward mobility or a way out of poverty.

African American, Latino, and American Indian women of all classes have current and historical experiences of discrimination based on their race and ethnicity. **Feminists,** who actively support the rights of women from these groups may feel forced to choose between

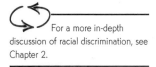

For a more in-depth discussion of racial discrimination, see Chapter 2.

a racial and a gender identity. Identification with one group may be prevalent in one setting, but not another. It is often a struggle to develop an identity that incorporates one's gender, ethnicity, race, sexual orientation, class, and religion into a whole with which one feels comfortable and self-assured. It is dangerous to assume that students will hold certain views or behave in gender-typical ways because of their ethnicity or class level. Individual families within those two cultural groups vary greatly in their support of gender-typical roles for men and women and their subsequent behavior along a continuum of gender identity.

Religions generally recognize and include masculine and feminine expectations as part of their doctrines. Regardless of the specific religion, rituals sometimes reflect and reinforce systems of male dominance. The more fundamentalist religious groups support a strict adherence to gender-differentiated roles. Their influence extends into issues of sexuality, marriage, and reproductive rights. They sometimes have successfully organized politically to

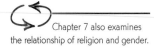

Chapter 7 also examines the relationship of religion and gender.

control state and federal policies on family and women's affairs. On the other hand, the more liberal religious groups may support the marriages of gays and lesbians, the right of a woman to choose abortion, and encourage both males and females to lead their congregations.

When a religious dogma declares that homosexuality is wrong, it is very difficult for its members to recognize homosexuality as normal and of equal status to heterosexuality. Awareness of the community and cultures within which schools are located will be essential as teachers ensure that they don't discriminate, support students as appropriate, and help all students develop their academic and social potential.

Sexual Orientation

Heterosexuality is the priviledged **sexual orientation** or sexual inclination in U.S. society and the world. It is so highly valued that laws and social practices have been written to prohibit **homosexuality**—the sexual attraction to members of the same sex. Laws in most states forbade sexual liaisons between members of the same sex until 2003 when the Supreme Court ruled in *Lawrence v. Texas* that all sodomy laws were unconstitutional, overruling the laws that still existed in 13 states (Miller, 2006). In many areas of the country where overt discrimination against homosexuals remains, gays and lesbians may not be able to find housing or jobs. They are not always admitted to "straight" clubs and are vulnerable to attacks on city streets. The Southern Poverty Law Center reports that antigay violence is now the most common hate-motivated crime in the country (Buchanan, 2005).

Many people have little knowledge about homosexuality. The actual term first appeared in Leipzig, Germany, in 1869 and became accepted in the professional literature by 1880. Over the next 100 years, the terms "homosexual" and "heterosexual" became identified with the sex of the two persons who were having sexual relations. Males were more pathologized than women for what was considered by many to be perverts (Lipkin, 1999). Many people viewed homosexuality as a sin, a moral failure, a sickness, or a crime. Even the American Psychological Association defined it as a mental illness until 1973.

One of the common questions about homosexuality is why some people are lesbian, gay, bisexual, or transgender (LGBT). Researchers are examining possible genetic causes, but have not yet identified a gene that controls sexual orientation. Hormone differences have been investigated, but the great majority of LGBT have hormonal levels that match

CRITICAL INCIDENTS IN TEACHING _____

Gay Parents

Maureen Flynn is a third-grade teacher in a suburban public school. Each year, she looks forward to Parents' Night, when she can meet the parents of her students. As she inspects her room one final time, the door opens and two nicely dressed women appear. "Good evening," they say, almost in unison. "Good evening. Welcome to the third grade. I'm Maureen Flynn." "We're Amy Gentry and Kirsten Bowers. We're Allison Gentry-Bowers' mothers." "Oh," says Ms. Flynn, trying not to show any surprise. "Let me show you some of Allison's artwork and where her desk is."

The rest of the evening is routine. Ms. Flynn introduces herself, welcomes the parents, and asks them to introduce themselves. As the parents exchange names and greetings, there are a few questioning looks as Allison's two mothers introduce themselves as her mothers. Ms. Flynn explains what the class is currently doing and what the goals and activities are for the remainder of the year. The parents and Ms. Flynn exchange pleasantries and then go home.

The next morning as class begins, Colleen Burke blurts out, "Miss Flynn, my mommy said that Allison has two mommies. How can that be? How can anyone have two mommies? Everyone is supposed to have a father and a mother." All of the students look to Ms. Flynn for her response.

Questions for Classroom Discussion

1. How should Maureen Flynn respond to Colleen's question?
2. Should she just evade the question? Why or why not?
3. Should she use the opportunity to discuss diverse family structures?

Building Teaching Skills

Go to the *Building Teaching Skills* section in Chapter 4 of MyEducationLab and select *Critical Incidents in Teaching: Gay Parents* to complete this exercise.

the heterosexual population. Environmental influences such as childrearing have also been proposed as a contributing factor (Lipkin, 1999).

Most researchers agree that sexual orientation is established early in life. As early as six years old, some boys and girls have a sense that they are sexually different than their peers. With the onset of puberty, they are likely to be attracted to a peer of the same sex (Johnson, 2006). Young people are identifying themselves as gay or lesbian at a younger age. In the 1960s the average age of self-identification was 20 for gays and 22 for lesbians. Today the average age of self-identification is 16 (National Gay and Lesbian Task Force, 2004).

The classroom teacher is likely to find students at different points along the gender identity continuum, both in their beliefs about female and male roles and in their actual behavior. Lesbian and gay adolescents are struggling with their sexual orientation and its meaning in a homophobic climate. Understanding the influence of students' cultural memberships will be important as teachers try to open up the possibilities for all of them, regardless of their gender and sexual orientation.

A Brief History of Homosexuality in the United States

Persons who have adopted the gender traits of the opposite sex in their dress and behaviors are often labeled by others as homosexual. Effeminate males stand out in this category, and were labeled "fairies" early in the twentieth century whether or not they were actually gay. Men who were gay but conformed to masculine gender traits were not usually identified as gay. Educator Arthur Lipkin (1999) reports that "Until World II the majority of homosexuals suppressed or hid their full identities and tried to live the lives that were expected of them in the communities where they had grown up" (p. 74). This lifestyle often included being married to someone of the opposite sex and raising a family as a heterosexual couple.

Until the 1970s many psychiatrists and psychologists saw homosexuality as a sickness. Others worried that exposure to homosexuals would have a negative impact on children and youth. Between 1927 and 1967, the state of New York did not allow what it called "sexual perversion" as a dramatic theme in plays. Similar bans were placed on movies. Nevertheless, noted writers continued to include gays and lesbians in their books and screenplays. In the 1950s Evelyn Hooker began to question these pathological explanations as a result of her study of gay men. She found that gay men were as well adjusted as straight men, and sometimes more so. Her findings set the stage to fight psychiatric treatments that often involved electroshock therapy (Miller, 2006).

In 1948 and 1953, biologist and zoologist Alfred Charles Kinsey released his books based on interviewing over 10,000 white women and men about their sexual behavior. He estimated that 10% of U.S. males and 8% of females were more or less exclusively homosexual for at least three years between the ages of 16–55 (Miller, 2006). The report was self-affirming for many gays and lesbians who realized that they were not the only ones whose sexual orientation did not match societal expectations. Kinsey's conclusions were widely attacked. Most people had believed that few people were homosexual, and they worried that the culture would be destroyed by them. Politicians and religious leaders became even more overt in their condemnation of those who deviated from the heterosexual model.

Beginning in 1950, the U.S. Senate called for a purge of homosexuals from the government. Within a year, the Federal Bureau of Investigation (FBI), under Director J. Edgar Hoover, had identified 406 of them. In 1953 President Eisenhower signed an Executive Order to dismiss homosexuals from the government (Miller, 2006). Lesbians and gays were being dismissed from the military at rates that rose to 3,000 annually in the early 1960s. In addition to losing their jobs, they were arrested by the hundreds in gay and lesbian bars, parks, and theaters as well as at parties in their own homes. In some communities, citizens were summoned to call out their homosexual neighbors and work colleagues (Lipkin, 1999). Many citizens confused homosexuality with pedophiles and child molesters and believed they would recruit others to their ranks. Homosexual demands for justice were ignored by most of the population. Civil rights groups did not intervene to support the gays and lesbians who were losing their jobs or being harassed in other settings (Lipkin, 1999). To support each other and their struggles for acceptance and equity in society, gays and lesbians began organizing in cities such as San Francisco and New York. One of their goals was to eliminate the pathological diagnosis that was prevalent in the dominant culture.

On June 27, 1969, a gay rights movement was born when police raided New York City's Stonewall Inn in Greenwich Village. Stonewall Inn was a refuge for gays who were not welcome in other bars. Its patrons were "cross-dressing street queens, hippies, obvious drug users, underage runaways and kids who had been kicked out of their homes" (Lipkin, 1999, p. 88). Police arrived that early summer night to close the bar because it was operating without a license, but raids on gay bars were not unusual. The bar was closed, employees arrested, and patrons pushed outside. As those arrested were placed in police wagons, the ousted patrons and crowd that had gathered began throwing coins at police. It soon escalated into a riot with everything in the bar being destroyed. This first riot lasted only 45 minutes, but participants had fought back against the police action. Crowds reconvened the following night at the Inn and on the street outside. They began shouting for "gay power" and cheering for gay liberation. It took police hours to disperse the crowd, which appeared again in smaller numbers the next night (Lipkin, 1999).

Gays had rioted earlier in Los Angeles and San Franciso against police raids, but those riots had been carefully organized by gay leaders. Stonewall Inn was different. Participants were gays who were rejected not only by society, but by more conservative gays who lived like they were heterosexual. At Stonewall the riot was spontaneous, full of emotion, and bloody (Lipkin, 1999). It became the symbol for fighting the inequities faced by LGBTs. Soon afterwards, the number of LGBT groups grew from 50 to over 800 (Lipkin, 1999).

As shown in Table 4.2, progress for gay rights and the elimination of discrimination against gays has occurred since 1969 although numerous obstacles periodically halted

TABLE 4.2   Milestones in the Movement for Gay Rights

June 28, 1969	Police raided Stonewall Inn, leading to a riot by its patrons.
1970	National Institute of Mental Health study group recommended civil rights protection for gays, but also supported prevention for gays who might be saved from homosexuality. Thousands marched in New York gay parade to celebrate the anniversary of the Stonewall Inn riot.
1970s	Civil Service Commission lifted its ban on employment of homosexuals. Police stopped raiding bars, but continued to pick up gays in other areas. Gay and lesbian caucuses were formed in professional associations.
1977	Save Our Children campaign initiated by former Miss America, Anita Bryant, worked to repeal protection for gays.
1978	A California proposal, the Briggs Initiative, would have banned gay teachers and their supporters from public schools. It was defeated.
1979	100,000 gay and lesbians participated in their March on Washington to call for gay rights.
1980	The Moral Majority organized to oppose homosexuality.
1981	Gays with a mysterious illness began appearing in emergency rooms. The disease was later identified as AIDS, which provided a uniting force for gays through the 1980s.
1982	Wisconsin passed a gay civil rights law, which was introduced by an openly gay legislator.
1987	Second gay and lesbian March on Washington in which the AIDS quilt was spread out on the Mall. ACT UP (AIDS Coalition to Unleash Power) was founded in New York City.
1989	Massachusetts passed a gay civil rights law sponsored by an open lesbian and closeted gay man.
1993	Third gay and lesbian March on Washington protested the military ban against gays and lesbians.
1996	U.S. Supreme Court ruled that states could not ban protection of gay rights outright in *Rohmer v. Evans*.
2000	Vermont approved civil unions between gays and lesbian couples.
2003	U.S. Supreme Court ended laws against sodomy in *Lawrence v. Texas*.
2004	Gay and lesbian couples were allowed to marry in Massachusetts.
2005	Connecticut approved civil unions.

significant changes. After the Stonewall riot, it became somewhat easier for gays and lesbians to openly admit their homosexuality, especially if they lived in cities. However, many still cannot be open because of community hostility and discrimination as evidenced by policies to prevent them from organizing clubs on some college campuses or openly declare their homosexuality in the armed services, schools, and religious organizations. Much work is still required to overcome prejudices and discrimination against those who are not heterosexual.

Even though a growing number of gays and lesbians are open about their sexual orientation, many still fear reprisal. In many areas of the country and in many classrooms, they are harassed and abused if they openly acknowledge their sexual orientation. It is not just other students who reject gay and lesbian students. A number of families, religious leaders, and teachers not only reject them, but label them as immoral and deviant. Unlike persons whose race can be easily identified by others, gays and lesbians can hide their identities from a hostile society. As a result, many of them suffer loneliness and alienation by not being able to acknowledge their homosexuality.

Many gay and lesbian educators separate their personal and professional lives for fear of losing their jobs. They worry that they might be accused of molestation or touching students inappropriately, charged of recruiting their students into being homosexual, or caught in a homosexual liaison (Lipkin, 1999). In addition, they worry about threats, harassment, vandalism to their cars and homes, and violence by students, parents, colleagues, and other members of the community. Although courts usually protect their jobs, they cannot provide the security and comfort that is needed by gay or lesbian teacher who openly acknowledges their homosexuality (Lipkin, 1999). Just like the military, a "don't ask, don't tell" policy operates in most schools.

Because lesbian and gay teachers are silent about their homosexuality, they neither serve as role models for gay and lesbian students nor provide the support needed by students who are usually not recognized by school officials. Heterosexual teachers who are willing to support gay and lesbian students also may face discriminatory retaliation by others.

Marriage between same-sex individuals was being tested in the 1990s. Hawaii's Supreme Court "ruled that the denial of marriage licenses to three same-sex couples represented discrimination on the basis of sex" (Miller, 2006, p. 530) and called on the state to demonstrate a reason for excluding these couples from marriage. The state legislature responded quickly by defining marriage as between a man and woman only. The voters of Hawaii agreed with the legislature's definition by ratifing it in 1998. At the same time Alaskan voters approved a constitutional amendment restricting marriage to a man and woman. In 2000 the Vermont legislature approved civil unions between gay and lesbian couples that would allow them the benefits and responsibilities of marriage without sanctioning marriage. Connecticut followed suit in 2005.

The movement for gay marriages received a boost when the Massachusetts Supreme Judicial Court in November 2003 declared that gay and lesbian couples had a right to marriage. By 2004 gay and lesbian couples were marrying in San Francisco, Portland (OR), and a few other cities. However, state legislators intervened, eventually declaring those marriage licenses void. On May 17, 2004, gays and lesbians were being married in Massachusetts. Other countries, particularly in Europe, have been more open to supporting gay marriages. They are legally recognized in The Netherlands, Belgium, Canada, and Spain; France, Germany, Finland, and Iceland have partnership laws that extend legal rights to same-sex couples.

Not all people supported the marriages in Massachusetts. Congress considered an amendment to the U.S. Constitution to ban same-sex marriages, but the Senate failed to adopt it in July 2004. States reacted quickly, placing the issue on the ballot during the 2004 national elections. Voters in 11 states overwhelmingly approved constitutional amendments limiting marriage to a man and woman (Miller, 2006). By 2006, 40 states had passed similar amendments (Johnson, 2006). Debates about civil unions and marriage continue in both religious and secular arenas. However, the public is becoming more accepting of gay and lesbian relationships. Most people in the United States support equal rights for gays in the workplace and most occupations. However, about half of the public supports a constitutional amendment against gay marriages. Liberals, young Americans, more educated people, less religious people, and Democrats are more likely to accept gay marriages (Gallup Organization, 2007).

Homophobia

An antigay movement is promoted by some white evangelical Christian leaders who have established groups such as the Traditional Values Coalition. They have now been joined in the gay bashing by some African American ministers who have identified "the so-called 'homosexual agenda'—not poverty, racism, gang violence, inadequate schools, or unemployment—as the No. 1 threat facing black Americans today" (Mock, 2007, p. 19). They generally believe that people are not born LGBT, but learn it from others. They believe that religion can help "save" their children from this plight.

Religious groups' views of homosexuality are also discussed in Chapter 7.

African Americans are more likely than other groups to support antidiscrimination legislation, even against gays, because of their commitment to equity. They and other groups of color have looked at homosexuality as a white, Western phenomenon that did not concern them (Lipkin, 1999). At the same time, African Americans in national polls are more likely than others to disapprove of homosexuality (Mock, 2007). Some African Americans resent gays using the civil rights movement to further their legal rights. Evangelical Christianity is not the only religious group that does not recognize homosexuals. Many fundamentalist religions around the world see it as a sin, sometimes resulting in severe punishment and ostracism.

Homophobia, which is actually **heterosexism,** can lead to harassment in schools, which is more common than most educators would like to admit. *The 2005 National School Climate Survey* by the Gay, Lesbian, and Straight Education Network (GLSEN) found that LGBT students face violence, bias, and harassment in schools. Nearly 40% of the students in the survey reported that they have been physically harassed at school. The majority of the students feel unsafe in school, and sometimes just don't go to school. The most common harassment is verbal abuse. Nine of 10 LGBT students

Observe and Learn
Lessons in Action

Homophobia

Go to the *Homework and Exercises* section in Chapter 4 of MyEducationLab and select *Observe and Learn: Lessons in Action* to view the video "Am I Blue?" and answer the accompanying questions. In this lesson, homophobia and sexual identity issues are presented in a poignant and funny short story about a teenager who gets beat up by a boy who suspects him of being gay. When his fairy godfather appears, the boy is treated to three wishes—one of which involves identifying anyone who is gay by a blue color.

1. How did students react to the story "Am I Blue?" Were you surprised by any of their comments?
2. Do you known any gay students or teachers? If so, how are they treated by classmates and/or colleagues? Do they hide their identity, or are they "out"?
3. Would you personally be able to teach this lesson in your future school? How might your views of the topic of homosexuality affect what you do in your future classroom?

report frequently hearing remarks such as "that's so gay" or "you're so gay." Three of four often hear remarks such as "faggot," or "dyke." LGBT students in high school report that students are called names based on their perceived or real sexual orientation. LGBT students of color are harassed because of both their race and sexual orientation.

Hostile climates for LGBT students affect their academic performance and college aspirations. When school officials and teachers are supportive of LGBT students, the students feel safer in school, miss fewer days of school, and are more likely to attend college. More than one-third of the students don't feel comfortable talking about LGBT issues with their teachers. The National School Climate Survey (GLSEN, 2005) study also found that LGBT students were safer in schools that had adopted policies against bias, violence, and harassment of LGBT students. A number of schools have now established student clubs such as Gay-Straight Alliances (GSAs) to provide support for and be allies to LGBT peers.

Suicide is sometimes related to homosexuality as discussed in Chapter 9.

Professional educators have the responsibility to provide a safe and inclusive environment at school by eliminating homophobia. High school is a difficult time for many adolescents, but it is particularly stressful for gays and lesbians as they struggle with the knowledge that they are members of one of the most despised groups in society. They have few, if any, support systems in their schools or communities. They are alone in making decisions about acknowledging their sexual orientation and facing attacks by others. Educators must not limit the potential of any student because of her or his sexual orientation or gender identity. Most faculty either never intervene or intervene only some of the time when homophobic remarks are being made (GLSEN, 2005). Teachers and administrators should confront colleagues and students who engage in name-calling and harassment. Classroom interactions, resources, extracurricular activities, and counseling practices must be evaluated to ensure that students are not being discriminated against because of their sexual orientation.

Pause to Reflect 4.3

Imagine you are teaching a high school class. You are leading a discussion about current events, and today's topic is AIDS. After several minutes of give-and-take discussion among students in the class, the following dialogue occurs:

Mary: I think it's too bad that all these people are so sick and are going to die. I just think. . .

Paul (interrupting): Those fags get what they deserve. What makes me mad is that we're spending money trying to find a cure. If we just let God and nature take its course, I won't have to worry about any queer bothering me.

Mary: I never thought about it that way before.

Mary then faces you and asks, "What do you think about Paul's comments?" How would you respond?

Go to the *Homework and Exercises* section in Chapter 4 of MyEducationLab and select *Pause to Reflect 4.3* to answer these questions.

Source: Sears, J. T. (1992). Educators, homosexuality, and homosexual students: Are personal feelings related to professional beliefs? In K. M. Harbeck (Ed.), *Coming out of the classroom closet: Gay and lesbian students, teachers, and curricula* (pp. 62–64). Binghamton, NY: Harrington Park Press.

The Women's Movement

Women have participated in a number of movements since the mid-nineteenth century to fight for gender equality. Some of the early feminists who were participating in the anti-slavery movements prior to the Civil War raised concerns about women's issues, including the right to divorce, property rights, the right to speak in public, abuse by husbands, work with little or no pay, and suffrage. At the Seneca Falls Convention in 1848, women organized to fight against their oppression. This effort involved some male supporters, including Frederick Douglass and white abolitionists who were fighting against slavery and for human and civil rights for all people. However, most women did not support the women's movement at that time. They did not view their conditions as oppressive and accepted their role as wife and mother as natural.

Later in the century, protective legislation for women and children was enacted. This legislation made some manual jobs inaccessible to women because of the danger involved and limited the number of hours women could work and the time at which they could work. Such legislation did little, however, to extend equal rights to women. During this period, most feminists segregated their fight for equal rights from the struggles of other oppressed groups and refused to take a stand against Jim Crow laws and other violations of the civil rights of ethnic and racial groups. Women's groups, which were predominantly European Americans, also pitted themselves against African American men in the fight for the right to vote.

The most significant advances in the status of women were initiated in the 1960s when feminists were able to gain the support of more women and men than at any previous time in history. As in the previous century, this movement developed out of the struggle for civil rights by African Americans. The 1963 Equal Pay Act required that men and women receive equal pay for the same job, but did not prevent discrimination in who was hired. In an attempt to defeat the Civil Rights Bill in Congress, a Southern congressman added the words "or sex" to Title VII, declaring that discrimination based on "race, color, national origin, or sex" was prohibited. This legislation, which was approved in 1964, was the first time that equal rights had been extended to women. Soon afterwards, President Lyndon Johnson signed an executive order that required businesses with federal contracts to hire women and persons of color, becoming the first affirmative action programs.

By 1983, political leaders were no longer disposed to extend full equal rights to women. Women's groups pushed for an Equal Rights Amendment (ERA) that read "Equality of rights under the law shall not be denied or abridged by the United States or by any state on account of sex." Although Congress passed the one-sentence Equal Rights Amendment, conservative groups concerned about family values lobbied state legislatures to reject the amendment. Although two thirds of the U.S. population supported the ERA, it was not adopted by the required number of states.

Women's movements have traditionally been dominated by middle-class white women. Limited to women's issues, the movement in the early days was not open to broader civil rights for all oppressed groups. This focus prevented the widespread involvement in the movement of both men and women of color. Support from the working class was also limited because the needs of neither these women nor women on welfare were part of the agenda. Lesbians and bisexuals did not feel that the women's movements addressed or highlighted their issues, leading to the establishment of separate groups to meet their needs.

The 1990s ushered in a change toward broader support for civil rights for all groups and greater inclusion of men and women from diverse ethnic groups in the feminist movement. As an example, the nations's largest feminist organization, the National Organization for Women (NOW), has added to its agenda fighting racism and supporting welfare reform, immigrant rights, and affirmative action. A growing number of articles and books on equity by feminists, sociologists, and critical theorists address the interaction of race, gender, and class in the struggle for equity for all groups.

Increasing numbers of men also support the equity agenda, including women's issues. Some men have established their own male liberation groups to promote choices beyond traditional male roles. However, unlike the women's movement, which became a social action agend, male liberation usually remains a personal, not a political, matter.

Why do equal rights for women, gays, and lesbians continue to be contested? People hold different views about the equality of the sexes. Feminists fight for equality in jobs, pay, schooling, responsibilities in the home, and the nation's laws. They believe that women and men should have a choice about working in the home or outside the home, having children, and acknowledging their sexual orientation. They believe that women should not have to be subordinate to men at home, in the workplace, or in society. They fight to eliminate the physical and mental violence that has resulted from such subordination by providing support groups and shelters for abused women and children, as well as by pushing the judicial system to outlaw and severely punish such violence. In addition, they promote shared male and female responsibilities in the home and the availability of child care to all families.

Some feminists think that there are few differences between males and females and that those differences are not linked to psychological traits or social roles. Their research concludes that differences are socially constructed. Others think that women's psyches and values do differ from those of men—that there are distinct female and male cultures. They believe that the world would be better served if traditional female values, rather than masculine values, guided society. They focus on the special qualities of being a woman and do not accept the adoption of male characteristics and values to succeed.

A vocal group of antifeminists that includes both men and women have fought against the ERA and women's equality. This group is led by political conservatives who believe that the primary responsibilities of a woman are to be a good wife and mother. Employment outside the home is viewed as interfering with these roles. They argue that homemaking and mothering are themselves viable careers that should be pursued. The male is to be the primary breadwinner in the family, and a woman's dependency on the husband or father is expected. They believe that feminism and equal rights will lead to the disintegration of the nuclear family unit. Homosexuality and abortion are rejected. The men and women who support these positions have effectively organized themselves politically to defeat legislation to provide greater equality of men and women. They promote abstinence programs and fight against the dissemination of information on sexuality in schools and health clinics.

Many young women take for granted the rights that have been won by women over the past century. The first feminists set the stage for recognizing women as equal to men, finally gaining the right to vote in 1919. Joining the civil rights movement in the last half of the twentieth century, the women's movement was renewed. These feminists fought for equal pay, equal opportunities for education and jobs, inclusion in medical tests, attention to breast cancer and other diseases affecting women, women's studies, **nonsexist education,** the right to choice, and the recognition of lesbianism. By the end of the century, most women were both working and raising families. The media was highlighting supermoms who held high-power jobs, but also attended PTA meetings, shuffled their children to

Pause to Reflect 4.4

Both males and females can support women's rights and fight together for equality. Think about your knowledge of women's issues.

- How much of a feminist are you? What feminist issues do you support?
- How have you been exposed to feminism and women's issues?
- What was the last book—not a textbook—by a woman that you read? Was the book about women or did it provide a woman's perspective?
- What was the last magazine you read? Was the content of the magazine focused on women's or men's issues?

Go to the *Homework and Exercises* section in Chapter 4 of MyEducationLab and select *Pause to Reflect 4.4* to answer these questions.

---

soccer and baseball, cooked breakfast and dinner, took care of themselves by exercising before their children were up in the morning, and returned to their e-mail after the kids had gone to bed. Of course, most women do not have high-power jobs, but they still have the greater responsibility for household work and childrearing.

Much has been accomplished over the past 35 years, but other struggles remain. The current movement is more inclusive, addressing the civil rights of women of color, women in poverty, and elderly women. A number of social issues have still not been embraced by political leaders. Thus, feminists continue to lobby for universal child care, safety nets for the nation's children, increasing the minimum wage for men and women workers, health care for women and children, and other laws and practices that support females. They also continue to fight to maintain the rights that have been won. Emphasizing the success of the women's movement, historian and journalist Ruth Rosen (2000) observed that "by the end of the twentieth century, feminist ideas had burrowed too deeply into our culture for any resistance or politics to root them out" (p. xv).

Sexism and Gender Discrimination

Only a century ago, most women could not attend college, had no legal right to either property or their children, could not initiate a divorce, and were forbidden to smoke or drink. Because these inequities no longer exist and laws now protect the rights of women, many people believe that men and women are treated equally in society. However, society's deep-rooted assumptions about how men and women should think, look, and behave can lead to discriminatory behavior based on gender alone.

When physical strength determined who performed certain tasks, men conducted the hunt for food while women raised food close to home. With industrialization, the pattern of men working away from home and women working close to home was translated into labor market activity for men and nonlabor market activity for women. Men began to work specific hours and to receive pay for that work. By contrast, women worked irregular and unspecified working periods in the home and received no wages for their work. Women's

Observe and Learn
Lessons in Action

Sexism and Gender Discrimination

Go to the *Homework and Exercises* section in Chapter 4 of MyEducationLab and select *Observe and Learn: Lessons in Action* to view the video "Rosalind Franklin: The Other Discoverer of DNA" and answer the accompanying questions. This lesson brings to light the inequities faced by women in science. Franklin is a role model for girls who are interested in science, as well as an example of the challenges that female scientist have faced throughout history.

1. How do the students in the video react to the revelation that Dr. Franklin was a woman? Is that reaction surprising to you?
2. As a student yourself, have you ever observed gender stereotyping in your high school? Your college?
3. How might your views regarding gender and equality of access to education and jobs affect what you do in your future classroom?

work at home was not as valued as the work of men, who contributed to labor market production.

Sexism is the belief that males are superior to females. Often, sexism is practiced by individuals in personal situations of marriage and family life, as well as in their occupational roles as manager, realtor, secretary, or legislator. Socialization patterns within the family may limit the potential of children when some are taught to be obedient, passive, and dependent, while others are encouraged to be aggressive, independent, exploring, and creative.

Many of us discriminate on the basis of gender without realizing it. Because we were raised in a sexist society, we think our behavior is natural and acceptable, even when it is discriminatory. Women often are not aware of the extent to which they do not participate equally in society, nor men the privilege that maleness bestows on them—a sign that the distinct roles have been internalized well during the socialization process. Most parents do not directly plan to harm their daughters by teaching them feminine roles. They do not realize that such characteristics may prevent their daughters from achieving social and economic success at the same levels as men. Young women are sometimes encouraged to gain fulfillment through marriage, rather than by their own achievement and independence.

Many individuals outside the family also practice gender discrimination. The kindergarten teacher who scolds the boy for playing in the girls' corner is discriminating. The personnel director who hires only women for secretarial positions and only men as managers is discriminating on the basis of gender. Educators have the opportunity to help students break out of group stereotypes and provide them opportunities to explore and pursue a wide variety of options in fulfilling their potential as individuals.

Gender discrimination not only is practiced by individuals but also has been institutionalized in policies, laws, rules, and precedents in society. These institutional arrangements benefit one gender over the other as described in the next sections.

Jobs and Wages

Regardless of their education, men are expected to work, but women sometimes have a choice about working. The amount of education obtained by women does little to close the gap between the earnings of men and women. For example, women with bachelor's degrees earn less than men with some college, but no degree. Women with bachelor's degrees or beyond have median incomes that are only 63% of the income earned by males with the same education (U.S. Census Bureau, 2006).

The difference in income between men and women generally increases with age as shown in Figure 4.1. Discrepancies in income are, in part, a result of the types of jobs held

FIGURE 4.1 Income of Year-Round, Full-Time Workers by Age and Gender.

From U.S. Census Bureau. (2006). *Statistical Abstract of the United States: 2007* (126th ed.). Washington, DC: U.S. Government Printing Office.

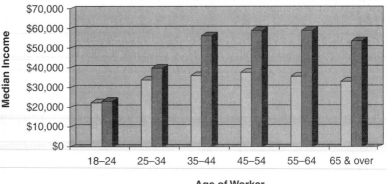

FIGURE 4.2 Female and Male Workers in Different Occupational Categories.

From U.S. Census Bureau. (2006). *Statistical Abstract of the United States: 2007* (126th ed.). Washington, DC: U.S. Government Printing Office.

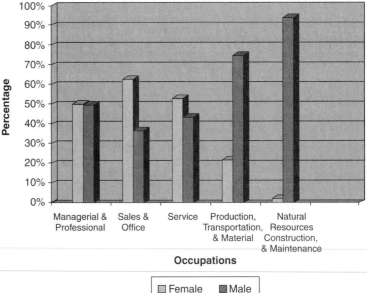

by the two groups. Women workers continue to be heavily concentrated in a few occupations that are accompanied by neither high prestige nor high income. Figure 4.2 shows the distribution of men and women in occupational categories. Women are underrepresented in management, business, and skilled jobs, but are overly represented as professionals, especially as teachers and nurses, and in sales, administrative support, and service occupations.

It has been difficult for women to enter administrative and skilled jobs in large numbers. These jobs have fewer entry-level positions than the less prestigious ones. The available openings are often for jobs that have short or nonexistent promotion ladders, few opportunities for training, low wages, few chances for stability, and poor working conditions. Clerical and sales positions are examples of such jobs, but even professions such as teaching

Women still work disproportionately in traditionally female jobs. For example, they make up more than 98% of the preschool and kindergarten teachers in the United States.

Krista Greco/Merrill

and nursing offer little opportunity for career advancement. To earn the comfortable living that is the American Dream requires women to seek either a traditionally male job or a husband with a good job.

When men enter traditionally female fields, they often do not hold the same positions as women in the field. In 2005, men comprised less than 3% of prekindergarten and kindergarten teachers and 18% of elementary teachers (U.S. Census Bureau, 2006), but were 45% of the elementary school principals (U.S. Department of Education, 2004). Over half of the high school teachers (U.S. Census Bureau, 2006), and 77% of the secondary principals were men (U.S. Department of Education, 2004). Male social workers are more often community organizers, rather than group workers or caseworkers. Although the percentage of men participating in traditionally female jobs has increased, they have become overrepresented in the higher status, administrative levels of these occupations. For example, 75% of public preschool through grade 12 teachers are women as compared with 43% of the college and university faculty (U.S. Census Bureau, 2006).

The gap between the participation of men and women in a number of high prestige professions has narrowed over a couple of generations, but not been eliminated. Women are still underrepresented in mathematics, science, and technology fields. In 1950, only 6.5% of all physicians were women; by 2005, 32% were women. The percentage of lawyers has increased from 4% to 30%, but only 10% of all engineers and 24% of architects are women (U.S. Census Bureau, 2006). The number of women in some professional jobs should continue to rise because they are receiving an increasing number of degrees in these fields. Women are now earning more than 45% of the professional degrees in medicine and law. In education, the percentage of female principals has increased from 20% in 1982 to 46% in 2000 (U.S. Department of Education, 2004). While the gap for women is closing in most fields, they are still receiving only 19% of the bachelor's degrees in engineering and 25% of the computer science degrees. Men completing bachelor's degrees are seriously underrepresented in the fields of health professions (14%), education (22%), and psychology (22%) (U.S. Census Bureau, 2006).

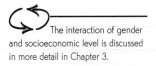

The interaction of gender and socioeconomic level is discussed in more detail in Chapter 3.

Although more women are entering the traditionally male-dominated fields, they continue to face discrimination in wages earned. In 1970, women working full-time earned 59 cents for every dollar earned by men; by 2005, they were doing better, but had not closed the gap with earnings that were 81 cents for every dollar earned by men (U.S. Bureau of Labor Statistics, 2006). This disparity is, in part, a result of the lower-status jobs held by many women. Although differences in the salaries of women and men in working-class jobs have decreased, many of these jobs do not pay enough to live much above the poverty threshold. Wages for these jobs have remained rather stagnant for men as well as women, not increasing at the same rates as jobs at the top end of the labor market (Blau & Kahn, 2006). Such discrimination greatly affects the quality of life for men and women, particularly those who are single heads of households, and their children.

A growing number of men are also suffering from the changing economic system that places them in competition not just with each other, but workers around the world. The policy publication, *Postsecondary Education Opportunity*, reports that "for decades men have been disengaging from the labor force, disengaging from the families with the children that they have fathered, getting into serious trouble with the law, disengaging from civic roles and responsibilities and even killing themselves at record rates" (The State of American Manhood, 2006, p. 1). Jobs in manufacturing industries, which were traditionally held by men, are being replaced with jobs in the service industry, which are held predominantly by women. Men are also underrepresented in other fast growing industries

VIDEO INSIGHTS
The Fairer Sex?

Although those fighting for women's rights have made great strides in the past several decades, women still earn only 81 cents for every dollar that men make, and they often pay more for things like consumer goods and medical care. In the video segment, a man and a woman decide to see for themselves whether men and women are treated differently in otherwise identical situations, such as buying a car, getting clothes dry cleaned, setting a tee time at a golf course, and interviewing for a job. Using hidden cameras, they document that women often suffer from a subtle and insidious kind of discrimination, the kind of discrimination that is difficult to quantify and even more difficult to prove.

1. Have you ever felt as though you suffered from gender bias?
2. Share with a group of male and female peers your own stories about how you believe your gender has affected your opportunities and life decisions. Note not only the differences in how men and women respond but also the differences in the way men and women in your group react to those differences.
3. What do the stories and responses that you've shared tell you about how entrenched cultural stereotypes about gender are?
4. What gendered behaviors do you think are developed through stereotyping, and what might be innate to each sex?

Go to the Video Insights DVD and watch *The Fairer Sex* video segment. Then, go to the *Homework and Exercises* section in Chapter 4 of MyEducationLab and select *Video Insights: The Fairer Sex?* to answer these questions.

such as hospitality, leisure, and financial activities (The State of American Manhood, 2006). The jobs that are available in the service industry are those that require more education than the traditional male occupations. They will require young men to become more engaged in learning and attend college at higher rates than today.

Data indicate that men with jobs are more likely to marry and be responsible fathers (The State of American Manhood, 2006). For men to be as economically successful as in the past will require them to have more education than in the past. Educators will need to find ways to engage boys and young men in education at higher levels than previously was required. More needs to be done to turn around the current trends of males dropping out of school, not completing high school, and not enrolling in college at the same rates as females. Their ability to get a job that will provide economic stability is key to the engagement of men in their families and communities.

Sexual Harassment

Sexual harassment of women has long existed in the workplace when women are the recipients of unwanted and unwelcome sexual behavior. Sometimes the perpetuator is in a position of power over the woman and uses that power to secure favors or to make sexual advances. In other cases, it is a coworker who makes unwanted advances. As in other areas related to gender socialization, schools mirror society in its perpetuation of sexual harassment. Students in high schools probably fare worse than adults in other settings. Both boys (79%) and girls (83%) report receiving unwanted sexual attention in schools. More than half of these students have themselves harassed other students (American Association of University Women [AAUW], 2001).

The study *Hostile Hallways: Bullying, Teasing, and Sexual Harassment in School* (AAUW, 2001) reports that sexual harassment occurs in public places, primarily in the halls and class-rooms of our schools. Seventy-six percent of the students had experienced nonphysical harassment; 68% had been physically harassed. Students are most upset when someone

- spreads sexual rumors about them (75%)
- pulls off or down their clothing (74%)
- says they are gay or lesbian (71%)
- forces them to do something sexual other than kissing (72%)
- spies on them as they dress or shower (69%)
- writes sexual messages or graffiti about them on bathroom walls, in locker rooms, etc. (63%). (AAUW, 2001, p. 5)

The most common excuse for sexual harassment is the "its just part of school life, a lot of people do it, or it's no big deal" (AAUW, 2001, p. 41). Some harassers (3 of 10) think that the victim liked it. Others (1 of 4) say their friends encouraged them to do it. Young men may be confused by accusations of sexual harassment, in part because the behavior has long been viewed as typical for male adolescents. Educators and parents alike may explain away sexual harassment as "boys will be boys" and attribute it to the perennial school bullies. It is not only boys who harass others; girls are also guilty, but less often. Teachers and other school personnel are the sexual harassers according to 38% of the students. Although a few of these are the well-publicized sexual assaults, most are nonphysical attacks.

Many principals and teachers either don't know that harassment is occurring in their school or ignore it. Most students say they are not comfortable reporting incidents to teachers or other school personnel. They usually tell a friend, but many, especially boys, tell no

Pause to Reflect 4.5

Many students report that they have been sexually harassed in school. However, not all teachers and school officials believe them. Think about your own experiences.

- Have you ever been a victim of sexual harassment? How did you feel at the time? Whom did you tell about it?
- Have you observed sexual harassment of other people? Why did you intervene or why didn't you?
- How could teachers help stop harassment among students?

Go to the *Homework and Exercises* section in Chapter 4 of MyEducationLab and select *Pause to Reflect 4.5* to answer these questions.

one. However, harassment and sex discrimination are social justice issues and are included under civil rights laws. Students who have suffered from such harassment are beginning to fight back through the courts. They argue that although the harassment has been reported to teachers, counselors, or administrators, no action has been taken to stop it.

School officials are no longer allowed to ignore the sexual harassment and abuse of students and may face the payment of damage awards if they do. Teachers, administrators, and staff need to become more alert to sexual harassment among students. In addition, they should monitor their own behaviors to ensure that they are not using their power as an authority figure to harass students. Policies and practices within schools may need to be revised, but discussions should involve the broader community of students and parents.

School should provide a safe environment for children and youth. For many students, schools are not safe, and sometimes they are dangerous. Educators can assist in the elimination of harassment, bullying, and other youth violence. Teachers should model appropriate behavior with their students by avoiding sexual references, innuendoes, and jokes. They cannot be passive bystanders; they must intervene when students are sexually harassing each other. They can also encourage students to form or join school leadership groups that work to educate others about and prevent sexual harassment.

Classroom Focus

Education is a key to upward mobility and financial security in adulthood. Therefore, the occupational roles that individuals pursue will influence the way they are able to live in the future. One's chances to pursue postsecondary education are greatly influenced by one's education in elementary and secondary schools. By the time students reach the secondary level, they have chosen, or been helped to choose, a college preparatory program, a general education program, or a specific vocational training program. When college students select a major, disproportionate numbers of males select engineering and computer science, which provide some of the highest salaries upon graduation. These early choices can make a great difference in later job satisfaction and rewards.

Girls appear to take better advantage of education than their male peers. Although males generally end up with better jobs and higher salaries, not all males are served well in schools. For example, the number of males classified as having a disability is disproportionately high especially for boys and young men of color and from low-income families (Wehmeyer & Schwartz, 2001). Young women, on the other hand, are more likely to graduate from high school and enroll in college. In 2004, 72% of recent high school completers who were female were enrolled in college as compared to 61% of the males; 58% of the persons earning bachelor's degrees were females. Women also earn the majority (58%) of master's degrees. Males, however, have a slim advantage in finishing first professional degrees (51%) such as law and medicine and doctorates (52%) (U.S. Census Bureau, 2006).

Tests and other assessments provide evidence of performance and learning throughout school. The assessments may assist teachers in knowing the gaps in student learning, allowing them to develop strategies that build on the prior experiences of students. Tests are also used to make high-stakes decisions that may dramatically affect a student's future. Differences between the scores of females and males have narrowed over the past few decades. Girls are slightly ahead in reading and writing; boys in mathematics. Males tend to do better than females on college admission examinations, in part because multiple-choice tests favor boys who take less time to guess when they do not know the answer. If the tests included more essay questions, the gap between the sexes would be reduced even further. The most recent data on test performance show that

- At grades 4 and 8, girls, on average, score higher than boys on national assessments of reading (U.S. Department of Education, 2006).
- At grades 4, 8, and 12, boys, on average, perform better than girls on national assessments of science (U.S. Department of Education, 2006).
- At grades 4 and 8, boys, on average, score slightly higher than girls on national assessments of mathematics (U.S. Department of Education, 2006).
- Males score higher than females on both the verbal and mathematics sections of the SAT (U.S. Census Bureau, 2006).
- Females score slightly higher than males on the English and reading sections of the ACT (U.S. Census Bureau, 2006).

Many people believe that if the school experiences of boys and girls are changed, differences in academic achievement will be eliminated, and both will have a chance for more equitable lives as adults. There is not common agreement, however, on how to accomplish this goal. Professional development programs on gender equity focus on changing the behavior of teachers toward students and the content of curriculum. Teachers, counselors, teacher aides, coaches, and principals all have roles in eradicating the inequities that result from sexism.

Women's studies programs in schools and universities allow men and women to study the history, culture, and psychology of women. These programs have promoted research on girls and women that support a gender equity agenda. Nonsexist classrooms in P–12 education incorporate curricula that include females as well as males, and support the learning of both sexes. A number of private schools, including colleges, enroll only female students. Some of the goals for these schools are similar to ethnocentric schools in that they help women develop the self-confidence to achieve at high levels. A number of public school systems have also established single-sex schools for the same purpose. A few school systems have a school whose enrollment is limited to gay students. The federal legislation, **Title IX,** makes it illegal for schools to discriminate against girls and women in any educational programs, including athletics. These approaches for providing gender equity in education are discussed in greater detail in the next sections.

Women's Studies

Women's studies programs are similar to ethnic studies programs in their attempt to record and analyze the historical and contemporary experiences of a group that has traditionally been ignored in the curriculum. Courses in women's studies include concepts of consciousness-raising and views of women as a separate group with unique needs and disadvantages in schools and other institutions. They examine the culture, status, development, and achievement of women as a group.

Women's studies have evolved in high schools, colleges, and universities as units in history, sociology, and literature courses; as separate courses; and as programs from which students can choose a major or minor field of study. Similar to the ethnic studies programs, the experiences and contributions of women and related concepts have been the focus.

Women's studies provide a perspective that is foreign to most students. Historical, economic, and sociological events are viewed from the perspective of a group that has been in a position subordinate to men throughout history. Until students participate in such courses, they usually do not realize that 51% of the population has received so little coverage in most textbooks and courses. These programs allow students to increase both their awareness and their knowledge base about women's history and the contributions of women. Sometimes women are taught skills for competing successfully in a man's world or for managing a career and family. In addition, many women's studies programs assist in developing a positive female self-image within a society that has historically viewed women as inferior to men. Psychological and career assistance to women is also a part of some programs.

Although the content of women's studies is needed to fill the gaps of current educational programs, it usually is a program set aside from the general academic offerings. Instead of being required, it is usually an elective course. Thus, the majority of students may never integrate the information and concepts of women's studies into their academic work. The treatment of women as a separate entity also subtly suggests that the study of women is secondary to the important study of a world that is controlled by males. All students should learn about a world in which the contributions of both males and females are valued.

Nonsexist Education

When women's studies programs are part of a nonsexist education, they become an integral part of the total education program, rather than a separate luxury. Knowledgeable teachers point out differences that exist between the genders, discuss how and why such inequities are portrayed, and supplement instructional materials with information that provides a more balanced view of the roles and contributions of both men and women. Required readings include the writings of women, as well as those of men. At a minimum, nonstereotypical male and female examples appear on bulletin boards and in teacher-prepared materials.

All students should be exposed to the contributions of women as well as men throughout history. History courses that focus primarily on wars and political power will almost totally focus on men; history courses that focus on the family and the arts will more equitably include both genders. Science courses that discuss all of the great scientists often forget to discuss the societal limitations that prevented women from being scientists. (Women scientists and writers of the past often used male names or gave their work to men for publication.) Students are being cheated of a wealth of information about the majority of the world's population when women are not included as an integral part of the curriculum. Because teachers control the information and concepts taught to students, it is their responsibility to present a view of the world that includes women and men and their wide ranges of perspectives.

It is also the responsibility of teachers to provide students the opportunity to reach their potential. If boys are stereotypically portrayed as more active, smarter, more aggressive, and exerting more control over their lives than girls, girls become the other with characteristics that may not serve them well in the future. Boys who are always expected to behave in stereotypically masculine ways also suffer.

Students are bombarded by subtle influences in schools that reinforce the notion that boys are more important than girls. This unplanned, unofficial learning—the hidden curriculum—has an impact on how students feel about themselves and others. Sexism is often projected in the messages that children receive in the illustrations, language, and content of texts, films, and other instructional materials. Sexism should be eliminated in the interaction of school authorities with male and female students and in the participation of the two sexes in sports and extracurricular activities. A school that is nonsexist is staffed by influential female and male role models who are sensitive to the importance of gender in the classroom and who model nonsexist and nonhomophobic behavior.

One of the goals of nonsexist education is to allow girls and young women to be heard and to understand the legitimacy of their experiences as females. Girls are often silenced as they enter adolescence and take on their more feminine roles, being less assertive and letting boys control discussions in the classroom. Young men are often not encouraged to break out of the expected masculine role with its own rules of what is required to be a man. They may become depressed and have lower self-esteem as they try to conform to the rules (Flood, 2001). Young men should have the opportunity to explore their privileged role in our inequitable society. They should learn to speak for the equity of girls and women. Teachers will not find this an easy task. Many females and males resist discussions of power relations and how they benefit or lose within those relations. However, the value to students and society is worth the discomfort that such discussion may cause students, and perhaps the teacher. The classroom may be the only place in which students can confront these issues and be helped to make sense of them.

Female Participation in Technology.   As indicated at the beginning of this section, girls do not perform as well on mathematics and science assessment as boys. Even though they are now more likely to complete advanced academic courses in science and mathematics than boys (U.S. Department of Education, 2004). However, advanced placement courses are not available to either girls or boys in a number of low-income schools, limiting their ability to compete with students from other schools. As educators, we may be able to improve participation in these areas by encouraging girls to develop positive attitudes about these subjects, and counseling them not only into advanced mathematics and science courses, but also computer science classes.

Although both girls and boys use computers at home and at school at about the same rate, girls are more likely to be involved with "computer 'tools,' such as databases, page layout programs, graphics, online publishing, and other 'productivity software'" (AAUW, 2000, p. 6). Boys, on the other hand, are more involved in programming and designing. The choices about courses taken in middle school and high school have an influence not only on achievement on standardized tests, but on one's future job options. For instance, technology jobs are among the fastest growing occupations with some of the highest salaries. Women and African Americans, Latinos, and American Indians are not preparing for jobs in this field at the same rate as European and Asian American men. Therefore, the participation of females in technology and computer science in schools deserves special attention.

Although girls and boys use computers at about the same rate, girls are less likely to take courses in computer programming and design. As a result, they are less likely to select computer science as a college major.

Lawrence Manning/Corbis RF

Different approaches to schooling and teaching may increase the participation rates of females. Girls report that computer work is very passive. They do not like the violence and redundancy of many computer games. They perceive programming as an uninteresting job in which their social interactions would primarily be with the computer. Girls need to be encouraged to become fluent in information technology, which requires skills in abstract reasoning, problem solving, and the interpretation and analysis of data. Girls are likely to be more interested in the field if they learn to solve real-world problems with technology (AAUW, 2000).

Interactions in the Classroom. An area over which all educators have control is their own interactions with students. Consistently, researchers find that educators treat boys and girls differently in the classroom, on the athletic field, in the hall, and in the counseling office. However, most teachers indicate that they do not discriminate in the way they respond to boys and girls. Once they critically examine their interactions, most find that they do respond differently. The most important factor in overcoming gender biases in the classroom is recognizing that subtle and unintentional biases exist. Once these are recognized, the teacher can begin to make changes in the classroom and in the lives of the students in that classroom.

One of the goals of a nonsexist education is to eliminate the power relationships based on gender in the classroom. Teachers should monitor the tasks and activities in which students participate in the classroom. Female and male students should share the leadership in classroom activities and discussions. Girls and young women may need to be encouraged to participate actively in hands-on activities, and boys may need encouragement in reading and writing activities. Research suggests that boys and girls provide leadership equally in middle school science activities, but girls begin to lose confidence in their science abilities. The problem observed in a number of science classes is that boys manipulate the equipment, usually delegating the girls in their group to note-taking and providing information (Jovanovic & King, 1998). Teachers need to intervene in these cases to ensure that girls are involved in all levels of the hands-on work.

If left alone, many girls and boys choose to sit with members of the same sex and participate in group activities with members of the same sex. To ensure that they work together in the classroom, the teacher may have to assign seats and groups. Small, heterogeneous, cooperative work groups reduce the emphasis on power relationships that characterize competitive activities. These activities can be designed to provide all students, even those who are often marginalized in the classroom, with the opportunity to participate at a more equitable level.

Nonsexist education does not ignore gender in the classroom. It does *not* require that boys and girls be treated the same in all cases. Gender may need to be emphasized at times to ensure equity. Instructional strategies should be varied to engage both girls and boys with the subject matter. Girls may be more comfortable than boys with cooperative group work, reading, listening, and seat work. Engaging more boys in the subject matter may require the use of spatial and graphic aids such as manipulatives in mathematics. Team competition, physical exercise, art, and music can also be used for instructional purposes to draw males into the subject (Gurian & Stevens, 2005). A wide repertoire of instructional strategies should include some that are more engaging to girls, others to boys, and others to both groups. Both girls and boys will learn to operate in the cultural spheres of each other while guaranteeing that one group is not engaged because the teacher uses only the instructional strategies that are more comfortable for the second group.

Nonsexist education is reflected in the school setting when students are not sorted, grouped, or tracked by gender in any aspect of the school program, including special education. The teacher can develop a curriculum that does not give preferential treatment to boys over girls or girls over boys; that shows both genders in aggressive, nurturing, independent, exciting, and emotional roles; that encourages all students to explore traditional and nontraditional roles; and that assists them in developing positive self-images about their sexuality. One's actions and reactions to students can make a difference.

Incorporating Sexual Orientation in the Curriculum

Educators also should incorporate factual information on sexual orientation in the curriculum. If it is discussed at all in schools, it is usually in health, sex education, and family life courses. It is generally a part of class discussions of HIV, sometimes being blamed for the spread of the disease. Sex education programs often become embroiled in controversy between families and school officials, especially when the curriculum includes discussion of sexual orientation. In many districts, parents can request that their children be excused from sex education classes when topics such as homosexuality or birth control are discussed.

Sexual orientation could be included in a number of other courses. Social studies could explore the privilege of heterosexuality in society and include a study of the history of LGBTs and their struggles for eliminating discrimination. Language arts and literature courses could include books and short stories by gay and lesbian authors. LGBT characters in readings can provide an understanding of the meaning of being different, discrimination against a population, and other topics. The contributions of gays and lesbians to society could be highlighted in these courses as well as courses in art, music, the sciences, and physical education.

Teachers can provide an environment for critically examining the dominant cultural norms that denigrate a different sexual orientation or gender identity. They can encourage an understanding of homosexuality through the presentation of facts, facilitation of discussions, and democratic debates in which everyone's opinion is respected. Homophobic name-calling by students could be used to provide facts and correct myths about gays, lesbians, and individuals with a gender identity different from their biological sex. If educators ignore homophobic remarks made by students or other adults, children and youth are quick to conclude that something is wrong with gays and they can be treated disrespectfully.

Teachers should learn to present information on LGBTs without embarrassment or condemnation. To be respected by LGBT and other students, teachers must guarantee respectful treatment of all students. This is difficult for some teachers. However, "in the public schools, religious conviction [as well as anti-gay beliefs or membership in hate groups] must surrender to democratic values" (Lipkin, 1999, p. 249). What should educators do to move to this level of acceptance of and comfortableness with sexual orientation? First, they should become familiar with the history, culture, and current concerns of LGBTs by reading or attending lectures and films about them. Second, they should create a safe and equitable classroom for all students as discussed earlier.

In addition to helping all students correct the myths they have about gays and lesbians, educators should promote the healthy development of self-identified homosexual youngsters in the school setting. Key to this approach is breaking the silence that surrounds the discussion of homosexuality. The classroom and school should provide a safe and supportive climate for children and adolescents who identify their sexual orientation. They should learn that they are not alone in figuring out their sexual orientation and sexuality.

Single-Sex Education

Single-sex schools focus on developing the confidence, academic achievement, and leadership skills of young women or men by using their unique learning styles and cultural experiences. Although most single-sex schools are for females, some private schools are for boys only. Schools in some urban areas have been established for young African American men. These schools often make their African American culture the center of the curriculum with the goal of developing self-esteem, academic achievement, and leadership of students who often confront a hostile environment.

Early in U.S. history, education for girls and boys was segregated, but by 1850, public schools had quietly become coed (Tyack, 2003). Since then, most single-sex schools and colleges have been private. Over time, the courts have required public men's colleges to open their doors to women. One of the most recent examples was the Virginia Military Institute, which admitted women for the first time in 1997. Public schools have also not been allowed to segregate schools or classes by sex. However, new federal regulations in 2002 provided greater flexibility to public schools in experimenting with single-sex education to improve the achievement of both girls and boys. A number of public schools and academies have now been established. A more common and expedient way to offer single-sex environments is to establish segregated courses within a coeducational school. A number of school districts have established or are experimenting with this approach.

Some research shows that girls are more likely to participate in advanced mathematics and science courses when they are in single-sex classes. They may feel less threatened when they are not competing with males in coeducational settings. Teachers are more likely to use strategies such as cooperative teaching. However, little is known about whether the instruction in single-sex courses and schools differs from that in coeducational settings. Reviews of the research show that students in single-sex settings do have a higher general self-esteem than their peers in coeducational settings. However, little or no differences in achievement and attitudes about the academic subject have been found (Campbell & Sanders, 2002; Haag, 2002). A recent study of female-only courses in mathematics and science found positive differences in performance and persistence in continuing to

FOCUS YOUR CULTURAL LENS: DEBATE
Should Girls Learn Technology in Classes Without Boys?

Only a few girls in your school are signing up for the information technology course that would prepare them with the basic skills for studying computer science in college. Overall, the girls in your school use the computer to write their papers. They use e-mail to communicate with their friends and to conduct research for school projects. They just don't seem interested in a technology career. A school district task force has recommended that your school try an experiment that would segregate boys and girls into separate courses next year. Teachers at your school have been asked to comment on the proposal. The following stances are being taken by your peers.

For

- Girls and boys have different learning styles that could be enhanced in separate classes.
- The teacher would have more time to spend with girls in a segregated class because he or she would not have to spend time disciplining the boys rather than teaching the content.
- Efforts to get girls involved in coeducational technology courses have not been successful.
- Girls will be less threatened by the technology if they are not competing with boys.

Against

- Research shows little or no difference in the achievement of girls or their attitudes to the subject when they are in girls-only or coeducational courses.
- Single-sex courses reinforce gender stereotypes.
- This approach just lets the teachers of coeducational courses off the book when the school system should be helping all teachers provide an equitable education for boys and girls.
- When girls go to college or enter the workforce, they most likely will be working with men. To be in a course with girls only does not mirror the real world.

Questions

1. What reasons for establishing a girls-only course in technology are the most compelling to you?
2. Even though the research on single-sex courses generally does not show significant improvement in the achievement of girls, are there other reasons that the approach may be viable? Why or why not?
3. Are you supportive of the task force recommendation? Why or why not?
4. What other strategies might encourage more girls to take this technology courses?

Go to the *Homework and Exercises* section in Chapter 4 of MyEducationLab and select *Focus Your Cultural Lens* to answer these questions.

Adapted from Campbell, P. B., & Sander, J. (2002). Challenging the system: Assumptions and data behind the push for single-sex schooling. In A. Datnow & L. Hubbard (Eds.), *Gender in policy and practice: Perspectives on single-sex and coeducational schooling* (pp. 31–46). New York: Routledge.

take mathematics and science courses (Shapka & Keating, 2003). Similar positive findings have been found for some male-only courses (Gurian & Stevens, 2005). Opponents to single-sex classes argue that teachers should learn to teach both girls and boys effectively and that girls should be encouraged throughout their schooling to enroll in advanced courses.

Title IX

Title IX of the 1972 Education Amendments addresses the differential, stereotypical, and discriminatory treatment of students on the basis of their gender. It protects students and employees in virtually all 16,000 public school systems and 2,700 postsecondary institutions in the United States. The law prevents gender discrimination in: (1) the admission of students, particularly to postsecondary and vocational education institutions, (2) the treatment of students, and (3) the employment of all personnel.

What does Title IX require of teachers and other educators in preschool through twelfth-grade settings? The law clearly makes it illegal to treat students differently or separately on the basis of gender. It requires that all programs, activities, and opportunities offered by a school district be equally available to males and females. All courses must be open to all students. Boys must be allowed to enroll in family and consumer science classes, and girls allowed in technology and agriculture courses. Regarding the counseling of students, Title IX prohibits biased course or career guidance; the use of biased achievement, ability, or interest tests; and the use of college and career materials that are biased in content, language, or illustration. Schools cannot assist any business or individual in employing students if the request is for a student of a particular gender. There can be no discrimination in the type or amount of financial assistance or eligibility for such assistance.

Membership in clubs and other activities based on gender alone is prohibited in schools, with the exceptions of YWCA, YMCA, Girl Scouts, Boy Scouts, Boys' State, Girls' State, Key clubs, and other voluntary and tax-exempt youth service organizations that have been traditionally limited to members of one gender who are 19 years of age or younger. Rules of behavior and punishments for violation of those rules must be the same for all students. Honors and awards may not designate the gender of the student as a criterion for the award.

The most controversial program covered by Title IX has been athletic programs. Provisions for girls to participate in intramural, club, or interscholastic sports must be included in the school's athletic program. The sports offered by a school must be coeducational with two major exceptions: (1) when selection for teams is based on competitive skill and (2) when the activity is a contact sport. In these two situations, separate teams are permitted but are not required. Although the law does not require equal funding for girls' and boys' athletic programs, equal opportunity in athletics must be provided. The courts apply a three-part test to determine equal opportunity. First, the percentage of male and female athletes is substantially proportionate to the percentage of females and males in the student population. Second, the school has a history of expanding opportunities for females to participate in sports. Third, a school fully and effectively meets the interest and abilities of female students even if it may not be meeting the proportionate expectation of the first requirement.

Although providing equal athletic opportunities remains controversial, this part of Title IX has resulted in major changes in schools. When Title IX was passed in 1972, 294,000 young women participated in high school sports. That number has increased by 904% with over 2.9 million females now participating in high school sports. Female athletes now comprise 41% of all high school athletes. The number of women in intercollegiate athletics

The number of women who participate in sports has increased dramatically since Title IX was passed in 1972.

has increased by 456% to 209,666 (National Coalition for Women and Girls in Education, 2007). Women comprise 55.8% of college students, but only 41.7% of the college athletes (Cheslock, 2007). At the same time, some groups charge that Title IX has led to the elimination of some college men's sports as women's sports are expanded. However, participation of college males has increased by 39% at the college level since 1972.

The law alone has not changed the basic assumptions and attitudes that people hold about appropriate female and male roles, occupations, and behaviors, but it has equalized the rights, opportunities, and treatment of students within the school setting. Experience has shown that once discriminatory practices are eliminated and discriminatory behavior is altered, even unwillingly, changes in prejudiced attitudes often follow. Equal treatment of students from preschool through college will more adequately encourage all students to explore available career and life options.

Pause to Reflect 4.6

Check your Title IX knowledge on the following items.

1. Title IX requires that a girl be allowed to play on the football team if she is good enough.   True   False
2. Title IX requires that all classes have both females and males in them.   True   False
3. Title IX requires that when there is a disproportionately small number of women principals, women must be promoted before men.   True   False
4. Title IX encourages special programs for pregnant girls.   True   False

5.	Title IX permits the use of separate vocational interest tests for females and males that provide occupational choices geared to the special interests of each sex.	True	False
6.	Title IX requires that there be female coaches for girls' sports.	True	False
7.	Title IX requires that as much money be spent on girls' as on boys' athletics.	True	False
8.	Title IX prohibits the use of gender-biased textbooks.	True	False
9.	Title IX requires that all club and extracurricular activities be coeducational.	True	False
10.	Title IX requires that schools pay victims of sexual harassment.	True	False

Go to the *Homework and Exercises* section in Chapter 4 of MyEducationLab and select *Pause to Reflect 4.6* to answer these questions.

Used with permission from Zittleman, K. (2007). Teachers, students, and Title IX: A promise for fairness. In D. Sadker & E. S. Silber, *Gender in the classroom: Foundations, skills, methods, and strategies across the curriculum* (pp. 73–107). Mahwah, NJ: Lawrence Erlbaum.

Summary

Researchers and theorists disagree about the importance of biology on the differences between males and females. Some argue that the differences are primarily culturally determined. Although girls and boys are members of multiple identity groups, the culture at large has different expectations of them solely on the basis of their gender. Children are socialized for their roles as male or female.

Individuals are biologically a female or male, but their gender identity is based on their feminine or masculine characteristics. The degree to which an individual adheres to a traditional gender identity varies as a result of past socialization patterns and is influenced by the family's ethnicity, race, and religion.

Gender discrimination has kept women in less prestigious and lower-paying jobs than men. Even the amount of education obtained by a woman does little to close the gap between the earnings of men and women—now at 81 cents earned by a woman for every dollar earned by a man. Such discrimination greatly affects the quality of life for families, single mothers, and children.

Women's studies, nonsexist education, and single-sex education represent educational approaches to combating sexism in schools and society. Women's studies programs attempt to record and analyze the historical and contemporary experiences of women and are usually offered as separate courses. Nonsexist education attempts to eradicate sexism in the school curriculum by incorporating content that reflects female as well as male perspectives. Single-sex education segregates boys from girls to help develop the self-esteem of the members of each group, improve their achievement in subjects in which they traditionally do not perform as well as the other sex, and help them develop positive attitudes about academic subjects. The federal government provides support for eliminating sexism in education through Title IX of the 1972 Education Amendments. This law protects against the differential, stereotypical, and discriminatory treatment of students on the basis of their sex.

PROFESSIONAL PRACTICE FOR EDUCATORS

Questions for Discussion

1. In what ways are differences between the sexes culturally, rather than biologically, determined?
2. How does socialization into stereotypical roles harm both females and males in our changing society?
3. Explain how gender discrimination has disproportionately affected women.
4. In what ways do men have power over women? Why is it difficult for men to see they have a privileged position in society?
5. Contrast women's studies and nonsexist education and explain the advantages of both.
6. How can teachers learn whether they are discriminating against students on the basis of gender?
7. How does homophobia manifest itself in schools? What can educators do toward eliminating prejudice and discrimination against gays and lesbians in their classrooms?
8. What are signs of sexual harassment in schools?
9. How can you as an educator help increase the participation of females and other underrepresented groups in computer science, mathematics, and science careers?
10. What impact has Title IX had on schooling during the past 30 years?

Portfolio Activities

1. Collect data on the number of boys and girls in mathematics, science, or technology courses in the schools you are observing. Describe the course-taking patterns by the level of the course (for example, general education and advanced placement). What, if any, differences exist between the course-taking of girls and boys? (INTASC Standards 2, 3, and 10)
2. Observe the differences between how boys and girls act in classrooms and interact with teachers. Analyze the differences and discuss how the teacher may reinforce stereotypical gender behavior. Describe teachers' responses to students that are most supportive of learning. Discuss how these responses differ for boys and girls. (INTASC Standards 3 and 6)
3. Observe classes using cooperative learning and other instructional strategies. Record the engagement of boys and girls in the different instructional approaches. Analyze your findings based on gender. Discuss whether the differences could be generalized to the sex of the students or whether differences existed within the same sex. (INTASC Standards 1, 3, 4, 5, 6, and 7)

Licensure Test Prep

1. A middle school teacher is trying to interest girls in the field of science. He has ensured that boys and girls work together in groups to conduct the day's experiment. Which of the following is a sign of inequitable participation of the girls and boys that may affect how they feel about science?
   A. All students appear engaged in planning the experiment and observing the results.
   B. Some of the boys are disengaged and a couple of girls are talking among themselves about social issues.
   C. Boys have gathered the equipment for the experiment and are conducting the experiment while the girls record notes about the steps and results.
   D. Girls and boys score about the same on the assessment related to the experiment.

Go to the *Homework and Exercises* section in Chapter 4 of MyEducationLab and select *Licensure Test Prep* to complete this exercise.

Suggested Readings

American Association of University Women Educational Foundation. (2000). *Tech-savvy: Educating girls in the new computer age*. Washington, DC: Author.
This report explores why girls are not using computers in the same way as boys and makes recommendations for increasing girls' participation in today's computer age.

Holladay, J. (2007). *The ABCs of sexual orientation*. Montgomery, AL: Southern Poverty Law Center. Retrieved on May 27, 2007, from www.tolerance.org/teach/activities/activity.jsp?ar+821
These activities help teachers understand antigay discrimination in schools and how to develop a safe and inclusive classroom and school.

Klein, S. S., Richardson, B., Grayson, D. A., Fox, L. H., Kramarae, C., Pollard, D. S., & Dsyer, C. A. (Eds.). (2007). *Handbook for achieving gender equity through education*. New York: Taylor & Francis.
This research-based summary of what is known about gender equity in education includes chapters on integrating it into subjects such as mathematics, science, social studies, communication, and physical education.

Lopez, N. (2003). *Hopeful girls, troubled boys: Race and gender disparity in urban education*. New York: Routledge.
Based on interviews with young adults from Dominican, West Indian, and Haitian families, the author explores their school experiences in New York City. The author learns that young women are optimistic about the promises of education while their male counterparts are ambivalent.

Marcus, Eric. (2002). *Making gay history: The half-century fight for lesbian and gay equal rights*. New York: Perennial.
This history walks through the past 50 years of the battle for gay and lesbian rights. The story is told by teenagers, grandparents, journalists, and housewives who participated at different stages of the struggle.

Orenstin, P. (2002). Anita Hill is a boy: Tales for a gender-free classroom. In *The Jossey-Bass reader on gender in education* (pp. 734–755). San Francisco: Jossey-Bass.
This chapter describes how one middle-school teacher has developed a gender-free classroom. Boys and girls in the class talk about what it

means to study women as well as men and be involved in girls' as well as boys' projects throughout the school year.

Ward, J. (2002). School rules. In *The Jossey-Bass reader on gender in education* (pp. 510–542). San Francisco: Jossey-Bass.

The experiences of African American girls in today's schools are explored in this chapter. The struggles they endure to maintain high self-esteem and high expectations for their academic performance are described with reflections from students and their parents. The accounts show how educators can limit and encourage learning.

References

American Association of University Women Educational Foundation, (2000). *Tech-savvy: Educating girls in the new computer age.* Washington, DC: Author.

American Association of University Women Educational Foundation, (2001). *Hostile hallways: Bullying, teasing, and sexual harassment in school.* Washington, DC: Author.

Blau, F. D., & Kahn, L. (2006). The gender pay gap: going, going . . . but not gone. In F. D. Balu, M. C. Brinton, & D. B. Grusky (Eds.), *The declining significance of gender?* (pp. 37–66). New York: Russell Sage Foundation.

Buchanan, S. (2005, Fall). Wave of anti-gay hate crimes reported. *Intelligence Report*, No. 119, p. 7.

Campbell, P. B., & Sanders, J. (2002). Challenging the system: Assumptions and data behind the push for single-sex schooling. In A. Datnow & L. Hubbard (Eds.), *Gender in policy and practice: Perspectives on single-sex and coeducational schooling* (pp. 31–46). New York: Routledge.

Cassidy, K. W. (2007). Gender differences in cognitive ability, attitudes, and behavior. In D. Sadker & E. S. Silber (Eds.), *Gender in the classroom: Foundations, skills, methods, and strategies across the curriculum* (pp. 33–72). Mahwah, NJ: Lawrence Erlbaum.

Cheslock, J. (2007). *Who's playing college sports? Trends in participation.* East Meadow, NY: Women's Sports Foundation.

Dolby, N., Dimitriadis, G., & Willis, P. E. (2004). *Learning to labor in new times.* New York: RoutledgeFalmer.

Flood, C. (2001). Schools fail boys too: Exposing the con of traditional masculinity. In H. Rousso & M. L. Wehmeyer (Eds.), *Double jeopardy: Addressing gender equity in special education* (pp. 207–236). Albany, NY: State University of New York Press.

The Gallup Organization. (2007). *Gallup's pulse of democracy: Constitutional amendment defining marriage as only between a man and a woman.* Princeton, NJ: Author.

Gay, Lesbian, and Straight Education Network. (2005). *The 2005 national school climate survey: The experiences of lesbian, gay, bisexual and transgender youth in our nation's schools.* New York: Author.

Gurian, M. (2001). *Boys and girls learn differently!: A guide for teachers and parents.* San Francisco: Jossey-Bass.

Gurian, M., & Stevens, K. (2005). *The minds of boys: Saving our sons from falling behind in school and life.* San Francisco: Jossey-Bass.

Haag, P. (2002). Single-sex education in grades K–12: What does the research tell us? In *The Jossey-Bass reader on gender in education* (pp. 647–676). San Francisco: Jossey-Bass.

Johnson, W. S. (2006). *A time to embrace: Same-gender relationships in religion, law, and politics.* Grand Rapids, MI: Eerdmans.

Jovanovic, J., & King, S. S. (1998, Fall). Boys and girls in the performance-based science classroom: Who's doing the performing? *American Educational Research Journal, 35*(3), 477–496.

Kindlon, D., & Thompson, M. (2000). *Raising Cain: Protecting the emotional life of boys.* New York: Ballantine.

Lipkin, A. (1999). *Understanding homosexuality, changing schools.* Boulder, CO: Westview.

Mansfield, H. C. (2006). *Manliness.* New Haven: Yale University Press.

Miller, N. (2006). *Out of the past: Gay and lesbian history from 1869 to the present.* New York: Alyson Books.

Mock, B. (2007, Spring). Face right: Black religious opposition to gays rising. *Intelligence Report*, No. 125, pp. 19–23.

National Coalition for Women and Girls in Education. (2007, May). *Title IX athletics policies: Issues and data for education decision makers.* Washington, DC: Author.

National Gay and Lesbian Task Force. (2004). *Youth.* Retrieved September 24, 2004, from www.thetaskforce.org/theissues/issue.cfm?issueID=13

Rosen, R. (2000). *The world split open: How the modern women's movement changed America.* New York: Viking.

Shapka, J. D., & Keating, D. P. (2003, Winter). Effects of a girls-only curriculum during adolescence: Performance, persistence, and engagement in mathematics and science. *American Educational Research Journal, 40*(4), 929–960.

Shaw, S. M., & Lee, J. (Eds.). (2007). *Women's voices, feminist visions: Classic and contemporary readings.* New York: McGraw Hill.

The State of American Manhood. (2006, September). *Postsecondary Education Opportunity,* No. 171.

Tyack, D. (2003). *Seeking common ground: Public schools in a diverse society.* Cambridge, MA: Harvard University Press.

U.S. Bureau of Labor Statistics. (2006). *Highlights of women's earnings in 2005* (Report 995). Washington, DC: U.S. Department of Labor.

U.S. Census Bureau. (2006). *Statistical abstract of the United States: 2007* (126th ed.). Washington, DC: U.S. Government Printing Office.

U.S. Department of Education, National Center for Education Statistics. (2004). *The condition of education 2004.* Washington, DC: Author.

U.S. Department of Education, National Center for Education Statistics. (2006). *The condition of education 2006.* Washington, DC: Author.

Wehmeyer, M. L., & Schwartz, M. (2001). Research on gender bias in special education services. In H. Rousso & M. L. Wehmeyer (Eds.), *Double jeopardy: Addressing gender equity in special education* (pp. 271–287). Albany, NY: State University of New York Press.

Chapter 5

EXCEPTIONALITY

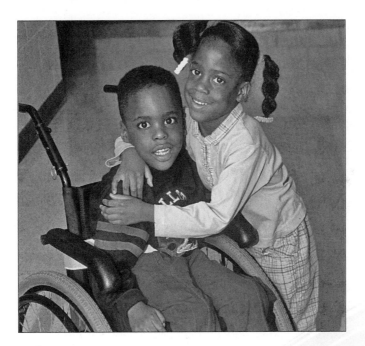

*N*o otherwise qualified handicapped individual in the United States . . .
shall, solely by reason of his [or her] handicap, be excluded from the
participation in, be denied benefits of, or be subjected to discrimination under
any program or activity receiving federal financial assistance.

SECTION 504, PL 93-112 (VOCATIONAL REHABILITATION ACT, 1993)

Calvin Behler, a third-grade teacher at the Martin Luther King Elementary School, has been asked to see the principal, Erin Wilkerson, after the students leave. Dr. Wilkerson explains that the school is expanding their **full inclusion** program in which children including those with severe disabilities are fully integrated into general education classrooms. Congruent with school district policy, King Elementary is enhancing its efforts to integrate special education students into general education settings. Behler's classroom is one of four additional general education classrooms, which will have special education placed in the next few weeks. "What this will involve, Cal, is two students with severe disabilities. One is a child with Down's syndrome who has **developmental disabilities** (characterized by severe delays in the acquisition of cognitive, language, motor, and social skills). He has some severe learning problems. The other child has normal intelligence but is nonambulatory, with limited speech and severe cerebral palsy."

"You will be assigned a full-time aide with a special education background. In addition, Bill Gregg, the inclusion specialist, will assist you with instructional plans and strategies. What is important is that you prepare the students in your class and the parents so that a smooth transition can be made when these students come into your class in January, in just two and a half months. I'd like you and Bill to map out a plan of action and give it to me in two weeks."

Reflections

1. What should Behler and Gregg's plan of action include?
2. When students with severe disabilities are integrated into general education classrooms, do they detract from the programming of nondisabled students?
3. Are the students with disabilities potentially a disrupting influence in the classroom?
4. Do general education teachers like Calvin Behler have adequate training and background to accommodate students with disabilities in their classrooms?
5. Should they be integrated, regardless of the degree of disability?

Students with Disabilities and Those Who Are Gifted and Talented

A significant segment of the population in the United States is made up of exceptional individuals. The Centers for Disease Control and Prevention (CDC, 2005) reports that the U.S. Census Bureau indicates that there are over 50 million individuals in the United States with some type of disability. The National Center for Education Statistics (2005) reports a total of approximately 6.3% or 3 million gifted and talented students. When we factor in adults, millions more would be added to the total. Every day, educators come into contact with exceptional children and adults. They may be students in our classes, our professional colleagues, our friends and neighbors, or people we meet in our everyday experiences.

Exceptional people include both individuals with disabilities and gifted individuals. Some, particularly persons with disabilities, have been rejected by society. Because of their unique social and personal needs and special interests, many exceptional people become part of a cultural group composed of individuals with similar exceptionalities. For some, this cultural identity is by ascription; they have been labeled and forced into enclaves by virtue of the residential institutions where they live. Others may live in the same communities or even neighborhood by their own choosing. This chapter will examine the exceptional individual's relationship to society. It will address the struggle for equal rights and the ways the treatment of individuals with disabilities often parallels that of oppressed ethnic minorities.

Definitions for exceptional children vary slightly from one writer to another, but Heward's (2006) is typical of most:

> Exceptional children differ from the norm (either below or above) to such an extent that they require an individualized program of special education and related services to fully benefit from education. The term exceptional children includes children who experience difficulties in learning as well as those whose performance is so superior that modifications in curriculum and instruction are necessary to help them fulfill their potential. Thus, exceptional children is an inclusive term that refers to children with learning and/or behavior problems, children with physical disabilities or sensory impairments, and children who are intellectually gifted or have a special talent. (p. 10)

This definition is specific to school-age children who are usually referred, tested to determine eligibility, and then placed in special education programs. Included in the process is the labeling of the child. At one end of the continuum are the **gifted and talented** children, who have extraordinary abilities in one or more areas. At the other end are children with disabilities (some of whom may also be gifted). Students with disabilities are categorized with labels such as having mental retardation, learning disabilities, speech impairment, visual impairment, hearing impairment, emotional disturbance (or behavioral disorders), or physical and health impairments.

If you completed a public school education within the past 10 to 15 years, there is a high likelihood that you experienced having a person with a disability in one or more of your classes.

Labeling

The categorizing and labeling process has its share of critics. Opponents characterize the practice as demeaning and stigmatizing to people with disabilities, with the effects often carried through adulthood. Earlier classifications and labels, such as moron, imbecile, and idiot, have become so derogatory that they are no longer used in a professional context. Some individuals, including many with learning disabilities and **mild mental retardation (MMR),** were never considered to have disabilities prior to entering school. The MMR individuals often have problems in intellectual functioning and in socially appropriate behaviors for their age group. The school setting, however, intensifies their academic and cognitive deficits. Many, when they return to their homes and communities, do not seem to function as individuals with disabilities. Instead, they participate in activities with their neighborhood peers until they return to school the following day, where they may attend special classes (sometimes segregated) and resume their role in the academic and social structure of the school as students with disabilities. The problem is so pervasive that it has led to the designation of "the 6-hour retarded child." These are children who spend 6 hours a day as children with mental retardation in our nation's schools. During the remaining 18 hours a day away from the school setting, they are not considered retarded by the people with whom they interact (President's Committee on Mental Retardation, 1969). Heward (2006) suggests that the demands of the school seem to "cause" the mental retardation. The labels carry with them connotations and stigmas of varying degrees. Some disabilities are socially more acceptable than others. Visual impairment carries with it public empathy and sometimes sympathy. The public has for years given generously to causes for the blind, as evidenced by the financially well-endowed Seeing Eye Institute, which produces the well-known guide dogs. The blind are the only group with a disability who are permitted to claim an additional personal income tax deduction by reason of their disability. Yet, the general public perceives blindness to be one of the worst afflictions imposed on humankind. In contrast, mental retardation, and to some extent emotional disturbance, is often linked to lower socioeconomic status and individuals of color. Both labels are among the lowest socially acceptable disabilities and perhaps the most stigmatizing. This is, in part, because of the general public's lack of understanding of these disabilities and the sometimes debilitating impact they can bring to the family structure.

Learning disabilities, one of the newest categories of exceptionality, is one of the more socially acceptable disability conditions. Whereas mental retardation is often identified with lower socioeconomic groups, those with learning disabilities often have middle-class backgrounds. Whether these perceptions are accurate or not, middle-class parents more readily accept learning disabilities than mental retardation as a cause of their child's learning deficits. This may also be the case with children with emotional disabilities or behavioral disorders as compared to children with attention deficit hyperactive disorders (ADHD). The former tends to be more stigmatizing while ADHD may have more social acceptance. What has been observed is a reclassification of some children from having mental retardation to being learning disabled. It has sometimes been said that one person's mental retardation is another's learning disability and still another's emotional disturbance. The sometimes fine line that distinguishes one of these disabilities from another is at times so difficult to distinguish that an individual could be identified as a student with emotional disturbance by one school psychologist and as a student with learning disabilities by another.

Although the labeling controversy persists, even its critics often concede its necessity. Federal funding for special education is predicated on the identification of individuals in specific disabling conditions. These funds, with $11.6 billion appropriated in 2005, are so significant that many special education programs would all but collapse without them, leaving school districts in severe financial distress. Consequently, the labeling process continues, sometimes even into adulthood, where university students may have to be identified with a disability in order to receive necessary accommodations to their learning needs. Vocational rehabilitation counselors often use labels more indicative of their clients' learning problems than their work skills. If their work peers become aware of these labels, it could stigmatize them and lead to social isolation.

Historical Antecedents

The plight of persons with disabilities has, in many instances, closely paralleled that of oppressed ethnic groups. The history of the treatment of those with disabilities has not shown a society eager to meet its responsibilities. Prior to 1800, with a few exceptions, those with mental retardation, for example, were not considered a major social problem in any society. Those with more severe retardation were killed, or they died early of natural causes (Drew & Hardman, 2007).

The treatment and care of people with mental and physical disabilities have typically been a function of the socioeconomic conditions of the times. In addition to attitudes of fear and disgrace brought on by superstition, early nomadic tribes viewed individuals with disabilities as nonproductive and as a burden, draining available resources. As civilization progressed from a less nomadic existence, individuals with disabilities were still often viewed as nonproductive and expendable (Drew & Hardman, 2007).

They were frequently shunted away to institutions designated as hospitals, asylums, and colonies. Many institutions were deliberately built great distances from the population centers, where the residents could be segregated and more easily contained. For decades, American society did not have to deal with its conscience with respect to its citizens with severe disabilities. Society simply sent them far away and forgot about them. Most Americans did not know of the cruel and inhumane treatment that existed in many facilities. Today, due to urban sprawl, many of these institutions are now close to or within population centers.

Individuals with mild disabilities were generally able to be absorbed into society, sometimes seeming to disappear, sometimes contributing meaningfully to an agrarian society, often not even being identified as having a disability. As society became more industrialized and educational reforms required school attendance, the academic problems of students with disabilities became increasingly more visible. Special schools and special classes were designated to meet the needs of these children. Thus, society segregated these individuals, often in the guise of acting in their best interests.

Society's treatment of some groups with disabilities, such as those with mental retardation, has frequently been questionable with respect to their civil rights. Although many Americans find the old miscegenation laws prohibiting intermarriage between different ethnic groups abhorrent, few realize that as recently as the latter part of the twentieth century, nearly half of the states had miscegenation laws that prohibited marriage between individuals with mental retardation.

In some instances, individuals with mild mental retardation were released from state institutions into society under the condition that they submit themselves to eugenic sterilization (Edgerton, 1967). The issue of marriage prohibitions and eugenic sterilization for persons with mental retardation raises serious social and ethical issues. The nondisabled segment of society, charged with the care and education of individuals with disabilities, apparently views as its right and responsibility those matters dealing with sexual behavior, marriage, and procreation. In a similar way, educators determine the means of communication for the deaf individual, either an oral/aural approach or a manual/total communication approach. Such decisions have profound implications because they determine not only how these individuals will communicate but also, to a great extent, with whom they will be able to communicate. Too often, society seeks to dehumanize people with disabilities by ignoring their personal wishes, making critical decisions for them, and treating them as children throughout their lives.

Litigation

Educational rights of individuals with disabilities were not easily gained. In many respects, the struggle for these rights paralleled the struggles of ethnic minorities for their rights to education. These rights were not handed to children with disabilities out of the concern or compassion of educators. Many educators were reluctant to extend educational rights to children with disabilities and when they finally did so, it was because their rights had been won in the courts and the education community was ordered by the courts to admit these students.

Some of the same court decisions, and many of the arguments that advanced the rights of African Americans and other oppressed groups, were used by the advocates of children with disabilities. However, in reality, the battles and the rights gained by the disability rights advocates followed years after similar rights were won by ethnic minority groups.

Attorneys for the children with disabilities and their parents utilized case law to fight their court battles. **Case law** is the published opinions of judges, which interpret statutes, regulations, and Constitutional provisions. The U.S. legal system relies on the value of these decisions and the legal precedents they established. Few cases result in published opinions and those that are published take on great importance.

Brown v. the Board of Education

As was with African American students, the initial struggles for children with disabilities involved the right to, or the access to, a public education. One of the most famous and important court decisions was the Supreme Court decision on *Brown v. Board of Education of Topeka* (1954). Historically, the Supreme Court of the United States had sided with the Louisiana District Court in *Plessy v. Ferguson* in 1896, which upheld the Constitutionality of Louisiana's Separate Car Act, that provided for separate but equal transportation facilities for African Americans. The *Plessy* verdict became a part of case law, and set a precedent segregating blacks from transportation, public facilities, schools, restaurants, and so on. This decision "legitimized" the establishment and maintenance of racially segregated "Jim Crow" schools, which were supposed to be separate but equal. As history clearly showed us, these schools were inherently unequal. This was the setting for the *Brown* case.

In 1950, Topeka student Linda Brown had to ride the bus to school five miles when a school was located just four blocks from her home. Linda met all of the requirements to attend the nearby school, but was prohibited from doing so because she was African American. Linda Brown's parents and 13 other black families filed suit against the Topeka Board of Education because of the district's refusal to admit their children in all-white schools. Linda Brown's name was the first name listed on the suit and the case became known as *Brown v. Board of Education*. The case eventually found its way to the United States Supreme Court. The rest became a major part of U.S. history.

The U.S. Constitution mandates that all citizens have a right to life, liberty, and property. They cannot be denied these without due process. *Brown* determined that education was a property right. Although there is no Constitutional guarantee of a free public education, in *Brown* the U.S. Supreme Court found that if a state undertakes the provision of free education for its citizenry, a property right of an education is established. The property (education) rights of Linda Brown and the other African American children had been taken without due process, a clear violation of the Fourteenth Amendment to the U.S. Constitution. The *Brown* decision overturned *Plessy* with regard to education (some of the other rights were not clearly gained until the Civil Rights Act of 1964), and began the integration of all children of color into American schools.

Brown did not involve children with disabilities, but as the precedent was set to guarantee equal educational opportunity for ethnic minority children, it too, set a precedent in the argument of guaranteeing the rights of students with disabilities. The Court had essentially ruled that what the Topeka School District had provided Linda Brown and the other African American children was not appropriate. Not only have the courts supported rights of students with disabilities to have a free education, but legislation has also sought to bring them the right to an appropriate education (Chinn, 2004).

The *Brown* decision found "separate but equal" education to be unequal. Separate education denied African American students an equal education. It mandated a fully integrated education, free from the stigma of segregation. Chief Justice Warren stated that segregation "generates a feeling of inferiority as to their (children) status in the community that may affect their hearts and minds in a way unlikely ever to be undone."

Throughout the history of special education in the United States, children with disabilities have faced a continuous uphill struggle to gain their right to attend public schools. Eventually some programs were instituted, but until the mid-1970s some children, particularly those with moderate to severe disabilities, were routinely excluded from public education. One of the arguments to deny admission to children with moderate and severe mental retardation was that they could not learn to read, write, and do arithmetic in the same manner that nondisabled

Brown v. Board of Education and other related cases are discussed in Chapter 2.

students learned. Learning these academic skills is education, it was argued. Since they were not educable, they did not belong in schools.

Parents and supporters of these children countered by arguing that learning self-help skills and other important life skills was indeed learning, and this was education. These children, along with children with severe physical disabilities could learn, particularly if support services were provided.

PARC v. The Commonwealth of Pennsylvania

In 1971, the Pennsylvania Association for Retarded Children (PARC) brought a class-action suit against the Commonwealth of Pennsylvania for the failure to provide a public supported education to students with mental retardation. The attorneys for the plaintiffs argued the following:

- Education cannot be defined as only the provision of academic experiences for children.
- All students with mental retardation were capable of benefiting from programs of education and training.
- Having undertaken a free public education for the children of Pennsylvania, the state could not deny children with mental retardation the same opportunities.
- The earlier the students with mental retardation were provided education, the greater the amount of learning could be predicted.

The Federal District Court ruled in favor of the plaintiffs, and all children ages 6 to 21 were to be provided a free public education. The court stipulated that it was most desirable to educate children with mental retardation in programs most like those provided to their peers without disabilities (Murdick, Gartin, & Crabtree, 2002; Yell, 2006).

Mills v. Board of Education

Following the *PARC* decision, another class action suit, *Mills v. Board of Education,* was brought before the Federal District Court in the District of Columbia, on behalf of 18,000 out-of-school children with behavior problems, hyperactivity, epilepsy, mental retardation, and physical problems. The court again ruled in favor of the plaintiffs and mandated the District of Columbia schools to provide a public supported education to all children with disabilities. In addition, the court ordered the following:

- The district to provide due process procedural safeguards.
- Clearly outlined due process procedures for labeling, placement, and exclusion.
- Procedural safeguards to include right to appeal, right to access records, and written notice of all stages of the process (Murdick, Gartin, & Crabtree, 2002; Yell, 2006).

While these two high-profile cases were being played out in their respective communities, other states were finding similar challenges. The PARC was a state chapter of the National Association for Retarded Children (NARC, now the Association for Retarded Citizens). The NARC and other national organizations, such as the Council for Exceptional Children, actively supported disability advocates throughout the country in preparing court briefs and in offering other means of support. Armed with their victories and case law favorable to their cause, parent groups in other states began taking on their legislatures and school districts and winning. Fresh with many court victories, disability advocates in the early 1970s were busy preparing for their next battleground, the U.S. Congress.

Pause to Reflect **5.1**

It took the legal actions of concerned and frustrated parents and the support of competent and caring professionals to finally bring the end of segregation and injustice to children with disabilities, who had been disenfranchised from a meaningful and appropriate education.

- How does this compare with the plight of African American children in the history of United States education?
- Would children with disabilities still be segregated had legal action not been taken?
- Why does it so often take legal action from American educators to do what is right?

Go to the *Homework and Exercises* section in Chapter 5 of MyEducationLab and select *Pause to Reflect 5.1* to answer these questions.

Legislation

Section 504 and Public Law 93-112

In 1973, Congress enacted **Section 504 of Public Law 93-112** as part of the Vocational Rehabilitation Act. Section 504 was the counterpart of Title VI of the Civil Rights Act of 1964. The language was brief, but its implications are far reaching:

> No otherwise qualified handicapped individual in the United States . . . Shall, solely by reason of his (or her) handicap, be excluded from the participation in, be denied the benefits of, or be subjected to discrimination under any program or activity receiving federal financial assistance.

Section 504 prohibits the exclusion from programs solely on the basis of an individual's disability. A football coach, marching band director, or a university admissions officer cannot deny participation solely on the basis of a disability. However, if a learning disability prevents a student from learning marching band formations even with accommodations, if test scores are clearly below the university admissions standards and indicative of likely failure, and if mental retardation inhibits a student's ability to learn football rules and plays, then exclusion can be justified. If denial of participation is unjustified, the school or agency risks the loss of all federal funds even in other programs in the institution that are not involved in the discriminatory practice (Murdick, Gartin, & Crabtree, 2002; Yell, 2006).

Public Law 94-142

In 1975, **Public Law 94-142, the Education for All Handicapped Children Act,** was signed into law. This comprehensive legislation provided individuals, ages 3 to 21, with the following:

- A free and appropriate education for all children with disabilities
- Procedural safeguards to protect the rights of students and their parents

CRITICAL INCIDENTS IN TEACHING

Meeting the Mandates and Challenges of Section 504

Larry Gladden is a junior high school social studies teacher and the head football coach for the eighth-grade team. With a poor turnout for his initial recruitment effort, Gladden has received permission from the principal to make another recruitment pitch over the school's public address system. Making a strong appeal for all interested able-bodied boys to come out, Coach Gladden sets a meeting time immediately after school. As the new prospects arrive, the coach is shocked to see Massey Brunson walk into the room. Recognizing Massey from the special education classroom adjacent to his own, the coach knows that Massey is a student with mild mental retardation. The others in the room know this, too. "Hi, Coach," says Massey. "You said you need strong, healthy players. That's me! I work out every day at the Nautilus Fitness Center, and I'm in great shape."

Massey is indeed a great physical specimen. He is among the tallest of the new recruits and very muscular. When the coach saw the other team prospects shaking their heads as Massey entered, he had serious doubts about how Massey might fit on the team. Would he be accepted by his teammates? Could he learn the plays and follow instructions?

Questions for Classroom Discussion

1. Is the coach obligated to allow Massey to try out? Why? Why not?
2. Should he discourage Massey from trying to play?
3. Should he treat Massey differently from other players?
4. Should he make special allowances for Massey?
5. If Massey is good enough to play, how should the coach foster his acceptance by other team members?

Building Teaching Skills

Go to the *Building Teaching Skills* section in Chapter 5 of MyEducationLab and select *Critical Incidents in Teaching: Meeting the Mandates and Challenges of Section 504* to complete this exercise.

- Education in the least restrictive environment
- Individualized Educational Programs
- Parental involvement in educational decisions related to their children with disabilities
- Fair, accurate, and nonbiased evaluations

These provisions forever changed the face of American education. Every child with a disability was entitled to a free public education, which is to be appropriate to his or her needs. The education is to be provided in the least restrictive environment, which means that the student is to be educated in a setting as close to a general or regular education class as is feasible. Parents are now to have an integral role in their child's education, and are to be involved in the development of the education program for their child and to share in other decisions relating to their child. When appropriate, the student is also to be involved. There are to be procedural safeguards, which the schools must follow to ensure that the

Parents now have by law, a significant voice in their special education child's education.

Scott Cunningham/Merrill

rights of the students and parents are observed by the schools. Each student must have an **Individualized Education Program (IEP),** which is designed to meet the student's unique needs. The identification and evaluation process is to be nondiscriminatory and unbiased, and multifactored methods used to determine eligibility and placement (Murdick, Gartin, & Crabtree, 2002; Yell, 2006).

Prior to the passage of P.L. 94-142, nearly half of the nation's 4 million children with disabilities were not receiving a public supported education. Many of the students who were in special education were often isolated in the least desirable locations within the schools (Losen and Orfield, 2002). In the first two special education teaching assignments (both prior to P.L. 94-142), which one of the authors of this text experienced, this was very much the case. In the first school, all three special education classes were located in the basement of the junior high school, isolated from the other students. In the second school, there were two lunch periods to accommodate the large student body. The special education students were required to eat in the school cafeteria between the two lunch periods, and were expected to leave the facility before any other students entered. When a new school building was completed next to the old, outdated facility, the special education class remained in the old facility, while the rest of the school moved.

Americans with Disabilities Act

President George H. W. Bush signed Public Law 101-336, the **Americans with Disabilities Act (ADA),** into law on January 26, 1990. ADA was the most significant civil rights legislation in the United States since the Civil Rights Act of 1964. ADA was designed to end discrimination against individuals with disabilities in private-sector employment, public services, public accommodations, transportation, and telecommunications.

Among the many components of this legislation, the following are a sampling of the efforts to break down barriers for individuals with disabilities:

- Employers cannot discriminate against individuals with disabilities in hiring or promotion if they are otherwise qualified for the job.
- Employers must provide reasonable accommodations for individuals with disabilities, such as attaching an amplifier to the individual's telephone.

- New buses, bus and train stations, and rail systems must be accessible to persons with disabilities.
- Physical barriers in restaurants, hotels, retail stores, and stadiums must be removed; if not readily achievable, alternative means of offering services must be implemented.
- Companies offering telephone services to the general public must offer telephone relay services to those using telecommunication devices for the deaf (Murdick, Gartin, & Crabtree, 2002; Yell, 2006).

Individuals with Disabilities Education Act (IDEA)

Congress passed Public Law 101-476, the **Individuals with Disabilities Education Act (IDEA),** in 1990 as amendments to Public Law 94-142. Key components of this amendment act included the addition of students with autism and traumatic brain injury as a separate class entitled to services. A **transition plan** was an added requirement to be included in every student's IEP by age 16. The transition plan includes a needs assessment and individual planning to transition the student with a disability successfully into adulthood. A far-reaching change in the new legislation included the change in language to emphasize the person first and the disability second. The title of the legislation included "Individuals with Disabilities," and not "disabled individuals." In nearly all of the newer literature you will now see "children with mental retardation, students with learning disabilities, individuals with cerebral palsy, and people with hearing impairments." Individuals with disabilities are people or individuals first. Their disability is secondary and at times inconsequential in their ability to perform the tasks they undertake. Referring to a person as a spina bifida student calls immediate attention to his or her disability rather than the student's many assets or abilities (Murdick, Gartin, & Crabtree, 2002; Yell, 2006).

IDEA Amendments.   In 1997, Congress passed **Public Law 105-17, IDEA Amendments.** The 1997 Amendments reauthorized and made improvements to the earlier law. It consolidated the law from eight to four parts and made significant additions, including the following:

- Strengthened the role of parents, ensured access to the general education curriculum, emphasized student progress by changing the IEP process
- Encouraged parents and educators to resolve their differences through nonadversarial mediation
- Gave school officials greater latitude in disciplining students by altering some procedural safeguards
- Set funding formulas (Murdick, Gartin, & Crabtree, 2002; Yell, 2006).

In 2004, Congress passed another amendment to IDEA (P.L. 108-446) referred to as IDEA 2004 or the Individuals with Disabilities Education Improvement Act. IDEA 2004 added new language about "academic and functional goals." IEPs must now include "a statement of measurable annual goals, including academic and functional goals. . . ." Another requirement of IDEA 2004 aligns IDEA with the No Child Left Behind requirement of "highly qualified teachers." Under IDEA requirements, emergency or provisional certificates do not qualify an individual (Weishaar, 2007; Yell, 2006). All students deserve highly qualified teachers. However, there has been and still is an acute shortage of fully certified or credentialed special education teachers throughout the country, and mandating highly qualified teachers will not make them suddenly appear for school districts to employ. As recently as 2000, California alone had a shortage of thousands of special education teachers; in addition, California had several thousand more teachers in special education classrooms teaching on waivers or hired as long-term substitutes without full licensure.

The shortages persist in California, and other states, but school districts can no longer employ individuals with emergency licensure. School districts must find ways to compensate for the lack of trained personnel by qualifying those previously hired under emergency licensure under creative new categories, such as internship programs or in creative instructional staffing for students with disabilities. Some school districts have created coteaching arrangements utilizing both qualified special education teachers with qualified general education teachers. In some other instances qualified special education teachers provide consultation to general education teachers. These arrangements may provide benefits of inclusion for students with disabilities. Even with the creative arrangements, shortages persist. When they do, the mandate does require the districts to notify parents if their child's teacher does not meet the appropriate standards. Individuals hired without full licensure must show progress toward completion. This provision while not immediately solving the problem of shortages, is holding school districts accountable and may in the future provide better qualified special education teachers for children with special needs. IDEA 2004 has brought some additional changes and these can be accessed on the web or in books on the suggested reading list.

IDEA Funding.   When Congress passed Public Law 94-142 in 1975, it mandated services for children with disabilities. This required states and school districts to provide extensive and often expensive services to these children. Congress set a goal to fund the mandate at 40% of the cost to educate children with disabilites. Often the classes for these children are smaller, many require additional staffing with aides, which increases the cost to the schools. Parents empowered by this mandate have rightfully insisted that their children receive the services to which they are entitled. From 1995 to 2005, Congress' appropriations for IDEA increased from $3,253,000,000 to $11,674,000,000 (Apling, 2005). While this is a very significant increase, special education programs have expanded and as recently as 2007, Congress' IDEA funding has barely reached the 18% funding level, less than half what it had promised. This leaves school administrators in a difficult quandary, trying to provide mandated appropriate services to all children, while doing so with the underfunded resources of IDEA.

Post P.L. 94-142 Litigation

Even with 30 years of legislation, amendments, and refinements, there are many aspects of special education law that remain unclear to the children, their parents and advocates, or to school district personnel. The laws are extremely precise in some areas, and deliberately vague in others. In addition, there are many other variables, which exacerbate the problem of interpreting and implementing the various laws and regulations.

Congress itself is part of the problem. It has mandated extensive provisions for children with disabilities. Many of these are time and staff intensive, and expensive to implement. Congress, however, has failed to meet its fiscal obligations to make IDEA fully viable. Yet, school districts are required to implement expensive mandates without the promised fiscal support. Thus when many states and school districts are experiencing budget shortfalls, special education can be a challenge for educators to find the necessary resources. Staffing is another serious problem facing most states. Even when school districts are committed to full compliance of the laws, the acute national shortage of qualified special education and related services personnel may preclude their ability to do so. Parents who are aware of the law's requirement of an appropriate education, are often angry and may feel that the schools have betrayed the best interests of their children, and have often successfully addressed their problems by taking legal action against the schools. At times the schools are at fault for deliberately ignoring the IDEA requirements, but their problems are often exacerbated by lack of funding.

Because IDEA does not provide a substantive definition for a "free and appropriate education," the issue has often been resolved in the courts. Parents, as might be expected, often view an appropriate education as the best possible education for their child. In 1982, *Hendrick Hudson School District v. Rowley* became the first case related to "an appropriate education" for a student with a disability to reach the U.S. Supreme Court. Amy Rowley was a student with a hearing impairment who was placed in a regular education kindergarten class. Several school personnel learned sign language to enable them to communicate with Amy. A teletype machine was placed in the school office to facilitate communication with Amy's parents who were also deaf. Amy was provided with a hearing aid by the school, and a sign language interpreter was assigned to her class. Amy completed kindergarten successfully and was found to be well adjusted and making better than average progress.

Following the kindergarten year, as was required by P.L. 94-142, an IEP was developed for the upcoming school year. The plan specified that Amy was to continue her education in a regular classroom. She was to continue the use of the hearing aid, and would receive speech and language therapy three hours a week. In addition she was to receive instruction an hour daily from a tutor who specialized in working with children with hearing impairments.

The parents disagreed with the IEP, as they believed that Amy should have a qualified sign language interpreter for all academic classes. The school district, however, concluded that a full-time interpreter was unnecessary and denied the request. As was their right under P.L. 94-142, the parents requested and were granted a due process hearing. The parents prevailed, and the case found its way through lower courts until it finally reached the U.S. Supreme Court.

The Court, noting that the absence in the law of any substantive standard for "appropriate," ruled that Congress' objective was to make a public education available to students with disabilities. The intent was to guarantee access on appropriate terms, but not to guarantee a particular level of education. The Court ruled that schools were not obligated to provide the best possible education, but a "basic floor of opportunity." It found that a free and appropriate public education (FAPE) standard could only be determined by a multifactorial evaluation on a case-by-case basis. This case essentially assured continued litigation to resolve "appropriate education" disputes (Murdick, Gartin, & Crabtree, 2002; Yell, 2006).

This case was significant in that it was the first case related to P.L. 94-142 to reach the Supreme Court. It set a standard for "appropriate education" to be more than simple access to education but less than the best possible educational program. It became part of case law, setting a precedent for similar cases that would follow (Murdick, Gartin, & Crabtree, 2002; Yell, 2006). Consequently, when a school can demonstrate that a student is making satisfactory progress (this too is open for debate), the district's position tends to prevail.

The courts have had to rule on other provisions of the law. For example, the courts have also ruled in favor of the child when parents have sought nonphysician support services necessary to sustain the student's ability to function in school (e.g., *Irving Independent School District v. Tatro*). Through the years there is a developing body of case law that provides both parents and advocates and school personnel with a better understanding of how the law should be implemented.

Public Law 94-142 provided students with disabilities their legal educational rights. However, some school districts too often have been found out of compliance, either deliberately, or due to the negligence of personnel. Over the past 30 years there have been numerous court decisions (e.g., Chandra Smith Consent Decree, Los Angeles Unified

Pause to Reflect 5.2

Many of us take for granted our ability to come and go as we please. With the exception of a few buildings, which are off-limits to the general public, we are free to enter any building we wish, whenever we wish. During the next week, keep track of the buildings you enter, the streets you cross, and the activities in which you participate.

- How accessible are these to persons who are in wheelchairs, blind, or hearing-impaired?
- Are the room numbers in your building labeled in Braille?
- Are the steps ramped or is there an accessible lift or an elevator?
- What areas have not been made accessible to these individuals?
- How does accessibility limit their participation in the activities in which you regularly participate?
- How could these areas be made more accessible to individuals with disabilities?

Go to the *Homework and Exercises* section in Chapter 5 of MyEducationLab and select *Pause to Reflect* 5.2 to answer these questions.

School District and Felix Consent Decree, Hawaii Department of Education) resulting in massive judgments costing districts far more in legal fees and staff time than if they had initially complied with the law.

More than ever, children and adults with disabilities are becoming an integral part of the nation's educational system and are finding their rightful place in society. Although the progress that has been made in recent years is indeed encouraging, society's attitudes toward individuals with disabilities have not always kept pace with their legal rights. As long as people are motivated more by fear of litigation than by a moral ethical response, we cannot consider our efforts in this arena a complete success.

Exceptional Individuals and Society

Even in modern times, the treatment and understanding of any type of deviance has been limited. Society has begun to accept its basic responsibilities for people with disabilities by providing for their education and care, but social equality has yet to become a reality.

Society's view of people with disabilities can perhaps be illustrated by the way the media portray our population with disabilities. In general, when the media wishes to focus on persons with disabilities, they are portrayed as (a) children, usually with severe mental retardation with obvious physical stigmata, or (b) persons with crippling conditions either in a wheelchair or on crutches. Thus, society has a mind-set about who the people with disabilities are. They are often viewed as children or childlike, and they have severe disabilities—mentally, physically, or both.

Because society often views those with disabilities as childlike, they are denied the right to feel and want like nondisabled individuals. Teachers and other professional workers can often be observed talking about individuals with disabilities in their presence, as if the individuals are unable to feel any embarrassment. Their desire to love and be loved is often ignored, and they are often viewed as asexual, without the right to the same sexual desires as the nondisabled.

Many religious groups now provide interpreters for individuals with deafness and other services for individuals with disabilities.

Patrick White/Merrill

Observe and Learn — Lessons in Action

Exceptional Individuals and Society

Go to the *Homework and Exercises* section in Chapter 5 of MyEducationLab and select *Observe and Learn: Lessons in Action* to view the video "FDR's Secret" and answer the accompanying questions. By viewing historic photos and political cartoons, students in this lesson examine the success of FDR's attempts to hide (or at least downplay) the extent of his physical disability. They also learn about attitudes toward those with disabilities as they discuss the reasons for Roosevelt's concealment.

1. How did the students in the video react to the idea of hiding a disability?
2. Do you know anyone who tries to hide a physical or learning disability? If so, why do you think they do this?
3. How might your views of people with disabilities affect what you do in your future classroom?

Contemporary American society places great emphasis on physical beauty and attractiveness. Individuals who deviate significantly from physical norms are subject to possible rejection, even if their physical deviations do not interfere with their day-to-day functioning.

Gliedman and Roth (1980) suggest that nondisabled individuals perceive those with disabilities as individuals who seldom hold good jobs, seldom become heroes in our culture, and are seldom visible members of the community. They further suggest that society systematically discriminates against many capable individuals with disabilities. They indicate that the attitudes of society parallel that of racism, which views disability as incompatible with adult roles. They state that society perceives a "handicapped person as mentally or spiritually inferior because he is physically different or that 'people like that' have no business being out on the streets with 'us regular folks'" (p. 23).

Gliedman and Roth (1980) suggest that, with respect to discrimination, individuals with disabilities are in some ways better off than African Americans in that there is no overt discrimination, no organized brutality, no lynch mob "justice," and no rallies by supremacist groups. In some ways, however, people with disabilities are worse off. African Americans and other groups have developed ethnic pride. It is unlikely that one has ever heard a "cerebral palsy is beautiful" cry. Society opposes racism with the view that blacks are not self-evidently inferior, but at the same time it takes for granted the self-evidently inferior status of those who have disabilities.

As we stereotype individuals with disabilities, we deny them a rightful place in society. The disability dominates society's perception of the person's social value, and creates a mind-set of deviance. Individuals with disabilities are viewed as vocationally limited and socially inept.

Persons with disabilities are too often tolerated and even accepted as long as they maintain the roles ascribed to them. They are often denied basic rights and dignity as human beings. They are placed under the perpetual tutelage of those more knowledgeable and more capable than they. They are expected to subordinate their own interests and desires to the goals of a program decreed for them by the professionals who provide services to them.

The general public may be required by law to provide educational and other services for individuals with disabilities. The public is prohibited by law against certain aspects of discrimination against our citizens with disabilities. No one, however, can require the person on the street to like persons with disabilities and to accept them as social equals. Many do not accept a person with a disability. Just as racism leads to discrimination or prejudice against other races because of the belief in one's racial superiority, handicapism leads to stereotyping of, and discrimination against, individuals with disabilities because of attitudes of superiority held by some nondisabled individuals.

Society tends to place behavioral expectations on both men and women. Males have specific masculine roles they are expected to fulfill. Boys are usually expected to be athletic. Physical impairments, however, may preclude athletic involvement. Unable to fulfill

VIDEO INSIGHTS

Jessica Parks Surmounts Her Obstacles

In this video, we have the opportunity to see the accomplishments of a truly remarkable young woman, Jessica Parks. Born without arms, she has accomplished more than many individuals without disabilities, and far more than her parents, physicians, and educators could have imagined. Educators (including special educators) often predetermine in their minds what children with disabilities will or will not be able to accomplish, and limit their access to educational programs. This is often a mistake, which can even lead to lawsuits.

In a well-known case, *Sacramento City School District v. Rachel Holland*, 1994, school district personnel denied general education placement to a student with mental retardation. They had determined that she could not benefit from such an educational placement. It was clearly demonstrated in court that the school district was very wrong in their assessment of the student's capabilities. In this video, we can see why the courts will almost always side with the student and his or her parents if the schools refuse to allow the student the opportunity to demonstrate the ability to perform in a general education class.

1. Are educators often biased against students with disabilities?
2. Do educators have preconceived notions of the limits of children's abilities?
3. What is the variable which educators often fail to fully consider? Answer: motivation

Go to the Video Insights DVD and watch the video segment *Jessica Parks Surmounts Her Obstacles*. Then, go to the *Homework and Exercises* section in Chapter 5 of MyEducationLab and select *Video Insights: Jessica Parks Surmounts Her Obstacles* to answer these questions.

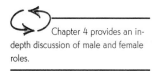
Chapter 4 provides an in-depth discussion of male and female roles.

this role, the young paraplegic male may develop devalued feelings of self-worth or a feeling that he is less than a man. Feminine roles are also assigned, and women with physical disabilities who are unable to assume these roles may suffer from feelings of inadequacy. With increased participation of women in athletics, and the success of the American women in recent Olympic competition, some females may also suffer the frustration of being unable to participate in athletic or other physical programs.

Exceptional Cultural Groups

Because of insensitivity, apathy, or prejudice, many of those responsible for implementing and upholding the laws that protect individuals with disabilities fail to do so. The failure to provide adequate educational and vocational opportunities for individuals with disabilities may preclude the possibility of social and economic equality. These social and economic limitations are often translated into rejection by nondisabled peers and ultimately into social isolation.

Not unlike many ethnic minority groups who are rejected by mainstream society, individuals with disabilities often find comfort and security with each other, and in some instances they may form their own enclaves and social organizational structures. Throughout the country, one can find groups of individuals, such as those who have visual or hearing impairments and those who have mental retardation. In some instances, they congregate in similar jobs, in the same neighborhoods, and at various social settings and activities.

Near Frankfort Avenue in Louisville, Kentucky, three major institutions provide services for individuals who have visual impairments. The American Printing House for the Blind, the Kentucky School for the Blind, and the Kentucky Industries for the Blind are all within close proximity of each other. The American Printing House for the Blind, the leading publisher of materials for individuals with visual impairments, employs a number of individuals who are blind. The Kentucky School for the Blind is a residential school for students with visual impairments, and it also employs a small number of individuals with visual

Pause to Reflect 5.3

State and Federal laws prohibit the discrimination against individuals with disabilities in our schools and in the workplace. However, no law can mandate how we treat or relate to these individuals on an individual and personal basis.

- Have you ever spent much time with a person with a disability?
- Do you have any friends with a disability?
- Are these individuals really any different from nondisabled individuals in matters that really count?
- What can the schools do to create a greater understanding and acceptance of students with disabilities?

Go to the *Homework and Exercises* section in Chapter 5 of MyEducationLab and select *Pause to Reflect 5.3* to answer these questions.

impairments, including teachers. The Kentucky Industries for the Blind operates as a sheltered workshop for individuals who are blind. With the relatively large number of persons who are blind employed by these three institutions, it is understandable that many individuals with visual impairments live in the surrounding residential area. Living in this area allows them to live close enough to their work to minimize the many transportation problems related to their visual limitations. It also provides a sense of emotional security for the many who, in earlier years, attended the Kentucky School for the Blind and lived on its campus and thus became part of the neighborhood. The neighborhood community can also provide social and emotional security and feelings of acceptance. A few years ago, a mailing was sent from the Kentucky School for the Blind to its alumni; 90% of the mailings had the same zip code as the school.

Individuals with visual impairments and hearing impairments are among the most likely to form their own cultural groups. Both have overriding factors that contribute to the need for individuals in these groups to seek out one another and to form cultural groups. Some of the blind have limited mobility. Living in cultural enclaves allows them easier access to one another. They share the same forms of communication—oral language, Braille, and talking books. Social and cultural interests created partly by their physical limitations can often be shared. The hearing impaired may have communication limitations within the hearing world. Their unique means of communication provides them with an emotional as well as a functional bond. Religious programs and churches for individuals with hearing impairments have been formed to provide services in total communication and social activities.

Individuals with physical disabilities may or may not become a part of a cultural group related to the disability. Some function vocationally and socially as part of the mainstream society. With adequate cognitive functioning and adequate communication patterns, normal social interaction is possible. Socialization, however, may depend on the degree of impairment and the individual's emotional adjustment to the disability. Some individuals with physical disabilities may function in the mainstream world and also maintain social contacts with others with similar disabilities. Social clubs for individuals with physical disabilities have been formed to provide experiences commensurate with functional abilities, as well as a social climate that provides acceptance and security. Athletic leagues for competition in sports, such as wheelchair basketball and tennis, have been formed. Many racing events (e.g., the Boston marathon) now include competition for wheelchair entries.

Many of the individuals with mild retardation live independently or in community-based and community-supported group homes. The group homes provide a family-like atmosphere, and house parents supervise the homes. Most of the individuals with moderate retardation who do not live in institutions tend to live at home. Many individuals with severe and profound retardation, and some with moderate retardation, are institutionalized and are thus forced into their own cultural group or enclave, isolated from the rest of society.

The gifted and talented usually do not experience the same type of discrimination and social rejection that many individuals with disabilities experience. Yet, like individuals with disabilities, they may suffer isolation from mainstream society and seek others with comparable abilities that may provide a feeling of acceptance as well as intellectual or emotional stimulation. The existence of Mensa, an organization whose membership prerequisite is a high score on an intelligence test, attests to the apparent need of some gifted individuals to be with others of their own kind.

Rejection of the gifted and talented may differ from that of individuals with disabilities because the roots may stem from a lack of understanding or jealousy, rather than from the stigma that may relate to certain disabilities.

CRITICAL INCIDENTS IN TEACHING

Placement of a Student with Epilepsy

Max Laird is a sixth-grade teacher in a middle-class suburban school. After school, Mr. Laird finds a note in his in-box, indicating that the principal and the special education resource room teacher want to meet with him the next day before the students arrive. At the meeting the next day, his principal, Dr. Gattelaro, explains to him that a new student, Chris Erickson, will be placed in the class the following Monday morning. He is informed that Chris is slightly above average in academics and a personable young man. However, Dr. Gattelaro wants Mr. Laird to know that Chris has epilepsy and occasionally has generalized tonic-clonic (previously called grand mal) seizures. Although the seizures are generally under control through medication, there is a possibility that sometime during the school year Chris will have a seizure in the classroom.

At this time, Ms. Chong, the special education resource room teacher, describes generalized tonic-clonic seizures. She explains that they are the most evident and serious type of epileptic seizure. They can be disturbing and frightening to anyone who has never seen one. Chris may have little or no warning that a seizure is about to occur. During a seizure, Chris' muscles will stiffen, and he will lose consciousness and fall to the floor. His whole body will shake violently, as his muscles alternately contract and relax. Saliva may be forced from his mouth, his legs and arms may jerk, and his bladder and bowels may empty. After a few minutes, the contractions will diminish, and Chris will either go to sleep or regain consciousness in a confused and drowsy state (Heward, 2006).

Stunned at this information, Mr. Laird sits in silence as Ms. Chong briefs him about the procedures to take if a seizure occurs in the classroom. She also explains to him that he should inform the other students that the seizure is painless to Chris and that it is not contagious.

Max Laird is aware that he has no option as to whether Chris will be in his class. He is determined to do the right thing and to make Chris' transition into his class as smooth as possible. He is also determined that he will help his class adjust and prepare for the likely seizure. Mr. Laird begins to map out a plan of action.

Questions for Classroom Discussion

1. What can Mr. Laird do with regard to his class?
2. What should be his plan of action?
3. Should he discuss Chris with his class?
4. Should he explain what epilepsy is?
5. Should he meet with the parents of his students? Why?
6. What should he say to Chris? What other actions can he take?
7. Who can teachers contact for help and guidance in these situations?

Building Teaching Skills

Go to the *Building Teaching Skills* section in Chapter 5 of MyEducationLab and select *Critical Incidents in Teaching: Placement of a Student with Epilepsy* to complete this exercise.

VIDEO INSIGHTS

abc NEWS

Against the Odds: Three Children with Autism

Autism is one of the fastest growing disorders among children. Among the behaviors seen in autistic children are apparent sensory deficits, severe affect isolation, self-multilatory behaviors, and behavior deficiencies. In this film we will see a family with three children with autism. The family has found a highly specialized treatment program, which has had a profoundly positive impact on these children. However, the program requires tuition of more than $170,000 a year for the three children. The family has exhausted their life savings on tuition. The Individuals with Disabilities Education Act (IDEA) requires schools to provide for the educational needs of children with disabilities. The U.S. Supreme Court has ruled that the schools are required to provide a basic floor of opportunity for children with disabilities, but are not required to provide them with the best possible education. With the private schooling, these three children seem to be thriving. The public schools are reluctant to pay the tuition to the private clinic.

1. Whose responsibility is the education of these children?
2. Should the taxpayers be responsible for making certain that these children receive the best possible education?
3. School districts have limited funds to spend on special education programming. If the parents prevail in due process and the district has to provide $170,000 for these children, there will be that much less to spend on other children with disabilities. Should the federal government be concerned with this?
4. Should the federal government, which has never met its financial obligations under IDEA be forced to do so?

Go to the Video Insights DVD and watch the video segment *Against the Odds: Three Children with Autism*. Then, go to the *Homework and Exercises* section in Chapter 5 of MyEducationLab and select *Video Insights: Against the Odds: Three Children with Autism* to answer these questions.

Disproportionate Placement in Special Education

The overrepresentation of students of color in special education classes has been one of the most problematic issues facing educators in recent years. Dunn (1968) reported that one third of the students in special education had been placed in classes for students with mild mental retardation. Dunn stated, "In my judgment, about 60 to 80 percent of the pupils taught by these teachers are children from low status backgrounds—including Afro-Americans, American Indians, Mexicans, and Puerto Rican Americans; those from nonstandard English speaking, broken, disorganized, and inadequate homes; and children from other non-middle class environments." Dunn has frequently been misquoted as stating that 60 to 80% of students in classes for the mild mentally retarded were students of color. Dunn stated that 60 to 80% of the students in these special education classes included (but were not limited to) students of color. As we do now know, some special education classes then and to some extent today had become a dumping ground for many culturally and linguistically diverse children.

The overrepresentation of students of color in special education classes is a major problem in education.

Anne Vega/Merrill

Artiles and Harry (2004) suggest that overrepresentation in special education placement is a problem when children are placed in special education classes when they do not have a disability. They also state that it is a problem if the placement in special education limits their opportunities for positive experiences (e.g., access to the general education curriculum, access to quality programs, obtaining a high school diploma). Similarly, Patton (1998) states that the misplacement of students in special education is problematic in that it is often stigmatizing to the individual and it can deny the student the high quality and life enhancing education to which he or she is entitled.

Overrepresentation in special education is a major problem in education. While overrepresentation in special education does not necessarily translate into inappropriate placement, it is indicative of either problems within the educational system, or society in general. It is possible that in some instances there may actually be more children of color in need of special education than their numbers or percentages in the general school population might suggest. If the child legitimately qualifies for special education services and is in need of such, it would be a disservice to him or her to not provide special education services because the numbers and percentages do not match. We are addressing the lives and education of children, and wrong decisions can have a lasting impact on their future. There are no doubts that there are inappropriate placements, which result in overrepresentation.

Mercer's research (1973) supported Dunn's earlier contentions. She found that Mexican American students in Riverside, California, were placed in classes for students with mild mental retardation at a rate four times that of the general school population. African American students were placed in the same special education classes at a rate three times what should have been expected given their numbers in the general school population. She stated that Mexican American students were ten times more likely to be placed in these classes than white students, while the likelihood of blacks was seven times greater.

In 1968, the Office of Civil Rights (OCR) began their biannual survey of student placement in special education classes. The data also provided racial backgrounds of the students in the broad categories of white, black, Asian/Pacific American, American Indian, and Latino. While the actual percentages have varied from survey to survey, one fact has remained consistent. African American students, particularly males, have been greatly overrepresented in classes for students with mental retardation and serious emotional disturbance. In some states, Latino students are overrepresented in classes for students with mild mental retardation. Another consistent finding is that African American, American Indian, and Latino students are greatly underrepresented in classes for the gifted and talented.

Reporting by Composition and Individual Risk

There are two valid means of reporting data related to the placement of students of color in special education classes: composition and individual risk (Artiles, Harry, Reschly, & Chinn, 2002). Composition gives us the percent of a program by group. It gives us the answer to a question: What is the percentage of African American students in classes for students with mental retardation? Of all of the students in classes for students with mental retardation, 32.34% are African Americans (U.S. Department of Education, 2004). The Office of Civil Rights reports special education enrollments by composition.

Individual risk gives us the percent of a group in a program. It provides us the answer to the question: What percent of African American students are in classes for students with mental retardation? In the entire United States, 2.58% of all African American students were placed in classes for students with mental retardation (U.S. Dept. of Ed., 2004).

With 2.58% of black students having been placed in these classes, the figures may appear to be small. However, it is problematic when we realize that the percentage of African Americans who are in classes of students with mental retardation is nearly five times greater than that of Asian/Pacific American students and twice that of white students. Also important is the fact that one third of African American students are not mentally retarded, as one might mistakenly assume from the OCR composition data. Rather, a little less than one third of those in classes for students with mental retardation are African American. This is a very important concept for the reader to understand.

Contributing Variables

While the majority of students in special education have most likely been carefully diagnosed and placed, educators and child advocates have raised concerns that it is also highly likely that many children are inappropriately placed in special education. The variables that contribute to the disproportionate special education placement are multifaceted. Some of the problems that contribute to the placement of these students are rooted in the social structure of the country. Other problems may be related to medical and genetic causes, particularly moderate and severe forms of disability, and may be beyond the ability of educators to remediate.

Poverty.   Dunn's 1968 findings that large percentages of students in classes for individuals with mental retardation were from backgrounds of poverty persist to this day. Poverty contributes to a significant number of problems. Pregnant women in poverty are provided less than optimal care during the prenatal period, as well as the period during and after birth. Physicians who provide medical care through government clinics are often burdened with excessive case loads and are unable to provide the quality of care that women are afforded from private physicians and managed care medical facilities. Appropriate nutrition and dietary supplements may be less available both to expectant mothers and to their children. Poverty may necessitate working late into term, even if it would be advisable to stop working and rest.

Children born preterm (those under normal gestation and less than 5 lbs 8 oz [2,500 grams]) may be at risk to develop cognitive and sensory disabilities (Drew & Hardman, 2007). Though more closely aligned with socioeconomic factors, preterm births have been associated with ethnicity. Younger women having children are more likely to have preterm babies, crack babies, and fetal alcohol syndrome children (Drew & Hardman, 2007), and teen births are disproportionately higher among the poor. Gelfand and Drew (2003) report that 51% of nonwhite births have complications as opposed to 5% of white upper-class births.

Lead Poisoning.   Nationally, about 434,000 children between the ages of 1 and 5 have elevated lead levels in their blood, according to the Centers for Disease Control and Prevention (Erickson, 2003). Lead poisoning can create problems for children such as reading and learning disabilities, speech and language disabilities, lowered IQ, neurological deficits, anemia, hearing loss, behavior problems, mental retardation, kidney disease, heart disease, stroke, coma, seizures, and even death (Davis, 2007; Erickson, 2003).

The primary sources of lead exposure to children in the United States are house dust contaminated by leaded paint and soil contamination. Both the residue of the leaded paint and decades of industrial and vehicle emissions have contaminated the soil. Leaded paint was in wide use in the 1940s, declined in use in the 1950s and 1960s, and was banned from residential use since 1978. However, older homes built before the ban are potentially a hazard to children. CDC reports that in a study, the children at greatest risk of lead poisoning are those living in pre-1946 homes with a prevalence of 8.6% with elevated lead levels. The high lead prevalence rate for children living in homes built between 1946 and 1973 was 4.6%, and dropped to 1.6% for children in homes built after 1973. The study found that the prevalence among low-income children was 16.4% as compared to children from middle-income (4.1%) and high-income families (0.9%) (Davis, 2007; Meyer et al., 2003). The latter finding is plausible given the fact that many of America's poor live in older homes.

Recently, there have been numerous recalls of millions of pieces of children's jewelry containing high concentrations of lead (e.g., bracelets, necklaces, and rings), much of which was manufactured in foreign countries. Parents should be particularly careful in purchasing such items even from well-known national chain stores. In 2007, millions of toys, including some well known brands were recalled due to excessive amounts of lead in their paint. Parents and educators must be vigilant in the selection of toys and educational materials, particularly those manufactured in other countries.

Over-referrals.   The individuals who are placed in classes for students with mild mental retardation and severe emotional disturbance are disproportionately male, African American, and from lower socioeconomic backgrounds. The first step in special education placement is referrals. Anyone (parents, doctors, educators) can make referrals. Teachers make most referrals in the elementary school years. These teachers are overwhelmingly female, white, and middle class. There is often incongruence between educators and culturally diverse students with respect to cultural values, acceptable behaviors in the school, and educational expectations. This may result in over-referrals to classes for students with disabilities and **under-referrals** to classes for the gifted and talented. In over-referrals, teachers tend to make excessive referrals of students of color for placement in special education classes for students with disabilities. In under-referrals educators fail to recognize potential giftedness and do not make referrals for placement in classes for gifted students. Ysseldyke, Thurlow, Graden, Wesson, Algozzine, and Deno (1983) suggest that a very large percentage of students who are referred to special education are eventually placed in special education programs.

Racial Bias.   Losen and Orfield (2002) suggest that undeniable intentional racial discrimination has been replaced by the soft bigotry of low expectations. There are numerous stories that can be told of students of color automatically placed in low academic tracks or in special education, particularly prior to the advent of IDEA. One such example involved a special education student athlete. At a football game many years ago, a high school principal recognized the backup quarterback, who had been called off the bench and who led the team to a come-from-behind victory. The quarterback was a special education student from an ethnic minority background who had been labeled as mentally retarded throughout his entire school years. The principal realized that the diagnosis and label had to be incorrect with the student's calling of complex plays and his clear gift for the game. The principal moved him out of special education and into regular classes where he was provided with extra help to adjust to the transition. He went on to earn a Ph.D., and is currently an associate dean in a Michigan University (Losen and Orfield, 2002).

Both ethnicity and gender are among the most consistent predictors of mental retardation and serious emotional disturbance identification by the schools. The Office of Civil Rights surveys have revealed persistent overrepresentation of students of color in certain disability categories (and underrepresentation in gifted and talented). We have already discussed the overrepresentation of African American children in classes for students with mental retardation. While the degree of disproportionate placement of African American males in classes for students with emotional disturbance is not to the extent which it is in classes for individuals with mental retardation, it is nevertheless at troubling levels. The placement percentage nationally for students in classes for students with emotional disturbance was .99%, while the percentage of African Americans in these classes was nearly at 1.5% (50% more than the general school population). Twenty-eight percent of the students in classes for students with emotional disturbance were African American (U.S. Dept. of Ed., 2004).

Assessment Issues.   Assessment of students of color is also a major concern as a contributing variable to the overrepresentation of these students in special education classes. Litigation in the 1970s (e.g., *Diana v. State Board of Education,* 1970, language minority Latino students, and *Larry P. v. Riles,* 1979, African American students) demonstrated the dangers of **biased assessment** instruments and procedures. Assessments, which favor certain cultural groups and discriminate in content, are considered biased. It is clear that some students in special education have central nervous system damage and that others have visual, auditory, orthopedic, and speech disabilities. There is no dispute regarding the appropriateness of the special education placement of these individuals. However, inappropriate placement of the students of color in the judgmental categories of mild mental retardation and severe emotional disturbance must be addressed if we are to have true equity in our educational system.

Unexplained Issues.   Losen and Orfield (2002) suggest that the differences in special education placement between Latino and African American students and between male and female African American students cannot be readily explained by either social background or in terms of measured ability. The poverty rates among Latinos and African Americans have been similar for a number of years. As previously stated, poverty is often listed as a variable that contributes to disability. However, we lack a clear explanation as to why placement rates in disability special education classes for Latinos are relatively low as compared to African American students. We also lack a clear understanding as to why black males and females have such disparate placement percentages when they come from the same socioeconomic backgrounds.

Perhaps one possibility is the fact that males and females are socialized differently regardless of the racial or ethnic backgrounds. Perhaps the socialized behaviors of African American males have a higher level of incongruence with educators' values than that of African American females, and elicit more negative attention.

When observing the placement differences between African Americans and Latinos, it might be noticed that some Latino students have more educational options open to them, including **bilingual education** and **English as a Second Language (ESL)** programs. Bilingual education, which utilizes both the home language and English in the instructional process, is designed to meet the needs of language minority students. ESL programs utilize only English with these students with a primary intent to teach them English. In addition Losen and Orfield (2002) suggest that racial, ethnic, and gender inequities could be a function of unconscious racial and class bias by school authorities. Unjustifiable reliance on IQ and other evaluation tools, high-stakes testing, and power differentials between minority parents and school officials may also be contributing variables.

Need for Disaggregated Data

While national data show trends for the various racial/ethnic groups, the data are often confusing because of the failure to disaggregate the various groups. For example, Asians and Pacific Americans are consistently shown to be underrepresented in disability categories and overrepresented in gifted and talented classes. There is considerable diversity within this category as it includes Asian groups such as the Chinese, Japanese, Koreans, Indians, and Vietnamese, while also including Pacific Americans such as Hawaiians, Samoans, and Tongans. There are considerable cultural differences between Asian groups and even greater differences between the Asians and Pacific Americans. Japanese Americans and Tongan Americans have little in common culturally. Yet they are grouped together for U.S. government reporting purposes. The same is true among Latinos. There are considerable cultural differences between Cuban Americans living in Miami and Central American immigrants living in East Los Angeles. They are also reported as one group.

When disaggregating data by states, or by ethnic groups, we often find considerable differences when compared to national data. For example, data from the Hawaii State Department of Education, shows that Hawaiian students are overrepresented in some categories of special education such as mental retardation. Yet, this cannot be determined from analyzing national data. Latinos or Hispanics are underrepresented in classes for students with mental retardation and emotional disturbance in the OCR national data. Yet in some states they are overrepresented, and Artiles, Rueda, Salazar, and Higareda (2002) found sixth- through twelfth-grade English language learners in 11 predominantly Latino urban school districts to be overrepresented in special education.

To explore the political and legal issues related to English language learners, see Chapter 6.

The inequities in special education raise concerns about the inequities in other areas of education and raise the prospect that there may be a relationship in these problematic issues. Special education overrepresentation often mirrors the overrepresentation seen in other categories and viewed by some as problematic: dropouts, low-track placements, corporal punishment, suspensions, and involvement in the juvenile justice system (Losen and Orfield, 2002).

The problem has persisted for decades and will not be easily ameliorated. It will take a concerted effort to eliminate all bias from the assessment process, a restructuring of teacher education curricula, and a commitment of the wealthiest nation to eliminate the insidious effects of poverty on our children.

Pause to Reflect 5.4

The overrepresentation of students of color is one of the most problematic issues facing special educators today. We have the knowledge and the ability to all but eradicate this problem.

- What steps would need to be taken to significantly reduce the problem of overrepresentation of students of color in special education?
- Do our educators and our legislators lack the will and the concern to take the necessary steps to ameliorate the problem?

Go to the *Homework and Exercises* section in Chapter 5 of MyEducationLab and select *Pause to Reflect 5.4* to answer these questions.

California Proposition 227 and Special Education

California's voters passed **Proposition 227** in 1998. This proposition, now a California law, requires all language minority students to be educated in **sheltered English immersion** programs, not normally intended to exceed one year. Sheltered English immersion is an instructional process in which English language acquisition for young children is structured so that all or nearly all classroom instruction is in English. However, one aspect will be addressed in this chapter. The proposition, which intended to dismantle bilingual education, sent waves of panic through California's bilingual education community. Those working with special needs students had even greater concerns because many believed that they were prohibited from using the home language with limited and non-English-speaking students (Baca and Cervantes, 2004). They were also concerned that the new law would require them to transition the students into general education classrooms after one year. Proposition 227 is a state law, as is a similar proposition in Arizona, and a similar law in Massachusetts. The federal law, IDEA, always takes precedence over a state law. Therefore, if the student's IEP requires bilingual education, it must be provided for as long as it is written.

A thorough discussion of Proposition 227 is presented in Chapter 6.

Classroom Focus

The educational implications for working with exceptional individuals are numerous and entire chapters could be devoted to each type of exceptionality. Educators should remember that exceptional children, those with disabilities and those who are gifted, are more like than unlike normal children. Their basic needs are the same as all children's. Abraham Maslow's theory on self-actualization is familiar to most students in education. To be self-actualized or to meet one's full potential, Maslow (1954) theorized, one's basic needs must be fulfilled: That is, to reach self-actualization, one's physiological needs, safety needs, belongingness or love needs, and esteem needs must first be met. Although many individuals with disabilities may never match the accomplishments of their nondisabled peers, they can become proficient at whatever they are capable of doing. Educators can assist them by helping to ensure that their basic needs are met, allowing them to strive toward self-actualization.

Teachers must be constantly cognizant of the unique needs of their exceptional children. The exceptional adult may choose, or may be forced by society, to become part of a cultural group. The interactions between educators and the exceptional child may not change what will eventually take place. Even if exceptional adults are part of a cultural group, they also will interact with the mainstream society on a regular basis. Efforts on the part of the educator to meet the needs of the child may ultimately affect the exceptional adult's interaction with society.

Teachers of children with physical and other health impairments may find it advantageous to check the student records carefully to determine potential problem situations with these students in the classroom. If a child has particular health problems that may surface in the classroom, the child's teachers need to be prepared so that they will know precisely what to do should the child have, for example, an epileptic seizure. The parents will most likely be able to provide precise instructions, and the school nurse could also provide additional recommendations. If the children are old enough to understand, they too can be a valuable source of information. Ask them what kinds of adaptations, special equipment, or teaching procedures work best for them. Teachers should not be afraid of their own uncertainties. They should feel free to ask the students when they won't or don't want help. Teachers should treat their students with disabilities as normally as feasible, neither overprotecting them nor giving or doing more for them than is needed or deserved. Allowing them to assume responsibility for themselves will do much to facilitate their personal growth.

Many variables affect the learning, cognition, and adjustment of individuals with disabilities. This is particularly evident for culturally and linguistically diverse learners who must cope with issues of language, culture, and values. Harry, Kalyanpur, and Day (1999) implore professionals who work with students with disabilities to take special note of the cultural values that may be embedded in their interpretation of a particular student's difficulties. They suggest that developing a sense of cultural self-awareness is crucial to effective interactions with students and families and that it will enable them to make appropriate decisions regarding services.

The range and variety of experiences imposed on, or withheld from, persons with disabilities may result in undue limitations. Too often, parents and teachers assume that a child's visual limitation precludes the ability to appreciate the typical everyday experiences of sighted children. Children who are blind may not be able to see the animals in a zoo, but they can smell and hear them. They may not be able to enjoy the scenes along a bus route, but they can feel the stop-and-go movements, hear the traffic and people, and smell their fellow travelers. The child who is deaf may not be able to hear the sounds at the symphony or the crowd's roar at a football game. Both events, however, offer the possibility of extraordinary sensory experiences to which the child needs exposure. The child with cerebral palsy needs experiences such as going to restaurants, even if there is difficulty using eating utensils in a socially acceptable manner.

Well-adjusted individuals with a sensory disability usually attain a balance of control with their environment. Individuals who depend completely on other members of the family and on friends may develop an attitude of helplessness and a loss of self-identity. Individuals with disabilities who completely dominate and control their environment with unreasonable demands sometimes fail to make an acceptable adjustment and could become selfish and self-centered.

It is critical to remember that children who are exceptional are, first and foremost, children. Their exceptionality, though influencing their lives, is secondary to their needs as children. They are more like than unlike nondisabled children. They therefore have the same basic needs as those children. Chinn, Winn, and Walters (1978) identify three of those needs: communication, acceptance, and the freedom to grow.

Communication Needs

Exceptional children are far more perceptive than many adults give them credit for being. They are sensitive to nonverbal communication and hidden messages that may be concealed in half-truths. They, more than anyone else, need to deal with their exceptionality, whether it is a disability or giftedness. They need to know what their exceptionality is all about so that they can deal with it. They need to know how it will affect their lives in order to adjust appropriately, to make the best of their lives, and to reach their full potential. They need straight, honest communication tempered with sensitivity.

Acceptance Needs

The society in which we live often fails to provide the exceptional child with a positive and receptive environment. Even the educational setting can be hostile and lacking in acceptance. The teacher can facilitate the acceptance of a child in a classroom by exhibiting an open and positive attitude. Students tend to reflect the attitude of the teacher. If the teacher is hostile, the students will quickly pick up these cues. If the attitude is positive, the students are likely to respond and provide a receptive environment for their classmates with disabilities.

> Jeff, a first-grade student who suffered from a hearing loss, was fitted with a hearing aid. When he came to school with the hearing aid, the students in the class immediately began whispering about the "thing" Jeff had in his ear. After observing the class behavior, the teacher assisted Jeff in a "show and tell" preparation for the next day. With the teacher's assistance and assurances, Jeff proudly demonstrated his hearing aid to the class. By the end of the demonstration, Jeff was the envy of the class, and any further discussion of the hearing aid was of a positive nature.

Freedom to Grow

Students with disabilities need acceptance and understanding. Acceptance implies a freedom for the exceptional child to grow. At times, it may seem easier to do things for a child, rather than to take the time to teach the child.

> Sarah was a nine-year-old girl who was blind and who had an orthopedic disability. She attended a state residential school for the blind. She wore leg braces but had a reasonable amount of mobility with crutches. To save time and effort, fellow students or staff members transported her between the cottage where she lived and the classroom building in a wagon. One day her teacher decided she needed to be more independent in her travel to and from her cottage. To Sarah's surprise, the teacher informed her after school that she would not ride back in the wagon but that he was walking her back. Angered, she denounced him as cruel and hateful in front of the entire class. She complained bitterly the full thirty minutes of their walk back to the cottage. After a few days the complaining subsided and the

travel time was curtailed. Within a few weeks Sarah was traveling on her own in ten minutes or less with newfound self-respect. (Chinn et al., 1978, p. 36)

At other times, it may be tempting for teachers and parents to make extra concessions for the exceptional child. Often, these exceptions preclude the emotional growth of the child and may later cause serious interpersonal problems.

Jimmy was a seven-year-old boy who was blind at the same state institution attended by Sarah. He was a favorite of the staff members because of his pleasant personality and overall adjustment. On a Sunday afternoon in the fall, he was assisting a staff member in making block prints for Christmas. The conversation turned to Christmas and Jimmy's wish for a transistor radio. This incident took place in 1960 when transistor radios were new on the market and very expensive. Since Jimmy had already made his request to his parents, the staff member was confident that the parents would not deny this child his wish. To the surprise of the staff, Jimmy returned after the holidays without a radio. He very philosophically explained to the staff that the radios were so expensive that had his parents granted his wish it would be at the expense of the other children in the family. Weeks later, when Jimmy returned from his birthday weekend at home, he entered his cottage with a transistor radio in hand, but in tears. He informed the staff that he and his younger brother Ralph had been fighting in the car on the way to the school and both had received a spanking. When a staff member went out to greet Jimmy's parents, his younger brother Ralph was also crying from the insult to his rear end. (Chinn et al., 1978, p. 36)

Jimmy's father was a laborer with a modest income. Although their child's disability created adjustment problems for everyone, they had resolved to treat him as an equal in the family. As such, he shared all of the family privileges. He also suffered the same consequences for inappropriate behavior. This attitude on the part of the parents was probably a primary factor in Jimmy's excellent adjustment to his disability.

Normalization and Inclusion

Much effort is directed today toward the concept of normalization. **Normalization** means "making available to all persons with disabilities or other handicaps, patterns of life and conditions of everyday living which are as close as possible to or indeed the same as the regular circumstances and ways of life of society" (Nirje, 1985, p. 67). Normalization was expanded and advocated in the United States by Wolfensberger (1972). He has subsequently suggested a rethinking of the term normalization and introduced the concept of **"social role valorization"**—giving value to individuals with mental retardation (Wolfensberger, 1983, 2000). He suggests that the "most explicit and highest goal of normalization must be the creation, support, and defense of valued social roles for people who are at risk of social devaluation" (Wolfensberger, 1983, p. 234).

Drew and Hardman (2007) suggest that normalization and social valorization have brought about an emphasis on deinstitutionalization, whereby individuals from large residential facilities for people with retardation are returned to the community and home environments. They add that the concept is not limited to movement away from institutions to a less restrictive environment; it also pertains to those individuals living in the community for whom a more "normal" lifestyle may be an appropriate goal.

The principles of normalization as they were first introduced were developed with individuals with mental retardation as the target group. In more recent years, the concept has broadened so that all categories of individuals with disabilities are now targeted. The

An increasingly larger number of students with disabilities are now being fully included in general education classrooms.

Krista Greco/Merrill

term "mainstreaming" now giving way to **"inclusion,"** seemed to undergo a natural evolutionary process from the concept of normalization. Turnbull, Turnbull, and Wehmeyer define inclusion allowing "students with disabilities to learn in general education classes and have a sense of belonging in these classes" (2007, p. 42). Tiegerman-Farber and Radziewicz (1998) further assert that in its "purest" form inclusion means that students with disabilities have a right to be integrated into general education classes regardless of their ability to meet "traditional" academic standards. Mastropieri and Scruggs (2007) differentiate between *inclusion* and *full inclusion* with the latter serving students with disabilities and other special needs *entirely within the general classroom.* This is an important difference, as students in full inclusion do not receive any of their education in segregated settings.

Initially inclusion was intended for students with mild disabilities. A more current movement, full inclusion, seeks to provide children with moderate to severe disabilities with similar opportunities. Although resistance to inclusion of students with mild retardation is far less intense than it once was, resistance from some educators still remains. The arguments against integrating children with severe disabilities have often been centered on the presumed inability of nondisabled children to accept their peers with disabilities. In reality, some of the reservations may be more a reflection of educators who themselves are unable or unwilling to accept the dignity and worth of individuals with severe disabilities.

Historically special education in the United States has offered a full continuum of placements for students with disabilities. These services have included the most restrictive placements such as residential schools and special schools, to the least restrictive settings, such as full inclusion into the general education classroom.

Federal special education law (IDEA) does not require inclusion. The law does require the least restrictive environment for students with disabilities. Herein lies the basis for considerable controversy in special education. The controversy is often fueled within special education itself, as special educators themselves are not in complete agreement regarding what is the least restrictive environment. **"Least restrictive environment"** means that children with disabilities are to be educated with nondisabled children whenever possible, in as normal an environment as possible. Few special educators would argue against the concept of inclusion. However, disagreement is centered on whether full inclusion is appropriate for every child regardless of the type of disability or the severity of the disability.

To some, and perhaps many of the advocates of full inclusion, the issue is not one of the efficacies of general education placement. Rather, it is a moral and ethical issue. Opponents of inclusion use many of the same arguments that segregationists used more than 50 years ago. Most Americans today would consider it unconscionable to segregate children in schools on the basis of race or ethnicity. This, we can agree, is morally and ethically wrong. Advocates for full inclusion find it equally repugnant to segregate children on the basis of a disability.

In reality, most (if not all) children with disabilities could be served in a general education classroom if adequate resources and supports were made available. Therein lies a primary problem. Special education resources are too often inadequate. There is seldom an adequate supply of certified or credentialed personnel in special education and in related services (e.g., school psychologists). General educators have many issues and concerns to address in inclusion. They may be concerned

- that the special needs student will detract from the attention normally provided other students.
- about the reception the nondisabled students will give to the students with disabilities.
- that if they are not provided with appropriate training to accommodate the students with disabilities, they will not be able to provide appropriate instructional services.
- that the younger students and those with more severe disabilities will require greater attention.
- that the promises of support in classroom personnel and other resources may not be kept.

A pragmatist would argue that there are not enough fiscal resources to provide the supports necessary for successful full inclusion for all children. We know that the courts will not accept, "we don't do it because there are inadequate resources." The courts may accept an argument that a particular program or service is not in the best interests of the student, but it must be clearly supported and documented. However, if full inclusion is warranted, the courts will order the schools (and they have consistently done so) to "get the resources and to do it."

Some who may question aspects of full inclusion may argue that some children are too disruptive and dangerous to themselves and to other students that they cannot be provided for in general education. Supporters of full inclusion can argue that given adequate resources, the student can be taught to stop disruptive and dangerous behaviors. Turnbull and his associates do suggest that there has been a progressive trend toward greater inclusion in the nation's schools. They indicate that prior to the 1984–1985 school year, only about a fourth of the students with disabilities spent a significant part of their day in general education classrooms. By the 1998–1999 school year, nearly half of the students were involved in general education most of the school day. There are some general conclusions, which we could draw from the issues raised:

- As long as Congress fails to meet its financial obligations in fully funding IDEA, school districts will continue to have difficulty in providing adequate resources for special education.
- Segregating students with disabilities from general education classes without justification is morally and ethically wrong.
- The debate over inclusion and full inclusion continues and is not likely to be fully resolved in the immediate future.

FOCUS YOUR CULTURAL LENS: DEBATE

Is Full Inclusion Feasible for All Children with Disabilities?

The Individuals with Disabilities Education Act is a federal law that requires the placement of students with disabilities in the least restrictive environment. This means that these students should be placed in settings in or as close to a general education setting as is feasible for them. What is the least restrictive setting for a child with a disability? Is it feasible to place every child with a disability in a general education setting? Are there realistically adequate resources to do this? Do we have the skill and the will to make it work?

For

- Full inclusion for all children with disabilities is a moral and ethical issue. It is as immoral to segregate a child because of his or her disability as it is to segregate children because of the color of their skin.
- The least restrictive environment that is feasible for every child is a general education classroom. We have the know-how to deliver quality educational services for every child in an inclusive general education classroom.
- The fact that we do not have adequate fiscal resources is not the fault of the child with a disability. If we don't have the resources, then we need to find ways to get them.

Against

- Full inclusion may work for some students with disabilities, but it makes no sense to insist on it for every student regardless of the disability or the degree of impairment.
- Some students with disabilities lack the maturity, the cognitive ability, the social skills, or adequate behaviors to function in general education.
- Until the Federal Government makes good on its commitment to fully fund IDEA, there will never be adequate resources to successfully implement full inclusion for all children with disabilities.
- Even if there were the fiscal resources, there simply are not enough professionally prepared personnel to provide the type of services needed for successful inclusion of every child.

Questions

1. Are there some students who should never be considered for general education placement?
2. If the Federal Government mandates special education for all children, commits itself to funding 40% of the cost, and continues to renege on the full funding, should school districts be forced to fully implement IDEA?
3. Is excluding children with disabilities from being fully included in general education morally and ethically comparable to excluding children because of race?

Go to the *Homework and Exercises* section in Chapter 5 of MyEducationLab and select *Focus Your Cultural Lens* to answer these questions.

Data is from VIDEO: Special Education Inclusion, Wisconsin Education Association Council, undated. Retrieved from www.weac.org/resource/june96/speced.htm

Pause to Reflect 5.5

Students with disabilities are sometimes forced into segregated settings for reasons beyond their control. For example, Kevin was a student who lived with his family on the side of a mountain in Appalachia. Kevin was blind, with no travel vision. It was a three-quarter-mile hike down the side of the mountain to the school bus stop. Kevin had good mobility skills and could negotiate the trail to and from the bus stop when weather conditions were good. The school was able to provide appropriate special education and general education services for him. During the winter, however, when snow covered the ground for the entire season, he could not get his bearings with his long cane and could not negotiate the trail. There was no one who could help him get to and from the bus stop, so during the winter he stopped going to school. The only school that could apparently meet his needs was the state school for the blind, which could provide him with residential services. The state residential school, however, is the most extreme form of a segregated setting for students with disabilities.

- Is segregating Kevin from his nondisabled peers inappropriate? Immoral? Unethical?

- Is the issue of full inclusion for students with disabilities similar to the issue of desegregation for all students of color into integrated classroom settings?

- When educators say they want a full continuum of services for students with disabilities that would permit inclusion for some and segregated classrooms for others or even institutionalization, is this a moral and ethical way to educate America's students? Is this an excuse for educators to discriminate against some?

Go to the *Homework and Exercises* section in Chapter 5 of MyEducationLab and select *Pause to Reflect 5.5* to answer these questions.

It is important for us as educators to see the parallels and differences that exist between the current debate regarding this group of students and the issues that *Brown* addressed more than 50 years ago. The two situations have similarities, but the groups are different. It is important that, as educators, we maintain an open mind so that perhaps we ourselves can be educated.

The legal mandates do not eliminate special schools or classes, but they do offer a new philosophical view. Instead of the physical isolation of individuals with disabilities, an effort to enable students with disabilities to assume a more appropriate place in the educational setting is being promoted. Still, many children with disabilities apparently may not benefit appreciably from an inclusive setting and may be better educated in a special setting. As attitudes become more congruent with the laws, people with disabilities may have more options in the decision to be a part of the mainstream or to segregate themselves into their own cultural groups.

Summary

The concerns related to the disproportionate placement of ethnic minorities, males, and students from low-income families in special education programs have been addressed to focus on a long-standing educational problem. The issues raised are not intended to negate the fact that there are students with retardation, serious emotional disturbance, and other disabilities in both majority and minority groups. Rather, they are raised to call attention to problems in referral and assessment, as well as to the problems associated with poverty.

Adults with disabilities often become part of a cultural group for individuals with disabilities by ascription or by individual choice. They do not choose to have a disability, and their situation often precludes full acceptance or integration into the world of those who are perceived to be physically, socially, or mentally normal. Their adjustment to their environment may be, in part, a function of the way they are perceived, treated, and accepted by educators. Consequently, teachers and other educators may have a greater influence on children with disabilities than they realize.

The Education for All Handicapped Children Act (EHA; P.L. 94-142), the Individuals with Disabilities Education Act (IDEA; P.L. 101-476), Section 504 of the Vocational Rehabilitation Act Amendments of 1973 (P.L. 93-112), and the Americans with Disabilities Act (ADA; P.L. 101-336) guarantee all exceptional children the right to a free and appropriate education and freedom from discrimination resulting from their disability. While thousands of children with disabilities are experiencing inclusive education in general education classes, many others are excluded because of bias, prejudice, or lack of understanding. Despite these mandates, equality still eludes millions of individuals with disabilities in this country. Until and unless the Federal Government fulfills its fiscal commitment to fully fund IDEA, full inclusion will continue to be a problematic and controversial issue for educators.

Insensitivity, apathy, and prejudice contribute to the problems of those with disabilities. Because of prejudice, institutionalization, or a desire to meet their own needs, some exceptional individuals form their own cultural groups and some their own enclaves, where they live and socialize with one another. The laws can force services for individuals with disabilities, but only time and effort can change public attitudes.

PROFESSIONAL PRACTICE FOR EDUCATORS

Questions for Discussion

1. What are some of the objections to labeling children with disabilities?
2. Why was *Brown v. Board of Education* (1954) important to special education?
3. What are the major implications for P.L. 94-142, IDEA, Section 504 of P.L. 93-112, and the Americans with Disabilities Act?
4. How do individuals with disabilities sometimes become a part of an exceptional cultural group?
5. Explain the difference of reporting placement in special education classes by composition and by risk.
6. What are some of the variables that contribute to the overrepresentation of students of color in special education classes?
7. What are the educational implications of California's Proposition 227 for students with disabilities?
8. What are some of the needs of exceptional children?
9. Explain the concepts of normalization and social role valorization.
10. What are the problems with providing full inclusion to all children with disabilities?

Portfolio Activities

1. Examine an entire building on your campus to determine its accessibility to individuals with wheelchair mobility. Make a notation of the following:
   a. Do curbs leading to the building allow wheelchair access?
   b. Is the entrance into the building accessible by wheelchair? Is it ramped?
   c. Are restrooms accessible with larger stalls to accommodate wheelchairs?
   d. Is the building multilevel, and if so, how does the student access the different floors?
   e. Are there Braille signs in appropriate places? (INTASC Standards 3 and 10)
2. Examine your campus to determine if it is accessible to visually impaired individuals. Determine if there are hazards on the campus, which endanger individuals who are blind (e.g., holes in the ground, posted metal sign at face height). (INTASC Standards 3 and 10)
3. Determine the percentage of students of color in the school in which you are working or student teaching. Determine the percentage of students of color in this same school who have placement in special education classes and determine if there is some degree of overrepresentation. This information is for your own use and possibly university classroom discussion. If you are a student teacher in the school, it may not be in your best interest to make an issue of overrepresentation with the school administration. (INTASC Standards 3 and 10)

Licensure Test Prep

Kyle Smith is a new teacher in a middle school. He has been assigned three students with disabilities in his class. One has mild mental retardation, two others have been diagnosed with learning disabilities.

Mr. Smith has been made acutely aware that there are federal and state laws that guarantee specific rights to students with disabilities as well as rights that are also extended to their parents. Mr. Smith wants to be certain that he follows the laws carefully. There are certain laws and facts that all teachers should be aware of.

Short Answer Questions

1. What is Section 504 of Public Law 93-112 and what is its relevance to educators?
2. What are the basic requirements of Public Law 94-142 (which has evolved into IDEA—Individuals with Disabilities Education Act)?
3. What is the Americans with Disabilities Act?

Go to the *Homework and Exercises* section in Chapter 5 of MyEducationLab and select *Licensure Test Prep* to complete this exercise.

Suggested Readings

Drew, C. J., & Hardman, M. L. (2007). *Intellectual disabilities across the lifespan* (9th ed.). Upper Saddle River, NJ: Pearson Education, Inc.

This is an excellent developmental approach to mental retardation. It includes a sensitive view of mental retardation and its impact on the family. It examines some of the early treatments of individuals with mental retardation. A chapter on legislative and legal issues related to individuals with mental retardation is also included.

Heward, W. L. (2006). *Exceptional children* (8th ed.). Upper Saddle River, NJ: Pearson Education, Inc.

This survey text is an overview of all exceptionalities that will provide a good basic understanding of the gifted and talented, as well as the various disabling conditions. It includes a chapter on culturally diverse exceptional students.

Losen, D. J., & Orfield, G. (2002). *Racial inequality in special education.* Cambridge, MA: Harvard Education Press.

This text is an excellent treatment in helping the reader to understand the problems of over-referral, overidentification, and overrepresentation of students of color (particularly African American) in special education classes. A thorough treatment of variables that contribute to the problems including bias, discrimination, poverty, and assessment issues is presented.

Turnbull, R., Turnbull, A., Wehmeyer, M. L. *Exceptional lives: Special education in today's schools* (5th ed.). Upper Saddle River, NJ: Pearson Education, Inc.

This is an excellent introductory text on exceptional children, which includes a very good treatment on inclusion.

Yell, M. L. (2006). *The law and special education* (2nd ed.). Upper Saddle River, NJ: Pearson Education, Inc.

This text provides an excellent overview of litigation and legislation in special education. It provides excellent insights into how litigation is developed and how it influences legislation, and also provides an explanation of legal terminology.

References

Americans with Disabilities Act of 1990, 42 U.S.C. 12101 *et seq.* (P.L. 101-336).

Apling, R. N. (2005). *Individuals with Disabilities Education Act (IDEA): Current funding trends.* Washington, DC: CRS Report to Congress, shelby.senate.gov/legislation/IDEA.pdf

Artiles, A. J., & Harry, B. (2004). *Addressing culturally and linguistically diverse student overrepresentation in special education: Guidelines for parents.* Denver, CO: National Center for Culturally Responsive Educational Systems.

Artiles, A. J., Harry, B., Reschly, D. J., & Chinn, P. C. (2002). Over-identification of students of color in special education: A critical overview. *Multicultural Perspectives* (4), 1, 3–10.

Artiles, A. J., Rueda, R., Salazar, J. J., & Higareda, I. (2002). English-language learner representation in special education in California urban school districts. In D. J. Losen & G. Orfield (Eds.), *Racial inequality in special education.* Cambridge, MA: Harvard Education Press.

Baca, L. M., & Cervantes, H. (2004). *The bilingual special education interface* (4th ed.). Upper Saddle River, NJ: Merrill/Prentice Hall.

Board of Education of the Hendrick Hudson School District v. Rowley, 458 U.S. 176 (1982).

Brown v. Board of Education of Topeka, 347 U.S. 483, 74 S.Ct. 686, 91, L.Ed. 873 (1954).

Centers for Disease Control and Prevention. (2005). *Disability and health in 2005: Promoting the health and well-being of people with disabilities.* Washington, DC: U.S. Department of Health and Human Services, www.cdc.gov/ncbddd/factsheets/Disability_Health_AtAGlance.pdf

Chinn, P. C. (2004). Brown's far reaching impact. *Multicultural Perspectives, 6* (4), 9–11.

Chinn, P. C., Winn, J., & Walters, R. H. (1978). *Two-way talking with parents of exceptional children: A process of positive communication*. St. Louis: Mosby.

Davis, T. (2007, February 4). Lead poisoning in kids a persistent problem. *AZ Daily Star* (Tucson, AZ), p. NA.

Diana v. State Board of Education, Civil Action No. C-7037RFP (N.D. Cal. Jan. 7, 1970 & June 18, 1973).

Drew, C. J., & Hardman, M. L. (2007). *Intellectual disabilities across the lifespan* (9th ed.). Upper Saddle River, NJ: Pearson Education.

Dunn, L. (1968). Special education for the mildly retarded: Is much of it justifiable? *Exceptional Children, 7,* 5–24.

Edgerton, R. B. (1967). *The cloak of competence.* Berkeley: The University of California Press.

Education for All Handicapped Children's Act of 1975, 20 U.S.C. 1401 *et seq.* (P.L. 94-142).

Erickson, S. (2003, April 17). Florida officials reach out to save children from lead poisoning. *Orlando Sentinel,* FL, pITEM03207051.

Gelfand, D. M., & Drew, C. J. (2003). *Understanding child behavior disorders* (4th ed.). Ft. Worth, TX: Harcourt Brace.

Gliedman, J., & Roth, W. (1980). *The unexpected minority.* New York: Harcourt Brace Jovanovich.

Harry, B., Kalyanpur, M., & Day, M. (1999). *Building cultural reciprocity with families: Case studies in special education.* Baltimore: Paul H. Brookes.

Heward, W. L. (2006). *Exceptional children* (8th ed.). Upper Saddle River, NJ: Merrill/Prentice Hall.

IDEA Funding Coalition. (2003). *IDEA funding: Time for a new approach.* Mandatory Funding Proposal, March 2003. Retrieved August 2, 2004, from www.aasa.org/government_relations/idea/Mandatory_2003_Proposal.pdf

Individuals with Disabilities Education Act of 1990, P.L. 101-476, 20 U.S.C. 1400 *et seq.* (1990).

Individuals with Disabilities Education Act Amendments of 1997, P.L. 105-17, 20 U.S.C. 1400 *et seq.* (1997).

Individuals with Disabilities Education Improvement Act of 2004, P.L. 108-446, 601 *et seq.,* 118 Stat. 2647 (2005).

Irving Independent School District v. Tatro, 468 U.S. 883 (1984).

Larry P. v. Riles, C-71-2270, FRP. Dis. Ct. (1979).

Losen, D. J., & Orfield, G. (2002). *Racial inequality in special education.* Cambridge, MA: Harvard Education Press.

Maslow, A. (1954). *Motivation and personality.* New York: Harper.

Mastropieri, M. A., & Scruggs, T. E. (2007). *The inclusive classroom: Strategies for effective instruction* (3rd ed.). Upper Saddle River, NJ: Pearson Education.

Mercer, J. (1973). *Labeling the mentally retarded.* Los Angeles: University of California Press.

Meyer, P. A., Privetz, T., Dignam, T. A., Homa, D. M., Schoonover, J., & Brody, D. (2003). Surveillance for elevated blood lead levels among children—United States, 1997–2001. *Morbidity and Mortality Weekly Report,* September 12, 2003/52 (SS10), 1–21. Atlanta, GA: Centers for Disease Control and Prevention.

Mills v. Board of Education, 348 F. Supp. 866 (D.D.C 1972).

Murdick, N., Gartin, B., & Crabtree, T. (2002). *Special education law.* Upper Saddle River, NJ: Merrill/Prentice Hall.

National Center for Education Statistics. (2005). *Digest of Education Statistics, 2005,* www.nces.ed.gov/programs/digest/d05/tables/dt05_053.asp

Nirje, B. (1985). The basis and logic of the normalization principle. *Australia and New Zealand Journal of Developmental Disabilities, 11,* 65–68.

Patton, J. M. (1998). The disproportionate representation of African Americans in special education: Looking behind the curtain for understanding and solutions. *The Journal of Special Education, 32*(1), 25–31.

Pennsylvania Association for Retarded Citizens v. Commonwealth of Pennsylvania, 343 F. Supp. 279 (E.D. Pa. 1972).

Plessy v. Ferguson, 163 U.S. 537 (1896). U.S. Supreme Court, caselaw.1p.findlaw.com/scripts/printer_friendly.pl?page=us/163/537.html

President's Committee on Mental Retardation. (1969). *The six-hour retarded child.* Washington, DC: U.S. Department of Health, Education and Welfare.

Rehabilitation Act of 1973, Section 504, 29 U.S.C. 794.

Tiegerman-Farber, E., & Radziewicz, C. (1998). *Collaborative decision making: The pathway to inclusion.* Upper Saddle River, NJ: Merrill/Prentice Hall.

Turnbull, R., Turnbull, A., & Wehmeyer, M. L. (2007). *Exceptional lives* (5th ed.). Upper Saddle River, NJ: Pearson Education.

U.S. Department of Education. (2004). *2004 civil rights data collection: Projected values for the nation.* Washington, DC: vistademo.beyond2020.com/ocr2004rv30/xls/nation-projection.xls

Weishaar, M. K. (2007). *Case studies in special education law.* Upper Saddle River, NJ: Pearson Education.

Wolfensberger, W. (1972). *Normalization: The principle of normalization in human services.* Toronto: National Institute on Mental Retardation.

Wolfensberger, W. (1983). Social role valorization: Proposed new form for the principle of normalization. *Mental Retardation, 21*(6), 234–239.

Wolfensberger, W. (2000). A brief overview of social role valorization. *Mental Retardation, 38*(2), 105–123.

Yell, M. L. (2006). *The law and special education.* Upper Saddle River, NJ: Merrill/Prentice Hall.

Ysseldyke, J. E., Thurlow, M., Graden, J., Wesson, C., Algozzine, B., & Deno, S. (1983). Generalizations from five years of research on assessment and decision-making: The University of Minnesota Institute. *Exceptional Education Quarterly, 4,* 75–93.

Chapter 6

LANGUAGE

To devalue his [her] language or to presume Standard English is a better system is to devalue the child and his [her] culture and to reveal a naiveté concerning language.

JOAN BARATZ, 1968

Theresa Roberts, a kindergarten teacher at Kaahumanu Elementary School in Honolulu, had just finished welcoming her new kindergarten class and introducing herself. As she wrote her name and the school's on the chalkboard, she felt a slight tug on the back of her skirt and heard a faint voice just above a whisper say, "Teacha, I like go pee." Turning around, she saw the pleading face of Nohea Kealoha. "What did you say?" Ms. Roberts said disgustedly. In a slightly louder voice, Nohea repeated herself, "I like go pee." With classmates beginning to giggle, Ms. Roberts exclaimed, "You will go nowhere, young lady, until you ask me in proper English. Now say it properly." "I no can," pleaded Nohea. "Then you can just stand there until you do." With the students still giggling and Nohea standing as ordered, Ms. Roberts proceeded with her lesson.

A few minutes later, the occasional giggle exploded in a chorus of laughter. As Ms. Roberts turned to Nohea, the child was sobbing as she stood in the middle of a large puddle of urine on the classroom floor.

Reflections

1. Do teachers have the right to expect and demand Standard English from their students?
2. How important is it for students to be able to speak Standard English?
3. If a student is able to communicate well enough in his or her nonstandard English for others to understand, why should educators be concerned about nonstandard English usage?

Language and Culture

The above incident took place in a school in Hawaii many years ago. Nohea (not her real name) described the incident as one of the most painful and humiliating in her life. When she entered school, she was unable to speak **Standard English** (language considered proper in a community); she could speak only pidgin English (a Creole of English with words and phrases from Hawaiian, Chinese, Japanese, etc.). The teacher knew precisely what the child was trying to say. The teacher's insensitivity, however, resulted in lasting emotional scars on a child, and now as an adult. This type of insensitivity, unfortunately, is not an isolated incident. Individuals in southeastern New Mexico have described similar incidents involving non-English-speaking Latino students entering school for the first time.

Language is a system of vocal sounds and/or nonverbal systems by which group members communicate with one another. It is a critical tool in the development of an individual's identity, self-awareness, and intellectual and psychological growth (Jay, 2003). It makes our behavior human. It can incite anger, elicit love, inspire bravery, and arouse fear. It binds groups of people together. Language and dialect serve as a focal point for cultural identity. People who share the same language or dialect often share the same feelings, beliefs, and behaviors. It provides a common bond for individuals with the same linguistic and same common heritage.

Meyerhoff (2006) suggests that language can play a key role in providing a national sense of identity. It may also be the means by which one group of people stereotypes another. Language and accents can usually be altered, whereas racial and physical appearance generally cannot. Through changing the style of one's language or even the language itself, individuals can shape other's impression of them (Dicker, 2003).

Most students enter school speaking Standard English. Some students, however, come to school barely speaking English. Some are bilingual, some speak a **nonstandard dialect** (the same language but a different dialect than that which is considered standard, e.g., Black English). A few students with hearing impairments may use sign language to communicate. As the scene changes from school to school, the languages and **dialects** (variations of a language usually determined by region or social class) spoken also change. The scene, however, is indicative of the multilingual nature of the United States, a result of its multi-cultural heritage. Because some students speak one or more languages, as well as dialects of these languages, they are part of another cultural group. Of course, not all African American children speak **Black English** (a **vernacular** or dialect of the majority of Black Americans), nor do all Latinos speak Spanish. Within most cultures, members will vary greatly in language or dialect usage.

Eurocentrism and Eurocentric curricula place Europeans and European Americans as the focus of the world with respect to culture, history, economics, values, lifestyles, worldviews, and so forth (Nieto, 2004; Smith, 2007). Because U.S. society has such strong Eurocentric roots, European languages and accents may be given higher status than those from non-European countries. French and German languages may be viewed as more academic, more sophisticated, and more prestigious in some segments of society. Children from these linguistic backgrounds may be viewed with greater esteem than immigrant children from Third World countries. Society and educators may stigmatize bilingual students or those from limited English backgrounds if they are from backgrounds of poverty. They may perceive them to be low status and educationally at risk. Too often some students from immigrant and language minority backgrounds have been discouraged by their teachers from seeking a college education.

Rather than value and promote the use of two or more languages, some educators expect students to replace their native languages with English. Unfortunately, in doing so, some students lose the home language in the process. Movements to establish English-only policies and practices may further devalue the immigrant student's home language.

Individuals who have limited English proficiency frequently suffer institutional discrimination as a result of the limited acceptance of languages other than English. Adger, Wolfram, and Christian (2007) assert that students in this group are frequently at great risk for school failure, despite the fact that they may not necessarily be categorized as disadvantaged. Garcia (1999) suggests that there may be adverse effects on students' cognitive development if their culture and native language are ignored or denigrated.

Language as a Socializing Agent

Language is much more than just a means of communication. It is used to socialize children into their linguistic and cultural communities, developing patterns that distinguish one community from another. Thus, the interaction of language and culture is complex but central to the socialization of children into acceptable cultural patterns. Although there are many theories regarding the development of language, exactly how a language is learned is not completely understood. Almost all children have the ability to learn one or more native languages. In part through imitating older persons, children gradually learn. They learn to select almost instinctively the right word, the right response, and the right gesture to fit the situation. By age 5, children have learned the syntax of their native language, and they know that words in different arrangements mean different things. This suggests that within their own communities, children develop impressive language skills, although these skills may vary greatly from school requirements (Adger, Wolfram, & Christian, 2007). At an early age, children acquire the delicate muscle controls necessary for pronouncing the words of the native language or for signing naturally if the child is deaf. As the child grows older, it becomes increasingly more difficult to make the vocal muscles behave in new, unaccustomed ways necessary to master a foreign language. All this tends to inhibit people from learning new languages and encourages them to maintain the one into which they were born.

Native speakers of a language unconsciously know and obey the rules and customs of their language community. Society and language interact constantly. A wrong choice in word selection may come across as rude, crude, or ignorant. Individuals who are learning a new language or who are unfamiliar with **colloquialisms,** the informal or conversational speech in a community, may make wrong choices or even be surprised at the use of certain words when such use is incongruent with their perceptions of what is proper. For instance, an Australian student in a southwestern U.S. university was shocked when a woman in his class responded to his query of what she had been doing during the summer: "Oh, just piddling around." Her response was meant to convey the message that she had been passing her time in idle activities. From his frame of reference, however, the Australian student understood her to say that she had been urinating. It is important for classroom teachers to recognize that students who are new to a language may not always be able to make appropriate word selections or to comprehend the meaning of particular dialects or colloquialisms. Although the United States is primarily an English-speaking country, many other languages are spoken here. Spanish, Chinese, French, German, Tagalog, Vietnamese, and Italian are the most commonly used languages other than English (U.S. Census Bureau, 2003).

In the 1930s, Fiorello La Guardia was the mayor of New York City. La Guardia, of Jewish and Italian ancestry, was fluent in Yiddish, Italian, German, and French as well as the New York dialect of English (NYC Mayors, 2004). La Guardia was known to vary not only the language, but his speech styles with each ethnic group. For example, when speaking to Italian audiences, he used broad, sweeping gestures, characteristic of the people of southern Italy. When speaking to Jewish audiences, he used the forearm chop identified with many of the Eastern European Jews. The example of La Guardia suggests not only that different ethnic groups have different communication styles but also that individuals adjust their communication style, whenever possible, to suit the needs of the intended audience.

Language Diversity

Among English-speaking individuals are numerous dialects—from the southern drawl to the Appalachian white dialect, to the Brooklyn dialect of New York. Each is distinctive, and each is an effective means of communication for those who share its linguistic style. The U.S. Census Bureau (2003) estimated that there were approximately 47 million non-English-speaking individuals living in the country in 2000. This figure does not include the millions of English-speaking individuals whose dialects are sometimes labeled as nonstandard. The U.S. Census Bureau (2003) also identified 329 languages spoken in the United States in 2000.

The advantage to being bilingual or multilingual is often overlooked because of our ethnocentrism, or belief in the superiority of our own ethnicity or culture. In many other nations, children are expected to become fluent in two or more languages and numerous dialects, enabling them to communicate with other groups and to appreciate language diversity.

The United States has become increasingly diverse linguistically, as evidenced by the various business signs we see in our communities.

Robert Brenner/PhotoEdit Inc.

Pause to Reflect 6.1

In many countries in Europe, Asia, and in other parts of the world, students are required to learn other languages other than the official language of their country. In the United States, except for our foreign-born students or those whose parents have immigrated from other countries, few of our students learn other languages.

• Why do you think bilingualism and multilingualism do not receive the same support in the United States?

• Are there advantages to being fluent in more than one language in the United States? If yes, what are they? Are there any disadvantages? If yes, what are they?

Go to the *Homework and Exercises* section in Chapter 6 of MyEducationLab and select *Pause to Reflect 6.1* to answer these questions.

The Nature of Language

There is no such thing as a good language or a bad language from a linguistic point of view. All languages have developed to express the needs of their users. In that sense, all languages are equal. It is true that languages do not all have the same amounts of grammar, phonology, or semantic structure. It is also true that society places different levels of social status on the different language groups. These judgments are based not on linguistic acceptability, but on social grounds (Adger, Wolfram, & Christian, 2007; Owens, 2005). All languages meet the social and psychological needs of their speakers and, as such, are arguably equal.

Cultural Influences

Language usage is culturally determined. In addition to influencing the order of words to form phrases, language influences thinking patterns. "Time" is described differently from culture to culture. Western societies view time as something that can be saved, lost, or wasted; punctuality is highly valued. In other societies, time assumes different values and is reflected in the language of the group. The language of the Lakota Sioux American Indians, for example, has no words to convey "late" or "waiting" (Samovar, Porter, & McDaniel, 2006).

Individuals from the southern United States may be accustomed to exchanging pleasantries and what they may consider "small talk," prior to substantive or business conversation. To do otherwise, might be considered rude by some individuals. Some Asians tend to be circular in their speaking patterns. They may not speak directly to the point, but provide broad background information on what they are trying to convey. One reason for this manner of speaking is the feeling that, for one to understand and appreciate the point to be made, a foundation or background must be fully laid out. In this manner, the point of the discussion is clearly in proper context. For others who are more accustomed to getting directly to the issue at hand, the point could be lost in the circular presentation of the concept.

For effective communication to take place, it is important that there are enough cultural similarities between the sender and the receiver for the latter to decode the message adequately. Even when one is familiar with a word or phrase, comprehension of the intended meaning may not be possible unless there is similarity in cultural backgrounds.

In certain cultural groups, words and phrases may assume a different meaning. "Bad" among some adolescent groups takes on an opposite meaning and may denote the "best." **Argot** is a more or less secretive vocabulary of a co-culture group. *"Turning a trick,"* is an example of argot used by a prostitute to indicate that he or she has or had a customer. **Co-cultures** are groups of people who exist and function apart from the dominant culture. Users of argot include prisoners, homosexuals, gang members, and prostitutes (Samovar, Porter, & McDaniel, 2006).

Language is very much cultural. It, together with dialects, is usually related to one's ethnic, geographic, gender, or class origins. Speakers from a particular background often downgrade the linguistic styles of others. For example, easterners may be critical of the speech of southerners, citing the use of slow, extended vowels and the expression "y' all." Southerners, on the other hand, may be critical of the speech and language patterns of some individuals from areas in New York, who seem to some to speak through their noses and to use such phrases as "youse guys." An Eastern dialect of English is appropriate in the East, the southern dialect appropriate in the South, and Black English, or **Ebonics,** the dialect of the majority of Black Americans, is appropriate in many African American communities.

Language systems are dynamic like most other cultural groups. They change constantly as society changes. Language change is inevitable and rarely predictable. For example, an elderly third-generation Japanese American born and raised in Maryland learned Japanese from both his grandparents and parents. On his first trip to Japan he spoke to the locals in what he considered his fluent Japanese. While he had no difficulty communicating, he was surprised that they were amused at his speech, which they thought archaic and representative of the late 1800s. The Japanese he had learned from his family was indeed the Japanese language of more than a hundred years earlier. In some areas, language

For more information on identity with cultural groups, see Chapter 1.

changes are so gradual that they go unnoticed. In other circumstances, changes are more easily noted. Expressions and words tend to be identified with a particular period. Sometimes the language is related to particular cultures for certain periods. For example, slang words and phrases

Pause to Reflect 6.2

Today, so many of our students are immigrants from countries other than the United States. As families become increasingly mobile, students move from one region of the country to another and bring with them unique speech patterns.

- Sit down with a group of your peers.
- Does anyone have a noticeable accent?
- How would you characterize it?
- Have you ever judged others on the basis of a dialect or an accent? If yes, when and how? Where was the person from?
- What kind of dialect do the people of your hometown have?

Go to the *Homework and Exercises* section in Chapter 6 of MyEducationLab and select *Pause to Reflect 6.2* to answer these questions.

such as *"24/7" "airhead,"* and *"iffy"* may be a part of our language for a time, only to be replaced by other expressions.

Language Differences

Literally thousands of languages are known in the world today. Most reference books suggest 4,000 to 5,000, but estimates are as high as 10,000 languages (Crystal, 1997). Vyacheslav Ivanov of the University of California, Los Angeles, indicates that there are at least 324 identified languages in Los Angeles County. In addition, many of these languages have different dialects (for example, Chinese Mandarin, Cantonese, Taiwanese, etc.). Professor Ivanov estimates that publications are locally produced in about 180 languages. There are 92 languages that have been specifically identified among students in the Los Angeles Unified School District (*Los Angeles Almanac,* 2004).

Social variables also contribute to language differences. Both class and ethnicity reflect differences in language. The greater the social distance between groups, the greater the tendency toward language differences. Upwardly mobile individuals often adopt the language patterns of the socially dominant group because it may, at times, facilitate social acceptance.

Bilingualism

Language diversity in the United States has been maintained primarily because of continuing immigration from non-English-speaking countries. In its relatively short history, the United States has probably been host to more linguistically diverse individuals than any other country. As new immigrants enter the country, they bring with them their own culture, values, and languages. As their children and grandchildren are born in this country, these immigrants witness with ambivalence, the loss of their home language in favor of English.

One aspect of **bilingualism,** the ability to speak two languages, in the United States is its extreme instability, for it is often a transitional stage toward **monolingualism** (ability to speak only one language) in English. As defined earlier, bilingualism is the ability to use two languages, and many children who are bilingual in their homes eventually lose the ability to utilize the home language in favor of the dominant language. In this, they become monolingual, with the ability to function in just one language. Schools have assisted in this process. Prior to World War I, native languages were used in many schools where a large number of ethnic group members were trying to preserve their language. In this country, the maintenance and use of native languages other than English now depend on the efforts of members of the language group through churches and other community activities. Now, our bilingual education programs are primarily designed to move students quickly into English-only instruction. However, a review of the research suggests that bilingual education in the United States is far more effective than a strictly monolingual approach (Corson, 1999).

Early language policies throughout this country were extremely narrow in focus, and failed to take into account the social-cultural problems inherent in language and learning (Corson, 1999). The acquisition of a second language is important when it serves one's own social and economic needs. Without English language skills, immigrants are often relegated to the most menial, lowest paying, and sometimes dangerous jobs in society.

During the civil rights movement of the 1960s, language-minority groups, especially Latinos, began to celebrate their native language traditions. Other ethnic groups decried the loss of their native languages over a few generations and blamed the school's Americanization process for the loss. Crawford (2004) suggests that while 175 indigenous languages are spoken in the United States, by 2050 only 20 of those languages will still be in use if current trends persist.

People hold different opinions about the degree of fluency required to be considered bilingual. Whereas some maintain that a bilingual individual must have native-like fluency in both languages, others suggest that measured competency in two languages constitutes bilingualism (Baca & Cervantes, 2004). Baca and Cervantes (2004) suggest that there are two types of bilingualism: **subtractive bilingualism** and **additive bilingualism.** Subtractive bilingualism occurs when a second language replaces the first. Additive bilingualism is the development of a second language without detriment to the first. The latter has the more positive effect on academic achievement, as the learner is able to acquire a high level of proficiency in both languages.

Accents

An **accent** generally refers to how an individual pronounces words. Because some monolingual Japanese speakers do not have the sound of an "*l*" in their language, many tend to pronounce English words that begin with the letter "*l*" as if they began with the letter "*r.*" Thus, the word *light* may be pronounced as if it were *right,* and *long* as if it were *wrong*. Note that an accent differs from the standard language only in pronunciation. A dialect, however, may contain changes both in pronunciation and in grammatical patterns of the language system. Teachers should be aware that persons who speak with an accent often speak Standard English but, at this level of their linguistic development, are unable to speak without an accent.

Dialects

In the United States, English is the primary language. Numerous English dialects are used throughout the country, however. There is no agreement on the number of dialects of English spoken in the United States. There are at least 11 regional dialects: Eastern New

VIDEO INSIGHTS
American Spoken Here

In this information age where everyone is a phone call, an e-mail, or a flight away from another, it would seem logical that the different accents and dialects around the country might merge into one, but research from the University of Pennsylvania tells a different story. In this video segment you will see how American accents are becoming more distinct from one another.

1. Are you able to detect different accents among your classmates when they speak?
2. Can you detect different dialects among your classmates?
3. Do some appear to be smarter or more sophisticated because of their accent or dialect than others?
4. When you hear someone with an English (as in British) accent do they seem more sophisticated than another person with a Spanish accent?
5. What kind of accent or dialect do you have?

Go to the Video Insights DVD and watch the video segment *American Spoken Here*. Then, go to the *Homework and Exercises* section in Chapter 6 of MyEducationLab and select *Video Insights: American Spoken Here* to answer these questions.

England, New York City, Western Pennsylvania, Middle Atlantic, Appalachian, Southern, Central, Midland, North Central, Southwest, and Northwest (Owens, 2005). While southern speech has frequently been denigrated in other parts of the country, the South is now the largest dialect area, with more Americans speaking "Southern" than any other regional dialect in the United States (MacNeil & Cran, 2005). Powerful southern politicians (e.g., John Edwards, Trent Lott) and popular television personalities (e.g., Paula Deen) increase the exposure and acceptance of southern speech or drawl.

Dialects are language rule systems used by identifiable groups that vary in some manner from a language standard considered ideal. Each dialect shares a common set of grammatical rules with the standard language and should be considered structurally equal (Adger, Wolfram, & Christian, 2007). Theoretically, dialects of a language are mutually intelligible to all speakers of the language; however, some dialects enjoy greater social acceptance and prestige. No dialect is better than any other, nor should a dialect be characterized as substandard, deviant, or inferior (Owens, 2005).

Certain languages are sometimes improperly referred to as dialects. Examples are the labeling of African languages as African dialects or the languages of the American Indians as Indian dialects. This improper practice would be synonymous with labeling French and German as dialects spoken in the different regions or countries in Europe.

Regional Dialects. Dialects differ from one another in a variety of ways. Differences in vowels are a primary means of distinguishing regional differences, whereas consonant differences tend to distinguish social dialects. Regional and social dialects cannot be divorced from one another, however, because an individual's dialect may be a blend of both. In northern dialects, for example, the *i* in words such as *time, pie,* and *side* is pronounced with a long-*i* sound that Wolfram and Christian (1989) describe as a rapid production of two vowel sounds, one sounding more like *ah* and the other like *ee.* The second sound glides off the first so that *time* becomes *taem, pie* becomes *pae,* and *side* becomes *saed.* southern and southern-related dialects may eliminate the gliding *e,* resulting in *tam* for *time, pa* for *pie,* and *sad* for *side.*

Social Dialects. In social dialects, consonants tend to distinguish one dialect from another. Common examples of consonant pronunciation differences are in the "*th*" sound and in the consonants "*r*" and "*l.*" In words such as *these, them,* and *those,* the beginning "*th*" sound may be replaced with a "*d,*" resulting in *dese, dem,* and *dose.* In words such as *think, thank,* and *throw,* the "*th*" may be replaced with a "*t,*" resulting in *tink, tank,* and *trow.* Adger, Wolfram, and Christian (2007) suggest that middle-class groups may substitute the "*d*" for "*th*" to some extent in casual speech, whereas working-class groups make the substitution more often.

In some groups, particularly the African American working class, the "*th*" in the middle or end of the word is not spoken. The "*th*" in author or tooth may be replaced with an "*f,*" as in *aufor* and *toof.* In words such as *smooth,* a "*v*" may be substituted for the "*th,*" resulting in *smoov.* In regional and socially related dialects, "*r*" and "*l*" may be lost, as in *ca* for *car* and *sef* for *self.*

Grammatical Differences. Among dialects, differences in various aspects of grammatical usage can also be found. Adger, Wolfram, and Christian (2007) suggest that nonstandard grammar tends to carry with it a greater social stigma than nonstandard pronunciation.

A common example of grammatical differences in dialect is in the absence of suffixes from verbs where they are usually present in standard dialects. For example, the *-ed* suffix to denote past tense is sometimes omitted, as in, "Yesterday we play a long time." Other examples of grammatical differences are the omission of the *s* used in the present tense to denote agreement with certain subjects. "She have a car" may be used instead of "She has a car." The omission of the suffix has been observed in certain Native Indian communities, as well as among members of the African American working class. In the dialect of some African American working-class groups, the omission of the *s* in the plural form of certain words and phrases, as in "two boy" rather than "two boys," has been observed. *Two* is plural, and an *s* to show possession after boy is viewed as redundant. Also often omitted in these dialect groups is the possessive *'s,* as in "my friend car" instead of "my friend's car."

Other Differences. Variations in language patterns among groups are significant when compared by age, socioeconomic status, gender, ethnic group, and geographic region (Adger, Wolfram, and Christian, 2007). For example, individuals in the 40- to 60-year-old age group tend to use language patterns different from those of teenage groups. Teenagers tend to adopt certain language patterns that are characteristic of their age group. Slang words, particular pronunciation of some words, and certain grammatical contractions are often related to the teenage and younger groups.

Social factors play a role in the choice of language patterns. The more formal the situations are, the greater the likelihood to use more formal speech patterns. The selection of appropriate speech patterns appears to come naturally and spontaneously. Individuals are usually able to "read their environment" and to select, from their large repertoire, the language or speech pattern that is appropriate for the situation.

Adger, Wolfram, and Christian (2007) also indicate that although the evidence is not conclusive, the range between high and low pitch used in African American communities is greater than that found in white communities. Such differences would, of course, be the result of learned behavior. African American males may tend to speak with raspiness in their voices. American women, it has been suggested, may typically have a greater pitch distribution over a sentence than do men.

Other differences in dialects exist as well. Because educators are likely to find dialect differences in the classroom, additional reading in this area may be appropriate. The "Suggested Readings" section at the end of this chapter includes some helpful resources.

Bidialecticism

Certain situations, both social and professional, may dictate adjustments in dialect. Some individuals may have the ability to speak in two or more dialects, making them **bidialectal.** In possessing the skills to speak in more than one dialect, an individual may have some distinct advantages and may be able to function and gain acceptance in more cultural contexts. For example, a large-city executive with a rural farm background may quickly abandon his Armani suit and put on his jeans and boots when visiting his parents' home. When speaking with the hometown folks, he may put aside the Standard English necessary in his business dealings and return to the hometown dialect, which validates him as the local town person they have always known.

Likewise, a school psychologist in Hawaii who speaks Standard English both at home and at work may continue to speak Standard English in her conference with working-class parents at the school. However, there may be an inflection or local variation of speech, which she may use to develop rapport and credibility with the parents. At times, this may happen spontaneously without deliberate planning or thought. This may convey to the parents that although she may be highly educated, and may be dressed professionally, she is still a local Island person and understands their needs and that of their child.

Children tend to learn adaptive behaviors rapidly, a fact that is often demonstrated in the school. Children who fear peer rejection as a result of speaking Standard English may choose to use their dialect even at the expense of criticism by the teacher. Others may choose to speak with the best Standard English they possess in dealing with the teacher but use the dialect or language of the group when outside the classroom.

Educators must be aware of children's need for peer acceptance, and balance this need with realistic educational expectations. Pressuring a child to speak Standard English at all times and punishing him or her for any use of dialects may be detrimental to the overall well-being of the child.

Perspectives on Standard English

With the wide variations of dialects, there are actually several dialects of Standard American English (Adger, Wolfram, & Christian, 2007). Although Standard English is often referred to in the literature, no single dialect can be identified as such. In reality, however, the speech of a certain group of people in each community tends to be identified as standard. Norms vary with communities, and there are actually two norms: informal standard and formal standard. The language considered proper in a community is the **informal standard.** Its norms tend to vary from community to community. **Formal standard** is the acceptable written language that is typically found in grammar books. Few individuals speak formal Standard English.

Because no particular dialect is inherently and universally standard, the determination of what is and what is not standard is usually made by people or groups of people in positions of power and status to make such a judgment. Teachers and employers are among those in such a position. These are the individuals who decide what is and what is not acceptable in the school and in the workplace. Thus, people seeking success in school and in the job market often tend to use the standard language as identified and used by individuals in positions of power. Generally speaking, Standard American English is a composite of the language spoken by the educated professional middle class.

Perspectives on Black English

Black English, sometimes referred to as Vernacular Black English, **African American English,** African American Vernacular English (AAVE), or Ebonics, is one of the best-known dialects spoken in the United States. It becomes controversial when schools consider using it for instruction. Its use is widespread and it is a form of communication for the majority of African Americans. It is a linguistic system used primarily by working-class African Americans within their speech community (Adger, Wolfram, & Christian, 2007; Owens, 2005).

Although there has been much debate regarding its nature and history, Black English is considered by most linguists and African Americans to be a legitimate system of communication. It is a systematic language rule system of its own and not a substandard, deviant, or improper form of English. Although differences are found between Black English and Standard English, they both operate with the same type of structural rules as any other type of language or dialect. Adger, Wolfram, and Christian (2007) assert that when comparing the linguistic characteristics of Black English and Standard English, we find far more common language features than distinctive ones. They dispute the theory by some linguists that Black English is increasingly evolving in a divergent path from other vernacular English dialects. In fact, there is considerable overlap among Black English, southern English, and southern white nonstandard English. Much of the distinctiveness of the dialect is in its intonational patterns, speaking rate, and distinctive lexicons (Owens, 2005). Jay (2003) contends that some individuals have used these differences to reinforce prejudice toward African Americans and their dialects.

Teacher bias against Black English is common among majority-group educators and among some African American educators as well. Although Black English is an ethnically related dialect, it is also a dialect related to social class. Dialects related to lower social classes, such as Appalachian English and Black English, are typically stigmatized in our multidialectal society. Unfortunately, many people attach relative values to certain dialects and to the speakers of those dialects. Assumptions are made regarding the intelligence, ability, and moral character of the speakers, and this can have a significant negative impact (Adger, Wolfram, & Christian, 2007). As such, the use of these dialects without the ability to speak Standard American English leaves the speaker with a distinct social, educational, and sometimes occupational disadvantage. The refusal to acknowledge Black English as a legitimate form of communication could be considered as another example of Eurocentric behavior. Insofar as teachers endorse this rejection, they are sending a message to many of their African American students that the dialect of their parents, grandparents, and significant others in their lives is substandard and unacceptable. The rejection of Black English as a legitimate form of communication has been detrimental to the academic development and achievement of students (Hecht, Jackson, & Ribeau, 2003).

The issue of requiring a standard American English dialect in the schools is both sensitive and controversial. Because of the close relationship between ethnic minority groups and dialects that are often considered nonstandard, this issue also has civil rights implications.

To require that Standard English be spoken in the schools is considered discriminatory by some who think that such a requirement places an additional educational burden on the

CRITICAL INCIDENTS IN TEACHING

Attitudes Toward Black English

Israel Martinez is the principal of Jackie Robinson Middle School. An appointment was made for him with Ms. Ruby Norton, the mother of a sixth grader. She declined to give Martinez's secretary any information on why she was coming. Martinez exchanges the customary greeting and then asks Ms. Norton what he can do for her. At this point, she calmly tells Mr. Martinez that his teachers need to stop being racist and to start respecting the culture of African American students.

Mr. Martinez is feeling defensive and tries to maintain his composure as he inquires about the nature of the complaint. "This white teacher of Trayson's says to my son to stop talking this Black English stuff because it is bad English and he won't allow it in his classroom. He says it's a low-class dialect, and if Trayson keeps talking like that, he ain't never going to amount to nothing, will never get into college, and won't never get a good job. That's just plain racist. That's an attack against all black folk. His granddaddy and grandmother talk that way. All my kinfolk talk that way. I talk that way. You mean to tell me that this school thinks we're all low-class trash? Is that what your teachers think of black folk?"

Questions for Classroom Discussion

1. How should Mr. Martinez respond to Ms. Norton?
2. Should he arrange a meeting between Ms. Norton and Aaron Goodman, Trayson's teacher?
3. What should be the school's position on Ebonics, or Vernacular Black English?
4. Is this a school district or individual school issue?
5. Is Mr. Goodman wrong to tell Trayson that his speech is a low-class dialect?
6. Is Mr. Goodman wrong to tell Trayson that if he speaks only Black English it will have negative educational and vocational consequences?

Building Teaching Skills

Go to the *Building Teaching Skills* section in Chapter 6 of MyEducationLab and select *Critical Incidents in Teaching: Attitudes Towards Black English* to complete this exercise.

nonstandard-English-speaking students. The insistence on Standard English could hinder the acquisition of other educational skills, making it difficult for these students to succeed.

Others argue that the school has the responsibility to teach each student Standard English to better cope with the demands of society. There is little doubt that the inability to speak Standard English can be a decided disadvantage to an individual in certain situations, such as seeking employment. MacNeil and Cran (2005) suggest that while Black English has played an important role in popular culture, it is also a barrier, which may limit prospects for advancement in education, employment, and housing.

Dialect differences in the school may cause problems beyond the interference with the acquisition of skills. A second problem tends to be subtler and involves the attitude of teachers and other school personnel toward students with nonstandard dialects. Too often, educators and other individuals make erroneous assumptions about nonstandard dialects, believing at times that the inability to speak a standard dialect reflects lower intelligence. Adger, Wolfram, and Christian (2007) suggest that unlike prejudice based on gender or ethnicity, which may often result in litigation and positive change, language prejudices are rarely challenged and, therefore, are much less likely to change.

Many individuals have distinct preconceived notions about nonstandard-English-speaking individuals. If teachers and other school personnel react in this manner to students, the consequences could be serious. Students may be treated as if they are less intelligent than they are, and they may respond in a self-fulfilling prophecy in which they function at a level lower than they are capable of reaching. In cases where children are tracked in schools, they may be placed in groups below their actual ability level. This problem surfaces in the form of disproportionately low numbers of African American and Latino children being placed in classes for the gifted and talented (U.S. Department of Education, 2004). School administrators cite the inability to appropriately identify these gifted and talented ethnic minority children as one of their biggest challenges. Teachers who have negative attitudes toward children with nonstandard dialects may be less prone to recognize potential giftedness and may be less inclined to refer these children for possible assessment and placement.

Teacher expectations and tracking are discussed in more detail in Chapter 3.

Educators have several alternatives for handling dialect in the educational setting. The first is to accommodate all dialects on the basis that they are all equal. The second is to insist that only a standard dialect be allowed in the schools. This second alternative would allow for the position that functional ability in such a dialect is necessary for success in personal, as well as vocational, pursuits. The third alternative is a position between the two extremes, and it is the alternative most often followed. Native dialects are accepted for certain uses, but Standard English is encouraged and insisted on in other circumstances. Students in such a school setting may be required to read and write in Standard English because this is the primary written language they will encounter in this country. They would not be required to eliminate their natural dialect in speaking. Such a compromise allows students to use two or more dialects in the school. It tends to acknowledge the legitimacy of all dialects while recognizing the social and vocational implications of being able to function in Standard English.

The issue that seems to be at stake with some supporters of the right to use nonstandard dialects is the recognition of the legitimacy of the particular dialect. Few, if any, will

Pause to Reflect 6.3

Some activists have suggested that the languages of instruction should be in the dialect of students' cultures. Others argue that Standard English should be the only acceptable language within the classroom.

- What are the advantages and disadvantages of each approach?
- Do you think teachers should at least be familiar with the dialects used by students in the classroom? Why or why not?
- How do you plan to respond to different dialects in your classroom?

Go to the *Homework and Exercises* section in Chapter 6 of MyEducationLab and select *Pause to Reflect 6.3* to answer these questions.

deny the social and vocational implications of dialects. Some parents may prefer to develop, or have their children develop, a standard dialect. However, the arrogant posture of some school officials in recognizing standard dialects as the only legitimate form of communication is offensive to many and may preclude rational solutions to this sensitive issue.

Sign Language

Some languages do not have a written system. Individuals who are deaf are not able to hear the sounds that make up oral languages and have developed their own language for communication. **American Sign Language (ASL)** is a natural language that has been developed and used by persons who are deaf. Just in the past 30 years, linguists have come to recognize ASL as a language with complex grammar and well-regulated syntax. A growing number of colleges and universities will accept fluency in ASL to meet a second-language requirement. The majority of adults who are deaf in Canada and the United States use ASL. Individuals who are deaf use it to communicate with each other. Like oral languages, different sign languages have developed in different countries.

Children who are deaf are able to pick up the syntax and rhythms of signing as spontaneously as hearing children pick up their oral languages. Both children who hear and children who are deaf who are born into deaf families usually learn ASL from birth. Most children who are deaf, however, have hearing parents and do not have the opportunity to learn ASL until they attend a school program for the deaf, where they learn from both their teachers and peers.

ASL is the only sign language recognized as a language in its own right, rather than a variation of spoken English. With its own vocabulary, syntax, and grammatical rules, ASL does not correspond completely to spoken or written English (Heward, 2006; Smith 2007). To communicate with the hearing, those who are deaf often use signed English. It is a system of signing that parallels the English language. Rather than have its own language patterns like ASL, **signed English** is a system that translates the English oral or written word into a sign. Few hearing individuals know ASL because they rarely observe it. When one sees an interpreter on television or at a meeting, it is usually signed English that is being observed.

Sign language is one component of the deaf culture that sets its users apart from the hearing world. Because of the residential school experiences of many individuals who are deaf, a distinct cultural community has developed. As a cultural community, they are highly endogamous, with in-group marriages estimated at between 85% of all marriages involving individuals who are deaf (News-Medical.Net, 2004). Although ASL is the major language of the deaf community, many individuals are bilingual in English and ASL.

Nonverbal Communication

Although most people think of communication as being verbal in nature, nonverbal communication can be just as important in the total communication process. Because it is so clearly interwoven into the overall fabric of verbal communication, nonverbal communication often appears to be inseparable from it.

Nonverbal communication can serve several functions. It conveys messages through one's attitude, personality, manner, or even dress. It augments verbal communication by reinforcing what one says: A smile or a pat on the back reinforces the positive statement made to a student. It contradicts verbal communication: A frown accompanying a positive

There is often as much or more communicated nonverbally as there is verbally.

Richard Hutchings/PhotoEdit Inc.

statement to a student sends a mixed or contradictory message. Nonverbal communication can replace a verbal message: A finger to the lips or a teacher's hand held in the air may communicate "Silence" to a class.

The total meaning of communication includes not only the surface message as stated (content) but also the undercurrent (emotions or feelings associated with that content). The listener should watch for congruence between the verbal message and the message being sent nonverbally.

How we appear to others is a form of nonverbal communication and can, therefore, be considered as a part of our communication or language. Research has supported the contention that definite prejudices are based on physical characteristics. For example, physical attractiveness plays a part in the way we perceive other people. If one has a bias against a particular group, individuals from that group could be perceived as unattractive, and can suffer from social rejection based on the perceptions and bias in the work situation (Hosoda, Stone-Romero, & Coats, 2003; McDonald, 2003; Seifert, 2001).

Cultural differences have profound implications on how individuals interact nonverbally with one another. Some cultural groups are more prone toward physical contact than others. Latinos and Native Hawaiians, for example, tend to be among the contact cultures. Consequently, one can often observe Latinos or Hawaiians greeting each other with a warm embrace. This is true among the men from these groups. As they meet their friends, it is certainly not uncommon to see these men embracing one another. On the other hand, however, it might be surprising to see Asian men embracing one another. Of course, the more acculturated Asian American men are likely to observe behaviors typical in the general society.

The usual conversational distance between Americans is about 20 to 36 inches (Haynes, 2004). A distance much greater than this may make the individuals feel too far apart for normal conversation and a normal voice level. Individuals of other cultural groups, such as Arabs, Latin Americans, and Southern Europeans are accustomed to standing considerably closer when they talk. In contrast with these contact cultures, Asians and Northern Europeans have been identified as noncontact cultures and may maintain a greater distance

Observe and Learn — Lesson in Action

Nonverbal Communication

Go to the *Homework and Exercises* section in Chapter 6 of MyEducationLab and select *Obeserve and Learn: Lession in Action* to view the video "Talking With Your Boby" and answer the accompying questions. Gestures are viewed as culture-specific in this lession. Students explore sign language and various gestures and discuss how they differ in a variety of cultural contexts.

1. What gestures did students share in the video? Did any of them surprise you? If so, which ones?
2. Are there any gestures that you use that you were surprised to find are considered rude in other cultures? What gestures that are acceptable in other cultures do you consider rude? Why do you think there is such a difference?
3. How might your understanding of world gestures affect what you do in your future classroom?

in conversation. Students maintain differential distances in cross-cultural relationships. White Americans tend to maintain a greater distance when conversing with blacks than when conversing among themselves. Women tend to allow a closer conversational space than do men. Straight individuals distance themselves more from conversational partners they perceive to be gay (Samovar, Porter, & McDaniel, 2006).

Educators need to be aware that different cultural groups have different expectations when it involves contact with a teacher. The differences may have implications for educators. Some groups may view a pat on the head of a child to be a supportive gesture. However, some Southeast Asians believe that the individual's spirit resides in the head, and a pat on the head of a child may very well be viewed as offensive by both the parents and child.

Other nonverbal issues may involve the facial expressions or behaviors of the student. American teachers typically expect a child to look at them while they are having a conversation. However, some groups consider it disrespectful for the child to look directly into the eyes of the teacher. Consequently, as a sign of respect, the child may look at the floor while either speaking to the teacher or being spoken to. The teacher, however, may view the behavior in an opposite manner than intended, and demand that the child look her or him in the eye.

Any discussion of nonverbal behavior has inherent dangers. As examples are given, you must realize that these are generalizations and not assume that any given behavior can immediately be interpreted in a certain way. Nonverbal communications are often a prominent part of the context in which verbal messages are sent. Although context never has a specific meaning, communication is always dependent on context.

Second Language Acquisition

With the arrival of new immigrants annually into the United States, the resulting effect is the addition of more language minority students in our schools. Most of these students are able to move from bilingual education programs to English-only instruction. Motivation is usually high. The acquisition of English skills serves both social and economic needs. Without linguistic acculturation, assimilation into mainstream society may be impossible. This, in turn, effectively keeps non-English speakers or **English language learners (ELL),** previously referred to as limited English proficient (LEP), out of many job markets. In the future teachers can anticipate increasing numbers of ELL students whose primary language is other than English.

We should clarify here that different terms are used to identify students from minority language groups. For our purposes, we will primarily use English language learners (ELL). Some writers use English learners (EL). ELL is the term now used in most of the professional literature and is taking the place of limited English proficient (LEP) used in most of the professional literature through the late 1990s. It is still used by the Federal Government today, particularly within the U.S. Office of English Language Acquisition, Language Enhancement, and Academic Achievement for Limited English Proficient Students (OELA). This office, within the U.S. Department of Education, was formerly the Office of Bilingual Education and Minority Language Affairs (OBEMLA). It was renamed with the George W. Bush administration, perhaps indicating a shift in the administration's de-emphasis in bilingual education programs. OELA's National Clearinghouse for English Language Acquisition & Language Instruction Educational Programs (NCELA), formerly the Bilingual Clearinghouse, was also renamed with the Bush administration.

The Role of First Language in Second Language Acquisition

Most children acquire their first language naturally through constant interaction with their parents or significant others. Knowledge of their first language plays an important role in the process of acquiring and learning a second language. Some concepts acquired through their first language (e.g., Spanish) can be transferred to a second language (e.g., English) when a comparable concept in the second language exists. However, English speakers should not think of Spanish, French, Chinese, or any other language as essentially English with Spanish, French, or Chinese words that, if translated, is basically the same language. There are words and concepts in all of these languages for which there is no English equivalent. There may be no exact English translation to convey the exact same meaning. For example, "*heung*" in the Chinese Cantonese dialect is translated into English as *"fragrant."* However, "*heung*" has no exact English translation. The Chinese have a very distinctive meaning, which not only conveys fragrance, but a multisensory experience. When Cantonese speakers say that food that they have placed in their mouths is "*heung,*" it may imply that it tastes, smells, and feels very special.

Corson (1999) suggests that early brain development of young children is shaped by the signs and symbols involved in first language acquisition. The failure of schools to build on a child's first language during these early years may have serious consequences in the learning process. The implications of these observed language behaviors suggest that ELL children should be allowed to develop a firm grasp of basic concepts in their home language prior to instruction of academic concepts in an English-only environment. Garcia (1999) advocates for a new **pedagogy** that is responsive and demonstrates respect for the skills and knowledge students bring to the classroom. Cummins (1996) maintains that we learn "by integrating new input into our existing cognitive structure or schemata" (p. 85). Consequently, a student's prior experience is the foundation for acquiring and interpreting new knowledge. Recent scientific research is challenging the hypotheses that early childhood is the optimum age to reach full proficiency in a second language (Crawford, 2004). In a study of second language acquisition, Hakuta, Bialystok, and Wiley (2003) concluded that in addition to age, socioeconomic factors and amount of formal education were important in predicting how well immigrants mastered English.

Language Proficiency.   Cummins (1996) found that many ELL students failed academically after completing English as a second language (ESL) training and being placed in monolingual English class settings. Many of these students were subsequently referred and placed in special education classes. In carefully studying the language characteristics of these students, Cummins found that in two years these students are able to acquire adequate English communication skills to suggest to their teacher that they were prepared to function in a monolingual English class placement. Cummins also found, however, that the basic language skills, which he labeled **"basic interpersonal communicative skills" (BICS),** are adequate everyday conversational skills, but are inadequate to function in high-level academic situations. Crawford (2004) suggests that a good example of BICS is "playground English," which relies on nonlinguistic cues and context, used to facilitate communication (for example gestures, and other nonverbal cues). BICS, he indicates, is primarily social rather than intellectual. It requires less knowledge of the language, and utilizes simpler syntax, and a more limited vocabulary than is needed in academic settings.

Although two years is adequate for everyday conversational usage, an additional five to seven years of school training is essential to develop the higher levels of proficiency required in highly structured academic situations. Cummins (1984) labeled this higher level of proficiency **"cognitive academic language proficiency" (CALP).** Crawford (2004) suggests that CALP is a level of linguistic proficiency that is required for abstract and analytical thinking and expressions with complex meaning. He further indicates that children need this level of proficiency, for example, in writing a journal entry, which describes what they have learned, or in making a persuasive oral presentation.

Professors, who were themselves ELL students in their earlier years, have shared with the authors their experiences in making professional presentations in foreign countries. For example, a Chinese American professor who was born in China and whose first language was Chinese, can carry on fluent conversations in both Mandarin and Cantonese. However, this professor insists on translators for her presentations in China because she does not consider herself proficient in academic Chinese. Other colleagues from non-English-speaking backgrounds have shared similar experiences. This may have some similarities to BICS-level students who have not yet developed academic-level English competence and who are thrust into English-only academic situations. Unfortunately, these students are not in a position to insist on translators.

Cummins' framework for conceptualizing language proficiency has been widely adopted by many ESL and bilingual special education programs and has profound implications for language minorities. Cummins (2000) suggests that there are two reasons why it takes much longer for ELL students to learn academic language than it does to learn basic conversational language. First, academic language is the language of subject matter (for example, science, math), literature, journals, and other scholarly materials. It is very different from conversational language. As students progress through successive grades, they encounter words that Cummins characterizes as "low frequency" words. These are words with Greek and Latin derivations. In addition, they are exposed to more complex syntax (for example, passive) and abstract expressions that are seldom if ever heard in everyday conversation. Secondly, academic language is what educators develop among native English speakers who are already fluent in conversational English when they enter school. Therefore, the ELL student is learning conversational English while classmates are at a higher level, learning academic English.

In discussing Cummins' theories, Crawford (2004) suggests that the language of instruction is not the most significant variable for ELL students. Cummins believes that sociocultural determinants of school failure for these students are more significant than linguistic factors. Schools must counteract the power relations, which exist in society, removing the racial and linguistic stigmas of being a minority group child. Cummins suggests that power and status relationships between majority and minority groups exert influence on the school performance of these students. He states that the lower the status of a group that is dominated, the lower the academic achievement (Cummins, 1996).

Hakuta, Butler, and Witt (2000) suggest that one of the most commonly asked questions regarding the education of language minority students is how long will they need specialized services such as bilingual education or English as a second language (ESL). Putting together the findings of studies of four different school districts in the San Francisco Bay area and from summary data from Canadian researchers, Hakuta and his associates came to conclusions that supported Cummins' earlier findings. The research findings suggest that oral proficiency takes three to five years to develop, and academic proficiency four to seven years.

Official English (English Only) Controversy

In 1981, U.S. Senator S. I. Hayakawa, a strong and harsh critic of bilingual education and bilingual voting rights, introduced a constitutional amendment to make English the official language of the United States. The measure sought to prohibit federal and state laws, ordinances, regulations, orders, programs, and policies from requiring the use of other languages. Hayakawa's efforts were made not only in support of English but also against bilingualism. Had the amendment been adopted, Hayakawa's proposal would have reversed the efforts that began in the 1960s to accommodate linguistic minorities in this country. The English Language Amendment died without a hearing in the 97th Congress (Crawford, 2003).

In 1983, Hayakawa helped found the organization called "U.S. English" and began lobbying efforts that resulted in a reported 1.8 million-member organization and an annual budget in the millions of dollars (U.S. English, 2004). The movement, also referred to as **"Official English"** or "English Only," supports only the limited use of bilingual education, and has mounted a major effort to lobby the U.S. Congress to pass legislation to make English the official language of the United States. By 2004, English as the official language has been adopted as statutes or state constitutional amendments in 27 states (Crawford, 1992; U.S. English, 2004). The organization favors sheltered English immersion, and it maintains its position that ELL students should be transitioned completely out of bilingual education and into mainstream English usage within a maximum of one or two years.

Official English has become a polarizing issue. For supporters of the English Only movement, English has always been the common language in the United States. Supporters of the English Only movement believe that it is a means to resolve conflict in a nation that is diverse in ethnic, linguistic, and religious groups. They also believe that English is an essential tool of social mobility and economic advancement (Crawford, 1992).

Crawford (2006) maintains that attempts to restrict languages other than English are never only about the language. He suggests that it also represents a negative attitude toward the speakers of other languages.

Classroom Focus

Language is an integral part of life and an integral part of our social system. The diversity and richness of the language systems in this country are a reflection of the richness and diversity of American culture. The ability of U.S. educators to recognize and appreciate the value of different language groups will, to some extent, determine the effectiveness of our educational system.

By the year 2026, it is estimated that there will be approximately 15 million students with limited proficiency in English enrolled in our schools. In California, 70% of the

TABLE 6.1   Elementary and Secondary Enrollment of ELL Students in U. S. 1994–95 to 2004–05

School Year	Total Enrollment	Growth from 1994–95	ELL Enrollment	Growth from 1994–95
1994–1995	47,745,835	0.00%	3,184,696	0.00%
1995–1996	47,582,665	−.34%	3,228,799	1.38%
1996–1997	46,714,980	−2.16%	3,452,073	8.40%
1997–1998	46,023,969	−3.61%	3,470,268	8.97%
1998–1999	46,153,266	−3.34%	3,540,673	11.18%
1999–2000	47,356,089	−.82%	4,416,580	38.68%
2000–2001	47,665,483	−.17%	4,584,947	43.97%
2001–2002	48,296,777	1.15%	4,750,920	49.18%
2002–2003	49,478,583	3.63%	5,044,361	58.39%
2003–2004	49,618,529	3.92%	5,013,539	57.43%
2004–2005	48,982,898	2.59%	5,119,561	60.75%

The Growing Number of Limited English Proficient Students, 1994/95–2004/05, The National Clearinghouse for English Language Acquisition and Language Instruction Educational Programs (NCELA), www.ncela.gwu.edu/

students will be nonwhite and Hispanic, and 50% of those will speak a language other than English when first entering the school system (Garcia, 1999). The U.S. Office of English Language Acquisition, Language Enhancement, and Academic Achievement for Limited English Proficient Students (OELA) reported that in the 2004–2005 school year, there were a total of 5,119,561 English language learners in U.S. schools. That number represents 10.45% of the 48,982,898 students reported by OELA in the general school population that year. This increase in ELL students also represented a growth rate of 60.76% between the 1994–1995 to the 2004–2005 school years. The estimated increase in the number of enrolled ELL students by school year is shown in Table 6.1. The greatest number of ELL students can be found in California, Texas, New York, Florida, Illinois, and New Mexico (National Clearinghouse for English Language Acquisition [NCELA], 2006). The California State Department of Education, for example, reported 1,570,424 ELL students in the 2005–2006 school year (California Department of Education [CDE], 2007). The highest density of ELL students is in Florida and in the western and southwestern U.S. states, where ELL enrollment is greater than 10% of the student population (NCELA, 2006).

All children bring to school the language systems of their cultures. It is the obligation of each educator to ensure the right of each child to learn in the language of the home until the child is able to function well enough in English. This may imply the use of English as a second language (ESL) or bilingual programs for ELL children. Research overwhelmingly demonstrates that encouraging the development of students' native language does not negatively impact the development of academic skills in English (Schechter & Cummins, 2003). Equally important, especially for educators, is the responsibility to understand cultural and linguistic differences and to recognize the value of these differences while working toward enhancing the student's linguistic skills in the dominant language. Although it is important to appreciate and respect a child's native language or dialect, it is also important that the teacher communicate the importance and advantages of being able to speak and understand Standard English in certain educational, vocational, and social situations.

Language and Educational Assessment

Few issues in education are as controversial as the assessment of culturally diverse children. The problem of disproportionate numbers of ethnic minority children in special education classes for children with disabilities has resulted from such assessment (Artiles, Harry, Reschly, & Chinn, 2002). The characteristics of language are directly related to the assessment of linguistically different children. Despite genuine attempts to accommodate the diverse backgrounds of students, many of the educational and intelligence tests used to assess ethnic and linguistic minority children are normed primarily on children from white, middle-class backgrounds. There is an expectation of cultural and linguistic uniformity in the development of assessment tests (Adger, Wolfram, & Christian, 2007). Therefore, such tests are often considered biased against the student who is not proficient in English or who speaks a dialect. Nieto (2002) estimates that approximately 100 million standardized tests are given every year with an average of 2.5 tests per student, per year. It is unlikely that there are any completely unbiased assessment instruments being used to test achievement or intelligence.

Most intelligence tests rely heavily on language. Yet, little attempt may be made to determine a child's level of proficiency in the language or dialect in which a test is administered. For example, a Latino child may be able to perform a task that is called for in an intelligence test, but may not be able to understand the directions given in English. Even if a Spanish translation was available, it might not be in a dialect with which the child is familiar. Using an unfamiliar Spanish dialect may place a student at an extreme disadvantage and may yield test results that are not a true indication of the student's abilities. The same may be true for Asians, African Americans, or Native Americans who are being tested. Rather than accurately testing specific knowledge or aptitude, all too often intelligence tests measure a student's competence in standard forms of the language (Adger, Wolfram, & Christian, 2007). Corson (1999) warns that one of the dangers of assessment tests is that they measure intelligence by those things that are valued within the dominant group and tend to exclude things that are culturally specific to minority children. Garcia (1999) contends that this bias calls into question the conclusions drawn from such tests regarding intelligence and ethnic background. Pence and Justice (2008) further caution that some students are misidentified with language disorders because of tests that were developed for Standard American English monolingual speakers. The introduction of standards-based instruction has resulted in an even more complex assessment process (Faltis, 2006). Refusal to acknowledge the value of linguistic differences has resulted in inadequate services and the inappropriate placement of children through highly questionable assessment procedures.

Several successful class-action lawsuits have been brought against school boards or school districts on behalf of children placed in special education classes on the basis of low scores on IQ tests. Typically the suits argue that biased and inappropriate test instruments were used on language minority students, which resulted in inappropriate special education placement. Among the cases often cited is *Guadalupe Organization, Inc. v. Tempe Elementary School District No. 3*, 587 F.2d 1022, 1030 (9th Cir. 1978), which was a suit filed in Arizona that resulted from the disproportionately high placement of Yaqui Indian and Mexican American children in classes for students with mental retardation. *Diana v. State Board of Education* was a suit brought on behalf of children of Mexican immigrants placed in classrooms for students with mental retardation on the basis of low IQ scores on tests argued to be discriminatory.

Bilingual Education

The definition of **bilingual education** that is generally agreed on is "the use of two languages as media of instruction" (Baca & Cervantes, 2004). Bilingual education has been supported, in part, by federal funds provided by the Bilingual Education Act of 1968, reauthorized in 1974, 1978, and 1984. The federal legislation views bilingual education more broadly than do Baca and Cervantes (2004), allowing and even encouraging methods other than the use of two languages.

Children who speak little or no English cannot understand English-speaking children or lessons that are presented in English. Not only are these children faced with having to learn new subject matter, but they must also learn a new language and often a new culture. It is likely that many of these children will not be able to keep up with the schoolwork and will drop out of school unless there is appropriate intervention. The school dropout rate for Latino students is disproportionately high. The high school dropout rate for Latino immigrants was 44.2% in 2001, versus 7.4% for all non-Latinos. The dropout rate for second-generation (children of immigrants) Latinos drops to 14.6% but holds at 15.9% for the third generation, almost double the non-Latino rate (Mehring, 2004). Most of the first-generation dropouts, however, had left school prior to immigrating to the United States (Rubin, 2003). Jeffries, Nix, and Singer (2002) indicate that the dropout rates for Native American students are also high. They cite a 1994 U.S. Department of Education report indicating a 25.4% dropout rate for Native American students. Although language differences may not be the sole contributor to the academic problems of these children, they are considered by many to be a major factor.

Lau v. Nichols.   In 1974, a class-action suit, *Lau v. Nichols* (1974), on behalf of 1,800 Chinese children was brought before the U.S. Supreme Court. The plaintiffs claimed that

A million new immigrants enter the United States annually. Many will be students in our schools who will need specialized instruction to help them acquire English.

the San Francisco Board of Education failed to provide programs designed to meet the linguistic needs of those non-English-speaking children. The failure, they claimed, was in violation of Title VI of the Civil Rights Act of 1964 and the equal protection clause of the Fourteenth Amendment. They argued that if the children could not understand the language used for instruction, they were deprived of an education equal to that of other children and were, in essence, doomed to failure.

The school board defended its policy by stating that the children received the same education afforded other children in the district. The position of the board was that a child's ability to comprehend English when entering school was not the responsibility of the school, but rather the responsibility of the child and the family. In a unanimous decision, the Supreme Court stated: "Under state imposed standards, there was no equality of treatment merely by providing students with the same facilities, textbooks, teachers, and curriculum; for students who do not understand English are effectively foreclosed from any meaningful education" (*Lau v. Nichols,* 1974). The Court did not mandate bilingual education for non-English-speaking or limited-English-speaking students. It did stipulate that special language programs were necessary if schools were to provide an equal educational opportunity for such students. Hence, the *Lau* decision gave considerable impetus to the development of bilingual education as well as ESL programs.

In 1975, the Education for All Handicapped Children Act (amended in 1990 as the Individuals with Disabilities Education Act [IDEA]) required each state to avoid the use of racially or culturally discriminating testing and evaluation procedures in the placement of children with disabilities. It also required that placement tests be administered in the child's native language. In addition, communication with parents regarding such matters as permission to test the child, development of individualized education programs (IEPs), and hearings and appeals must be in their native language. The IEP specifies the programming and services children with disabilities will receive and requires the participation of the parents in its development.

Throughout the 1970s, the federal government and the state courts sought to shape the direction of bilingual education programs and mandate appropriate testing procedures for students with limited English proficiency. The *Lau* remedies were developed by the U.S. Office of Education to help schools implement bilingual education programs. These guidelines prescribed transitional bilingual education and rejected ESL as an appropriate methodology for elementary students. With a change of the federal administration in 1981, a shift to local policy decisions began to lessen federal controls. Emphasis was placed on making the transition from the native language to English as fast as possible. The methodology for accomplishing the transition became the choice of the local school district. Thus, ESL programs began to operate alongside bilingual programs in many areas. Although the future level of federal involvement in bilingual education is uncertain, there is little doubt among educators that some form of bilingual education is needed.

The primary goal of bilingual education is not to teach English or a second language per se, but to teach children concepts, knowledge, and skills in the language they know best and to reinforce this information through the use of English (Baca & Cervantes, 2004). Two philosophies currently shape programs in bilingual education: the transitional approach and the maintenance approach.

Transitional programs emphasize bilingual education as a means of moving from the culture and language most commonly used for communication in the home to the mainstream of U.S. language and culture. It is an assimilationist approach in which the ELL student is expected to learn to function effectively in English as soon as possible. The native language of the home is used only to help the student make the transition to the English language. The native language is gradually phased out as the student becomes more proficient in English.

Bilingual education can be justified as: (a) the best way to attain maximum cognitive development for ELL students, (b) a means for achieving equal educational opportunity and/or results, (c) a means of easing the transition into the dominant language and culture, (d) an approach to educational reform, (e) a means of promoting positive interethnic relations, and (f) a wise economic investment to help linguistic minority students become maximally productive in adult life for the benefit of society and themselves (Baca & Cervantes, 2004).

Bilingual educators strongly support the use of bicultural programs even within the transitional framework. A bicultural emphasis provides students with recognition of the value and worth of their families' cultures and enhances the development or maintenance of a positive self-image. Crawford (2004) warns that cultural loss for students may also result in negative academic consequences.

A comprehensive study from 1982 to 1996 of 700,000 language minority students from a number of large school districts found that in all content areas students receiving bilingual education completed their schooling with average scores exceeding the 50th national percentile. In contrast, those language minority students who received only ESL-pullout instruction, typically completed school "with average scores between the 10th and 18th national percentile" (Nieto, 2002). Krashen and McField (2005) report that studies confirm that students in bilingual programs either outperform students in all-English programs, or perform just as well on tests of academic achievement in English. These are the precise skills that immigrant children need in order to perform well in school (Crawford, 2006).

Advocates of bilingual education see the advantages in being bilingual. Although bilingual education programs have primarily been established to develop English skills for ELL students, some offer opportunities for English-speaking students to develop proficiency in other languages. In addition, bilingualism provides an individual with job market advantages. As the United States becomes less parochial, the opportunity for business and other contacts with individuals from other countries increases, providing decided advantages to bilingual individuals. Crawford (2006) reminds critics of bilingual education that the United States has always been linguistically diverse. He further suggests that given that language diversity is common throughout the world, Americans are at a distinct disadvantage if they embrace a monolingual philosophy. In the post 9/11 era, the United States clearly stands to benefit from an increase in proficiency in other languages.

Bilingual education as it currently exists has many problems and many critics. Research has provided evidence that well-developed and well-delivered bilingual education programming can deliver positive results. Critics have also provided ample evidence that some children in bilingual education programs have fared poorly and many have dropped out of school. What should be recognized is that there is an acute national shortage of qualified bilingual educators. Being bilingual does not necessarily qualify an individual as a bilingual educator. Many who fill bilingual education positions are not fully qualified in their preparation and training. When these individuals fail to deliver desired results, bilingual education is often unfairly characterized as being programmatically unsound.

English as a Second Language

English as a second language (ESL) is a program often confused with bilingual education. In the United States, learning English is an integral part of every bilingual program. But teaching English as a second language in and by itself does not constitute a bilingual program.

Both bilingual education and ESL programs promote English proficiency for ELL students. The approach to instruction distinguishes the two programs. Bilingual education accepts and develops native language and culture in the instructional process. Bilingual education may use the native language, as well as English, as the medium of instruction. ESL instruction, however, relies exclusively on English for teaching and learning. ESL programs are used extensively in this country as a primary medium to assimilate ELL children into the linguistic mainstream as quickly as possible. Hence, some educators place less emphasis on the maintenance of home language and culture than on English language acquisition, and they view ESL programs as a viable means for achieving their goals.

In some school districts there may be ELL students from several different language backgrounds, but too few in some groups to warrant a bilingual education class (e.g., Cantonese, Farsi, Russian). In such a situation, an ESL may be the most logical approach to providing appropriate services for these students.

California's Proposition 227.   U.S. English members have vigorously supported California **Proposition 227,** a state ballot initiative, which passed in 1998 by a margin of 61 to 39%. This law was intended by its supporters to put an end to bilingual education in the state. This proposition is often referred to as the Unz initiative after its co-author, Ron Unz. Operating under the organization, One Nation, Unz and his supporters cite numerous examples of bilingual education failures. The proposition requires all language minority students to be educated in sheltered English immersion programs, not normally intended to exceed one year. Sheltered English immersion or structured English immersion involves a classroom where English language acquisition is accomplished with nearly all instruction in English, but with the curriculum and presentation designed for children who are learning the language. During this time, ELL students are temporarily sheltered from competing academically with native English-speaking students in mainstream classes. At the completion of the year, the students are transferred to English language mainstream classrooms (Education Commission for the States, 2004; Unz & Tuchman, 1998). The law allows parents to seek waivers and, if granted, the child's education may continue in a bilingual classroom. If schools or teachers fail to implement a child's education as prescribed by the law, they may be sued.

As might be expected, supporters of bilingual education have vigorously attacked the proposition with concerns that the Unz initiative will spread to other states. Proposition 227 opponents argue that the Unz initiative was not backed by research or scientific data. Rather, they argue, it was based on observations of the high failure and dropout rate of ELL students, primarily Latino. It was also based on observations that most ELL students are able to grasp the fundamentals of speaking English in a year. They support their arguments against the proposition by citing research (e.g., Cummins, 1984), which suggests that only basic conversational skills can be acquired in such a limited time and not the necessary academic language skills, which take years to develop adequately. Opponents of Proposition 227 contend that the law is a "one size fits all" approach to educating students and that it cannot have lasting benefits. Further, they argue, that during K–4 years in school, it is extremely difficult for parents to obtain waivers to keep their children in bilingual education. Parents, they contend, have no appeal rights, and the law intimidates teachers and administrators and inhibits them from doing what they know is educationally appropriate for students (National Association for Bilingual Education [NABE], 2000).

Proposition 227 Revisited.   The results of the California SAT-9 test scores for the 1998–1999 academic year provided the achievement test scores for the first ELL students to be tested after the implementation of Proposition 227. Unz and his backers declared the initiative a success as evidence by the test scores in California's Oceanside City Unified School District, which had faithfully implemented the mandates of the proposition. The scores for second-grade ELL students had increased by 11 percentile points over the previous year. The scores for the following year were also positive, adding to the Proposition's supports claim of victory and validation.

Hakuta and his bilingual education research associates at Stanford University (Hakuta, 2001a, 2001b; Hakuta, Butler, & Bousquet, 1999; Orr, Butler, Bousquet, & Hakuta, 2000) examined the achievement test results for three years following the implementation of Proposition 227. In the first two academic years of testing 1998–1999 and 1999–2000, SAT-9 test scores improved somewhat across the board in the state, particularly in grades 2 and 3. Scores rose for ELL students in both English-only classrooms and in bilingual education classrooms.

Hakuta and his associates found that districts, such as Vista Unified, Santa Ana Unified, and Ocean View Unified, which had maintained various forms of bilingual education experienced similar increases to that of Oceanside Unified. They found that the Oceanside students had started at a lower baseline (12th percentile) than the Vista (18th percentile), Santa Ana (17th percentile), or Ocean View students (17th percentile). They strongly suggested that a statistical phenomenon known as **regression to the mean** had been in operation for the Oceanside students. Regression to the mean implies that scores at the extreme ends of the statistical distribution move toward the population average (mean), with low scores moving higher and high scores moving lower. They also point to class size reduction, which had just taken place in California schools, as contributing to the improved scores. While the test scores for ELL students had improved, they point to the fact that they were still low.

Hakuta and his associates also made the following observations. Educators were very aware that they were part of an "experiment," and under close scrutiny. They were likely highly motivated to do their best to improve learning and enhance test scores (Hakuta et al., 1999; Orr et al., 2000; UCLMRI Newsletter, 2003).

By 2001, the Oceanside School District's percentile scores for ELL students had stalled and in some instances dropped. That year, ELL third-grade reading scores were one percentile point below the state's ELL percentile score. District-wide ELL test scores in more than half the schools had declined compared to the previous year, contrary to the rising state ELL test scores.

The American Institutes of Research (AIR) was commissioned by the California Department of Education in 2000 to conduct a five-year study on the effects of Proposition 227 on the education of ELL. The third-year report released in late 2003 indicated that since the passage of 227, almost all students across all language groups had experienced gains in math, reading, and language as measured by the SAT-9 achievement test. However, Crawford (2004) suggests that careful review indicates problems with the methodology of the AIR study. Student performance can be a function of a number of variables, which can vary from school site to school site, and are probably difficult to control for research purposes. These may include factors such as (1) leadership, (2) a clear instructional plan, (3) accountability and assessment, (4) schoolwide climate, (5) instructional strategies, (6) staff development, and (7) family involvement (AIR & WestEd, 2003).

As indicated in the most recent data in Table 6.2, supporters of Proposition 227 have in part been successful in their efforts to dismantle bilingual education in California. In the school year prior to Proposition 227, there were 409,879 students enrolled in bilingual education programs. By the following academic year, 1998–1999, the bilingual education enrollment had dropped to 169,440. This represented a drop in the bilingual education

TABLE 6.2   Effects of Proposition 227 on California's Bilingual Education Student Enrollment

Academic Year	Numbers Enrolled	Percent Enrolled ELL
1997–1998*	409,879	29%
1998–1999**	169,440	12%
2001–2002	151,836	9.7%
2004–2005	111,920	7.0%
2005–2006	95,155	6.1%

*Year prior to the implementation of Proposition 227
**Year following the implementation of Proposition 227

Adapted from Crawford, (2007). The Decline of Bilingual Education: How to Reverse a Troubling Trend. International Multilingual Research Journal, 1(1), 33–37.

student enrollment of 29% of the ELL enrollment to 12%. Since 2001–2002, there has been a steady and alarming decline.

In 2002, the State Board of Education in California allowed principals and educational staff, as well as parents, to make the decision on whether children should be placed into bilingual education programs. This significantly weakened the mandates of Proposition 227 (Rossell, 2003).

Other Efforts to Dismantle Bilingual Education.   English language learners are often caught in the middle of politics. Both sides of the English Only movement believe strongly that their positions are best for language minority immigrant students. Ron Unz and his supporters continue their efforts to bring what they consider a success in California (both the passage of Proposition 227 and the educational results) to other parts of the country. They were successful with similar measures (Proposition 203) in Arizona in 2000 (Crawford, 2001), and in Massachusetts in 2002 (*Boston Globe,* 2003), but were unsuccessful in Colorado.

Opponents of the English Only movement readily agree on the importance of learning English. However, they view their adversaries as individuals trying to force Anglo conformity by ending essential services in foreign languages. They view the attacks on bilingual education as unjustified because good bilingual education has been shown to be effective. Bad bilingual education, they concede, is ineffective and is seldom bilingual education,

Pause to Reflect 6.4

In spite of research by respected scholars showing the effectiveness of properly implemented bilingual education, it has been attacked from many fronts including high-ranking individuals in both some state and the federal government.

- What is the attitude toward bilingual education in your state?
- What lessons can be learned from the results of achievement test scores?

Go to the *Homework and Exercises* section in Chapter 6 of MyEducationLab and select *Pause to Reflect 6.4* to answer these questions.

FOCUS YOUR CULTURAL LENS: DEBATE

Curtailing Bilingual Education

With the Supreme Court decision in the *Lau v. Nichols* case in 1974, bilingual education came to the forefront in American education and was give a greater sense of legitimacy. While *Lau v. Nichols* did not mandate bilingual education, it required schools to address the linguistic needs of their students from diverse backgrounds.

Over the past 30 years, the road for bilingual education has often been bumpy. Although some researchers continue to affirm the value, others conclude that while not harming students, bilingual education provides no particular advantage (Krashen & McField, 2005). Some critics have attacked it as a colossal failure, and advocate for English immersion classes and the discontinuation of bilingual education. Even the federal government in the George W. Bush administration appears to be de-emphasizing bilingual programs. The name of the U. S. Office of Bilingual Education and Minority Language Affairs has been renamed as the Office of English Language Acquisition, Language Enhancement, and Academic Achievement for Limited English Proficient Students (OELA).

For

- Opponents of bilingual education advocate sheltered English immersion limited to one year, while they have no research to back the efficacy of what they propose.
- Research by Cummins and Hakuta has clearly shown that ELL students cannot become proficient in English for academic purposes in one year's time.
- The problems in bilingual education have been rooted in the lack of qualified personnel trained in bilingual education techniques, lack of adequate resources, and the lack of commitment both at the federal and state levels.
- Research has clearly demonstrated that bilingual education, properly implemented, is highly effective.

Against

- Over 400,000 California students began the school year as non-English proficient, and prior to Proposition 227, at the end of the school year, only 5% had learned English.
- Prior to California's Proposition 227, English language learners studied grammar, reading, writing, and all other academic subjects in their own native language—almost always in Spanish—while receiving only small amounts of English instruction.
- Achievement test scores for immigrant children are low and dropout rates are high.
- Bilingual education in California, Arizona, and Massachusetts has been reduced to a fraction of what it used to be. The same should happen throughout the United States.

Questions

1. What should programmatic decisions (for example, what type of program should be offered for ELL?) be based on?
2. Are the attacks on bilingual education justified?
3. What has the research shown with respect to language acquisition and ELL?

Go to the *Homework and Exercises* section in Chapter 6 of MyEducationLab and select *Focus Your Cultural Lens* to answer these questions.

From http://onenation.org/unz101997.html and www.standford.edu/~hakuta/docs/howlong.pdf

except in name. Opponents of bilingual education, they argue, have seen to it that these programs fail by giving inadequate support or resources, by staffing programs with unqualified personnel, by obtaining faulty test results on bilingual education students, by testing them in English, and by other means that cast negative outcomes on bilingual education (Fillmore, 1992). In the post–Proposition 227 era, the Los Angeles Unified School District, the largest in the state of California, assigns most English Language Learners to a phonics-intensive reading program specifically designed for native English speakers (Crawford, 2006).

The backlash against bilingual education is clearly reflected in the fact that between 1992 and 2002, the number of K–12 English Language Learners increased by 72% nationwide, while enrollment in bilingual programs declined from 37% to 17% (Crawford, 2006).

The passage of the No Child Left Behind Act of 2001 dealt a further blow to bilingual education. By holding schools accountable and instituting high-stakes testing in English, Crawford (2006) maintains that schools are encouraged to favor an all-English approach to instruction. He suggests that it is particularly unfair to English Language Learners to be tested in a language they have not mastered, resulting in substantial punishment to schools based on unreliable assessments. It is true that many earlier immigrants did not have the benefit of bilingual education programs. Thrust into sink-or-swim situations, they ended up swimming, succeeding in school, and finding their niche in society. It is also true, however, that many students were unable to swim and sank in their efforts to acculturate in school. Since the number of language minority students today has increased dramatically, we can ill afford a sink-or-swim system, which could result in an education breakdown for massive numbers of students who are unable to succeed.

In spite of their differences, the majority of the individuals who support bilingual education, as well as those who are opposed to it, are well-intentioned individuals who want to enhance the educational opportunities for immigrant children. If all interested parties would be less concerned with the politics of the issue and would base their programmatic preferences on sound, well-documented research, the students would be the ultimate winners.

Nonverbal Communication in the Classroom

As discussed earlier in this chapter, cultural differences in nonverbal communications between students and teachers can be very frustrating to both. To begin to overcome such differences, a teacher must try to analyze particular nonverbal communications when students, especially those from a different cultural background, are not responding as the teacher expects. What the teacher perceives as inattention on the part of the students, interruptions by the students at times considered inappropriate by the teacher, or even a tendency on the part of the students to look away from the teacher while being addressed may, in fact, be due to cultural differences.

In most school settings, students from subordinate groups are expected to become bicultural and adopt the nonverbal communication patterns of the dominant group while in school. A more sensitive approach is for teachers also to learn to operate biculturally in the classroom.

Teachers should reflect on what is occurring in the classroom when communications are not as expected. The first step is to become more aware of the nature of the difficulty. In the school setting, students should sometimes have access to teachers, counselors, or administrators who are from a culturally similar background. Teachers can make an effort to learn what the cultural cues of students mean and to react appropriately. A more effective approach, however, is to be able to analyze what is happening in the classroom and to respond on the basis of what is known about the student and his or her cultural background.

Summary

The *Lau* decision of 1974 ensures non-English-speaking children the right to an appropriate education that meets their linguistic needs. Even with a legal mandate, appropriate services may not always be delivered because of lack of tolerance or insensitivity to language or dialects that are not considered Standard English. Because nonstandard dialects tend to have a negative stigma attached to them, some educators may refuse to view them as legitimate forms of communication. Although they may indeed be legitimate forms of communication and may serve the speaker well in certain contexts, nonstandard English dialects may preclude certain social and vocational opportunities.

Bilingual education has both its supporters and its detractors. Through proper educational programming, however, children with limited English proficiency can have the education to which they are entitled. Our responsibility as educators is to recognize the linguistic diversity of our nation's students, and to recognize the value of the family's unique cultural and linguistic background. As students become bilingual and bidialectal, they will find themselves in the position of being able to navigate through a greater variety of social, academic, and vocational settings.

PROFESSIONAL PRACTICE FOR EDUCATORS

Questions for Discussion

1. How is language a function of culture?
2. What are the advantages of being bilingual in the United States?
3. How is bilingualism encouraged and discouraged within educational settings?
4. What are dialects? What factors generally determine whether an individual becomes bidialectal?
5. Why is Black English a controversial issue in education? How should it be handled in the classroom?
6. Why is it important to be sensitive to nonverbal communications between teacher and student and among students?
7. Why might it be unwise to assume that a student is ready for academic instruction in English as soon as he or she has some basic English conversational skills?
8. What is the relationship between language and educational assessment?
9. Contrast maintenance and transitional bilingual education. Which do you think is more appropriate? Why?
10. When might an ESL approach be the most appropriate strategy to use in a classroom?

Portfolio Activities

1. Survey your students (where you teach, student teach, or are involved in a practicum) to find out how many different languages or dialects they speak. Ask them when and

where they feel comfortable speaking a different dialect or language other than Standard English. (INTASC Standard 3)

2. Check with your local school district office and find out how many different language groups are served in the district. (INTASC Standard 3)

3. Find out what type of programs are used in your district to facilitate English language acquisition of English language learners in the schools. (INTASC Standard 3)

4. Survey the teachers who have language minority students in their classes and find out what type of programming they favor for their students and why. (INTASC Standard 3)

Licensure Test Prep

Lupe Gomez is a third grade teacher in the Los Angeles Unified School District. She has three special education students who are part of the district's special education inclusion program. All three are immigrants from Mexico and Central America who speak Spanish in the home and have extremely limited English-speaking skills. Mr. Gomez is bilingual and has an adequate bilingual education background to carry out the IEP.

Since Ms. Gomez teaches in California and is under the mandate of Proposition 227, which prohibits her from teaching in Spanish, she is concerned about the three students special education IEP, which specifies a bilingual approach to their instruction.

Short Answer Questions

1. If Ms. Gomez instructs the three special education students in English, is she risking disciplinary action and possible fines as Proposition 227 stipulates?

2. What does the research by Cummins indicate with respect to the amount of time students need to acquire a new language to be able to function academically?

3. What are the implications of this research for special education students and other English Language Learners (ELL)?

Go to the *Homework and Exercises* section in Chapter 6 of MyEducationLab and select *Licensure Test Prep* to complete this exercise.

Suggested Readings

Adger, C. T., Wolfram, W., & Christian, D. (2007). *Dialects in schools and communities* (2nd ed.). Mahwah, NJ: Lawrence Erlbaum Associates.
This is an excellent overview of dialects by well-recognized authorities in the field of dialects. The text addresses language variations in the United States, and defines and explains dialects and the sources of language differences. It also addresses communicative interactions and cultural styles in the classroom, and explains why language differences do not mean language deficits.

Baca, L. M., & Cervantes, H. (2004). *The bilingual special education interface* (4th ed.). Upper Saddle River, NJ: Merrill/Prentice Hall.

An excellent overview of bilingual special education, this book contains basic but important information on general bilingual education, including litigation and legislation related to the rights of children with limited English proficiency.

Crawford, J. (2004). *Education of English learners: Language diversity in the classroom* (5th ed.). Los Angeles: Bilingual Educational Services.

Written by the former Washington Editor of *Education Week,* and current Executive Director of the National Association for Bilingual Education,

the text provides an excellent overview of bilingual education. Among several issues addressed are language policies in the United States, the politics surrounding bilingual education, and an overview of research on language acquisition.

Samovar, L. A., Porter, R. E., & McDaniel, E. R. (2006). *Communication between cultures* (6th ed.). Belmont, CA: Wadsworth.

An excellent treatment of language and culture, this book includes chapters on intercultural communication and the communication of a nonmainstream group.

References

Adger, C. T., Wolfram, W., & Christian, D. (2007). *Dialects in schools and communities* (2nd ed.). Mahwah, NJ: Lawrence Erlbaum Associates.

American Institutes of Research (AIR) & WestEd. (2003). Effects of the implementation of Proposition 227 on the education of English learners, K–12, Year 3 Report. Submitted to the California Department of Education, October 29, 2003.

Artiles, A. J., Harry, B., Reschly, D. J., & Chinn, P. C. (2002). Over-identification of students of color in special education: A critical overview. *Multicultural Perspectives* (4), 1.

Baca, L. M., & Cervantes, H. (2004). *The bilingual special education interface* (4th ed.). Upper Saddle River, NJ: Merrill/Prentice Hall.

The Boston Globe (via Knight Ridder Tribune Business News). (2003, April 27). Second bilingual education battle gears up in Massachusetts.

California Department of Education (CDE). (2007). *Number of English learners by language.* Educational Demographics Unit. Retrieved June 10, 2007, from http://dq.cde.ca.gov/dataquest/LEPbyLang1.asp?cChoice=LepbyLang1&cYear=2005-06&cLevel=State&cTopic=LC&myTimeFrame=S&submit1=Submit

Corson, D. (1999). *Language policy in schools: A resource for teachers and administrators.* Mahwah, NJ: Lawrence Erlbaum Associates.

Crawford, J. (Ed.). (1992). *Language loyalties.* Chicago: University of Chicago Press.

Crawford, J. (2001). Bilingual education: Strike two, Arizona voters follow California's lead and mandate English-only programs. *Rethinking Schools, 15* (2).

Crawford, J. (2003). *Issues in U.S. language policy, language legislation in the U.S.A.* http://ourworld.compuserve.com/homepages/jwcrawford/langleg.htm

Crawford, J. (2004). *Education of English learners: Language diversity in the classroom* (5th ed.). Los Angeles: Bilingual Educational Services.

Crawford, J. (2007). *The decline of bilingual education: How to reverse a troubling trend. International Multilingual Research Journal, 1(1) 33–37.*

Crystal, D. (1997). *The Cambridge encyclopedia of language* (2nd ed.). Cambridge, UK: Cambridge University Press.

Cummins, J. (1984). *Bilingualism and special education: Issues in assessment and pedagogy.* San Diego: College-Hill Press.

Cummins, J. (1996). *Negotiating identities: Education of empowerment in a diverse society.* Los Angeles: California Association for Bilingual Education.

Cummins, J. (2000). *Language, power and pedagogy: Bilingual children in the crossfire.* Clevedon, England: Multicultural Matters.

Diana v. State Board of Education, Civil Action No. C-7037 RFP (N. D.Cal. Jan. 7, 1970 and June 18, 1973).

Dicker, S. J. (2003). *Languages in America: A pluralistic view* (2nd ed.). Bristol, PA: Multilingual Matters.

Education Commission for the States. (2004). *Bilingual/ESL.* Retrieved August 5, 2004, from www.ecs.org/ecsmain.asp?page=/html/issues.asp

Faltis, C. J. (2006). *Teaching English language learners in elementary school communities: A joinfostering approach* (4th ed.). Upper Saddle River, New Jersey: Pearson Prentice Hall.

Fillmore, L. W. (1992). Against our best interest: The attempt to sabotage bilingual education. In J. Crawford (Ed.), *Language loyalties.* Chicago: University of Chicago Press.

Garcia, E. (1999). *Student cultural diversity: Understanding and meeting the challenge* (2nd ed.). Boston: Houghton Mifflin.

Hakuta, K. (2001a). *Silence from Oceanside and the future of bilingual education.* Retrieved August 5, 2004, from www.stanford.edu/%7Ehakuta/ SAT9Silence%20from%20Oceanside.htm

Hakuta, K. (2001b). *Follow-up on Oceanside: Communications with Ron Unz.* Retrieved August 5, 2004, from www.stanford.edu/%7Ehakuta/ SAT9Silence%20from%20Oceanside%202.htm

Hakuta, K. (2002). *What can we learn about the impact of Proposition 227 from SAT-9 scores?* Retrieved August 5, 2004, from www.stanford.edu/ %7Ehakuta/SAT9/index.htm

Hakuta, K., Bialystok, E., & Wiley, E. (2003). Critical evidence: A test of the critical-period hypothesis for second-language acquisition. *American Psychological Society, 14, (1).*

Hakuta, K., Butler, Y. G., & Bousquet, M. (1999). *What legitimate inferences can be made from the 1999 release of SAT-9 scores with respect to the impact of California's Proposition 227 on the performance of LEP students.* Retrieved August 5, 2004, from www.stanford.edu/%7Ehakuta/SAT9/NABE

Hakuta, K., Butler, Y. G., & Witt, D. (2000). *How long does it take English language learners to attain proficiency?* Santa Barbara, CA: University of California Linguistic Minority Research Institute Policy Report 2000-1.

Haynes, J. (2004). *Proxemics and U.S. culture* Retrieved August 5, 2004, from www.everythingesl.net/ inservices/proxemics_elevator.php

Hecht, M., Jackson, R., II, & Ribeau, S. (2003). *African American communication: Exploring identity and culture* (2nd ed.). Mahwah, NJ: Lawrence Erlbaum Associates.

Heward, W. L. (2006). *Exceptional children* (8th ed.). Upper Saddle River, NJ: Merrill/Prentice Hall.

Hosoda, M., Stone-Romero, E. F., & Coats, G. (2003, Summer). The effects of physical attractiveness on job-related outcomes: A meta-analysis of experimental studies. *Personnel Psychology, 56* (2), 431–432.

Jay, T. (2003). *The psychology of language.* Upper Saddle River, NJ: Prentice Hall.

Jeffries, R., Nix, M., & Singer, C. (2002, February–March). Urban American Indians "dropping" out of traditional high schools: Barriers and bridges to success. *High School Journal, 85* (3), 38–39.

Krashen, S., & McField, G. (2005, November–December). What works? Reviewing the latest evidence on bilingual education. *Language Learner.* 1(2): 7–10.

Lau v. Nichols, 414 U.S., 563–572 (Jan. 21, 1974).

Los Angeles Almanac. (2004). Retrieved August 5, 2004, from www.losangelesalmanac.com/LA/ la10b.htm

MacNeil, R., & Cran, W. (2005). *Do you speak American?* New York: Nan A. Talese/Doubleday.

McDonald, J. J., Jr. (2003, Fall). Civil rights for the aesthetically-challenged. *Employee Relations Law Journal, 29* (2), 118.

Mehring, J. (2004, August 2). Latinos' education gap; High-school dropout rates remain high. *Business Week,* i3894, 28.

Meyerhoff, M. (2006). *Introducing sociolinguistics.* New York: Routledge.

National Association for Bilingual Education (NABE). (2000). *The Unz intiative: Extreme, irresponsible, and hazardous to California's future.* Washington, DC: Author.

National Clearinghouse for English Language Acquisition (NCELA). (2006). *Growing numbers of limited English proficient students.* www.ncela.gwu.edu/ policy/states/reports/statedata/2004LEP/ GrowingLEP_0405_Nov06.pdf

News-Medical.Net. (2004, April 27). *A high rate of marriage among deaf individuals can explain the increased frequency of connexin deafness in the United States.* Retrieved August 5, 2004, from www.news-medical.net/print_article.asp?print= yes&id=911

Nieto, S. (2002). *Language, culture, and teaching: Critical perspectives for a new century.* Mahwah, NJ: Lawrence Erlbaum Associates.

NYC Mayors. (2004). *Fiorello Henry LaGuardia.* Retrieved August 5, 2004, from www.nyc.gov/html/ nyc100/html/classroom/hist_info/mayors. html#laguardia

Orr, J. E., Butler, Y. G., Bousquet, M., & Hakuta, K. (2000). What can we learn about the impact of Proposition 227 from SAT-9 scores? *An Analysis of Results from 2000.* Retrieved August 5, 2004, from www.stanford.edu/%7Ehakuta/SAT9/SAT9_2000/ analysis2000.htm

Owens, R. E., Jr. (2005). *Language development* (6th ed.). Needham Heights, MA: Allyn & Bacon.

Pence, K., & Justice, L. (2008). *Language development from theory to practice.* Upper Saddle River, NJ: Pearson/Merrill Prentice Hall.

Rossell, C. H. (2003). *Dismantling bilingual education, implementing English immersion: The California initiative.* San Francisco: Public Policy Institute of California, August 20, 2002.

Rubin, H. G. (2003, June 19). Hispanic dropout rates lower than feared. *Education Daily, 36* (116), 4.

Samovar, L. A., Porter, R. E., & McDaniel, E. R. (2006). *Communication between cultures* (6th ed.). Belmont, CA: Wadsworth.

Schechter, S., & Cummins, J. (Eds.). (2003). *Multilingual education in practice: Using diversity as a resource.* Portsmouth, NH: Heinemann.

Seifert, M. W. (2001, July 20). Appearances count to the point of bias? *Austin Business Journal, 21* (18), 21.

Smith, D. D. (2007). *Introduction to special education: making a difference (with MyLabSchool)* (6th ed.). Needham Heights, MA: Allyn & Bacon.

UCLMRI Newsletter. (2003, Fall). *Has Proposition 227 reduced the English learner achievement gap?* Santa Barbara, CA: University of California Minority Research Institute.

Unz, R. K., & Tuchman, G. M. (1998). *Initiative statute: English language education for children in public schools.* Palo Alto, CA: Author. (Available: www.nabe.org/unz/text)

U.S. Census Bureau. (2003). *Statistical abstract of the United States: 2003* (123rd ed.). Washington, DC: U.S. Department of Commerce.

U.S. Department of Education. 2004 civil rights data collection: projected values for the nation, Washington, D.C. vistaademo.beyond 2020.com/ocr2004rv30/xls/nation-projection.xls

U.S. English. (2004). Retrieved August 5, 2004, from www.us_english.org/inc/

Wolfram, W., & Christian, D. (1989). *Dialects and education: Issues and answers.* Upper Saddle River, NJ: Prentice Hall.

Chapter 7

RELIGION

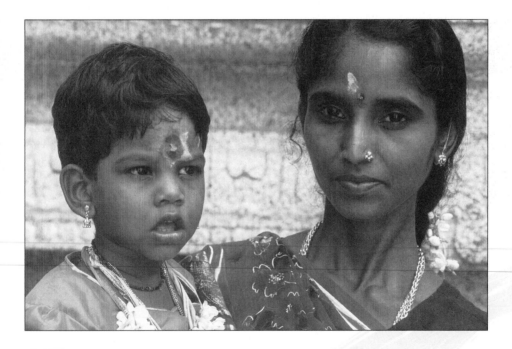

*C*ongress shall make no law respecting an establishment of religion, or prohibiting the free exercise thereof; or abridging the freedom of speech, or of the press; or the right of the people peaceably to assemble, and to petition the Government for a redress of grievances.

FIRST AMENDMENT TO THE UNITED STATES CONSTITUTION, 1791

The teachers and administrators of the Edison Onizuka Middle School near San Francisco had put the finishing touches on their plans for the school's honors convocation and had selected Ramakrishnan Gupta and Rebecca Rose who were tied with the highest grades in the eighth grade to be recognized in a convocation ceremony and asked to make a 7- to 10-minute speech on the value of an education. Because the faculty and Dr. Hovestadt wanted the district superintendent to be part of the ceremony, they had agreed to schedule the event at 3:00 p.m. on the fourth Saturday in May, the superintendent's only available time.

Dr. Hovestadt, the principal, called the Gupta and Rose families to inform them of their children's selection as convocation speakers. As expected, both sets of parents were delighted at the news of their son and their daughter's accomplishments and selection. Mr. Rose indicated, however, that Saturday was quite impossible because it was the **Sabbath** for their family, who were **Orthodox Jews**. The Sabbath, a day of religious observance and rest among Jews is from sundown on Friday until sundown on Saturday. Orthodox Jews are a conservative branch of Judaism, which strictly observes religious law. The event had to be rescheduled to any other day but the Sabbath. It was impossible, Dr. Hovestadt pleaded. All the plans were made, and no satisfactory alternate dates were available. "Would you plan the event on a Sunday?" Mr. Rose exclaimed. "I would not ask you to. Then why do you schedule it on our Sabbath? You must change the day." At an impasse, Dr. Hovestadt knew he had to come up with an alternative plan in a hurry.

Reflections

1. Is Mr. Rose being unreasonable?
2. What if the event in question took place in a homogeneous community that was primarily Christian and the Rose family was one of only two Jewish families in the community? In a democracy, does the majority always rule?
3. Does the thought that one family can create such chaos in the careful planning of a school event irritate you?
4. How would you feel if you were a Christian living in a non-Christian community, and a major event that you were expected to attend was scheduled on Christmas Day?
5. Should the majority always rule?
6. Do the rights of every individual have to be considered?

Religion and Culture

In 2003, Alabama's chief Supreme Court Justice, Roy Moore, was removed from office for his defiance of a federal district court order to remove a monument of the Ten Commandments. After his election to the high court, Moore had the monument installed in the rotunda of the Alabama Judicial Building. A U.S. District Court judge found Moore's actions to be a violation of the doctrine of separation of church and state and ordered the monument removed. This resulted in the standoff, which eventually led to Moore's removal from his position (Johnson, 2003).

Moore had indicated that it was not only his right, but also his obligation to acknowledge God in his courtroom. When Moore campaigned to become his state's ranking judicial officer, he vowed to restore the moral underpinnings of the law (Johnson, 2003).

Moore's defiance was hugely popular among his fellow citizens. Seventy-five percent of those in Alabama supported his position. He also received support from others outside the state. Moore indicated that the U.S. Government stamps "In God We Trust" on our coins and imprints the same on our currency. Yet, he was denied the right to put "God's Commandments" on display. This, he indicated, is an inconsistency at best. Moore's right to his beliefs or his desire to enhance morality was never in question. What was in question was the use of his public office to foster religious concepts in a public area. Even though he was supported by a vast majority, the Court and the judicial panel ruled that the minority, no matter how small, had a right not to be subjected to his (and that of others') beliefs.

Justice Moore was likely aware of the consequences of his actions, however he was apparently willing to give up the highest judicial position in his state to adhere to his religious convictions (Johnson, 2003). Every student should have the security in knowing that they will not have anyone else's religious dogma imposed on them.

Influence of Religion on Education

In the United States, 90% of the population claims a preference to some religious group (Winseman, 2005). As can be seen in Figure 7.1, about 43% of adults attend a church or synagogue in an average week (Gallup Poll, 2006). Individuals who belong to the more conservative Protestant groups and members of the Church of Jesus Christ of Latter-Day Saints (Mormons) tend to attend church most frequently (Gallup Poll, 2006). Religion is clearly an important aspect of the lives of many people. Although it may have little impact on the lives of some people, it influences the way many other people think, perceive, and behave. The forces of religious groups are far from dormant. They can influence the election of school board members as well as the curriculum and textbooks used in schools. Principals, teachers, and superintendents have been hired and fired through the influence of religious groups. This chapter provides an overview of religion in the United States and its influence on the individual and on the educational system.

The religious pluralism of the school in which one teaches will be determined, in great part, by the geographic region of the United States. Because of various immigration and migration patterns throughout history, different ethnic and religious groups have settled

FIGURE 7.1   Weekly or Almost Every Week Attendance at Church or Synagogue.

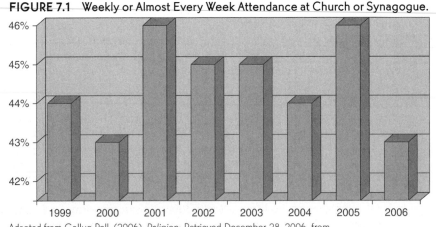

Adapted from Gallup Poll. (2006). *Religion*. Retrieved December 28, 2006, from http://www.galluppoll.com/content/?ci=22414&pg=1

in different parts of the country. Although a few areas remain totally homogeneous, families that strongly identify with a particular ethnic group may dominate a school community. More often, families identify strongly with the religious orientation of one or more denominations in the community. The perspective of a particular religious doctrine often influences what a family expects from the school and, therefore, from the teacher. In an area where the religious perspectives and school expectations differ greatly, educators face numerous challenges. A look at the religious composition of schools in various sections of the country will provide a sense of the diversity one might face throughout a career in education.

For example, a consolidated rural high school in the South may be primarily comprised of students whose families are conservative Southern Baptist, Church of Christ, or Pentecostal. The United Methodist students may be less conservative than the others. The church serves as the center of most community activities, and many families spend several nights a week at church or serving the church. Sex education may not be allowed in the public school curriculum. Teachers may face harsh criticism if they teach about evolution or lifestyles that conflict with those acceptable in that community. Textbooks and assigned readings are often scrutinized to ensure that the content does not stray far from the beliefs of this conservative community.

At a middle school in northeastern Indiana, most students are from the same European background, but they dress and behave differently. Some students are from a local **Old Order Amish** community with strict codes for the behavior and dress of its members, whereas the majority of other students are **Mennonites**. Both the Amish and the Mennonites are part of conservative Christian groups with Swiss and Dutch origins. The Amish students are very respectful and well behaved, but some may experience ridicule by their non-Amish peers because of their conservative attire and overall appearance. After completing the eighth grade, the Amish students are no longer part of the school system because their families withdraw them to work full-time on their farms, which utilize neither electricity nor motorized vehicles. The Mennonites, though not as conservative as the Amish, share some of the same origins as the Amish. The early Amish were a group that separated from the Mennonites.

Students from Catholic, Jewish, Protestant, Muslim, Hindu, and Buddhist (these religious groups are described in this chapter within the section on religious pluralism in the United States) families attend a suburban school on the West Coast. Some students are from families with no religious affiliation. Although the religious backgrounds of the students differ, they seem to share many of the same values. The school projects a generally liberal curriculum that includes sex education, ethnic studies, and religion courses. Except for the students' observance of various religious holidays, religion seems to have little impact on the students or the school.

At an inner-city school in an East Coast city, the religious backgrounds of students vary greatly. Some students attend Catholic services; others attend Baptist churches or storefront Pentecostal churches; and others have no religious affiliation. There are a few **atheists** and **agnostics** in this community as there are in other communities throughout the country. The atheists believe that there is no God, while the agnostics argue that we do not and cannot know God or gods exist. Some students are involved in religious activities during their nonschool time. The school reflects little of these diverse religious perspectives in the curriculum or school environment.

In Utah, the educator will find a school in a moderate-size community dominated by members of the Church of Jesus Christ of Latter-Day Saints (LDS, or Mormons, are described in this chapter within the section on religious pluralism). Many Mormon families participate in their ward activities several nights every week, and socialize almost exclusively with other Mormon families. LDS beliefs do not permit smoking or the drinking of alcohol, coffee, or tea. In that Utah community, this religious group controls most major institutions and businesses. Religion itself is not and cannot lawfully be taught as part of the school curriculum, but the perspective of the dominant religious group in this community is reflected in school and curriculum practices (e.g., what is and is not lawfully taught in the schools). The vast majority of teachers and school administrators are LDS Church members. Their daily behaviors, their orientation toward life, morality, politics, and social issues reflect their religious beliefs. This in turn either directly or indirectly influences the topics they select for classroom discussions, and the treatment of the discussions.

Many students leave during school hours to receive religious instruction at a Mormon seminary adjacent to the school. Many of the boys and some of the girls will leave home following high school or shortly after to serve on a church mission for two years. Most of the elected officials are members of the Mormon Church; therefore state and local laws affecting education reflect a Mormon influence.

People differ greatly in their beliefs about the role that religious perspective should play in determining school curriculum and environment. Like all other institutions in the United States, schools have a historical background of rural, white, Protestant domination. Such influence has determined the holidays, usually Christian holidays such as Christmas, which are celebrated by most public schools. Moreover, the dominant Protestant groups have often determined the moral teachings that have been integrated into the public schools.

Pause to Reflect 7.1

The first European settlers in what has become the United States were primarily devout Christians. The Founding Fathers of the country were primarily Christians. Until recent years school prayer was permitted in our schools, and at school athletic and other events. In recent years we have seen what many complain is a moral decay in the country. Today, the vast majority of the citizens of this country are Christians. The majority of them would like prayer returned to the schools and for the schools to instill in the students the basic morality, which is reflected in the Ten Commandments.

- If the majority of the individuals living in your community are Christians and the parents of students want the return of school prayer and the Ten Commandments posted on every classroom wall, how can that harm any children in the school?
- Would the school and the community not benefit from a greater emphasis on morality?
- What would be the harm of daily prayer if the prayers did not make mention of God or Jesus?
- Individuals are elected to public office by receiving the most or the majority of votes. Should the majority rule in matters of religion?

Go to the *Homework and Exercises* section in Chapter 7 of MyEducationLab and select *Pause to Reflect 7.1* to answer these questions.

The First Amendment and the Separation of Church and State

The First Amendment quoted at the beginning of this chapter clearly states that Congress is prohibited from making laws establishing a religion or prohibiting religious worship. This has been consistently interpreted by the courts as affirming the principles of separation of church and state. While one of the most valued parts of our Constitution it is also one of the most controversial. Throughout the history of this country, various individuals and groups tend to interpret this amendment to meet their own needs and interests. For some people, religious emphasis is appropriate in the public schools as long as it is congruent with their own religious persuasion. These same people, however, may be quick to cite the constitutional safeguards for separation of church and state if other groups attempt the infusion of their religious dogmas. Equity and propriety are often in the eye of the beholder, and one's religious orientation may strongly influence one's perception of what constitutes objectivity, fairness, and legality.

Since the removal of prayer from the schools by a 1963 Supreme Court decision, parent groups have continued to fight to restore prayer in the schools through state and federal legislation. Parent groups have fought on religious grounds to prevent the teaching of sex education and evolution. Coming from different religious backgrounds, parents have fought verbally and physically over what books their children should read in literature courses and what curriculum should be used in social studies and science classes. Members of more liberal Protestant, Catholic, and Jewish denominations often argue that they want their children exposed to the perspectives of different religious and ethnic groups. Members of the more conservative groups argue that they do not want their children exposed to what they consider immoral perspectives and language inherent in such instructional materials. They object to what they consider **secular humanism** in the curriculum, which they believe emphasizes respect for human beings and de-emphasizes or ignores God. Community resistance to cultural pluralism and multicultural education has, at times, been led by some individuals associated with conservative religious groups. Because cultural pluralism inevitably involves religious diversity, multicultural education is sometimes viewed as an impediment to efforts to maintain the status quo or to return to the religious values of the past.

Multicultural education is sometimes maligned as a bedfellow of the secular humanist movement, which emphasizes the dignity and worth of the human being rather than the belief in the supernatural (discussed in the section on censorship in this chapter). Multicultural education is erroneously accused of supporting movements that detract from basic moral values. Multicultural education, however, provides a basis for understanding and appreciating diversity and minimizes the problems inherent in people being different from one another.

Of all the cultural groups examined in this book, religion may be the most problematic for educators. In one school, the religious beliefs of students appear to have little influence on what is taught in a classroom; in fact, the teacher is expected to expose students to many different perspectives. In another school, the teacher may be attacked for discussing evolution.

Educators themselves vary in their beliefs about the role of religious perspective in education. If one shares the same religion or religious perspectives as the community, there will probably be little conflict between one's own beliefs and the beliefs reflected in the school. If the educator is from a religious background that is different from that prevalent in the community or has a perspective about the role of religion that differs from that of the community, misunderstanding and conflicts may arise that prevent effective instruction.

If an educator does not understand the role of religion in the lives of students, it may be difficult to develop appropriate instructional strategies, or even retain one's job.

On the following pages, we examine religion's impact on a student's life, some of the more prevalent religions in the United States, the degree to which individuals identify with a particular religious doctrine, and the educational implications of religion.

Religion as a Way of Life

Many religions are particularistic in that members believe that their own religion is uniquely true and legitimate and all others are false. Other religious groups accept the validity of various religions that have grown out of different historical experiences.

Although the separation of church and state is an integral part of our heritage, the two usually support each other. In many churches, the American flag stands next to the church flag, and patriotism is an important part of religious loyalty. God has been mentioned in all presidential inaugural addresses except Washington's second address, and it is not uncommon for politicians and preachers to refer to the United States as the "promised land." The secular ideas of the American dream also pervade many religions in this country. In fact, many religions reflect the dominant values of our society.

The purpose of this chapter is to assist you in understanding how religion can be an important part of the cultural makeup of an individual, rather than to provide a comparative review of all religions. We will briefly examine the larger religious groups within the United States and a few of the smaller ones. It is impossible to address every religious group or sect in a single chapter. Our decision to limit the groups or denominations discussed is not to suggest that they are not important. All religions and religious groups are important, especially to those who belong to them. We will discuss here some of the most prevalent religious groups educators may see in their schools. Considerable coverage in this edition will be devoted to evangelical Christians because of their influence on the political process and the focus of some within the evangelical movement to influence educational systems.

In this edition as in the previous edition there will also be a focus on Islam. The events of September 11, 2001, the conflicts in Afghanistan, and Iraq, and the growth of Islam in the United States and throughout the world are some of the obvious reasons for our focus on this religion.

The Importance of Religion in Our Lives

As seen in Figure 7.2, 57% of Americans in 2006 regarded their religious beliefs to be very important, while another 27% indicate that religion is fairly important to them (Gallup Poll, 2006). These findings suggest that religion is important to more than four out of every five Americans. The importance of religion to an individual correlates with age groups, gender, education level, income level, race, and region in which one lives as can be seen in Figure 7.3.

Sixty percent of Americans believe that religion can answer all or most of today's problems (Gallup Poll, 2006). Although less than half of the population attends church weekly, most people identify with a religious perspective that is reflected in their daily living. It may affect one's dress, social activities, and dietary habits, including alcohol consumption and smoking.

FIGURE 7.2   The Importance of
Religion to Americans.

Adapted from Gallup Poll. (2006). *Religion.*
Retrieved December 28, 2006,
from http://www.galluppoll.com

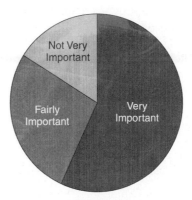

FIGURE 7.3   Characteristics of Americans Who Say Religion Is Very Important to Them.

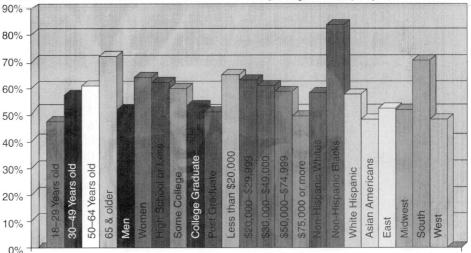

Adapted from Newport, F. (2006d). *Religion Most Important to Blacks, Women, and Older Americans.* Gallup News
Service, November 29, 2006. Retrieved from www.galluppoll.com/content/?ci=22414&pg=1

Religious behavior is learned as a normal part of the socialization pattern. The church
or religious center is sometimes not only a place of worship but also a social center.
Religion and religious differences are important in our study of this pluralistic nation
because it is a way of life for many people. In many areas of the United States, going to
church is a primary family function. Following church services, families may go out to
restaurants or enjoy their main meal of the week in their home. This is particularly true in
the South, where church attendance is highest.

If the religious group is tightly knit, a member may have little chance to interact on a
personal level with anyone other than another member of the same religion, especially if
attendance at a religious school is involved. Tight control over criteria for membership in
the group and little contact with those who are not group members are often key factors
in maintaining the integrity of religious sects. The Amish have been able to survive in this
way. Mormons, a much larger group, were able to grow with little outside interference
once they were established in Utah. Even in suburban areas, friendship patterns are largely
based on religious preference.

Churches and their religious programs serve as a strong socialization mechanism in the transmission of values from one generation to another. Rituals, parables, and stories reinforce these values, and Sunday schools serve as primary agents for transmitting these values. Religious institutions are also responsible for reinterpreting social failure in spiritual terms, compensating for the lack of value realization, and functioning as an agent of social control by reward and punishment.

Religiosity

Religiosity appears to be a function of culture. Age, gender, geographical background, and political affiliation appear to influence the religious nature of a person. As seen in Figure 7.4, Carroll (2004) found that older Americans (50 plus) were more likely to be church members and attend religious services than their younger counterparts. Regular religious attendance was also a function of gender, political affiliation, geographical background, income, and religious affiliation.

Attendance at religious services by different religious groups can be seen in Figure 7.5.

FIGURE 7.4   Characteristics of Americans Attending Religious Services Weekly or Almost Weekly.

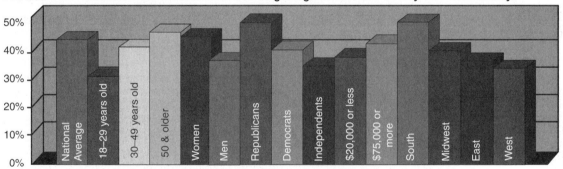

Adapted from Carroll J. (2004, March 2). American Public Opinion About Religion. *Gallup Tuesday Morning Briefing.*

FIGURE 7.5   Weekly or Almost Weekly Attendance at Religious Services by Religious Group.

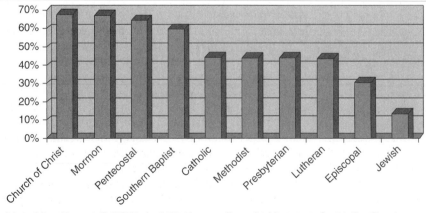

Adapted from Newport, F. (2006b, April 27). *Mormons, Evangelical Protestants, Baptists Top Church Attendance List.* Retrieved from www.galluppoll.com/content/?ci=22414&pg=1

Religious Pluralism in the United States

Five decades ago, few Americans would have envisioned their country led by a Catholic President or foreseen William H. Gray, an African American minister, being elected as the majority whip in the U.S. House of Representatives (1989–1991). In 1988, Pat Robertson, a popular televangelist, was a serious candidate for the Republican Party's presidential nomination and received strong support financially and otherwise. In 2004, Senator Joseph Lieberman, a Jewish American, was the Democratic nominee for Vice President of the United States. On January 4, 2007, Henry "Hank" Johnson (D-GA) and Mazie Hirono (D-HI) were sworn in as the first two Buddhists, and Keith Ellison (D-MN) became the first Muslim elected to Congress. Ellison took his oath of office on a copy of the Koran, once owned by Thomas Jefferson.

Religion in the United States is dynamic, as it is constantly changing. A Korean minister and leader of the **Unification Church** (considered by some to be a cult and an adaptation of Christianity, which believes in a cosmic struggle between the forces of good and evil) has led thousands of young people, many who are white, into his church's membership. African Americans have left traditional African American Protestant churches and joined the ranks of the Black Muslims. Tens of thousands of Latinos have left the Roman Catholic Church for Pentecostal churches, and some college students have embraced Buddhism (Black Muslims and Buddhism are described later in this chapter).

Some conservative Christian groups, such as the Mormons and Jehovah's Witnesses, do not classify themselves as **Protestants**, although some nonmembers often classify them as such. These two groups and the Seventh-Day Adventists tend to stand out from some other religious groups because their religious practices thoroughly pervade their way of life. Members of both the Mormon and Jehovah's Witness groups proselytize as a part of their commitment to their beliefs. Jehovah's Witnesses distribute the publication *Watchtower* widely in communities, and Mormon missionaries often work door-to-door. Members are unrelenting in their beliefs and in their commitment to prepare themselves for future fulfillment in the establishment of a latter-day sainthood and a life in heaven (Mormons), in life after the Armageddon (Jehovah's Witnesses), or in the millennium after Christ's Second Coming (Adventists).

Americans tend to identify not only with major groups, such as Protestants, Catholics, or Jews, but also with smaller groups or denominations within these major religious groups. For example, former President Jimmy Carter, a Southern Baptist, identifies himself as a "born again" Christian. Others may identify themselves as charismatic Catholics. It is important to note that within each major group is considerable heterogeneity.

Religious demographic data is often problematic. The U.S. Census Bureau does not gather information on religious membership or preferences. However, it is important to note that most denominations have remained in their traditional regional strongholds, with Catholics in the Northeast, liberal and moderate Protestants in the Northeast and Midwest, and conservative Protestants in the South. Some groups, however, have expanded their base considerably. For example, Episcopalians, Presbyterians, and members of the United Church of Christ are no longer as concentrated in the Northeast as they once were; some numerical base shifts have been made into the Sun Belt, primarily the southern and southwestern regions. Conservative Protestants, such as the Southern Baptists, are growing in all regions, including the Northeast and the West. Mormons have extended their influence far beyond the borders of Utah, Idaho, and Nevada. Their presence is felt in every state, as well as in many other countries. The Jewish population tends to be located in metropolitan areas throughout the country, with large concentrations in the mid-Atlantic region.

The data that is available is often self-reported by each religious group. The groups that do report do not always do so regularly. Of the U.S. population, 77% identify themselves as belonging to Protestant, Catholic, Jewish, or Latter-Day Saints (Gallup Poll, 2006). Until early in the twentieth century, however, Protestantism was by far the dominant religious force in the country. In 2006 Protestants were the largest religious group in the United States, with 49% of the population; 24% of the population identify themselves as Catholic, 2% Mormon, 2% Jewish, 1% Orthodox (Carroll, 2004), 11% indicated no religious affiliation (Gallup Poll, 2006), and 1% to 2% are Muslim (Council on American-Islamic Relations [CAIR], 2007). The estimates of Muslims living in the United States vary considerably from low estimates of around 2 million to as many as 7 million, with Islamic organizations providing the higher estimates. While Islam, in recent years, has grown rapidly in the United States, and may by now have become the third largest religious group, much of the literature still lists Judaism as one of the three major religious groups. This may be due to the fact that Judaism has been a driving force in the country for such a long period of U.S. history, and because Jewish individuals have provided so much leadership in the cultural, economic, and political landscape of the country.

Some denominational differences have their origin in ethnic differences. The English established the Anglican (Episcopalian) and Puritan (later Congregational) churches here; the Germans established some of the Lutheran, Anabaptist, and Evangelical churches; the Dutch, the Reformed churches; the Spanish, French, Italians, Poles, and others, the Roman Catholic churches; and the Ukrainians, Armenians, Greeks, and others, the Eastern Orthodox churches. Over time, many of these separate ethnic denominations have united or expanded their membership to include other ethnic groups.

Although religious pluralism has fostered the rapid accommodation of many American religious movements toward acceptability and respectability by society, groups such as Jehovah's Witnesses and Seventh-Day Adventists have maintained their independence. The smaller groups that maintain their distinctiveness have historically been victims of harassment by members of mainstream religious groups. Christian Scientists, Jehovah's Witnesses, Children of God, and the Unification Church are minority groups that have been subjected to such treatment.

Conflict among the four major faiths (Protestantism, Catholicism, Judaism, and Islam) has also been intense at different periods in history. Anti-Semitic, anti-Muslim, and anti-Catholic sentiments are still perpetuated in some households and institutions. Although religious pluralism in our past has often led to conflict, the hope of the future is that it will lead to a better understanding and respect for religious differences. In the following sections, we examine in greater detail the four major faiths and a few other faiths that the educator may find in various U.S. schools.

Protestantism

The Western Europeans who immigrated into this country in large numbers brought with them their various forms of Protestantism. While claiming 49% of the population (Gallup Poll, 2006), Protestants in the United States no longer constitute the dominant numerical majority in previous decades, but continue their influence in society and institutions.

To understand the differences that exist in Protestantism and that are often reflected in the classroom, the faith may be divided into two broad categories—liberal and conservative.

Liberal Protestants attempt to rethink Christianity in forms that are meaningful for a world dominated by science and rapid change. They stress the right of individuals to determine for themselves what is true in religion. They believe in the authority of Christian experience and religious life, rather than in dogmatic church pronouncements of the Bible. They are likely to support and participate in social action programs because of their belief that what individuals become depends greatly on an environment over which they have little control. They may or may not believe in the virgin birth of Jesus, and may not believe the Bible to be inerrant, as do their conservative counterparts. Some may not accept the miracles cited in the Bible to be factual. The United Church of Christ and Episcopalian churches are examples, although the degree of liberalism depends on the individual congregation. Methodists and Disciples of Christ represent more moderate denominations within this category.

Conservative Protestants generally believe that the Bible is inerrant, that the supernatural is distinct from the natural, salvation is essential, and that Jesus will return in bodily form during the Second Coming. They emphasize personal morality, rather than social ethics.

Effect of Protestants on Education.   Differences in beliefs among Protestants themselves have resulted in many court cases to determine what can or cannot be taught to or asked of students in the public schools. In addition to the previously discussed efforts by some **fundamentalist Christians** instituting the teaching of creationism, there has been other litigation. Jehovah's Witnesses have had confrontations with the schools because their children have refused to salute the flag. The Amish have fought in courts to remove their children from public schools after they have completed the eighth grade. Some religious groups continue to fight against the 1963 Supreme Court decision that disallowed prayer in school. Protestants have had a long history of involvement in both public and private educational programs. Some of their influence in the public schools is discussed in the section on evangelicals.

Ten Connecticut clergymen founded Yale, the nation's third oldest university, in 1701. Now considered as a nonsectarian institution, Yale still maintains some religious influence with its prestigious Yale Divinity School. Baylor University (Southern Baptist), Southern Methodist University (United Methodist), Goshen College (Mennonite), and Centre College (Presbyterian) are a few examples of the hundreds of Protestant institutions of higher education in the United States that have educated and influenced the lives of millions of American and international students.

Evangelicals.   As religion begins to play an increasing role in American society and politics, the general public is often exposed by the media to the terms "evangelical," the "Religious Right," and "fundamentalists." The general public often views these terms synonymously. However, this is not true as discussed below. Evangelicals are Protestants, but not all Protestants are evangelicals (Zorba, 2005).

The term **fundamentalist** can apply to any religious group: Christian, Jewish, Islamic, and others who represent an extremely conservative element of their religion. For the purposes of our discussion in this section, we will also try to explain what the term *evangelical* encompasses, and attempt to differentiate between the terms "evangelicals" and "the Religious Right." We will use Religious Right and fundamentalists interchangeably in this section, as different writers use either term.

Who Are the Evangelicals?   Newport (2005a) indicates that while approximately 80% of Americans identify themselves as Christians, there is no easy way to determine what part of that group can be considered evangelicals. He states that there are two basic and different means to determine who is an evangelical. Newport reported that 42% of Americans responded affirmatively when asked, "Would you describe yourself as a 'born again' or evangelical?" If these percentages are accurate, approximately 120 million Americans could be considered evangelicals.

The second means to identify oneself as an **evangelical** is to answer affirmatively to three questions: (1) if you have been "**born again**" or have had a "born again experience," (2) if you have encouraged other people to believe in Jesus Christ, and (3) if you believe the Bible is the actual word of God. Twenty-two percent of Americans qualified as evangelicals with these criteria (Newport, 2005a). Those who are considered to have been "born again," are believed to have a Christian conversion experience with a spiritual rebirth into a new life.

Evangelicals and Mainline Protestants. Many evangelical churches have become mega churches with weekly attendance of 2,000 or more. Some mega churches have attendance that exceeds 10,000 and even 20,000 or more on a Sunday. Mainline Protestant churches are the traditional and historical denominations, which are among the larger ones established in the United States. Some mainline churches, which have not embraced the evangelical movement, have had difficulty in maintaining their congregations. Marsden (2006) suggests that by the end of the 1970s some of the mainline Protestant denominations such as the United Methodists, American Baptists (formerly Northern), Presbyterians, Episcopalians, and the United Church of Christ had declining memberships due in part to their loss of older members, and the inability to attract comparable numbers of young members. This was due in part to the leadership of these groups moving toward the moderate left politically and theologies viewed as ethically centered. In the 1980s and 1990s, conservatives or fundamentalists took control of the largest Protestant denomination, the Southern Baptist Convention by gaining control of both the central boards of the denomination and the theological seminaries (Marsden, 2006).

Evangelicals strongly support the nuclear family and place great emphasis on individual morality and responsible personal behavior. Pro-choice issues are in direct conflict with their beliefs (Green, 2004). Marsden (2006) states that by the early 1980s, anti-abortion had become the centerpiece of the Catholic-Protestant alliance for militants. Hundreds if not thousands of crisis pregnancy centers have opened throughout the country. Often they open next to planned-parenthood centers or are even located in the same building to counter the work of the pro-choice advocates.

Homosexuality goes against the values of the evangelicals and they strongly believe that one can overcome what they believe is a sin by being converted and abstaining and even changing their behavior with the help of God and the religious community (Green, 2004). Evangelicals strongly believe that humanity was established in God's image as the centerpiece and heterosexual relationships as God's model. Both abortion and gay rights are contrary to what evangelicals believe is God's intention for humanity (Zorba, 2005).

See Chapter 4 regarding issues related to sexual orientation and rights.

With evangelicals assuming a major role, religion has become even more central to many local and national elections and has in some instances helped shape public policies. Religion has influenced the direction of many local school boards, has had profound impact on judicial appointments, and has provided strong support for the country's involvement in Iraq.

Evangelical Moderates. Evangelicals cast a very broad umbrella, forming a very diverse group of individuals who often have different beliefs and agendas. In recent years there has been an increasing division between conservative or fundamentalist evangelicals and their moderate counterparts. Adam Hamilton, a moderate evangelical minister has been quoted as saying, "Our task is not to go around judging people—Jesus didn't do that" and has expressed compassion for homosexuals (Miller, 2006). Hamilton feels that conservative evangelicals have lost their focus on the spirit of Jesus and have separated the world into black and white, when the world is much grayer. He states that it is hard to imagine Jesus carrying signs at an anti-gay rally (Miller, 2006).

Hamilton, Rick Warren, and Jim Wallis are noted evangelicals who have large follow-ings and are representative of the moderates in the evangelical movement. Miller (2006) indicates that there is a new generation of evangelical believers pressing beyond the reli-gious right trying to broaden the movement to focus on social and economic justice rather than the wars on sex.

While leaders among the Religious Right have openly called for support of Republican candidates, other evangelicals such as Wallis (2005) state that God is neither Republican nor Democrat. Wallis further states that poverty, the environment, war, truthfulness, human rights, response to terrorism, and human life are all religious issues. He empha-sizes those political candidates' decisions to pursue war or peace must be respectful of international law in responding to real global threats. Political candidates are obligated to be truthful in justifying war and other foreign and domestic policies. Further he cautions that candidates use language judiciously when speaking on the war against terrorism and not confuse the roles of God and church.

Others tiring of the divisive politics of religion are also embracing a wider ranging agenda, emphasizing reaching out to the poor and disenfranchised. While embracing typical evangelical values condemning abortion and stem cell research, Warren and his congregation have demanded an end to the atrocities in Darfur and have denounced the torture of individuals in that country. Other moderates are now addressing the issues related to global warming, reminding their congregations that they must assume stewardship for the welfare of the environment.

Fundamentalists and Their Political Influence. We should reiterate here that Protestant fundamentalists are evangelicals, however, they are a smaller subgroup, and have narrower and stricter criteria for inclusion.

While evangelicals believe the Bible to be the word of God, the **Religious Right** or fundamentalist Protestants accept it literally. Some evangelicals believe that there is metaphor and poetry in the Bible and that there is truth in the metaphors and poetry (Green, 2004). All evangelicals, or "born again Christians," believe that Jesus is the son of God, that he died to redeem mankind for their sins, and that they will have eternal life (life after death) if they believe in Jesus in this manner. In their conversion process of believing that Jesus, the son of God died for their sins, they are "born again," in a spiritual life. Green also indicates that many if not most fundamentalists believe that Jesus will someday return to earth, and it will mark the end of human history, as we know it. Some of the evangelicals do not accept the return of Jesus seriously or the end of the earth as believed by the fundamentalists.

Marsden (2006) suggests that the Religious Right includes fundamentalist militants who come from the entire spectrum of evangelicals. Issues related to family, sexuality, gay rights, and abortion have forged coalitions between Catholics, Mormons, and conservative Protestants.

Much of the fundamentalist leadership has come from Southerners such as Pat Robertson, James Robison, and the late Jerry Falwell. Their national impact became possible as the turmoil of the civil rights movement receded and the South joined the rest of the nation in integration. Marsden (2006) indicates that the fundamentalist movement had some of its impetus from the confrontations over what was being taught in the public schools. The **Moral Majority** emerged in 1979 with Rev. Jerry Falwell, a televangelist, and his associates. It consisted of conservative Christian action committees that campaigned for issues and candidates, which they believed supported Christian moral law. They believed they represented the majority of the people's opinion, thus the name of "Moral Majority." The organization lobbied for prayer and the teaching of creationism in public schools, while opposing the Equal Rights Amendment, homosexual rights, abortion, and the U.S.-Soviet Strategic Arms Limitation Treaty (SALT). They strongly supported Ronald Reagan and were in part responsible for his election to the presidency. The Moral Majority was officially dissolved in 1989, but much of its work continues through the Christian Coalition network initiated by Rev. Pat Robertson (*Columbia Encyclopedia*, 2001–2005b).

Marsden (2006) contends that fundamentalists are militant evangelicals who are waging battles on two fronts. They are struggling against the theological modernism in mainline denominations. Fundamentalists are also fighting against what they view as alarming changes in culture, such as issues of gender, sexuality, and the family. They are distressed over changing sexual standards, the ordination of women, birth control, divorce rates, the decline in family authorities, ban on prayer in schools, and the teaching of biological evolution in public schools. Marsden also notes that while fundamentalists typically believe that church leaders and public spokespersons should be male, women in the fundamentalist movement defend their subordinate roles and exercise considerable influence in the movement.

Fundamentalism within American Protestantism militancy does not typically lead to personal undertaking of physical violence, although on rare occasions, some individuals have made attacks on abortionists or their clinics. However, fundamentalists have often provided open support for military warfare on the part of the nation against what has been perceived as the forces of evil (Marsden, 2006). Newport (2003) suggests that most religions advocate a doctrine of love and acceptance, antithetical to hostile and violent means of solving conflicts. However, throughout history, religious individuals have supported some wars as necessary, moral, and justifiable. In early 2003, when support for military intervention in Iraq was still popular with the American public, Newport found the greatest support for military action came from the Religious Right, and evangelicals.

Noted fundamentalist media personalities such as Dr. James Dobson, and previously mentioned Rev. Pat Robertson and the late Rev. Jerry Falwell have or have had millions of followers supporting their ministries, their moral/religious positions, and their politics. They and other evangelical leaders were instrumental in rallying both moderate evangelicals and religious conservatives (including Protestant, Catholic, and Jews) in electing Ronald Reagan, George H. W. Bush, and George W. Bush. They played a prominent role in the Republican Party's gaining control of Congress in the 1994 midterm elections, and indirectly contributed to the appointment of conservative federal appointments both at the Supreme Court (e.g., Chief Justice Roberts and Justice Alito) and other levels of the federal judiciary. The impact of these conservative appointments to the bench have had and will continue to have an impact on the interpretation of federal laws for decades.

Evangelicals and Education. Evangelical Christians also have differing views on education. Some of the more conservative evangelicals prefer to send their children to private Christian schools, while some others prefer to homeschool their children. Some believe it is their responsibility to take over the schools and to infuse the curriculum with a Christian orientation. The fundamentalist Citizen's for Excellence in Education (CEE)

Pause to Reflect 7.2

The evangelical Christians and other conservative religious groups formed effective political alliances, which enabled them to elect a conservative President and gain control of both houses of Congress. This in turn allowed for the appointments of conservatives to the federal courts and to gain control of the Supreme Court, which will have a lasting impact on how the laws are interpreted.

- What role should religion play in politics?
- Why do some people think that religious groups should not be involved in political elections?
- How do religious politics influence curriculum and instruction in schools?

Go to the *Homework and Exercises* **section in Chapter 7 of MyEducationLab and select** *Pause to Reflect 7.2* **to answer these questions.**

---

with their accompanying National Association for Christian Education advocates the removal of Christian children from public schools to rescue them from what they believe is an indoctrination in inappropriate and harmful curricula. An alternative approach to education by this group is for committed Christians to take over the school boards and to infuse the schools with Christian morality. CEE has been successful in some school districts and has developed a publication on how this can be accomplished.

Fundamentalist evangelicals are distressed by what they consider the negative influence of secular humanism. They are concerned with the staffing of homosexual and lesbian teachers, and also with curricula, which they view as harmful to America's children because it lacks a Christian influence.

School prayer remains an important issue among many of the evangelicals. Tuition tax credits are another issue, which is often raised, especially among those individuals who have removed their children from the public schools in favor of private Christian schools. These issues are addressed later in this chapter in a section on controversial issues.

The majority of evangelicals see their role in schools as just being there and providing a positive influence by their behaviors. Many do not criticize the public schools but focus on the failings of the family in not meeting the responsibility of instilling morality and values. Some do support the schools instilling a common core of values and morality, which most in the country would support. They want the schools to focus on basic academics, reading, writing, and mathematics rather than on social concerns (e.g., poverty, human rights violations, gender equity, ethnic studies, etc.). They are concerned with what they view as unfair discrimination against religious views in the schools such as creation science or intelligent design (Smith, 2000).

Today a significant number of Americans continue to reject Charles Darwin's view of evolution. Newport (2006c) found that 46% of Americans surveyed believe that God created humans about 6,000 years ago in essentially their current form. Another 36% believe that man evolved with God guiding the process. Only 13% believe that God had no part of the process. These findings should give educators a clear understanding why the teaching of evolution has often come under attack in the schools and why some parents insist that other theories of the origins of man be provided in the schools.

Evangelicals are firmly behind the movement to either rid the schools of evolution in the curriculum or to provide alternative theories. The most often cited alternative theory is that of **creation science**. Creation science accepts creation of all living things in six days, literally as presented in the Bible (Moore, 2005). As might be expected, opponents of creation science suggest that it is not a science, but a theory based on a story as told in the Bible.

A third theory has been proposed: **intelligent design**. Supporters of intelligent design suggest that only an intelligent being could have created a natural world, which is so complex and so well ordered. Some scientists and evolutionists suggest that intelligent design is creationism veiled in this relatively new term (Carlson, 2005). President George W. Bush fueled the debate by suggesting that "intelligent design" should be taught along with evolution in the schools (Moore, 2005). In reality, while most supporters of intelligent design likely support creationism, an individual could believe in both evolution and intelligent design, theorizing that God, the intelligent being, guided the evolutionary process. It is important for educators to understand that supporters of both sides of the issue are often passionate about their beliefs and opinions. It is essential to know one's community in deciding the curriculum related to these issues and the manner in which it is presented in both the classroom and to the community.

Evangelicals may be a numerical minority in the United States, but they are an influential force in our society. Their efforts affect politics, our judicial system, our legal system, and our schools. Those who disagree with their beliefs, their practices, and their efforts to bring change to the country often resent them. Whether educators agree or disagree with the views and practices of evangelicals, it may be helpful to understand that what they ultimately want for the country is no different from what other religious persuasions seek. They envision a more moral and safer America, one free of drugs, crime, and violence that plague our schools and our streets. Their views on how to accomplish this may or may not agree with you as an educator, but it may be helpful to understanding what they hope to accomplish. This can help you in being respectful of their values, and may minimize the likelihood of conflict over curriculum and student assignments.

Political Influence of Protestants and Other Religious Groups.   The political leadership in the country often reflects the influence of various religious groups. Table 7.1 shows the religious affiliation of members of the U.S. Congress. In 2007, as in the past,

VIDEO INSIGHTS

Battle Between Faith and Science

The American public is very much split on Darwin's Theory of Evolution. This is not merely a matter of philosophical difference. This involves religion, and religion is a matter viewed very seriously by a majority of Americans. This video painfully shows how a community can be split by religious differences.

1. Why do individuals feel so strongly about an issue such as evolution?
2. Could anything have been done to avoid the contentious situation as shown in the video?
3. What are the attitudes toward evolution in your community?

Go to the Video Insights DVD and watch the video segment *Battle Between Faith and Science*. **Then, go to the** *Homework and Exercises* **section in Chapter 7 of MyEducationLab and select** *Video Insights: Battle Between Faith and Science* **to answer these questions.**

TABLE 7.1   Religious Affiliation of Members of the U.S. Congress in 2007

	U.S. Senate	U.S. House of Representatives	
	Percent	Number	Percent
Buddhist	0%	2	0.5%
Catholic	24%	126	29%
Christian (Unspecified)	3%	23	5%
Jewish	13%	30	7%
LDS (Mormon)	5%	10	2%
Muslim	0%	1	0.2%
Orthodox	1%	4	1%
Protestant	51%	220	51%
Unitarian	1%	1	0.2%
None Indicated	2%	18	4%

Adapted from *Congressional Yellow Book.* (2007, Spring). New York: Leadership Directories, Inc.

Protestants led in Congress with 50.65%, as compared to the 49% of the general population who indicated they were Protestants that year. **Roman Catholics** followed with 28.3%, which is higher than the Gallup findings of 24% for the general population. Jewish congressional members made up 8% of the House and Senate seats, which is considerably higher than the 2% of the general population. Mormon presence in Congress was 2.8%, also higher than their presence in the overall population (*Congressional Yellow Book,* 2007; Gallup Poll, 2006).

Members of more liberal churches (e.g., Episcopalians, Presbyterians) and Jewish members may be disproportionately overrepresented in Congress because, historically, they have felt a responsibility for social issues. Another factor is probably related to the social class of members of these various denominations. Because seeking political office can be quite costly, religious groups whose members are typically upper middle class tend to be overrepresented in political offices. For example, a study by Sacerdote and Glaeser, (2001) revealed that the educational level of Jewish individuals was the highest among the religious groups studied, followed by Presbyterians and Episcopalians. Lutherans and Methodists were in the next highest educated religious groups followed by Roman Catholics. The two groups with the lowest education level were the "other denomination Protestants" (which included fundamentalists), and the Baptists at the lowest overall education level. While educational level does not always translate into higher income, there is often a correlation between the two. In a report indicating differential per capita contributions of various denominations, the per capita contribution for Southern Baptists was $582; Methodists, $611; Episcopalians, $1,091.05; and Presbyterians, $1,183 (Lindner, 2004). While some could argue that each group may have its own culture toward giving, this logic does not explain the differences in these particular groups. Some of the conservative religious groups such as the Southern Baptists and Latter-Day Saints strongly encourage their members to tithe (giving a tenth of their income).

Protestantism maintains not only the major religious influence on society but also on political leadership. Because Protestants continue to represent such a large segment of the population, such influence is to be expected. Pluralism increasingly forces the sharing of power and resources, however, among diverse groups of people in society.

Catholicism

Although the doctrine and pattern of worship within the Catholic Church are uniform, individual parishes continue to differ to some extent according to the race, ethnic background, and social class of their members. Individual dioceses also may differ with the more conservative or liberal (progressive) views of the presiding bishop. Unlike the Protestant faith, however, which includes denominational pluralism, the **Catholic** faith is one denomination under a Pope, which has authority over all Catholics throughout the world.

With approximately 24% of the U.S. population identifying with the Roman Catholic Church (Gallup Poll, 2006), the *Yearbook of American and Canadian Churches* (2006) reported Catholic Church membership to be 67,820,833 million.

Today, the Catholic Church in the United States is the wealthiest national church in the Roman Catholic world and contributes approximately half of its income to the Church in Rome. The increasing number of American cardinals and American priests appointed to important posts in Rome attests to the growing importance of the Catholic Church in the United States (Corrigan & Hudson, 2004).

Similarities Among Diversity.   The movement toward conservatism has not been limited to Protestants. Some Catholics have objected to changes in liturgy and other areas of modernization by their church. In many instances, conservative Catholics have joined forces with conservative Protestants on such issues as abortion and sexual morality. Some Catholics have even abandoned their traditional support of the Democratic Party to support conservative Republican candidates. On the other end of the continuum, some Catholics have protested the conservative position of their church regarding the limited participation of women in leadership roles and some support the pro-choice movement. In the 1960s, Roman Catholics, including some priests, engaged in political activism and joined radical elements in opposing the Vietnam War.

Membership in U.S. Catholic churches involves many different ethnic groups. Some parishes are predominantly Irish, while others are predominantly Italian, Polish, Mexican, Puerto Rican, and so on. A parish may choose to conduct services in the predominant language group of its parishioners or may have individual masses for different language groups. Cultural events of the ethnic groups may be incorporated into the daily activities of the particular parish (for example, Quinceniera for Latino females reaching the age of 15, as seen in the photo on p. 253).

Effect on Education.   In addition to its phenomenal numerical growth, the Roman Catholic Church in the United States has developed the largest private educational system in the world. In many communities, Catholic parochial schools often offer quality educational options to both Catholic and non-Catholic students at a relative lower cost than most other private institutions.

With thousands of elementary and secondary schools from Vermont to Hawaii and such internationally recognized universities as Notre Dame, Creighton, and Loyola, Roman Catholic schools and universities have educated millions of Americans and greatly influenced the culture of the country.

A thirteen-year-old Jewish female observes her Bat mitzvah by reading from the Torah in Hebrew. The event marks her entry into religious adulthood. In a Los Angeles area church a fifteen-year-old Mexican American female observes mass in celebrating her entry into womanhood.

Political Influence.   In 1928, Alfred Smith, the Democratic nominee, was the first Roman Catholic to run for the office of President. There were two major issues in that campaign—prohibition and religion. Attacks were made against Smith, claiming that if elected he would make Catholicism the national religion. In the 1960 presidential election, similar attacks were made against John F. Kennedy and his Catholic background. However, Kennedy was elected. John Kerry, a Catholic, was the unsuccessful Democratic candidate for the office of President. During the 2004 campaign, some conservative Catholics voiced objections to Kerry because of his pro-choice position on abortion.

By becoming a uniquely American church, members of the Catholic Church have not rejected the belief that they belong to the one universal church. Instead, they have accepted the fact that U.S. society is intrinsically pluralistic and that their religion is one of the four major faiths that exists together with Protestantism, Judaism, and Islam.

Judaism

Judaism is one of the oldest religions known to humanity and provides the historical roots of both Catholicism and Protestantism. Primarily as a result of Jews from many countries amalgamating under the identification of Jewish American, Judaism has become one of the four major faiths in this country. While Judaism represents only about 2% of the population, the contributions of Jewish Americans to the fields of medicine, science, academia, business, economics, entertainment, and politics in the United States has been profound.

In the nineteenth century, large numbers of Jews emigrated from Germany and many began moving from Jewish enclaves along the East Coast to other parts of the country.

Religious persecution in countries such as Russia and Germany brought additional Jewish refugees to the United States in the twentieth century.

The *2006 American Jewish Yearbook* estimated the U.S. Jewish population to be approximately 6,400,000 or 2.2% of the U.S. population (PR Newswire, 2006). Compared with the Protestant and Catholic populations, the Jewish population has not grown substantially, partly as a result of intermarriage and low birthrates. Yet, as a group, they remain a distinctive, identifiable religious minority whose social standing and influence are disproportionate to their numbers.

Later generations changed the entire picture of American Jewry and Judaism in America; ethnic and an American religious identity emerged. The lifestyle evolved into a microculture of the American middle class. Education, including higher education, played an important role in the Jewish community by advancing young people from the working class into white-collar and professional positions.

Similarities Among Diversity.   Judaism's long and varied history makes it difficult to define a Jewish person. There is no Jewish race. Jewish identity is blended in historical, religious, and ethnic variables. Early Jewish settlers in the United States found it difficult, if not impossible, to practice Judaism in the traditional ways that they had experienced in Europe. Jewish religious practices and patterns were modified to meet the needs of the immigrants and in ways that made them characteristically American.

While some Jewish families have maintained their ties to Orthodox and Conservative Judaism, the majority of American Jews affiliated with Reformed Synagogues. Reformed Jews represent the more liberal end of the continuum. For example, according to Jewish law, one who is born to a Jewish mother, or who converts to Judaism is considered a Jew. Reformed Jews also accept children born to non-Jewish mothers as Jews. At the other end of the continuum from the reformed Jews are the conservative and the Orthodox Jews. They tend to hold firm to Jewish law, including diet and dress.

In addition to differences in religious adherence to traditional Jewish law, American Jews come from diverse backgrounds. There are two major groups of Jews who immigrated into the United States. The Ashkenazim came from Jewish communities of central and Eastern Europe. The Sephardim were Jews from Spain, Portugal, or other Mediterranean countries and the Middle East. Other groups of Jews include those from Jewish communities of Ethiopia and India. These different groups brought much of the culture of their countries of origin when they immigrated to the United States. Some of the Sephardic Jews from Spain settled in Hispanic communities in areas such as New Mexico. Many blended in with their Hispanic neighbors and became an integral part of their communities.

Although most Jews strongly identify with their religion, the Jewish practice of religion is relatively low regarding synagogue attendance and home religious observance. Nevertheless, the U.S. synagogue is the strongest agency in the Jewish community. Although they may not attend services as regularly as their Catholic and Protestant counterparts, a large percentage of Jews retain some affiliation with a synagogue. Some believe that Jewish identity does not require regular attendance at the synagogue. Attending religious services and studying Jewish texts hold little interest for much of the Jewish population. Attendance on High Holidays such as Rosh Hashanah, Yom Kippur, and Passover, however, is always high. The synagogue in the United States serves not only as a place of religious worship but also as a primary base for Jewish identity and survival.

Effect on Education.   Many of the Jewish temples or synagogues throughout the country operate private schools. Some schools operate only at the elementary grades, while others are more comprehensive. In some of the larger Jewish communities, particularly among the Orthodox groups, yeshivas, or private religious schools, have been established to provide high-quality instruction in both academics and in-depth religious studies. Jewish universities such as Yeshiva University in New York, and Brandeis University in Massachusetts have made significant contributions to higher education in the United States.

For decades American schools observed the Christian holiday, Christmas. In the last 30 or 40 years, educators have become increasingly more sensitive to the diversity of the students in their schools. December is also the time of the year when Jewish families observe Chanukah (Hanukkah), when there is usually gift giving for the children. In the spirit of inclusiveness and sensitivity, December school recess and any holiday parties should be referred to as holiday parties or December recess in school. The families choosing to do so can then observe religious observances at home.

Political Influence.   While the Jewish population in the United States is relatively small (about 2.2%), the group's political influence is significant (see Table 7.1). Jewish representation in political office is disproportionately high.

Anti-Semitism.   Jews in the United States and throughout the world have been the targets of prejudice and discrimination, sometimes leading to attempted annihilation of the population. During World War II, the Jewish Holocaust, which resulted in the deaths of millions of European Jews, was systematically conducted by one of the most economically and technically advanced nations of the period. The civilized world cannot ignore the fact that despite overwhelming evidence of what was being done by the Nazis, nothing was done to stop one of the greatest atrocities ever committed against humankind. Now in the twenty-first century, neo-Nazis, the President of Iran, and others suggest that the Jewish Holocaust was a myth that never happened. The Gallup Poll over the years has found from 2% to 9% of Americans doubting that the Holocaust ever took place (Newport, 2005b). Other attempts at genocide persist in various places in the world. It is the responsibility of educators to help their students understand that, even today, other holocausts have taken place in places such as Europe and Africa.

Anti-Semitism is rooted in Jewish-Gentile conflicts that have existed for centuries. In the United States, Jews and Catholics were also targets of the Ku Klux Klan especially in the 1920s and 1930s when anti-Semitic newspapers and radio commentators proliferated (Johnstone, 2007). Discrimination has occurred in both occupational and social life. In some instances, Jews have often been denied high-level corporate management positions and have had limited access or have been barred from membership in social clubs (Hemeyer, 2006). The form and degree of anti-Semitism vary with world and national events; when non-Jews believe that events are the result of Jewish action, prejudices resurface in work and deed. Events in the Middle East that involve Israel often initiate these reactions. Examples of continued anti-Semitic hate crimes persist with the burning of synagogues and the attack on a Jewish day care center in Los Angeles in recent years.

Islam

As a religious term, **Islam** means to surrender to the will or law of God. Islam is one of the major religions of the world, with over 1 billion adherents worldwide. Islam is also one of the fastest growing religions in the United States. The U.S. Census Bureau does not compile data on religious preference, and there has been no creditable scientific survey

Educators will continue to see increasing numbers of religious minority group students in their classrooms reflecting the religious diversity of the United States.

to determine the actual number of Muslims in the United States. Estimates range from a low of 1.1 million to as many as 6 to 7 million followers (CAIR, 2007; Huda, 2006), and 1,209 mosques located throughout the country (U.S. State Department, 2004). While many Americans think Islam is primarily a Middle Eastern religion, only a small portion of the world's Muslims lives in that region. Indonesia, Pakistan, and India all have larger Muslim populations than any Middle Eastern country.

More than a hundred years ago, a group of immigrants from the Middle East settled in Cedar Falls, Iowa. They were among the first Muslims to settle in this country. The descendants of these immigrants have maintained the religion of their ancestors, built a new mosque, and have become an integral part of their community. As everyday citizens, businesspeople, and professionals, they dress, talk, and act like any other American. Only their religion distinguishes them from their Christian and Jewish neighbors.

Islamic Beliefs. Those who practice Islam are **Muslims**. Islam is both a belief system and a way of life for individuals and entire societies. Islam is based on the holy writings of the **Qur'an**, or **Koran**. Muslims believe that the Qur'an consists of the exact words that were revealed by God through the Angel Gabriel to the prophet Muhammad (A.D. 570–632). The Qur'an's basic theme is the relationship between God and His creatures. It provides guidelines for a society that is just with proper human conduct, and an economic system that is equitable. Muslims believe that Islam began with Adam and continued through the line of prophets including Abraham, Moses, Jesus, and Mohammad. The basic tenets of Islam include:

1. *Faith:* belief in one God and Mohammad as his last messenger.
2. *Prayer:* five times daily, facing Mecca.
3. *Charity:* contributing to the poor.
4. *Fasting:* without food or water from sunrise to sunset during Ramadan (9th month of the Islamic year).
5. *Pilgrimage:* a visit to Mecca once in a lifetime, performing the Hajj (Ellwood & McGraw, 2005).

The pilgrimage to Mecca is an obligation to those who are physically and financially able. The rites of the Hajj (pilgrimage) begin in the 12th month of the Islamic lunar year.

They include circling the Ka'ba seven times and joining in prayer for God's forgiveness. Muslims believe that the Ka'ba is the place of worship that **Allah,** the Arabic word for God, commanded Abraham and Ishmael to build. Muslims worship the same God as Christians and Jews. Christian Arabs also refer to God as Allah (Denny, 2006; Ellwood & McGraw, 2005).

Among Westerners, **jihad** is one of the most misinterpreted concepts in Islam. It is often mistakenly translated as "holy war," evoking images of terrorists and Osama bin Laden. The word "jihad" comes from the Arabic *jahada*, meaning "struggle," "effort," or "striving" in the way of God (Burkholder, 2002; Denny, 2006). Burkholder suggests that in a theological context it can encompass any kind of struggle which has spiritual significance, such as giving up smoking, and controlling one's temper. It can mean a physical struggle in building or cleaning of a mosque, a struggle to avoid religious persecution, or even the struggle against human passions and instincts, which inhibit one from doing the work of God. It can also mean an armed struggle against forces of injustice. Muslim scholars teach that only defensive wars are truly jihad (Hopfe & Woodward, 2007).

Observe and Learn — Lesson in Action

Islam

Go to the *Homework and Exercises* section in Chapter 7 of MyEducationLab and select *Observe and Learn: Lessons in Action* to view the video "Geometry and Tessellation in Islamic Art" and answer the accompanying questions. Through the lesson, students gain an understanding of how the Muslim world uses geometry and tessellation as a means of making meaning of the natural world. The resulting images are used to decorate houses of worship, homes, and community buildings in the Muslim world and can be said to reveal religious and spiritual beliefs.

1. In what ways did students in the class connect to the art shown at the start of the lesson?
2. In what ways did the creation of student drawings deepen an understanding of the principles of Islamic art for students?
3. What do you know about Islam? Where do you get your information?
4. How might your understanding of a variety of religions affect what you do in your future classroom?

Attitudes Toward Islam.   The tragic destruction of the World Trade Center on September 11, 2001, the airliner crash in Pennsylvania, and the damage to the U.S. Pentagon resulted in the loss of thousands of lives and focused world attention on Muslim extremists. Since then, the United States has been in almost continuous conflict with Muslim extremists in Afghanistan and Iraq. Around the world, in countries such as Spain, the Philippines, Great Britain, and Indonesia, hundreds of lives have been lost at the hands of Islamic extremists. At times it is difficult to separate the actions that are politically motivated from those actually motivated by an individual's religion. Educators, however, should be mindful of the fact that there are extremists in almost every religious group, and the vast majority of Muslims in the United States and throughout the world are peace-loving individuals who abhor violence.

When acts of terrorism occur, such as the Oklahoma City bombing in 1995, Muslim Americans often are blamed and become the targets of hate crimes. As feared, local and national news media incorrectly speculated that Muslim terrorists perpetrated the Oklahoma City bombing. Educators have the responsibility to assist our students in understanding that their Muslim classmates and their families are no more responsible for these acts than were German Americans responsible for the Holocaust.

The continued conflicts in both Iraq and Afghanistan have drawn daily attention to both Arabs and Islamic extremists. By midyear 2007, more than 3,500 American servicemen and women had lost their lives in Iraq, with thousands more wounded. The casualties of these conflicts are reported daily in almost all forms of media. It is therefore, important for us as educators to understand how the American public views Islam. Since the events of 9/11, the Gallup Poll has twice conducted surveys to determine Americans' perception of Muslims. Saad (2006) found that 22% of Americans indicated that they would not want a Muslim as a neighbor, 18% indicated that they would be nervous if they notice a Muslim woman on their airline flight, and 31% expressed the same sentiments if there were a Muslim man on their flight. Nearly 40% admit to harboring feelings of prejudice, while nearly 60% indicate they do not. The 41% of Americans who reported that they knew someone who is a Muslim provided some positive hope, as these individuals tended to report a positive perception of their Muslim acquaintances (Saad, 2006). Educators can help to create a more positive attitude for their students by introducing them to positive personal experiences with individuals of Islamic faith.

In September 2005, a Danish newpaper published an article "The Face of Muhammad." The article consisted of 12 cartoons (of which only some depicted Muhammad). The articles and accompanying cartoons received a very negative reaction by Danish Muslims, and that in part led to the reprinting of the cartoons by over 50 newspapers in other countries. This resulted in both peaceful and violent protests and rioting, particularly in Muslim countries.

The newspapers and defenders of the cartoon publishing cited the right of "freedom of expression" and "freedom of the press." Esposito (2006), a Gallup senior scientist, suggests that the printing and reprinting of the cartoons by newspapers may have been "as much about profits as about the prophet, of Islam. Respected European newspapers have acted more like tabloids" (p. 1). Esposito states that the cartoons seek to test and provoke by mocking Muslims' most sacred symbols and values. He further states that defaming the prophet and Islam is inflammatory and enforces Muslim grievances, humiliation, and social marginalization. Further, it drives a wedge between the West and moderated Muslims. The newspapers unwittingly played directly into the hands of Muslim extremists. France's Rabbi Joseph Sitruk was quoted by the Associated Press: "We gain nothing by lowering religions, humiliating them, and making caricatures of them. It's a lack of honesty and respect. Freedom of expression is not a right without limits." Esposito concludes that the pluralism and tolerance today demand greater mutual understanding and respect from non-Muslims and Muslims alike.

Similarities Among Diversity. Believers are of two major groups. Sunni Muslims, who comprise 85% of Islam, believe that the rightful leadership began with Abu Bakr and that the succession has passed to *caliphs,* or political leaders. Shi'i or Shi'ite Muslims are a smaller but highly visible group. Shi'ite Muslims believe that Muhammad intended the succession of leadership to pass through the bloodline of his cousin and son-in-law, 'Ali. Shi'ite Muslims have attracted considerable world attention in recent years because of their insistence of adherence to Islamic law by their countries' governments (Denny, 2006; Hopfe & Woodward, 2007).

In 1979, a group of Shi'ite Muslims, followers of the Ayatollah Kohmeni, overthrew Shah Reza Pahlavi of Iran and later gained international attention by seizing American hostages. Some of the religious/political Shi'ite leaders view Western culture as antithetical to Islam and have strongly resisted U.S. and other Western influences on their countries. This has often led to fierce political battles between the two groups and has occasionally resulted in acts of terrorism against Western countries. Saddam Hussein, who

CRITICAL INCIDENTS IN TEACHING

Who Is an American?

Nadar Hoseini is a third grader in a suburban community in northern Virginia. Nadar's parents emigrated from Iran in the mid-1970s and are now naturalized citizens. Nadar was born in Virginia, where his father is a chemist for a large manufacturer. During recess, Ms. Nash, Nadar's teacher, notices that Nadar is sitting alone and is visibly upset. After some probing into an apparent problem, she learns that Nadar's friends have shunned him.

"Michael," he tells Ms. Nash, "told the group that his father says the World Trade Center was destroyed by Muslims who are all fanatics trying to blow up America and kill innocent Americans. 'Your friend Nadar is one of them Muslims, and you had better not let me catch you playing with him again. We ought to ship all of them Muslims back where they came from!'" Michael quotes his father.

Protesting, Nadar insists that he was born in the United States and that he and his family are American. The protest falls on deaf ears as Nadar's classmates join Michael in ostracizing him. Ms. Nash is determined to help Nadar's situation but at the moment is at a loss as to how she will approach the problem.

Questions for Classroom Discussion

1. What should Ms. Nash say to Nadar?
2. Should Ms. Nash go directly to Michael and the other boys involved?
3. How can she change perceptions of the boys without seeming to attack Michael's father?
4. What sensitivity activities can she conduct in the class?

Building Teaching Skills

Go to the *Building Teaching Skills* section in Chapter 7 of MyEducationLab and select *Critical Incidents in Teaching: Who Is an American?* to complete this exercise.

led Iraq for many years, was a Sunni Muslim. He and his Sunni followers dominated the numerically superior Shi'ites in his country by force and at one time waged war with the Shi'ite government in Iran. The sectarian violence within Iraq, which the United States has sought to control, has involved these two warring factions, along with the involvement of outside groups.

Black Muslims.   While U.S. **Black Muslims** have primarily aligned themselves with the Sunni form of Islam, they form a unique identity of their own. Although a few black slaves may have been Muslims, the origins of the Black Muslims in the United States likely began with Timothy Drew or Noble Drew Ali (1886–1927), who taught that blacks were from Asia and, therefore, Moors or Muslims.

Elijah Poole (1875–1975), who became known as Elijah Muhammad, led the Nation of Islam into national visibility. In the early 1960s, Malcolm X (1925–1965) became the most articulate spokesperson for the Nation of Islam. Born Malcolm Little, he renounced his "slave" name *Little* and adopted *X,* which symbolized identity lost when his ancestors were forcibly taken from their homeland as slaves (Ellwood & McGraw, 2005; Fisher 2008).

Malcolm X and other Black Muslims sought to use the Nation of Islam to engage African Americans in economic nationalism and to instill in them a sense of pride and achievement. This was accomplished through the rejection of Christianity, which they taught to be a symbol of white oppression in America.

In 1964, following a rift with Elijah Muhammad, Malcolm X broke with the Nation of Islam and formed the Organization of Afro-American Unity (OAAU). In that same year, he made a pilgrimage to Mecca and embraced traditional Sunni Islam, which he believed offered a superior religious path based on inclusiveness, rather than divisiveness and antagonism (Lincoln, 1994). In 1965, Malcolm X was assassinated.

Wallace Deen Muhammad became the leader of the Nation of Islam after the death of his father, Elijah Muhammad, in 1975. Under his leadership, the Nation of Islam embraced traditional Sunni Islam and changed its name to the American Muslim Mission. "During the 1970s and 1980s, W. D. Muhammad, as he is known, slowly dispensed with the racist rhetoric of his sect's past and led his followers toward orthodox Koranic Islam" (Kosmin & Lachman, 1993, p. 136). As a result, the group often supports conservative causes such as the free market. Hard work, personal responsibility, and family values are expected of members (Fisher, 2008; Kosmin & Lachman, 1993).

The well-known leader of Black Muslims, Louis Farrakhan, led a splinter movement in the 1980s that resumed the use of the original name, Nation of Islam, and the black separatist position. He continues to receive considerable attention from the press and political leaders because of his sometimes-inflammatory rhetoric as well as appeal to many African Americans who are not Muslims. This influence was demonstrated in his ability to mobilize an interfaith coalition that drew nearly 1 million African American men together for the One Million Man March in Washington, DC, in 1996. Members have become role models in many inner cities as they establish businesses. They often serve as visible neighborhood guardians against crime and drug abuse, and have assumed an important role in the rehabilitation of individuals released from prison (*Columbia Encyclopedia,* 2001–2005a; Fisher, 2008; Johnstone, 2007).

Islam is one of the fastest growing religions in the U.S., as evidenced by the increasing number of mosques and Islamic Centers in many communities.

© Clayton Sharrard/PhotoEdit Inc.

Effect on Education.   The vast majority of Muslim students in the United States and Canada attend public schools. The September 11, 2001, attacks enhanced concerns of some Muslim students in U.S. schools for their personal safety and fear that traditional attire (e.g., head covering for women) could draw unfavorable attention to themselves (Vyas, 2004). Taggar (2006) interviewed Muslim high school students and found that the majority reported that Muslims have been labeled in stereotypical ways and were particularly concerned with the media's portrayal of their culture and religion. Taggar urges culturally responsive teaching requiring educators to examine their own attitudes and beliefs before they attempt to educate their students. Taggar further urges creating a school environment, which is emotionally and physically safe for all students.

In the United States, about 15,000 students attend 200 Islamic schools. These schools are designed to provide full-time educational programs "to help a child grow into an Islamic personality with the ideals and images which can help him and her achieve the best in this world and the best in the Hereafter" (Johnstone, 2007; SoundVision, 2004). Many of these schools are located in Islamic Centers throughout the country. In addition, another half million Muslim students attend weekend religious training in weekend Islamic schools (SoundVision, 2004).

Buddhism

Buddhism is one of the world's major religions with estimates ranging from a quarter of a billion to a third of a billion members worldwide. Immigration of Asians each year from countries such as China, Taiwan, Korea, Thailand, Japan, and Tibet brings thousands of additional Buddhists into the United States, changing further the religious landscape of the country. Estimates of more than 1 million Buddhists in the United States appears to be conservative given the fact that there are now approximately 12 million Asians in the country, with over half having immigrated from predominantly Buddhist countries.

With the Buddhists coming from so many regions of the world, there are invariably different forms of Buddhism practiced. Consequently there is tremendous diversity in both beliefs and in practice, just as there is diversity among the various Christian faiths we have discussed. Buddhist schools of thought or belief are united in a twofold orientation toward existence: a fundamental negative attitude toward life and a pessimistic approach to ordinary existence. Buddhists view existence itself as the problem with life. As long as there is existence, there is suffering. The second common orientation of all Buddhists is that Buddha provides a solution to the frustrations of life. Each school of Buddhism provides a pathway to overcome the meaninglessness of life. Buddha is the solution to life's dilemma (Fisher, 2008; Young 2005).

The Fo Kuang Shan Hsi Lai Temple in Hacienda Heights, California, is the largest Buddhist temple in the Western hemisphere.

Buddhism teaches that the secret to enlightenment is neither through a life of luxury nor through self-deprivation, but through the middle way, away from the extremes. The key to salvation is to let go of everything. Salvation and enlightenment occurs when one realizes his or her place of non-self in the world. Nonexistence is the reality and self-extinction is the reality. With enlightenment comes the state of nirvana, meaning "blown out" (Hopfe & Woodward, 2007; Young, 2005).

Teachings of Buddha.   Buddha taught four "noble truths":

- To live is to suffer
- Suffering is caused by desire
- One can eliminate suffering by eliminating desire
- Desire is eliminated by an eightfold path

The Eightfold Path to Eliminating Desire

1. The right belief (understanding the truths of existence)
2. The right aspiration (willing to achieve enlightenment)
3. The right speech
4. The right conduct
5. The right means of livelihood
6. The right endeavor (effort)
7. The right mindfulness (meditating properly)
8. The right meditation (or concentration) (Young, 2005)

To know that your student is from a Buddhist family may or may not tell you much about the family belief structure or religious practices. While one might expect belief in the four noble truths and practice of the eightfold path from a Buddhist priest or monk, the layperson may take bits and pieces of the religion into his or her everyday life. Chinese, Japanese, Korean, and Vietnamese individuals are often influenced by Confucian philosophy, which directs daily behaviors in much the same way that a religion can. Thus some individuals may be Buddhist with a strong philosophical overlay of Confucianism. It may be somewhat difficult to clearly separate the religious from the cultural and philosophical backgrounds of a Buddhist layperson from Taiwan, one from Tibet, and another from Japan.

Hinduism

Hinduism is the major religion of India and the world's third largest religion after Christianity and Islam. There are approximately 837,000,000 adherents in the world, representing 13% of the world's population. The number of Hindus in the United States ranges from between 766,000 to 1,100,000. Generally regarded as the world's oldest organized religion, it differs from Christianity and other Western religions in that it does not have a single founder (Robinson, 2006b). Its roots date back to prehistoric times in India. Neither does it have a single system of morality or a central organization. Robinson (2006b) suggests that it consists of thousands of different religious groups that evolved out of India since 1500 B.C.E. (Before the Common Era, same as B.C.). Hinduism is credited with influencing the development of both Buddhism and Jainism.

As with most other religions, Hinduism has basic beliefs about divinities, life after death, and how followers should conduct their lives. Unlike Judaism, Christianity, and Islam, Hinduism does not limit itself to a single book or writing. Hinduism has several sacred writings, which contribute to the basic beliefs of Hinduism. The most important writings are known as the Vedas, the Puranas, the Ramayana, the Mahabharata, the Bhagavad-Gita, and the Manu Smriti. These sacred writings include prayers, hymns, philosophy, myths, epics, discussions of the meaning of nature and existence, and Hindu religious and social law. Part of the latter includes the basis of the caste system. The caste system was legally abolished in 1949, but its influence remains to this day. Each follower of Hinduism belonged to one of the communities, which were grouped into one of four social castes that included the following:

- Brahmins, the priests and academics
- Kshatriyas, the rulers and military
- Vishyas, the farmers, landlords, and merchants
- Sudras, the peasants, servants, and workers in nonpolluting jobs

The Dalit represented a fifth group, who were considered outcasts and not a part of one of the castes. They worked in what was considered polluting tasks (e.g., tanning hides) and are, therefore, untouchable by members of the other four castes. Even their shadow could not fall on one of the caste members. Although the caste system is now illegal in India, and has lost much of its influence in the cities, it remains a way of life in some of the rural areas. Consequently, some of the Dalit have left Hinduism and have converted to Buddhism or Christianity (Ellwood & McGraw, 2005; Robinson, 2006b).

Teachings of Hinduism.   There are many deities in Hinduism. However, there are three gods that are generally considered the most important. They include Brahma, the creator of the universe; Vishnu, its preserver; and Shiva, the destroyer.

Hinduism teaches that the soul never dies. When the body dies, the soul is reincarnated. The soul may be born into an animal or another human being. The law of karma states that every action taken by an individual influences how he or she will be reincarnated. Those who live a good life will be reincarnated into a higher state. Those who do evil will be reincarnated in lower forms such as a worm. Reincarnation continues until a person reaches spiritual perfection. The soul then enters a new level of existence referred to as moksha, from which it never returns (Ellwood & McGraw, 2005).

Other Denominations and Religious Groups

In addition to the four major faiths in the United States, what other religions might an educator encounter in a community? They include Christian religious groups, which do not fall into the discrete categories of Protestantism, Catholicism, Judaism, or Islam.

Latter-Day Saints.   The Church of Jesus Christ of Latter-Day Saints (LDS or Mormon) is a rapidly growing group that is neither Catholic nor Protestant. In the early 1830s, Joseph Smith founded the LDS Church in western New York State. By his own account, Smith was instructed to translate a history of ancient inhabitants of North America written on tablets of gold, which had been stored in a nearby hillside. The translations were published in 1830 as the Book of Mormon, which together with the Old and New Testaments and some of Smith's later revelations became the sacred scripture of Mormonism (Hemeyer, 2006).

Smith and his followers met strong opposition from established Protestant groups, and he and his followers were harassed and violently driven out of various communities. The Mormon practice of polygamy (the Church discontinued the practice of plural marriage in 1890) exacerbated their rejection by other groups, and in 1844, Smith and his brother were killed by a mob in Carthage, Illinois. With the death of Smith, Brigham Young became the new leader of the group and led them to Utah, now the religious center of the Mormons. The Mormons aggressively proselytize, and as a result have grown to a membership of 5.4 million in the United States, and 11.7 million worldwide (Young, 2005).

Eastern Orthodoxy.

The Eastern Orthodox Church is another Christian religion that does not fall into the two major groupings of Protestant or Roman Catholic. Eastern Orthodoxy probably claims about one fourth of all Christians worldwide. One reason that the Eastern Orthodox Church is less well known in this country may be that its members, from Syria, Greece, Armenia, Russia, and the Ukraine, only immigrated during the last century. Although they split with the Roman Catholic Church in 1054 over theological, practical, jurisdictional, cultural, and political differences, to many outsiders they appear very similar to the pre-Vatican II Catholic church.

Worldwide, the Eastern Orthodox Churches together have an estimated combined membership of 214,000,000 to 300,000,000 (Robinson, 2006a). The actual and reported memberships in Eastern Orthodox Churches in the United States vary considerably. The churches themselves have in recent years reported membership of approximately 4,000,000. The Hartford Research Institute suggests that the actual number of adherents is approximately 1,200,000 (Hartford Research Institute, 2002). The Institute suggests that the discrepancy is due to the common practice of equating the number of members to the number of members of the corresponding ethnic groups. This practice does not take into consideration the second- and third-generation descendants of the original immigrant church members who are not currently involved with the respective churches.

Christian Science and Unitarian Universalists.

At least two other religions have a Christian heritage but seem to fall through the cracks of discrete categorization because of their precepts—the Christian Scientists and Unitarian Universalists. The Christian Scientists are one of these groups, with probably fewer than a half million members.

Christian Scientists believe that all that God creates is good, as a good God would not create that which is not good. They rely on the power of God to heal rather than traditional medicine. Adherents are not prohibited from utilizing traditional care, though reliance on the power of God is encouraged, as they believe that the cause and cure of illness is spiritual. Believing that the body is the temple of the Holy Spirit, Christian Scientists advocate healthy habits including exercise, good nutrition, and abstaining from alcohol and tobacco use. Many are vegetarians. Their publication, *Christian Science Monitor,* is a highly respected general newspaper (Hemeyer, 2006).

The second group that defies categorization is the Unitarian Universalists—a church that connotes liberalism to most people. Their membership has included several U.S. presidents (William Howard Taft, Thomas Jefferson, John Adams, and John Quincy Adams) and several New England writers (Henry Wadsworth Longfellow, James Russell Lowell, and William Cullen Bryant), helping make the church an influence beyond that expected of a relatively small group. Unitarians are often found in suburbs, small towns, and college communities; many members could be described as political liberals. Although many members have the highest respect for Jesus Christ, the church is "most open to the wisdom of non-Christian religions and may draw many of its readings from scriptures of Buddhism, Hinduism and religious philosophies" (Marty, 1975, p. 217). As an expression of this openness, Unitarianism houses both Christian and non-Christian wings. The denomination follows no imposing standards of dogma or membership. Thus, their worship services appear extremely simple and are often experimental (Corrigan & Hudson, 2004; Marty, 1975).

Native American Religions.   Native Indian religions are among the most difficult to describe or characterize, as there are 314 federally recognized tribes or groups and each is likely to have its own distinctive views on religion. A New York City University religious identification survey (2001) estimated that there are about 103,000 practitioners of Native American religion. There are a few general characteristics that are universal or tend to transcend across tribal boundaries. Traditional Native American religions recognize three levels of spiritual beings—a supreme god, nature spirits, and ancestor spirits. Superior spirits with god-like characteristics also factor into the religious equation. Tribes differ in their emphasis of the different spirits. *Wakan* or *orenda* apply to the spiritual power found in all entities. They are found in grass, rocks, animals, and spiritual beings. Each plant, rock, or even body of water may be sacred. Some may even inform a deer of its impending fate before killing it in a hunt in order to maintain harmony with the natural world (Corduan, 1998).

Shamans are men and women who heal through their contact with spirits. Individuals become shamans through supernatural calling. Frequently this happens when one vows to become a shaman if they are healed from an illness (Corduan, 1998). Among some tribes, much importance is placed on receiving and implementing visions. Visions are attained in different ways. Sometimes they may come after a tranquil moment or after great stress. Fasting, self-imposed exposure to climatic extremes, or injury may induce a vision. Individuals from some tribes may experience a vision where an animal enters the body. A person or a group of individuals may come to an individual in order to deliver a message. The recipient of a vision can anticipate success because of it (Corduan, 1998).

Jainism.   Jainism evolved out of India in the sixth century B.C.E. Both Jainism and Buddhism grew out of Hindu traditions. Jains observe the "three jewels" of right faith, right knowledge, and right conduct. They emphasize peacefulness and moderation, and refuse to injure animals. Their philosophy of nonviolence had a profound influence on Gandhi. There are an estimated 4,000 Jains in North America (Corduan, 1998; Ellwood & McGraw, 2005).

Sikhism.   **Sikhism** was founded in the fifteenth or sixteenth century B.C.E. in India. Sikhism draws from the elements of Hinduism and Islam, stressing a universal single God. Union with God is accomplished through meditation and surrender to divine will. Sikhs believe in reincarnation, karma, and the destruction and rebuilding of the universe. Male Sikhs are initiated into a religious brotherhood called the Khalsa, vowing to never cut their hair or beard, to wear special pants, an iron bangle, a steel dagger, and a comb. There are an estimated 490,000 Sikhs in North America (Corduan, 1998; Ellwood & McGraw, 2005).

Baha'ism.   Baha'ism was founded in Persia (Iran) in the late nineteenth century. Its founder, Baha'ullah claimed to be the divine manifestation of God and the last of a line of divine figures including Zoroaster, Buddha, Christ, and Muhammad. Bahai emphasizes the principles of equality of sexes, races, and religious adherence. Bahai believers advocate for peace, justice, racial unity, economic development, and education. There are an estimated 300,000 or more members in the United States (Corduan, 1998; Ellwood & McGraw, 2005).

New Age Spirituality.   The **New Age** movement began around the early 1980s. New Age has roots in nineteenth-century spiritualism and in the counterculture movement of the 1960s, rejecting materialism and favoring spiritual experience to organized religion. The movement emphasizes, among many of its followers, reincarnation, biofeedback, shamanism, the occult, psychic healing, and extraterrestrial life. It is a movement that is difficult to define as evidenced by the multitude of the movement's publications on a wide range of topics, viewpoints, and paraphernalia, from crystals to tarot. Much of the emphasis of the various groups is on the paranormal or parapsychology. It involves such experiences as meditation, visualization, dream interpretation, self-improvement, extrasensory perception, telepathy, clairvoyance, divination, precognition, out-of-body experiences, channeling spirit guides, angels, regression analysis of past lives, and so forth. It has influences from Eastern religions such as Buddhism, Sufism, Taoism, and Hinduism (Brown, 2008; Chryssides, 1999).

Some New Agers believe Christianity to be a thing of the past. New Agers tend to reject highly structured institutionalized religion, such as the organized Christian religious authority of the Roman Catholic Church. There is no formal institutional structure for the New Age movement, nor is there any agreed upon creed. There is no authoritative hierarchy, and it is unclear precisely what the New Age groups are and what they are not. (Brown, 2008; Chryssides, 1999).

Wicca.   Wicca, considered by some to be a neo-pagan religion, is sometimes referred to as witchcraft. Although still relatively small compared to mainstream religions, it is by percentage of growth, the fastest growing religion in the United States. The adherents (referred to as Wiccans) increased from 8,000 in 1990 to 134,000 in 2001 (City University of New York [CUNY], 2001). Wiccans have experienced comparable growth in Australia, Canada, and elsewhere in the world.

Wicca is a modern revival of the old religion of witchcraft. Wiccans believe that all nature is alive with the sacred and that humans are interconnected with nature as is all else in the world. Member wiccans form their own small groups or covens of 12 or 13 members, with no hierarchy or authoritarian priesthood. All members are witches. Rituals generally focus on the goddess, who appears in triple form. The wiccan movement has focused on feminist spirituality and the sacred meaning of women's lives. The movement has attracted adolescents as well as adults and both men and women (Ludwig, 2006).

Cults.   The term *cult* evokes a wide variety of reactions from positive to contempt on the part of members of mainline religious groups. Ellwood and McGraw (2005) define cults as "Minority religions characteristically centered on a charismatic leader, who requires strict adherence to beliefs and practices of the group. Generally, the cult contains teachings and practices from several sources and often requires adherents to sever ties with people who are not a part of the cult" (p. 494). Johnstone (2007) further suggests that cults tend to be transitory and short lived. When the cult's charismatic leader dies, leaves, or is discredited, the cult usually disbands or disappears, as in the case of People's Temple and its leader, Jim Jones. At times the cult grows, develops a structure, and develops a leadership succession. The cult may then develop into a denominational status. In this sense, during its early years, Christianity might have been characterized as a cult. Likewise, the Mormon Church could have been considered a cult in its early years, prior to becoming a sizable denomination with over 10 million members worldwide.

Young people in many communities practice religions based on an Eastern religious tradition. This grouping includes the Hare Krishna, the Divine Light Mission, and the

Unification Church. Members of some of these groups are very visible to the public. The Hare Krishna can sometimes be seen dancing with tambourines on sidewalks in larger cities.

These various religions are practiced by a small minority of the population, but their presence in a community is often exaggerated beyond that warranted by their numbers. This notoriety often stems from the fact that their doctrine and practices are viewed as heretical by members of the major faiths, especially fundamentalist Christians. In addition, members of the majority faiths, especially parents, fear the attraction of some of these groups, some of which are considered cults, because they allegedly practice some degree of mind control.

As mentioned above, the term *cult* will generally evoke negative reactions that may range from fear, to contempt, to disgust on the part of many individuals. The term may kindle thoughts of brainwashing or that which is most feared by families—suicide. During the past 25 or so years, there have been a number of highly publicized mass suicides among the so-called "Suicide Cults." Among those most publicized involving Americans were the People's Temple, the Branch Davidians, and the Heaven's Gate groups.

Interaction of Religion with Gender, Homosexuality, and Race

Religion and Gender

In an era of gender equality in the general society in the United States, where major corporations are sued for gender discrimination, issues of gender equality are often raised in religious institutions. In many of the more conservative religious bodies, the role of women is clearly defined and limited. There are no female priests in the Roman Catholic Church and Eastern Orthodox Churches, no women can attain the priesthood in the Mormon Church, and very few fundamentalist churches or denominations have or are willing to ordain women ministers. The same can be said about many other religious groups. At the 2000 annual convention of the Southern Baptist Convention, the 16,000 delegates voted on an explicit ban on women pastors. This action followed an earlier action by the Baptists to support the submission of women to their husbands.

Although Gomes (1996) indicates that Lydia, Phoebe, and Priscilla were women mentioned in the New Testament as having prominent roles in the formative days of early Christianity, other biblical passages are used to delimit the participation of women in leadership roles in religious activity. In supporting the ban or limitations of female leadership and wifely submission, these groups cite the fact that Jesus did not call on women to serve as his disciples. Biblical verses (e.g., I Corinthians 14:34–35) admonish women to submit themselves to their husbands and indicate that the husband is the head of the wife.

Van Leeuwen (1990) suggests that some biblical interpreters believe that God gave men, through Adam (Genesis 1:26–27), dominion over Eve and, therefore, over women. At the same time, some biblical scholars argue that such an interpretation is incorrect and that both Adam and Eve (man and woman) were given dominion over every other living thing. Groothuis (1997) indicates that in addition to the examples provided by Gomes (1996), there are numerous other biblical examples of women who were leaders or prophets (e.g., Deborah, Judges 4–5). Groothuis indicates that Deborah was a prime example of a woman called to lead by God and questions how her female leadership could be considered a violation of moral principles if ordained by God. Traditionalists counter that Deborah was an extreme exception to the long-standing precedent of male authority.

Other traditionalists counter that Deborah's position of leadership was less authoritative than that of male prophets. The participation of women in leadership roles in both Protestantism and Judaism is a function of where the particular denomination is on the liberal to conservative continuum. Liberal Protestants (e.g., Episcopalians) ordain women as priests. Likewise the Reformed Jewish movement has ordained women as rabbis for more than 30 years. The Conservative Jewish seminaries are also training women to be rabbis, but the Orthodox Jewish movement does not.

Limitations on participation of females in religious activities are by no means the sole province of Judeo-Christian groups. Islam and other religions either limit the participation of females or typically rest leadership in the hands of men. Islam views women as equal but different from men. They do not worship alongside the men in their mosques, but in separate areas. They are expected to observe all pillars of Islam including the five daily prayers and fasts during Ramadan. They are, however, exempted from five daily prayers and fasts of Ramadan during their menses and in pregnancy.

In 2006, the Gallup World Poll did a survey of Islamic countries to determime attitudes toward women holding leadership positions. The survey included residents in the eight Islamic countries of Jordan, Saudi Arabia, Egypt, Iran, Pakistan, Turkey, Morocco, and Lebanon. In all countries, except Saudi Arabia, the majority of the individuals responded affirmatively to the statement, "Women should be allowed to hold leadership positions in the cabinet or national council" (Newport, 2006a). Women in some Middle Eastern countries have severe limitations placed on them (e.g., working, attending school, driving a car, face covering). These limitations are more a function of the culture of the country or region than the mandates of Islam.

Due to the diversity of the backgrounds of its adherents as well as the society in which they live, many Islamic women in the United States function differently than Islamic women in some other parts of the world. This includes the extent to which they are allowed to work outside the home, assume active roles in Islamic centers and community life, and interact with the non-Muslim community (Peach, 2002).

The importance of religion in determining male and female roles is also discussed in Chapter 4.

Not only is religion used to define the parameters of religious participation of males and females, but religion may also be used to prescribe male and female roles outside the religious context. Such prescriptions may be done either directly or indirectly. In religious groups in which women are given a less prominent status, this may carry over into general family life and other aspects of society as a natural course. In other instances, the pronouncements may be more direct. Religious writings with great importance, such as the Bible, are continuously interpreted, studied, and analyzed. In the United States, the Bible (or at least the Old Testament) is viewed as very sacred by most of its citizens who claim church membership. Consequently, the Bible and other religious writings, such as the Koran, have a profound influence on many Americans.

Religion and Homosexuality

Homosexuality is one of the most controversial issues in religious institutions today. Attacks on homosexuality in the religious context are often justified through biblical interpretation or other religious writings. Some argue that the textual interpretation and, in some cases, translation of biblical passages regarding homosexuality are not clear and may be subject to misinterpretation and misguided beliefs. Others argue that the Bible is clear on the issue of homosexuality, as in the book of Genesis where God destroyed Sodom and Gomorrah because of the sinful behaviors, including homosexuality, of the inhabitants.

The debate is serious, as are the consequences. Conservative Christians and other conservative religious groups tend to view homosexuality as a matter of choice, a sin, and an abomination. More liberal religious groups tend to believe that the only choice is in whether or not the individual engages in homosexual behavior. They contend that the individual is born homosexual or predisposed to that life.

Because some conservative Christians, as well as members of other religious bodies, view homosexuality as a sin, they believe the AIDS epidemic is God's retribution for the gay life. Other Christian groups have willingly accepted gays and lesbians into their congregations, and some have even been ordained into leadership positions, often creating controversy within the respective churches or denominations.

Views toward homosexuality vary considerably in other religious groups. There are often intergroup as well as intragroup differences. The Roman Catholic position on homosexuality is congruent with that of many other conservative groups. These groups view homosexuality as "*objectively disordered*" and view homosexual practices as very serious "*sins gravely contrary to chastity*" (Robinson, 2006e).

The issue of adolescent suicide as related to homosexuality is discussed in Chapter 9.

The Catholic Church, however, has had to address the issues related to homosexuality among its own clergy. The unfortunate clergy abuse scandals, which have surfaced in recent years, have caused great spiritual and economic concerns in various dioceses. Even though the abuses have been linked to a minority of priests, the scandal has caused immense problems for the Church.

The 2004 elevation of Rev. V. Gene Robinson to Bishop in the Episcopal Diocese of New Hampshire, as the first openly gay Episcopal bishop, has created considerable divisiveness among Episcopalians. Some Episcopal congregations have split away over what they view as excessively liberal practices (Altamirano, 2007).

The views toward homosexuality among Jewish groups tend to mirror those of Christians and are typically a function of where the group lies on the continuum of liberal to conservative. Reformed Judaism tends to view homosexuality as the normal behavior of a minority of adults. Orthodox Judaism views it as abnormal and condemned by God (Robinson, 2006d).

Homosexuality in Islam is viewed as lewd and sinful. There are two primary references to homosexuality in the Qur'an (Qur'an 7:80–81 and Qur'an 26:165). Both address homosexuality negatively. In Southern and Eastern Asian Islamic countries, no physical punishment for homosexuality is considered warranted. However, some Arabic Islamic countries tend to deal with it more harshly, especially in Iran and in Afghanistan when under the rule of the Taliban (Robinson, 2005b).

Robinson (2005a) indicates that with the many schools and sects within Buddhism, there is, as with Christianity, no consensus regarding homosexuality within the religion. Buddha did not provide any teachings regarding homosexuality. Buddhism, Robinson states, is more concerned with good intentions and good actions. Because of the relative lack of homophobia in some sects of Buddhism, it has attracted some gay men and lesbian women.

Young (2005) indicates that the mention of homosexuality is rare in classical Hindu texts, and where they do occur, the practice is not viewed positively. Homosexuality is seen as fundamentally incompatible with the goals of duty and material well-being among Hindus. Young further states that the major Hindu deities (e.g., Shiva) have both masculine and feminine aspects, which contribute to a more tolerant attitude toward homosexuality and bisexual orientation in India, which has the world's largest Hindu population.

Pause to Reflect 7.3

Historically, many religions have treated men and women differently. Today, there are still many religions that do not allow women to assume their highest religious and spiritual leadership positions. This often carries into society in general. In 1966, Indira Gandhi became the first female Prime Minister of India, a predominantly Hindu country. In 1988, Pakistan's Benazir Bhutto made history by becoming the first woman to head the government of a Muslim-majority state in modern times. While women have held the highest elected office in predominantly Christian countries (e.g, Margaret Thatcher, Great Britain), no woman has to date been elected President of the United States. On January 4, 2007, history was made in the United States Congress, when Representative Nancy Pelosi (D-CA) assumed the position of Speaker of the U.S. House of Representatives. This made Speaker Pelosi, second in line to the Presidency, the first woman in history to rise to this position and arguably the highest ranking woman ever in the United States Government.

- If you teach in a public school setting what is your responsibility to your male and female students?
- Are there any differences in the way you can or should treat gender bias in private, church related schools?
- What should you do if a student makes inappropriate gender biased statements in your class?

Go to the *Homework and Exercises* section in Chapter 7 of MyEducationLab and select *Pause to Reflect 7.3* to answer these questions.

It is important to understand that clergy and other church and religious authorities have considerable influence on the people they lead. They, the writers and theologians who influence others, often get their inspiration or their justification for their positions through religious scriptures. These writings are then interpreted for laypersons and may be used to shape their perceptions of self and others. Children growing up in a religious environment may learn to condemn or to practice tolerance. They may learn that homosexuality is an abomination, or they may learn that homosexuality is an innate and natural sexual orientation for some. Hopefully they will learn to respect all individuals as valued members of society. For more information, visit the Religious Tolerance website **(www.religioustolerance.org),** which provides the views toward homosexuality of the various Christian groups or denominations, Jewish groups, and other religious groups.

Religion and Race

As with gender issues, religion has had a profound impact on race and ethnic diversity issues. Gomes (1996) notes that Christians seek to establish the kingdom of God on the earth. In doing so, they seek guidance from the Bible on how to conduct themselves in

See Chapter 2 for further details on race with other cultural groups.

society. When individuals misinterpret biblical scriptures or interpret them to justify aberrant behavior, the consequences can be severe. Gomes points out that at their 1995 meeting, the Southern Baptist Convention, which is the country's largest Protestant denomination, in an unprecedented act of contrition apologized for the role it had played in the justification of slavery and in the maintenance of a culture of racism in the United States.

Slavery and Racism.   Historically, many religious groups had found justification for the practice of slavery in the Bible. The Bible does not condemn slavery, and its practice can be found throughout both the Old and New Testaments. In the New Testament, there is no record of either Jesus or Paul specifically condemning the practice of slavery, which was a common practice during that period. Paul returned a slave to his master rather than providing refuge as was required by Jewish law (Deuteronomy 23:15–16). Therefore, proponents of slavery believed that this institution was built on a solid biblical foundation.

Gomes (1996) suggests that the Catholic king of Spain and his ministers viewed it as their divine right and obligation to enslave and Christianize or slaughter the natives of Latin America. Both Cortés and Pizarro operated under papal and governmental authority as they enslaved and killed thousands of natives and justified their behavior with biblical texts.

Anti-Semitism can also find many of its historical roots in the Bible and other religious works. Gomes (1996) further suggests that Bach's *Passion of St. John,* though musically beautiful and inspiring, is filled with strong anti-Semitic German lyrics. Biblical passages are often used to justify anti-Semitic behaviors (e.g., Matthew 27:25–26, Romans 3:1). It is ironic that those, especially Christians, who justify their anti-Semitic behaviors through religious doctrines and sacred writings, may have failed to recognize that Jesus and his earliest followers were themselves Jews.

Role of Black Religious Groups.   Historically, African Americans often organized their own religious institutions due to racism, which either prohibited or limited their membership, participation, or attendance. Black churches and religious institutions have served their people in different ways. Some provide food, shelter, and occasional employment opportunities. Others, such as the Black Muslims, have provided a sense of Black Nationalism, pride, and a self-help philosophy. They have encouraged education and black entrepreneurship. Other black religious leaders have solicited philantropic assistance from the white community (Johnstone, 2007).

Civil Rights Movement and Black Churches.   The modern civil rights movement was centered in Southern African American churches. Many of the civil rights leaders were or are ministers or church leaders (e.g., Martin Luther King, Jr., Ralph Abernathy, Andrew Young, and Jesse Jackson). From their pulpits, these religious leaders were able to direct boycotts and organize civil disobedience and nonviolent confrontations.

In earlier times, spirituals provided comfort, hope, or a promise of a better life after death. Today, many of these spirituals are still sung in the churches, but the people who sing them and the people who listen to them seek a more immediate response to the demands for equity. Clearly, African American churches deserve much credit for bringing about many of the civil rights gained in the last three or four decades. Alienated and disillusioned by mainstream politics, few African Americans registered to vote in the past. African American clergy nationwide have advocated church involvement in social and political issues. In recent years, black churches have been extremely successful in registering millions of voters and in doing so, becoming an important voice in the electoral process.

Disenchantment Among Younger Generations.   Johnstone (2007) suggests that some young blacks have become increasingly disenchanted with their black churches. They have turned to secular organizations, which deal more directly with their life situations and with the social problems they face. Johnstone emphasizes that this situation does not mean the demise of the black church. While some will remain because of habit, others would be unwilling to give up the important associations and relationships available to them in their respective churches. The historical nature of the black church as the center of the black community life, makes it unlikely that the masses will abandon it.

In some religious groups, African Americans were permitted membership but prohibited from attaining the higher positions of church leadership. These prohibitions were justified through biblical interpretations or through divine revelations received by church leaders. Although nearly all such racial limitations on membership and church leadership have been removed in recent years, the effects of these religious prohibitions remain to be seen. Many individuals who read or listened to leaders justifying segregation or bans against leadership positions cannot readily dismiss some of the attitudes developed through years of prolonged exposure to negative points of view.

Changing Attitudes. Like the gender issues that have become a center of religious debate, racial issues have been debated for decades. As the courts and society as a whole have turned their backs on segregation and racially limiting practices, so too have most religious bodies taken an official position of openness. Although the official position and the actual positions may differ somewhat, at least in churches that express brotherly love the two may be moving to a higher level of congruence.

It is important to note that society in general often reflects the positions of religious institutions. We are still experiencing the lingering effects of the proslavery and prosegregationist view of religious groups. Women who are not permitted leadership roles in their churches find the same attitudes in other areas of society where few are encouraged to seek leadership roles in school, work, or politics. The influence of religious beliefs on the everyday behavior of individuals can be considerable. Religion has often inspired goodness and charity. Unfortunately, in some instances, some people have used it to justify inflicting pain and suffering on others.

Individual Religious Identity

Most Americans are born into the religion of their parents, later joining that same body. Within the context of the religious freedom espoused in the United States, however, individuals are always free to change their religion or to choose no religion. The greatest pressure to retain membership in the religious group in which one was born usually comes from the family and from other members of that same religious group. Often, it is more difficult for individuals to break away from their religious origins than to make breaks from any of the other cultural groups of which they are members.

Although a person's ethnicity, class, or gender may have a considerable influence on behavior or values, religion may well be the primary microculture with which many individuals identify. When ethnic identity is very important to an individual, it is often combined with a religious identification such as Irish Catholic, Russian Jew, or Norwegian Lutheran. Understanding the individual's relationship to both ethnic and religious microcultures is important in understanding the individual.

The region of the United States in which one lives also affects the strength of identification with a specific religious group. For example, in parts of Alabama, many people will have the same or similar views; religious diversity may be limited. In many areas of the country, any deviation from the common religious beliefs and practices is considered heretical, making it very difficult for the nonadherent to be accepted by most members of the community. In other areas, the traditionally religious individual may not be accepted as a part of a community that is religiously liberal. Educators, as well as students, are usually expected to believe and behave according to the mores of the community—mores that are often determined by the prevailing religious doctrine and the degree of religious diversity.

Most communities have some degree of religious diversity, although the degree of difference may vary greatly, depending on the community. Often, students whose beliefs are different from those of the majority in the community are ostracized in school and social settings. For instance, Jews, atheists, Jehovah's Witnesses, and Pentecostals are among those groups whose members are sometimes shunned and suffer discrimination for their beliefs. Educators must be careful that their own religious beliefs and memberships do not interfere with their ability to provide equal educational opportunity to all students, regardless of their religious identification.

Classroom Focus

Testing the First Amendment

School districts and various state legislators who seek to circumvent the principle of Separation of Church and State continually test the First Amendment. It would be difficult to believe that state legislators, many of whom are attorneys, are not aware that laws requiring a form of religion are not intended to create a government sponsored religious activity. It is likely that these legislators or school officials believe it their responsibility to infuse morality and ethics into school activity or curriculum. The Supreme Court, however, has the responsibility to rule on the constitutionality of such directives. The following are examples of Supreme Court rulings related to education, the First Amendment, and the principle of the Separation of Church and State:

- *Engel v. Vitale.* 82 S. Ct. 1261 (1962) [New York]. The Court ruled that any type of prayer, even that which is nondenominational is unconstitutional government sponsorship of religion.
- *Abington School District v. Schempp.* 374 U.S. 203 (1963) [Pennsylvania]. The Court found that Bible reading over the school intercom was unconstitutional and in *Murray v. Curlett,* 374 U.S. 203 (1963), the Court found that forcing a child to participate in Bible reading and prayer was unconstitutional.
- *Epperson v. Arkansas.* 89 S. Ct. 266 (1968). The Court ruled that a State statute banning teaching of evolution was unconstitutional. A state cannot set a course of study in order to promote a religious point of view.
- *Stone v. Graham.* 449 U.S. 39 (1980) [Kentucky]. The Court ruled that the posting of the Ten Commandments in schools was unconstitutional.
- *Wallace v. Jaffree.* 105 S. Ct. 2479 (1985) [Alabama]. The Court ruled that the State's moment of silence in a public school statute was unconstitutional as a legislative record revealed that motivation for the statute was the encouragement of prayer.
- *Edwards v. Aquillard.* 107 S. Ct. 2573 (1987) [Louisiana]. The Court found it was unconstitutional for the state to require teaching of "creation science" in all instances in which evolution is taught. The statute had a clear religious motivation.

Pause to Reflect 7.4

It has already been stated that it is important for you to be aware of your religious beliefs and that of your community. It is also important that you reflect on where you lie on the religious continuum with respect to being religiously liberal or religiously conservative. As stated before, it is your right to believe as you wish. However, it is not your right to impose your religious orientation to your students in a public school setting. The nation is unfortunately polarized in some of the issues related to religion and the public schools. The sides typically feel passionately about their perspectives. Again, this is their right to do so. It is neither their right nor your right to bring it into the classroom. It is your responsibility as an educator to make every child feel welcome and safe in your classroom and in your school.

• What are the religious affiliations of people in the community in which you now reside?
• How does the religious diversity differ from where you grew up?
• How would you classify the majority groups on a scale of conservative to liberal?
• What influence might these religions have on what you teach in the classroom?

Go to the *Homework and Exercises* section in Chapter 7 of MyEducationLab and select *Pause to Reflect 7.4* to answer these questions.

• ***Lee v. Weisman.***   112 S. Ct. 2649 (1992) [Rhode Island]. The Court ruled it to be unconstitutional for a school district to provide any clergy to perform nondenominational prayer at elementary or secondary school graduation. It involves government sponsorship of worship.

Nationally, adherence to the principle of Separation of Church and State has been schizophrenic, at best. Oaths are typically made on Bibles and often end with the phrase "so help me God." U.S. coins and currency state "In God We Trust." We have military chaplains and congressional chaplains, and we hold congressional prayer breakfasts. The Pledge of Allegiance includes the words, "under God." This has been interpreted by some to mean that the separation of church and state simply means that there will be no state church.

Complete separation of church and state, as defined by strict constitutionalists, would have a profound effect on social-religious life. It is likely that the American public wants some degree of separation of these two institutions, but it is equally likely that the public would be outraged if total separation were imposed. Total separation would mean no direct or indirect aid to religious groups, no tax-free status, no tax deductions for contributions to religious groups, no national Christmas tree, no government-paid chaplains, no religious holidays, no blue laws, and so on. The list of religious activities, rights, and privileges that could be eliminated seems almost endless.

Religious groups place different emphases on the need for education and have different expectations of what children should be taught. For instance, the Amish usually want to remove their children from formal schooling after they complete the eighth grade in order to work with their families. Catholics, Lutherans, Episcopalians, Seventh-Day Adventists, and some Fundamentalist Christian groups have established their own schools to provide both a common education (the general, nonreligious skills and knowledge) and a religious education.

Public schools are supposed to be free of religious doctrine and perspective, but many people believe that schools without such a perspective do not provide a desirable values orientation for students. Debate about the public school's responsibility in fostering student morality and social responsibility is constant. A major point of disagreement focuses on who should determine the morals that will provide the context of the educational program in a school. Because religious diversity is so great in this country, that task is nearly impossible. Therefore, most public schools incorporate commonly accepted American values that transcend most religions. In response, some students are sent to schools operated by a religious body; other students attend religion classes after school or on Saturdays; and many students receive their religious training at Sunday School.

Although the U.S. Constitution requires the separation of church and state, this does not mean that public schools and religion have always been completely separated. Until 1962 and 1963, when Supreme Court decisions [i.e., *Engel v. Vitale,* 82 S. Ct. 1261 (1962) and *Abington School District v. Schempp,* 374 U.S. 203 (1963)] determined that these practices were unconstitutional, some schools included religious worship and prayer in their daily educational practices. Although schools should be secular, they are greatly influenced by the predominant values of the community. Whether evolution, sex education, and values clarification are taught in school is determined, in great part, by the religious beliefs of a community. Educators must be cognizant of this influence before introducing certain readings and ideas that stray far from what the community is willing to accept within their belief and value structure.

VIDEO INSIGHTS

Standing Alone

Although the Supreme Court voted in 1963 to remove prayer from schools, the issue is still not settled. In some areas of the country, where religious diversity is minimal, this ruling is effectively ignored. Other districts have agreed to a "moment of silence" for the purpose of moral reflection. Still others are locked in battle over this issue, like the high school choir in Utah, an area with a large Mormon population, that refused to honor the wishes of Rachel, its single Jewish member, to sing fewer religious songs.

Rachel's parents accused the choir director of insensitivity to their concerns, offering a "Jewish song" to appease them.

Rachel's father encouraged the protests, and wrote letters to add to the protest.

1. Consider how you would have reacted to Rachel's request if you were the choir director.
2. As an educator, is it your responsibility to represent various religious viewpoints, even if the majority of your students share the same religious beliefs?
3. Did Rachel's father act in her best interest by his involvement and by encouraging her to take issue with a popular school position? Should an individual (and parents) stand up for a principle even if it will lead to rejection, social isolation, and harassment?
4. How will you handle similar issues in your own classroom?

Go to the Video Insights DVD and watch the video segment *Standing Alone.* Then, go to the *Homework and Exercises* section in Chapter 7 of MyEducationLab and select *Video Insights: Standing Alone* to answer these questions.

Controversial Issues

School Prayer. Among the controversial issues that surround the efforts of the Religious Right and fundamentalist religious groups are school prayer, school vouchers, and censorship. Despite the 1962 and 1963 Supreme Court decisions regarding school prayer, conservative groups have persisted in their efforts to revive school prayer in the schools. The law now is, in essence, a voluntary prayer law. The law in no way precludes private prayer in school. The Supreme Court decisions do not prevent teachers or students from praying privately in school. Any teacher or student can offer his or her own private prayer of thanks before the noon meal or meditate or pray between classes and before and after school. The law forbids public group prayer. Advocates of school prayer sometime advance their efforts under the term *voluntary* prayer. The interpretation of what constitutes voluntary school prayer has become a main issue in the prayer controversy. Some proponents of school prayer advocate mandated school prayer, with individuals voluntarily choosing to participate or not participate. It is likely that if such laws were ever enacted, the considerable social pressure to participate would be particularly difficult for younger children to resist.

In 2000, the Supreme Court ruled against a Texas school district, which had permitted prayer at a football game over the public address system. The district maintained that the football games were extracurricular, and students were not required to attend and be a part of the prayer (*Santa Fe Independent School District v. DOE,* 2000). Prayers and invocations have been a long-standing tradition at many high school games to invoke the protection against harm for all of the football players and typically ask for good sportsmanship. Seldom has the practice been challenged in the past because it had the support of the vast majority of students and parents. However, the Court has ruled that this is a violation of the separation of church and state. Lyons (2002) reports Americans continue to provide support for public school prayer and other religious activities. Lyons suggests that in the last few decades consensus appears to have shifted away from the view that government should be able to require such expressions. Furthermore, a majority of Americans indicate that they would oppose public school prayer if it offended a large proportion of parents (Lyons, 2002).

Since 1962, the Supreme Court has ruled several times against school prayer, and other state sponsored religious activities (Lyons, 2002). With public sentiment favoring prayer in the schools, it is understandable why continued attempts are made to change or to circumvent the Supreme Court's decision.

School Vouchers. Various groups raise school voucher initiatives periodically. Vouchers are intended to provide parents with a choice of schools for their children, public, or private. Secretary of Education Rod Paige in the first George W. Bush administration supported voucher programs in what he said would help low-income parents and children to escape low performing schools (Gordon, 2002). The funds for vouchers come from tax monies and usually range between $2,500 and $5,000, with around $3,000 typical. Voucher initiatives are often strongly supported by religious factions, particularly those who send their children to private religious schools. Parents and others who support these initiatives point to the failure of the public schools to educate their children adequately. They point to the states' low national rankings in student math proficiency, reading proficiency, SAT scores, class size, teacher/student ratios, computer availability, and per pupil spending (38 YES-School Vouchers, 2000). They also point to falling system-wide test scores and to the moral decline in schools as evidenced by school violence, drugs, and teen pregnancies. They believe that school vouchers will make it possible to send their children to the schools of their choice.

Proponents of voucher programs argue that vouchers will not require any further appropriations since school districts can provide vouchers to students who are not using their services, thereby decreasing their expenses. They argue that when parents redeem a school voucher, part of the expense that would otherwise cost the school to educate the student can remain in the public schools. The voucher program will enable all parents to ensure the quality education that they wish for their children.

Opponents to voucher initiatives maintain that vouchers will indeed take away needed funds from the public schools. School districts have many fixed costs and already are suffering from inadequate funding. Opponents also suggest that voucher systems will create a fiscal crisis in the public school system, and there will be a need for additional state support to even maintain the status quo. They further state that the $3,000 or $4,000 provided by the vouchers will not enable any child to go to any school of choice. Many private schools have annual tuitions of $14,000 to $20,000, or more, and the $3,000 or $4,000 vouchers will not even begin to cover the cost of the full tuition. While some schools may grant partial scholarships to deserving students with financial need, it will not be possible to provide support to all. Private schools tend to be located in the more affluent areas of the community. Transportation will be a major problem for students who live in areas distant from the preferred schools. Opponents also contend that the primary beneficiaries of the school voucher programs will be the wealthy who can afford the private schools and already enroll their children in them, and the few borderline families who can send their children to private schools only with the help of vouchers. The American public (43% to 54%) tends to be against spending public funds to assist low-income children to attend religious schools (Gordon, 2002).

Censorship.   The discussion of censorship is included in this section because the censorship movement tends to be heavily influenced by many individuals from fundamentalist and conservative religious groups. In most cases, a censor is a concerned citizen who sincerely seeks to improve society or protect children. At other times censorship may take place to forward one's own religious or political agenda (American Library Association, 2004).

Individuals or groups may be self-appointed and pressure school districts or libraries, video stores, publishers, art galleries, and so forth not to stock or show, publish, or distribute the targeted materials. Censorship may also take place with committees appointed by a state or school district as textbook selection committees. Censorship of textbooks, library books, and other learning materials in education has become another major battleground in education for the Religious Right and other fundamentalist groups.

The impact of censorship in the public schools cannot be underestimated. It is a serious matter. Censorship or attempts at censorship have resulted in the dismissal or resignation of administrators and teachers. It has split communities and has the potential of creating much controversy as did the desegregation of schools. Few can doubt the sincerity of censors and their proponents. They feel passionately that the cause they support is just and morally right. Censors believe that they are obligated to continue their fight to rid schools of objectionable materials that contaminate supple minds and that contribute to the moral decay of society.

At the other end of the continuum, opponents to the censors also tend to share a conviction that they are the ones in the right and that censors infringe on academic freedom, seeking to destroy meaningful education. Opponents to the censors believe that their

FOCUS YOUR CULTURAL LENS: DEBATE

School Vouchers

With every report of declining achievement test scores or school violence, we can expect to hear the cry for school vouchers. Some view vouchers as the answer to ineffective schools. Typically in the range of $3,000 to 4,000, parents can use the vouchers to choose and offset the cost of private schools. Presumably, the districts would save the cost of educating students who opt for private schools, and these savings can be used by the districts to pay for the vouchers. Opponents see vouchers as damaging to the public school system as well as a way to finance the education of students in church operated schools.

For

- School districts spend $7,000 or more a year to educate each student.
- With the typical voucher in the $3,000 range, this will save the school districts $4,000 or more a year for each student who withdraws from a public school utilizing the voucher.
- Vouchers will improve the quality of education in public schools.
- They will create a healthy competition and force the schools to improve or close.
- Most important is the fact that parents and students would then have an opportunity to select a school that will provide a quality education.

Against

- Voucher programs will require taxpayers to support religious education or to support students to attend private racially segregated schools.
- Students already attending private schools will seek vouchers.
- When students leave the public schools with their vouchers, most of the schools' fixed costs would remain.
- Vouchers will drain the resources of school districts and exacerbate the fiscal problems most schools already face.
- Many inner-city students will not be able meet the entrance requirement of the better private schools.
- Even if they can, they may have difficulty with transportation or in paying the balance of the tuition beyond the value of the voucher.
- Vouchers are likely to benefit primarily the wealthy and those whose children already attend church related schools.

Questions

1. If the parents are paying taxes, why shouldn't they get some support to send their children to the school of their choice even if it is a church related school or one that is segregated?
2. If the public schools can't compete adequately with private schools, shouldn't they be closed?

Go to the *Homework and Exercises* section in Chapter 7 of MyEducationLab and select *Focus Your Cultural Lens* to answer these questions.

Adapted from Citizens for Educational Freedom, *Frequently Asked Questions*, www.educational-freedom.org/faq.html; *Myth Conceptions about School Choice*, www.schoolchoices.org/roo/myths.htm; National Education Association, *Vouchers*, www.nea.org/issues/vouchers/; Anti-Defamation League (ADL), *School Vouchers: The Wrong Choice for Public Education*, www.adl.org/vouchers/vouchers_main.asp

antagonists thrive on hard times, such as when schools come under fire because of declining Scholastic Aptitude Test (SAT) scores, rising illiteracy rates, escalating costs of education, and increasing concern about violence and vandalism in the schools. Other factors that prompt the activities of censors are the removal of school prayer; teaching methods that are branded as secular humanism; and programs such as values clarification, drug education, and sex education. Books written specifically for teenagers about subjects that are objectionable to some parents and in language that others consider too realistic are often a source of concern. The emergence of African American literature, sometimes written in the black vernacular, is sometimes the source of irritation or concern.

Censorship occurs when expressive materials such as books, magazines, films, videos, or works of art are removed or kept from public access, including the removal of materials from textbook adoption lists. Censorship may be based on the age of or other characteristics of the potential user. Targets for the censors are books and materials that are identified as disrespectful of authority and religion, destructive of social and cultural values, obscene, pornographic, unpatriotic, or in violation of individual and familial rights of privacy. Books written by gays and lesbians are frequently attacked. Other materials attacked by censors may be those that are considered nonracist or nonsexist. In a conservative community, teachers may be surprised to find that magazines such as *Time, Newsweek,* and *U.S. News and World Report* are sometimes attacked because they publish stories about war, crime, death, violence, and sex. In this same community, a teacher can anticipate a negative reaction to the teaching of evolution without presenting the views on creationism. In addition, certain dictionaries with words and definitions described as offensive have been forced off book adoption lists.

One can understand the concern of parents who are often influenced by censors. These parents believe that unless they choose sides and act, their children will be taught with materials that are anti-God, anti-family, anti-authority, anti-country, anti-morality, and anti-law and order. The failure to communicate effectively with parents is a contributing source of alienation between educators and parents. Failure to communicate the objectives of new curricula and to explain how these programs enrich the educational experience may cause suspicion and distrust. Many administrators and librarians indicate that communication with parents is more crises oriented than continuous. Information about programs, policies, and procedures tends to be offered in response to inquiries or challenges, rather than as part of an ongoing public relations effort.

Often controversy develops when parents do not understand what educators are including in their children's curriculum. Controversy can be avoided or minimized when time and care is devoted to clearly explaining curricular content and its purpose before the instructional process is undertaken. Showing parents how the curriculum will support rather than conflict with basic family values can avoid potential conflict.

Secular Humanism.   Secular humanism has been a direct target of the censors, particularly those affiliated with Fundamentalist religious groups. The emphasis in secular humanism is a respect for human beings, rather than a belief in the supernatural. Its objectives include the full development of every human being, the universal use of the scientific method, affirmation of the preciousness and dignity of the individual person, personal freedom combined with social responsibility, and fulfillment through the development of ethical and creative living (Robinson, 2006c).

Because many Secular Humanists feel that the role of religion throughout history has been profoundly negative, and because some humanists regard God as a creation of mankind rather than the reverse, they are often targets of conservative Christians. Secular humanism is not an organized religion like Roman Catholicism, Protestantism, and Judaism. It does not have rituals, a church, or professed doctrines. Its existence is in the minds of individuals who align themselves with these perspectives. The specific beliefs and manifestations of beliefs vary from one believer to another.

Conservative Christians tend to view Secular Humanism as a religion, and one that has taken over the public school systems. This may be unlikely since the majority of teachers in the public schools are from Christian backgrounds. The principle of Separation of Church and State requires public schools to base their curriculum on secular or nonreligious foundations. In mathematics, reading, writing, chemistry, and physics there is no conflict. However in subjects such as human sex education, biology, sociology, and history, the secular approach often comes into conflict with conservative Christian theology. Consequently, books and materials viewed as Secular Humanist in orientation are often targets for censorship (Robinson, 2006c). Materials and topics infused into the curriculum that address issues such as abortion, corporal punishment of children, death penalty, enforced prayer in schools, homosexuality, and physician-assisted suicide will typically draw the attention of censors who view them as secular humanist objectionable material. Writings by individuals such as B. F. Skinner, Abraham Maslow, Carl Rogers, and Mary Calderone would likely be targets of some censors who identify them with secular humanists.

Teachers new to the profession or new to a community should never underestimate the determination of those involved in the censorship movement. Teachers would be well advised to make certain that they are fully aware of the climate within the community before introducing new, innovative, or controversial materials, teaching strategies, and books. Experienced colleagues and supervisors can usually serve as barometers as to how students, parents, and the community will react to the new materials or teaching techniques. With this type of information, the new teacher can proceed with a more realistic anticipation of the reception that can be expected.

Classroom Implications

Although religion and public schooling are to remain separate, religion can be taught in schools as a legitimate discipline for objective study. A comparative religion course is part of the curriculum offered in many secondary schools. In this approach, the students are not forced to practice a religion as part of their educational program. They can, however, study one or more religions.

Guidelines for Teaching About Religion

The Fairfax County Schools in Virginia have provided teachers with a handout titled *Religion and Public Schools: The Path Between Too Much and Too Little*. In the handout are guidelines for teaching about religions. This important advice will assist teachers in understanding how religion can be taught while maintaining the all-important separation of church and state:

- The school may sponsor the study of religion, but may not sponsor the practice of religion.
- The school may expose students to all religious views, but may not impose any particular view.
- The school's approach to religion is one of instruction, not one of indoctrination.

- The function of the school is to educate about all religions, not to convert to any one religion.
- The school should study what all people believe, but should not teach a student what to believe.
- The school should strive for student awareness of all religions, but should not press for student acceptance of any one religion.
- The school should seek to inform the student about various beliefs, but should not seek to conform him or her to any one belief. (Becker, undated)

As part of the curriculum, students should learn that the United States (and indeed the world) is rich in religious diversity. Educators show their respect for religious differences by their interactions with students from different religious backgrounds. Understanding the importance of religion to students and their families is an advantage in developing effective teaching strategies for individual students. Instructional activities can build on students' religious experiences to help them learn concepts. This technique helps students recognize that their religious identity is valued in the classroom and encourages them to respect the religious diversity that exists.

At the same time, educators should avoid stereotyping all students from one denomination or church. Diversity is found within every religious group and denomination as mentioned earlier in this chapter. Within each group are differences in attitudes and beliefs. For example, Southern Baptists may appear to be conservative to outsiders. Among Southern Baptists, however, some would be considered part of a liberal or moderate group, whereas others would be identified as conservative. Some Southern Baptist churches may hold services so formal in nature that they might even be described as resembling an Episcopalian service.

It is the responsibility of educators to be aware of the religious diversity and the influence of religion in the community in which they work. They must also understand the influence of religion on the school's curriculum and climate in order to teach effectively. Finally, educators must periodically reexamine their own interactions with students to ensure that they are not discriminating against students because of differences in religious beliefs. It is imperative that educators recognize how influential membership in a religious microculture is in order to help students develop their potential.

Summary

Educators should never underestimate the importance that Americans place on religion. For some individuals, their religion takes precedent over all other microcultures. People have been willing to die for their religion; some have been willing to inflict great pain on others because of their beliefs. We live in a society that has become increasingly diverse. Along with increasing ethnic diversity has come increasing religious diversity. The United States has operated under Judeo-Christian principles for more than two centuries. When new religions threaten established religions, however, controversies and challenges arise.

Educators would do well to inform themselves of the religious groups in their community and in their school. In doing so, they greatly enhance their ability to function in the classroom, mindful and respectful of the religious rights of all students.

One's religion has considerable impact on how one functions on a day-to-day basis. For example, an individual's education may be greatly influenced by religious groups.

Some private schools are established on religious principles and, in those schools, religion is an integral part of the curriculum. Even in public schools, attempts by religious groups to influence the system are made regularly. The degree of religious influence in the schools varies from one community to another. Educators should not underestimate the influence and strategies of both conservative and liberal religious groups and would be well advised to know their community before introducing controversial materials.

PROFESSIONAL PRACTICE FOR EDUCATORS

Questions for Discussion

1. Discuss how the religious majority in a community can influence curriculum and instructional methodology. Does the majority rule? Can and should the majority religious group in a community be able to mandate what is taught in the schools?

2. What is the relationship of religion to public office? Why are some groups disproportionately represented in Congress?

3. What are the current trends with respect to membership in conservative, moderate, and liberal religious groups? What are the implications of these trends for the political and legal directions of the country?

4. How have Protestantism, Catholicism, and Judaism influenced American culture?

5. In what ways does gender affect religion and religion affect gender issues?

6. How do the perceptions about gay and homosexual individuals differ between religious conservatives and liberals? What are the responsibilities of the schools toward gay and lesbian students?

7. What is the First Amendment to the Constitution? Explain the concept of Separation of Church and State. Does it mean that no religion can be taught in public schools?

8. What do laws permit with respect to school prayer? How and why does the Religious Right want to change these laws? Do religious conservatives have valid concerns about our public schools?

9. What are the issues surrounding school vouchers?

10. What is secular humanism? What objections does the Religious Right have against secular humanism in the schools?

Portfolio Activities

1. Form a group to work on a project to determine religious or theological implications of parents having a child born with a disability. Divide your assignments so that the group can interview (if your community is large enough) at least two or three Catholic priests, Protestant ministers (from different denominations), Jewish rabbis, Mormon bishops, and Islamic center directors. Ask them what information they would provide parents of a newborn child with a disability when they ask what God's reason was for bringing a child with a disability into the world. As a group formulate a report

looking at the similarities and differences of each religious group or denomination. (INTASC Standards 3, 8, and 10)

2. Utilizing various sources including legal documents and search engines, find and summarize the court cases in your state in the last 25 years involving challenges to the First Amendment and public schools. (INTASC Standard 10)

3. Write a plan of action for meeting with parents and explaining to them how you will be addressing evolution in your class. Show what steps will be taken to avoid conflict with parental religious views. (INTASC Standards 3 and 10)

Licensure Test Prep

Ms. Sinclair is a public school sixth-grade teacher in both a politically and religiously conservative community. In a state-adopted textbook that her class uses, there is a section that briefly specifically discusses the theory of evolution. Ms. Sinclair is adamantly opposed to this theory as she believes firmly that the earth and all of its inhabitants were created in six days precisely as her church teaches. She feels strongly that the students should at least have the creation point of view if evolution is to be imposed on them. She knows that she is not alone in her feelings, other teachers she has spoken to share her beliefs.

Short Answer Questions

1. Can Ms. Sinclair add creationism or "creation science" into her lessons on her own?

2. Do public school teachers have academic freedom to teach what they wish as many college professors do?

3. Since she is teaching the evolution theory, which the textbook provides along with creationism, is she providing "equal time," and therefore, relieved of any legitimate criticism?

4. What would be the prudent steps she should take before deciding on what to teach her class on this subject?

Go to the *Homework and Exercises* section in Chapter 7 of MyEducationLab and select *Licensure Test Prep* to complete this exercise.

Suggested Readings

Corrigan, J., & Hudson, W. S. (2004). *Religion in America* (7th ed.). Upper Saddle River, NJ: Prentice Hall.
A look at the history of religion in this country and its profound influence on the formation of culture in America. It includes a discussion of the pluralistic nature of religion today.

Ellwood, R. S., & McGraw, B. A. (2005). *Many people, many faiths.* Upper Saddle River, NJ: Prentice Hall. This text provides the conceptual, sacred, and social elements of the various religions. It also

provides an examination of the role of women in the world's religions.

Gallup Poll.
The Gallup Organization provides an Internet reporting each week of the results of their research. The service provides a look at the nation's pulse, so that you can see what Americans think, feel, and what they are doing. There is always information on politics, the economy, and religion. This is a subscription service, which has an annual $95 fee.

Hopfe, L. M., & Woodward, M. R. (2007). *Religions of the world* (10th ed.). Upper Saddle River, NJ: Prentice Hall.

This work provides comprehensive and concise descriptions of the world's great religions as well as the smaller and less well-known religions. It explores the historical and cultural factors related to religions as well as their teachings and current status in the world.

Johnstone, R. L. (2007). *Religion in society* (8th ed.). Upper Saddle River, NJ: Prentice Hall.

This text provides an examination of religions from a sociological perspective. It includes but is not limited to chapters on religious politics, religion and economy, and women and religion.

Peach, L. J. (2002). *Women and world religions.* Upper Saddle River, NJ: Prentice Hall.

This text provides an excellent coverage of how women are viewed and treated in the various religious traditions.

Van Leeuwen, M. S. (1990). *Gender and grace.* Downers Grove, IL: InterVarsity Press.

This volume is an excellent examination of gender issues in a Christian biblical context. It was written several years ago, but it is still relevant.

Wallis, J. (2005). *Why the right gets it wrong and the left doesn't get it.* New York: HarperCollins.

This book is written from the perspective of a "moderate" evangelical, who provides a lengthy discussion of the problems he views with the extreme ends of the continuum, the Religious Right, and the liberals in Protestantism.

Zorba, W. M. (2005). *The Beliefnet guide to evangelical Christianity.* New York: Doubleday.

This is a short and concise book that provides a good overview of evangelicals.

References

Altamirano, N. (2007, February 2). Episcopal church faces threat. *Washington Times.* Retrieved from www.washtimes.com/metro/20070201-105012-3624r.htm

American Library Association. (2004). *Intellectual freedom and censorship Q & A.* Chicago: American Library Association, www.ala.org/ala/oif/basics/intellectual.htm#ifpoint3

Barna Update. (2007). *Survey explores who qualifies as an evangelical.* Barna Group, January 18, 2007. Retrieved from www.barna.org/FlexPage.aspx?Page=BarnaUpdates & BarnaUpdateID=263

Becker, B. (undated). *Religion and public schools: The path between too much and too little.* Springfield, VA: Fairfax County Schools.

Brown, M. F. (2008). The New Age and related forms of contemporary spirituality. In R. Scupin (Ed.), *Religion and culture: An anthropological focus* (2nd ed.). Upper Saddle River, NJ: Prentice Hall.

Burkholder, R. (2002). *Jihad—"Holy War," or internal spiritual struggle?* The Gallup Poll, December 3, 2002. Retrieved from www.galluppoll.com/content/?-ci=7333&pg=1

Carlson, D. K. (2005). *Americans weigh in on evolution vs. creationism in schools.* Gallup Poll, May 24, 2005. Retrieved from www.galluppoll.com/content/?ci=16462&pg=1

Carroll, J. (2004, March 2). American public opinion about religion. *Gallup Tuesday Morning Briefing.*

Chryssides, G. D. (1999). *Exploring new religions.* London: Cassell.

City University of New York (CUNY). (2001). *American religious identification survey 2001.* Retrieved from www.gc.cuny.edu/faculty/research_studies.htm#aris_1

The Columbia Encyclopedia (6th ed.). (2001–2005a). Louis Farrakhan. Retrieved from www.bartleby.com/65/fa/Farrakhn.html

The Columbia Encyclopedia (6th ed.). (2001–2005b). The Moral Majority. Retrieved from www.bartleby.com/65/e-/E-MoralMajo.html

Congressional Yellow Book. (2007). New York: Leadership Directories, Inc.

Corduan, W. (1998). *Neighboring faiths.* Downers Grove, IL: InterVarsity Press.

Corrigan, J., & Hudson, W. S. (2004). *Religion in America* (7th ed.). Upper Saddle River, NJ: Prentice Hall.

Council on American-Islamic Relations (CAIR) (2007). *American Muslims: Statistics.* Retrieved from www.cair.com/asp/populationstats.asp

Denny, F. M. (2006). *An introduction to Islam* (3rd ed.). Upper Saddle River, NJ: Prentice Hall.

Ellwood, R. S., & McGraw, B. A. (2005). *Many people, many faiths.* Upper Saddle River, NJ: Prentice Hall.

Esposito, J. L. (2006). *Muslims and the West: A culture war?* Gallup Poll, February 13, 2006. Retrieved from www.galluppoll.com/content/?ci=21454

Fisher, M. P. (2008). *Living religions* (7th ed.). Upper Saddle River, NJ: Prentice Hall.

Gallup Poll. (2006). *Religion*. Retrieved December 28, 2006, from www.galluppoll.com/content/?ci=1690&pg=1

Gomes, P. (1996). *The good book*. New York: Morrow.

Gordon, G. (2002, July 9). Beyond vouchers: Fixing public schools. *Gallup Tuesday Morning Briefing*.

Green, J. (2004). *Frontline:* The Jesus Factor: Interview with John Green. Retrieved from http://149.48.228.121/wgbh/pages/frontline/shows/jesus/interviews/green.html

Groothuis, R. M. (1997). *Good news for women: A biblical picture of gender equality*. Grand Rapids, MI: Baker Books.

Hartford Research Institute. (2002). *A quick question: How many Eastern Orthodox are there in the USA?* Retrieved on November 24, 2007 from http://hirr.hartsem.edu/research/quick_question17.html

Hemeyer, J. C. (2006). *Religion in America* (5th ed.). Upper Saddle River, NJ: Prentice Hall.

Hopfe, L. M., & Woodward, M. R. (2007). *Religions of the world* (10th ed.). Upper Saddle River, NJ: Prentice Hall.

Huda, Q. (2006, February). *Diversity of Muslims in the United States*. United States Institute of Peace, Special Report 159. Retrieved from www.usip.org/pubs/specialreports/sr159.pdf

Johnson, J. (2003, November 14). Panel removes Alabama's "Ten Commandments judge." *Los Angeles Times*, pp. A1, A34.

Johnstone, R. L. (2007). *Religion in society: A sociology of religion* (8th ed.). Upper Saddle River, NJ: Prentice Hall.

Kosmin, B. A., & Lachman, S. P. (1993). *One nation under God: Religion in contemporary American society*. New York: Harmony.

Lincoln, E. E. (1994). *The Black Muslims in America* (3rd. ed.). Grand Rapids, MI: Eerdmans.

Lindner, E. W. (2004). *2004 yearbook of American and Canadian churches*. Nashville: Abingdon Press.

Ludwig, T. M. (2006). *Sacred Paths, The: Understanding the Religions of the World*, 4th ed. Upper Saddle River, NJ: Prentice Hall.

Lyons, L. (2002, December 10). The Gallup brain: Prayer in public schools. *Gallup Tuesday Morning Briefing*.

Marsden, G. M. (2006). *Fundamentalism and American culture* (2nd ed.). New York: Oxford University Press.

Marty, M. E. (Ed.). (1975). *Our faiths*. Royal Oak, MI: Cathedral Publications.

Miller, L. (2006, November 13). An evangelical identity crises. *Newsweek, CXLIII*(20), 32–37.

Moore, D. W. (2005). *Most Americans tentative about origin-of-life explanations*. Gallup Poll, September 23, 2005. Retrieved from www.galluppoll.com/content/?ci=18748&pg=1

National Catholic Reporter. (2004, March 26). Membership figures reported—USA—the 10 largest churches in the United States. According to the National Council of Churches.

Newport, F. (2003, February 27). Support for war modestly higher among more religious Americans. *Gallup Tuesday Morning Briefing*.

Newport, F. (2005a). *Who are the evangelicals?* Gallup Poll, June 24, 2005. Retrieved from www.galluppoll.com/content/?ci=17041&pg=1

Newport, F. (2005b). Iran on Holocaust. *The Gallup Poll Daily Briefing* (video). Retrieved from www.galluppoll.com/videoArchive/?ci=20467&pg=

Newport, F. (2006a). *The issue of women in government in Islamic countries*. The Gallup Poll, March 30, 2006. Retrieved from www.gallupworldpoll.com/content/?ci=22180&pg=1

Newport, F. (2006b). *Mormons, evangelical Protestants, Baptists top church attendance list*. Retrieved from April 14, 2006, from www.galluppoll/content/?ci=22414&pg=1

Newport, F. (2006c). *Almost half of Americans believe humans did not evolve*. Gallup Poll, June 5, 2006. Retrieved from www.galluppoll.com/content/?ci=23200&pg=1

Newport, F. (2006d). *Religion most important to blacks, women, and older Americans*. Gallup News Service, November 29, 2006. Retrieved from www.galluppoll.com/content/?ci=25585&pg=1

Newport, F., & Carroll, J. (2003, March 6). Support for Bush significantly higher among more religious Americans. *Gallup Tuesday Morning Briefing*.

Peach, L. J. (2002). *Women and world religions*. Upper Saddle River, NJ: Prentice Hall.

PR Newswire. (2006). *2006 American Jewish yearbook population survey finds 6.4 million American Jews*. Retrieved from http://sev.prnewswire.com/publishing=information=services/20061222/UNTH01421122006-1.html

Robinson, B. A. (2005a). *The Buddhist religion and homosexuality*. Ontario Consultants on

Religious Tolerance. Retrieved on February 11, 2007, from www.religioustolerance.org/hom_budd.htm

Robinson, B. A. (2005b). *Islam and homosexuality*. Ontario Consultants on Religious Tolerance. Retrieved on February 11, 2007, from www.religioustolerance.org/hom_isla1.htm

Robinson, B. A. (2006a). *Eastern Orthodox churches*. Ontario Consultants on Religious Tolerance. Retrieved on March 7, 2007, from www.religioustolerance.org/orthodox.htm

Robinson, B. A. (2006b). *Hinduism, the world's third largest religion*. Ontario Consultants on Religious Tolerance. Retrieved on February 10, 2007, from www.religioustolerance.org/hinduism.htm

Robinson, B. A. (2006c). *Humanism and the humanist manifestos*. Ontario Consultants on Religious Tolerance. Retrieved from www.religioustolerance.org/humanism.htm

Robinson, B. A. (2006d). *Policies and teachings about homosexuality in Judaism*. Ontario Consultants on Religious Tolerance. Retrieved from www.religioustolerance.org/hom_judaism.htm (retrieved October 15, 2007)

Robinson, B. A. (2006e). *Roman Catholics and homosexuality*. Ontario Consultants on Religious Tolerance. Retrieved on November 24, 2007 from www.religioustolerance.org/hom_rom.htm

Saad, L. (2006). *Anti-Muslim sentiments fairly commonplace*. The Gallup Poll, August 10, 2006. Retrieved from www.galluppoll.com/content/?ci=24073&pg=1

Sacerdote, B., & Glaeser, E. L. (2001, March). *Education and religion*. Harvard Institute of Economic Research, Discussion Paper 1913. Retrieved from http://econweb.fas.harvard.edu/hier/2001papers/HIER1913.pdf

Santa Fe Independent School District v. DOE (99–62) 16 F.3d 806 (June 19, 2000).

Smith, C. (2000). *Christian America? What evangelicals really want*. Berkeley, CA: University of California Press.

SoundVision. (2004). *Education, educating our future!* Retrieved on July 15, 2004, from www.soundvision.com/info/education/

Taggar, S. V. (2006). Headscarves in the headlines! What does this mean for educators? *Multicultural Perspectives, 8*(3), 3–10.

38 YES-School Vouchers 2000. Retrieved on July 15, 2004, from www.vouchers2000.com

U.S. State Department. (2004). *Muslim life in America*. International Information Programs. Retrieved on July 15, 2004, from http://usinfo.state.gov/products/pubs/muslimlife/

Van Leeuwen, M. S. (1990). *Gender and grace*. Downers Grove, IL: InterVarsity Press.

Vyas, S. (2004). "We are not all terrorists!" Listening to the voices of Muslim high school students in the post September 11 era. *Ejournal/Ejournal, 1*(2). Vyas.pdf, www.subr.edu/coeducation/ejournal/EJournal

Wallis, J. (2005). *Why the right gets it wrong and the left doesn't get it*. New York: HarperCollins.

Winseman, A. L. (2005, December 6). *Religion in America: Who has none*. Retrieved from Gallup Poll, www.galluppoll.com/content/?ci=20329&pg=1

Yearbook of American and Canadian Churches. (2006). New York: National Council of Churches in the U.S.A.

Young, W. A. (2005). *The world's religions* (2nd ed.). Upper Saddle River, NJ: Pearson Prentice Hall.

Zorba, W. M. (2005). *The Beliefnet guide to evangelical Christianity*. New York: Doubleday.

Chapter 8

GEOGRAPHY

The reality of any place is what its people remember of it.

CHARLES KURALT, TV JOURNALIST

In November a new student, Jack Williams, appeared at Mark Polaski's classroom door. He appeared to be just another white student whose family had moved to the neighborhood last week. Mr. Polaski assigned him a desk, asked him to introduce himself, and continued with the lesson.

Before a month had passed, Mr. Polaski noticed that other students had not accepted Jack. In fact, they were making fun of his mannerisms and dialect. He overheard a couple of the boys calling him a hillbilly. As he thought about Jack's involvement in the class up to that point, Mark realized that Jack had been very quiet, not actively participating in the lively discussions that were encouraged. He was performing as well as most other students on the few tests that had been given, and he had turned in the required short paper on time just after Thanksgiving. Mr. Polaski tried to recall where Jack said he had last attended school. He was sure it was in a rural area of the state.

Reflections

1. Why was Jack not fitting into this diverse suburban school?
2. What differences might exist between a rural and suburban school?
3. How does growing up in a different part of the country or world affect one's experiences in school?
4. How could Mr. Polaski learn more about Jack's cultural background?
5. If you were Mr. Polaski, how would you get the students to stop picking on Jack?

Geography and Culture

Our identities are closely linked to the geographic area in which we grew up and now live. One of the first questions asked when meeting someone new is "Where are you from?" The answer will indicate whether we share a common background and experiences. Although our membership in other groups may have a great impact on our identity, the place or places in which we have lived provide a cultural context for living.

Because we have grown up in the same or similar geographic areas does not mean we have experienced the places in the same ways as our neighbors or friends. Some members of the community have lived there much longer than others and have different histories and experiences that sometimes lead to conflict with more recent arrivals. The area takes on a different meaning based on a member's race, ethnicity, religion, age, and language, and how membership in those groups is viewed by other members of the community. One's job and educational background may take on different significance in one geographic area as compared to another. For example, almost all adults in one suburban neighborhood have postbaccalaureate degrees and work as professionals or managers. Farming and related jobs are common in one area, logging and fishing in another, and manufacturing in yet another.

The natural surroundings and climate make a difference in the way we work, relax, and interact. People from Hawaii, Alaska, the mountains of Colorado, and the prairies of Nebraska adapt to their space in different ways. People in new environments may find that the "natives" use unfamiliar dialects and phrases and react to events somewhat differently than they are used to. Jack in the opening scenario, for instance, has a dialect and mannerisms that are different from other students in his new school. This strangeness is particularly noticeable when we travel outside the United States, but it also appears to some degree in different parts of the same city and from one region of the United States to another.

Different individuals and groups interpret places differently (Massey, 1997). Some find the locale as the ideal place to live and raise a family; others feel isolated or crowded or entrapped. Mountains are critical to the well-being of some; others feel the need to be near bodies of water or the desert or greenery. Wide-open spaces in which one can live for long periods of time with little interaction with others provide freedom for some, but boredom and confinement for others. Cities can be exciting and stimulating places for some, but stifling and impersonal to others. Thus, the places in which we live provide complex multiple identities for the people who live in them. Understanding the place, including the part of the city or county, from which our students have come helps us know the context of their everyday experiences.

What Is Geography?

You probably studied geography in elementary school as you learned about different parts of the world and memorized state capitals. Yet, newspaper headlines declare "Global goofs: U.S. youth can't find Iraq" (CNN, 2002). We are enticed to learn more about a country when a disaster occurs such as the tsunami in Indonesia, or the massacre in Rwanda. But, generally our knowledge of places in the world is rather limited. People who are lucky enough to travel to other parts of the country and world become familiar with geographical, cultural, and language differences. People who are place-bound and unable to travel much beyond their own neighborhoods will have to learn about these differences in books, the media, and the Internet.

Geography comes from the Greek word *geōgraphia,* which means a description of the earth's surface. It is the study of places, cities, countries, savannahs, mountains, deserts, rural areas, oceans, continents, and communities. Geographers try to figure out why places are the way they are. They not only explore the physical features of a place but they examine the economic activities, human settlement patterns, and cultures of the people who live there. The place where one lives is the space or land area that is distinct and has meaning or symbolism for the people who live there.

Physical geography is the study of the physical features of the earth such as the climate, soils, vegetation, water, and landforms. **Human geography**, on the other hand, is the study of the economic, social, and cultural systems that have evolved in a specific location. It encompasses many of the topics that are discussed in this book such as classism, racism, ethnicity, poverty, language, sexual orientation, religions, exceptionalities, and age differences.

Geographers use a number of tools to record and track the physical and human geography of a place. Maps are the most common as you probably remember from your study of geography. With today's technologies, geographers are able to understand an area in great and intricate detail through the use of computers, global positioning system (GPS) devices, and satellite images. Throughout this chapter we will use maps to understand the differences in the places our students live or used to live and the difference that location can make in one's everyday life.

Our Place in the World

Placing the United States within the world provides a context for understanding where we and others live. First, people are concentrated in certain areas since few choose to live in the earth's cold and dry areas. Three of every four people currently live in the Northern Hemisphere—the area north of the equator (Bergman & Renwick, 2005). As you can see

Pause to Reflect 8.1

Think about the geographic area in which you grew up (or one of them if you have moved from one area to another).

- How would you describe the geographic landscape that influenced the way the people you know lived?
- What stories were told when you were growing up that detailed someone's experience with the land or weather?
- How do you think the place where you were raised has impacted your values and way of living?

Go to the *Homework and Exercises* section in Chapter 8 of MyEducationLab and select *Pause to Reflect 8.1* to answer these questions.

in Figure 8.1, of the 10 countries with the largest populations, Brazil is the only one located south of the equator. Over half of the world's population lives in Asia (Population Reference Bureau, 2006). The United States, by contrast, had a population of over 302 million by mid-2007 (U.S. Census Bureau, 2007) or just less than 5% of the world's population.

North America has a culturally diverse population, most of whom have immigrated from other parts of the world over the past 400 years. It is a resource-rich region that has experienced a great deal of economic development over the past 200 years. Its **metropolitan** areas are technology-rich and oriented to a global economy in which U.S. corporations have offices and employees in many parts of the world. The region is very consumer oriented, buying up the latest versions of the products its businesses produce. Although it is an affluent area, many of its citizens live in poverty.

Poverty in the United States is discussed in Chapter 3.

FIGURE 8.1 Countries with the Largest Populations in 2006.

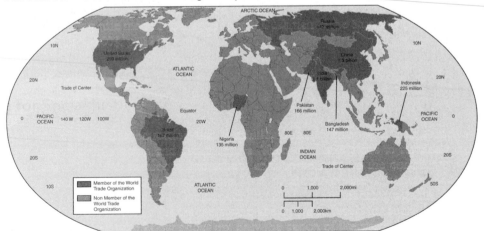

From Population Reference Bureau. (2006). *2006 world population data sheet.* Washington, DC: Author.

Regional Diversity in the United States

Regional differences become apparent to educators as they move from one area to another to work. Sometimes local and regional differences will hardly be noticeable. At other times, they will lead to a number of adjustments in the way one lives, the content that can be taught in the classroom, and interactions in the community. For example, religion plays a more important role in some regions of the country than others, which could influence a teacher's approach to teaching sex education or evolution. Not only teachers move around the country and globe, so do students and their families, especially if they are in the military or on a fast track at a multinational corporation. Students like Jack in the scenario that opened the chapter may experience cultural shock that should be considered as they settle in a new school. To meet the needs of students, educators need to be aware of the influences of geography and space on the culture of the people who live there, especially school-aged children.

The diversity of the population differs across regions of the United States as shown in Figure 8.2. Whites are less than half of the population in California, the District of Columbia, Hawaii, New Mexico, and Texas. However, the diversity in these and other states differs.

FIGURE 8.2 Degree of Diversity by State.

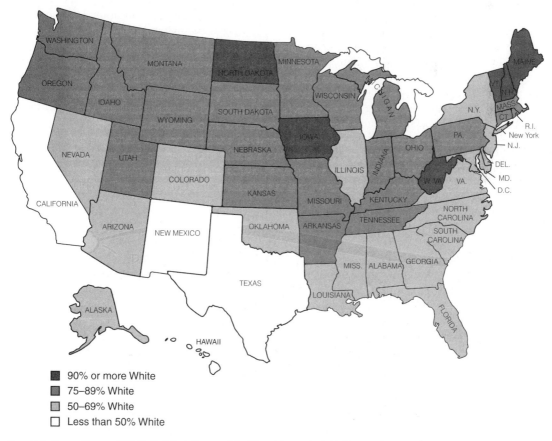

- ■ 90% or more White
- ■ 75–89% White
- ■ 50–69% White
- □ Less than 50% White

From U.S. Census Bureau. (2006). *Statistical Abstract of the United States: 2007* (126th ed.). Washington, DC: U.S. Government Printing Office.

African Americans are the majority in the District of Columbia and over one fourth of the population in Mississippi (37%), Louisiana (33%), Georgia (30%), South Carolina (29%), Maryland (29%), and Alabama (26%). Asian Americans are the majority in Hawaii with the largest numbers being from Japanese and Chinese heritages. Latinos comprise 43% of New Mexico and 35% of the California and Texas populations. The largest numbers of American Indians live in California, Arizona, Oklahoma, New Mexico, North Carolina, Washington, and New York (U.S. Census Bureau, 2006).

From 1892 to 1954 new immigrants entered the country by boat at Ellis Island on the East Coast. By the end of the twentieth century they were entering through airports in New York City, Los Angeles, and Seattle. They established or moved to ethnic enclaves that were similar to areas they had just left. In these communities they did not have to assimilate into the dominant culture and could continue to use their native language. A larger percentage of more recent immigrants are joining family members who live in the **suburbs** or in small towns. Some, especially refugees, have been sponsored by churches or community agencies in nonurban areas. Others have been attracted to the Midwest and South for jobs in meatpacking and farm industries. Still others have chosen rural areas because they think the values and lifestyle are closer to their own than living in urban areas.

Whites represent many ethnic groups with different cultures and experiences, some who emigrated from Europe several centuries ago and others who are new immigrants. Whites in the South and New England are predominantly from Anglo backgrounds, but the ethnic diversity within the white population is increasing with migration from other states. The Mid-Atlantic and Midwest states have a greater mix of European ancestry from Great Britain, Ireland, Germany, Italy, Poland, and other eastern European countries. A large portion of the population in the central Great Plains states is German American. Swedes and Norwegians settled in the northern states of this region (Clawson, Johnson, Haarmann, & Johnson, 2007).

Characteristics of the population and land on which they live can be used to group geographic areas with similar landscapes and histories. The racial, ethnic, and religious diversity varies from one region to another, both in the amount of diversity and the groups that have settled there. The interests and perspectives of those who live in various geographic regions often are reflected in their stands on state and federal issues as seen when national elections are reflected by red (Republican) and blue (Democrat) states. We will explore some of these regional differences in this section.

The South

Outsiders identify southerners by their distinctive dialect, but may know little else about the region other than its involvement in the Civil War. The area includes 12 southeastern states shown in Figure 8.3, but the culture extends into the states that border them as well— east Texas, east Oklahoma, southern Missouri, southern Illinois, southern Indiana, southern Ohio, the eastern shore of Maryland, and southern Delaware. Not all states in the region share the same southern culture. For example, south Florida with its Cuban and Jewish populations does not fit the traditional southern culture and language patterns. Many northerners and others from outside the region inhabit Atlanta, one of the largest southern cities. Others from northern states have retired in the region or spend the winter months there.

Dialects are discussed in greater detail in Chapter 6.

Nearly one of four of the nation's residents lives in the South (U.S. Census Bureau, 2006). The region has a number of major cities—Atlanta, Nashville, Charlotte, Orlando, Miami, and New Orleans. Around 35% of the population lives in rural areas or small towns (U.S. Census Bureau, 2006) where families may have known each other for generations.

FIGURE 8.3   The South.

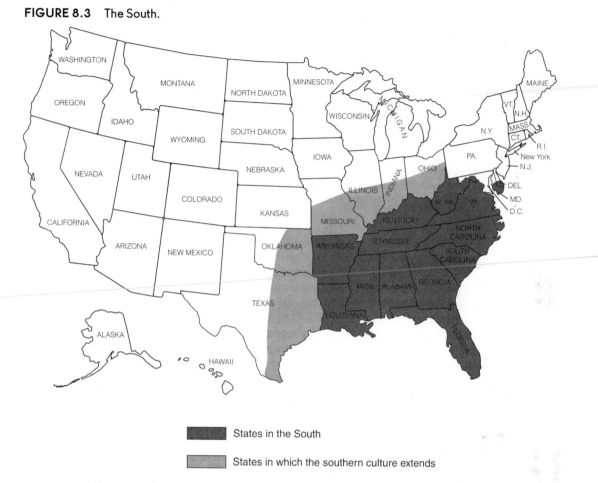

States in the South

States in which the southern culture extends

Historical Context.   Among the early European settlements were the coastal regions of Virginia and North Carolina. The settlers quickly learned that their wealth could be built on the cultivation of subtropical crops such as tobacco, cotton, indigo, and rice. They moved throughout the southern states, establishing plantations and smaller farms to produce crops that could be exported north and across the ocean to Europe. Production depended on a large labor force, which was filled by purchasing African slaves. Because American Indian tribes across the South were unwilling to sell their land to European settlers Congress passed legislation in the 1830s to forcibly remove them from the southern states to the Oklahoma territories. After the Civil War, segregation and Jim Crow laws divided the population into white and persons of color.

Following the Civil War (1861–1865), race became a defining feature of the South, legalizing Jim Crow laws to separate blacks and whites and limiting the benefits to which African Americans were entitled. The state of Virginia, for example, passed the Racial Integrity Law in 1924 to identify its residents as either white or colored. The state declared that American Indians were white. The law was not repealed until 1968 (Wilson & Ray, 2007). Before and after the Civil War, the population in the South was not just black and white. American Indians had always lived across the region. Cubans were making cigars in Key West by 1831 and established cigar manufacturing in Tampa in the 1880s.

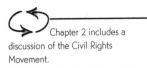

Chapter 2 includes a discussion of the Civil Rights Movement.

Because of its racist policies and practices, the South became the battleground for the civil rights struggle in the 1950s and 1960s. The continued use of the Confederate flag in many settings remains controversial. To many it is a reminder of past and continuous discriminatory and racist treatment of African Americans, Jews, and other powerless groups across the region.

By the 1970s, the population of the South had begun to grow, especially in metropolitan areas such as Atlanta, Birmingham, Charlotte, and Huntsville (AL). Manufacturing industries and corporation headquarters were enticed to move to the South because of lower wages and low rates of unionization. Retirees were attracted to the warmer climate and recreational opportunities. The region became known as the Sun Belt, pulling young families from the North to new jobs.

Characteristics of the South.   Native southerners are generally proud of their southern culture and traditions, which are highlighted and promoted through books and magazines. However, there is not a single southern culture across the region. It includes many subregions such as the Delta of Mississippi, the Low Country of South Carolina, south Florida, the Piedmonts of North Carolina and Georgia, the Ozarks of Arkansas, and the Bluegrass Country of Kentucky—all with their own distinctive cultures. Traditional cultures have been maintained by American Indian tribes and other groups such as the Gullah and Geechees of South Carolina and Georgia, and the Cajuns of Louisiana. The southern culture has evolved from the mixing of its numerous American Indian, European, and African cultures—a process of **creolization.**

More African Americans continue to live in the South than any other region of the United States. Twenty-two percent of the population is African American; 67% is white (U.S. Census Bureau, 2006). Until recently, most white southerners were Protestants of English, Irish, or Scottish descent. The population is much more diverse today. The *Encyclopedia of Southern Culture* lists 34 American Indian and 54 other ethnic groups (Wilson & Ray, 2007). Since the 1970s, a growing number of Asian Americans have settled in the South with the largest numbers being Filipinos, Korean, Vietnamese, Hmong, and Asian Indians. Larger numbers of Latinos began to move into the southern states in the 1990s. During this same period, the number of Middle Easterners doubled in Florida, North Carolina, Texas, and Virginia.

As businesses moved to the nonunion South, northerners moved with them, leading to an influx of outsiders who are not as familiar, and perhaps not as appreciative of the culture as those born there. One of the major concerns of staunch southerners is that their distinctive culture is being destroyed as the population swells with outsiders.

Similar to other rural areas, income is relatively low in the South. With the exception of Virginia, per capita income, which is $27,876, is below the national average of $31,071 (U.S. Census Bureau, 2006). Only Florida and Virginia's poverty rates are lower than the United States as a whole (U.S. Census Bureau, 2006).

Education in the South.   Schools were slow to develop in the South and when they did, they were primarily for the children of landowners. It was illegal to teach slaves and their children. Nevertheless, they taught themselves and established their own schools years before the government provided support for them. For this reason, literacy among African Americans grew dramatically after the Civil War. Most schools across the South were segregated by race until a decade or more after the 1954 *Brown* decision. During the period in which schools were being desegregated, many European American families established their own private schools—many of them Christian schools—or moved from cities to rural or suburban areas to avoid attending schools with African Americans. At the

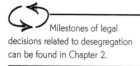

Milestones of legal decisions related to desegregation can be found in Chapter 2.

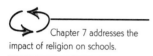

Chapter 7 addresses the impact of religion on schools.

same time, many school districts did become more integrated, sometimes extending desegregation plans beyond city borders into the suburbs.

Religion is an important cultural component for many southerners. The role of religion and prayer in schools has led to numerous school board debates and the enactment of legislation in some states and school districts. Controversies at the beginning of this century included the posting of the Ten Commandments in schools and practices that are sometimes close to promoting prayer or religion in schools.

Average teacher salaries range from $37,924 in Mississippi to $48,300 in Georgia as shown in Table 8.1 (National Education Association, 2007).

TABLE 8.1   Average Teacher Salaries in 2005–2006

District of Columbia	$61,195	Wisconsin	$44,299
Connecticut	$59,499	North Carolina	$43,922
California	$59,345	Idaho	$43,390
Michigan	$58,482	Florida	$43,302
Illinois	$57,819	South Carolina	$42,207
New Jersey	$57,707	Arkansas	$42,093
New York	$57,354	Tennessee	$42,072
Massachusetts	$56,587	Kentucky	$41,903
Maryland	$54,486	New Mexico	$41,637
Delaware	$54,264	Kansas	$41,369
Alaska	$53,553	Nebraska	$41,026
Rhode Island	$53,473	Texas	$41,009
Pennsylvania	$53,258	Iowa	$40,877
Hawaii	$51,599	Maine	$40,737
Ohio	$48,692	Wyoming	$40,392
Minnesota	$48,489	Alabama	$40,347
Oregon	$48,330	Louisiana	$40,253
Georgia	$48,300	Utah	$39,965
Indiana	$47,255	Missouri	$39,922
Washington	$45,724	Montana	$39,832
Colorado	$45,616	West Virginia	$38,360
New Hampshire	$45,263	Mississippi	$37,924
Virginia	$44,763	Oklahoma	$37,879
Arizona	$44,672	North Dakota	$36,449
Vermont	$44,535	South Dakota	$34,040
Nevada	$44,426		

Adapted from National Education Association. (2007). *Teacher salaries: State by state.* Retrieved March 1, 2007, from www.nea.org/student-program/about/state.html#alaska; www.nea.org/student-program/about/state2.html#kentucky; and www.nea.org/student-program/about/state3.html#northdakota

With the exceptions of Arkansas and Virginia, high school graduation rates across the South remain lower than other regions of the country (U.S. Department of Education, 2006a).

Appalachia

The region of the country called Appalachia follows the Appalachian Mountain chain, crossing many states from its northern projection into New York through northern Maryland and all of West Virginia; through western parts of Virginia, North Carolina, South Carolina, and Georgia along with eastern Kentucky and Tennessee; and into northern Mississippi and Alabama, as shown in Figure 8.4. Appalachia has been described in numerous fiction and nonfiction publications over the past century as mountainous and backwards, not maintaining progress with other parts of the country. A commission convened by President John F. Kennedy in 1963 brought to public attention the severe poverty prevalent in the region at that time.

Historical Context.   Early Spanish and French explorers traded in the Appalachian area with the Cherokee, Iroquois, Creek, Mohawk, Oneida, Onondaga, Cayuga, Seneca,

FIGURE 8.4 The Appalachia Region.

From Appalachia: A History by John Alexander Williams. Copyright © 2002 by the University of North Carolina Press. Used by permission of the publisher. www.uncpress.unc.edu

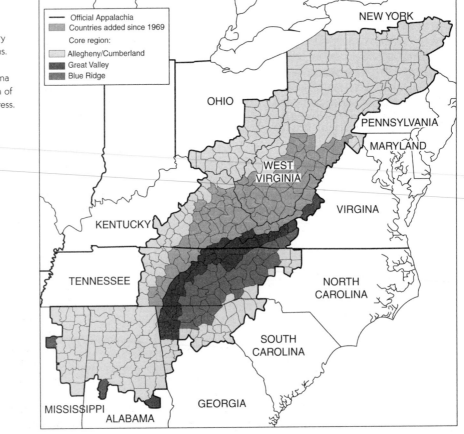

Shawnees, and other American Indian tribes. European Americans settled on the eastern side of the mountains with little resistance, but faced bloody conflicts with American Indian tribes as they moved to the western side of the mountain. By the Revolutionary War, German and Irish immigrants had settled the Appalachian area as far west as the Ohio Valley and as far south as the Carolinas and Georgia (Williams, 2002).

The twentieth century was characterized by large government projects that changed the courses of rivers, flooded farmland, and displaced residents as dams were built by the Tennessee Valley Authority to construct hydroelectric plants. The U.S. Forest Service also had to relocate Appalachians as it purchased land for national forests and parks throughout the core of Appalachia. Coal had become an essential resource for making steel, and the mountains were the primary source. Coal miners were involved in bitter fights with owners over wages, safety issues, and the establishment of unions. State and local governments sided with owners, protecting the convicts and other strikebreakers while engaging in gun battles with the strikers. Although the textile industry was based in the South, it was attractive to unemployed Appalachians who left the mountains for work where they also found themselves in different labor battles.

Characteristics of Appalachia.   The people of Appalachia have been stereotyped as mountaineers or hillbillies. The mountaineer is usually seen as a rugged and independent individual who has mastered the mountains. The hillbilly is a caricature of a person from the backcountry. These stereotypes have been promoted in popular cartoon strips like *Li'l Abner* and *Snuffy Smith* and television shows like the *Beverly Hillbillies* and *Dukes of Hazzard*. Appalachians have been projected as living in poverty, feuding with neighbors, operating moonshine stills, using violence to settle disputes, and being lazy (Billings, Norman, & Ledford, 1999). However, the poverty rate in Appalachia today is about the same as in other rural areas of the country with the exception of eastern Kentucky, West Virginia, and northern Mississippi, where it remains below the national average. (Clawson et al. 2007). When the report of the President's Appalachian Regional Commission was released in 1964, one of three Appalachians lived in poverty (Appalachian Regional Commission, n.d.a). By the 2000 census, it had been reduced to 14% and the general standard of living had risen across the area as a result of changing their dependence on farming and manufacturing to a service-dependent economy (Black & Sanders, 2004).

Although bordered by Atlanta, Pittsburgh, and Cincinnati, Appalachia is primarily rural. Chattanooga and Knoxville (TN), Charleston (WV), and Asheville (NC) are its largest cities. Although more of the population lives in rural areas than in most other parts of the country, the majority lives in metropolitan areas and participates in the related commerce and labor markets. **Subsistence farming** continues to exist in some parts of Central Appalachia, but it is not common (Isserman, 1996).

The native population worries about the number of residents who have had to move out of Appalachia to find employment. At the same time, retirees and community activists have moved into the area, replacing long-time residents and driving up prices. Although coal mines still operate in the region, tourism leads its economic growth. It is home to the Blue Ridge Parkway and Shenandoah and Great Smoky Mountains National Parks. The natural resources have supported the development of water "rafting, rock climbing, mountain biking, skiing, hang gliding, and diving" (Williams, 2002, p. 359). The folkways of the European settlers have led to the establishment of folk schools, folk festivals, and Centers of Folk Music and Crafts.

Appalachia has limited diversity. The population is predominantly white and reflects the general religious and ethnic background of the South. African Americans comprised

8% of the population in 2000, residing primarily in Pennsylvania and the northern counties of Alabama, Georgia, and Mississippi (Hayden, 2004). An increasing number of Latinos, primarily of Mexican origin, are providing an ethnic flavor to some areas. They now make up 2% of the population (Hayden, 2004).

Education in Appalachia.   Historically, school attendance in the rural and mountain regions of Appalachia was lower than other parts of the country. It has improved dramatically since the 1960s. West Virginia, for example, has a high school graduation rate similar to the rest of the country as shown in Figure 8.5. However, the percentage of the adult population in the most rural, isolated areas of the region have finished high school and college at lower rates than the rest of the U.S. population (Appalachian Regional Commission, n.d.b).

The region also has a history of providing higher education opportunities. For example, Berea College, located in Berea, Kentucky, was founded in 1855 as a co-education institution, which has a primary focus of serving students with financial need from Appalachia. While students are accepted from all over the United States and from other countries, the vast majority of students are from Appalachia. All students attend school on a full time basis

FIGURE 8.5   High School Completion Rates: 2002–2003.

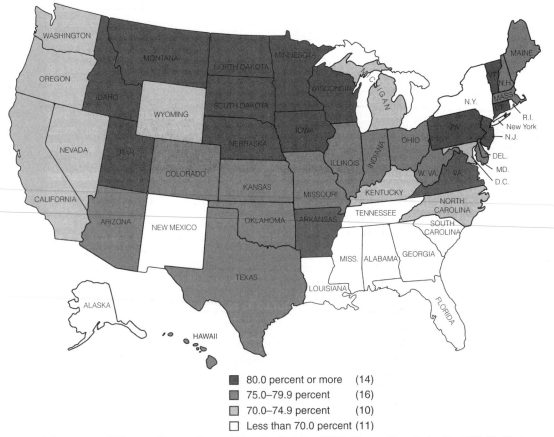

■ 80.0 percent or more	(14)
■ 75.0–79.9 percent	(16)
■ 70.0–74.9 percent	(10)
□ Less than 70.0 percent	(11)

From U.S. Department of Education. National Center of Education Statistics. (2006). *The condition of education 2006.* Washington, DC: Author.

with full academic scholarships. In return for their scholarship, each student works 10 hours a week in school-owned operations including weaving, woodcraft, a bakery, laundry, printing shop, and the historic hotel, Boone Tavern. With its high academic standards, many of Berea College graduates have gone on to professional and graduate schools.

New England and the Mid-Atlantic

The northeastern states that comprise New England and the Mid-Atlantic were home to the early political centers of the European settlers. As shown in Figure 8.6, the six states in New England include Connecticut, Maine, Massachusetts, New Hampshire, Rhode Island, and Vermont. Except for their major cities near the coast, such as Boston, Providence, and Hartford, the number of residents is rather sparse. Dialects of New Englanders differ from area to area, but help distinguish them. The Mid-Atlantic states of Delaware, the District of Columbia, Maryland, New Jersey, New York, and Pennsylvania are more populous with major cities such as New York City, Philadelphia, Pittsburgh, Baltimore, and Washington, DC.

Historical Context.   The New England and Mid-Atlantic areas are steeped in the earliest history of European settlements. The political and religious dissidents who were the early leaders in the area planted the seeds for a Protestant work ethic based on hard work.

FIGURE 8.6   New England and the Mid-Atlantic.

☐ States in New England

☐ States in the Mid-Atlantic

New England towns are recognizable by their architecture.

They also preached the importance of thrift and religion. Residents of part of New England continue to participate in town meetings as a participatory form of local government.

Although the early settlers in New England were farmers, the land was not easily cultivated. In addition to developing a fishing and logging industry, New England was successful in establishing nonagricultural industries. As a result, the area became more urbanized with Boston being a hub for distributing the products of the new industrial enterprises. The population of the area is older than most of the rest of the country and continues to decline.

The Mid-Atlantic states were the site of early settlements by the English, Dutch, German, Scots-Irish, and Swedish. They developed a mixed agricultural system that included raising hogs and cattle and crops like corn. These patterns were transferred to the Midwest and Appalachia as settlers migrated west. This area has always been home to the nation's capital and is home to many national and international organizations.

Characteristics of New England and the Mid-Atlantic.   New England is among the least racially diverse areas of the country. Eighty-two percent of the population is white, 7% Latino, 6% African American, 3% Asian American, and 3% American Indian. The greatest diversity exists in Connecticut, Massachusetts, and Rhode Island. Over 94% of the population in Maine, New Hampshire, and Vermont is of European descent (U.S. Census Bureau, 2006). In some areas French is the first language of students and their families.

Fourteen percent of the U.S. population lives in the Mid-Atlantic. It is the most diverse of the regions east of the Mississippi River. The population is 67% white, 17% African

American, 11% Latino, 5% Asian American, 1% two or more races, and 0.4% American Indian. Most (85%) of the population in these two regions lives in a metropolitan area. In contrast, Maine and Vermont are primarily rural. The Atlantic Coast is an important commerce center for these areas, and tourism flourishes. Companies with a high-technology focus have established roots in a number of these metropolitan areas.

Per capita income in 2005 was highest ($49,397) in the District of Columbia, which also had the highest poverty rate in the region, indicating a wide difference between the income and standard of living of the rich and poor in that city. Connecticut had the next highest per capita income at $42,959. Incomes in Maine ($28,076) and Vermont ($29,940) are more similar to other rural states. Poverty rates in New England are below the national average at 8% in Connecticut and Vermont to 13% in Rhode Island. They are larger in the Mid-Atlantic states ranging from 9% in New Jersey to 19% in DC.

Education in New England and the Mid-Atlantic.   Cities in this region have been home to many new immigrants for centuries. Concerns were raised in colonial days about the cultures and language of German immigrants changing the Anglo culture. German was the language used in some schools and churches. By the mid-1880s, Catholics complained that the Protestant bible was used in public schools. These religious debates led to riots in some cities of this region and the eventual move to the establishment of Catholic schools and a more secular curriculum in public schools. Whose culture will be taught in schools and other assimilation policies such as English immersion continue to be debated across this and other regions today.

New England and the Mid-Atlantic are home to some of the country's oldest and most prestigious colleges and universities. Harvard University was established in 1641, the College of William and Mary in 1693, Yale University in 1701, and Princeton University in 1746. The first elementary and secondary schools were also established there with the purpose of teaching the scriptures to develop moral citizens.

Teacher salaries in this region are higher than the rest of the country with the highest being in the District of Columbia and Connecticut at $61,195 and $59,400, respectively (National Education Association, 2007). High school graduation rates are among the highest in the nation in the New England states. Except for New York and the District of Columbia, graduation rates are above the national average in the Mid-Atlantic states. However, even in most of these states 20 to 25% of the students who enter as freshmen are not graduating within four years.

The Great Plains and Midwest

The Great Plains lie between the Rocky Mountains and the Great Lakes of Ohio as shown in Figure 8.7. They extend into central Texas on the south and into the Canadian provinces of Manitoba, Saskatchewan, and Alberta on the north. This region is often called the nation's breadbasket, producing enough grain to feed several nations. It is among the flattest surfaces on earth, interrupted only by the Black Hills of South Dakota and the Ozarks in Missouri.

The Midwestern states connect the Mid-Atlantic and Great Plains. The five states of Illinois, Indiana, Michigan, Ohio, and Wisconsin are all connected to the Great Lakes and rivers that lead to the Mississippi. This access to waterways and later the interstate highways that crossed them allowed these states to develop industries whose products could easily be shipped to distant markets. As a result, these states are more populous with their major industrial cities of Chicago, Detroit, Milwaukee, Cleveland, Columbus, and Indianapolis. Less than one of four residents in the Midwest lives outside of a metropolitan area.

FIGURE 8.7 The Great Plains and Midwest.

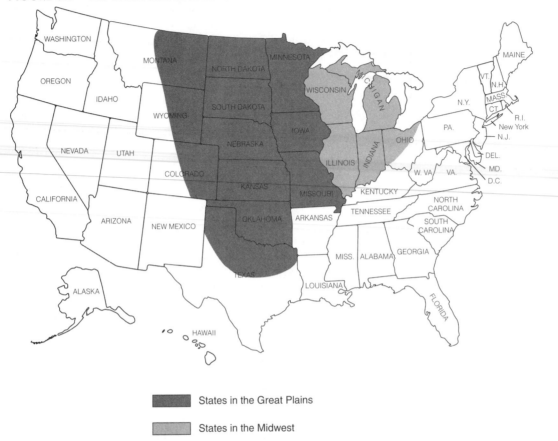

■ States in the Great Plains

■ States in the Midwest

Historical Context. The Great Plains states west of the Mississippi River joined the United States when the French sold the American Indian lands to the federal government in 1803. The Midwestern states of Ohio, Indiana, Illinois, Michigan, and Wisconsin attracted German, English, and Scottish migrants from the East, who were able to transplant their experiences with mixed agriculture into this fertile region of the country. However, travel was difficult in the nineteenth century. European Americans crossed the country by walking, riding an animal, or being pulled in a wagon. The Great Plains west of Illinois were sparsely settled, in part, because of the unpredictable weather, the treeless landscape, and the difficulty of toiling the land before equipment became mechanized.

During this period, the federal government surveyed the land, dividing it into rectangular plots for sale. One of the plots in each of the six-mile-square townships was set aside for a school. European Americans became more interested in settling the western plains as agriculture became more mechanized and commercialized as railroads transported products to faraway trading centers. Automobiles and highways in the twentieth century made it easier for farmers and ranchers to move their products to market.

The climate of the Great Plains varies with the seasons, becoming very cold in the northern winters and very hot in the summer. Tornadoes invade the prairies in the spring and summer, with blizzards in the winter. Farmland is sometimes flooded, destroying crops and property. The extreme lack of rain, which occurs every 20 years or so, leads to serious droughts that affect the economy. For example, beginning in 1931, the Great Plains and Arkansas had little rain for eight years. The severe drought and overplowed and over-grazed lands led to dust storms that caused diseases and made it very difficult to live in the area, and nearly impossible to make a living. Over half a million farming families left the region, often traveling west to seek employment (Public Broadcasting Service [PBS] n.d.).

Characteristics of the Great Plains and Midwest.

To the city dweller, the western Great Plains may appear uninhabitable. One of three people in this area lives in a rural area of 2,500 people or less; Alaska is the only area that is more rural. Kansas City, St. Louis, and Oklahoma City are the area's urban areas; Dallas borders the area on the south. Smaller cities exist in the midst of farms, ranches, and small towns. A family may travel long distances to shop or visit neighbors. The population is sparse with 30% of the region's population living in Missouri. The population of North Dakota and South Dakota is less than 1 million, which is less than a number of U.S. cities. This large area in the center of the country houses less than 6% of the nation's population (U.S. Census Bureau, 2006).

The Midwestern states have greater diversity. Seventy-eight percent of the population is European American. The percentage of African Americans ranges from 15% in Illinois to 6% in Wisconsin. Illinois has the largest number of Latinos and Asians, comprising 14% and 4% of its population (U.S. Census Bureau, 2006).

The Great Plains is home to a number of American Indian tribes. American Indians comprise 9% of South Dakota's population. In Oklahoma, Montana, and North Dakota they are 8, 6, and 5%, respectively. Reservations in this region are home to over 380,000 American Indians. Oklahoma has the greatest diversity in this region with an African American and Latino population of 8 and 7%, respectively. The percentage of African Americans in the region ranges from 11% in Missouri to less than 1% in Montana, North Dakota, and South Dakota. Eight percent of Kansas' population is Latino, and Asian immigrants have taken jobs in the area's meatpacking industry. However, European Americans comprise 83% of the region's population, about the same as New England. The population of this region is also older than other regions of the country (U.S. Census Bureau, 2006).

As might be expected in a primarily rural area, the per capita income in the Great Plains is among the lowest in the country with the exception of Minnesota. The Midwestern states are somewhat higher, but less than the national average in all states except Illinois. At the same time, most states in these two regions have a lower than average poverty rate.

Education in the Great Plains and Midwest.

As the West was settled by Europeans during the nineteenth century, schools were established in sod houses and log cabins across the plains. Because of the great distances between farms and the sparsely populated area, most schools in those early days were one-room schools where teachers taught all subjects to students from the first to eighth grades and sometimes beyond. One-room schools still exist in some of these communities today.

Salaries of teachers in the Great Plains are below the national average. With the exception of Minnesota, salaries are $3,000–$17,000 more in the Midwest. At the same time, student to teacher ratios in schools are lower than in other parts of the country, and they have a higher high school graduation rate than any other region of the country.

Although the region has less ethnic and racial diversity than other areas of the country, a growing number of school districts have implemented bilingual and ESL programs to serve students who speak an American Indian language, Spanish, Russian, Vietnamese, or other Asian, African, or European languages of recent immigrants. Communities strongly support the local control of schools and sometimes resent the perceived intrusion of the state or federal government in local school issues.

The Southwest

The Mexican and American Indian influences are prevalent in the culture, architecture, and commerce of the Southwest. The southwestern states shown in Figure 8.8 include Arizona, New Mexico, southern California, and western Texas.

Historical Context.   This region was part of Mexico until it was annexed by the United States after the Mexican-American War ended in 1848. Although the Mexican citizens were promised by the government that they would become citizens of their new country, it was 1866 before legislation was passed to extend citizenship to all persons born in the country except American Indians. They were physically driven out of some Texas cities and counties (Spring, 2001). Mexican American students were classified as nonwhite, sometimes placing them in segregated schools. In 1930 the attorney general of California classified them as American Indian because "the greater portion of the population of Mexico are Indians" (Spring, 2001, p. 171). Race—not being white—was important in the status and education of the native populations across the region.

FIGURE 8.8   The Southwest.

States in the Southwest

VIDEO INSIGHTS

abc NEWS

Immigration Wars

The 2,000-mile border between Mexico and the United States serves as the entry point into the United States for undocumented persons from Mexico and Central America. The U.S. Border Patrol annually arrests over a million people crossing the border without documentation, but nearly half a million make it across the border daily. A number of residents are so unhappy with these numbers that they have armed themselves as minutemen patrolling the border. President George W. Bush responded with a proposal to improve security at the long border by deploying thousands of National Guard troops to assist Border Patrol agents with administrative duties so that agents would have more time to enforce the law. Not all politicians and Southwest residents agree with the minutemen. Tension is high among groups living on both sides of the border.

1. Why are over a million undocumented persons crossing the southwest border into the United States annually?
2. Why has this issue become such a political sore spot for people on different sides of the issue?
3. Where do you stand on the issue of developing a path for the undocumented population to become citizens?
4. What impact do these crossings have on the student population in schools across the Southwest?

Go to the Video Insights DVD and watch the video segment *Immigration Wars*. Then, go to the *Homework and Exercises* section in Chapter 8 of MyEducationLab and select *Video Insights: Immigration Wars* to answer these questions.

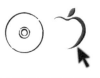

The border between Mexico and the United States is an ever-present reality in these states, having an impact on politics and economics in the region. Border patrols search for undocumented immigrants. Latinos from all walks of life are regularly stopped and searched by government authorities. Power struggles among powerful and oppressed groups, landowners and migrant workers, and potential industries and the owners of water rights dominate the landscape.

Characteristics of the Southwest. Over half of the population in California, New Mexico, and Texas has national origins other than Europe. Forty-three percent of New Mexico's population is Latino; 10% is American Indian. Nearly 30% of Arizona's population is Latino and 5% is American Indian. Over 35% of Californians are Latino. California is also home to over 5 million Asian Americans, more than eight times the number who live in Hawaii. Around 35% of the population of Texas is Latino. The African American population across these states ranges from 2% in New Mexico to 12% in Texas. The population in the Southwest is younger than the rest of the country, which results in a growing number of students in schools (U.S. Census Bureau, 2006).

Most (83%) of the Southwest population lives in metropolitan areas. New Mexico has the largest proportion (25%) of its residents living in rural areas (U.S. Census Bureau, 2006). The Four Corners area where Utah, Arizona, New Mexico, and Colorado meet is a part of the largest American Indian reservation in the country. It is about the size of West Virginia and is home to the Navajo or Dineh nation with over 175,000 American Indian residents (U.S. Census Bureau, 2006). Members of many other tribes live in the small towns and rural areas as well as on smaller reservations in the Southwest.

The sun, dry climate, desert, and mountains attract retirees and working people looking for a change. Per capita income is low in the southwestern states, being similar to the Great Plains. The percentage of persons in poverty is higher in New Mexico than in any other state in the region—around 6% higher than the national rate. The poverty rate in Arizona and Texas is also above the national average.

Education in the Southwest.   The use of Spanish and American Indian languages in instruction has been controversial for over 150 years. In 1855 California required that instruction be in English only. Texas soon followed, and by 1918, made the use of Spanish in schools a criminal offense. School segregation was common, especially in California and Texas until mid-century. American Indian students in this and other regions were sometimes removed from their homes to attend boarding schools, which were supported by the labor of the students.

Bilingual education continues to be debated across the Southwest and other regions of the country. The public does not fully agree on the need for bilingual education as shown in voter referenda against it in some states. Some local school boards have reprimanded teachers for teaching Chicano history and the histories of other oppressed groups. The Navajo Reservation operates its own educational system. Some schools in the region have been established to place American Indian history and traditions at the center of the curriculum rather than building on the traditional Eurocentric approach to schooling.

Teacher salaries are similar to those in the Great Plains, being among the lowest in the country. High school graduation rates in Arizona and Texas are similar to most of the rest of the country. However, graduation rates in New Mexico are among the lowest in the country.

The West

For this discussion, the West is the area from the Pacific Ocean to the Rocky Mountains and other mountain ranges from northern New Mexico through Montana and into Canada. It includes the Pacific Coast states of Alaska, California, Oregon, Washington, and Hawaii as shown in Figure 8.9. It also includes the mountain states of Colorado, Idaho, Nevada, Utah, and Montana. The landscape is quite varied from the highest mountains in the country to mountain plateaus to deserts and the long Pacific Coast that reaches to Alaska.

Historical Context.   Mexicans, many of them Catholic, and American Indians inhabited the area west of the Rocky Mountains when settlers from the east side of the mountains began arriving in large numbers in the nineteenth century. The area was very attractive to explorers and speculators who joined the California gold rush in the 1840s. By 1849, Chinese laborers, who were mostly men, began arriving on the West Coast for jobs in farming, mining, and building transcontinental railroads (Takaki, 1993). As the transcontinental railroads were finished in the late nineteenth century, the region opened up to a growing number of European Americans.

The West continues to attract migrants from the East and includes some of the fastest growing metropolitan areas in the country such as Las Vegas, Phoenix, Salt Lake City, Tucson, and Boise. Its growth has been fueled by new jobs in high-technology industries and services as well as the many recreational and scenic attractions that draw retirees and tourists.

FIGURE 8.9   The West.

▉	States in the coastal West
▉	States in the mountain West

However, life is not perfect in the West. Water is in short supply in many populous areas. It is moved from one area of the region to another for irrigation, industry, and meeting the needs of metropolitan areas.

Characteristics of the West.   Almost one of five U.S. residents now lives in these western states. California has by far the largest population in the country, with a population almost twice as large as the second largest state, New York. People in this region are more likely to live in metropolitan areas than any other part of the country. The region is home to the nation's second largest city, Los Angeles, and other major cities along the West Coast. Only 10% of the residents live in rural areas.

The population of the West is more diverse than the rest of the country. Fifty-one percent of the coastal states, including Alaska and Hawaii, is white; 75% of the landlocked states is white. Hawaii's population is 42% Asian American, 20% two or more races, 9% Hawaiian and other Pacific Islanders, 8% Latino, 2% African American, and 24% European Americans. Alaska Natives comprise 16% of Alaska's population. In Oregon, Utah, Idaho, and Wyoming, whites make up over 80% of the population. The percent of African Americans in the West ranges from 8% in Nevada to less than 1% in Wyoming. Latinos have the largest representation in California, but they also make up 24% and 20% of the populations in Nevada and Colorado. More than half of California's population is persons of color as shown in Figure 8.10.

FIGURE 8.10   Ethnicity of California's
Population.

From the U.S. Census Bureau. (2006). *Statistical Abstract
of the United States: 2007* (126th ed.). Washington, DC:
U.S. Government Printing Office.

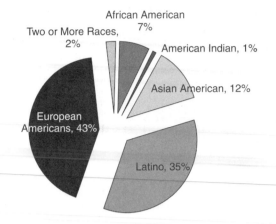

Except for Hawaii, Oregon, Idaho, and Utah, the per capita income is higher than the national average. Poverty rates in Idaho, Oregon, and California are also higher than the national average.

Education in the West.   A number of Catholic mission schools, which had been established by Spanish priests, existed in California by the time of the Revolutionary War. The goal was to Christianize the local American Indian population, in the process teaching the converts the Spanish way of life. The Mexican government tried to secularize the missions in the early 1800s, but the influence of Catholicism on the culture remains in the cities that evolved from those early missions.

Like other regions of the country, American Indian, Mexican American, and Asian American students were categorized as nonwhite. In many communities, they were required to attend segregated schools until the mid-twentieth century. As in the Southwest, the use of native languages for instruction continues to be debated. Along the Pacific Coast, native languages are even more diverse than in the Southwest because of the large number of Asian Americans, many of them foreign-born or second-generation immigrants.

Lau v. Nichols on the use of native languages is discussed in Chapter 6.

Pause to Reflect 8.2

Now that you have a brief introduction to six regions of the United States, think about cultural characteristics that may be different than your own.

- In what region did you grow up? How were you influenced by the culture of that region?
- What are some of the characteristics of the culture of the region in which you now live?
- In what region of the country do you think Jack, the new student in the chapter's opening scenario, had lived before moving to this suburban school?
- In which region would you like to teach? Why?

Go to the *Homework and Exercises* section in Chapter 8 of MyEducationLab and select *Pause to Reflect 8.2* to answer these questions.

Teacher salaries are around or above the national average in all of the coastal states except Washington. California has the highest salary at $59,345. Salaries are below average in all of the interior states ranging from $39,965 in Utah to $45,616 in Colorado. High school graduation rates for the coastal states, Nevada, and Wyoming are below the national average. Utah and Idaho have among the highest graduation rates in the country.

Rural, Urban, and Suburban Areas

Now that we have explored regions of the United States, let's examine differences within each region that also influence our lives. The way we experience life and our culture is greatly influenced by the people who share the space and place in which we live. They give meaning to the space and, in turn, are affected by it. We become very familiar with the place in which we live and know what is expected of us and others. This comfortableness is a reason why many teacher candidates indicate that they want to teach in or near the area in which they grew up.

Seventy-nine percent of the U.S. population lives in towns, cities, and metropolitan areas with 2,500 people or more (U.S. Census Bureau, 2006). Teaching in an isolated rural area hundreds of miles from a shopping center is very different than teaching in a wealthy suburban area with access to a wide range of cultural and sporting events. Let's examine the characteristics of rural, urban, and suburban areas that may help you determine where you would like to teach.

Rural Areas

In 1900, 60% of the U.S. population lived in rural areas. Beginning early in the twentieth century, large numbers of rural workers migrated to cities for employment. Today, rural areas are the location of choice for 21% of the U.S. population and many people around the world. They may choose to live in rural areas because they enjoy the wide open space, the stars in the sky, the outdoors, fewer people with whom to contend, and the freedom to have more control of one's life. Most have grown up in rural areas, but a growing number have moved from cities to escape the crowding, crime, and bureaucracies of city life— to recapture a quality of life that they think provides a healthier environment for raising children. Some people who live in cities because of job opportunities long to return to the country for its peacefulness, calmness, and less stressful conditions.

Working the land is the vocational goal of most farmers and ranchers. Most were probably raised on the land and have honed their skills through informal apprenticeships with family members and neighbors. However, the population of rural areas is more than the people who work the land or raise cattle, hogs, sheep, chickens, or fish. The massive areas of land are dotted with small towns and villages, some of which serve as the county seats for government purposes. The residents of these towns may work in a nearby city or in local manufacturing establishments. They may provide services to the farming communities as the managers and laborers at grain elevators, where the process of distributing grain to national and world markets begins. Businesses sell supplies needed to raise crops or animals, buy and sell meat products at the stockyards, and produce and deliver gas and oil required for farming. Grocery stores and other retail stores serve farm and small town residents although they sometimes must drive many miles to the nearest mall with larger stores and options.

Population of Rural Areas.   The rural population across the country is predominantly of European background; 47% of the nation's farmers and fishermen are white; 40% are Latino. Twenty-two percent of the U.S. farm operators are women. One of five American Indians lives on reservations or trust lands (U.S. Census Bureau, 2006).

The foreign-born population makes up approximately 5% of the rural population and are most likely to be Latino (Lichter & Johnson, 2006). They are attracted to jobs in meat-packing, food processing plants, and agriculture. Immigrants to rural areas today are more likely to be married adults than children or elderly persons. Although these immigrants are more likely to be working than their urban counterparts, they are more likely to be in poverty (Jensen, 2006).

Economics in Rural Areas.   Not all is idyllic in rural living. The rural workforce earns less than its urban counterparts, and the poverty rate is higher than in other places. Over a fourth of rural residents who work earn only enough to place them just over the poverty line. The percent of rural children in poverty has increased by 3% since 2000 (O'Hare & Savage, 2006). The rural economy is sensitive to fluctuations in manufacturing and export rates. Farm production can fluctuate with the weather and prices controlled by the world economy.

Successful farmers today use technology and business principles, as well as their knowledge about agriculture, to manage a farm. In addition to watching the weather, they are monitoring the market to determine the best time to sell. They must be prepared to store products during times of low prices, requiring storage facilities and adequate finances to sustain families during that period. The nature of the business is making it difficult for small farmers to make it. They often cannot afford to hold products to sell at higher prices because loan payments won't wait. In this environment, the number of individual and family farmers has decreased over the past few decades. Although families still own the majority of farms in the country, corporations own a growing proportion of the farmland as shown in Figure 8.11.

Multinational corporations have moved manufacturing jobs that were once available in rural areas to cheaper labor markets in other parts of the country or world. Processing

FIGURE 8.11   Farm Owners in 2002.

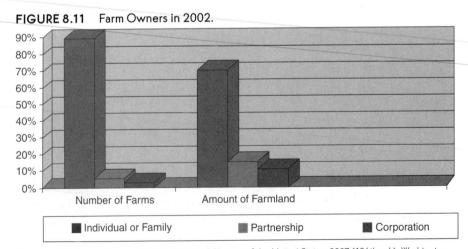

From the U.S. Census Bureau. (2006). *Statistical Abstract of the United States: 2007* (126th ed.). Washington, DC: U.S. Government Printing Office.

plants for meat and fish continue to be located near the source of the raw product, but the work is dangerous and laborers are poorly paid. New immigrants have been filling a number of these jobs in areas that have had little racial or ethnic diversity in the past.

Rural Schools and Their Issues.   Are you interested in teaching in a rural area? There are advantages and limitations. Schools in rural areas are smaller than in suburban and urban areas, meaning that there are fewer students to manage and a better chance of knowing students' families.

The lower enrollment in rural schools usually results in a relatively low student to teacher ratio, allowing more individual attention for students. One of the problems in small schools is that teachers often must teach some subjects for which they were not prepared (for example, physics, chemistry, and biology). Schools often do not have the resources or adequate number of students to offer foreign languages, technology education, music, art, or advanced placement courses. However, satellite connections in some rural areas have allowed students to take these courses via distance learning.

School consolidation can be a contentious issue in rural communities. In rural and even urban areas at times, schools have student enrollments that are very small. Debates about the values and realities of closing a school almost always ensue. Not only parents and students are involved in these discussions. Alumni are not comfortable with the disappearance of their school, which was an important part of their personal histories.

Proponents for consolidation argue that the curriculum could be expanded to include subjects not available in a small school, buildings upgraded with educational equipment and technology, and students better served when small schools are combined into a single school. Opponents argue that the local neighborhood school is an important social and academic cornerstone of the community. Moving students to a school located many miles away will limit the participation of parents and students in school activities. As classes become larger in a consolidated school, teachers may not be able to give students the same individual attention that they had in the smaller school. Teachers and the principal will not know all of the students and families as in small schools. Additionally, students may be required to spend additional time—sometimes over an hour—on school buses to and from school each morning and afternoon.

Urban Areas

Some people choose to live in urban areas because of the excitement and access to the symphony, theater, opera, and other amenities. Large cities are abundant in professional jobs and have sports complexes, numerous libraries, colleges and universities, recreational activities, restaurants that vary greatly in cuisine and price, and clubs with entertainment. Others live in the city because they grew up or accepted a job there. They may choose to remain in the city because they like it or it adequately meets their needs. Others have no choice because of family or economic obligations or just don't have the opportunity to break loose from the grip of the city. Many who live in the city have never attended the activities that attract others to the city, mainly because of their limited income.

Geography plays a role in defining the conditions of a city. The upper middle class and rich live together in one or more areas of the city; the middle class and low-income families live in other areas of the city. The homeless are usually shepherded into specific areas so that others do not see them. Housing is more expensive than other places and the cost of living is high in most major cities. A small two-bedroom condominium can cost over $500,000 in or very near the city. Low rental housing is limited and often in disrepair.

Most cities do not have enough public housing to meet their needs. Owning a car and paying insurance may be exorbitant. Public buses and subway systems serve as a major means of transportation.

Some people like living in the city because life can be lived without the prying eyes of neighbors. Neighbors often don't know each other, let alone anything about the families or roots of those who live around them. One is able to live alone within a great mass of humanity. On the other hand, there are communities within cities in which people do know their neighbors and work together on community projects. The city does not allow for a single stereotype that fits all of its residents. Economic conditions, ethnicity, race, and language sometimes divide cities into neighborhoods such as Little Italy or Chinatown that clearly distinguish one group from another.

Population of a City.   One half of the world's population lives in mega-cities. New York City is the largest city in the United States with a population of around 8.1 million (U.S. Census Bureau, 2006), which grows to 21.8 million when extended into the metropolitan area that includes its suburbs (City Population, 2006). Figure 8.12 shows how New York City compares in size to other major cities around the world.

The power relations between these cities differ greatly. Cities in **developing nations** have limited means or resources to provide housing, sanitation, or a healthy environment for their growing populations. Not all new immigrants and migrants in the United States have access to adequate and inexpensive housing, leading to multiple families sharing the same, very small homes or apartments, usually in violation of city ordinances. Some families end up homeless.

Fifty metropolitan areas in the United States have over 1 million residents (U.S. Census Bureau, 2006). They range in size from the New York area with over 21 million to Salt Lake City with just over 1 million. The ethnic and racial diversity is usually greater in cities than in other areas, in part, because many new immigrants from around the world initially settle in urban areas. Latinos are the majority population in San Antonio and over 25% of the population in Texas' other largest cities. They are also a large proportion of the population in many California cities, including Los Angeles (44%), Riverside (43%), San Diego (29%),

FIGURE 8.12   Population of Major Metropolitan Areas in the World.

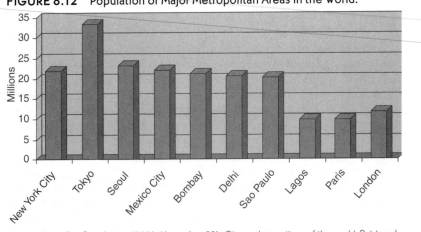

Data are from City Population. (2006, November 22). *City agglomerations of the world.* Retrieved on March 9, 2007, from www.citypopulation.de/World.html

and San Jose (26%). The largest proportion of Asian Americans lives in San Jose, San Francisco, and Los Angeles. African Americans are over 30% of the population in the metropolitan areas of Memphis, New Orleans, Atlanta, Richmond, Virginia Beach, and Washington, DC (U.S. Census Bureau, 2006).

Contradictions of Cities.   Cities are centers of extremes and contradictions. They are places where persons from different cultural backgrounds intermingle. An expensive, elite restaurant may be on one block and a food kitchen on the street behind it. Some of the highest salaries in the world are earned in the corporate headquarters housed in or near the city while large proportions of African Americans, Puerto Ricans, Mexican Americans, and women workers are being paid so little that their families live in poverty. The unemployment of young people of color is also high.

While the city provides the creative energy for many, it becomes oppressive and dangerous for others. Many city residents live in safe and comfortable environments with good schools, parks, and recreational facilities. Others live near waste dumps that have contributed to disproportionately high incidents of asthma and other diseases. The night—and sometimes the daylight—is interrupted by gunshots, ambulances, and police raids in some sections of the city in which the dropout rates for high schoolers is over 50% (Orfield, Losen, Wald, & Swanson, 2004) and funerals for young people are common occurrences.

Some new immigrants may be trying to become American as defined by the dominant culture, but others would like to maintain their culture within the American context. Immigrant parents are raising their children in the cultural context with which they are most familiar, using their native language or their developing English. Children are often trying to shed the immigrant ways to be accepted by their American counterparts, often leading to conflict between children and parents.

Oppressed people in the city sometimes resist the dominant values that have not served them effectively. The hope, joy, and freedom of living in cities have not been the experience of many people. Many who are better advantaged and living comfortably in the city view these sections of the city as places of chaos and immorality. City leaders find it difficult to raise the resources necessary to improve city services, ensure that the population has housing and food, make schools of the same quality across the city, and pay enough to attract and retain highly qualified teachers. Low-income and public housing almost never is built in or near economically advantaged areas of the city.

Urban Schools.   Forty-three percent of the nation's students attend schools in the largest 500 school districts. Nearly one in four are in the largest 100 school districts. Enrollment in the largest 100 school districts (see Figure 8.13) ranged from 46,594 in 50 schools in the Cherry Creek School District outside of Denver to over 1 million in 1,225 schools in New York City (Dalton, Sable, & Hoffman, 2006). Students of color are in the majority in 60% of these school districts. Students in these largest school districts represent diverse ethnic, racial, and language diversity with 29% of their students being African American, 7% Asian American, and 34% Latino. Nearly half of them are eligible for free lunch; 12% have one or more disabilities; and 12% are enrolled in English language programs (Dalton et al., 2006).

Not all schools in a city are equal. Parents in schools in upper-middle-class neighborhoods are able to donate funds to hire teachers of art and music. They can pay for tutors to ensure that their children have the knowledge and skills necessary for entrance into desirable colleges and universities. These and a number of low-income parents are engaged actively in their children's education. They talk with teachers; they try to ensure that their

FIGURE 8.13   The 100 Largest School Districts in the United States and Jurisdictions: School Year 2003–2004.

From Dalton, B., Sable, J., & Hoffman, L. (2006). *Characteristics of the 100 largest public elementary and secondary school districts in the United States: 2003–2004* (NCES 2006-329). Washington, DC: U.S. Department of Education, National Center for Education Statistics.

children are in classes with the best teachers; they encourage their children to be involved in extracurricular activities; and they monitor their children's performance to ensure that they are performing well on standardized tests. Most low-income parents do not have the same cultural capital. They do not have the income that allows them to support school activities and may be unable to volunteer to work in schools because their employers do not give them time off. They may not feel comfortable interacting in English or with the well-educated teachers.

Urban schools are sometimes characterized as highly centralized, authoritative, and bureaucratic. However, a number of urban school districts are now electing their school boards, have reduced the bureaucracy, become decentralized, and allowed the establishment of alternate schools. At the same time, mayors have taken over the management of their schools in cities such as New York City and Washington, DC.

Magnet schools, in which the curriculum emphasizes a particular subject or field such as performing arts or mathematics and science, are popular in urban areas. Six percent of the schools in the 100 largest school districts are magnet schools, enrolling 9% of their districts' students (Dalton et al., 2006). Advantaged and well-educated families seek admission to select magnet schools, especially if their neighborhood does not meet their standards.

A number of school districts allow parents, teachers, community groups, and entre-preneurs to establish **charter schools.** Within public school systems, charter schools make up 4% of the schools in a district and 2% of the student population (Dalton et al., 2006). High schools are more likely to be large (that is, over 900 students) in cities than other areas of the country (U.S. Department of Education, 2003). However, the Bill and Melinda Gates Foundation has been supporting the establishment of small schools in many urban areas to better serve students with great needs. Although the average student to teacher ratio in urban schools is only slightly higher than in suburban schools (Anderson & Summerfield, 2007), research shows that small classes may be more critical in the inner city to assist students in meeting standards.

The students in inner-city schools have the greatest need for support and care in society. They may have a sick grandmother at home for whom they are responsible. A father who could help them learn to navigate the community and school is in jail. A mother is too sick to work and help with homework. These are major problems that children do not usually face in economically advantaged communities.

School may be a refuge for a number of students, but some inner schools meet in less than desirable classrooms such as basement corridors or storerooms without windows. Jonathan Kozol (2000) reminds us that "There should not be a narrow gate for children of the poor, a wide and open gate for children of the fortunate and favored. There should be one gate. It should be known to everyone. It should be wide enough so even Pineapple [a low-income student] can get in without squeezing" (p. 296).

Suburban Areas

In the 1930s only 17% of the U.S. population lived in the suburbs. Today, over half of the population lives there. After World War II, the suburbs offered affordable single-family houses with yards in an area that seemed safer than the city and more desirable for raising

Pause to Reflect 8.3

Urban areas usually have a large number of teaching jobs available annually. Sometimes, it is the only place a new teacher can find a job. Test your knowledge of urban schools by indicating whether the statements below are true or false.

1. A Title I school is designed to serve students with disabilities.   **True**   **False**
2. All teachers in a Title I school must be highly qualified, which requires
   passing the state licensure test and being fully licensed by the state.   **True**   **False**
3. Urban schools must provide bilingual education for their English language
   learners.   **True**   **False**
4. A large proportion of students in urban schools will be eligible for free
   or reduced lunch.   **True**   **False**
5. The majority of students in the largest school districts are white.   **True**   **False**

Go to the *Homework and Exercises* section in Chapter 8 of MyEducationLab and select *Pause to Reflect 8.3* to answer these questions.

CRITICAL INCIDENTS IN TEACHING

Teacher Expectations

Apryl, a petite African American teenager, walks into an urban school's Spanish class 15 minutes late. The teacher, Mr. Roth, informs her that she cannot sit with her friends. Apryl proceeds to seat herself in the corner with her friends. Mr. Roth declares that he is going to call Apryl's counselor to come to class and talk to Apryl, and that he will give Apryl none of the worksheets the class is required to complete until Apryl moves to her seat. As Mr. Roth circulates the room, he makes no eye contact with Apryl. Apryl freezes anytime Mr. Roth comes within earshot of her desk. Otherwise, she leans back in her chair, engages in conversation with the boys around her, and rearranges the papers in her backpack.

Apryl raises her hand to ask for the worksheets about 30 minutes into class, but is told she cannot have the worksheets until she moves. Apryl's conversation with the boys around her gets louder and more animated. She pulls food and drink out of her bag and starts eating and drinking. She gets out of her seat every 5 or 10 minutes to stand at the window to see what is going on outside. She starts a couple of exchanges with students across the room. Every once in a while, Mr. Roth shouts at Apryl, "You cannot talk in class." Apryl replies either that she "ain't talking, give me the work" or that she is "waiting for her counselor," and Mr. Roth starts ignoring Apryl again.

Fifty minutes into the 110-minute class, a boy near Apryl gets so disruptive that Mr. Roth starts filling out the paperwork to have security remove him from the classroom. Apryl starts packing her backpack. When security shows up at the door 10 minutes later, Apryl runs towards the door and begs the guard to remove her from the classroom. The guard cannot remove Apryl without a teacher request. Mr. Roth finally tells the guard to take both of them.

Questions for Classroom Discussion

1. What are some reasons why Apryl may not be engaged in the assigned work?
2. How is the worksheet assignment, which was the assignment for the full 110-minute period, related to Apryl's world?
3. How did Mr. Roth's interactions with Apryl support or not support her learning of Spanish?
4. Do Mr. Roth's responses to Apryl suggest he has high expectations for her? Why or why not?
5. Based on this limited information, would you say that Mr. Roth has a caring relationship with Apryl? Why or why not?

Building Teaching Skills

Go to the *Building Teaching* Skills section in Chapter 8 of MyEducationLab and select *Critical Incidents in Teaching: Teacher Expectations* to complete this exercise.

Adapted from Anderson, L. (2003). Ain't doin' that: Why "doing good in school" can be so hard. In L. Darling-Hammond, J. French, & S. P. Garcia-Lopez, *Learning to teach for social justice* (pp. 103 115). New York: Teachers College Press.

children. The wage earner—mainly fathers at that time—commuted to the city daily to work. Most wives stayed at home to care for children and became involved in developing a community.

Development of the Suburbs.

Home ownership is a major reason for the mid-century development of suburbia. Forty-six percent of U.S. families were homeowners in the 1920s, but a smaller proportion of the families in cities could afford a home of their own. Cities need rental property and low-cost housing projects to provide shelter for families whose incomes vary greatly. However, profits in these housing projects were not high enough to attract investors. Developers, builders, bankers, the lumber industry, and the media worked together to convince the public and government that individual home ownership was critical to maintain the "American way of life" (Baxandall & Ewen, 2000). Advertising campaigns for new houses in the suburbs were directed to white World War II veterans.

Most of the suburbs during the 1920s were racially and economically homogeneous. While African Americans established their own suburbs in a few places, neither they nor members of other ethnic groups of color were encouraged to buy in the suburbs. Racist governmental policies and business practices at the time exacerbated racial and class inequalities and guaranteed that suburbia was almost exclusively white. At the same time, programs for public housing, urban renewal, and replacement of homes with highways were undermining the stability and vibrancy of African American neighborhoods in the cities. In addition, they were being denied mortgages to buy their own homes (Freund, 2006).

Although these official policies were dismantled years ago, **redlining** still occurs to limit the geographic areas in which diverse populations are able to live in urban as well as suburban communities (Baxandall & Ewen, 2000). Zoning policies in many suburbs continue to be used to maintain class and racial homogeneity. Zoning can restrict housing to single-family homes or require lots of a certain size. Homeowner associations can also require houses to be a certain size and design, limiting the families who can meet the requirements to those who are economically advantaged.

Suburbia initially provided a place for the middle class with all of the consumer trappings—a new house, a new car, new appliances, a new television. However, it did not last long as just a bedroom community for people who worked in the city. Grocery stores, gas stations, parks, community services, schools, and churches were needed to support families. Soon malls with many varieties of retail stores emerged. Two incomes became a necessity to meet the financial commitments of families. As the suburbs became more like extended cities and the cost of housing more expensive, migration moved to areas even further from the city (Lalasz, 2006).

By the 1980s, the suburb was a metropolis. Shopping malls had been joined by office complexes, high-tech and landscaped industrial parks, and an extensive network of highways. Wage earners no longer had to go to the city for work; factories and other businesses existed in their own backyards. Along with these changes came the problems that others had tried to escape by leaving the city—unemployment, homelessness, AIDS, drugs, and crime. Many suburbs had not developed the governmental structures or other support systems to handle the resulting economic and social diversity (Baxandall & Ewen, 2000).

By 1990 the efforts of the building industry had paid off. Home ownership was the highest ever. However, the major problem remains—the dearth of new large-scale affordable housing that more families could afford. The fastest growing housing option today is the gated community in which diversity may be limited and the perceived need for security and protection is of prime importance.

Most suburbs are economically, racially, ethnically, linguistically, and religiously diverse. Diversity within some communities is actively solicited and celebrated. In others, little is done to encourage it. Today, immigrants from Central America, South America, Asia, and the Middle East are sometimes bypassing cities and moving directly into the suburbs.

Software, electronic, and biotechnology companies found the suburban business centers, sometimes called "**edge cities**," ideal for their development and research. They attracted entrepreneurs and professionals who moved into elite housing developments near their jobs. These office and research parks developed into what some researchers called "cities of knowledge." They began to interact academically, economically, and socially with research universities and both public and private groups to develop and use their products. The employees of these companies represented the upper stratum of the upper middle class. To ensure that their neighborhoods are limited to people with the same economic advantages, the production of their products (for example, silicon chips) usually occurs in other places (O'Mara, 2006).

Suburban Schools.   The quality of schools is often one of the reasons that families move from cities to the suburbs. Because the suburbs are fairly new, its schools are not as old as many that are in disrepair in urban areas. Wealthy suburbs are more likely to have beautiful schools with the latest technology, qualified teachers, advanced placement courses, gifted and talented programs, and numerous extracurricular activities. Sometimes, high schools are sprawling campuses in park-like settings.

However, not all suburban schools are of this high quality. Those that predominantly serve students with limited English skills, from low-income families, and from backgrounds other than Europe are likely to be the older schools in the region. One school district next to Washington, DC, for example, has had a very difficult time recruiting qualified and licensed teachers, usually beginning the school year with far too many teachers who are not qualified. In this case, teacher salaries are not competitive and school conditions are not conducive to the most effective teaching. This district serves a diverse, but predominantly African American population. On the other side of the city is a school district in one of the wealthiest counties in the country. Qualified teachers are waiting for jobs, sometimes substituting for several years before a full-time job becomes available. Teacher salaries in this district are among the highest in the country.

The size of schools in the suburbs are, on the average, slightly less than urban schools, but nearly 40% of the high schools have 900 or more students (U.S. Department of Education, 2003). The school population is diverse. Overall, students' families have higher incomes than in other areas. Only one of three students is eligible for free or reduced-price lunch as compared to over half of the students in urban schools. A major difference is the higher academic performance of suburban students on standardized tests (U.S. Department of Education, 2005).

Magnet schools are also popular in the suburbs. Upper-middle-class families are very supportive of gifted and talented programs in their schools, in part to separate their children from the immigrant, low-income, and limited English proficient students in the school (Jones-Correa, 2006). It is not uncommon that calls for improving the diversity of students in those programs meet with resistance from the more advantaged families in the school district.

The problems of urban schools affect many suburban schools as well, especially drugs, student-on-student harassment, and lack of attention to students who may need it the most. Not all suburban schools have the resources to adequately support counselors, social workers, and others who can help students deal with the complexity of today's life. Additionally, not all suburban schools have the computers and technology that are important in preparing students for their future work world.

High schools in some upper middle class communities are large attractive complexes.

Spencer Grant/PhotoEdit Inc.

Migration

The diversity of a geographic area varies because of history, immigration, and migration. Although the United States annually receives more immigrants than any other country, immigration is not only a U.S. phenomenon; it is worldwide. Three percent of the world's population lives in countries in which they were not born (Smith, 2003). About half of the world's immigrants has emigrated to countries in the developed world. The other half has moved to countries with industrial, mining, or oil economies in the less developed world (Rowntree, Lewis, Price, & Wyckoff, 2006). The foreign-born population in the United States was 12% of the population in 2005 (U.S. Census Bureau, 2006). It is much higher in other parts of the world. For example, the majority of the population in Kuwait and the United Arab Emirates is foreign-born (Ueda, 2007).

Migration refers to moving from one place to another while immigration indicates that a person has moved into a country with the goal of permanently settling in the new country. Political and religious persecution drives people out of the countries of their birth. Economic conditions that lead to the lack of jobs, subsistent wages, and starvation are other common reasons for leaving. What factors are considered in determining the country to move to? Sometimes people have no choice. The best they can do to escape oppression and possible death is to cross into a contiguous country. When they have a choice, they are likely to choose a country with job opportunities or religious and political liberty.

Migration Worldwide

In much of the world, migration refers to people crossing borders temporarily. The host country views them as temporary guest workers who will eventually return to their homeland. They sometimes have been forced out of their homelands because of civil war, persecution, or economic depression, and may be living in refugee camps rather than working in the new country. They may later return home after economic and political conditions are stable. However, many migrants never return to their original homeland.

Much of the world's population lives in squalid conditions on the edge of major cities in developing nations. Educational opportunities are limited or non-existent for most of these children.

Mark Edwards/Still Pictures/Peter Arnold, Inc.

The worldwide trend is the migration from rural to urban areas. This trend is particularly salient in less developed countries where families can no longer sustain themselves in rural areas. They hope they can find jobs and greater economic stability in an urban area. The problem is that most cities in developing countries are unable to provide necessary services for a rapidly growing population. Housing, food, water, waste treatment, and jobs do not exist. As a result, large numbers of migrants are living in shanty villages on city borders without adequate clean water and sanitation. When they can find work, it is often in the informal economy of selling wares on the street, gathering items to sell from garbage dumps, or participating in illegal activities. Death rates are high, and the number of years expected to live is low. Schooling for children in these areas is very limited or nonexistent.

Migration in the United States

As the government expanded its territory in the nineteenth century, the population of the early colonies migrated west. Some groups like the Cherokees and other American Indian tribes were forced by the government to move to lands west of the Mississippi River. In the 1920s, the 1940s, and the 1950s, large numbers of African Americans moved from the South to northern and western industrial areas to fill jobs that were then open to them.

Throughout the twentieth century, groups of people moved to new areas primarily because of crippling economic conditions where they lived and the possibility of jobs in another location. The stock market crash on October 29, 1929, triggered the Great Depression. People lost their jobs and their homes as they desperately sought ways to make a living. During the 1930s, the Dust Bowl in the Great Plains drove out many farming families. They were not always welcome in other parts of the country. Many cities and some states considered them "undesirables," taking legal actions to try to bar them from entering (PBS, n.d.).

Other migrations resulted from coal mines being closed in Appalachia. As factories closed or moved to other countries, families across the Northeast, Mid-Atlantic, and Midwest have moved south and west. As farmers with small plots of land find it difficult to maintain a desired standard of living or the bank forecloses on their farm, they move to town or a metropolitan area. Today, it is not only the working class who is affected by layoffs. As companies merge and move their headquarters, the jobs of middle-class workers and managers are also displaced. If a major business closes, not enough jobs remain in the community to absorb all of the workers. As a large number of families migrate, both the place they left and the one they enter change.

Advantaged families in the United States today move from one place to another for a better or different job, better schools, or a larger, more desirable, housing unit. Low-income families may be forced to move because they can no longer afford the rent or mortgage payment. The most recent major migration occurred as a result of Hurricanes Katrina and Rita that displaced everyone in New Orleans and many people across southern Louisiana and Mississippi in 2005. Although some people are returning to these areas, others have settled in new places across the country.

Many people in the United States have moved in a direction different from the worldwide trend. They are more likely to move from urban to rural areas and smaller towns (Rowntree et al., 2006). U.S. residents also continue to move from cities to the suburbs. Some cities are drawing people back into the city as areas are gentrified or rebuilt for people with higher incomes than those who had been living in the neighborhood. One of the concerns about this migration is that these developments often lead to low-income people being displaced and forced to another decaying part of the city or suburbs.

In the past 25 years, the states in New England and the Mid-Atlantic have lost more of their population than other areas of the country as their inhabitants moved to the Sun Belt states between the Mississippi River and the Atlantic Ocean, especially to Florida. The populations in a number of western states are growing at a fast rate. Arizona and Nevada lead the race, but Idaho and Washington are growing at a faster pace than most states outside of the South. By 2010, 60% of the U.S. population will live in the South and West, compared to 48% in 1970. One of four residents will live in California, Florida, and Texas alone. Simultaneously, California and New York have the largest numbers of people migrating out of the state (U.S. Census Bureau, 2006).

Public school enrollment is projected to decrease in the Northeast and Midwest as their population becomes older. The South and West will experience increases of as much

Pause to Reflect 8.4

Children change schools as their families move into a new community within their school district or into a different school district in the next county or state. Students are not always happy with these moves and may have a difficult time adjusting in the new setting. Can you relate to such a change in their lives?

• Have you ever had to change schools because your family moved?

• What was most difficult about moving to a new school? How did you respond?

• How could teachers and schools make this change easier for new students?

• How will you ensure that you do not stereotype a new student based on where she or he last attended school?

Go to the *Homework and Exercises* section in Chapter 8 of MyEducationLab and select *Pause to Reflect 8.4* to answer these questions.

as 36%. The largest increases in enrollment over the next decade are projected to occur in the following states:

- Nevada (36%)
- Arizona (32%)
- Texas (23%)
- Georgia (19%)
- Idaho (18%)
- Utah (17%)
- Florida (17%)

(Hussar & Bailey, 2006)

Globalization

The realities of the twenty-first century call for us to not only know the places where we live, but also the places where others live. We are connected to other countries through economic, political, environmental, and cultural systems. One of five students in our schools has a foreign-born parent. We live in a global world that is becoming more controlled by international conglomerates.

The early stages of **globalization** occurred when European nations began to colonize the Americas, Africa, and India in the late fifteenth century. They wanted both the raw materials and labor of these countries, usually taking them by force and sending them back to their home country. The colonizers followed a policy of **manifest destiny** in which they saw their own cultures as superior to all others and destined to rule over others. After the United States became independent of England, it became a colonizer itself, making and breaking treaties with American Indian tribes and gaining land by annexing it or winning it in wars with Mexico and Spain. By the mid-1800s, the Europeans had colonized Indonesia, Indochina, and all of Africa except for Ethiopia and Liberia. They controlled the crops that would be produced, and limited industrial development. Globalization during this period moved resources primarily one way—from the colonized country to Europe or America.

It wasn't until after World War II that these countries were able to become independent from their colonizers. However, the colonizers quickly centralized their power in 1948 by establishing the GATT (General Agreement on Tariffs and Taxes), which later became the World Trade Organization (WTO). With a membership beyond the European colonizers, the goal of the WTO was to reduce barriers of trade so that goods and labor could move more easily across national borders. The International Monetary Fund and World Bank were established to help defend the world's monetary system and make investments through loans in the infrastructure of developing countries. Not to give up their control of global economic and political issues, the old colonizing countries (Germany, Great Britain, France, and Italy) joined the other economically and politically powerful countries (United States, Canada, Japan, and Russia) to form the Group of Eight (G-8) to oversee the world's future development, which will affect the lives of both the richest and poorest people of the world.

Globalization also impacts the ability of the world's population to live without famine, debilitating and killing diseases, and brutality brought on by poverty, religious beliefs, or war. The United Nations Educational, Scientific and Cultural Organization (UNESCO) and other international organizations see the education of children and women as critical in changing their economic status and ability to be self-sufficient. The 1989 United Nations Convention on the Rights of the Child identified early childhood care and education, especially for the most needy children, as its top goal and collects data to track the progress of countries in meeting this goal (UNESCO, 2006).

Economics

Events in one country can affect other countries around the world. For example, when adjustments are made to the stock market in China, the stock markets drop or rise in Japan, Europe, and the United States. When rainforests are depleted in Ecuador, the natural production of oxygen for the world is reduced, and the indigenous groups depending on the rainforests lose their livelihood. When a hurricane like Katrina wipes out a city and scatters its population across the country, the gross national product is negatively affected. The movement of factories from U.S. communities to Mexico, Vietnam, and Thailand provides jobs at low wages for workers in the new locations while workers in the original city become unemployed.

Work is international. Professionals in multinational companies have work visas allowing them to work in different countries. Workers around the world cross borders legally and illegally to work. Global cities serve as connectors and centers for global decision-making. New York City, Miami, Chicago, Los Angeles, and Seattle are major links to other global centers, governmental agencies, and multinational companies. Multinational corporations and financial institutions make decisions that affect nations and their people.

Many U.S. companies are known around the world as employers as well as for their products. McDonald's, Burger King, and Kentucky Fried Chicken are found in cities as diverse as Beijing, Moscow, Singapore, and Nairobi (Rowntree et al., 2006). General Electric, Coca-Cola, Intel, Proctor and Gamble, AT&T, IBM, Nike, and many clothing chains are well-known products around the world. These companies also provide employment at low wages in many countries outside the United States. Products are sometimes produced by children or women in sweatshops under conditions that would be illegal in this country. Consumerism of U.S. products is promoted around the world, and cheaper products from other countries are consumed here as imports grow. The managers and large owners of corporations have profited greatly from their global connections.

Even though economic growth remains strong in the old industrialized countries and is becoming strong in developing countries such as India and China, many people in the world are struggling to live from day to day. Absolute poverty in developing countries is defined as having a daily income of $1 or less. Over one of five people in these countries live in absolute poverty, often being undernourished and without clean water and sanitation. In developed nations such as the United States and Europe, many groups of color and new immigrants have not benefited from the economic growth of their countries, sometimes living in poverty and sometimes in conditions similar to those in developing countries. Across the world, the disparities between the rich and poor continue to increase.

Technology is both changing the job market and opening communications across national borders. It provides the opportunity to connect people around the world. The use of computers and cellular phones around the globe has increased dramatically over the past decade (Worldwatch, 2006). The Internet is allowing direct communications across national, political, and geographical boundaries. However, the digital revolution is not reaching the majority of the world's population, especially in developing nations (Worldwatch Institute, 2006).

Environment

The environment is also greatly influenced by global conditions, changes, and decisions. A volcano, explosion, fire, or oil spill in one country can impact the environment and economy of many other countries as ash or pollutants are spread by wind or water around the earth. A number of factors contribute to the degradation of the environment and the world's **ecosystem.** As the world's population increases, the need for food, clean water, sanitation, and jobs also increases. Rapid economic growth, which will draw on natural resources, is expected in countries such as China and India. Another factor is the increased consumption of natural resources and produced goods by the populations of industrialized countries.

Although the destruction of the environment is a global problem, some countries contribute much more to the problem than others. Industrialized nations are the greatest contributors, using more than their equitable proportion of natural resources and adding more than their share of pollutants to the environment. The United States tops the list of offenders as shown in Figure 8.14. Although the U.S. population is only 5% of the world, we consume 25% of the oil produced and emit 25% of the carbon dioxide emissions (Worldwatch, 2006). The United States is also the third largest consumer of water, behind China and India (Rowntree et al., 2006).

Although the discussion above may sound like the world is doomed, most scientists think that the damage can be halted and steps taken to dramatically improve the environment. Such a change in direction requires a global commitment from multinational corporations, local companies, policymakers, and the public to do things differently. Industrial leaders have traditionally argued against environmental control because it may cost more money, hurting their competitiveness and profits. However, the tide may be turning. A number of companies are marketing sustainable development. A growing number of cities are enforcing their own greening policies to support a sustainable environment. In 2006 the state of California adopted the strictest control on carbon dioxide in the United States; it plans to cut emissions 25% by 2020.

FIGURE 8.14   Consumption Per Person by Hectares, 2006.

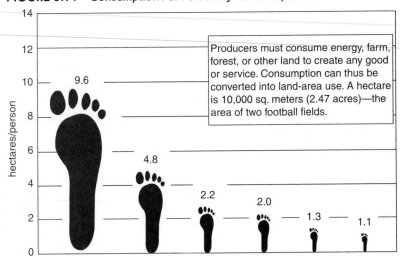

Data is from Global Footprint Network. (2006). *Ecological footprint and biocapacity* (2006 ed.). Retrieved on March 12, 2007, from http://www.footprintnetwork.org/webgraph/graphpage.php?country=usa

Resistance by Indigenous People

Not all people are excited about the globalization that opens up the world to the interests of corporations, investors, and politicians. Skeptics do not believe that these groups have the best interests of the people and the environment in mind as they make decisions that affect their profits and own economic and social well-being. Indigenous people are most severely affected by global decisions, but they have had limited or no voice in the decisions that dramatically change their lives.

Indigenous people may be a small fraction of the world population, but some are living on the natural resources that others desire. Approximately 350 million people live in an estimated 5,000 indigenous societies around the world (Mander, 2006). They are spread around the world in the Amazon jungles; the mountains of the Andes; the tundras of the far north; the forests of Canada, Siberia, and Indonesia; the small islands of the Pacific; the agricultural lands of the Philippines, Guatemala, Mexico, and the United States; and the grasslands and deserts of Africa (Mander, 2006). They face immediate threats to their cultures and lives as others seek their natural resources.

The value system of indigenous people is antithetical to that of dominant groups with political power in the G-8 and most other nations. Community values are central to their perceptions of a people. The dominant group, on the other hand, values its individual freedom and the right of the individual to accumulate his or her own wealth and power.

Another core value of indigenous people is their reciprocal relationship with nature (Mander, 2006). As the earth gives them the gifts of water, food, and protection, they must give back to the earth and take care of it. To them, globalization has given the powerful the right to dominate both people and the earth for the purpose of making money with no commitment to take care of either. These strangers who want to destroy the land on which the natives have lived for thousands of years do not have a relationship with the land. The land and its produce have much more meaning to the natives than providing the substance for living. Winona LaDuke of the Anishinabeg (Ojibwe) people describes the contradiction: "For us, rice is a source of food and also wisdom. For the globalizers, it is just a commodity to be exploited for profit. The paradigms are at loggerheads" (LaDuke, 2006, p. 25). Most indigenous groups practice subsistence living in which they produce enough food for their communities to survive, but do not accumulate food or money for private use.

Collective ownership is another core value of indigenous groups (Mander, 2006). Their colonizers believed that individuals should own land, which can be bought, sold, and accumulated. For example, European settlers in the 1830s tried to convince the Cherokees to divide their lands in Southeastern United States into private plots that would be owned by individual Cherokees. The intent of the European settlers, however, was then to buy the property plot by plot from the owners, thus removing the Cherokees from the land that the new settlers desired. The Cherokees resisted individual ownership, which resulted in them being moved forcibly from their homes by federal troops. Indigenous peoples are constantly confronted with others trying to exploit their collective ownership.

Many indigenous groups have suffered from the invasion of their lands by highways and pipelines. They have been relocated to make way for hydroelectric dam projects that flood their lands and destroy their livelihoods. They have become ill because of the contamination from the dumping of oil and chemicals into the water. They are not immune to diseases and problems such as alcohol abuse that arrive with industrial development. When people are removed from their land and subsistence living, they are forced to enter the capitalistic economy in which they have to sell their products to buy the necessities for life. The indigenous society begins to fall apart as family members have to find jobs away from their land (Lloyd, Soltani, & Koenig, 2006).

Students from indigenous groups usually have a different worldview than other students. Teachers should understand and respect the differences.

Today, groups of indigenous people are fighting successfully in the courts and public forums for their rights to sovereignty, self-governance, and collective ownership. They do not want to assimilate into the dominant society. They desperately want to protect their languages, cultures, religions, artifacts, and traditional knowledge and sciences (Mander, 2006). They are fighting to prevent global corporations and organizations from getting a patent on the seeds and medicines that their community has developed. They fight against the deforestation that will destroy their environment and many of the living organisms that have made the ecosystem work effectively for them. They fight the globalization that could destroy their family and community.

Pause to Reflect 8.5

A 2007 report from scientists from around the world reported that the climate was warming (Eilperine, 2007). The snow and ice cover in the North was already decreasing at alarming rates. The Barrier Reefs off of the Australian coast are disappearing. Not everyone, including scientists, agree with the report.

- Why do some people disagree with the scientists' description of global warming?
- Why has the United States not provided leadership in acknowledging global warming and other environmental destruction?
- How do indigenous groups define their responsibility for the environment? How is this in conflict with most world leaders?
- What responsibility do you think you have for taking care of the environment?

Go to the *Homework and Exercises* section in Chapter 8 of MyEducationLab and select *Pause to Reflect 8.5* to answer these questions.

Classroom Focus

Students and their families may have lived in the community served by the school for all of their lives and generations before. But some may have recently moved from another part of the city or another area of the state or another country as occurred in this chapter's opening scenario. The local protocols for behavior in schools and social settings may be strange to these newcomers. Students may speak a language or dialect for which they are teased or harassed. Teachers should recognize that these differences are not shortcomings on the part of students. Instead they are an outgrowth of their own histories and experiences outside of the local community. Educators may have to become acquainted with other cultures to serve the new students effectively. Meeting with parents and listening to the students' own narratives of their lived experiences will help in providing a context for effective teaching and learning.

One way that local and regional differences are reflected is in the school traditions that develop over time. The mascots and slogans of schools distinguish them from others. The sports valued and supported in communities vary. Rivalries develop across schools and communities that last for some graduates far into adulthood. Students and adults develop symbols connected to their group memberships and locale. Many thrive on the connections to a place like high school and community. Others escape as soon as possible to a place where they can establish their own identity outside the confines of the dominant and powerful groups in their community.

Teaching Immigrant Students

Immigrant students, especially at the high school level, tend to be overlooked by their teachers and other officials. Their education is affected by a number of factors that impact their families. A large number of immigrant students are living in segregated, low-income communities. The parents of some Mexican American students are undocumented immigrants who worry about being deported and separated from their families. Some students in rural areas will be in the school a short time as their parents participate in seasonal agricultural work and then move to another area of the country where they can be employed. Many immigrant students will be English language learners who are participating in one of the language programs discussed in Chapter 6.

Older students in urban areas may be assigned to a special newcomer school or program that is designed to help them learn English and adjust to the U.S. school culture. Younger students are more likely to be assigned to a class where the majority of students are native-born. Most rural schools and many urban and suburban school districts will not have special schools or programs for older immigrant students. Instead, they will be integrated into current classrooms with or without support to help them adjust to their new settings.

Where should you begin if an immigrant student is assigned to your class? First, you should be welcoming and supportive of the student. Second, you should find out from a school administrator what support the school district offers for immigrant students. You should learn whether the district has translators or student advocates who can assist you in working with the student and his or her parents. If the student is an English language learner and you have no background in ESL or bilingual education, enroll in a staff development or local university course. Courses may be available online to provide you with assistance. Talk with other teachers in your building or school district who have been successful at integrating immigrant students into their classrooms and helping them be academically successful. In some cases, a school district will not have support systems for either the student or the teacher. You will have to learn on your own.

Most immigrant parents strongly believe that education is critical in their children's future success and will be supportive of the teacher's efforts to help their children learn. In many cultures, the parents respect the role of teachers and trust them to have the best interest of their children in mind. You should consider the family an ally.

As you work with immigrant students, you should make it clear that you have high expectations for them and do everything you can to help them meet those expectations. Although Latino parents are more likely than most other parents to want their children to go to college, their children do not always have the appropriate academic preparation for college and have not had appropriate advice on college requirements (Immerwahr, 2003). Teachers can be very helpful in steering students to the courses they will need for college admission.

You should be conscious of the ethnic identification of immigrant students. They may be at very different stages of assimilation, which means that they cannot be thought of as a homogeneous group. Some students will identify strongly with the dominant group. Others will be transcultural or successfully figuring out how to fuse the culture of the dominant society with their native culture. Still other students will strongly identify with their native cultures and even resist or develop opposition to the dominant culture. A number of researchers have found that the longer immigrant students are in school, the more negative about the value of education they become (Suárez-Orozco & Suárez-Orozco, 2007). If you understand where they are, you can better understand how to use their native cultures to help them learn and possibly retard their opposition to academic achievement.

Honoring Family Cultures

Students' cultural backgrounds should be reflected in the examples used to teach. Rural students do not relate to riding a subway to school or work, nor do inner-city students easily relate to single-family homes with large yards and no other houses around them. If students seldom see representations of themselves, their families, or their communities in

Pause to Reflect 8.6

You have a student in your class whose family emigrated from Iraq the previous year. You know that you should bring the family's culture into the classroom. Are you ready?

- What language is the student's family likely to speak?
- What religion is the family likely to be?
- Why did the family immigrate to the United States?
- What is the family's immigration status likely to be?

Go to the *Homework and Exercises* section in Chapter 8 of MyEducationLab and select *Pause to Reflect 8.6* to answer these questions.

Drawing on students'
cultures in the classroom is discussed
in Chapter 10.

the curriculum, it becomes difficult to believe that the academic content has any meaning or usefulness for them. It will appear to them that the subject matter has been written and delivered for someone else. At the same time, they can still learn about other lifestyles based on different cultural backgrounds and experiences, but not as the only ones to which they are ever exposed. The teacher's repertoire of instructional strategies should relate content to the realities of the lives of students.

The teacher who understands the experiences of students from different cultural backgrounds can use that knowledge to help students learn subject matter. A teacher's sensitivity to those differences can be used to make students from oppressed groups feel as comfortable in the class as those from the dominant culture.

Incorporating Global Perspectives

Because our world has become so interdependent and will become even more so in the future, it is important that students have an understanding of global connections and how they impact on their lives. As you plan lessons, think about how you can integrate worldwide events and actions. A natural disaster such as a tsunami, earthquake, or volcanic eruptions provides an opportunity to learn about the part of the world in which the disaster occurred and the people affected by it. Students can learn more about the areas in which the United States is at war or involved in peacekeeping missions, who lives there, and how they are affected. A lesson on manufacturing should investigate where around the world products are being made and who is working in the factories or sweatshops. Students could study child-labor laws and how children are involved in the production of products that they buy. A lesson on music could explore the influence of U.S. music around the world and the influence of music from other countries on the United States. How could you bring other parts of the world into the subject that you plan to teach?

Another strategy for incorporating global issues into the curriculum is to help your students think about topics from the perspective of different classes of people in another country. Their perspectives on an issue could be the same or quite different from those of students in your classroom. Globalization itself will look quite different from the perspective of a less developed nation than from a developed nation. Indigenous people look at the environment in a very different way than oil companies. Presenting different perspectives will help students clarify the issues and understand why different people think quite differently about the same issue.

With the Internet your students could connect to students in classrooms around the world. Some schools connect their students as pen pals to students in other countries. Students in different countries could work on projects together to learn more about each other or an issue or project in which both countries are engaged. Students from all kinds of schools participate in exchange programs with families around the world. Teachers sometimes sponsor trips for students to visit other countries. The possibilities for interacting with people from other countries will continue to expand as we learn how to use technology to work together.

Working with Families and Communities

After working in Alaska, in historically black and predominantly white universities, and in the South Pacific country of Papua, New Guinea, Delpit (2006) concluded,

FOCUS YOUR CULTURAL LENS: DEBATE

Incorporating Global Perspectives in the Curriculum

When a number of teachers in John F. Kennedy High School began to realize the impact that globalization was having on their community, they began to talk to their colleagues about more systematically incorporating global perspectives across the curriculum. Some of the other teachers agreed. They clearly saw that a number of parents had lost their jobs when several factories relocated to Southeast Asian cities. And all around them they could see that they and their students were wearing clothing and buying goods that were made outside the United States. The latest threats to food were due to imports from China.

Other teachers thought it was nonsense to change their curriculum to integrate global issues and perspectives. One teacher was overheard saying "Who do these young radicals think they are? All they want to do is convince these kids that the U.S. is an imperialist country that only cares about filling corporate pockets. The country will be ruined with suck talk." The principal, however, likes the idea of students developing a greater global awareness. She thinks that it might gain community support and provide a unique branding for the school.

For
- The study of globalization will help students understand how different nations are connected.
- It will help students understand which people are benefited by globalization and which ones lose as a result.
- Students will learn to think more critically about the changes that are occurring in the country as a result of globalization.
- Projects in some classes could help students become more involved in their communities by organizing to fight against inequalities.

Against
- Social studies courses already cover global issues.
- The approach must present a balanced view of the importance of globalization for our economy.
- Including global perspectives in the curriculum will politicize the curriculum.
- The curriculum should concentrate on preparing students for college or jobs.

Questions

1. Why do faculty members disagree about how globalization should be addressed in the curriculum?
2. Why do the proponents feel that it is important to help students not only understand globalization, but to understand the negative impact it is having on many of their students as well as children around the world?
3. Where do you stand on including global perspectives throughout the curriculum? How could they be integrated into the subject that you will be teaching?

Go to the *Homework and Exercises* section in Chapter 8 of MyEducationLab and select *Focus Your Cultural Lens* to answer these questions.

"If I want to learn how best to teach children who may be different from me, then I must seek the advice of adults—teachers and parents—who are from the same culture as my students" (p. 102).

Not all parents feel welcome in schools, in part because most schools reflect the dominant culture and language, rather than their own. Therefore, school personnel may need to reach out to parents, rather than simply waiting for them to show up at a meeting. A true collaboration requires that parents and teachers become partners in the teaching process. Teachers need to listen to parents and participate in the community to develop a range of teaching strategies that are congruent with the home cultures of students. Parents can learn to support their children's learning at home but may need concrete suggestions, which they will seek from teachers who they believe care about their children.

Educators must know the community to understand the cultures of families. In a school in which a prayer is said every morning regardless of the Supreme Court's decision forbidding prayer in public schools, one should not teach evolution on the first day of class. In that school setting, one may not be able to teach sex education in the same way it is taught in many urban and suburban schools. In another school, Islamic parents may be upset with the attire that their daughters are expected to wear in physical education classes and may not approve of coed physical education courses. Jewish and Muslim students wonder why the school celebrates Christian holidays and never their religious holidays.

Because members of the community may revolt against the content and activities in the curriculum does not mean that educators cannot teach multiculturally. It does suggest that they know the sentiments of the community before introducing concepts that may be foreign and unacceptable. Only then can educators develop strategies for effectively introducing such concepts. The introduction of controversial issues should be accompanied by the education of parents and by the presentation of multiple perspectives that place value on the community's mores.

In addition, the community becomes a resource in a multicultural classroom. We can learn much about cultures in the community through participation in activities and by inviting community members into the school. Community speakers and helpers should represent the diversity of the community. Speakers also should be selected from different roles and age groups. Not only will students learn about other cultural groups, so will you.

Summary

The places in which we live influence our culture and our experiences. We have common understandings of everyday life and events with people who attended the same school and lived in the same neighborhood. When we are in another country, we share a culture and understanding with other U.S. citizens who are there.

Within the United States, people live in six regions of the country that help define who they are. The regions have different historical contexts, characteristics, and populations that impact on their culture and education. Educational issues differ across regions as do the student population and teacher salaries.

Each region has rural, urban, and suburban areas that provide different experiences for families and their children. Schools in rural areas usually have fewer students, contributing to a lower teacher to student ratio. Urban schools vary in size and quality across a city with a large number of students of color, English language learners, and students from low-income families. Overall, suburban schools have students of a higher socioeconomic level and teachers who are better qualified than the nearby city.

Families around the world move not only from school to school, but from state to state and from one country to another. In most of the rest of the world, more people move from rural to urban areas, placing stress on cities in developing nations. In the United States, people are more likely to move from an urban to a rural or suburban area.

The world today is very interdependent with events in one country having an impact on many other countries. For example, globalization affects the economics of U.S. citizens as jobs move from this country to another with lower wages and fewer regulations. It also affects the environment. Not all people support globalization that can dramatically change their economic status and quality of living. For example, indigenous populations have been destroyed as their lands are taken over by international conglomerates.

Schools and teachers must determine how they will integrate students from around the world into their educational environment. These strategies include honoring the cultures of new families and drawing on them to teach. Because the families of most of these students understand the importance of their children becoming educated, teachers need to become their allies. Finally, teachers should bring the world to the classroom, introducing students to global perspectives from around the world.

PROFESSIONAL PRACTICE FOR EDUCATORS

Questions for Discussion

1. How does where one lives (geography) help determine one's cultural identity?
2. What historical events have had a great impact on the education of students in the South?
3. How would you describe the geographic landscape of Appalachia? How has it impacted its families and children over the past 50 years?
4. What influence have educators in New England had on education in the United States?
5. Why do you think students in the Great Plains finish high school at higher rates than other regions of the country?
6. What are the major educational issues debated at the political level in the West and Southwest?
7. What are the major differences in teaching in a rural, urban, and suburban school district?
8. What impact does a family's moving from one school district to another have on their children? How can teachers provide a welcoming environment to a new student?
9. Why should global perspectives be included in the P–12 curriculum?
10. How should a teacher integrate immigrant students into the classroom and assist them in learning at a level similar to other students?

Portfolio Activities

1. Observe teachers several times in a rural and urban or suburban school. As you observe, make notes of the diversity of students and teachers in the different schools, the relationship of students and teachers, and the interactions of students across groups. Contrast the two schools in a paper or matrix and discuss your findings.

2. Visit a school with a number of immigrant students to determine the approaches being used to integrate the students and help them learn. Talk with teachers about the instructional strategies they are using to most effectively serve these students and their families. Write a summary of your findings for your portfolio with recommendations about how you will work with new immigrant students when you begin teaching.

Licensure Test Prep

At their faculty department meeting, high school English teachers were discussing strategies for helping their immigrant students who spoke limited English understand an English text. A number of teachers agreed that the best way for them to learn English was to imitate the way the English-speaking students speak. Ms. Clarke said that their fluency in English would improve as they developed their reading skills in English. Therefore, she was focusing on helping them read. Mr. Bishop said that he was asking his students to read aloud in English so that he could correct errors in their pronunciation.

Short Answer Questions

1. What principle of second-language development does Mr. Bishop's approach fail to take into account?
2. What is the advantage of the approach used by Ms. Clarke?

Go to the *Homework and Exercises* section in Chapter 8 of MyEducationLab and select *Licensure Test Prep* to complete this exercise.

Suggested Readings

Bigelow, B. (2006). *The line between us: Teaching about the border and Mexican immigration.* Milwaukee, WI: Rethinking Schools.
This resource provides the context for undocumented workers coming to the United States within a global community. It includes a curriculum for a course on global studies, lesson plans, readings, and student handouts.

Bigelow, B., & Peterson, B. (2002). *Rethinking globalization: Teaching for justice in an unjust world.* Milwaukee, WI: Rethinking Schools.
This resource for middle level and high school teachers provides a wealth of information to help students and teachers think about the unequal ways we are affected by globalization. It includes essays, interviews, poems, stories, cartoons, lesson plans, and hands-on activities.

Delpit, L. (2006). *Other people's children: Cultural conflict in the classroom.* New York: The New Press. Sharing her experiences in cultures new to her in Papua, New Guinea, and Alaska, Lisa Delpit helps us understand that we need to listen to the families and communities of our students to understand how to teach. The book forces us to look at ourselves and our beliefs about how other people's children learn.

Waters, M. C., & Ueda, R. (Eds.). (2007). *The new Americans: A guide to immigration since 1965.* Cambridge, MA: Harvard University Press. This comprehensive guide describes the major immigrant groups that arrived from around the world over the past 45 years. It also addresses major issues related to immigration, ethnic and racial identity, assimilation, religion, and education.

References

Anderson, P. M., & Summerfield, J. P. (2007). Why is urban education different from suburban and rural education? In S. R. Steinberg & J. L. Kincheloe (Eds.), *19 urban questions: Teaching in the city* (pp. 29–39). New York: Peter Lang.

Appalachian Regional Commission (n.d.a). *Appalachian region: Economic overview.* Retrieved on March 4, 2007, from www.arc.gov/index.do?nodeId=26

Appalachian Regional Commission. (n.d.b). *Education—high school and college completion rates in Appalachia, 2000.* Washington, DC: Author.

Baxandall, R., & Ewen, E. (2000). *Picture windows: How the suburbs happened.* New York: Basic Books.

Bergman, E. F., & Renwick, W. H. (2005). *Introduction to geography: People, places, and environment* (3rd ed.). Upper Saddle River, NJ: Pearson Prentice Hall.

Billings, D. B., Norman, G., & Ledford, K. (Eds.). (1999). *Confronting Appalachian stereotypes: Back talk from an American region.* Lexington, KY: The University Press of Kentucky.

Black, D. A., & Sanders, S. G. (2004, September). *Labor market performance, poverty, and income inequality in Appalachia.* Washington, DC: Appalachian Regional Commission.

City Population. (2006, November 22). *City agglomerations of the world.* Retrieved on March 9, 2007, from www.citypopulation.de/World.html

Clawson, D. L., Johnson, D. L., Haarmann, V., & Johnson, M. L. (2007). *World regional geography: A development approach* (9th ed.). Upper Saddle River: Pearson Prentice Hall.

CNN.com/Education. (2002, November 22). *Global goofs: U.S. youth can't find Iraq.* Retrieved July 8, 2007, from http://archives.cnn.com/2002/EDUCATION/11/20/geography.quiz/

Dalton, B., Sable, J., & Hoffman, L. (2006). *Characteristics of the 100 largest public elementary and secondary school districts in the United States: 2003–2004* (NCES 2006-329). Washington, DC: U.S. Department of Education, National Center for Education Statistics.

Delpit, L. (2006). *Other people's children: Cultural conflict in the classroom.* New York: The New Press.

Eilperine, J. (2007, February 3). Humans faulted for global warming: International panel of climate scientists sound dire alarm. *The Washington Post,* pp. 1, 8.

Freund, D. M. P. (2006). Marketing the free market. In K. M. Kruse & T. J. Sugrue (Eds.), *The new suburban history* (pp. 11–32). Chicago: The University of Chicago Press.

Hayden, W. J. (2004). Appalachian diversity: African-American, Hispanic/Latino, and other populations. *Journal of Appalachian Studies, 10* (3), Table 8.

Hussar, W. J., & Bailey, T. M. (2006). *Projections of Education Statistics to 2015* (NCES 2006-084). U. S. Department of Education, National Center for Education Statistics. Washington, DC: U.S. Government Printing Office.

Immerwahr, J. (2003, June). *With diploma in hand: Hispanic high school seniors talk about their future* (National Center Report #03-2). San Jose, CA: National Center for Public Policy and Higher Education and Public Agenda.

Isserman, A. M. (1996). *Appalachia then and now: An update of the realities of deprivation,* reported to the President in 1964. A report prepared for the Appalachian Regional Commission.

Jensen, L. (2006). *New immigrant settlements in rural America: Problems, prospects, and policies.*

Durham, NH: Carsey Institute, University of New Hampshire.

Jones-Correa, M. (2006). Reshaping the American dream: Immigrants, ethnic minorities, and the politics of the new suburbs. In K. M. Kruse & T. J. Sugrue (Eds.), *The new suburban history* (pp. 183–204). Chicago: The University of Chicago Press.

Kozol, J. (2000). *Ordinary resurrections: Children in the years of hope.* New York: Crown.

LaDuke, W. (2006). The people belong to the land. In J. Mander, V. Tauli-Corpuz, and International Forum on Globalization. *Paradigm wars: Indigenous peoples' resistance to globalization* (pp. 23–25). San Francisco: Sierra Club Books.

Lalasz, R. (2006, May). *Americans flocking to outer suburbs in record numbers.* Retrieved on February 4, 2007, from www.prb.org/Articles/2006/AmericansFlockingtoOuterSuburbsinRecordNumbers.aspx.

Lichter, D. T., & Johnson, K. M. (2006). Emerging rural settlement patterns and the geographic redistribution of America's new immigrants. *Rural Sociology, 71*(1), 109–131.

Lloyd, J., Soltani, A., & Koenig, K. (2006). Infrastructure development in the South American Amazon. In J. Mander, V. Tauli-Corpuz, & International Forum on Globalization. *Paradigm wars: Indigenous peoples' resistance to globalization* (pp. 89–94). San Francisco: Sierra Club Books.

Mander, J. (2006). Introduction: Globalization and the assault on indigenous resources. In J. Mander, V. Tauli-Corpuz, & International Forum on Globalization. *Paradigm wars: Indigenous peoples' resistance to globalization* (pp. 3–10). San Francisco: Sierra Club Books.

Massey, D. (1997). Space/power, identity/difference: Tensions in the city. In A. Merrifield & E. Swyngedouw (Eds.), *The urbanization of injustice.* New York: New York University Press.

National Education Association. (2007). *Teacher salaries: State by state.* Retrieved March 1, 2007, from www.nea.org/student-program/about/state.html#alaska; www.nea.org/student-program/about/state2.html#kentucky; and www.nea.org/student-program/about/state3.html#north dakota.

O'Hare, W. P., & Savage, S. (2006, Summer). *Child poverty in rural America: New data show increase in 41 states* (Fact Sheet No. 1). Durham, NH: Carsey Institute, University of New Hampshire.

O'Mara, M. P. (2006). Uncovering the city in the suburb: Cold war politics, scientific elites, and high-tech spaces. In K. M. Kruse & T. J. Sugrue (Eds.), *The new suburban history* (pp. 57–79). Chicago: The University of Chicago Press.

Orfield, G., Losen, D., Wald, J., & Swanson, C. B. (2004). *Losing our future: How minority youth are being left behind by the graduation rate crisis.* Cambridge, MA: The Civil Rights Project at Harvard University. Contributors: Urban Institute, Advocates for Children of New York, and The Civil Society Institute.

Population Reference Bureau. (2006, September). *Quick facts: America at 300 million.* Retrieved on February 4, 2007, from www.prb.org/Articles/2006/QuickFactsAmericaat300Million.aspx

Public Broadcasting Service (PBS). (n.d.). *Timeline of the dust bowl: 1931–1939.* Retrieved on July 11, 2007, from www.pbs.org/wgbh/amex/dustbowl/timeline/

Rowntree, L., Lewis, M., Price, M., & Wyckoff, W. (2006). *Diversity amid globalization: World regions, environment, development* (3rd ed.). Upper Saddle River, NJ: Pearson Prentice Hall.

Smith, D. (2003). *The Penguin state of the world atlas* (7th ed.). New York: Penguin.

Spring, J. (2001). *The American school: 1642–2001* (6th ed.). Boston: McGraw-Hill.

Suárez-Orozco, C., & Suárez-Orozco, M. (2007). Education. In M. C. Waters & R. Ueda, *The new Americans: A guide to immigration since 1965* (pp. 243–257). Cambridge, MA: Harvard University Press.

Takaki, R. (1993). *A different mirror: A history of multicultural America.* Boston: Little, Brown & Co.

Ueda, R. (2007). Immigration in global historical perspective. In M. C. Waters & R. Ueda (Eds.), *The new Americans: A guide to immigration since 1965* (pp. 14–28). Cambridge, MA: Harvard University Press.

U.S. Census Bureau. (2006). *Statistical Abstract of the United States: 2007* (126th ed.). Washington, DC: Author.

U.S. Census Bureau. (2007). *Population Clocks.* Retrieved on July 1, 2007, from www.census.gov/

U.S. Department of Education, National Center for Educational Statistics. (2003). *The condition of education 2003* (NCES 2003-067). Washington, DC: Author.

U.S. Department of Education, National Center for Educational Statistics. (2005). *The condition of education 2005* (NCES 2005-094). Washington, DC: Author.

U.S. Department of Education, National Center for Educational Statistics. (2006a). *The condition of education 2006* (NCES 2006-071). Washington, DC: Author.

United Nations Educational, Scientific and Cultural Organization. (2006). *Education for all global monitoring report 2007.* Paris: Author.

Williams, J. A. (2002). *Appalachia: A history.* Chapel Hill, NC: The University of North Carolina Press.

Wilson, C. R., & Ray, C. (2007). Ethnicity. In *The new encyclopedia of southern culture* (Vol. 6). Chapel Hill, NC: The University of North Carolina Press.

The Worldwatch Institute. (2006). *Vital signs 2006–2007.* New York: W. W. Norton.

Chapter 9

AGE

*I*f *people learn to love and learn to share in early adulthood, they will be able to care for and guide the next generation effectively.*

FERGUS P. HUGHES AND LLOYD D. NOPPE (1991)

Mark McKenzie was a tenth grader in an affluent school district in a Southwestern suburban community. The community is essentially a new town. The town, which 40 years ago had fewer than 50,000 residents, had grown to more than 250,000. Most homes in Mark's neighborhood were in the $400,000 to $550,000 price range. Crime in this community has been almost nonexistent. At least one fourth of the students in high school drive their own cars, including several luxury late-model cars.

Mark moved into this community with his family just two years ago. His father was an engineer in a large high-tech company, and his mother was a successful realtor. His brother was in the eighth grade and his sister in the sixth grade. Mark's parents were extremely fond of their children, but time commitments to their successful careers precluded extensive time and interactions with them. Mark had been promised a car for his next birthday. When Mark and his family moved from their previous home in the Midwest, Mark had begun to demonstrate occasional periods of depression. He had left two very close friends that he had grown up with, and he had objected vehemently to the move.

Since moving to the new home, Mark had made some casual friends, but none as close as the friends in his previous community. In the fall of Mark's sophomore year, he became more withdrawn, attended no school social events, and spent most of his nonschool hours in his room, behind closed doors.

In a conversation with two classmates the next spring, he stated that death brought peace and tranquility. He expressed the same sentiment in a poem written for his English class. His teacher considered the poetry good and passed off his expressions as a teenager's glamorization of death.

A month after writing the poem, Mark began giving away some of his prized possessions. He gave the baseball card collection that he had started 5 years before, and had always valued, to his brother along with his portable DVD player; he gave his treasured I-Pod to his younger sister. When questioned by his parents, he replied only that he had paid for these out of his own money and thought it was his prerogative to do what he wanted with them. "Besides," he stated, "I'm no longer interested in the cards, movies, or music." Later, Mark gave his $300 guitar to his brother, along with his baseball glove. He gave other personal items to his sister and a few to friends at school.

Shortly after giving away his possessions, Mark's depression seemed to dissipate and his behavior was such that it could be described as euphoric. His parents were pleased, and his father remarked, "Mark's finally got his act together." A week later, Mark's body was found in a wooded area less than a half mile from his home. He had died of a self-inflicted gunshot wound. Mark had become one of nearly 2,000 teenagers who would end their own lives that year.

Reflections

1. Was Mark's death the fault of his parents who had forced the family move on their children?
2. Was it the fault of the parents who seemed to be too wrapped up in their careers to spend more time with their children?
3. What were some signs of Mark's impending action?
4. Why had he become euphoric when he was about to take such drastic action on himself?
5. What should the school do after Mark's death?
6. Should a school memorial service be held? Why? Why not?

Age and Culture

Each person who lives long enough will become a part of every age group. Without choice, we must all go through the various stages in life and eventually join the ranks of the aged. Like other cultural groups, we feel, think, perceive, and behave, in part, because of the age group to which we belong. In this edition, we are focusing on school-age groups and the age cohort that many young preservice students and beginning teachers belong to, young adulthood. We include the young adults so that the reader can see how many in this age group tend to function or are perceived to function by others. We examine how ethnicity, gender, social status, and other determinants of culture interface with these periods in an individual's life. We examine how peer pressure affects behavior in some age groups. Critical issues such as child abuse, childhood obesity, adolescent substance abuse, and adolescent suicide are examined. Finally, we examine how an understanding of age groups can affect the educational process.

An understanding of the various age groups is helpful in understanding and providing appropriately for the needs of students. A student's classroom behavior may be a function of his or her relationship with parents, siblings, and significant others. As these family members and significant others move through various age stages in their lives, their behavior, as well as their relationship to the student, may change. Consequently, the student's behavior may, in part, be influenced by the age changes of the significant people in his or her life.

How we behave is often a function of age. Although many adolescents behave differently from one another, the way they think, feel, and behave is at least partly because they are adolescents. At the same time, age does not stand alone in affecting the way a person behaves or functions. Ethnicity, socioeconomic status, religion, and gender interact with age to influence a person's behavior and attitudes.

A Fort Worth, Texas, child in her preschool years, for example, may eat the type of food she does partly because her age and a related health condition require eliminating certain foods from her diet. But her socioeconomic status may determine, to some extent, the foods her parents can afford to buy, and her ethnicity and the fact that she lives in Texas may determine her choices in foods. Her gender, language, disability/nondisability status, and religious background may not influence eating habits to any significant degree, unless she belongs to a religious group with dietary restrictions. These other cultural variables, however, along with her age, may influence other types of behavior and functioning. From the time of birth through the last days of life, a person's age may influence perceptions, attitudes, values, and behavior.

In this chapter, we do not attempt to examine all developmental stages of the various age groups. This information can be obtained through a human development text. Instead, we examine some critical issues related to various age groups. Because it is impossible to address all critical issues affecting each age group, we selectively address issues affecting schools directly or indirectly.

Childhood

Social Class and Poverty

One of the most critical issues that educators routinely face is that of social class and poverty. Today, 18% of the children in the United States live in poverty (Cauthen & Fass, 2007), and teachers in the inner city may find that nearly all of the children in their classrooms live in poverty. Poverty creates numerous problems for children. In many instances, children live with a single parent, typically the mother. When the father is absent, children often lack adequate male role models, and the mother often bears the entire burden of discipline and financial support. Single mothers living in poverty must often work outside the home to provide for their families.

Some mothers from middle and upper socioeconomic groups may not need to work outside the home. Those who choose to do so can often be selective in their choice of a day care setting to ensure an environment congruent with family values. Day care settings are often important variables in the socialization process because many of a child's early behaviors are learned from peers and caregivers. Parents from less affluent groups, however, may have limited choices for their children's day care environment. In some instances, older siblings, themselves children, may be required to assume family child care responsibilities while their parents work at outside jobs.

In 2005, the percentage of the U.S. population living in poverty was estimated to be 10.8%. However, the 20.2% poverty estimates for children under the age of five, was particularly alarming (U.S. Census Bureau, 2006). Poverty statistics are generally based on individuals living below the federal poverty guidelines, which change annually. In 2006 the poverty threshold or level for a family of four was $20,794 (U.S. Census Bureau, 2007). This means that a family of four, which has a combined income of $20,800, is technically not considered to be living in poverty. While the federal government does provide a differential threshold for the high cost of living states of Alaska and Hawaii, there are no allowances for areas of the country where the cost of living is extremely high. Even with the declining real estate market in 2007, the reported median price of a single-family home in California was over $580,000. If one were to factor in the high income tax rates in California and one of the highest energy costs in the nation, it would appear highly unlikely that a family of four could live even modestly with an income double the poverty threshold.

The National Center of Children in Poverty (NCCP) emphasizes a more realistic category to view families who live at risk economically. NCCP reports that research suggests that on an average, families require an income equal to twice the federal poverty threshold in order to meet their most basic needs (Cauthen & Fass, 2007). This center refers to children whose families fall below these criteria as low-income children. There were an estimated 28.4 million children (39%) in the United States in 2006 living in low-income families. Younger children are particularly vulnerable. Forty-two percent of those under age 6 were classified as low-income. Sixty-one percent of Latino (8.8 million) and sixty percent African American (6.5 million) children were also in low-income families. Fifty-seven percent (7.0 million) of children of immigrant parents were designated to be in the low-income category as compared to 35% of children of native-born parents (Douglas-Hall, Chau, & Koball, 2006).

NCCP takes issue with income as the sole criteria for determining poverty. Housing costs, food, child care, health insurance, transportation, payroll taxes, and other necessities should be factors in determining basic needs. These expenses vary from region to region and community to community, and these differences, NCCP suggests, should be factors in determining poverty or low income. NCCP provided an example of the minimal basic costs in these seven areas for New York City and estimated that it would take a minimum of $55,000 or 2.75 times the poverty threshold level for a family of four to meet their most basic needs (Cauthen & Fass, 2007).

Many of these low-income children suffer from inadequate housing, nutrition, and medical care. Many of their homes have inadequate heating or cooling, which affects their sleep and physical well-being. Homes are often old and in neighborhoods where residents live in fear for their personal safety. The National Center for Health Statistics found that children living in poverty were 3.6 times more likely to have fair or poor health. They

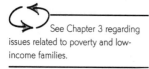

See Chapter 3 regarding issues related to poverty and low-income families.

are also 2 times more likely to die from birth defects and 5 times more likely to die from infectious diseases (Free the Children, 2003). Children who suffer from physical problems are less likely to function academically at their highest potential. Eamon (2001) suggests that poverty in children can contribute to depression, lower levels of sociability, initiative, problematic peer relations, and disruptive classroom behavior.

One of the best sources for determining the conditions for children in the nation and in each individual state is the Annie E. Casey Foundation. The Foundation publishes its *Kids Count* report annually, ranking states in 10 different at-risk areas:

- Low-birth-weight babies
- Infant mortality
- Child deaths rate
- Teen deaths by accident, homicide, or suicide
- Teen birthrates
- Teen high school dropouts
- Teens not in school and not working
- Children with parents without full-time, year-round employment
- Children living in poverty
- Children in families headed by single parent (Annie E. Casey Foundation, 2007)

By going to the Foundation's website (www.aecf.org/) you can see how your state compares to national scores and other states in the various at-risk categories.

As children enter school, they begin to recognize socioeconomic differences. Although the choice of friends may or may not be a function of socioeconomic levels, the type of playmates available may be. Most children in their earlier years attend schools that are somewhat homogeneous in terms of socioeconomic level. Neighborhood playmates are even more homogeneous. During this period, however, an increasing awareness develops regarding the differences in material possessions found in different homes. Children whose families lack financial resources are often unable to acquire clothing considered important to the peer group. Around the ages of 6 to 8, children begin to understand what is meant by rich and poor.

Pause to Reflect 9.1

After looking at the *Kids Count* data for your state on the Annie E. Casey Foundation report, think about the children in your state or the state you plan to teach in. Even if your state is among the highest ranked states, such as Minnesota, there are still too many infant deaths, teen deaths, children living in poverty, and so forth.

- What should society be doing to make life better for these children?
- What do you want to do when you are teaching to make a difference?

Go to the *Homework and Exercises* section in Chapter 9 of MyEducationLab and select *Pause to Reflect 9.1* to answer these questions.

Immigrant Children

The immigrant child who enters an American school for the first time may experience a culture shock resulting from the loss of self-identity and the loss of familiar language and the social structure to which the child is acquainted. If the child immigrates to an area where there are many other children with similar backgrounds, the transition may not be as difficult or as traumatic as it could be if moving to very unfamiliar surroundings.

Each year there are thousands of non-English-speaking immigrants who enter California primarily from Asia and Latin America. Some schools are predominantly Hispanic and many familiar surroundings provide a welcoming atmosphere for the immigrant student. However, if the immigrant child moves to an area of the country in which there are few if any other students from the same background, there may be an immediate feeling of isolation. These may be the children at greatest risk, and school officials need to make a concerted effort to facilitate the child's adjustment. Immigrant children seeking peer acceptance may wish to become more acculturated than what is considered acceptable by parents seeking to maintain traditional cultural values. The conflicting values may emanate from teachers, as well as from peers. It is not uncommon to find immigrant children in their early school years resisting the language of the home, as well as family values related to dress and behavior. During the early school years, children begin to identify with significant adults in their lives who serve as role models. This identification allows children to strengthen, direct, and control their own behavior in such a way that it approximates the behavior of those they hold in esteem. Educators often serve as role models for children, and their influence can be profound. Educators who are sensitive to diverse cultural and family values can assist children from immigrant families in becoming bicultural, rather than having to choose between the culture of the home and that of the school.

See Chapter 1 regarding children, acculturation, maintaining cultural identity, and so on.

Children, Ethnic Awareness, and Prejudice

After years of work in improving race relations in this country, the 1980s and 1990s saw growing optimism that the United States had turned the corner on race relations. The hate crimes and racial violence, which have emerged in recent years, however, remind us that the ugly head of racism continues to surface. Although we as educators may expect to see racism among adults and, to some extent, adolescents, we are sometimes shocked and often dismayed when it is evidenced in the behavior of some young children.

Aboud (1988) defines ethnic awareness as a "conscious recognition of ethnicity in individuals or groups . . . being able to assign correctly the labels to the actual faces or pictures of various people indicates a basic form of perceptual ethnic awareness" (p. 6). Among young children, ethnic awareness and prejudice tend to increase with age. At some point, prejudice may decline but ethnic awareness may remain high. Although it may be necessary for a child to be aware of ethnic differences before he or she can develop prejudice, ethnic awareness in itself is not bad in a child. Attempts to discourage children from noticing that people are different, that they have different pigmentation, have different hair and eye colorization, or speak differently denies an accurate perception of reality in children (Aboud, 1988).

To recognize differences in others, a child must also be involved in self-identification because the child must be aware of what he or she is like before recognizing how another child differs. Children, as young as 3, are able to identify with others of the same color or racial group, and those who are different from themselves (Aboud, 1988; Sleek, 1997).

Prejudice is also discussed in Chapter 1.

Between the ages of 4 and 5, a significant number of children are able to make ethnic identifications.

Dan Floss/Merrill

At 4 and 5 years of age, a significant number of children (about 75%) are able to correctly identify ethnic groupings. By ages 6 and 7, children are able to make the identification at close to 100% accuracy. Some children of color demonstrate an early preference for whites, and some white children indicate a preference for their minority group peers (Aboud, 1988). By the age of 5, some children have developed high levels of prejudice toward other racial groups (Bigler & Liben, 1993; Doyle & Aboud, 1995). It is often assumed that children who hold biased attitudes toward other groups are simply reflecting their parents' attitudes.

Variables Affecting Attitudes and Prejudice

People assume that children who are prejudiced were taught these attitudes by their parents. Aboud and Doyle (1996a, 1996b) concluded that such assumptions are unjustified. There appears to be no strong evidence that children are influenced by the attitudes of parents or peers. Children under the age of 7 are often more prejudiced than their parents and often do not adopt the open and unbiased attitudes of their parents. Parents tend to have greater influence with their children over the age of 7. However, others influence the biases they develop in addition to their parents (Aboud, 1988).

One proposed theory of prejudice in children is the social reflection theory. This theory suggests that the prejudice we see in children is a reflection of the values of society. Research studies, in general, have shown that the higher-status and in-groups in society are preferred by both white and some children of color. European Americans or whites are typically the higher-status and in-group in society. Where social stratification occurs in a community, young children develop negative attitudes toward the lower-status and out-groups. This tends to be true even if the parents hold positive or open attitudes toward minority groups who are typically the lower-status or out-groups (Aboud, 1988).

Tatum suggests (1997) that many white individuals never consider their own ethnic group membership, as they view themselves as the societal norm. European American children, therefore, may grow up with this perception. If whiteness is the norm, then are those who are not white abnormal? Tatum states that white children are often unaware of their white privilege, which is conferred upon them by society simply for being white or European American. In contrast, children of color often grow up aware that they are not perceived as part of this norm. Many if not most become aware of the institutional racism which exists, but to which most white children are oblivious. Children of color often observe or hear discussions by their elders regarding daily discrimination in employment, in being served (or inappropriately served) in restaurants, and in housing.

Over 50 years ago, the Supreme Court ordered U.S. schools to desegregate. To facilitate the desegregation of the schools, the courts mandated school busing in the 1970s. However, by 1999 and 2000, many school districts began to abandon both mandated and voluntary busing. Some parents complained of the long daily bus trips for their children and others felt that their children's distant schools precluded parental involvement. Thus school racial and ethnic compositions again tend to reflect neighborhood composition. Schools in minimally integrated neighborhoods are racially homogeneous.

Children are influenced by what those around them think, do, and say. Even when parents model tolerance, children may still be exposed to the racist behaviors of others. They observe how some individuals do not associate with members of certain groups (Anti-Defamation League [ADL], 2004). They may observe how some of the European American teachers tend to sit only with other European American teachers in the cafeteria. They may see that a particular teacher's table is filled primarily with individuals of color. Unwittingly, the teachers are modeling behaviors for the students. If students look through their books and notice the pictures of American Presidents, they can quickly observe how all are European American and all are male. In some communities, their television news anchors may be European American, their school principal and their superintendent may also be white, and often male. While we are seeing greater diversity in school leadership positions, there are still communities where diversity in management or administration is the exception. These same children may hear older children or adults putting down some groups in jokes. If no one addresses this behavior, the children may grow up believing that this is acceptable and normal behavior (ADL, 2004).

Children are greatly influenced by the media. They watch television and they observe their parents watching television. They have easy access to movies on television and those that family members rent on DVD. They see pictures in newspapers and in the magazines their parents have in the home. There is hardly a day that goes by without children being exposed to stereotyping, misinformation, or exclusion of important information (ADL, 2004).

For the past few years, children have been exposed to the horrors of war in Afghanistan and Iraq, as well as bombings in Indonesia, Spain, and other parts of the world. They have heard or seen the news of American military personnel killed daily by people of color, usually Arabs who are Muslims. They continually hear expressions of justifiable anger directed toward terrorists and suicide bombers, who are almost always described by race and/or religion.

The popular media has always had its villains. From the American Indians to the Japanese and Germans in the Second World War, villains of choice have evolved into the Russians, then Latin American drug lords, and now Arabs and Muslims. It is easy to see how children, particularly European American children can grow up having prejudicial attitudes toward certain groups of individuals. This is especially so when there is so little effort to show that the majority of the people in these groups are good, law-abiding, loyal Americans.

The ADL (2004) suggests that children with poor self-images are prone toward developing prejudices. By targeting individuals they can put down, they may perceive this as a means to bolster their own self-worth. It enables them to feel more important and powerful than those they attack. At other times, children may exclude or ridicule other children because they perceive this to be a popular thing to do. They may feel that this behavior can enhance their standing among their peers (ADL, 2004).

Because prejudice appears to be somewhat prevalent among young children (ages 4 to 7) and because children are cognitively capable of becoming less prejudiced, it would appear to be very appropriate to develop activities that have been shown to reduce prejudice during the early years of elementary school.

Child Abuse

Each year, hundreds of thousands of child abuse cases are reported. **Child abuse** is the physical or psychological mistreatment of children. The American Academy of Pediatrics indicates that more than 2.5 million cases of child abuse and neglect are reported each year. http://www.aap.org/publiced/BKφ_ChildAbuse.htm retrieved October 23, 2007. There were 906,000 victims. It is estimated that 1,500 children died of abuse and neglect, with thousands more suffering from permanent physical or emotional injuries (Centers for Disease Control and Prevention [CDC], 2007a). Some experts believe the reported numbers are unrealistic and estimate that the number of children who die from abuse each year is three times greater than the number reported to authorities (Bartollas & Miller, 2005).

Table 9.1 provides some of the Centers for Disease Control and Prevention's 2006 key findings of child abuse or maltreatment.

The majority (59.3%) of the child abuse perpetrators were women; and one or both parents were responsible for 80.9% of the children who were abused (National Clearinghouse on Child Abuse and Neglect Information, 2004).

Child abuse or maltreatment is usually categorized as physical abuse, physical neglect, sexual abuse, or emotional abuse. The Federal Child Abuse Prevention and Treatment Act defines child abuse as:

- Any recent act or failure to act on the part of a parent or caretaker, which results in death, serious physical or emotional harm, sexual abuse or exploitation; or
- An act or failure to act, which presents an imminent risk of serious harm (U.S. Code: Title 42, 5106g. Definitions)

TABLE 9.1   Child Maltreatment: Key Findings

- 906,000 children were victims of child abuse or neglect
- Sixty-one percent of child victims experienced neglect
- Ten percent were sexually abused
- Nineteen percent were physically abused
- Five percent were emotionally or psychologically abused
- An estimated 1,500 children were confirmed to have died from maltreatment.
  - 36% of these children died from neglect
  - 28% from physical abuse
  - 29% from multiple forms of maltreatment
- Shaken-baby syndrome (resulting from violent shaking of infant or child) affected 1,200 to 1,600 children

From Centers for Disease Control and Prevention. *(2007). Child maltreatment: Fact sheet.* Retrieved from www.cdc.gov/ncipc/cmprfact.htm

Physical Abuse. **Physical abuse** refers to nonaccidental injury inflicted by a caretaker. There is often a fine line between physical abuse and discipline through physical punishment. In the United States, physical punishment is common in many families as a childrearing practice. Physical abuse ranges from minor bruises to severe fractures or even death as a result of punching, beating, kicking, biting, shaking, throwing, stabbing, choking, hitting (with a hand, stick, strap, or other object), burning, or otherwise harming a child. These injuries are considered abuse whether or not the caregiver intended to injure the child (Child Welfare Information Gateway, 2006).

Physical Neglect. **Physical neglect** involves the deliberate neglect or extraordinary inattentiveness to a child's physical well-being. When it becomes necessary for both parents to work, older siblings may be called upon to assume child care responsibilities. When the older siblings are considered by authorities to be too young to provide responsible care, this by law may be considered neglect. This is particularly problematic in cities with large immigrant populations. Some children who suffer from neglect may exhibit poor hygiene, may be inappropriately dressed for weather conditions, or may suffer from hunger. Children who suffer from neglect may have medical or dental needs, which have not been attended to. At times, the practices of some religious groups can come into conflict with the law regarding parental decisions for addressing illness and refusing conventional medical care. The courts have, in some instances, intervened and overturned parental rights when children were considered to be at extreme risk. According to the Child Welfare Information Gateway (2006), neglect may be:

- Physical (e.g., failure to provide necessary, food, shelter, supervision)
- Medical (e.g., failure to provide medical or mental health treatment)
- Educational (e.g., failure to educate a child or tend to special education needs)
- Emotional (e.g., inattention to a child's emotional needs, failure to provide psychological needs, or permitting a child to engage in substance abuse)

Sexual Abuse. **Sexual abuse** refers to the involvement of children or underage adolescents in sexual activities. It also includes practices that violate the social mores of one's culture as they relate to family roles. Sexual abuse is usually found in familial abuse or incest; extrafamilial molestation or rape; exploitation through pornography, prostitution, sex rings, or cults; or institutional abuse (e.g., day care centers). Children who are sexually abused may become withdrawn or secretive. Some may do poorly in school. While physical injury does not usually result from sexual abuse, research does indicate that the emotional impact is both serious and long term; including socioemotional behavior, low self-esteem, depression, and substance abuse (Lotz, 2005).

Emotional Abuse. Children who are emotionally abused are chronically belittled, humiliated, or rejected, or they have their self-esteem attacked. **Emotional abuse** "is a pattern of behavior that impairs a child's emotional development or sense of worth. This may include constant criticism, threats, or rejection, as well as withholding love, support, or guidance" (Child Welfare Information Gateway, 2006). Children who are emotionally or psychologically abused may exhibit a low self-esteem by continually demeaning themselves. Some become self-destructive through the use of drugs, develop eating disorders, or even become suicidal. Some children exhibit withdrawal behaviors; others may exhibit destructive behaviors.

Abusive behavior can have a long-lasting effect on a child. The scars may persist into adulthood. Petersen (2004) reports that youth who are both physically and sexually abused are four times more likely to participate in a gang than youth who are not maltreated. Bartollas and Miller (2005) further assert that research continues to demonstrate that children who are victims of maltreatment are placed at a greater risk for arrest. More than one third of women in prisons reported being abused as children, as compared to 12 to 17% of women in the general population. Fourteen percent of male prison inmates reported abuse as children, as compared to 5 to 8% of men in the general population (Childhelp Inc., 2003).

Table 9.2 provides some of the key signs of child abuse. Child abuse is everyone's problem. It is the responsibility of each teacher to report known or suspected cases of child abuse to the school supervisor. The supervisor, in turn, is responsible for reporting these problems or concerns to professionals who are mandated by state and federal laws to bring the matter to the attention of appropriate protective agencies. These professionals are referred to as "mandated reporters." Every state has mandated laws requiring the reporting of child abuse. State laws differ in that one state has no penalties for failure to report, whereas others impose fines and even jail terms. Some states stipulate that a report must be made if there is suspicion of abuse; others stipulate accountability for failure to report if there is "reasonable cause to believe." Beyond the legal mandates, educators have a professional and ethical obligation to make reports to protect children from abuse.

TABLE 9.2   Recognizing Child Abuse

The following signs may be indicative of child abuse or neglect.

The Child

- Shows sudden changes in behavior or school performance.
- Has not received help for physical or medical problems brought to the parent's attention.
- Has learning problems (or difficulty concentrating) that cannot be attributed to specific physical or psychological causes.
- Is always watchful, as though preparing for something bad to happen.
- Lacks adult supervision.
- Is overly compliant, passive, or withdrawn.
- Comes to school or other activities early, stays late, and does not want to go home.

The Parent

- Asks teachers or other caretakers to use harsh physical discipline if the child misbehaves.
- Sees the child as entirely bad, worthless, or burdensome.
- Demands a level of physical or academic performance the child cannot possibly achieve.
- Looks primarily to the child for care, attention, and satisfaction of emotional needs.

The Parent and Child

- Rarely touch or look at each other.
- Consider their relationship entirely negative.
- State that they do not like each other.

From Child Welfare Information Gateway. (2006). *Recognizing child abuse and neglect: Signs and symptoms.* Washington, DC: U.S. Department of Health and Human Services, www.childwelfare.gov/pubs/factsheets/spsigns.cfm
For more detailed indicators of physical abuse, neglect or sexual abuse, see the Child Welfare Information Gateway website above.

Childhood Obesity

The Centers for Disease Control and Prevention (CDC) (2007b) reported the prevalence of overweight and obesity in the United States has increased markedly in both adults and children in the last 30 years. Increases of overweight and obesity have affected children at all levels from preschool through high school with the worst increase in the 12 through 19 age group from 5 to 17.4%.

Bad nutrition habits in adulthood are often formed during youth. Nearly a third of U.S. adults are overweight or obese. Overweight adolescents have up to an 80% chance of becoming overweight or obese adults. It is estimated that obesity has a $117 billion impact on health care costs and loss of productivity. Childhood obesity alone is costing as much as $14 billion a year in direct health care costs to treat overweight children (U.S. Newswire, 2007).

The CDC suggests that being overweight or obese can have serious consequences. This increases the risk for numerous diseases or health conditions including (CDC, 2007b):

- Hypertension
- Dyslipidemia (e.g., high cholesterol or triglycerides)
- Type II diabetes
- Coronary heart disease
- Stroke
- Gallbladder disease
- Osteoarthritis
- Sleep apnea and respiratory problems
- Some cancers (e.g., endometrial, breast, and colon)

The physical consequences of overweight and obesity are often obvious, however there are other consequences that may not be as easy to identify. Prejudice and discrimination toward overweight children may be another consequence, which may have serious implications for children. Overweight children may find discrimination from peers as well as educators. The social rejection can have lasting effects on the individual.

While parents may view their "chubby" child as cute with "just baby fat," the evidence appears to be fairly conclusive that infants who are overweight tend to be overweight as they grow older. The American Alliance for Health, Physical Education, Recreation and Dance (JOPERD, 2007) cited a study of 1,042 children. Those who were considered overweight between the ages of 2 to 4.5 years (body mass exceeding the 85 percentile for age group) were five times as likely to be overweight at age 12 as those who had not been overweight during their earlier years.

The cause of overweight problems in both children and adults is multifaceted. There is probably no single cause we can attribute to the problem. Among the contributing factors are:

- Food and marketing
- Parental influences on eating behavior
- Dietary intake
- Lack of physical activity or exercise

Unfortunately for many individuals the foods that seem to taste the best are the ones that are often unhealthy. The youth in the United States (and other parts of the world) have grown up in a culture where fast foods are an integral part of daily life. Much of it may be tasty but often high in saturated fats. Until recent harsh criticism against the fast-food industy, many in the industry encouraged consumers to "supersize" or to increase the portions of their food orders for a modest additional cost. In addition to the availability of these fast-food establishments throughout the community, many schools included these foods in their offerings. Many of these foods considered unhealthy by nutritionists have been referred to as "junk" foods. Some school cafeterias and school vending machines readily dispense sugar-filled soft drinks, chips, cookies, and other unhealthy items.

Parents may exacerbate the problem by encouraging or even forcing their children to eat all of their food and clean off their plates, even if they are already satiated. Other parents, also hooked on unhealthy foods, purchase unhealthy food items and serve them in their homes. Both quality and quantity are clearly issues of concern.

Another concern is the sedentary lifestyle that many of our youth have adopted. Again, parental modeling is often flawed. Today's youth have more entertainment options than earlier generations when there was no or limited television, video games, and computers. The lack of physical activity among many of today's youth is a major contributor to the obesity and lack of physical conditioning.

Health care professionals, state legislatures, and even the U.S. Congress are beginning to address the problem. The Institute of Medicine, a part of the National Academy of Sciences, recommended that junk foods such as potato chips, doughnuts, chocolate-covered ice cream, and sugary drinks should be banned from K–12 schools. A bipartisan effort in the U.S. Congress has initiated legislation to create a federal ban (Burros, 2007).

States such as Washington have already enacted laws requiring schools to address the nutritional content of foods sold in all schools. Parents in some instances have collaborated with school officials in drafting school food policies. In one Washington school district, cafeteria buffets now offer fresh fruits and vegetables, low-fat potato chips, whole-wheat buns, and few if any desserts. Vending machines mostly are stocked with water, 100% fruit juices, and more nutritious snacks such as granola bars (Woodward, 2006).

The sale of food from vending machines as well as junk foods sold in cafeterias is often a major source of revenue for schools. If educators, administrators, and school boards are sincere in advocating for the welfare of their students, they will not place profit over health. We must educate our students in the benefits and ways to maintain good nutrition and eliminate unhealthy foods from our schools.

Pause to Reflect 9.2

The variables that contribute to childhood obesity are obvious. Many of our children do not get enough exercise, their eating habits are terrible, and many are addicted to junk foods, which taste good to them but are filled with saturated fats and calories. Many of our schools contribute to the problem by selling sodas and junk foods.

- What can you do in your classroom to help the problem?
- Is there anything you can do to help educate parents as to the steps they can take to help their children choose healthier and more nutritious foods?
- Is there anything you can do to voice your concern to the school authorities without seriously jeopardizing your position?

Go to the *Homework and Exercises* section in Chapter 9 of MyEducationLab and select *Pause to Reflect 9.2* to answer these questions.

Adolescence

Adolescence, approximately ages 13 through 18, is perhaps one of the most challenging times in the life of an individual and the family. It is a long transitional period (6 years or so) during which the individual is "suspended" between childhood and adulthood. During adolescence, emancipation from the primary family unit is the central task of the individual. It is a difficult period for the young person, who is attempting to be free from the role of a child but is not fully equipped to assume the responsibilities of adulthood.

Relationship with Parents

As the adolescent shifts emotional ties from the family to peers, a restructuring may take place in the parent-adolescent relationship. Parents may be viewed more objectively. Parents may become more concerned about peer influence as they have increasingly less interaction with their child. These changes have the potential for turning the period of adolescence into one of dissonance and alienation from parents and other members of the family. One need only observe a few adolescent-family situations, however, to realize that the degree of dissonance and alienation varies greatly.

The attitude of the parents may contribute to the alienation. Parents who expect problems with their children in the adolescent period sometimes fall into the trap of a self-fulfilling prophecy. Their expectation of alienation generates a hostile attitude on their part. In contrast, parents who have confidence in their children may promote a feeling of confidence and trust. These children often develop sufficient self-confidence to resist peer pressure when it is appropriate.

Alienation is disturbing to families, to adult members of the community, and to the adolescents themselves. In their efforts to achieve autonomy, sexual functioning, and identity

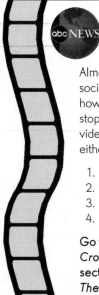

VIDEO INSIGHTS

The In Crowd and Social Cruelty

Almost anyone can remember the popular kids in school and those who were treated as social outcasts. From an early age children can be incredibly cruel. This video clearly shows how children are bullied. One teen was bullied in spite of repeated pleas by parents to help stop the cruel behavior. As we can see in the video she eventually took her own life. The video indicates that bullying takes place in the playground every day. Yet teachers seem to either ignore it or are oblivious to it.

1. Were you popular in school?
2. Were you treated badly by other students?
3. Have you seen children bullied in your school?
4. What can you and other educators do to stop children from mistreating one another?

Go to the Video Insights DVD and watch the video segment *The In Crowd and Social Cruelty*. Then, go to the *Homework and Exercises* section in Chapter 9 of MyEducationLab and select *Video Insights: The In Crowd and Social Cruelty* to answer these questions.

in order to become productive, self-sufficient individuals, some adolescents think they must turn away from the family. As adolescents assert their rights to assume adult behaviors, they sometimes are unable to assume complementary adult-like responsibility. Recognizing this shortcoming, parents are understandably reluctant to grant adolescents adult privileges; this further adds to the alienation.

At-Risk Youth and High-Risk Behavior

It is important to differentiate between the terms adolescent **"at risk"** and "high-risk." At-risk youth are those who live in a disadvantaged status. This may be due to conditions such as poverty, discrimination, family instability, genetic or constitutional factors, parental neglect or abuse, or major traumatic events. **High-risk behaviors** are those that youth engage in that make them or others vulnerable to physical, social, or psychological harm or negative outcomes. Youth deemed "at risk" do not necessarily engage in high-risk behaviors. These categories of high-risk behaviors include the use of harmful substances such as alcohol or other drugs, and sexual behaviors leading to unwanted pregnancies or sexually transmitted diseases. These behaviors are initiated during adolescence, are frequently interrelated, and often extend into adulthood.

Substance Abuse

The use of harmful substances, primarily by children and adolescents, has been one of the most problematic areas faced by parents, schools, communities, and law enforcement agencies in the past two decades. It will inevitably continue to be a major problem in the next decade. **Substance abuse** is the use of banned or illegal drugs and substances or the overuse of legal substances. The problem is a national phenomenon, and many of the problems of adult substance abuse have their roots in adolescence.

Substances are abused to produce altered states of consciousness. The adolescents who use them often seek relief, escape, or comfort from stress. The social institutions, to which the adolescents must relate, including family and particularly the educational system,

Experimentation with smoking, alcohol, and drugs often occurs during adolescence at the urging of peers.

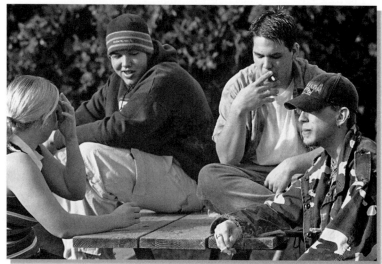

George Dodson/PH College

may be perceived as unresponsive or openly hostile. Their inability to focus on long-range goals, their desire for immediate gratification, and their lack of appreciation for the consequences of their behavior may contribute to some adolescents' misuse of substances.

There are two broad categories of adolescent drug users: the experimenters and the compulsive users. Experimenters make up the majority of adolescent drug users. A few progress from experimenters to compulsive users. Although most experimenters eventually abandon such use, the fear of progression to compulsive use is a serious concern of parents and authorities. Recreational users fall somewhere between experimenters and compulsive users. For them, alcohol and marijuana are often the drugs of choice. Use is primarily to achieve relaxation and is typically intermittent. For a few, however, the goal is intoxication, and these individuals pose a threat to themselves and others.

Nationally, 38.4% of students reported that they had tried marijuana once or more during their lifetime. Twenty percent of students had used marijuana one or more times during the 30 days preceding the CDC Youth Risk Surveillance Survey (Eaton, 2006).

The data obtained between October 2004 and January 2006 found that 43.3% of students grades 9–12 had at least one drink of alcohol in the 30-day period preceding the CDC Youth Risk Surveillance Survey. However, one alarming statistic in the survey was that nationwide, 25.6% of students had drunk alcohol (other than a few sips) for the first time before age 13.

The CDC reported that nationally 7.6% of high school students had tried some form of cocaine one or more times, with 3.4% using the drug in the 30 days prior to the CDC Youth Risk Surveillance Survey. The Surveillance report also indicates that 8.5% of students had used hallucinogenic drugs (e.g., LSD, acid, PCP, angel dust), 2.4% had used heroin, 6.2% of students had used methamphetamines ("speed," "crystal," or "ice"), and 6.3% of students had used ecstasy one or more times during their lifetime (Eaton, 2006).

Numerous problems related to substance abuse affect the community at large. Intravenous drug users are one group at high risk for AIDS. The spread of the deadly HIV virus among adolescents had, by the 1990s, affected thousands of the country's youth.

Substance abuse, while a concern among all youth groups, is no more problematic for minority youth than among their majority group counterparts. Figure 9.1 shows these

FIGURE 9.1 Substance Abuse by High School Students.

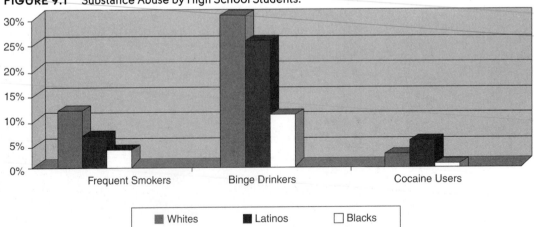

From Centers for Disease Control and Prevention. (2005). *Youth risk behavior surveillance—United States, 2005.* Retrieved from www.cdc.gov/mmwr/preview/mmwrhtml/ss5505al.htm

risk behaviors by racial group. As can be seen in this figure, and in Table 9.3, high-risk behaviors affect all groups. The data also show that all three of these racial groups "take their turn" at being at the top of risky behaviors.

It is a complex problem that deserves more attention by educators than the brief coverage here. The problem can and must be dealt with through the home, school, and law enforcement authorities, as well as through social agencies and responsible media.

Adolescent Sexual Behaviors

The 2005 CDC Youth Surveillance Survey indicates that while 6.2% of students reported their first sexual intercourse prior to age 13, 46.8% of high school students and 63.1% of seniors had sexual intercourse at least once in their lifetime. Among these students 33.9% of students had had sexual intercourse with one or more partners during the 3 months preceding the survey. Nearly half (49.4%) of high school seniors reported that they were currently sexually active. Slightly more than half of the 33.9% sexually active high school students indicated that they or their partners had used some form of birth control prior to their previous sexual intercourse. Among the sexually active, 62.8% reported that either they or their partner had used a condom during their last sexual intercourse. These statistics clearly suggest that America's high school students are involved in activities that can lead to pregnancy and sexually transmitted diseases (STDS) including HIV infection. The report also suggests that not enough preventative measures are being taken by many of the students to prevent either pregnancy or infections, some of which can have lethal consequences.

Table 9.3 shows the high school students who are sexually active by racial groups. This high-risk behavior and the accompanying teen pregnancies often have a high correlation with poverty and with states and regions with high levels of poverty (e.g., Washington, DC). Consequently, there is a higher birthrate among teens of color who are significantly impacted by poverty. When compared across poverty groups, teen birthrates among poor whites and poor African Americans are more similar. Children born to young mothers face a substantially greater risk of low birth weight, and of serious disabilities.

The Centers for Disease Control and Prevention does not provide disaggregated data for adolescents who have been diagnosed with HIV/AIDS. Rather, the CDC (2005) groups the adolescents with individuals up to the age of 24 in the category of young people ages 13–24. The CDC advises that young people (13–24) in the United States are at risk for HIV infection. This risk is especially notable for youth of minority races and ethnicities. In 2004, an estimated 4,883 young people aged 13–24 were diagnosed with HIV/AIDS in the 33 states reporting to the CDC. This represented about 13% of the persons diagnosed that year (CDC, 2007c).

TABLE 9.3   High School Students Sexually Active

Racial Groups	Percent Sexually Active
African Americans	47.4%
Hispanics	35.0%
Whites	43.2%

From Centers for Disease Control and Prevention (2005). *Youth risk behavior surveillance—United States, 2005*. Retrieved from www.cdc.gov/mmwr/preview/mmwrhtml/ss5505a1.htm

Pause to Reflect 9.3

It is quite obvious, whether we approve or not, that half or more of our nation's teenagers are involved in sexual activity. The problems are at least twofold. They are risking the possibility of pregnancies, and many (about half) are having unprotected sex and risking the possibility of contracting sexually transmitted diseases (STDs).

- Whose responsibility is this? The students? The parents? The school? Public health agencies?
- Does providing free condoms to junior high and high school students encourage them to be sexually promiscuous?
- If they are going to be involved in sexual activity anyway, should we protect both them and society?

Go to the *Homework and Exercises* section in Chapter 9 of MyEducationLab and select *Pause to Reflect 9.3* to answer these questions.

As indicated by the CDC (2005), studies have found a correlation between higher AIDS incidence and low income. The CDC further states that poverty contributes to the lack of access to quality health care, directly or indirectly increasing the risk of HIV infection. In addition school dropouts are more likely to become sexually active at younger ages and fail to use contraception.

Despite an impressive decline (30% over the past decade), the birthrate for teenagers in the United States is still significantly higher compared with other industrialized countries. Most impressive was the report that the teen birthrate for African Americans had been cut in half since 1991 (CDC, 2003a). However, the pregnancy rate for African American teens is twice the rate of white teens (CDC, 2003a).

Adolescent Suicide

Many of America's youth are apparently troubled, some depressed to the point of thoughts of suicide and some who actually carry through with the act. During the 12-month period preceding the 2005 CDC Youth Surveillance Survey, 28.5% of students nationwide indicated that they had felt sad or hopeless almost every day for two or more weeks. Nationally 16.9% indicated that they had seriously considered suicide, and 13% indicated that they had made a plan as to how they would attempt suicide, and 8.4% indicated that they had attempted suicide once or more the preceding 12 months (Eaton, 2006). Although the overall rate among teenagers has declined since 1992, suicide remains the third leading cause of death among young people, surpassed only by car accidents and homicide. It is estimated that annually in the United States nearly 2,000 young people commit suicide (CDC, 2006b). In all likelihood, the actual number of adolescent deaths due to suicide is higher than that which is reported. Some suicides are likely reported as accidents; especially high-speed automobile crashes where no suicide notes are recovered. Likewise, some gunshot deaths may be reported as accidents.

One encouraging statistic is that the CDC reported that the overall suicide rate for those ages 10 to 19 fell from 6.2 deaths per 100,000 in 1992 to 4.6 in 2001. Restrictions on the access to fire arms and decreased stigma over sexual orientation were suggested variables contributing to the decrease. Television programming today about gays and lesbians has increased. This, combined with increasing numbers of individuals including celebrities, who have acknowledged their sexual orientation, has likely saved a lot of lives (*Los Angeles Times,* 2004).

Numerous theories have been advanced for the adolescent suicide phenomenon. Among the reasons offered are the decline in religion, tension between parents, the breakup of the nuclear family, family tensions and conflict, and the competitiveness in school.

Because of their youth and lack of experience in making accurate judgments, depressed adolescents may be more prone to respond to the suggestion of suicide than an adult. Adolescent depression is a function of a wide range of situations, perhaps involving failure, loss of a love object, or rejection. It can also be a function of biochemical imbalances in the brain or the loss of a parent through death, divorce, separation, or extended absence. The widespread availability and use of both legal prescription and illegal drugs may be another contributing factor.

There are a number of warning signs, which adolescents may manifest when contemplating suicide. The observant educator can often see these signs and solicit appropriate intervention. Some of these sign are listed in Table 9.4.

Adolescents who are unable to conform to expected sexual behavior patterns are at considerable risk. It is estimated that gay and lesbian youth constitute 30% of the completed suicides in their age group. Approximately 30% of a surveyed group of gay and bisexual males indicated that they have attempted suicide at least once (American Academy of Pediatrics, 2004). The American Academy of Pediatrics (2004) found homosexual

TABLE 9.4   Warning Signs of Adolescents Contemplating Suicide

- Changes in eating and sleeping habits
- Withdrawal from others and routine activities
- Aggressive and hostile behaviors including running away
- Unusual passive behavior
- Substance abuse
- Neglecting personal appearance
- Personality changes
- Persistent boredom, difficulty concentrating, or a decline in the quality of schoolwork
- Frequent complaints about physical symptoms, often related to emotions (e.g., stomachaches, headaches, etc.)
- Loss of interest in pleasurable activities
- Loss of interest in schoolwork and activities
- Complaints of being a bad person or feeling badly inside
- Providing verbal hints with statement suggesting that they will no longer be a problem, that things no longer matter, or that they will not be around much longer
- Giving away or throwing away valued possessions and other behaviors suggesting that the individual is putting affairs in order
- Exhibiting euphoria following depression
- Expressions of hopelessness and helplessness
- Unusual reckless, life-endangering behaviors (e.g., speeding)

Adapted from Teen Suicide. *(2004). The American Academy of Child and Adolescent Psychiatry, No. 10. Updated July 2004, from http://aacap.org/page.ww?name=Teen+Suicide&section=Facts+for+Families; from Griffin M. E. & Felsenthal, C. (1983). A cry for help. Garden City, NY: Doubleday; and from WebMed, Depression: Recognizing the warning signs of suicide. Retrieved from http://www.webmd.com/depression/guide/depression-recognizing-signs-of-suicide*

youth were two to seven times more likely to attempt suicide than their heterosexual peers. They also are two to four times more likely to be threatened with a weapon at school, and are more likely to engage in the use of drugs and alcohol.

Risk factors for suicide completion include:

- Previous suicide attempts
- Mental disorders or co-occurring mental and alcohol or substance abuse disorders
- Family history of suicide
- Stressful life event or loss
- Easy access to lethal methods, especially guns
- Exposure to suicidal behaviors of others
- Incarceration (Youth Violence Prevention Resource Ctr., 2004)

Suicide attempts are often more of a desperate attempt to be heard and understood than a true intent to end life. Those who contemplate suicide but do not follow through with an attempt often report that their plans were changed by someone's simple act of concern.

Youth Violence

Violence is one of the greatest problems facing young Americans today. Although the violent crime rate in the United States has declined in recent years, this trend has not been evident in the juvenile violent crime rate (Petersen, 2004). Champion (2004) reports that while youths ages 13 to 18 constitute approximately 10% of the population in the United States, this age group actually accounts for 20% of all arrests. The CDC (2007d) reported that 1,938 youth between the ages of 15 and 19 died from homicides in 2003. Another 321 under the age of 15 also died from homicides.

Bartollas and Miller (2005) suggest that the actual number of youth homicides in the United States may actually be as high as 5,000 a year. In a study of the top industrialized nations in the world, it was determined that the United States was responsible for 73% of all child homicides (Prothrow-Stith & Spivak, 2004).

Due to media coverage, the nation has become well conditioned to school violence. In reality, less than 1% of all homicides among school-aged children (5–19 years of age) occur in or around school grounds or on the way to and from school. Since the 1992–1993 school year, incidents of school-related homicides (the majority of which involved firearms) have been on a steady decline. However the incidents involving multiple victims have been on the increase, with an average of five such occurrences per year (CDC, 2000).

Everyone in the United States was shocked and stunned when the images of the April 1999 shootings at Colorado's Columbine High School reached their TV screens or by the shooting rampage at Virginia Tech University, eight years later. In a few brief moments two outcast students shot and killed 12 of their classmates and a popular teacher/coach at Columbine High School, then killed themselves. On the Blacksburg, Virginia, campus, a solitary, troubled student gunman took 32 lives, wounding many more before taking his own. The odds were certainly against such a scenario taking place at either school serving these comfortable and otherwise peaceful communities.

Columbine students are overwhelmingly white, and only one of the victims was black. The school served the affluent community of Littleton. Perhaps even more alarming was the intent of the two assailants who had planted at least 30 bombs in the school with the intention of killing even more of their classmates. Fortunately the bombs never detonated.

CRITICAL INCIDENTS IN TEACHING _____

Gay Student

Elizabeth Harvey is a 10th-grade English teacher in a suburban middle-class school, in a predominantly white, southern community. It is after school, the hallways are cleared of students, and she is on her way to the office from her classroom to check on mail, notices, and other things before going to her car. In a darkened small hallway off the main hallway, she hears what sounds like sobs and whimpering. Investigating she sees John Cameron, one of her English students, curled up in a near fetal position, his face bruised and cut, with tears running down his face.

Harvey gets on her knees and carefully cradles his head in her arms. "What is it, John?" she asks. He shakes his head and replies, "Nothing. I slipped and fell." "You and I both know that isn't true, John. I want to know who did this to you and why. We will get to the bottom of this and make sure that whoever did this will be punished." John shakes his head and emphatically says, "No! It would only make it worse for me if you do something to them." "Who and why?" she asks. "It doesn't really matter who, Mrs. Harvey. It is everybody. They called me a dirty faggot, and said to get out of this school."

Gathering her composure, Harvey asks him in a gentle manner, "Is it true, John? I mean that you are gay?"

"Yes, I guess so. I've never even admitted it to my parents. My father would probably kick me out of the house if he knew. He is Mr. Macho and has always wanted me to be the same. I wish I were dead. It's not worth living anymore."

Elizabeth Harvey is a devout Evangelical Christian. She believes that homosexuality is a sin, and a matter of choice. She believes that John can be cured through prayer and faith. Her first inclination is to tell him this and to tell him that she and others in her church love him, would welcome him, and will help him to change and to be normal.

Harvey, however, is also a devoted professional educator. The thoughts that are now racing through her mind are what is the appropriate thing for her to do for John in her professional role.

Questions for Classroom Discussion

1. What should Elizabeth Harvey do with John at this time?
2. Should she take him into her principal's office and together with John discuss the incident with the site administrator in charge?
3. Should the school contact John's parents and tell them what has happened, informing them that their son is gay?
4. Should the school seek out and punish the students who attacked John?
5. Should the school seek out someone better qualified than they are in issues such as this to assist them in this matter?

Building Teaching Skills

Go to the *Building Teaching Skills* section in Chapter 9 of MyEducationLab and select *Critical Incidents in Teaching: Gay Student* to complete this exercise.

The Littleton incident was but one of a string of violent attacks against students and teachers across the United States in recent years. Most of these high-profile shootings involved young males, most of who are viewed as alienated individuals or outcasts. Often, their peers had ridiculed them, and they associated with other disaffected individuals in outcast groups. This was the case of the assailant in a Pearl, Mississippi, school who complained of "mistreatment every day." Another school killer in the Jonesboro, Arkansas shooting, allegedly boasted openly "individuals will die" (Cannon, Streisand, & McGraw, 1999).

The Columbine assailants had provided ample warning signs of their troubled lives and potential to do harm. Authorities apparently ignored or paid little heed when advised of a hate-filled website and death threats against another student. They intensely disliked the school athletes, who allegedly mocked and harassed them. Not unlike other suicidal teens, these were individuals who were troubled, and who gave out warning signs to those who would pay heed. Unfortunately no one who might have prevented the tragedy in this instance, and in so many other situations, paid heed.

The March 2001 school shooting in Santee, California, is particularly troubling since several friends and associates of the alleged shooter admitted that he had told them the weekend before that he was planning the incident. They did not report it because they said he later laughed it off as a joke, and as one said, he did not want to get his friend into trouble. It is essential that teachers, students, and the community be trained to take all talk of this nature seriously and to report it to the proper authorities.

Many of these warning signs of potentially aggressive behavior overlap with the warning signs of individuals considering suicide (e.g., depression). Whether or not the presence of these signs is indicative of suicide consideration or imminent danger to others, it is a potential warning of a troubled individual. Parents, teachers, and school authorities cannot risk taking such situations lightly.

VIDEO INSIGHTS

abcNEWS

Action, Reaction, and Zero Tolerance

With the tragic school shootings at Columbine High School in Colorado and other schools in the country, school authorities are understandably cautions to the point of establishing zero tolerance rules. Some of the rules are so stringent that as we can see in the video, some students are reported and arrested for actions that were not intended for arrest, discipline, or punishment.

1. Have the schools and authorities gone too far in the effort to protect students?
2. Can more reasonable rules be established to protect our children and at the same time avoid frivolous reporting?
3. Should school authorities and law enforcement be given more discretion to determine what is truly intended and dangerous behavior and what behaviors should be ignored or dismissed?

Go to the Video Insights DVD and watch the video segment *Action, Reaction, and Zero Tolerance*. Then, go to the *Homework and Exercises* section in Chapter 9 of MyEducationLab and select *Video Insights: Action, Reaction, and Zero Tolerance* to answer these questions.

FOCUS YOUR CULTURAL LENS: DEBATE
Zero Tolerance

Because of the increasing violence in the schools, officials have instituted zero tolerance regulations in which specific behaviors and items are banned from the school. In general, violators are dealt with immediately and sometimes harshly (e.g., immediate expulsion) regardless of the intent, age of the offender, or the severity of the offense. Often administrators have no discretionary powers to make exceptions. The tough rules are designed to ensure that the schools will be safer, with every violation having a mandatory punishment.

For
- Seemingly harsh punishment for infractions is a small price to pay for keeping our schools and children safe.
- Students and their parents know what the rules are. If they break the rules then they must suffer the consequences.
- Zero tolerance means that there are consequences for every infraction.
- Good zero tolerance policies do not require the maximum punishment for every offense.

Against
- Young children are expelled simply for forgetting some minor item.
- Zero tolerance has gone too far. Innocent children are treated like criminals, scarring them for life.
- Unless administrators are give more discretion, these ridiculous laws need to be scrapped.

Questions
1. If we don't institute zero tolerance policies, then what can the schools do to make students and parents realize that they are serious in curbing violence?
2. Should there be more flexibility for administrators in dealing with grade school offenders than older students?
3. Is zero tolerance really zero tolerance if administrators have discretionary powers and can make exceptions?

Go to the *Homework and Exercises* section in Chapter 9 of MyEducationLab and select *Focus Your Cultural Lens* to answer these questions.

Adapted from Cauchon, D. (1999). Zero Tolerance policies lack flexibility. *USA Today*, www.usatoday.com/educate/ednews3.htm; California Department of Education. (2004). *Zero Tolerance*. www.usatoday.com/educate/ednews3.htm.

Depression does not necessarily indicate the likelihood of violent behaviors; however, violent behavior is often the function of depression. If you have reason to suspect that a student is depressed, refer the individual to a school counselor or to an appropriate authority.

Educators must not allow such behavior to go on without intervention. The stakes are far too high. The problems associated with school violence are actually greater than the reported incidents.

The CDC 2005 Youth Risk Surveillance Survey (Eaton, 2006) had some very disturbing findings. Nationally 6% of students had stayed home from school one or more times during the 30-day period preceding the survey because they felt unsafe at school or on the way to or from school. As troubling as this finding may be, it should not be surprising given the results from the CDC survey. During the 12 months preceding the survey:

- 29.8% of students had property stolen or deliberately damaged on school property one or more times.
- 7.9% of students nationwide had been threatened or injured with a weapon (e.g., a gun, knife, or club) on school property one or more times.
- 13.6% of students had been in a physical fight on school property one or more times.
- 6.5% of students had carried a weapon (e.g., a gun, knife, or club) on school property one or more times (in 30 days preceding survey).

While the reasons for such untoward violent behaviors are multifaceted, the American Academy of Pediatrics (2000) reports that by the age of 18, the average American child will have viewed about 100,000 acts of violence on television alone. The level of violence on Saturday morning cartoons exceeds that of prime time. There are 20 to 25 acts of violence an hour on Saturday morning as compared with 3 to 5 during prime time. Some of the most popular prime-time network shows are crime shows (e.g., *CSI, Cold Case*, etc.). Though highly entertaining to some viewers these shows provide graphic violence and are unsuitable for young children and perhaps even for younger adolescents. Parents should use considerable discretion before allowing children to view such violent programming. With such continuous exposure to violence, is it possible that our children have become desensitized to senseless violent acts?

Prothrow-Stith and Spivak (2004) argue that there is substantial evidence of the connection between exposure to violence on television and aggressive or violent behavior in children. Media violence affects children in the following ways:

- Increasing aggressiveness and antisocial behavior
- Increasing the fear of becoming a victim
- Making them less sensitive to violence and victims of violence
- Increasing their appetite for more violence in entertainment and real life

Some of the variables that contribute or predispose youth to violence are obvious. Among industrialized countries, few provide their youth easier access to firearms and drugs than the United States. Many of our youth, particularly those in poverty living in the inner city are recruited into street gangs. Poor, or inadequate parenting, a dysfunctional family life, and lack of adequate role models, particularly male, are other frequently cited contributing variables.

The CDC (2006b) reports that homicides are the leading cause of youth deaths among African Americans and the second leading cause among Hispanics. In 2004, homicides accounted for 2,803 deaths among black youth 15–24, more than the 2,126 white youth who died in that manner even though whites greatly outnumbered blacks in the general population.

Lotz (2005) argues that the higher rates are primarily the result of the social conditions in the daily lives of African Americans. They are more likely to live in neighborhoods with conditions that contribute to criminal activity. The literature also suggests that African American youth receive differential treatment from the juvenile justice system. They are more likely to be arrested, convicted, and incarcerated than white youth for similar offenses. The poor typically have court appointed attorneys and the trial and subsequent incarceration is often a mere formality. Youth from middle-class backgrounds may have the

Graffiti may be an indication of street gangs marking their turf.

Scott Cunningham/Merrill

benefit of privately retained attorneys who may be able to secure probation or reduced sentences. Incarceration severely impacts the future of these individuals, limiting educational opportunities, employment opportunities, and income (Drakeford & Garfinkel, 2007; Justice Policy Institute, 2005).

Street Gangs

Juvenile gang activity in the United States can be documented as far back as the mid-1800s. Prior to the 1980s, gang activity and violence tended to affect only those in their immediate communities. Middle-class white Americans had few concerns with respect to street gangs. By the 1970s, however, and especially the 1980s, gang organizations had become more sophisticated and their activities had begun to affect a wider range of people (Kratcoski & Kratcoski, 2004). Because of the sensationalized portrayal of gangs on television, film, and in the news media, gangs and violence have become nearly synonymous with violent crime. Research suggests that youth become involved in gangs for a variety of reasons. These include family stress, protection against victimization, and emotional fulfillment (Petersen, 2004). For many gang members, affiliation with a gang is their means of achieving status in a community. The gangs acquire power in a community through violent behavior and the fear that such behavior generates. Some of today's gangs are well armed, and in some areas either match or exceed the police with firepower. In Los Angeles County and in other Southern California communities, street gangs have grown in size much faster than the resources to combat them. In Los Angeles County there was an estimated 12,000 gang members in 1973. Today police have identified 720 street gangs in the city of Los Angeles, with 39,315 members (McGreevy & Winton, 2007). Neither the Los Angeles Police Department nor the Los Angeles County Sheriff's Department has come close to matching the growth of the gangs. In addition, due to budgetary constraints, other resources such as gang prosecution, prevention, and intervention have been cut or have fallen short of keeping up with gang growth (Barrett & Browne, 2004).

With the expiration of the federal ban against assault weapons in 2004, law enforcement and other officials fear that gang members will have greater access to high-powered sophisticated weaponry. Even when gang members cannot legally obtain these weapons, they are readily available through other means. Gang members consider guns essential for passing through the turf of others. The problem of gun ownership is not limited to a few "bad apples"; rather, it is typical in the impoverished inner city and is spreading outward. For many, assault rifles are the weapon of choice. With weapons such as these, drive-by shootings have become commonplace among gang members struggling for turf, avenging an insult, or retaliating a rival gang's previous assault. Drive-by shootings claim the lives of almost as many innocent bystanders as intended victims.

In communities such as Los Angeles, the number of innocent bystanders injured or killed each year is in the hundreds. Los Angeles police estimate that members of street gangs are involved in more than 90% of all drive-by shootings (Petersen, 2004). These acts of violence generate the fear that, in turn, gives gangs power in the community.

While not all gangs are violent, violent gang activity is a growing problem in the country. These gangs draw the attention of the media, offenses have become more violent and more lethal weapons are being used, resulting in more serious injuries and death. While gangs are certainly a part of the problem, it is unclear whether the problems are primarily due to organized street gangs, law-breaking youth groups, or nongang–related youth. Gangs have moved eastward from the West Coast. The rival gangs, the Bloods and Crips have migrated from the Los Angeles area to 45 or more Western and Midwestern communities. It is uncertain if this migration is due primarily to family migration or deliberate gang relocation and expansion. There is ample evidence to indicate that some gang members are involved in drug use and have been involved in narcotics trafficking and drug-related killings. What is uncertain is whether the gang involvement is an organized effort, or primarily the acts of individuals who happen to be gang members. Most gang on gang violence is the result of turf disputes and some of the violence attributed to drug wars may be more related to turf wars.

The variables that contribute to gang membership and the reasons for the violent nature of many of the gangs are multifaceted. So too are the means to combat the problem. Either the solutions to ending gang membership have not yet been found, or the will to solve the problems has not yet been resolved.

Gang membership is usually structured by race or national origin. Actual estimates of gang membership vary, but indications are that whites comprise less than 15%, with the majority of members being African Americans or another group of color—usually Hispanic (Petersen, 2004).

Most visible among these gangs are Latino, African American, and Asian gangs, and Jamaican posses. Latino gangs tend to operate out of barrios and are some of the older gangs in existence. Some gang members belong to the same gangs that their fathers did before them. Among the best-known gangs are the African American Bloods and the Crips. The Crips began in the Los Angeles area as high school youth who extorted money from classmates and were involved in other violence. Both gangs have extended well beyond Los Angeles, spreading as far north as Alaska and as far east as Washington, DC, and making inroads in communities across the country.

Asian gangs are most prominent in Chinese and Vietnamese communities. Among the Chinese gangs, the Yu Li, Joe Boys, and Wah Ching are the most prominent. In Massachusetts, the Asian Boyz, Asian Crips, Asian Family/AR-Z, and Blood Red Dragons are comprised primarily of individuals with Southeast Asian backgrounds (Cambodian, Laotian,

Vietnamese). Asian gangs are, by their own choice, less visible but capable of the same levels of violence as the other ethnic gangs. It is believed that some Asian gangs have ties to organized crime groups in Asia, such as the Hong Kong and Mainland China triads. They also have spread across the United States and Canada (Lindberg, 2002). These Asian gangs typically target other Asians who are distrustful of law enforcement and reluctant to participate in attempts to prosecute. Their typical activities include gambling, extortion, theft of luxury cars to ship overseas, and smuggling of illegal immigrants.

Gang members are usually identifiable by their clothing, communication, graffiti, and tattoos. Bloods and Crips often wear bandannas on their heads. The color of the Bloods is red; the Crips, blue. Clothing may identify individuals as gang members. Gang-specific clothing may include jackets or sweatshirts with gang names. Tattoos on the hands, arms, and shoulders are common among Latino gang members but are not usually displayed by African American gang members. Hand signs may identify an individual with a specific gang.

Graffiti used by gangs can provide considerable information. African American and Latino gang graffiti differ from one another: Black gang graffiti often contains profanity and other expressions that are absent from Latino gang graffiti. Latino gang graffiti has more flair and more attention to detail. Gangs use graffiti to stake a claim to turf. If the graffiti is crossed out and new graffiti written, another gang is challenging the former's claim to the turf. Through careful observation, law enforcement can determine the sphere of influence a gang has. Graffiti will indicate where the gang has unchallenged influence and where challenges begin and by whom.

Gang Violence and America's Schools.   In inner-city schools, gang members may be involved with student extortion and teacher intimidation. Violence occasionally erupts on school campuses. The presence of several gang members in the same class may be intimidating to teachers, as well as to other students. Discipline in such classes may be a considerable challenge.

The emergence of street gangs over the past three decades has become a major challenge for educators. In some instances, schools have become scenes of violence resulting in the installation of metal detectors and the hiring of security guards at the schools. If law enforcement is unable to stem the growth of gang violence, it is unlikely that educators are any better equipped to do so. As with other issues related to youth, gang participation is often a function of poverty. It disproportionately affects individuals of color because they are disproportionately affected by poverty. Calhoun and Chapple (2003) argue that poor family relationships frequently are one characteristic of gang youth. Compared to nongang youth, gang members are more likely to experience family conflict, live in single-parent homes, and to receive poor supervision. There are white gangs as well. Some of the white gangs are involved in hate groups, such as the "skinheads." Gang membership gives the disenfranchised perceived visibility and status. It provides a sense of acceptance and, at times, a substitute for family. It may even provide the individual an income from illegal activities. Somehow, society has failed to provide better alternatives than gang membership. Perhaps that is one of the major challenges for education.

The Hip-Hop Culture

Already accounting for billions of dollars in sales, music, clothing, and related industry giants seek to entice hip-hop enthusiasts into buying their products. Rap and rap music are a major part of the **hip-hop culture.** Rap may be described as a rhythmic delivery of rhymes, with or without music. Snoop Doggy Dogg and Kanye West are among the better-known rap artists. Rap artists have been under increasing criticism for their frequent use of sexist, racist, and violence-laced verbiage and lyrics. Another aspect of the rap music culture is **breakdancing** (a.k.a. b-boying, b-girling), an improvised form of dancing with intricate and sometimes acrobatic moves. Michael Jackson used breakdancing in some of his music videos.

Young Adulthood

Young adulthood is typically defined as ages 18 to 24 (Jekielek & Brown, 2005). Young adulthood is a critical period in the life of an individual because it is the time when one's hopes and aspirations begin to take shape or for some, when one's dreams are shattered. The latter is often the case for the millions of low-income and disenfranchised young Americans. We include this section here because this is the period when many who seek careers in education begin their preservice preparation, and for some others, begin their teaching careers.

To some people, the young adult years represent the best years of their lives. To others, it is a time of important decision making, coupled with stress and sometimes pain. Young adults are often under pressure to make some of the most important decisions they will ever make in their lives. Some decisions are awesome because of the impact they may have on the rest of an individual's life. Decisions must be made about education beyond high school; vocational choices must be made; and decisions regarding a mate, marriage, and children may be made during this period. It can be extremely stressful for an 18- to 20-year-old to make a decision of what college he or she wants to attend and what career choice they will pursue, which can have an impact on their entire life.

Physical vitality, the acquisition of new knowledge on the college campus, the making of new lifelong friends, the excitement of courtship and marriage, the planning or the actual birth of children, and new careers can bring considerable pleasure to individuals during this period of life. At the same time, unwise choices in education or vocation along with frustration in courtship and in relationships can bring frustration and emotional pain. To many Americans in poverty, young adulthood brings the reality that they are among the disenfranchised in this country. If they are among the minority groups frequently targeted for discriminatory practices, life can be particularly difficult. Lack of financial resources may make the reality of a higher education elusive. Good jobs are particularly difficult to find because preference is often given to members of the dominant group and to individuals from more favored minority groups. During a recession, these individuals tend to be the most affected. They may suffer from abject poverty, unemployment, and poor living conditions and are not likely to escape from this life. Frustration and anger appear to be inevitable, along with an intense feeling of impotence.

Those with strong family support and connections are often able to gain entrance in prestigious colleges and universities and upon graduation receive generous and sometimes highly satisfying employment options. While we hear examples of the individuals who succeed in spite of humble backgrounds, they are more often the exception rather than the rule.

Jekielek and Brown (2005) provide a snapshot of young adults in the United States at the time of the 2000 U.S. Census. At the time of the last census there were 27.1 million individuals ages 18 to 24 living in the United States, representing 9.6% of the total population. If this same percentage holds, for 2008, we could expect the total to be around 29,000,000. Over a fourth (27%) of these young adults live in just three states, California, New York, and Texas.

Sixty-two percent of young adults are white, 17% Hispanic, 14% black, 4% Asian/ Pacific Islanders, and less than 1% American Indian/Alaskan Native. Among young adults 21 to 24, 18% had not graduated from high school, with the foreign-born accounting for a third of this group (Jekielek & Brown, 2005).

Fourteen percent of young adults were disconnected from productive activities (e.g., school, employment, military) with no more than a high school diploma or GED. One in four black, Hispanic, and American Indians ages 18 to 24 were disconnected (Jekielek & Brown, 2005).

Over half of the young adults no longer lived with their parents or other relatives. Twenty-seven percent had formed their own households and 24% were living in a household with a nonrelative (e.g., roommates, unmarried partner, in college dorm). Among those in this group 18.5% report being married in 2000. Those who married as teens were two to three times more likely to divorce compared to those who married later (Jekielek & Brown, 2005).

Generation Y

Generation Y are the children of baby boomers, and the younger siblings of **Generation X.** Martin and Tulgan (2001) describe members of Generation Y (Yers) as the fourteenth generation of Americans. There is no clear-cut definition for Generation Y. For our purposes, we will use one of the definitions cited by Amour (2005) that Generation Y includes individuals born between 1978 and 1989. This group would likely include at least 60 million Americans. With this definition, the youngest are just finishing high school and entering college or possibly have already entered the workplace, where their presence will grow for many more years. In addition to being tagged Generation Y, they have been called Echo Boomers because they echo their parents' generation. They may also be called the Millennium Generation.

This cohort of young Americans has grown up in a society identified with crack cocaine, designer drugs, and an AIDS epidemic. While growing up, the older members of this cohort watched on TV the Los Angeles riots following the Rodney King incident, the O. J. Simpson trial, the Branch Davidian standoff, the Oklahoma City bombing, Atlanta's Olympic Park bombing, the Columbine and Virginia Tech shootings, the destruction of the World Trade Center, and the wars in Afghanistan and Iraq. While they have never been concerned about the Russians dropping a nuclear bomb on the United States, they are aware of possible Iranian and North Korean nuclear capabilities, have had to avoid areas of known street gang banging (activity), go through airport security, and consider the threat of a terrorist attack.

Martin and Tulgan (2001) describe the Generation Y group as more positive about their future than Generation X. Most have an optimistic outlook on life and work and expect to be better off financially than their parents. This is in sharp contrast to Generation Xers, who had been told that they would be the first generation in the history of the country to be worse off than their parents.

Martin and Tulgan (2001) describe the Yers as the "self-esteem generation." Because humanistic theories of childrearing permeated parenting efforts, this group reaped the benefits of greater involvement of both parents. In addition, this group has ended up the most technologically astute group that parents and educators have seen. Their ability to utilize technology and access information leaves many in the older generations in awe. They are the first generation to grow up with 500 TV channels including high definition, to design their own websites, and to have the ability to access people worldwide through their computers. I-Pods, MySpace, and YouTube are an everyday part of their lives.

This group of young Americans may be the most education-minded generation in history. Between the influence of their boomer parents who tend to value education, and the workplace, which demands it, Yers generally have embraced education. Martin and Tulgan (2001) report that 90% of high school seniors indicate that they will attend college, 70% expect to have professional positions, 70% believe that a college degree is essential to meet their career goals, and 40% of college freshmen indicated that they plan to pursue a master's degree.

One of the most encouraging characteristics of Generation Yers is that they are perhaps the most tolerant generation in this country's history. Because they themselves are products of interracial or multicultural marriages or are friends of those who may be, they tend to rail against racism, sexism, and homophobia.

A *60 Minutes* segment (2004) characterized them as overachieving, overmanaged, and pressured. Their parents have felt that they needed structure, so they were or are heavily programmed with organized activities. Because, as a group, they have been so highly valued by their parents, they view themselves as special. They in turn tend to be very close to their parents, and many consider their parents to be their best friends. Unlike some earlier generations they prefer rules to rebellion, and choose teamwork to individualism. Violent crime, substance abuse, and teen pregnancy are all down with most in this generation (*60 Minutes,* 2004).

Twenge, Konrath, Foster, Campbell, and Bushman (2007) suggest that parental efforts to boost the self-esteem of their children may have backfired. Generation Y as a group have become more narcissistic than their older Generation X siblings. Twenge with other researchers across the country studied 16,000 college students who were given psychological surveys to determine if they had narcissistic personalities. The study found that

Pause to Reflect 9.4

We have often seen children from Generation Y and now Generation Z with highly structured lives. Parents are involving their children in one organized activity after another, from weekly matches during soccer season to basketball leagues for both boys and girls. We also see parents freer with praise than earlier generations. University professors frequently complain of grade inflation and students expecting "A's" and no less than a "B" simply because they attend a class. If some of the literature is accurate indicating that these young people are naïve and entering the workplace with unrealistic expectations, are we doing our children a disservice?

- Do we need to temper our praise more realistically?
- Are we indeed experiencing grade inflation?
- Do we need to prepare our children better for the real world of hard work and competition?

Go to the *Homework and Exercises* section in Chapter 9 of MyEducationLab and select *Pause to Reflect* 9.4 to answer these questions.

other important persons in their lives. Knowledge can eliminate fear of the unknown as students begin to move into different age groups at different times in their lives. It is important that issues related to age groups be appropriately introduced into the curriculum because students need to understand the concept of ageism. Just as the school assists students in understanding the problem of racism, the school should be responsible for helping students understand the aged and dispel the myths related to this group. Field trips to retirement homes or visits to the class by senior citizens may provide useful experiences. As students become aware of the nature and characteristics of each age group, they will develop perceptions of each individual, regardless of age, as being an important and integral part of society.

It is critically important for educators to understand age as it relates to both students and their parents. Understanding the particular age group characteristics and needs of students can assist the educator in better understanding and managing age-related behavior, such as reactions or responses to peer-group pressure. Understanding the nature of parents, siblings, and other important individuals (e.g., grandparents) will assist the educator in parent-teacher relationships and in helping students cope with their interactions with others. For example, as an elderly grandparent moves into the family setting, this event may affect a child and his or her classroom behavior.

The school is perhaps in the best position of any agency in the community to observe the effects of child abuse. The classroom teacher is an important agent in detecting and reporting abuse and in all states is required by law to do so. To do this, the teacher must be aware of the problem of abuse, the manifestations of abuse, and the proper authorities to which abuse is reported. If the teacher's immediate supervisor is unresponsive to the reporting of a potential abuse problem, the teacher should then continue to seek help until competent and concerned individuals in positions of authority provide it.

The single most important factor in determining possible child abuse is the physical condition of the child. Telltale marks, bruises, and abrasions that cannot be adequately explained may provide reason to suspect abuse. Unusual changes in the child's behavior patterns, such as extreme fatigue, may be reason to suspect problems. The parents' behavior and their ability or lack of ability to explain the child's condition and the social features of the family may be reason to suspect abuse. Although physical abuse or neglect may tend to have observable indicators, sexual abuse may occur with few, if any, obvious indicators. Adults may be unwilling to believe what a child says and may be hesitant to report alleged incidents. There is no typical profile of the victim, and the physical signs vary. Behavioral manifestations are usually exhibited by the victims but are often viewed as insignificant or attributed to typical childhood stress. Chronic depression, isolation from peers, apathy, and suicide attempts are some of the more serious behavioral manifestations of the problem.

The number of children and youth infected by the HIV virus and other sexually transmitted diseases is a national tragedy. Prevention efforts must be multifaceted if these diseases are to be eradicated. The school has a major role to play, and there are specific steps, that can be taken. School-based programs are critical in reaching youth before they engage in risky behaviors. Topics such as HIV, STDs, unintended pregnancy, and tobacco and other drug abuse should be integrated into the curriculum and should be an ongoing program for all students, kindergarten through high school. The development of these programs should be done carefully and should take into consideration parent and community values.

The majority of suicides are planned and are not committed on impulse, and most suicide victims mention their intentions to someone. Often, a number of warning signs can alert teachers, other professionals, and parents. Educators should take these signs seriously (see Table 9.4).

If teachers or other school personnel suspect trouble, friendly, low-key questions or statements may provide an appropriate opening: "You seem down today" or "It seems like something is bothering you." If an affirmative response is given, a more direct and probing (but supportive) question may be asked. If there is any reason whatsoever to suspect a possible suicide attempt, teachers and other school staff should alert the appropriate school personnel. Teachers should recognize their limitations and avoid making judgments. The matter should be referred to the school psychologist, who should, in turn, alert a competent medical authority (psychiatrist) and the child's parents. Assistance can also be obtained from local mental health clinics and suicide prevention centers. Prompt action may save a life.

Our coverage of adolescent substance abuse has been brief. But the importance of the problem is such that every educator should be aware of the problem and work toward providing children at an early age with appropriate drug education. No agency, group, or individual can wage an effective campaign against substance abuse alone. Only with a united effort can an effective battle be waged. Possible symptoms of alcohol or drug abuse among adolescents often overlap with those of individuals who are at risk for suicide. The Partnership for a Drug Free America (2006) provides some possible physical symptoms of individuals involved in substance abuse:

- Change in sleeping patterns
- Bloodshot eyes
- Slurred or agitated speech
- Sudden or dramatic weight loss or gain
- Skin abrasions/bruises
- Neglected appearance/poor hygiene
- Sick more frequently
- Accidents or injuries

Some possible behavioral symptoms of substance abuse include (Dorsey, Jaffe, Slotnick, Smith, & Segal, 2007):

- Negative schoolwork changes
- Increased secrecy about possessions or activities
- Use of incense, room deodorant, or perfume (to hide smoke or chemical odors)
- Subtle changes in conversations with friends (more secretive, using "coded" language)
- "New friends"
- Increase in borrowing money
- Frequent use of mouthwash or breath mints (covering up alcohol)

In the event these signs are observed in the classroom, the school nurse should be notified immediately. If none is available, then someone trained in CPR should be summoned. It would be advisable for a list of all personnel with CPR training to be made available to all teachers and other staff.

As parents hurry children into adulthood, educators may also contribute to the hurrying process. Teachers, administrators, and support personnel should be cognizant of the fact that the children they teach and work with are children, and not miniature adults. Children have but one opportunity to experience the wonders of childhood. In comparison with adulthood, childhood and adolescence are relatively short periods of time, and these young people should have every opportunity to enjoy these stages of their lives to the fullest extent possible.

Summary

The study of age as a function of culture is important to educators because it helps them understand how the child or adolescent struggles to win peer acceptance and to balance this effort with the need for parental approval. In some instances, the pressures from peers are not congruent with those from the home.

As each child develops into adolescence, we observe a growing need for independence. Adolescence for some is a time of storm and stress; for others, it passes with little or no trauma.

Young adulthood is one of the most exciting times in life. It is a time for courtship, marriage, children, and career choices. It is a time when individuals reach their physical and occupational prime. Young adulthood can also be a threatening time because choices made at this time often have a lifetime impact on the individual.

PROFESSIONAL PRACTICE FOR EDUCATORS

Questions for Discussion

1. Explain why child abuse is a problem, and cite some of the signs of child abuse.
2. When does ethnic identification begin in children, and how is it manifested?
3. Describe some variables that contribute to prejudice in children.
4. What are the variables that contribute to childhood obesity, why is it a problem, and what can the schools do to help the problem?
5. What are the sources of alienation between adolescents and their families?
6. What is the extent of substance abuse among adolescents, and what are some of the underlying causes of substance use in this age group?
7. What are the causes of adolescent suicide, and what are the warning signs?
8. How does Generation Y differ from Generation Z?

Portfolio Activities

1. Interview three teachers from three different schools and ask them what their school policy is in reporting suspected child abuse of their students. (INTASC Standard 10)
2. Interview teachers or administrators from schools to find out what their policy is on zero tolerance or if there is no zero tolerance policy, what measures are taken for students who carry weapons or drugs to school. (INTASC Standard 10)

Licensure Test Prep

Ms. Narzisi is a middle school teacher in an urban school district. Nearly all of her students come from low-income families and it is not uncommon for her to observe some of her students with various health problems, which sometimes seem to be prolonged. Whenever she is particularly concerned about a student, she contacts the school nurse. Because there is only one nurse and the school is large, there is a limit to what can be done.

One student, however, is of particular concern to Ms. Narzisi. The student has been coming to school with marks and bruises on her face, arms, and legs. There are some other suspicious behaviors that alarm the concerned teacher.

Short Answer Questions

1. What are some of the telltale signs of possible abuse to a child?
2. In this day of enlightened childrearing practices, how realistic is it to think a child might actually be physically abused?
3. Should Ms. Narzisi call the child's mother and express her concern?
4. What prudent steps should the teacher take?
5. Is she required to report her concerns or wait a while and hope that the matter will resolve itself?

Go to the *Homework and Exercises* section in Chapter 9 of MyEducationLab and select *Licensure Test Prep* to complete this exercise.

Suggested Readings

Centers for Disease Control and Prevention. www. cdc.gov/.
This government website provides a wealth of information on issues such as adolescent sexual behaviors, suicide, child maltreatment and abuse, substance abuse, and so forth.

References

Aboud, F. (1988). *Children and prejudice.* Cambridge, MA: Basil Blackwell.

Aboud, F., & Doyle, A. B. (1996a). Does talk of race foster prejudice or tolerance in children? *Canadian Journal of Behavioral Science, 28* (3), 1–14.

Aboud, F., & Doyle, A. B. (1996b). Parental and peer influence on children's racial attitudes. *International Journal of Intercultural Relations, 20,* 371–383.

American Academy of Pediatrics. (2000). *Some things you should know about media literacy.* Retrieved September 3, 2004, from www.aap.org/advocacy/childhealthmonth/media.htm

American Academy of Pediatrics. (2004). Committee on Adolescence. *Homosexuality and adolescence.* Retrieved September 3, 2004, from wwww.medem.com/search/article_display.cfm?path=\\TANQUERAY\M_ContentItem&mstr=/M_ContentItem/ZZZUHJP3KAC.html&soc=AAP&srch_typ=NAV_SERCH

Amour, S. (2005, November 6). Generation Y: They've arrived at work with a new attitude. *USA Today,* www.usatoday.com/money/workplace/2005-11-06-gen-y_x.htm

Annie E. Casey Foundation. (2007). *Kids count.* Baltimore, MD: Author.

Anti-Defamation League. (2004). *What to tell your child about prejudice and discrimination.* Retrieved September 3, 2004, from wadl.org/what_to_tell/whattotell_intro.asp

Barrett, B., & Browne, P. W. (2004, September 27). Gangs outnumber police. *San Gabriel Valley Tribune,* p. A1, A6.

Bartollas, C., & Miller, S. (2005). *Juvenile justice in America.* Upper Saddle River, NJ: Prentice Hall.

Beloit College Mindset List: Class of 2010. (2007). Retrieved June 2, 2007, from www.beloit.edu/~pubaff/mindset/2010.php

Bigler, R., & Liben, L. (1993). A cognitive development approach to racial stereotyping and reconstructive memory in Euro-American children. *Child Development, 64,* 1507–1519.

Burros, M. (2007, April 26). Panel suggests junk food ban in schools to help fight obesity. *The New York Times,* p. A22 (L).

Calhoun, T. C., & Chapple, C. L. (2003). *Readings in juvenile delinquency and juvenile justice.* Upper Saddle River, NJ: Prentice Hall.

Cannon, A., Streisand, B., & McGraw, D. (1999, May 3). Why? *U.S. News and World Report, 26*(17), 16–19.

Cauthen, N. K., & Fass, S. (2007). *Measuring income and poverty in the United States.* New York: National Center for Children in Poverty, www.nccp.org/publications/show.php?id=707

Centers for Disease Control and Prevention. (2000). *Facts about violence among youth and violence in schools.* Retrieved September 3, 2004, from www.cdc.gov/ncipc/factsheets/schoolvi.htm

Centers for Disease Control and Prevention. (2003a). *U.S. pregnancy rate down from peak; births and abortion on the decline.* Atlanta, GA: Author

Centers for Disease Control and Prevention. (2005). *HIV/AIDS among youth.* Retrieved from www.thebody.com/content/whatis/art17110.html

Centers for Disease Control and Prevention. (2006a). *Child maltreatment: Facts at a glance.* Retrieved from www.cdc.gov/ncipc/factsheets/cmfacts.htm

Centers for Disease Control and Prevention, National Center for Injury Prevention and Control. (2006b February 8). Web-based Injury Statistics Query and Reporting System (WISQARS) [online]. Retrieved from http://www.cdc.gov/ncipc/wisqars

Centers for Disease Control and Prevention. (2007a). *Child maltreatment: Fact sheet.* www.cdc.gov/ncipc/cmprfact.htm

Centers for Disease Control and Prevention. (2007b). *Overweight and obesity introduction.* Retrieved May 22, 2007, from http://www.cdc.gov/nccdphp/dnpa/obesity/index.htm

Centers for Disease Control and Prevention. (2007c). *Sexual risk behaviors.* Retrieved from www.cdc.gov/HealthyYouth/sexualbehaviors/index.htm

Centers for Disease Control and Prevention. (2007d). *Healthy youth: Unintentional injuries, violence, and the health of young people.* Retrieved January 3, 2007, from www.cdc.gov/healthyyouth/injury/facts.htm

Centers for Disease Control and Prevention. (2007e, Winter). *Youth violence: Facts at a glance.* Retrieved from www.cdc.gov/ncip/dvp/dvp.htm

Champion, D. (2004). *Juvenile justice system: Delinquency, processing, and the law* (4th ed.). Upper Saddle River, NJ: Prentice Hall.

Childhelp, Inc. (2003). *National child abuse statistics.* Retrieved September 3, 2004, from www.childhelpusa.org/pdf/stats2003.pdf

Child Welfare Information Gateway. (2006). *What is child abuse and neglect?* Washington, DC: U.S. Department of Health and Human Services, www.childwelfare.gov

Department of Health and Human Services (DHHS) (US), Administration on Children, Youth, and Families (ACF). (2005, April 5). *Child maltreatment 2003* [online]. Washington DC: U.S. Government Printing Office. Retrieved from http://www.acf.hhs.gov/programs/cb/pubs/cm03/index.htm

Dorsey, J., Jaffe, J., Slotnick, J., Smith, M., & Segal, R. (2007). *Drug abuse and addiction: Signs, symptoms, and effects.* HelpGuide.org. Retrieved from www.helpguide.org/mental/drug_substance_abuse_addiction_signs_effects_treatment.htm#signssymptoms

Douglas-Hall, A., Chau, M., & Koball, H. (2006). *Basic facts about low-income children birth to age 18.* New York: National Center for Children in Poverty, www.nccp.org/publications/pub_678.html

Doyle, A. B., & Aboud, F. E. (1995). A longitudinal study of white children's racial prejudice as a social cognitive development. *Merrill-Palmer Quarterly, 41,* 210–220.

Drakeford, W., & Garfinkel, L. F. (n.d.). *Differential treatment of African American youth.* Retrieved May 2007, from The National Center on Education, Disability and Juvenile Justice, http://www.edjj.org/Publications/pub_06_13_00_2.html

Eamon, M. K. (2001, July). The effects of poverty on children's socioemotional development: An ecological systems analysis. *Social Work, 46* (3), 256.

Eaton, D. (2006). *Youth risk behavior surveillance—United States, 2005*. Centers for Disease Control and Prevention. Retrieved from www.cdc.gov/mmwr/preview/mmwrhtml/ss5505a1.htm

The Federal Child Abuse and Treatment Act, 1972 (amended 1978, 1984, 1988, 1992, 1996, 2003) US. Code: Title 42, 5106g. definitions

Free The Children. (2003). *Child poverty in the U.S.* Retrieved September 3, 2004, from www.freethechildren.org/youthinaction/child_poverty_usa.htm

Geck, C. (2006, February). The generation Z connection: Teaching information literacy to the newest net generation. *Teacher Librarian, 33*(3), 19(5).

Jekielek, S., & Brown, B. (2005). *The transition to adulthood: characteristics of young adults ages 18 to 24 in America*. Baltimore: Annie E. Casey Foundation, Population Reference Bureau, and Child Trends.

Journal of Physical Education, Recreation and Dance (JOPERD). (2007). Early childhood obesity deserves attention, *78* (4), 3(1). Author.

Justice Policy Institute. (2005, October 3). *Crime, race, and juvenile justice policy in perspective*. Retrieved from www.justicepolicy.org/FTC_Crime_race_juvenile05.doc

Kratcoski, P. C., & Kratcoski, L. D. (2004). *Juvenile delinquency* (5th ed.). Upper Saddle River, NJ: Prentice Hall.

Levine, M. (2004). Echo boomers. Interview on *60 Minutes* [Television series episode]. October 3, 2004, CBS, Steve Kroft, narrator.

Lindberg, R. C. (2002). *Spotlight on Asian organized crime*. Schaumburg, IL: Search International. Retrieved September 3, 2004, from www.search-international.com/WhatsNew/WNasiangangs.htm

Los Angeles Times [Associated Press]. (2004, June 11). Suicide Among Young Down 25%, p A 31.

Lotz, R. (2005). *Youth crime in America: A modern synthesis*. Upper Saddle River, NJ: Prentice Hall.

Martin, C. A., & Tulgan, B. (2001). *Managing Generation Y*. Amherst, MA: HRD Press.

McGreevy, P., & Winton, R. (2007, January 10). L.A. shifts tactics against gangs. *Los Angeles Times*, p. B1, B8.

National Clearinghouse on Child Abuse and Neglect Information. (2004). *Child maltreatment 2002: Summary of key findings*.

The Partnership for a Drug Free America. (2006). *Signs someone is using drugs or alcohol—physical signs*. Retrieved from www.drugfree.org/Intervention/Articles/Signs_Someone_Is_Using

Petersen, R. D. (2004). *Understanding contemporary gangs in America: An interdisciplinary approach*. Upper Saddle River, NJ: Prentice Hall.

Prothrow-Stith, D., & Spivak, H. R. (2004). *Murder is no accident: Understanding and preventing youth violence in America*. San Francisco: Jossey-Bass.

Sixty (60) Minutes. (2004, October 3). Echo boomers [Television series episode]. 2004, CBS, Steve Kroft, narrator.

Sleek, S. (1997, October). People's racist attitudes can be unlearned. *APA Monitor*, 38.

Tatum, B. D. (1997). *Why are all the black kids sitting together in the cafeteria?* New York: Basic Books.

Twenge, J. M., Konrath, S., Foster, J. D., Campbell, W. K., & Bushman, B. J. (2007). *Egos inflating over time: A cross-temporal analysis of the Narcissistic Personality Inventory*. Unpublished manuscript.

U.S. Census Bureau. (2006). *People in families by family structure, age, and sex, iterated by income-to-poverty ratio and race: 2005—Below 100% of Poverty—all races*. Retrieved from http://pubdb3.census.gov/macro/032006/pov/new02_100_01.htm

U.S. Census Bureau. (2007). *Poverty thresholds 2006*. Retrieved from www.census.gov/hhes/www/poverty/threshld/thresh06.html

U.S. Newswire. (2007, April 4). Robert Wood Johnson Foundation announces $500 million commitment to reverse childhood obesity in U.S., p. NA. Author.

Woodward, H. (2006, September 3). A lunchroom without junk food: South Sound schools offering more nutritious options. *Olympian* (Olympia, WA), p. NA.

Youth Violence Prevention Resource Center. (2004). Youth Suicide fact sheet. Retrieved September 3, 2004 from http://www.safeyouth.org/scripts/facts/suicide.asp

Chapter 10

EDUCATION THAT IS MULTICULTURAL

We must be the change we wish to see in the world.

MAHATMA GANDHI

Natisha Loftis had not said a word to any of her teachers since the beginning of school. It's not that she was a "bad" student; she turned in assignments and made Bs. She certainly didn't cause her teachers trouble. Therefore, the high school counselor, Mr. Williams, was somewhat surprised to hear that she was dropping out of school. He had been Natisha's advisor for more than two years, but he didn't really remember her. Nevertheless, it was his job to conduct interviews with students who were leaving school for one reason or another.

Natisha described her school experiences as coming to school, listening to teachers, and going home. School was boring and not connected at all to her real life, in which she had the responsibility for helping her father raise five brothers and sisters. She might even be able to get a job with the same cleaning firm that her dad worked for. For sure, nothing she was learning in school could help her get a job. And she knew from more than 10 years of listening to teachers and reading textbooks that her chances of becoming a news anchorwoman or even a teacher were about the same as winning the lottery. The last time a teacher had even asked about her family was in the sixth grade, when her mom left. The only place anyone paid attention to her was in church.

School had helped silence Natisha. Classes provided no meaningful experience for her. The content may have been important to the teachers, but she could find no relationship to her own world.

Reflections

1. Why has Natisha decided to drop out of school?
2. How can the curriculum be made more meaningful to students who are not middle-class white?
3. How can teachers make a student like Natisha excited about learning?

Initiating Multicultural Education

After learning the sociopolitical aspects that provide the framework for multicultural education in the first nine chapters of this book, you are probably wondering how you put it all together to provide education that is multicultural. There is no recipe book that indicates how to respond to students from different cultural groups. For one, differences within groups can be as great as differences among groups. Therefore, the recipe would work for some students, but not all of them. This chapter is designed to provide some suggestions for delivering multicultural education, incorporating the multiple identities of your students into your teaching, and becoming more multicultural yourself.

It is no easy task to incorporate cultural knowledge throughout teaching. In the beginning, you must consciously think about it as you interact with students and plan lessons and assignments. You should approach teaching multiculturally as an enthusiastic learner with much to learn from students and community members who have cultural identities different from your own. You may need to remind yourself that your way of believing, thinking, and acting evolved from your own culture and experiences, which may vary greatly from that of the students in your school. You will need to listen to the histories and experiences of students and their families and integrate them into your teaching. Students' values need to be validated within both their in-school and out-of-school realities—a process that is authentic only if you value the cultures of your students.

Educators are often at a disadvantage because they do not live, or have never lived, in the community in which their students live. Too often, the only parents with whom they interact are those who are able to attend parent-teacher meetings or who have scheduled conferences with them. In many cases, they have not been in their students' homes nor been active participants in the community. How do we begin to learn others' cultures? Using the tools of an anthropologist or ethnographer, we could observe children in classrooms and on playgrounds. We can listen carefully to students and their parents as they discuss their life experiences. We can study other cultures. We can learn about the perspectives of others by reading articles and books written by men and women from different ethnic, racial, socioeconomic, and religious groups. Participation in community, religious, and ethnic activities can provide another perspective on students' cultures.

Our knowledge about our students' cultures will allow us to make the academic content of our teaching more meaningful to students by relating it to their own experiences and building on their prior knowledge. It should help us make them and their histories the center of the education process in our effort to help them reach their academic, vocational, and social potentials. In the process, students should learn to believe in their own abilities and become active participants in their own learning. Students should be able to achieve academically without adopting the dominant culture as their own. They should be able to maintain their own cultural identities inside and outside the school.

Teaching multiculturally requires the incorporation of diversity throughout the learning process. If race, ethnicity, class, and gender are not interrelated in the curriculum, students do not learn that these are interrelated parts of a whole called self. Although Chapters 2 through 9 addressed membership in these cultural groups separately, they should be interwoven throughout our teaching. For example, if activities are developed to fight racism but continue to perpetuate sexism, we are not providing multicultural education. At the same time, we must integrate the experiences of women of color and women in poverty when discussing the impact of sexism and other women's issues.

All teaching should be multicultural and all classrooms should be models of democracy, equity, and social justice. To do this, educators must do the following:

1. Place the student at the center of the teaching and learning process.
2. Promote human rights and respect for cultural differences.
3. Believe that all students can learn.
4. Acknowledge and build on the life histories and experiences of students' group memberships.
5. Critically analyze oppression and power relationships to understand racism, sexism, classism, and discrimination against persons with disabilities and gays, lesbians, the young, and the elderly.
6. Critique society in the interest of social justice and equality.
7. Participate in collective social action to ensure a democratic society.

Teachers and other school personnel can make a difference. Making one's teaching and classroom multicultural is an essential step in empowerment for both teachers and students. Now that you know about the multiple groups to which you and your students belong, how can you put it all together to help students learn? Education that is multicultural incorporates the educational strategies described in Chapters 2 through 9, but moves beyond them to a holistic approach to teaching all students and confronting the barriers that prevent many students from being able to access the education that is so critical to their future.

Remember that multicultural education is for all students, not just English language learners or students of color. European American students also belong to a racial and ethnic group and need to understand how their group has been privileged in schools. A strength of multicultural education is that we learn about our similarities and differences as we struggle to provide equity for all people. Students who are in segregated classrooms or in communities with little religious, language, ethnic, and racial diversity need to learn about the pluralistic world in which they live and the role they can play in providing social justice in their communities and beyond. Social justice and equity are part of our commitment to a democratic society.

Focus on Learning

Multicultural teachers care that all of their students learn regardless of the obstacles they face because of their disabilities or economic conditions that limit their social capital. These teachers recognize when some students are not learning, reach out to them, and try different pedagogical strategies to help them learn. They do not allow students to sit in their classroom without being engaged with the content. They do not ignore the students who are withdrawn, depressed, or resistant to classroom work. They do everything they can to help students see themselves as learners and value learning.

The focus on learning is not limited to the basic literacy and numeracy skills that all people need to function effectively in society. Multicultural educators help students understand the **big ideas,** the concepts that undergird a subject. They encourage students to question what is written in textbooks and the newspaper and what they see on television and in movies. They do not treat students as receptacles in which knowledge is poured. They help students learn by doing through hands-on activities, community projects, collecting data from their neighborhoods, and testing their ideas.

The Center for Research on Education, Diversity, and Excellence (CREDE) (Viadero, 2004) at the University of California, Santa Cruz, has identified the following five standards as critical to improving the learning of diverse students:

1. ***Teachers and Students Working Together.*** Use instructional group activities in which students and teacher work together to create a product or idea.
2. ***Developing Language and Literacy Skills Across All Curriculum.*** Apply literacy strategies and develop language competence in all subject areas.
3. ***Connecting Lessons to Students' Lives.*** Contextualize teaching and curriculum in students' existing experiences in home, community, and school.
4. ***Engaging Students with Challenging Lessons.*** Maintain challenging standards for student performance; design activities to advance understanding to more complex levels.
5. ***Emphasizing Dialogue over Lectures.*** Instruct through teacher-student dialogue, especially academic, goal-directed, small-group conversations (known as instructional conversations), rather than lecture. (CREDE, 2004, p. 1)

Researchers at CREDE have tested and refined these standards in a number of schools with diverse populations. Lesson plans and multimedia resources for using the standards, as well as research reports, can be found at CREDE's website at www.crede.ucsc.edu/. These five standards are key in culturally responsive teaching, which is discussed in the next section of this chapter.

A key to helping students learn is to connect the curriculum to their culture and real-world experiences. They should be able to see themselves in the curriculum to provide meaning for their own lives. Otherwise, they may resist the curriculum and learning, which are seen as the dominant culture's way of denigrating their culture. The remainder of this chapter proposes pedagogies or teaching strategies that will help educators deliver education that is multicultural education.

Pause to Reflect 10.1

The most important goal of teaching is to help students learn. The problem is that some teachers do not accept this challenge, encouraging some students to learn at high levels while allowing other students to learn little.

- How will you know that students are learning?
- Do you believe that all students can learn? Why or why not?
- How will you relate the subject that you are teaching to the lives of your students?

Go to the *Homework and Exercises* section in Chapter 10 of MyEducationLab and select *Pause to Reflect 10.1* to answer these questions.

Supporting Dispositions

Education that is multicultural requires teachers and other school personnel to have dispositions that support learning for students from diverse populations. **Dispositions** are the values, commitments, and professional ethics that influence teaching and interactions with students, families, colleagues, and communities. An educator's dispositions affect student learning, motivation, and development as well as the educator's own professional growth. They are guided by beliefs and attitudes related to values such as caring, fairness, honesty, responsibility, and social justice (National Council for the Accreditation of Teacher Education, 2002). If a teacher's interaction with students is disrespectful and disparaging of the student's culture and experiences, the teacher will be incapable of delivering multicultural education. Educators with the dispositions outlined in Chapter 1 will be able to build on the cultures and experiences of students from diverse backgrounds to support and extend academic learning.

A list of professional dispositions can be found in Chapter 1.

One of the characteristics of teachers who are successful in working with students from diverse populations is caring. As part of their caring, they have high expectations for academic achievement and push students to achieve at those levels.

Anne Vega/Merrill

Culturally Responsive Teaching

Culturally responsive teaching is an essential component of education that is multicultural. This pedagogy affirms the cultures of students, views the cultures and experiences of students as strengths, and reflects the students' cultures in the teaching process. It is based on the premise that culture influences the way students learn (Darling-Hammond, French, & García-Lopez, 2002; Gay, 2000). It also moves beyond the dominant **canon** of knowledge and ways of knowing. "Students are taught to be proud of their ethnic identities and cultural backgrounds instead of being apologetic or ashamed of them" (Gay, 2000, p. 34).

In this section we will explore elements of the teaching-learning process that should be considered and developed to become a culturally responsive teacher. Begin now to incorporate these practices into your own lesson plans and work in classrooms. Look for evidence of these practices as you observe teachers in schools and identify others who support culturally responsive teaching.

Multicultural Curriculum

The curriculum should define the knowledge and skills that students are expected to learn in a course or program. It is also political. Whose story, whose culture, and whose values will be reflected in the curriculum being taught and the supporting textbooks and readings that are assigned? Will students be pushed to assimilate the dominant culture, making its stories their own? Or will the curriculum value the students' cultures and teach them their histories and experiences along with those of the dominant culture? A **multicultural curriculum** supports and celebrates our diversity in the broadest sense; it includes the histories, experiences, traditions, and cultures of students in the classroom. In classrooms with limited diversity, the curriculum introduces them to the major cultural groups in the state or nation.

Regardless of the grade level or subject being taught, the curriculum should be multicultural. The students in your classroom should be able to see themselves and their

Pause to Reflect 10.2

One of the goals of culturally responsive teaching is to validate the cultures of students as you teach. They should see themselves in the curriculum. Think about the following issues:

- How would you feel if you never saw yourself, your family, or your community in the curriculum except in a negative way? What groups are seldom seen in textbooks?
- How could you incorporate the cultures of your students into the subject that you plan to teach?
- Who are some of the women and persons of color who have made outstanding contributions to the subject that you will teach?

Go to the *Homework and Exercises* section in Chapter 10 of MyEducationLab and select *Pause to Reflect 10.2* to answer these questions.

experiences in the curriculum. It is as important for students in a homogeneous setting as for those in more diverse settings to acknowledge and understand the diversity in the United States and the world. Because students in settings with limited diversity do not have the opportunities to interact with persons from other cultural groups, they should learn to value diversity, rather than fear it. They should come to know that others have different perspectives on the world and events that are based in different experiences. The Internet could facilitate interacting with and getting to know persons from other cultures.

Although communities are not always rich in ethnic diversity, they all are diverse. Educators need to determine the cultural groups that exist in the community. Schools that are on or near American Indian reservations will include students from the tribes in the area, as well as non-American Indians. Urban schools typically include multiethnic populations and students from different socioeconomic levels and religions; inner-city schools have a high proportion of low-income and immigrant students. Rural schools include low-income and middle-class families. Teachers who enter schools attended by students from different groups than that of the teacher will need to learn about other cultures. Otherwise, both students and teachers could suffer.

The current traditional curriculum is based on the histories, experiences, and perspectives of the dominant group. The result is the marginalization of the experiences of other groups. Multicultural teaching should tell it as it is. Diversity existed in the United States when Europeans arrived and became greater with each passing century. To teach as if only one group is worthy of inclusion in the curriculum is not to tell the truth. Instructional materials and information about different groups are available to students and teachers. It may be more difficult to find resources on groups where the membership is small or somewhat new to the United States, but it is not impossible. Both students and teachers can use the Internet to locate information, including personal narratives, art, music, and family histories. Although teachers cannot possibly address each of the hundreds of ethnic and religious groups in this country, they should attempt to include the groups represented in the school community, whether or not all of them are represented in the school.

In western Pennsylvania, a teacher should include information about and examples from the Amish. This approach will signal to other students that the diversity in their community is valued. In schools in the Southwest, the culture of Mexican Americans and American Indians should be integrated throughout the curriculum. In other areas of the country, the curriculum should reflect the histories, experiences, and perspectives of Mormons, Muslims, Vietnamese Americans, Lakotas, Jamaican Americans, African Americans, Chinese Americans, Puerto Ricans, and other groups as appropriate. Students should find themselves in the curriculum; otherwise, they are marginalized and do not see themselves as an integral part of the school culture.

Educators are cautioned against giving superficial attention to groups. Multicultural education is much more than food, festivals, and fun, or heroes and holidays. Even celebrating African American history only during February or women's history during March is not multicultural education. It is much more complex and pervasive than setting aside an hour, a unit, or a month. It should become the lens through which the curriculum is presented.

The amount of specific content about different groups will vary according to the course taught, but awareness and recognition of the nation's diversity can be reflected in all classroom experiences and courses. No matter how assimilated students in a classroom are, it is the teacher's responsibility to ensure that they understand diversity, know the contributions of members of both dominant and other groups, and hear the voices of individuals and groups who are from cultural backgrounds different from the majority of students.

Multiculturalism is not a compensatory process to make others more like the dominant group. As an educator integrates diversity into the curriculum, the differences across groups must *not* become deficits to be overcome. Teachers who believe that their own culture is superior to students' cultures will not be able to build the trust necessary to help all students learn. When one first begins to teach multiculturally, extra planning time will be needed to discover ways to make the curriculum and instruction reflect diversity. With experience, however, this process will be internalized. The teacher will begin to recognize immediately what materials are not multicultural and will be able to expand the standard curriculum to reflect diversity and multiple perspectives.

Reflecting Culture in Academic Subjects.

Knowledge about students' cultures is important in teaching subject matter in a way that students can learn it. Culturally responsive teaching increases academic achievement because the subject matter is taught within the cultural context and experiences of the students and the communities served. In this approach, the subject begins to have meaning for students because it relates to their lives and what they know. It validates their experiences.

Teachers must know a subject well to help students learn it. Subject matter competence alone, however, does not automatically translate into student learning. Without an understanding of students' cultures, teachers are unable to develop instructional strategies that can be related to students' life experiences. Interviews with African American teachers who have successfully taught mathematics to black students who speak a dialect confirmed that the use of cultural context and students' prior experiences is essential in helping students learn. One teacher interviewed by Delpit (2006) reported that:

> He found that the same problem that baffled students when posed in terms of distances between two unfamiliar places or in terms of numbers of milk cans needed by a farmer, were much more readily solved when familiar locales and the amount of money needed to buy a leather jacket were substituted. (p. 65)

Including Multiple Perspectives.

It is important for students to learn that individuals from other ethnic, religious, and socioeconomic groups often have perspectives on issues and events that are different from their own. Most members of the dominant group have not had the negative and discriminatory experiences that people of color have had with schools, with the police, in government offices, or in shopping centers. They do not understand the privilege they experience based solely on their skin color. These experiences and the histories of groups provide the lens for viewing the world. Thus, perspectives vary for good reasons. Understanding the reasons makes it easier to accept that most other perspectives are just as valid as one's own. At the same time, perspectives and behaviors that degrade and harm members of specific groups are unacceptable.

Culturally responsive teaching requires examining sensitive issues and topics. It requires looking at historical and contemporary events from the perspective of European American men, African American women, Puerto Ricans, Japanese Americans, Central American immigrants, Jewish Americans, and Southern Baptists. Reading books, poems, and articles by authors from diverse cultures is helpful because it exposes students to the perspectives of other groups.

The community and students may view as untrustworthy teachers and others who are unable to accept alternate perspectives. An example is the inability of whites to see racism in almost everything experienced by African Americans. Even when African American

CRITICAL INCIDENTS IN TEACHING

Teaching About Thanksgiving

Michele Johnson was observing a kindergarten class in a school near her campus during the fall semester of her junior year. She was taking a class in multicultural education at the same time and was expanding her knowledge base regarding groups of color. The week before Thanksgiving, the teacher she was observing gave her materials for students to color for their discussion of the meaning of Thanksgiving. When she looked through the materials, she discovered that the kindergartners were to cut out and decorate headbands that some of them would wear with feathers to give gifts to the pilgrims for Thanksgiving. She was appalled that the teacher was perpetuating stereotypes of First Americans and their relationships with the European settlers. She worried that the students were already learning stories about cultural groups that were inaccurate.

Questions for Classroom Discussion

1. Why does Michele think the project to teach about Thanksgiving is not appropriate?
2. How would you teach kindergartners about Thanksgiving? How would you project First Americans and the pilgrims in relationship to each other?
3. Should Michele say something to the teacher who might later be evaluating her performance? Why or why not?

Building Teaching Skills

Go to the *Building Teaching Skills* section in Chapter 10 of MyEducationLab and select *Critical Incidents in Teaching: Teaching About Thanksgiving* to complete this exercise.

students point out a racist action, many white teachers and students cannot see it, in part, because they have no experience of knowing or feeling racism. Instead of acknowledging it, they often argue that the reporter misinterpreted the action or that the action was not meant to be racist. As a result, many African Americans learn that whites are really not interested in eliminating racism because they never recognize it or choose to ignore it (Tatum, 1997). Immigrant students, other students of color, students with disabilities, and girls and young women have similar narratives that are given little or no credit by many members of the dominant group.

Holding High Expectations

Some teachers respond differently to students because of the students' group identities. They have low expectations for the academic achievement of students of color and students from low-income families. Low expectations are often based on negative generalizations about a group. When these generalizations are applied to all or most students from those groups, grave damage can be done. Students tend to meet the expectations of the teacher, no matter what their actual abilities are. Self-fulfilling prophecies about how well a student will perform in the classroom are often established early in the school year, and both student and teacher unconsciously fulfill those prophecies. Thus, educators should develop strategies to overcome negative expectations they may have for certain students and plan classroom instruction and activities to ensure success for all students.

Cultural group membership cannot become an excuse for students' lack of academic achievement. Empathy with a student's situation (for example, being homeless) is appropriate, but we must prevent it from subsequently lowering our expectations for achievement.

Not all expectations are low. Teachers often expect high achievement from Asian American students. Upper-middle-class students are placed disproportionately in high academic tracks, whereas low-income students are disproportionately placed in low academic tracks. Even when students have no differences in ability, academic tracks reflect race, gender, and class differences. Students who end up in the low-ability classes have limited academic mobility; they rarely are perceived to achieve at a level high enough to move them to the next highest level (Weinstein, 1996). Teaching behavior for high-ability groups is much different than for low-ability groups. Middle-ability groups usually receive treatment more similar to that of high-ability groups. Students in the lowest tracks are often subject to practice and review drills. At the high end of the track, students are engaged in interesting and motivating intellectual activities.

To a large degree, students learn to behave in the manner that is expected of the group in which they are placed. Through tracking, educators have a great influence not only on directing a student's potential but also on determining it by their initial expectations for that student. The sad reality is that tracking does not appear to work, especially if the goal is to improve learning.

Tracking is discussed in more detail in Chapter 3.

Heterogeneous grouping is more helpful in improving academic achievement for students from low-income and oppressed groups. Contrary to popular belief, such grouping does not limit the academic achievement of the most academically talented students, especially when the instruction is geared to challenging them. The students who suffer the most from tracking practices are those from groups who are disproportionately placed in the low-ability groups. Compared with students in other tracks, these students develop more negative feelings about their academic potential and future aspirations. Educational equity demands a different strategy. It requires that all students be academically challenged with stimulating instruction that involves them actively in their own learning.

Caring

One of the complaints of students is that their teachers don't know them and do not care about them. Students indicate that they are more willing to work and perform better when they feel the teachers care about them (Cushman, 2003). However, caring does not mean that teachers are easy on students or permissive, letting them do what the students want. It is not enough to just like the students. A caring teacher has high expectations for students, and pushes students to meet those high expectations.

Caring requires honoring the students and their families. Caring teachers have overcome their racial biases and do not stereotype students because they do not know their father, their parents are gay, their mother is on drugs, or they wear the same clothes day after day. They do not punish students because they do not conform to the dominant culture's expectations for normalcy. They do not label students or "find them unlovable, problematic, and difficult to honor or embrace without equivocation" (Gay, 2000, p. 46) because they have different group memberships than the teacher.

What are the characteristics of caring teachers? They are patient, persistent, and supportive of students. They listen to students and validate their culture. They empower their students to engage in their education. Caring teachers don't give up on their students. They understand why students may not feel well on some days or are having a difficult time outside of school. Nevertheless, these teachers do not accept failure.

"Uncaring [teachers] are distinguished by impatience, intolerance, dictations, and control" (Gay, 2000, p. 47). Natisha, whose story began this chapter, did not have teachers who tried to learn why she was silent. Her teachers did not care enough about her to reach out and engage her in her education.

Encouraging Student Voices

Teaching must start from the students' life experiences, not the teacher's life experiences. Multicultural teachers seek, listen to, and incorporate voices of students, their families, and communities. Students are encouraged to speak from their own experiences, to do more than regurgitate answers that the teacher would like to hear. Teaching that incorporates the student voice allows students to make sense of subject matter within their own lived experiences or the realities that they know because they have themselves experienced them. Listening to students helps teachers understand their prior knowledge of the subject matter, including any misinformation or lack of information that suggests future instructional strategies. Student voices also provide important information about their cultures.

Most schools today legitimate only the voice of the dominant culture—the Standard English and world perspective of the European American middle class. Many students, especially those from oppressed groups, learn to be silent or disruptive, and/or they drop out, in part because their voices are not accepted as legitimate in the classroom. Culturally responsive teaching requires educators to recognize the incongruence between the voice of the school and the voices of students. Success in school should not be dependent on the adoption of the school's voice.

Teachers could use an approach in which instruction occurs as a dialogue between teacher and students' which is the fifth CREDE standard mentioned earlier in this chapter. Rather than depend on a textbook and lecture format, the teacher listens to students and directs them in the learning of the discipline through dialogue. It incorporates content about the diverse backgrounds of students, as well as those of the dominant society. It requires discarding the traditional authoritarian classroom to establish a democratic one in which both teacher and students are active participants.

Introducing student voices to the instructional process can be difficult, especially when teacher and students are from different cultural backgrounds. The teacher may face both anger and silence, which in time will be overcome with dialogue that develops tolerance, patience, and a willingness to listen. Although this strategy increases the participation of students in the learning process, some teachers are not comfortable with handling the issues that are likely to be raised. Too often, teachers ignore students' attempts to engage in dialogue and, as a result, halt further learning by many students.

In addition to dialogue between students and teacher, student voices can be encouraged through written and artistic expression. Some teachers ask students to keep journals in which they write their reactions to what is occurring in class. The journals make the teacher aware of learning that is occurring over time. To be effective, students must feel comfortable writing whatever they want without the threat of reprisal from the teacher. The dialogues developed through these approaches can help students understand the perspectives brought to the classroom by others from different cultures. The resulting dialogues can help students relate subject matter to their real world, encouraging them to take an interest in studying and learning it.

Engaging Students

Culturally responsive teaching encourages student participation, critical analysis, and action. Classroom projects focus on areas of interest to students and the communities in which they live. As they participate in these activities, they apply and extend the mathematics, science, language arts, and social studies that they have been learning. Teachers and students in these classrooms have developed a vision for a more egalitarian and socially just society. Projects often engage students in collective action to improve their communities.

After conducting research and collecting and analyzing data, students sometimes move their recommendations through the democratic processes of their local communities to make changes for improving conditions. In one Nebraska school, students and their teacher became very concerned about the treatment of new immigrants in the local community and businesses. They drafted legislation requiring the study of race in social studies across the state. Facing opposition from some, they lobbied the state legislature on behalf of the bill and were successful in having it adopted. Students in this social studies class not only were able to affect school curriculum through their actions, but also learned the legislative process of their state through hands-on experience.

A group of teenagers from across the country shared their views of how teachers can keep students engaged, motivated, and challenged in the book, *Fires in the Bathroom: Advice for Teachers from High School Students*. These students from diverse populations suggest that teachers get and keep students motivated by:

- Being passionate about your material and your work.
- Connecting to issues they care about outside school.
- Giving them choices on things that matter.
- Making learning a social thing.
- Making sure they understand.
- Responding with interest when they show interest.
- Caring about them and their progress.
- Helping them keep on top of their workload.
- Showing your pride in their good work.
- Providing role models to inspire them. (Cushman & the Students of What Kids Can Do, Inc., 2003, p. 122)

Teaching for Social Justice

As a part of providing education that is multicultural, teachers and their students confront inequities in schools and communities. Then they take steps to eliminate existing inequities within the classroom and school and, sometimes, in the community. Teaching for social justice requires what the 2005 president of the American Educational Research Association, Marilyn Cochran-Smith (2004) calls "teaching against the grain." She identifies the dilemma for teachers who are trying to teach for social justice: "How to educate children who know about not only the canon of literature, language, and history, but also their own history, language, and literature; not only how to negotiate their

As part of social justice education, teachers establish learning communities among students to encourage them to work together in the learning process. The learning communities with members from different cultural groups can also promote cross-cultural interactions and understandings.

Anthony Magnacca/Merrill

way through the system's gatekeepers but also how to work to dismantle the inequities of the system" (p. 63).

Teaching for social justice requires a disposition of caring and social responsibility for persons who are not advantaged. Socially just educators believe that the country's resources should be somewhat equitably distributed. They also believe that all people have the right to decent housing, health insurance, education, and adequate food and nutrition, regardless of their ethnicity, race, socioeconomic status, sexual orientation, or disability. They confront inequity by critically analyzing oppression in society.

Socially just classrooms are democratic, engaging both students and teachers in learning together. Power relations between students and teachers are enacted in classrooms. Teachers and other school officials can use their power to develop either democratic settings in which students are active participants or autocratic settings controlled totally by adults. The problem with authoritarianism, which is the concentration of power in one

Pause to Reflect 10.3

Many teacher education programs indicate that social justice is part of their conceptual framework. As a result, they expect teacher candidates to develop proficiencies related to the social justice.

- What is a conceptual framework? What is the conceptual framework for the program in which you are enrolled?
- Does your program's conceptual framework include social justice or some aspect of social justice? What are you expected to know and be able to do related to social justice?
- Why do some conservative critics think that universities should not be teaching social justice?
- What does social justice mean to you?

Go to the *Homework and Exercises* section in Chapter 10 of MyEducationLab and select *Pause to Reflect 10.3* to answer these questions.

person, is that it undermines democratic education (hooks, 2003). Establishing a democratic classroom helps overcome the power inequities that exist. It challenges the authoritarianism of the teacher and breaks down the power relationships between teacher and students. Students become active participants in governing the classroom and in critically analyzing school and societal practices related to equity and social justice.

Developing Critical Thinking

As a result of being taught multiculturally, students learn to think critically about what they are learning and experiencing. **Critical thinking** challenges the status quo, encourages questioning of the dominant canon and culture, and considers alternate views to the inequitable structure of society. Students should be supported in questioning the validity of the knowledge presented in textbooks and other resources. They should be encouraged to explore other perspectives. Developing the skills to think critically about issues helps students make sense of the events and conditions that affect their lives.

Multicultural teaching requires students to investigate racism, classism, and sexism and how societal institutions have served different populations in discriminatory ways. Even though we may overcome our own prejudices and eliminate our own discriminatory practices against members of other cultural groups, the problem is not solved. It goes beyond what we individually control. The problem is societal and is imbedded in historical and contemporary contexts that students must be helped to understand.

Most students accept the information written in their textbooks as the absolute truth. However, critical thinkers do not automatically accept the content of textbooks as truth. They understand that authors write from their own perspectives with their own biases. The presentation is usually from the perspective of the dominant culture rather than persons who have been oppressed because of events and practices supportive of the dominant culture. Teaching for social justice encourages students to question what is written in textbooks or appears in multimedia materials. Students are expected to conduct research that provides other facts and perspectives that might negate the content in the textbook.

Educators can help students examine their own biases and stereotypes related to different cultural groups. These biases often surface during class discussions or incidents outside the classroom. They should not be ignored by the teacher. Instead, they should become one of those teachable moments in which issues are confronted and discussed. Accurate information can begin to displace the myths that many hold about others.

Addressing Inequity and Power

Many teachers have a difficult time addressing the issue of race in the classroom. Yet, it affects the work of schools. Most European American students probably don't believe that racism is a factor in their lives; they may even question its existence. Most persons of color, on the other hand, feel the pressure of racism all around them. They don't understand how their white peers and teachers could possibly miss it. To ignore the impact of racism on society and our everyday worlds is to negate the experiences of students and families who suffer from its negative impact. Can we afford to ignore it because it is complex, emotional, and hard for some students to understand and handle? As teachers incorporate diversity throughout the curriculum, there should be opportunities to discuss the meaning of race in this country and the debilitating effect racism (as well as sexism, classism, etc.) has on large numbers of people in this country and the world.

Confronting racism in classrooms is also discussed in Chapter 3.

FOCUS YOUR CULTURAL LENS: DEBATE

Critical Thinking: At What Age Should We Teach the War?

The School Board in one school district passed a resolution that all middle level and high schools dedicate one class period and one after-school event to studying the war in Iraq. The resolution indicated that age-appropriate materials should be used by teachers and diverse perspectives presented. When the resolution was adopted, one teacher in the district was already discussing the war with her fourth-grade students. As part of social studies, these students were studying Iraq, "discussing what factors led to the current conflict, and listening to diverse perspectives on the impending war from people around the world." They were not limiting their discussion to one class period. Is it appropriate to discuss political issues with young children?

For

- Young children need to know the critical issues that are affecting the lives of their families (e.g., they or their classmates may have family members serving in Iraq).
- Young children should be helped to understand different perspectives on the political issues that they see on television.
- Without discussing war critically with younger students, they learn that war is an acceptable response to conflict.
- A critical discussion of war may help young students understand why they should not hate the Iraqis, other Arabs, or other Arab Americans.

Against

- Talking about war may scare young children.
- Young children are not able to understand the complexity of war and other controversial political issues.
- Discussing war contributes to the development of extreme patriotism and hate against the citizens of another nation.
- Teachers should not be influencing student's perspectives on the Iraq war. It is the role of parents to help them understand the war.

Questions

1. Should teachers help students see the war with Iraq from the perspectives of the Iraqi people and their leaders as well as the United States and its allies? Why or why not?
2. How old should students be to begin the critical study of political issues?
3. Why should teachers help students think critically about war and other political issues?
4. Thinking critically about issues fits naturally into social studies. How can teachers help students think critically about mathematics, science, and literacy?

Go to the *Homework and Exercises* section in Chapter 10 of MyEducationLab and select *Focus Your Cultural Lens* to answer these questions.

Adapted from Dawson, K. (2003, Summer). Learning from the past, talking about the present: A fourth-grade teacher reflects on her own schooling and poses hard questions to her students about the war. *Rethinking Schools, 17*(4), 17.

VIDEO INSIGHTS
The Reunion

While European Americans were resisting integration of schools in the South in the 1960s, a group of African and European American parents in Shaker Heights, Ohio, decided to work at maintaining an integrated community. They voluntarily integrated their neighborhood elementary school. At this reunion of the students in this experiment, they talk about being best friends across races in and out of school when they were young. Relationships changed when they moved to a junior high school with students from formerly segregated schools. At the height of the Civil Rights Movement, they began to segregate themselves as they developed their identities with their own ethnic groups. They realized they had grown up in a protected cocoon that didn't sustain itself as they interacted with youth outside their neighborhood.

Now, switch to a Shaker Heights high school 40 years later. European and African American students talk about race in their school and how members of the two groups interact. This video provides the opportunity to explore the progress that has been made.

1. What changed over the past 40 years in Shaker Heights?
2. Have race relations improved in this town? Explain how or how not.
3. How integrated were the neighborhood and school in which you were raised? Were your experiences similar to either of the groups interviewed in this video? Why or why not?
4. What do the experiences of Shaker Heights residents suggest for race relations in this country?

Go to the Video Insights DVD and watch the video segment *The Reunion*. Then, go to the *Homework and Exercises* section in Chapter 10 of MyEducationLab and select *Video Insights*: *The Reunion* to answer these questions.

There is value in racial and ethnic groups working together to overcome fears and correct myths and misperceptions. This healing cannot occur if educators are unwilling to facilitate the dialogue about race. Discussions of race often challenge the teachers' and students' deeply held beliefs about the topic. Some students react with anger; others are defensive and feel guilty. At the beginning, many white students resist reexamining their worldviews, acknowledging the privilege of whiteness, and accepting the existence of discrimination.

These changes do not occur overnight. They take months, and sometimes years, of study and self-reflection. Some people never accept that racism exists and needs to be eliminated. The dialogue about race and racism should occur in all schools, not just those with diverse populations.

Another difficult topic to analyze critically is poverty, especially its causes. Too often, families and individuals are blamed for their own poverty. It is difficult for many, especially those advantaged by the current economic conditions, to acknowledge that our system does not provide the same opportunities for all whites and persons of color.

Poverty and income differences are the focus of Chapter 3.

Teachers can help students explore the contributions of the labor class as well as the rich and powerful. They can examine various perspectives on eliminating jobs in one area of the country and moving them to cheaper labor markets in another part of the country or world. Students could examine the changing job markets to determine the skills needed for future work. They could discuss why companies are seeking labor outside the United States for high-tech jobs as well as low-paying jobs in meat processing companies and agriculture. They could critique different perspectives on seeking labor outside the country rather than ensuring that U.S. students have the necessary skills for the growing technology fields.

Fostering Learning Communities

Numerous studies show that interactions and understandings among people from different racial and ethnic groups increase as they work together on **meaningful projects** inside and outside the classroom. In social justice education, these meaningful projects address equity, democratic practices, and critical social issues in the community.

Teachers should ensure that students are integrated in cooperative groups and group work. **Cooperative learning** is a popular strategy for supporting learning communities. It is a strategy for grouping students to work together on a project to support and learn from each other. It minimizes competition among students and encourages sharing the work required to learn. They can establish opportunities for cross-cultural communications and learning from each other, but teachers should ensure that groups are racially mixed.

School Climate

Another area in which commitment to multicultural education can be evaluated is the general school climate. Visitors entering a school can usually feel the tension that exists when cross-cultural communications are poor. They can observe whether diversity is a positive and appreciated factor at the school. If only students of color or only males are waiting to be seen by the assistant principal in charge of discipline, visitors should wonder whether the school is providing effectively for the needs of all of its students. If bulletin boards in classrooms are covered with only European Americans, visitors should question the appreciation of diversity in the school. If the football team is comprised primarily of African Americans and the chess club of European Americans, they should wonder about the inclusive nature of students from a variety of groups in extracurricular activities. If school administrators are primarily men and most teachers are women, or if the teachers are European American and the teacher aides are Latino, the visitors could envision discriminatory practices in hiring and promotion of staff. These are examples of a school climate that does not reflect a commitment to multicultural education.

Staffing composition and patterns should reflect the diversity of the country. At a minimum, they should reflect the diversity of the geographic area. Women, as well as men, should be school administrators; men, as well as women, should teach at preschool and primary levels. Persons of color should be found in the administration and teaching ranks, not primarily in custodial and clerical positions. Faculty, administrators, and other staff see themselves as learners enhanced and changed by understanding, affirming, and reflecting cultural diversity. Teachers and administrators are able to deal with questions of race, intergroup relations, and controversial realities on an objective, frank, and professional basis.

When diversity is valued within a school, student government and extracurricular activities include students from different cultural groups. Students should not be segregated on the basis of their membership in a certain group. In a school where multiculturalism is

Adults in the community can be valuable resources in discussions of cultural differences. When community members trust school officials, they become partners with teachers in improving students' learning.

Scott Cunningham/Merrill

valued, students from various cultural backgrounds hold leadership positions. Those roles are not automatically delegated to students from the dominant group in the school.

If the school climate is multicultural, it is reflected in every aspect of the educational program. In addition to those areas already mentioned, assembly programs reflect multiculturalism in their content, as well as in the choice of speakers. Bulletin boards and displays reflect the diversity of the nation, even if the community is not rich in diversity. Cross-cultural communications among students and between students and teachers are positive. Different languages and dialects used by students are respected. Both girls and boys are found in technology education, family science, calculus, bookkeeping, physics, and vocational classes. Students from different groups participate in college preparatory classes, advanced placement classes, special education, and gifted education at a rate equal to their representation in the schools. Differences in academic achievement levels disappear between males and females, dominant and oppressed group members, and upper-middle-class and low-income students. The school curriculum incorporates the contributions of many cultural groups and integrates multiple perspectives throughout it. Instructional materials are free of biases, omissions, and stereotypes.

The school climate must be supportive of multicultural education. When respect for cultural differences is reflected in all aspects of students' educational programs, the goals of multicultural education are being attained. Educators are the key to attaining this climate.

Hidden Curriculum

In addition to a formal curriculum, schools have a hidden curriculum that consists of the unstated norms, values, and beliefs about the social relations of school and classroom life that are transmitted to students. Because the hidden curriculum includes the norms and values that support the formal curriculum, it must also reflect diversity if education is to become multicultural. Although the hidden curriculum is not taught directly or included in the objectives of the formal curriculum, it has a great impact on students and teachers alike. It includes the organizational structures of the classroom and the school, as well as the interactions of students and teachers.

Pause to Reflect 10.4

The school climate is an indicator of whether diversity and equality are respected and promoted in a school. Take an inventory of: (a) a school that you may be observing; (b) the school, college, or department of education that is responsible for preparing teachers at your college or university; or (c) the college or university itself.

- What is the diversity of the faculty? How diverse is the student body?
- How does the diversity differ between administrators and faculty?
- In what activities do white students and students of color participate?
- How reflective of diversity are displays on the walls and in display cases?
- What is the diversity of students on the honor roll or dean's list?
- What positive and negative characteristics do you observe?

Go to the *Homework and Exercises* section in Chapter 10 of MyEducationLab and select *Pause to Reflect 10.4* to answer these questions.

Students must take turns, stand in line, wait to speak, wait for the teacher to provide individual help, face interruptions from others, and be distracted constantly by the needs of others. They must develop patience in order to be successful in the school setting. They must also learn to work alone within the crowd. Even though they share the classroom with many other students, they usually are not allowed to interact with classmates unless the teacher permits it. These same characteristics will be encountered in the work situations for which students are being prepared. They are not part of the formal curriculum but are central to the operation of most classrooms.

Messages Sent to Students

Unknowingly, educators transmit biased messages to students. Most educators do not consciously or intentionally stereotype students or discriminate against them. They usually try to treat all students fairly and equitably. We have learned our attitudes and behaviors, however, in a society that is ageist, ableist, racist, sexist, and heterosexist. Some biases have been internalized to such a degree that we do not realize we have them. When educators are able to recognize the subtle and unintentional biases in their behavior, positive changes can be made in the classroom.

Students of color are often treated significantly different from white students. Because many white students share the same European and/or middle-class culture as the teacher, they also share the same cultural cues that foster success in the classroom. Students who ask appropriate questions at appropriate times or who smile and seek attention from the teacher at times when the teacher is open to such gestures are likely to receive encouragement and reinforcement from the teacher. In contrast, students who interrupt the class or seek attention from the teacher when the teacher is not open to providing the necessary attention do not receive the necessary reinforcement.

As a result of the teacher's misreading of the cultural cues, ethnic or racial boundaries are established within the classroom. This situation is exacerbated when students from the dominant group receive more opportunities to participate in instructional interactions and receive more praise and encouragement. Low-income students and students of color receive fewer opportunities to participate, and the opportunities usually are of a less-substantive nature. They also may be criticized or disciplined more frequently than European American students for breaking the rules.

Unless teachers can critically examine their treatment of students in the classroom, they will not know whether they treat students inequitably because of cultural differences. Once that step has been taken, changes can be initiated to ensure that cultural identity is not a factor for automatically relating differently to students. Teachers may need to become more proactive in initiating interactions and in providing encouragement, praise, and reinforcement to students from cultural groups different from their own.

Teachers usually evaluate students' academic performance through tests and written and oral work. Much more than academic performance is evaluated by teachers, however. Student misbehavior occurs when classroom rules are not adequately obeyed, which usually results in some sort of punishment. Discipline varies by the infraction and student, but sometimes is influenced by the gender, race, and class of the student. Similarly, students who have been assigned a low-ability status often receive negative attention from the teacher because they are not following the rules, rather than because they are not performing adequately on academic tasks.

In addition to evaluations based on academic performance and institutional rules, teachers make evaluations based on personal qualities. Students are sometimes grouped according to their clothes, family income, cleanliness, and personality, rather than academic abilities. This practice is particularly dangerous because most tracking perpetuates inequities.

Another aspect of the hidden curriculum is that of unequal power. In many ways, this is a dilemma of childhood. By the time students enter kindergarten, they have learned that power is in the hands of adults. The teacher and other school officials require that their rules be followed. In addition to the institutional rules, teachers may require that students give up their home languages or dialects to be successful academically or at least to receive the teacher's approval. Instead, students should be encouraged to be bicultural, knowing both their home and dominant cultural language and patterns.

How can the hidden curriculum reflect multicultural education? A first step is to recognize that it exists and that it provides lessons that are valuable in life. However, the rules are known to the members of the dominant culture. They don't have to think about them. Too often, the requirements of the classroom place more value on following the rules than on learning. Our interactions with students should be evaluated to ensure that we are actually supporting learning, rather than preventing it.

Student and Teacher Relations

Although the development and use of culturally responsive materials and curricula are important and necessary steps toward providing multicultural education, alone they are not enough. The interactions between teachers and students determine the quality of education. Teachers send messages that tell students they have potential and they can learn. Teachers who know their subject matter, believe that all students can learn, and care about students as individuals can have a great impact on students and their learning. Teenagers recommend that teachers show respect, trust, and fairness by:

- Letting them know what to expect from you and from the class.
- Knowing your material.
- Pushing them to do their best—and push them equally.
- Doing your part.

- Making sure everyone understands.
- Grading them fairly.
- Understanding that they make mistakes.
- Not denigrating them.
- Keeping your biases to yourself.
- Not treating them like little kids.
- Listening to what they think.
- Caring what's going on with them.
- Not betraying their confidences. (Cushman, et al., 2003 p. 35)

The teacher who is enthusiastic about culturally responsive teaching will be more likely to use multicultural materials and encourage students to develop more egalitarian views. Research studies have found that warmer and more enthusiastic teachers produce students with greater achievement gains. These teachers solicit better affective responses from their students, which leads to classrooms with a more positive atmosphere. Students from low-income families and students of color "do especially well with teachers who share warm, personal interactions with them but also hold high expectations for their academic progress, require them to perform up to their capabilities, and see that they progress as far and as fast as they are able" (Brophy, 1998). Teachers need to carefully assess the needs of individual students in the classroom, however, to develop effective teaching strategies.

Teachers do make a difference in student learning. They can make students feel either very special or incompetent and worthless. After reviewing the research on teacher interactions with students of color, Gay (2000) concluded that

> students of color, especially those who are poor and live in urban areas, get less total instructional attention; are called on less frequently; are encouraged to continue to develop intellectual thinking less often; are criticized more and praised less; receive fewer direct responses to their questions and comments; and are reprimanded more often and disciplined more severely. (p. 63)

These factors are critical in promoting students' learning. When teachers respond to students of color in this way, they are limiting their possibilities for high achievement.

To provide the greatest assistance to all students, teachers cannot provide the same treatment for each student because they should be working toward meeting individual needs and differences. Teachers must be sure they are not treating students differently, however, based solely on students' group membership. With the elimination of bias from the teaching process and the emergence of proactive teachers who seek the most effective strategies to meet the needs of individual students, the classroom can become a stimulating place for most students, regardless of their cultural identities, abilities, and experiences.

How can teachers analyze their own classroom interactions and teaching styles? If equipment is available, teachers can videotape or audiotape a class and then systematically record the interactions as they view or listen to the tape later. An outside observer could be asked to record the nature of a teacher's interaction with students. An analysis of the data would show teachers how much class time they spend interacting with students and the nature of the interactions. These data would show any differences in interactions based on gender, ethnicity, or other characteristics of students. Such an analysis would be an excellent starting point for teachers who want to ensure that they do not discriminate against male or female students or students from different ethnic or socioeconomic groups.

Every effort must be made to ensure that a teacher's prejudices are not reflected in his or her interactions with students. Teachers must continually assess their interactions with boys, girls, and students from dominant and oppressed groups to determine whether the interactions provide different types of praise, criticism, encouragement, and reinforcement based on the culture of the students. Only then can steps be taken to equalize treatment.

Student and Teacher Communications

Lack of skill in cross-cultural communications between students and teachers can prevent learning from occurring in the classroom. This problem is usually the result of misunderstanding cultural cues when students have cultural identities different from that of the teacher.

Just as cultures differ in the structure of their language, they also differ in the structure of oral discourse. Moves made in teaching-learning discourse, who is to make them, and the sequence they should take vary from culture to culture. These rules are not absolute laws governing behavior; in fact, they are learned in their interactions within our own cultural groups. But when these patterns differ from the culture-of-teacher to culture-of-child, serious misunderstandings can occur as the two participants try to play out different patterns and assign different social meanings to the same actions.

These differences are likely to prevail in schools with large numbers of students from oppressed groups. Miscommunications occur when the same words and actions mean something different to the individuals involved. When students are not responding appropriately in the classroom, teachers should consider the possibility that their communication cues do not match those of their students.

Direct and continuous participation in cultures that are different from our own can improve our competency in other communication systems and should help us be more sensitive to differences in cultures with which we are not familiar. Teachers who are aware of these differences can redirect their instruction to use primarily the communications that work most effectively with students. At the same time, the teacher can begin to teach students

Effective cross-cultural communications between students and teachers promote student learning. When the cultural cues between students and teachers are not understood, communications and learning often are affected adversely.

Pearson Learning Photo Studio

how to interact effectively in the situations with which they are uncomfortable. This approach will assist all students in responding appropriately in future classroom situations that are dominated by interactions with which they are not familiar.

Developing Multicultural Proficiencies

Educators should undertake a number of actions to prepare to deliver education that is multicultural. First, they should know their own cultural identity and the degree to which they identify with the various groups of which they are members. Second, they should accept the fact that they have prejudices that may affect the way they react to students in the classroom. When they recognize these biases, they can develop strategies to overcome or compensate for them in the classroom.

Know Yourself and Others

One of the first steps to becoming multicultural is knowing your own cultural identity. Many European American students have never identified themselves as ethnic or racial (Weinstein, Tomlinson-Clarke, & Curran, 2004). They have not thought about their privilege in society. Students of color may have thought little about their multiple identities because their race or ethnicity has been the center of their identity.

Refer to Chapter 2 for a more in-depth discussion of ethnicity.

In addition to knowing yourself, you need to learn about groups other than your own. You might read about them, attend ethnic movies or plays, participate in ethnic celebrations, visit different churches and ethnic community groups, and interact with members of different groups in a variety of settings. If you enjoy reading novels, you should select authors from different cultures. The perspective presented may be very different from your own. Novels may help you understand that other people's experiences lead them to react to situations differently from the way you would. It is often an advantage to discuss one's reactions to such new experiences with someone else to clarify and confront your own feelings of prejudices or stereotypes.

You should make an effort to interact with persons who are culturally different from you. Long-term cultural experiences are probably the most effective means for overcoming fear and misconceptions about a group. You must remember, however, that there is much diversity within a group. You cannot generalize about an entire group on the basis of the characteristics of a few persons. In direct cross-cultural contacts, you can learn to be open to the traditions and ways of the other culture in order to learn from the experience. Otherwise, your own traditions, habits, and perspectives are likely to be projected as better, rather than as just different. If you can learn to understand, empathize with, and participate in a second culture, you will have a valuable experience. If you learn to live multiculturally, you are indeed fortunate.

Teachers also should take a critical look at their own interactions with students and communities of color. Many teachers have not critically examined the meaning of race and racism and their role in maintaining the status quo. If educators are unable to acknowledge the existence of racism and understand the effect it has on their students, it will be difficult to serve communities of color effectively and nearly impossible to eliminate racism in either schools or society.

Reflecting on Your Practice

To provide education that is multicultural, professional educators need to continually reflect on their practice in the classroom. Multicultural educators care that the content of textbooks and district-wide curriculum accurately portray diversity and perspectives beyond the dominant culture. They ask questions about school practices that lead to disproportionate numbers of students of color who are suspended from school; the disproportionate numbers of Asian Americans and upper-middle-class white students in gifted and talented programs; and the disproportionate numbers of low-income males and English language learners in low-ability classes. They recognize racism, sexism, homophobia, and ableism and confront students and colleagues who are not treating others with respect. They correct their own behavior when they learn that their prejudices are showing.

As you begin working with students and other professional educators in schools, continue to observe how you and others interact with students, parents, and colleagues who are from different cultures than your own. Think about ways you can use the students' cultures to help them learn the subjects and skills you are teaching. By reflecting on what works and does not work in the classroom, you can continuously improve your teaching for all students.

Teaching as a Political Activity

Teachers who have made their teaching multicultural confront and fight against racism, sexism, and other discrimination in schools and society. They develop strategies to recognize their own biases and overcome them. They use their knowledge and skills to support a democratic and equitable society.

Politically active teachers become advocates for children who have been marginalized by society. They may become active in political campaigns, supporting candidates who have a positive agenda for children and for adults with the greatest needs. They become involved in local political action to improve conditions in the community. They are teachers who work for equity, democracy, and social justice.

Pause to Reflect 10.5

Good teachers reflect on their practice as they work with students. They wonder why a student isn't learning a concept or a skill. They make mental notes about a student who is not attentive and experiment with a new way of engaging the student. In addition, they like to ask others to observe them and provide feedback with the goal of improving their teaching and student learning.

- How do you plan to analyze your interactions with students when you student teach?
- What are the advantages and disadvantages of videotaping your teaching?
- Are you comfortable with asking one of your classmates to observe you teaching lessons? Why or why not?

Go to the *Homework and Exercises* section in Chapter 10 of MyEducationLab and select *Pause to Reflect 10.5* to answer these questions.

Summary

Multicultural education is a means for using diversity positively in the total learning process. Culturally responsive teachers help students increase their academic achievement levels in all areas through the use of teaching approaches and materials that are sensitive and relevant to students' cultures and experiences. The voices of students and the community are valued and validated in the process. Teachers should make an effort to know all of their students, to build on their strengths, and to help them overcome their weaknesses.

A multicultural curriculum incorporates the culture of the community and students in the classroom. Students learn to think critically. They study the social and historical realities of U.S. society, and gain a better understanding of the causes of oppression and inequality, including racism and sexism. Multicultural education starts where people are, builds on the histories and experiences of the community, and incorporates multicultural resources from the local community.

Positive student and teacher interactions can support academic achievement, regardless of gender, ethnicity, age, religion, language, sexual orientation, exceptionality, or where one lives. Oral and nonverbal communication patterns between students and teachers can be analyzed and changed to increase the involvement of students in the learning process. Teachers must be sure, however, that they do not treat students differently solely on the basis of the students' group memberships. Teachers should regularly evaluate their academic expectations for students and their biases to ensure that they are helping all students learn.

One of the first steps in becoming a multicultural educator is to examine and clarify one's own cultural identity. In addition, teachers should become familiar with the cultures of others through studying them and participating in them. To provide education that is multicultural throughout one's career will require continuous reflection on one's teaching to determine what is working and what needs to be changed to help all students learn.

PROFESSIONAL PRACTICE FOR EDUCATORS

Questions for Discussion

1. What is the relationship of multicultural education and culturally responsive teaching?
2. How can a student's culture be used to teach academic content? Give examples that apply to the subject area that you plan to teach.
3. If the textbook you have been assigned to use includes no information or examples pertaining to groups other than European Americans, what can you do to provide a balanced and realistic view of society to students?
4. How can you incorporate student voices into the subject that you plan to teach?
5. What teacher behaviors and attributes positively support the delivery of education that is multicultural?
6. How might you structure group work in your class to facilitate cross-group interactions?

7. What are the characteristics of socially just classrooms? How do they differ from most classrooms?
8. Why is teaching for social justice controversial in some school systems?
9. What characteristics would determine that a school is committed to education that is multicultural?
10. What do you need to do to prepare yourself to understand and use the culture of students in your own teaching?

Portfolio Activities

1. Select a school and write a case study of its multicultural orientation. Describe the diversity of the students and teachers in the school. Describe the inside and outside of the school. Describe how the school addresses multicultural education based on interviews with selected teachers and students. (INTASC Standard 3)
2. Develop a lesson plan in your subject area that relates the subject to a real-life community issue (for example, social services, care of the elderly, or environment issues). (INTASC Standards 3, 7, and 10)
3. Write your own biography, describing your multiple cultural identities and the impact they have on who you are. (INTASC Standard 3)
4. Develop a personal plan for increasing your knowledge about and experiences with groups that are different than your own. How will you assess your progress at becoming more aware of cultural differences? (INTASC Standard 3)

Licensure Test Prep

Faculty at the Beckett Child Development Center are discussing how they can help the diverse class of 3- and 4-year-olds develop strong, positive self-concepts. Carmen Martinez argues that the teachers need to provide a wide range of multicultural materials, especially books and pictures about children from different countries. Alex Morgan thinks the teachers should figure out ways to ensure that the students play with different groups of students and learn to be courteous to each student regardless of their racial and ethnic background. Mary Thompson talks about how her last school invited parents to an international night in which they could share traditional foods from their ethnic culture. Janet Whitehorse said that all of these activities could be helpful, but she thinks they should affirm the cultures of all their students and make sure they can see their family's culture somewhere in the classroom. The students could even learn to say "good morning" in the native languages of the immigrant families.

Short Answer Questions

1. Which of the strategies suggested by these early childhood teachers is a critical component of culturally responsive teaching?
2. Why is the strategy that you chose more appropriate than the other three?

Go to the *Homework and Exercises* section in Chapter 10 of MyEducationLab and select *Licensure Test Prep* to complete this exercise.

Suggested Readings

Christensen, L. (2000). *Reading, writing, and rising up: Teaching about social justice and the power of the written word.* Milwaukee, WI: Rethinking Schools.

The author describes how reading and writing are political acts. This practical, inspirational book offers essays, lesson plans, and a collection of student writing, all rooted in an unwavering focus on language arts teaching for justice.

Cushman, K. and the Students of What Kids Can Do, Inc. (2003). *Fires in the bathroom: Advice for teachers from high school students.* New York: New Press.

Forty teenagers provide advice to teachers on building mutual understanding and respect, classroom behavior, group work, language difficulties, and homework.

Langer de Ramirez, L. (2006). *Voices of diversity: Stories, activities, and resources for the multicultural classroom.* Columbus, OH: Merrill Prentice Hall.

This teacher's handbook includes narratives by students, teachers, and parents for understanding the topics discussed in this book. The cartoons and activities push the reader to think deeply about important issues and conditions faced by schools today.

Multicultural Perspectives. (Published by the National Association for Multicultural Education, 733 15th Street, NW, Suite 430, Washington, DC 20005; nameorg@nameorg.org).

This quarterly magazine features articles by scholars and practitioners in the field of multicultural education. It also includes promising practices, multicultural resources, and book and film reviews.

Nieto, S. (2003). *What keeps teachers going?* New York: Teachers College Press.

Experienced teachers who have been successful with culturally diverse students in urban schools identify the challenges of helping these students learn. The book offers an alternative vision of what's important in teaching and learning.

Rethinking Schools. (Published by Rethinking Schools, 1001 E. Keefe Ave., Milwaukee, WI 53212; www.rethinkingschools.org).

Advocating the reform of elementary and secondary schools, this quarterly newsletter promotes educational equity and supports progressive educational values. Teachers, parents, and students are the regular contributors.

Schniedewind, N., & Davidson, E. (2006). *Open minds to equality: A sourcebook of learning activities to affirm diversity and promote equity* (3rd ed.). Milwaukee, WI: Rethinking Schools.

Chock-full of classroom activities and resources for teachers, this book provides an inclusive framework for thinking about diversity and working with diverse populations. It is sequenced from building awareness and understanding to experiencing collective responsibility.

References

Brophy, J. E. (1998). *Motivating students to learn.* Boston: McGraw-Hill.

Center for Research on Education, Diversity, and Excellence (CREDE). (2004). *Five standards.* Retrieved November 2, 2004, from www.crede.ucsc.edu/

Cochran-Smith, M. (2004). *Walking the road: Race, diversity, and social justice in teacher education.* New York: Teachers College Press.

Cushman, K. and the Students of What Kids Can Do. (2003). *Fires in the bathroom: Advice for teachers from high school students.* New York: New Press.

Darling-Hammond, L., French, J., & García-Lopez, S. P. (2002). *Learning to teach for social justice.* New York: Teachers College Press.

Delpit, L. (2006). *Other people's children: Cultural conflict in the classroom.* New York: New Press.

Gay, G. (2000). *Culturally responsive teaching: Theory, research, and practice.* New York: Teachers College Press.

hooks, b. (2003). *Teaching community: A pedagogy of hope.* New York: Routledge.

National Council for the Accreditation of Teacher Education. (2002). *Professional standards for the accreditation of schools, colleges, and departments of education.* Washington, DC: Author.

Tatum, B. D. (1997). *Why are all the black kids sitting together in the cafeteria? And other conversations about race.* New York: Basic Books.

Viadero, D. (2004, April 21). Keys to success: Researchers identify methods to help 'nonmainstream' pupils make academic gains. *Education Week,* 28–31.

Weinstein, C. S., Tomlinson-Clarke, S., & Curran, M. (2004, January/February). Toward a conception of culturally responsive classroom management. *Journal of Teacher Education, 55*(1), 25–38.

Weinstein, R. S. (1996, November). High standards in a tracked system of schooling: For which students and with what educational supports? *Educational Researcher, 25*(8), 16–19.

Glossary

accent   How an individual pronounces words.

acculturation   Adoption of the dominant group's cultural patterns by a new or oppressed group.

acting white   A label used by some people to describe persons of the same race who take on the behaviors, values, and attitudes of the dominant white culture.

additive bilingualism   Occurs when two languages are of equal value and neither dominates the other.

adequate yearly progress (AYP)   A minimum level of improvement—measurable in terms of student performance—that school districts and schools must achieve within specific time frames specified in the law *No Child Left Behind*.

adolescence   Approximately ages 13 through 19.

African American English   Another term for Black English, Vernacular Black English, and Ebonics. A dialect used by many African Americans and used primarily by those in working-class families.

Afrocentric curriculum   Curriculum centered on or derived from African history, culture, and traditions.

agnostic   One who believes that the existence of God can neither be proven or unproven. An agnostic does not believe in a God or Goddess.

alienation   Estrangement or disconnected from oneself or others.

Allah   God in Arabic. It is the term used for God by Muslims and Arab Christians.

American Sign Language (ASL)   A natural language that has been developed and used by persons who are deaf using a system of manual gestures.

Americans with Disabilities Act (ADA)   Public Law 101-336 passed on January 26, 1990, which was designed to end discrimination against individuals with disabilities in private-sector employment, public services, public accommodations, transportation, and telecommunications. It was intended to complete what Section 504 was unable to do. The greater accessibilities in buildings, in public transportation, sidewalk curbs, etc., can to a great extent be credited to ADA.

argot   Somewhat secret vocabulary of a co-culture group.

ascribed status   Characteristics such as ethnicity, race, socioeconomic level, and gender with which children are born or assigned at birth. Most of these characteristics match those of their families.

assimilation   Process by which groups adopt or change the dominant culture.

asylees   Individuals who travel to the United States from another country and ask for asylum or protection from being persecuted in their native country.

at risk   Children and youth who are economically disadvantaged to a degree that can affect their educational opportunities.

atheist   One who positively does not believe in the existence of a God or Goddess.

authenticity   Relates the curriculum and activities to real-world applications with meaning in the lives of students.

authoritarian   The concentration of power in one figure, usually the teacher or principal in schools.

basic interpersonal communications skills (BICS)   Basic, everyday conversational skills, which English Language Learners can develop in approximately two years.

biased assessments   Assessments that favor one group over another group. One example is tests that, in the past, were typically developed and normed on white, middle-class children. Children of color, particularly African American and Latinos, have been and often still are at a disadvantage in testing because test items are more familiar to white, middle-class children. The bias may be in the instrument, the administration of the assessment, or the interpretation of test results.

bicultural   A person who is competent in two cultures and educational programs that recognize the value and worth of both the dominant culture and the culture of a student's family, enhancing the development or maintenance of a positive self-image.

bidialectical   An individual who has the ability to speak or utilize two or more dialects.

big ideas   The major concepts that support a subject such as mathematics or English language arts.

bilingual education   "The use of two languages as media of instruction" (Baca & Cervantes, 2004). It accepts and develops native language and culture in the instructional process to learn English and to learn academic subject matter. Bilingual education may use the native language, as well as English, as the medium of instruction.

bilingualism   The ability to function in two languages. While some contend that bilingualism implies native-like fluency, others measure competency in two languages as adequate to be considered bilingual.

Black English   Another term for African American English, Vernacular Black English, and Ebonics. A dialect used by many African Americans and used primarily by those in working-class families.

Black Muslims   A group of African Americans who now align themselves primarily with the Sunni form of Islam. Black Muslims in the United States likely had their early beginnings in the late 1800s, but at that time had little in common with traditional Islam. In the 1970s Elijah Muhammad led them into national visibility.

blue-collar   Jobs or workers characterized by manual labor that is usually mechanical and routine.

born again   Christians who have had a conversion experience with a spiritual rebirth into a new life.

breakdancing   An improvised form of dancing with intricate and sometimes acrobatic moves.

Buddhism   The fourth largest religion in the world. Founded in 535 B.C. by Siddhartha Gautama, who was believed to be a prince of India. Buddhists believe in reincarnation and emphasize virtue, good conduct, morality, concentration, meditation, mental development, discernment, insight, wisdom, and enlightenment.

canon   The principles, rules, standards, values, or norms that guide a Western European education.

case law   Published opinions of judges, which interpret statutes, regulations, and constitutional provisions.

caste   A distinction imposed at birth to justify the inequitable social distribution of power and privilege on a group.

Catholic   Members of the Roman Catholic Church who believe that the Pope in Rome is God's visible lieutenant on earth and the rightful leader of Christianity.

charter schools   Public schools that are exempt from many of the bureaucratic regulations of traditional public schools.

child abuse   The physical or psychological mistreatment of children.

civil rights   The rights of personal liberty guaranteed by the 13th and 14th Amendments to the U.S. Constitution and by acts of Congress.

class   A group sharing the same economic and social status.

classism   The view that one's class level (e.g., middle class or upper class) makes one superior to members of classes perceived below one's own.

co-cultures   Groups of people who exist and function apart from the dominant culture (e.g., street gangs, drug dealers, prostitutes).

cognitive academic language proficiency (CALP)   The higher levels of proficiency required in highly structured academic situations.

colloquialisms   The informal or conversational speech in a community (e.g., Texas colloquialism, "I like to got hit by that car" meaning "I was almost struck by that car").

color blindness   Claim that one does not see a person's race and treats everyone equally regardless of race.

compensatory education   The provision of special services to students who have limited economic or educational advantages with a goal of reducing the educational gap between them and more advantaged students.

conservative Protestants   Protestants who believe in the virgin birth of Jesus, the Bible being inerrant, and Jesus as the son of God as essential to salvation.

cooperative learning   Strategy for grouping students to work together on a project or activity to support and learn from each other.

creation science   The term advocated by conservative Protestants who support the teaching of the Biblical account of creation in public schools in addition to or in place of the theory of evolution.

creolization   The result of European Americans, African Americans, and American Indians intermarrying and developing unique cultures, languages, and dialects.

critical thinking   An effort to see an issue clearly and truly to judge it fairly without a preset bias.

cultural borders   A boundary based on cultural differences that may limit an individual's understanding of persons from a different cultural background.

cultural capital   Endowments such as academic competence, language competence, and wealth that provide an advantage to an individual, family, or group.

cultural pluralism   The maintenance of cultures as parallel and equal to the dominant culture in a society.

culturally responsive teaching   A pedagogy that affirms the cultures of students, views the cultures and experiences of students as strengths, and reflects the students' cultures in the teaching process.

culture   Socially transmitted ways of thinking, believing, feeling, and acting within a group. These patterns are transmitted from one generation to the next.

curriculum   A sequence of courses offered by educational institutions.

de facto segregation   The separation of groups that occurs as people choose to live in different neighborhoods or participate in different clubs and social groups.

de jure segregation   The separation of groups of people that has been mandated by city, state, or federal government policies.

deductive   A way of thinking and reasoning that begins with general principles to reach conclusions about particular details.

democracy   A government in which power is vested in the people and exercised by them directly or indirectly through elected representatives.

developing nations   Countries that have lower per capita income, greater poverty, and much less capital development than the nations that wield global economic power such as the United States, Japan, and European countries.

developmental disabilities   Mental or physical impairments during birth or by the adolescent years. Typically, functional limitations in at least three areas of major life activities such as self-care, language, learning, mobility, independent living, etc.

dialects   Variations of a language usually determined by region or social class (e.g., southern drawl).

discrimination   The arbitrary denial of the privileges and rewards of society to members of a group.

dispositions   Values, attitudes, and commitments that guide the work of teachers and other school professionals.

dominant culture   The cultural group whose values and behaviors have been adopted by most institutions in society, such as schools. In the United States, it is the middle class, white, English-speaking, heterosexual Christian culture with its historical roots in Europe.

Ebonics   Another term for Black English, Vernacular Black English, and African American English. A dialect used by the majority of African Americans and used primarily by those in working-class families.

ecosystem   The natural system of animals, plants, and microorganisms functioning together in the physical and chemical environment in which they are located.

edge cities   Suburban centers that include businesses, residences, shopping centers, schools, churches, entertainment complexes, and other amenities common in cities.

egalitarianism   A belief in social, political, and economic rights and privileges for all people.

emigrate   To leave one's native country to relocate in another country.

emotional abuse   A pattern of behavior that impairs a child's emotional development or sense of worth.

enculturation   Process of acquiring the characteristics of a given culture and becoming competent in its language and ways of behaving and learning.

endogamy   Marriage within the same ethnic, cultural, or religious group.

English as a Second Language (ESL)   Educational strategy that relies exclusively on English for teaching and learning the English language. ESL programs are used extensively in this country as a primary medium to assimilate English Language Learners (ELL) into the linguistic mainstream as quickly as possible.

English Language Learners (ELL)   Students who have limited or no English skills and who are in the process of learning English.

equality   State of being equal in that one cultural group is not inferior or superior to another and that all groups have access to the same benefits of society regardless of their group memberships.

ethnic group   Membership based on one's national origin or the national origin of one's ancestors when they immigrated to the United States.

ethnocentrism   View that one's cultural group is superior to all others.

Evangelicals   Conservative Christians who fall under a broad umbrella. Some are considered more moderate within the group and focus on social action agendas in addition to their religious agenda. Another group tends to be more conservative and focuses on issues such as pro-life and an anti-gay agenda. Evangelicals generally agree in three areas: (1) one must have a "born again" conversion experience, (2) one must encourage others to believe in Jesus Christ as the son of God, and (3) the Bible is the actual word of God.

feminists   Persons who actively support the rights of women.

formal standard   The acceptable written language that is typically found in grammar books.

freedom   Not being unduly hampered or constrained in choice or action by others.

full inclusion   Serving students with disabilities and other special needs entirely within the general classroom. This is an important difference from inclusion, as students in full inclusion do not receive any of their education in segregated settings.

fundamentalist   The most conservative wing of a religious group, whether Protestant, Catholic, Jewish, Islamic, etc. These are often groups that dig in their heels to protect their faith from external forces they perceive as attacking their faith and morality.

fundamentalist Christians   Conservative Christians who advocate the teaching of creation as presented in the Bible as opposed to the theory of evolution. There are many different groups of fundamentalist Christians. Each has their own unique set of differences, which sets them apart from other groups.

gender   The characteristics of femininity and masculinity determined by culture.

Generation X   The generation born between 1965 and 1976.

Generation Y   The children of baby boomers, and the younger siblings of Generation X, who were born between the early 1980s and 1994.

Generation Z   The age cohort of individuals born after 1990.

geography   Study of the earth's surface, why people live where they live, how the place in which one lives affects the lives of its residents, and how regions of a country and the world impact on each other.

gifted and talented   Students with very high intelligence or such unusual gifts and talents in the arts that they require special educational programming to reach their full potential.

globalization   A system that connects countries economically, politically, environmentally, and culturally through a global economy supported by free trade, international corporations, and worldwide labor markets.

heterosexism   An irrational fear of or aversion to homosexuals that leads to prejudice, discrimination, and sometimes violence against them. Although heterosexism is the more accurate term, *homophobia* is more commonly used.

high-risk behaviors   Actions such as drug use or premarital sex, which could lead to alcohol or drug dependency, teenage pregnancy, sexually transmitted diseases, etc.

Hinduism   The major religion of India and the third largest religion in the world, with over 750,000 adherents and as many as 1 million in the United States. Unlike Christianity and Islam, Hinduism does not limit itself to a single religious book of writings, or to one God. Hinduism relies on a number of sacred writings and a number of gods. They believe that the goodness of an individual's life will determine how he or she will be reincarnated.

hip-hop culture   A subculture created by African American youth on the street, but now has worldwide appeal, resulting in massive marketing in clothing, music, and rap.

homophobia   An irrational fear of or aversion to homosexuals that leads to prejudice, discrimination, and sometimes violence against gays, lesbians, bisexuals, and transgendered persons.

homosexuality   Sexual attraction to persons of the same sex.

human geography   The study of the economic, social, and cultural systems that have evolved in a specific location of the world.

IDEA amendments   Congressional improvements to Public Law 105-17 (1997), strengthening the role of parents and giving school officials more latitude in discipline. The 2004 Amendments, Public Law 108-446, requires IEPs to include a statement of academic and functional goals and aligns IDEA with No Child Left Behind.

immigration   To enter a country in which one was not born for the purpose of becoming a permanent resident.

inclusion   The placement of special education students in general education settings. *(See also full inclusion)*

income   Amount of money earned in wages or salaries.

indigenous   Population that is native to a country or region. In the United States, American Indians, Hawaiians, and Alaska Natives are the indigenous populations.

individualism   Dominant feature of Western culture that stresses the rights, freedom, and importance of individuals over groups.

Individualized Education Program (IEP)   A written program required for all children with disabilities under IDEA. It includes statements of the student's present performance, annual goals, short-term objectives, specific educational services needed, relevant dates, participation in regular education, and evaluation procedures. Parents should participate in the development of the IEP and sign the document.

Individuals with Disabilities Education Act (IDEA)   Public Law 101-476 that emphasized the individual first and the disability second, and forever changed how individuals with disabilities are referred to in the literature (e.g., *students with mental retardation* took the place of *mentally retarded students*).

inductive   A way of thinking and reasoning that begins with specific facts or details to reach a general conclusion.

inequality   Marked distinctions in economic success, educational achievement, educational credentials, and power among groups of people.

informal curriculum   Rules that guide the expected behaviors and attitudes of students in schools.

informal standard   The language considered proper in a community.

intelligent design   A theory that only an intelligent being could have created a natural world so complex and well ordered as ours. Some, if not most supporters of the evolution theory, view intelligent design as a new term for creationism or creation science.

involuntary immigrants   Immigrants who did not choose to emigrate from their native countries, but were forced to or conquered by the country in which they are living.

Islam   The second largest religion in the world, which is still growing in numbers and influence. "Islam" means to submit to the will of Allah or God and is derived from the same Arabic word as "peace." Islam offers hope and salvation to the righteous and God-fearing individuals of all religions. Muslims believe that the Qur'an (Koran) is the final message delivered to his prophet Muhammad. The holy writing contains laws, moral precepts, and narratives guiding the lives of nearly one fifth of the world's population.

Jihad   The Arabic word for Muslims, which means the struggle in the path of Allah or God. It can mean the struggle against human passions and instincts, which inhibit one from doing the work of God. It can also mean an armed struggle against forces of injustice. Muslim scholars teach that only defensive wars are truly jihad. It is often mistakenly interpreted by non-Muslims to mean a holy war, evoking images of terrorists.

Jim Crow laws   Legal restrictions preventing persons of color from sharing public accommodations with whites.

Koran   The Koran is the holy writings of Islam, believed by Muslims to be the exact words revealed by God or Allah to the prophet Muhammad. It is also written as Qur'an in English.

language   Written or spoken human speech. It is a system that enables people to communicate with one another and to share their thoughts and ideas with one another.

least restrictive environment (LRE)   The educational setting closest to a regular school or general education setting in which the child with a disability can be educated. For many children, this may mean a general education classroom. Others may require a less inclusive setting to best meet their needs.

liberal Protestants   Protestants considered to be on the liberal end of the religious continuum who view Christianity in ways meaningful in a world of science and continual change. They stress the right of the individual to determine what is true in religion. They may or may not believe in the virgin birth of Jesus and may or may not believe the Bible to be inerrant.

lived experiences   Realities that individuals know because they have themselves experienced them.

magnet schools   Schools in which the curriculum emphasizes a particular subject or field such as performing arts or mathematics and science. Generally, students from anywhere in a school district can apply to attend these schools.

maintenance programs   Programs in bilingual education that teach ELL students to function effectively in both the native language and English. Students become bilingual and bicultural in the process, with neither language surfacing as the dominant one. The student's native language and culture are taught concurrently with English and the dominant culture.

manifest destiny   A policy in which a nation or culture believes they are superior to all others and are destined to rule over other nations and cultures.

marginalization   Relegation to a position that is not part of the mainstream nor accepted by most people.

McKinney-Vento Homeless Assistance Act   The federal legislation that outlined the education rights and protections for homeless children and youth.

meaningful projects   Student projects that address equity, democratic, and social justice issues in the community.

median income   The number of persons, families, or households who earn more than this income is the same as the number who earn less than this income.

Mennonites   Protestants who adhere to a simple lifestyle and simple forms of worship. They base their beliefs on the Bible, particularly the New Testament, and place much focus on the Sermon on the Mount (Matthew 5-7). They believe the Bible forbids them from going to war, swearing oaths, or holding offices that require the use of force. Their origins were in Switzerland in the early 1500s. Some settled in Pennsylvania in the late 1600s and early 1700s and became part of the group known as the Pennsylvania Dutch. In the 1870s some moved to Canada and the Great Plains States.

meritocracy   A system based on the belief that an individual's achievements are based on their own personal merits and hard work and that the people who achieve at the highest levels deserve the greatest social and financial rewards.

metropolitan   A geographic area that includes a city with a substantial population and adjacent communities that are economically connected to the city.

middle class   Group whose members earn annual incomes that allow them to have a standard of living that includes owning a home and car. Members are usually white-collar workers, professionals, and managers.

mild mental retardation   A label for individuals with limited intellectual or cognitive abilities, which often inhibit their academic functioning and socialization. Those with mild mental retardation are the highest functioning of those individuals with mental retardation and can generally master some basic academic skills.

miscegenation   Marriage between persons of different races.

monolingualism   The ability to speak only one language.

Moral Majority   A conservative religious group founded by Rev. Jerry Falwell in 1979 consisting of a Christian action committee who campaigned and supported political candidates who supported Christian "moral law," believing that they supported the majority of people's opinions. They lobbied for school prayer and the teaching of creationism in public schools.

multicultural curriculum   Coursework in schools that incorporates the histories, experiences, traditions, and cultures of students in the classroom and supports and celebrates diversity in the broadest sense.

multicultural education   An educational concept that addresses cultural diversity and equity in schools. It incorporates the different cultural groups to which individuals belong, with an emphasis on the interaction of race, ethnicity, class, and gender in students' lives.

multiethnic curriculum   A course of studies that reflects accurate and positive information about the history, experiences, contributions, and perspectives of the ethnic groups that comprise the U.S. population.

MySpace   A social networking website where individuals can place personal profiles, photos, blogs, music, and videos.

Muslims (or Moslems)   The adherents of Islam. Estimates of Muslims are as high as 1.3 billion in the world, and the highest estimates of Muslims in the United States are approximately 7 million. Only about 20% of the world's Muslims live in the Middle East. India and Indonesia have the largest numbers of Muslims, with about 175 million each.

nationalism   National identity based on a common language, common culture, and loyalty and devotion to a nation.

nativism   Policy favoring assimilated ethnic groups over more recent immigrants.

net worth   Amount of money remaining if all owned property was converted to cash and all debts were paid.

New Age   A spiritualistic movement that began in the early 1980s. New Age has roots in nineteenth-century spiritualism and in the counterculture movement of the 1960s, rejecting materialism and favoring spiritual experience to organized religion. New Age emphasizes reincarnation, biofeedback, shamanism, the occult, psychic healing, and extraterrestrial life. The movement is difficult to define, as there are so many variations of followers.

nonsexist education   Education that attends to the needs of girls and boys equitably by incorporating females as well as males in the curriculum, ensuring that girls and boys achieve at the same levels in all subjects, and encouraging girls and boys to choose subjects which they traditionally would not have selected.

nonstandard dialect   A dialect of the same language (e.g., English), that is not considered standard (e.g., Black English).

Nordic race   Germanic people of northern Europe who are white with a tall stature, long head, light skin and hair, and blue eyes.

normalization   Making available to all persons with disabilities or other handicaps, patterns of life and conditions of everyday living which are as close as possible to or indeed the same as the regular circumstances and ways of life of society.

official English   A position supported by U.S. English, a citizen's action group, which is seeking to have English declared by Congress as the official language of the United States. Individuals who support this movement believe that all public documents, records, legislation and regulations, as well as hearings, official ceremonies, and public meetings should be conducted solely in English.

Old Order Amish   Also referred to simply as the Amish. They had their origins with the Swiss Mennonites but broke away in the 1690s because of disagreements over church discipline. Like the Mennonites, they are forbidden to go to war, swear oaths, or hold any public offices. They require their members to maintain themselves as separated from the rest of the world as possible. Men wear dark clothes and wide-brimmed hats, and women wear plain long dresses and bonnets. They prohibit the use of electricity, telephones, and mechanical equipment in their homes and farms. They farm with equipment drawn by horses, and they travel by horse-drawn carriages. Children are allowed to attend school only to the age of 15.

Orthodox Jews   The oldest, most conservative, and most diverse form of Judaism. Orthodox Jews look upon every word in their sacred texts as being divinely inspired. They adhere to a strict dietary law (kosher), which requires the use of special ingredients and preparation. Kosher usually refers to food, but may refer to anything ritually fit or proper by Jewish law.

otherness/others   Cultural groups that are different from our own.

patriarchal   Social organization in which the father controls the family, and the wife and children are legally dependent on him. It also refers to men having a disproportionately large share of power in society.

pedagogy   Art or science of teaching, which includes instructional strategies and methods.

physical abuse   The nonaccidental injury inflicted by a child's caretaker.

physical geography   The study of the physical features of the earth.

physical neglect   The deliberate neglect or extraordinary inattentiveness to a child's physical well-being.

prejudice   Negative attitudes about a group of people.

privileged   Individuals or groups whose socioeconomic status, race, native language, gender, or other group memberships give them advantages and power over others in society.

proficiencies   Knowledge, skills, and dispositions that students or teachers acquire to meet standards.

Proposition 227   An initiative passed by California voters in 1998 that required all language minority students to be educated in sheltered English immersion programs, not normally intended to exceed one year. Although it has not completely succeeded, Proposition 227 was designed to eliminate bilingual education from California's schools.

Protestants   The general name given to an extremely diverse group of Christians, who may differ slightly or greatly from one another. Together, they form the second largest Christian group in the world after Roman Catholics. Protestants are centered primarily in Europe and North America. The hundreds of Protestant groups evolved out of the Reformation in the 1500s led by Martin Luther against the Catholic Church. Protestants share some important beliefs and values with Roman Catholics, such as the belief in only one God and the Trinity (God the Father, God the Son, and God the Holy Spirit). They differ in their views of the authority of the Pope and the ways that people relate to God.

Public Law 94-142, Education for All Handicapped Children Act   A comprehensive legislation signed into law in 1975 that guaranteed all children ages 3–21 with disabilities a free and appropriate education in the least restrictive environment.

Public Law 105-17, Individuals with Disabilities Act Amendments (1997)   Amendments that consolidated the law from eight parts to four parts, strengthened parental roles, encouraged parents and educators to resolve differences through mediation, gave schools more latitude in the discipline of students with disabilities, and set funding patterns.

Qur'an   The Qur'an is the holy writings of Islam, believed by Muslims to be the exact words revealed by God or Allah to the prophet Muhammad. It is also written as Koran in English.

racism   Belief that one race has inherent superiority over all others and thereby has the right to dominate.

redlining   The withholding of mortgages or insurance to oppressed groups limiting their ability to move into less depressed neighborhoods.

refugees   Persons recognized by the U.S. government as being persecuted or legitimately bearing persecution in their home country because of race, religion, nationality, or membership in a specific social or political group.

regression to the mean   A statistical phenomenon that implies that scores at the extreme ends of the statistical distribution move toward the population average (mean), with low scores moving higher and high scores moving lower.

Religious Right   Fundamentalist Protestants who accept the Bible literally as the word of God. The group may include fundamentalist militants who strongly oppose gay rights and abortion rights.

Roman Catholics   Members comprise the largest Christian church in the world with over 1 billion adherents. Most believers live in Europe, South America, and North America. The numbers of Catholics in Africa and Asia have been growing in recent years. Catholics believe that Jesus founded their Church and that the Apostle Peter was the first in the line of bishops leading to the current Bishop of Vatican City. The Pope is the spiritual and political leader of Roman Catholics.

Sabbath (or Shabbat)   A day of rest and holiness observed by Jews and a minority of Christian denominations (e.g., Seventh Day Adventists). It is observed from sunset on Friday night until nightfall on Saturday. Most Christian groups observe Sunday as the Sabbath.

Section 504 of Public Law 93-112   Part of the Rehabilitation Act of 1973 designed as a counterpart law for individuals with disabilities to the Civil Rights Act of 1964. It requires reasonable accommodations for those with disabilities, and prohibits the denial of participation in any program receiving federal funds solely on the basis of one's disability.

secular humanism   A nonreligiously based philosophy promoting man as the measure of all things. Typically rejects the concept of a personal God and regards humans as supreme. Secular humanists tend to see God as a creation of man, rather than man being a creation of God.

self-fulfilling prophecy   A teacher's projection of a student's academic achievement based on socioeconomic, social, and cultural factors that do not indicate a student's academic potential.

sexism   The conscious or unconscious belief that men are superior to women that results in behavior and action to maintain the superior, powerful position of males in society and families.

sexual abuse   The involvement of adults with children or underage adolescents in sexual activity.

sexual harassment   Unwanted and unwelcome sexual behavior that interferes with the victim's life.

sexual orientation   One's sexual attraction to persons of the same or opposite sex or both sexes.

sheltered English immersion   An instructional process in which English language acquisition is structured so that nearly all instruction is in English. This is the instructional method mandated by California Proposition 227 and is normally limited to one year.

signed English   A system that translates the English oral or written word into a sign.

Sikhism   A religion founded by Guru Nanak during the fifteenth or sixteenth century B.C.E. in India. He drew from the elements of Hinduism and Islam, and stressed a universal single God. Union with God, he said, is accomplished through meditation and surrender to divine will. He believed in reincarnation, karma, and the destruction and rebuilding of the universe, but he rejected the Hindu belief in the caste system.

social justice   A philosophy that expects citizens to provide for those persons in society who are not as advantaged as others.

social role valorization   Giving value to individuals with mental retardation.

social stratification   Ranking of persons and families based on specific characteristics such as income, education, occupation, wealth, and power.

socialization   Process of learning the social norms and expectations of a culture.

socioeconomic status (SES)   Composite of the economic status of families or persons on the basis of occupation, educational attainment, income, and wealth.

Standard English   The English spoken by a particular group of individuals in a community. Typically this group is the professional educated middle class and the group with a high degree of influence and prestige in the community.

stereotyped   Application of generalizations, many of which are negative, about a group without consideration of individual differences within the group.

stereotypes   Exaggerated and usually biased views of a group.

structural assimilation   Assimilation of groups to the point that they share primary relationships, intermarry, and have equality with the dominant group.

subcultures   Subsocieties connected to cultural group memberships such as gender, race, ethnicity, socioeconomic status, religion, exceptionalities, language, and age.

subsistence living   A socioeconomic system in which people produce enough food for their communities to survive, but do not accumulate food or money for private use.

subsocieties   Systems of values, attitudes, and behaviors of social groups within society. Examples are gangs, groupies, and skinheads.

substance abuse   Use of drugs or alcohol to a level of addiction or other at-risk behaviors.

subtractive bilingualism   Occurs when a second language replaces the first.

suburbs   The communities that surround a city and are home to many of the city's workers.

Title IX   Legislation passed by Congress in 1972 to provide females equal access to all aspects of education.

tracking   The practice of separating students based on their perceived academic abilities for instruction that is supposed to be most appropriate to their abilities.

transgender   Persons of one sex who have or adopt characteristics of the opposite sex.

transition plan   A needs assessment and planning to transition from student into adulthood. Transition plans became a requirement for all children with disabilities by the age of 14 years in IDEA 1990.

transitional programs   Programs that emphasize bilingual education as a means of moving from the culture and language most commonly used for communication in the home to the mainstream of U.S. language and culture. The native language of the home is used to help the student make the transition to the English language. The native language is gradually phased out as the student becomes more proficient in English.

under-referrals   Disproportionately low referrals by teachers of children for specific programs or activities. These often include the disproportionately low numbers of children of color (particularly African American, Latino, and American Indian) in classes for the gifted and talented or advanced placement classes.

Unification Church   A religion founded in Korea in 1954 by the Rev. Sun Myung Moon. Individuals outside of the faith refer to the group's adherents as "Moonies," considered derogatory by its members. Members refer to themselves as Unificationists. Rev. Moon moved to the United States in 1972 and began a major effort to proselytize members into his church.

upper class   Group whose members earn the highest annual incomes and have great wealth.

upper middle class   Group whose members are the affluent middle class who are highly educated professionals, managers, and administrators.

values   Qualities or principles that are considered desirable and important.

Vernacular Black English   Another term for Black English, African American English, and Ebonics. A dialect used by the majority of African Americans and used primarily by those in working-class families.

wealth   Accumulated money and property such as stocks, homes, and cars that can be turned into money.

white-collar   Jobs or workers characterized by nonmanual labor in offices, retail stores, and sales.

working class   Group whose members work at manual jobs that do not usually require post-secondary education, except for the more skilled jobs.

young adulthood   Individuals between the ages of 18 and 24.

YouTube   A website where users can upload, view, and share videos.

Author Index

Subject Index